READERS AND WRITERS IN PRIMARY GRADES

A Balanced and Integrated Approach

K–4

Third Edition

Martha Combs

Marian College

University of Nevada, Reno
Professor Emerita

PEARSON

Merrill
Prentice Hall

Upper Saddle River, New Jersey
Columbus, Ohio

Library of Congress Cataloging in Publication Data

Combs, Martha.
    Readers and writers in primary grades: a balanced and integrated approach/Martha
Combs.—3rd ed.
        p. cm.
    Includes bibliographical references and indexes.
    ISBN 0-13-118486-5
        1. Language arts (Primary) 2. Reading (Primary) 3. English language—Composition and exercises—Study
and teaching (Primary) 4. Language experience approach in education. I.
Title.

LB1528.C64 2006
372.6′ 044—dc22

2005043885

Vice President and Executive Publisher: Jeffery W. Johnston
Senior Editor: Linda Ashe Montgomery
Senior Editorial Assistant: Laura Weaver
Senior Production Editor: Mary M. Irvin
Design Coordinator: Diane C. Lorenzo
Production Coordination: Norine Strang, Carlisle Publishers Services
Design: Carlisle Publishers Services
Cover Designer: Ali Mohrman
Cover Image: Adam Lorenzo, age 6
Photo Coordinator: Valerie Schultz
Production Manager: Pamela D. Bennett
Director of Marketing: Ann Castel Davis
Marketing Manager: Darcy Betts Prybella
Marketing Coordinator: Brian Mounts

This book was set in Cheltenham by Carlisle Communications, Ltd. It was printed and bound by Hamilton
Printing. The cover was printed by Phoenix Color Corp.

Photo Credits: Andy Brunk/Merrill: 3; Anne Vega/Merrill: 6, 9, 138, 217, 267, 280, 429; Patrick White/Merrill: 25;
Laima Druskis/PH College: 31, 341; Scott Cunningham/Merrill: 75, 177, 180, 248, 293, 296, 335; Anthony Magnacca/
Merrill: 103, 129; Todd Yarrington/Merrill: 357; David Mager/Pearson Learning Photo Studio: 397.

Pearson Prentice Hall™ is a trademark of Pearson Education, Inc.
Pearson® is a registered trademark of Pearson plc
Prentice Hall® is a registered trademark of Pearson Education, Inc.
Merrill® is a registered trademark of Pearson Education, Inc.

Pearson Education Ltd.   Pearson Education Australia Pty. Limited
Pearson Education Singapore Pte. Ltd.   Pearson Education North Asia Ltd.
Pearson Education Canada, Ltd.   Pearson Educacíon de Mexico, S.A. de C.V.
Pearson Education—Japan   Pearson Education Malaysia Pte. Ltd.

10 9 8 7 6 5 4 3 2
ISBN: 0-13-118486-5

To my sister, Debbie.
May you find joy and inspiration
as a teacher.

Preface

Every child has the right to know firsthand the power and possibility that come from being a literate individual! For almost 40 years, I have been a teacher of children and adults, and during that time I have learned that effective teachers have at least two things in common—a belief that all children can learn and a commitment to providing the assistance necessary for every child to become literate. There is much that we must know about children, language, and literacy if we are to support all children as learners. This book is a beginning toward that effort.

Imagine that we are helping a young child learn to ride a bike. At first we provide a great deal of support, patiently demonstrating the parts of bike riding that the child needs to know and seems ready to learn. Teaching this child to ride requires repetition, redirection, and careful observation of his or her responses. Slowly, as the child demonstrates new levels of skill, we adjust the amount and types of support we provide, until the child is riding without our support. There may be spills along the way, even regressions, but we intervene only as the child demonstrates need because we want the child to become independent.

This story about riding a bike could just as easily be a story about helping a child learn to read and write. Young children who learn to read and write early usually do so with the support of a responsive adult, an adult who listens to them, talks with them, reads with them, and writes with them. This is what we want for every child, a responsive adult who supports their acquisition of literacy skills and strategies, because our goal for children is independence! To this end, this book is organized around teaching strategies that can help each of us be responsive to the literacy needs of young children.

A LITERACY FRAMEWORK

This third edition of *Readers and Writers in Primary Grades* focuses on a balanced and integrated approach to literacy, meshing theory and practice in every chapter. The figure shown on the next page clearly identifies the components of our literacy framework. Each chapter focuses on one or more components, providing the theory base for the component as well as illustrations of effective classroom practices using the component.

DEVELOPING NEW KNOWLEDGE . . .

- *Chapter 1* provides an overview of language and literacy development, principles of teaching and learning, a framework for a balanced and integrated approach to literacy, and the diversity of today's classrooms. It examines our role as responsive adults in the literacy process.

	Reading Aloud and Guided Literature Study	
Shared Reading		Shared and Interactive Writing
Guided Reading and Guided Literature Study	**Balanced and Integrated Literacy Framework**	Guided Writing and Writer's Workshop
Independent Reading and Reader's Workshop		Independent Writing
	Word Study	

- *Chapters 2 and 3* build background for children's transition from oral to written language. We begin with phonological awareness, the basis for success in reading and writing. Then we develop our understanding of both phonics and the structure of words that enable us to "break the code" of written language.
- *Chapter 4* introduces the foundation for building comprehension of text, reading aloud to children. This component is a powerful tool that is often overlooked for its instructional value. In this chapter we explore ways of engaging children in read-aloud experiences to enhance language development and knowledge of what print has to offer. We also examine ways to engage children in the whole-class study of literature.
- *Chapter 5* provides an examination of shared reading experiences, in which teachers model reading processes for children and support the initial development of skills and strategies in whole-class settings.
- *Chapter 6* focuses on guided reading, which should be at the heart of any primary-grade literacy program. Guided reading with children in small groups provides an intermediate step on the way to independence, with assistance as needed to extend children's learning that began in read-aloud and shared reading.
- *Chapter 7,* Independent Reading and Reader's Workshop: Encouraging Independence, is the culmination of discussion about the reading components in our literacy framework because independence for children should be our goal as teachers. It is only when we step back to observe children's independent levels of functioning that we are truly able to see the impact of our instruction.

🍎 *Chapter 8* shifts the focus from reading to writing, with an in-depth examination of shared and interactive writing. Shared writing, like shared reading, provides teacher support in learning to compose in the safety of the whole-group environment. Shared writing becomes interactive when we share the pen and let children write. With our support, interactive writing enables children to demonstrate their developing understandings about written language.

🍎 *Chapter 9* completes our journey to develop an understanding of writing within our literacy framework by focusing on guided and independent writing. In guided writing we support children as they attempt to use their knowledge of writing to communicate their thoughts for themselves or to communicate with others. As with independent reading, it is important that we also take time to step back to let children demonstrate what they have internalized about written language.

INTEGRATING AND APPLYING WHAT WE LEARN . . .

🍎 *Chapter 10* provides the opportunity to apply an understanding of our literacy framework to the realities of teaching with a basal reading/language arts series. Many school districts require teachers to use a commercial reading/language arts program as a main instructional resource. Our challenge as teachers is to use that program wisely, in ways that benefit our students. Only we can know what is most appropriate for the students in our classrooms.

🍎 *Chapter 11* provides an overview of a second-grade thematic unit about amphibians and serves as a culminating opportunity to observe how four second-grade teachers link instruction in literacy through their use of all of the components in our framework. Reading this classroom illustration along with Chapter 1 provides a more comprehensive overview of our literacy framework. Rereading this section periodically provides continued clarification of the possibilities for components.

TEXT FEATURES

Literacy is a field that is constantly influenced by forces from within education, as well as from outside groups that are concerned about schools and what students learn. This edition of *Readers and Writers in Primary Grades* responds to the changing demographics of the United States and to the role of the federal government in education through enactment of No Child Left Behind in 2001. A number of features in the text are provided to support your learning:

🍎 *Literacy Framework*—Each chapter opens with a graphic organizer that identifies the literacy focus for the chapter. Throughout the text, this organizer serves as a reminder of the components of our framework for literacy instruction.

- *In this chapter . . .* —This feature identifies the major concepts, issues, and ideas on which the chapter will focus. It provides an opportunity to think ahead about familiar ideas that might appear in the chapter.
- *Focus Literature*—Specific texts used in a chapter are identified on the opening pages. Familiarity with the literature enhances understanding of chapter activities.
- *Looking into Classrooms . . .* —Each chapter opens with a classroom vignette that provides a practical connection to a real classroom in which the focus component is being practiced. Typically, the teachers featured in the vignette reappear later in the chapter as we focus in more depth on classroom practice and application.
- *Building a Theory Base . . .* —Following *Looking into Classrooms . . . ,* we turn our attention to the particular background knowledge needed to implement the literacy component(s) we focus on in each chapter. To be able to innovate new applications on the ideas of others, we must understand the theories the ideas are based upon.
- *Putting Theory into Practice . . .* —The remainder of each chapter provides extensive applications of theory to classroom practices. Classroom dialogues, expanded illustrations, and assessment features appear in each chapter.
- There is increased attention to the needs of *English language learners (ELL)* in this edition. Within the discussion of each component, ELL issues are highlighted. Chapter 1 also includes a discussion of second-language acquisition.
- Issues of *assessment* and *respecting diversity* are integrated into each chapter, as they apply to the literacy focus component. Discussions of assessment and diversity are easy to find, as they are the final two sections of each chapter.
- *Margin Notes* call attention to definitions of important terms, websites that might be useful in building more background about a topic, and issues related to English language learners.
- *Making Connections . . .* —At various times throughout a chapter you will be encouraged to pause to consider your own learning. To retain new ideas we must re-collect and re-construct our ideas to make them our own. The activities suggested in the *Making Connections . . .* sections are usually most effective if completed with someone else. Sharing ideas and teaching each other helps us refine and solidify our thinking.
- A **Handbook of Children's Literature,** Appendix A, provides an overview of genre and literary elements to support planning for the use of children's literature, particularly in read-alouds and literature study.
- Sample *pictures* and *word lists* for word study activities are provided in Appendix B and Appendix C.

ACKNOWLEDGMENTS

First and foremost to my husband, Randy. Thank you for eveything! To the teachers and teacher education students in Nevada and Wisconsin, especially at Roger Corbett Elementary, who are a constant source of joy and inspiration.

Many thanks to those at Merrill/Prentice Hall who work their magic to make books come to life—especially Linda Montgomery, Laura Weaver, Jeff Johnston, Mary Irvin, and Kirsten Balayti. My thanks also to each of the reviewers who provided helpful ideas and constructive criticism for this third edition: Cindy Dooley, Western Illinois University; Carol J. Fuhler, Iowa State University; Barbara Pettegrew, Otterbein College; Bonnie Piller, California State University, San Bernardino; Linda Ray, Florida Gulf Coast University; and Sam Sebesta, University of Washington. And finally, thank you to the readers who breathe life into the ideas on these pages, and, I hope, draw upon them to touch the lives of children. Thank you.

Martha Combs

Educator Learning Center:
An Invaluable Online Resource

Merrill Education and the Association for Supervision and Curriculum Development (ASCD) invite you to take advantage of a new online resource, one that provides access to the top research and proven strategies associated with ASCD and Merrill—the Educator Learning Center. At **www.educatorlearningcenter.com**, you will find resources that will enhance your students' understanding of course topics and of current educational issues, in addition to being invaluable for further research.

How the Educator Learning Center Will Help Your Students Become Better Teachers

With the combined resources of Merrill Education and ASCD, you and your students will find a wealth of tools and materials to better prepare them for the classroom.

Research
- More than 600 articles from the ASCD journal *Educational Leadership* discuss everyday issues faced by practicing teachers.
- A direct link on the site to Research Navigator™ gives students access to many of the leading education journals, as well as extensive content detailing the research process.
- Excerpts from Merrill Education texts give your students insights on important topics of instructional methods, diverse populations, assessment, classroom management, technology, and refining classroom practice.

Classroom practice
- Hundreds of lesson plans and teaching strategies are categorized by content area and age range.
- Case studies and classroom video footage provide virtual field experience for student reflection.
- Computer simulations and other electronic tools keep your students abreast of today's classrooms and current technologies.

Look into the Value of Educator Learning Center Yourself

A four-month subscription to Educator Learning Center is $25 but is **FREE** when packaged with any Merrill Education text. In order for your students to have access to this site, you must use this special value-pack ISBN number **WHEN** placing your textbook order with the bookstore: 0-13-195970-0. Your students will then receive a copy of the text packaged with a free ASCD pincode. To preview the value of this website to you and your students, please go to **www.educatorlearningcenter.com** and click on "Demo."

Contents

Part I   Literacy Methods for K–4 Classrooms   1

Chapter 1   Foundations of Language and Literacy   2

Looking into Classrooms . . .   3

Building a Theory Base . . .   4

Literacy Issues in the 21st Century   4
Defining Literacy   4
Current Achievement Levels in Reading and Writing   5
Concerns about Literacy Instruction   5
Who Are Today's Students?   7
Principles to Guide Teaching and Learning   8
Principle 1: Language and Literacy Development   9
Language and Literacy in Preschool Years   10
Language and Literacy in the Primary Grades, K–4   13
Principle 1: Learning English as a New Language   14
Preproduction Stage   14
Early Production Stage   14
Speech Emergence Stage   14
Intermediate Fluency   15
Advanced Fluency   15
Principle 2: Teaching-Learning Relationships   15
Learning in the Zone of Proximal Development   16
Scaffolding Children's Learning   16
Guidance toward Self-Regulated Behaviors   16
Principle 3: Meaningful Learning Environments   17
Encouraging Independence   17
Respecting and Valuing Individuals   17

A Framework for Literacy Teaching and Learning   18
    Components of the Framework   *18*
    Instructional Strategies in the Framework   *19*

Chapter 2 **Learning about Words I: Making the Transition to Print** **24**

Looking into Classrooms . . .   ***25***

Building a Theory Base . . .   ***26***

An Overview of the Emergent Stage   26
Developing a Schema for Words and Print   28
Concepts about Print   29
    Permanence of Print   *30*
    Directionality of Print   *30*
    Language to Talk about Print   *31*
Principles of Written Language   32
    Recurring Principle   *32*
    Generative Principle   *33*
    Sign Concept   *33*
    Flexibility Principle   *33*
    Directionality   *34*
Foundations for Decoding Print   34
    High-Frequency Sight Words   *34*
    Context   *36*
    Phonics and Morphemic Analysis   *37*
Decoding in the Emergent Stage   38
    Rhyming   *39*
    Syllable Units   *40*
    Onset and Rime   *41*
    Phonemes   *42*
Recognizing Letters of the Alphabet   43
    Letter Names   *43*
    Letter Shapes   *44*
Connecting Letters to Sounds   45
Writing Alphabet Letters   47

Putting Theory into Practice . . .   ***48***

Using Music to Focus on Sounds   49
    Rhyming   *49*
    Blending Syllables   *50*

Blending Phonemes   *50*
Splitting Syllables   *51*
Onset and Rime   *51*
Matching Phonemes   *52*
Changing Phonemes   *52*
Games   53
Sorting Activities   53
Sorting Phonemes   *53*
Sorting by Letters   *56*
Using Sound Boxes   58
Say-It-and-Move-It   *58*
Say-It-and-Write-It   *59*
Using Environmental Print to Focus on Letters and Sounds   60
Environmental Print Books   *60*
Environmental Word Wall   *60*
Using Children's Literature to Focus on Sounds and Letters   61
Alphabet Books   *61*
Feed the Hungry Thing   *62*
Assessment: Monitoring Early Concepts of Sounds and Letters   64
Phonological Skills   *64*
Alphabet Recognition   *65*
Letter-Sound Relationships   *66*
Concepts about Print (CAP)   *67*
Keeping Records of Children's Development   *70*
Respecting Diversity in Development of Word Knowledge   70
Experience Sets Children Apart   *73*
Language of Instruction   *73*

Chapter 3   **Learning about Words II: Phonics and Morphemic Analysis**   **74**

Looking into Classrooms . . .   **75**

Building a Theory Base . . .   **76**

Who Are the Developing Readers and Writers?   76
Who Are the Transitional Readers and Writers?   77
The Importance of Learning about Words   77
How Do Children Learn about Words?   78
Phonics in the Developing and Transitional Stages   79
Consonants   *79*

Vowels   *80*

What Do Children Need to Learn about Phonics?   82

What Are Morphemes?   83

  Free and Bound Morphemes   *85*

  Base Words and Roots   *85*

  Affixes   *86*

What Do Children Need to Learn about Morphemes?   87

Instruction in the Developing and Transitional Stages   88

  *Instruction in the Developing Stage (Early/Mid-First-Grade
  to Early-Third-Grade Reading Level)*   *89*

  *Instruction in the Transitional Stage (Third- through Sixth-Grade
  Reading Level)*   *89*

Guiding Principles for Instruction   91

  Systematic Instruction   *92*

  Explicit Instruction   *92*

  Embedded Instruction   *93*

Putting Theory into Practice . . .   **94**

Building Words—A Whole-Class Approach to Word Study   94

  Selecting a Focus for Building Words   *95*

  Preparing Materials   *95*

  Basic Procedures for Building Words   *96*

  Building Phonetic Words   *97*

  Building Morphemic Words   *98*

Sorting Words—A Small-Group Approach to Word Study   101

  Guiding Small-Group Word Study   *103*

  Forming Developmental Groups for Word Study   *104*

Selecting Words for Study   105

  Words Have Multiple Possibilities   *105*

  Patterns Have Levels of Complexity   *106*

Types of Sorts   106

Using a Word Study Notebook   108

Assessment: Monitoring Growth in Word Knowledge   112

Assessing Word Knowledge in Reading   115

  Miscues in Oral Reading   *115*

  High-Frequency Sight Words   *115*

  Phoneme and Word Recognition   *116*

Assessing Word Knowledge in Writing   116

  Unfocused Writing Sample   *116*

  Focused Writing Sample   *118*

Keeping Records of Word Knowledge Development   122

Respecting Diversity in Learning Words   122

Chapter 4   Reading Aloud to Children: Foundations for Comprehension of Text   **128**

Looking into Classrooms . . .   *129*

Building a Theory Base . . .   *130*

Why Read and Study Quality Literature?   131

Literature Comes in a Variety of Genres   131

    Multicultural Literature   *132*

Comprehension of Text—Learning to Think Like a Reader   133

    A Reader's Intentions   *133*

    An Author's Intentions   *134*

Comprehension of Text—Ways of Thinking about Written Language   134

    Literal Comprehension—Text-Explicit Thinking   *134*

    Inferential Comprehension—Text-Implicit Thinking   *134*

    Personal and/or Critical Comprehension—
    Scriptal Thinking about Text   *135*

    Assessing Children's Comprehension of Text   *136*

Putting Theory into Practice . . .   *137*

Reading to/with Children—An Invitation into Literature   138

    Create a Comfortable Environment   *138*

    Expose Children to New Literature   *138*

    Provide Time to Revisit Old Favorites   *139*

    Encourage Responses to Literature   *139*

    Help Children Interpret and Appreciate Literature   *140*

Guiding Children's Comprehension of Text   140

Comprehension of Narrative and Expository Texts   142

Guiding Comprehension of Narrative Text—*A Chair for My Mother*
by Vera B. Williams   144

Guiding Comprehension of Expository Text—*Trains* by Gail Gibbons   148

    Sample Mediated Read-Aloud with Expository Text—Trains
    by Gail Gibbons   *149*

Extending Comprehension of Text—Rereading and Revisiting Texts   153

    Developing Vocabulary and Book Language   *154*

    Enhancing Understanding and Appreciation of Text   *154*

Building Comprehension through Retelling   155

Retelling with Text Illustrations   155
Retelling with a Story Map   156
Retelling with Drawings   156
Retelling with a Flannel Board   157
Retelling through Writing   157
Retelling through Drama   158
Building Comprehension through Response   158
Response in Journals   159
Response with Chants and Rhythms   160
Response with Creative Movement   161
Response with Art   161
Read-Aloud Literature Study   162
Focusing Literature Study   163
Read-Aloud Literature Study—Picture Books   164
Read-Aloud Literature Study—Chapter Book   166
Chocolate Fever by Robert Kimmel Smith   166
Developing Discussion Skills   169
Assessment: Monitoring Comprehension during Read-Aloud   171
Respecting Diversity during Read-Aloud   171

Chapter 5   **Shared Reading: Participating in a Community of Readers**   **176**

Looking into Classrooms . . .   **177**

Building a Theory Base . . .   **178**

Texts for Shared Reading   179
Big Books   179
Enlarge a Book Using an Overhead Projector   179
Charts: Songs, Poems, Chants, Letters, and Recipes   180
Shared Writing or Language Experience Charts   182
Using a Pocket Chart   183
Scripts for Reader's Theater   183
Multiple Copies of a Text   184
Criteria for Selecting Quality Texts   185
Quality of Illustrations   185
Size and Amount of Print   185
Structure or Predictability of Text   186

Shared Rereading 187
Why Do Shared Reading? 189
Confidence and a Sense of Control 189
Concepts about Print 189
Decoding Skills 190
Developing Vocabulary 190
Comprehension of Text 190
Fluency 190

Putting Theory into Practice . . . **191**
Planning Shared Reading Experiences 191
Clear Goals/Purpose(s) for Instruction 191
Analyzing the Demands of Text 192
Observing What Children Know 192
Organizing Shared Reading Experiences 193
First Shared Reading 193
Shared Rereadings 194
Sample Shared Reading: Big Book 194
Sample Shared Reading: Experience Chart 197
Extending Shared Reading Experiences 201
Retelling and Responding to a Shared Reading 202
Using Enlarged Text to Create Wall Stories 202
Creating Floor Puzzles 203
Preparing for Reader's Theater 203
Shared Reading of Challenging Text 204
Developing Word Knowledge through Shared Reading 206
Concepts about Print 206
High-Frequency Sight Words 207
Using Context Clues 207
Decoding Words 209
Integrating Writing with Shared Reading 209
Assessment: Monitoring Development in Shared Reading 211
Concept of Word (COW) 211
Respecting Diversity through Shared Reading 213
Safety and Support of a Group 214
Support through Modeling and Guided Participation 214
Language Support through Predictability 214
Extending Learning through Sheltered Text 214

Chapter 6 **Guided Reading: Scaffolding Children's Reading** **216**

Looking into Classrooms . . . *217*

Building a Theory Base . . . *218*

What Is Guided Reading? 218
Matching Children and Texts 219
    Reading Potential *220*
    Frustration Level *220*
    Instructional Level *220*
    Independent Level *221*
    Comparing Levels of Text *221*
    Stages of Development and Levels of Difficulty *221*
Selecting Appropriate Texts 222
    Length of the Text *223*
    Size of the Print and Layout on the Page *223*
    Illustration Support *223*
    Genre and Text Structure *223*
    Language Structures and Concepts *224*
    Predictability and Pattern *224*
    Linking Learning Experiences *224*
The Need for Flexible Grouping 225
Developing Strategies for Self-Monitoring 226
    Meaning Cues *226*
    Language Cues *226*
    Visual Cues *226*
    Becoming a Strategic Reader *227*

Putting Theory into Practice . . . *228*

Planning for Guided Reading 228
    Setting Up Flexible Groups *228*
    Selecting Texts for Guided Reading *229*
    Guiding the Reading of a Text *230*
Engaging Children in Guided Reading Experiences 231
    Guided Reading of More Challenging Text *235*
Selecting Teaching Points for Guided Reading 239
Guided Literature Study in Small Groups 240
    Guided Literature Study: Picture Books *241*
    Guided Literature Study: Chapter Books *243*

Organizing for Guided Chapter Book Study   *246*

Teaching Skills/Strategies through Mini-Lessons   249

Assessment: Monitoring Growth in Guided Reading   250

    Scripted Reading Record   *253*

    Unscripted Reading Record   *257*

    Assessing Fluency   *261*

    Keeping Accurate Records   *263*

Respecting Diversity through Guided Reading   263

    Children Vary in Their Reading Interests   *263*

    Children Vary in Reading Ability   *263*

    Text Can Influence Comprehension   *263*

Chapter 7   **Independent Reading and Reader's Workshop: Encouraging Independence**   **266**

Looking into Classrooms . . .   **267**

Building a Theory Base . . .   **268**

What Is Independent Reading?   268

What Is Reader's Workshop?   269

    Time   *270*

    Choice   *270*

    Response   *270*

    Community   *270*

    Structure   *271*

Moving toward Independence   271

Putting Theory into Practice . . .   **272**

Promote a Reading Atmosphere   272

    Book Boxes or Tubs   *273*

    Teach Children How to Select Books   *273*

    Ensure Adequate Reading Time   *274*

Plan for Independent Reading   276

    Make a Predictable Time to Read   *276*

    Meet the Range of Reading Levels and Interests   *276*

    Build an Inviting Classroom Library   *276*

    Observe Children's Progress   *277*

Reader's Workshop: Independent Reading as the Centerpiece   278

    Help Children Select Literature   *278*

    Promote Silent Reading   *279*

Conference with Children	*280*
What Happens in a Conference?	*280*
Instruction In Reader's Workshop	284
Mini-Lessons	*284*
Flexible Groups	*285*
Extending Engagement with Books in Reader's Workshop	286
Using Literature Response Logs	*286*
Independent Book Extensions	*288*
Assessment: Monitoring Children's Growth in Independent Reading	288
Reading Records	*288*
Focus Students	*289*
Conferences	*289*
Samples of Student Work	*289*
Respecting Diversity during Independent Reading and Reader's Workshop	290
Pursuing Personal Reading Interests	*290*
Learning about Oneself as a Reader	*290*
The Continuing Need for Self-Monitoring	*290*
The Need to Be a Kid-Watcher	*290*

Chapter 8 Shared and Interactive Writing: Participating in a Community of Writers   292

Looking into Classrooms . . .	***293***
Building a Theory Base . . .	***294***
What Is Shared Writing?	295
When Does Shared Writing Become Interactive Writing?	297
Why Use Shared/Interactive Writing?	299
Thinking about Written Language	300
Retaining Experience	*300*
Re-Collecting Experience	*300*
Re-Creating Experience	*301*
Re-Constructing Experience	*301*
Re-Presenting Experience	*302*
How Is Writing Used in Classrooms?	302
Writing as a Code	*303*
Writing as a Medium	*303*
Writing as a Product	*303*

Writing as an Active Process — *303*

The Value of Functional Writing — 304

Lists — *305*

Ordered Lists — *305*

Descriptions — *305*

Clusters — *306*

Annotated Drawings — *307*

Charts — *307*

Graphs — *308*

Explanations — *308*

Putting Theory into Practice . . . — **308**

Possibilities for Shared and Interactive Writing — 309

Composing as Expressions of Learning — *309*

Composing as Organization of Thinking — *310*

Grouping for Shared and Interactive Writing — 313

Procedures for Shared/Interactive Writing — 314

Meaningful Shared Experiences — *315*

Talking about Experiences and Ideas — *315*

Shared Composition and Modeled/Interactive Writing — *315*

Shared Reading, Discussion, and Rereading of Text — *316*

Extending Interaction with Text — *316*

Exploring Composition Processes — 317

Exploring Various Forms of Writing — 319

Extending Interaction with Shared/Interactive Compositions — 320

Building Background before Reading — *321*

Making Predictions before Reading — *321*

Responding to the Text — *321*

Retelling the Text — *321*

Innovating with the Text — *321*

Group Literature Log — *322*

Mini-Lessons — *322*

Making Strategy Use Explicit — *322*

K-W-L Charts — *322*

Adapting Difficult Informational Texts — *323*

Developing Labeled Drawings — *323*

Extending Interactions with the Original Text — 324

Editing Text — *324*

Concept of Word in Print — *324*

Guided Rereading — *324*

Use Context, Written Cloze 325
Reinforcing Sight Words 325
Reinforcing Alphabet Recognition 325
Reinforcing Phonics Patterns 326
Reinforcing Morphemic Patterns 326
Extending Interactions with Duplicated Text 326
Rereading Text 327
Reconstructing Text 327
Class-made Big Book 327
Individual Books 327
Sentence Building 327
Word Building 328
Word Sorts 328
Word Bank Books 328
Magic Window Words 329
Word Hunts 329
Word Posters 329
Picture Dictionary 329
Word Wall 329
Games 329
Art 330
Assessment: Monitoring Children's Development in Shared/Interactive
Writing 330
Respecting Diversity with Shared/Interactive Writing 331
Respecting the Language of the Learner 331
Respecting Special Learning Needs 333
Respecting the Thinking of the Learner 333
Respecting Experiential Background 333

Chapter 9   Guided and Independent Writing   334

Looking into Classrooms . . .   335

Building a Theory Base . . .   337

Writing—Guiding Children's Journey in Thinking 337
Getting Started 338
Finding a Focus 338
Composing 338
Editing for Meaning and Correctness 339
Re-Presenting the Writing 341

Moving toward Independence as Writers 341

Putting Theory into Practice . . . **343**

Getting Started in Writer's Workshop—A Visit to Peggy's Classroom 343
Organizing a Writer's Workshop 350
Whole-Class Opening Meeting 351
Demonstrations of Writing: Mini-Lessons 351
Demonstrations of Writing: Shared/Interactive Writing 354
Making Plans for the Day 355
Writing Time 356
Individual Writing 356
Writing Conferences 356
Response Partners/Groups 358
Editing Partners/Groups 359
Whole-Class Closing Meeting 359
The Author's Chair 360
Closure for the Day 360
Moving toward Independence as Writers 361
Trying out a Variety of Journals 361
Learning Logs 365
Trying on Different Forms of Writing 366
Extending Personal Narratives 366
Experimenting with Fiction 368
Exploring Poetry 371
Exploring Informational Writing 375
Independent Writing in Activity Centers 380
Extending Writing through Bookmaking 381
Accordion Books 381
Fan-Page Books 381
Pocket Books 383
Pop-up Books 383
Sequence Books 383
Shape Books 383
Helping Children Develop Legible Handwriting 383
Assessment: Monitoring Children's Development as Writers 385
Observing Writers at Work 385
Evaluating Writing Traits 386
Conferencing with Writers 388
Collecting Samples of Writing 389

Respecting Diversity in Writing Development   392
   Honoring Children's Thinking   *393*
   Supporting Independence   *393*

Part II   Making Connections: Linking Children's Learning Experiences within a Balanced Literacy Program   **395**

Chapter 10   Teaching a Basal Reading/Language Arts Series: Integrating Instruction to Maximize Children's Learning   **396**

Looking into Classrooms . . .   *397*

Building a Theory Base . . .   *398*

What Is a Basal Reading/Language Arts Series?   398
   A Little History   *398*
   A Call for Change   *400*
Teacher Decision Making and the Basal Series   401

Putting Theory into Practice . . .   *401*

What Is in a Basal Reading/Language Arts Series?   402
How Is a Theme Organized in a Basal Series?   403
What Is Included with Each Literature Selection?   404
   Practice and Resource Materials   *405*
   Lesson Planner   *405*
   Cross-Curricular Centers   *406*
Teaching a Basal Literature Selection   408
Whole Group: Oral Language and Word Work (40 to 60 Minutes)   409
Small-Group/Independent Work: Reading (60 to 90 Minutes)   411
Whole Group: Language Arts (30 to 45 Minutes)   416
Assessment: Monitoring Children's Progress in a Basal Series   422
Respecting Diversity in Basal Instruction   424

Chapter 11   Integrating Elements in a Literacy Framework: Teaching about Amphibians in Second Grade   **428**

Looking into Classrooms . . .   *429*

Putting Theory into Practice . . .   *430*

Setting the Stage 430
Meet the Teachers 430
Getting Started with Planning 431
   Academic Standards in Language Arts *431*
   Academic Standards in Science *432*
Making Instructional Decisions 432
   Shared Reading—Poem of the Week (15–20 Minutes) *433*
   Mediated Read-Aloud (20 Minutes, Twice Each Day) *434*
   Guided Literature Study (20 Minutes) *434*
   Shared/Interactive Writing (15–20 Minutes) *434*
   Guided Writing (30–40 Minutes) *435*
   Word Study (15–20 Minutes) *435*
   Guided Reading Block (60–90 Minutes) *435*
   Independent Reading (15–20 Minutes) *436*
   Independent Writing (Time Varies) *438*
Planning Key Features of the Unit 438
Putting the Pieces Together 438
Lesson Plans for Week 1—Introduction to Amphibians 442
   Poem of the Week—"Frogs and Toads" *442*
   Morning Mediated Read-Aloud (Informational Text) *443*
   Interactive Writing—T-Chart of Facts *443*
   Shared Writing—Narrated Drawing *443*
   Shared Writing—Compare/Contrast Chart *445*
   Interactive Writing—Summarize Differences *445*
   Guided Writing—Learning Logs *446*
   Word Study *446*
   Guided Reading Block *449*
   Afternoon Mediated Read-Aloud (Fiction) *451*
Lesson Plans for Week 2—Salamanders and Amphibian Life Cycles 451
   Poem of the Week—"Salamanders, Salamanders" *451*
   Morning Mediated Read-Aloud (Informational Text) *451*
   Interactive Writing—Salamander Characteristics and Life Cycle *454*
   Interactive Writing—Summarize Amphibian Characteristics and Life Cycles *456*
   Guided Writing—Learning Logs *456*
   Word Study *459*
   Guided Reading Block *461*
   Afternoon Mediated Read-Aloud (Fiction) *461*

Lesson Plans for Week 3—*Frog and Toad Are Friends* and Group Reports   464
    Poem of the Week—"Tadpoles, Tadpoles"   464
    Guided Literature Study—Frog and Toad Are Friends   464
    Interactive Writing—Character T-Chart   465
    Shared Writing—Response to Frog and Toad's Friendship   466
    Guided Writing—Group Reports   466
    Word Study   467
    Afternoon Mediated Read-Aloud (Informational Text)   472
Lesson Plans for Week 4—Versions of *The Frog Prince*   473
    Poem of the Week—"Five Little Bumpy Toads"   473
    Guided Literature Study—Versions of The Frog Prince   474
    Shared Writing—Story Elements Chart   474
    Shared Writing—Venn Diagram   475
    Shared Writing—Summarize Comparison   475
    Guided Writing—Literature Logs   475
    Word Study   478
    Guided Reading Block   479
    Afternoon Mediated Read-Aloud (Fiction)   479
Assessment: Monitoring Children's Learning in a Thematic Unit   480
    Documenting Student Learning   480

Appendix A   Handbook of Children's Literature   **485**
Appendix B   Sample Word Lists and Word Sorts   **506**
Appendix C   Pictures for Sorting Activities   **520**
References   **551**
Name Index   **559**
Subject Index   **563**

Part I
Literacy Methods
for K-4 Classrooms

Aa Bb Cc Dd Ee Ff Gg Hh Ii Jj Kk Ll Mm

C H A P T E R

1

Foundations of Language and Literacy

	Reading Aloud and Guided Literature Study	
Shared Reading	**Balanced and Integrated Literacy Framework**	Shared and Interactive Writing
Guided Reading and Guided Literature Study		Guided Writing and Writer's Workshop
Independent Reading and Reader's Workshop		Independent Writing
	Word Study	

In this chapter, we learn about . . .

- 🍎 Literacy issues in the 21st century
- 🍎 Diversity of children in today's classrooms
- 🍎 Principles of teaching and learning
- 🍎 Language and literacy development
- 🍎 Learning English as a new language
- 🍎 Teaching-learning relationships
- 🍎 Meaningful learning environments
- 🍎 A framework for literacy teaching and learning

2

Looking into Classrooms . . .

It is October in Carmen's first-grade classroom, and the children have gathered on the floor near the painting easel that also serves to hold their favorite songs, poems, and big books for shared reading. Jeremy holds the pointer and confidently touches each word on the chart the class has made of "Old MacDonald Had a Farm" as the children sing along. Jeremy's face shows the pleasure that he has in being the "pointer" for that day. Following cries of "Let's do it again!" Jeremy places the pointer at the beginning of the song, and in a loud voice begins to sing, "Old MacDonald had a . . . " as he points to each word.

Later that morning the children are allowed to choose activities as part of their morning work. Jasmine sits at the small table in the corner by the mouse cage, which holds a mother mouse and her four new pink babies. The cage bears the label "Minnie Mouse." As Jasmine writes, she looks intently at the cage and also up to the wall that displays words the class uses frequently in reading and writing. Jasmine puts the finishing touches on a birth announcement for the baby mice:

> Come see the babez
> Minnie Mouse haz 4 babez

As she writes the last word on her announcement, Jasmine says aloud with great pleasure, "There! Now everyone will know about the babies." Carmen encourages Jasmine to tape the birth announcement outside the classroom door so that neighboring classes can read the news.

At the end of the day, Carmen pins a note on Ruben's shirt. "What's this say?" he demands, pulling at the note. "Read it to me. Is my mom gonna be happy or mad?" As Carmen unpins the note and opens it, Ruben sees some letters and the drawing of a happy face and smiles. He has had a note like this before. Carmen reads the note, "Ruben helped a friend on the playground today. I am proud of him."

3

BUILDING A THEORY BASE . . .

Like the children in Carmen's classroom, becoming literate enables each of us to "read and write the world to meet our needs and interests, taking from and making of the world what we will" (Shannon, 1992, p. 1). As we strive to make meaning in our lives, we are able to:

- experience satisfaction in our work,
- communicate important feelings and ideas to others,
- resolve personal problems,
- satisfy our desire to know,
- experience vicariously what we may never know in real life,
- escape, through the narratives of others' lives, the stresses of our own,
- record and save our thinking in written form for a later time, and . . .

What would you add to this list? What does it mean to you to be a literate individual, a member of a literate community?

 ## LITERACY ISSUES IN THE 21ST CENTURY

Defining Literacy

Historically, literacy has been defined in ways that reflect the nature of the times. Each historical period lends new meaning to the term. In the 1700s, literacy might have been defined only as the ability to read and write one's own name, or in the early 1900s as simply the basic ability to read and write. The National Literacy Standards for Language Arts (1996) suggest that "a much more ambitious definition of literacy today includes the capacity to accomplish a wide range of reading, writing, speaking, and other language tasks associated with everyday life" (p. 73). To be literate today requires that we understand and use diverse sources and forms of information in meaningful ways. Today the word

Read here to find a definition of *literacy*.

literacy describes competence in technical fields, such as computer literacy, numerical literacy, and scientific literacy. Each of us is typically skilled in areas that require some type of technical knowledge, but we must also be able to negotiate with others in a range of specialized fields to solve life's problems.

As we consider definitions of literacy we should remember that words are mere "inkspots on paper until a reader transforms them into a set of meaningful symbols" (Rosenblatt, 1978, p. 25). We have learned from research that reading is "a high-speed, automatic, simultaneous operation of complex linguistic and cognitive processes. At any moment, a reader of any level of proficiency must keep in mind story meaning, sentence meaning, sentence syntax, and some metacognitive awareness of fit, while simultaneously perceiving and identifying words, word-parts, and punctuation marks" (Jones, 1995, p. 44). Skillful readers transform the symbols on a page to make and share meanings "as ways of exploring and understanding what it means to live" (Thomson, 1987, p. 13). Similarly, writers use this knowledge of language and symbols to construct messages that communicate their meanings for various purposes. As adults who will guide and support children's acquisition of literacy skills, we must develop a keen awareness of the issues and challenges that surround current concerns about children's literacy.

Current Achievement Levels in Reading and Writing

Being literate enables us to have greater access to the benefits of citizenship in a technological society. Yet, each year we are reminded by reports in the media and from government agencies that large numbers of children are not functioning at adequate levels of literacy. The 2002 and 2003 results of the National Assessment of Educational Progress (NAEP) document reasons for continued concern about children's literacy development in the United States. In addition, substantial disparities continue to exist between White students and students of ethnic minorities. Since the first NAEP results were reported in 1971, a disproportionate number of minority children and children of low socioeconomic status have demonstrated limited literacy ability. Within this group of students who are not achieving at their potential are English language learners, K–12 students who are learning English as an additional language and must acquire sufficient skill in English to learn academic subjects.

The NAEP is first administered in fourth grade. Recent results for fourth-grade students across the United States in reading and writing document the following:

Find out more about the NAEP assessment and The Nation's Report Card at *http://www.nces.ed.gov/ nationsreportcard.*

Reading Levels in Fourth Grade

- 37% function below a basic level of literacy,
- 32% function at a basic level of literacy, and
- only 32% function at or above a proficient level.

Writing Levels in Fourth Grade

- 14% function below a basic level of literacy,
- 58% function at a basic level of literacy, and
- only 28% function at or above a proficient level. (NAEP, 2003)

Concerns about Literacy Instruction

The failure of some children to reach their literacy potential, however, is not a recent phenomenon. Literacy research reveals that children with normal intelligence frequently have difficulty learning to read and write proficiently. Growing out of the struggles that some children endure when learning to read and write, early literacy development and instruction continues to be the subject of national education policy:

For a more in-depth discussion of the "reading wars," see *http://www.nrrf.org/article_ anderson6–18–00.html.*

- From the late 1980s through the 1990s there were national "reading wars" between proponents of various instructional techniques, most notably between phonics (which emphasizes word-decoding skills before textual meaning) and whole language (which emphasizes textual meaning). The "reading wars," as they were characterized, were part of

To learn more about the No Child Left Behind Act and Reading First, visit *http://www. nochildleftbehind. gov, http://www.ed.gov/ print/programs/readingfirst/ index.html,* and *http://www. nwrac.org/reading/*.

the debates between traditional and progressive pedagogy in America's schools (Anderson, 2000).

- In 1985, a report of the Commission on Reading, *Becoming a Nation of Readers,* called for a balance between explicit instruction in word recognition (phonics) and comprehension, as well as daily opportunities to read and write meaningful, connected text (Anderson, Hiebert, Scott, & Wilkinson, 1985).

- In 1998, the report of the Committee on the Prevention of Reading Difficulties in Young Children identified the need to balance instruction that emphasizes meaningful reading and writing with specific attention to the features of print, particularly the features of the alphabetic system of English (Snow, Burns, & Griffin, 1998).

- In 2000, the National Reading Panel issued a controversial report of research-based reading instruction that became the cornerstone of U.S. federal reading education policy. The report concluded that sound reading instruction helps children to figure out words, to read fluently, and to think effectively about what they read (National Institute of Child Health and Human Development).

- Most recently, in January of 2002, the No Child Left Behind Act (NCLB) was signed into law and requires that teachers be highly qualified and work stridently to close the achievement gap between groups of children, such that all children make adequate yearly progress in learning to read. The research-based components identified by NCLB are phonemic awareness, phonics, vocabulary, fluency, comprehension, and writing.

- The No Child Left Behind Act established *Reading First* as a new, high-quality evidence-based program for the students of America. The Reading First initiative provides federal funds to help state and local school districts eliminate the reading deficits that exist for many

Students in today's classrooms bring many varied experiences as learners.

students by establishing high-quality, comprehensive reading instruction in kindergarten through grade 3.

Making Connections . . .

How do you define literacy? What factors influence your definition? You might also want to interview teachers you know concerning their definitions of literacy. Be curious about how those teachers have developed their definitions.

WHO ARE TODAY'S STUDENTS?

As we begin to examine the issues that surround literacy development of young children, it is important to consider the students who are in today's classroom. The United States is a nation of diverse racial and ethnic groups, each with a rich cultural heritage of language, values, and traditions. The United States is the nation that it is because of the unique contributions that each group has made to the nation's way of life (Ramirez & Ramirez, 1994). What we have in common is that we all belong to a democratic society that in turn has its own values and traditions. Somewhere in the mingling of culture and citizenship, it is important that we all have a place in which we are valued and respected.

As you think about the children who will enter your classroom, consider the words of Asa Hilliard (1994), an expert in multicultural education:

> Diversity is the norm in our society, even when homogeneity appears on the surface. . . . When educators do not notice diversity, when they give negative notice, or when they lose the opportunity to give positive notice of the natural diversity that is always there, they create a bogus reality for teaching and learning. (p. x)

Historically, there has always been diversity among individuals in our society—diversity of gender, social class, ethnic group membership, religion, learning styles, physical or mental abilities, personal interests, and the like. In today's classrooms there is also greater likelihood of diversity in the languages that children speak.

Gender differences have always existed in our classrooms. Boys and girls are not only different physiologically, but are also socialized differently into a culture. To see this process in action one only need look at the portrayal of male and female roles in advertisements, literature, or television and film. Similarly, differences in social class have always existed because the capitalistic system of the United States traditionally produces an economically stratified society. The opportunities for life that are determined by economics affect the experiences and outlook that children from different social groups bring to the classroom. The conditions associated with poverty help to explain much of the variation in achievement among individuals (White, 1982).

In any group of children, there is diversity in preferred learning style, in physical, intellectual, social, and emotional abilities, and in personal interests. Sometimes this diversity in children has been identified, for example, by inclusion in a special education or compensatory program such as Title I. Sometimes children are segregated from others based on their differences. More recently,

For more information about diversity of students in schools, see *http://www.ed.gov/offices/OSERS/Policy/IDEA/overview.html*).

the trend has been toward inclusivity, accommodating these differences within the least restrictive educational environment (Individuals with Disabilities Education Amendments Act, Public Law 105-17, 1997).

Finally, the 2000 census revealed that the foreign-born population of the United State reached 31.1 million people, or 11.1% of the population. This figure is 57% greater than in 1990. By 2004, the foreign-born population numbered 34.2 million, or 12% of the total U.S. population, an increase of 2.3% over 2003. Within the foreign-born population, 53% were born in Latin America, 25% in Asia, 14% in Europe and the remaining 8% in other regions of the world, such as Africa and Oceania (Australia, New Zealand and all of the island nations in the Pacific) (U.S. Census Bureau, 2005). It is highly likely that you will have children in your classroom who speak a language other than English outside of school while they are learning to speak, read, and write a new language in school.

Making Connections . . .

As you participate in classrooms, what have you observed about the diversity of today's classrooms? What thoughts do you have about how these factors may affect your ability as a teacher to help children learn to read and write?

PRINCIPLES TO GUIDE TEACHING AND LEARNING

Theories of development provide the principles for learning and teaching that support the development of competent readers and writers. From Lev Vygotsky (1978) we learn that:

> From the very first days of the child's development his activities acquire a meaning of their own in a system of social behavior and, being directed towards a definite purpose, are refracted through the prism of the child's environment. The path from object to child and from child to object passes through another person. This complex human structure is the product of a developmental process deeply rooted in the links between individual and social history. (p. 30)

In this text, three principles of learning and teaching are the basis for developing an understanding of literacy. These principles should become the basis for the decisions that you will make as a teacher as you develop and organize an effective literacy framework to support the learning of all children, regardless of their backgrounds.

Principle 1: Language and Literacy Learning
   Children learn by using language and their senses, and by being actively involved in constructing meaning from their experiences and communicating that meaning to others.

Principle 2: Teaching-Learning Relationships
   Children learn through the modeling of more knowledgeable others, through appropriate and scaffolded levels of challenge, and through encouragement and opportunity to learn how to monitor and regulate their own learning.

Children need our guidance as they move toward independence as readers and writers.

Principle 3: Learning Environments

Children learn in environments that are meaningful and nonthreatening, where they feel valued and respected as individuals, and where they are encouraged to become independent, self-regulated learners.

In the next several sections we consider each of the three principles and how they might contribute to our framework for teaching and learning.

PRINCIPLE I: LANGUAGE AND LITERACY DEVELOPMENT

Effective teaching of young children requires that teachers have an understanding of language and its role in literacy learning. "Language is a gateway to new concepts, a means of sorting out confusions, a way to interact with people, or to get help, a way to test out what one knows. It enters into every activity we can envisage" (Clay, 1998, p. 11). Learning language involves the negotiation of meaning between two or more persons: between speaker and listener, between writer and reader. These negotiations require the knowledge of multiple skills and strategies that enhance understanding by another and personal interpretations that are appropriate to a particular context. Language is a universal cultural tool used in many contexts to solve problems and is central to becoming literate:

> Learn more about milestones in speech and language development at *http://www.nidcd.nih.gov/health/voice/speechandlanguage.asp.*

> As a cultural tool, language is a distillation of the categories, concepts, and modes of thinking of a culture . . . . Language allows the acquisition of new information: context, skills, strategies, and processes. While not all learning involves language, complex ideas and processes can only be appropriated with the help of language . . . . Language delays impact on other areas of development: motor, social, and cognitive. (Bedrova & Leong, 1996, p. 96)

Children's developing brains are marvelous at learning language (Clay, 2004). Language development begins on the day a child is born, and for a short time every child becomes a linguistic genius and with great creativity learns to construct his or her first language (Lindfors, 1987). Children receive stimulation and communication from other humans in their environment. Slowly they develop the physical ability to respond and make their needs and desires known. They learn to use language to interpret and negotiate meaning with others in their environment.

When speech and thinking merge, a special kind of speech ensues, called private speech (Vygotsky, 1962). Although private speech is audible, it is directed to the self rather than to other people and is used to inform and regulate one's own behavior or learning. Children use private speech as they rehearse new skills that have been modeled by a more knowledgeable person, such as a parent or older sibling. Adults also use private speech when faced with a new and challenging task as a means of support and self-regulation. As development proceeds, private speech becomes inner speech, then verbal thinking. When tasks are familiar we are able to engage ourselves with verbal thinking, without needing to talk aloud to ourselves.

Over time and experience these internal mental processes become automatic and enable humans to think and function at higher cognitive levels. By the time children enter school they know a great deal about using their first language to comprehend and interpret their own world (Halliday, 1975). They have command of their native language and can communicate using complex sentence structures.

Children who are learning English as an additional language will need many rich language interactions to develop the language competence demonstrated by native English speakers. As their teacher, you must remember how children learn language and provide a rich language-learning environment in your classroom.

Language and Literacy in Preschool Years

What children know about language is quite dependent on the environment in which they develop. "For the first five years a child's language growth is entirely dependent on what people say to him—on how much they speak to him, about what things, in what dialect or language, and in what manner, whether gentle and explaining or peremptory and imperative" (Clay, 1991, p. 70). Depending upon socioeconomic status and the educational background of the adult(s) in the home, some children receive more scaffolding, or support, for thinking and learning language than do others. There can be large differences in the quality of language interactions that children experience as a function of social class (Hart & Risley, 1995).

Language Is Acquired through Interactions

Through interactions with others during the preschool years, most children acquire the sounds and structures of the language spoken around them. Although there are commonalities among speakers of a language such as English, it is also possible that individuals will develop unique ways of using that language in their lives. The same possibilities for language variation exist between members of different neighborhoods in the same city, between people living in different regions of a country, and between people of different cultural groups.

Rules of language are learned through children's interactions with others, particularly caregivers. Language use is influenced by the dialect used within the child's home and community. There is no formal curriculum for learning language, only situations when adults enter into conversations with children because they have a desire to help children learn to communicate. Language, whether it is a first or second language, is best acquired through many meaningful social interactions (Cummins, 1981). Without formal training, many adults seem to know how to adjust the level of language to a level that is useful to children. Adults make language available and easy by listening to children, responding to what they say, repeating words and phrases, altering sentence structures, and encouraging children to produce language at whatever level is comfortable. As children produce more language, the adults produce less. The learning of a new language, such as English for new immigrants, proceeds in much the same way.

Children learn to negotiate meaning with those around them through their interactions. Every sentence construction is based on a child's intuitive hypotheses about language (Chomsky, 1975). Children constantly test out their hypotheses about how they think other speakers structure language. Through their interactions, children are able to judge the correctness of their thinking. Because they want to be understood, they ask questions, search for more information, revise their concepts, and work to connect ideas.

Responsive adults help to expand the language capabilities of children. When children's hypotheses about language structure are not correct, responsive adults provide a more complete model, not merely correction. This model may be the correct pronunciation of a particular word or the conventional organization of words within a sentence, but the message to children emphasizes the important role of language in communicating intentions clearly and accurately in order to be understood. When language interactions occur in a nonthreatening environment, children will try out new words and structures as they communicate. They will enlist the help of a more knowledgeable language user in order to acquire the language needed to communicate their needs and desires.

Literacy Is Acquired through Interactions

Children's natural desire to understand leads them to explore and emulate what the significant people in their lives show them about language and print (Teale, 1986). Prior to school entrance, responsive adults encourage, support, and extend literacy behaviors by encouraging children to:

- reread favorite books with an adult,
- practice reading-like behaviors by "reading" favorite books to stuffed animals or to self,
- "write" a note to a grandparent,
- talk about favorite books during bedtime reading,
- learn to write their name,
- recognize signs that indicate familiar foods, such as cereal, at the grocery store,
- leave a message for a family member using magnetic letters on the refrigerator,

- recognize the sign that shows which building is the place for their favorite foods, or
- play word games, chant rhymes, or sing songs with an adult while riding in the car.

Such activities typically grow out of meaningful interactions between young children and more knowledgeable readers and writers who encourage children's interest in language and print.

One of the most powerful activities in these early years is bedtime stories, when adults read aloud to children and share the sounds and rhythms of language in print. They engage in rich discussions and animated conversations with children about the images of the world that are presented in books. As they do so, adult and child work out the meaning of a text (Morrow, 2005). During bedtime story reading, adults model skillful reading and bring the words in books to life. They demonstrate that reading is both pleasurable and worthwhile. Children begin to learn about book language and the type of meaning-making associated with comprehending text through participation in book-reading experiences with adults or older peers at home (Elster, 1998).

At bedtime adults read and reread children's favorite stories. Children can be very persuasive with their requests for rereading. The more familiar the book, the more children participate in the rereading. Familiarity breeds confidence. Children use the illustrations and their recollections of the text to help in the rereading. They join in with the phrases they remember, such as "Run, run, as fast as you can. You can't catch me I'm the Gingerbread Man." They delight in telling what will happen just before it actually does. This knowledge of what is in a book brings a feeling of confidence and a sense of power for children.

Engagement with books also presents new language-learning opportunities. Although children negotiate meaning and understanding quite well in daily conversation, encountering ideas in print can present a challenge for making meaning. Daily conversation takes place in a familiar context that children understand and make interpretations about. If they lack understanding, they are able to interact with the speaker to clarify or gain other needed information. In addition, voice intonation, facial expressions, and body language of a speaker provide additional support for understanding the message.

In contrast to speech, text is written in such a way that the reader must attempt to reconstruct the author's message, without the benefit of the author being present to help clarify ideas. While children listen to stories, they can begin to develop an ear for written language. Constructing and reconstructing meaning with written text is not necessarily a natural task that will develop through immersion in print-rich environments.

With the assistance of a responsive adult, however, children can come to understand concepts about written language, such as:

- All books are not the same. For example, "Once upon a time" signals make-believe rather than a true story.
- Pictures can help to tell the story.
- Books can help us learn about new people, places, things, and ideas.

🍎 "Book talk" is different than "face-to-face" talk; for example, authors must tell who is talking and how the words sound (e.g., Lucinda shouted, "Don't do that!").

As children listen to stories they begin to discover the symbolic power of language, in contrast to the concrete world in which they live. This power will "create a possible or imaginary world through words by representing experience in symbols that are independent of the objects, events and relationships symbolized and that can be interpreted in contexts other than those in which the experience originally occurred, if indeed it occurred at all" (Wells, 1986, p. 203). The long-term effects of this discovery can be seen in children's learning as they read and write in meaningful ways. Strong positive correlations exist between storybook reading during preschool years and subsequent vocabulary and language development, children's interest in reading, and early success in reading (Sulzby, 1985).

To enhance your background knowledge of language development during the preschool years, visit http://www.childdevelopmentinfo.com/development/language_develpment.shtml.

Language and Literacy in the Primary Grades, K–4

Language has its beginning within the social setting of the home and within a particular cultural context. Given the diversity within American society, it is likely that the home language of many children will differ from the language you will use for instruction in school. Such differences may be found in the sounds, accent, or intonation of children's language; vocabulary used; grammatical forms the children know; and type and range of sentence forms they use (Clay, 1991). Most children typically have a vocabulary of approximately 5,000 words when they enter school (Morrow & Gambrell, 2004). Many of the words will be similar for a classroom of children, but there will also be variety depending upon children's experiences prior to school.

Regardless of the range of differences, we must remember that children have already learned *how* to learn language. If we assist children in expanding their language knowledge, they *will* be able to do so. Marie Clay (1991) states:

> The child may not know as much about language as some of his peers, or he may find the rules for talking in school are different from those of his culture or ethnic group, or he may see little similarity between talking in his family and the more formal teacher-pupil talk of the classroom, or he may even speak a different language from the teacher's. Yet in all these cases the child has already learned how to learn language.(pp. 26–27)

Learning experiences in school must assist children in successfully using what they already know about language and adding to that knowledge as they acquire literate behaviors and the academic language for studying school subjects. Like the responsive caregiver, we must continually work to expand children's language knowledge and scaffold their learning experiences as they strive to use their knowledge of oral language as a foundation for experiences with written language.

As teachers, we must always remember how children learn their first language and use that knowledge to provide a rich language-learning environment in the classroom. That means that children must practice new language skills by

To learn more about language development in the elementary grades, visit http://www.childparenting.about.com/cs/childdevelopment/a/languagedevelop.htm.

engaging adults and peers in meaningful conversations. We must provide a learning environment that entices children to want to learn about written language to expand their ability to communicate with others.

PRINCIPLE I: LEARNING ENGLISH AS A NEW LANGUAGE

Nearly 10% of K–12 students in the United States are learning English as an additional language. Federal regulations (e.g., Title VI of the Civil Rights Act of 1964; *Lau* v. *Nichols,* affirmed by the U.S. Supreme Court in 1970) require school districts to take steps to help students overcome language barriers and to ensure that they can participate meaningfully in the district's educational programs. Therefore, as we examine the development of literacy skills and processes in children we must understand some basics of learning a new language that is not one's native language.

All children who are learning English as a new language will progress through the same stages to acquire this new language. These stages are similar to the stages of acquiring a first language and are identified as:

- 🍎 silent/receptive or preproduction,
- 🍎 early production,
- 🍎 speech emergence,
- 🍎 intermediate language proficiency, and
- 🍎 advanced language proficiency. (Northwest Regional Educational Laboratory, 2004)

Preproduction Stage

This stage can last from 10 hours to 6 months. Learners in this stage have a receptive vocabulary of about 500 words that they can understand, but may not yet be comfortable using in speech situations. Though learners in this "silent period" may not speak, they can indicate understanding through physical responses such as pointing and gestures, or nodding simple yes/no responses.

Early Production Stage

This stage can last an additional 6 months after the preproduction stage. By this time, learners have developed a vocabulary of about 1,000 words that they are able to understand and use. Learners are usually able to speak in short phrases and can demonstrate their comprehension by giving answers to simple yes/no, either/or, and who/what/where questions.

Speech Emergence Stage

This stage can last an additional year beyond the early production stage. Learners typically have developed about 3,000 words they use in short phrases and simple sentences to communicate. As learners experiment with longer sentences, they will often make grammatical errors with language structures they do not yet understand.

Intermediate Fluency

Intermediate fluency may take another year beyond the speech emergence stage. By this time learners usually know about 6,000 words and are beginning to construct complex sentences that share their thoughts, state opinions, or ask for more information or clarification.

Advanced Fluency

Becoming proficient in a second language can take from 5 to 7 years for most learners (Cummins, 1981). Recent studies suggest that it may actually take 7 to 10 years to acquire the sophisticated academic language structures required for success in educational settings, including the university (Rameriz, Pasts, Yuen, Billings, & Ramey, 1991).

For more information see Teaching English to Speakers of Other Languages (TESOL) at *http://www.tesol.org* and *http://www.nwrel.org/request/2003may/overview.html.*

Though the stages of development through which children will pass are predictable and sequential, the length of time that they spend in each stage can vary greatly. Contextual factors, such as opportunities to speak the new language with more expert language users, will affect the rate at which children will acquire skill in English.

It is important to have an understanding of the language diversity of your students. As a teacher, you are/will be accountable for the academic language learning of your students. Under the federal No Child Left Behind Act (2001) English language learners are expected to meet specific annual targets of Adequate Yearly Progress (AYP) just like native speakers are expected to meet AYP targets. Therefore, it is important to understand both first- and second-language acquisition/learning to better serve the needs of culturally and linguistically diverse students (Fillmore & Snow, 2000). Being a culturally responsive teacher focuses on making learning relevant to students' experiences and frames of reference by recognizing children's home culture and providing for continuity between children's home life and school literacy experiences (Ladson-Billings, 2001; Neuman, 1999).

Making Connections . . .

What are your current beliefs about the role of language in learning to read and write? What experiences have influenced your current view? Take time to record those beliefs. Throughout your study of children's literacy development you should continually revisit and reevaluate your beliefs because they will influence how you engage children in learning.

PRINCIPLE 2: TEACHING–LEARNING RELATIONSHIPS

The interactions that facilitate children's development are most likely to occur when teachers present tasks that are within a child's reach if assistance is provided by a more knowledgeable other. Without assistance, there are many forms of thinking that children would not discover, either alone or through interaction with their peers. Input that teachers provide to all students, including English language learners, must be comprehensible and lead to student understanding.

If you are unfamiliar with Lev Vygotsky, visit *http://www.psy.pdx.edu/ PsiCafe/KeyTheorists/ Vygotsky.htm, http://www. sk.com.br/sk-vygot.html,* or *http://www.kolar.org/ vygotsky/.*

Learning in the Zone of Proximal Development

A child's ability to learn something new exists within a zone of proximal development (ZPD). A child's ZPD is:

> The distance between the actual developmental level as determined by individual problem solving and the level of potential development as determined through problem solving under adult guidance or in collaboration with more capable peers. The zone of proximal development defines those functions that have not yet matured but are in the process of maturation, functions that will mature tomorrow but are currently in an embryonic state. (Vygotsky, 1978, p. 86)

Children learn how to perform tasks appropriately within their ZPD by interacting with a teacher who provides hints and prompts on an as-needed basis.

We know that a child's learning of a new skill begins on a social plane, between child and teacher, before we see that skill within the child's independent functioning. Learning is regulated socially by a teacher before it is self-regulated by the child. The amount and type of regulation given by the teacher depend on the age of the child and the nature of the task.

Scaffolding Children's Learning

Early in learning a new task or skill, children's understanding of what is to be learned and why may be very limited. Initially a teacher offers explicit directions or modeling and the children respond in an imitative way. Gradually the children come to understand the relation between parts of the activity, or come to understand the meaning of the performance. This understanding typically develops through the conversation that occurs during the performance of the task. Teachers may guide children through questions, or further cognitive structuring such as suggesting a strategy to try. When teachers assist in this fashion they provide a scaffold for children's learning (Wood, Bruner, & Ross, 1976). Like the scaffolding of a building under construction, responsive teachers provide support to the development of children's concepts that are under construction.

Learning to talk is an excellent example of how adults scaffold, or assist children, within their ZPD:

- Adults pay close attention to what children are trying to communicate, provide models of how speech sounds are structured, and at appropriate times assist children with the vocabulary and sentence structures they are trying to use to be understood.
- Over time, children gain control of certain vocabulary and are able to use it accurately and without adult assistance.
- As children gain inner control over particular speech patterns and structures, the range of that zone moves upward, toward more complex speech patterns for which adults continue to provide assistance as needed by the child.

Guidance toward Self-Regulated Behaviors

Through doing a task with support, children eventually perform the task without assistance, having internalized the kind of thinking that was previously supported by the teacher. To accomplish this move toward self-regulation, teachers gradually remove support as children demonstrate the ability to control the task themselves. Eventually, children take over the actual structuring of the task for themselves. At this level, the children are capable of redirecting themselves using such strategies as talking themselves through a task, similar to the support previously offered by the teacher. Eventually performance of the task is smooth and integrated, internalized and automatic. They no longer need teacher assistance for the task.

It is important to remember that "For every individual, at any point in time, there will be a mix of other-regulation, self-regulation, and automatized processes" (Tharp & Gallimore, 1988, p. 38). Throughout a person's life, learning is made up of the same regulated sequences recurring again and again for the development of new capacities.

PRINCIPLE 3: MEANINGFUL LEARNING ENVIRONMENTS

As each of us strives to meet our personal needs and interests, the environments in which we live take on great importance. The social context of the classroom plays a central role in the continued development of mental processes in young children (Bedrova & Leong, 1996), especially the more formalized thinking required in academic learning (Vygotsky, 1978). The environment teachers promote in the classroom affects children's views about the nature and importance of reading and writing in their lives and in the lives of significant others. Interaction and exploration through oral and written language provide tools with which young children begin to develop higher mental functions.

Encouraging Independence

Learning environments that are meaningful for children help them move toward independence as learners. Parents instinctively foster independence when they encourage children to talk, walk, eat, and dress themselves. Often without deliberate planning or conscious knowledge, parents provide a meaningful learning environment that fosters children's natural desire to learn and be independent. A teacher's goal for children in school should also be independence, because independent learners are confident and more proficient in the control over their own abilities and skills.

Learning complex processes such as reading and writing occurs slowly and requires much time and practice. As learners, we are more likely to practice when we are in an environment in which our own needs and desires can drive our learning. The amount and intensity of our practice is regulated best by our own motivation (Holdaway, 1979). If a teacher takes over the function of regulating practice for a child, the child may become less motivated to learn. In addition, the child's self-confidence to make decisions about learning may be jeopardized.

Respecting and Valuing Individuals

When children are encouraged to exercise control over their own learning, they are well aware of their level of effort and have a sense of the progress they are making. If someone else controls the learning, children tend to look outside of themselves for evaluation. A primary goal of meaningful learning environments is for learners to develop the ability to be self-corrective, and ultimately to be self-evaluative. For children to learn self-regulation as a way of thinking about learning, they must participate in a learning environment in which their teacher supports and respects their attempts to learn and treats them as worthwhile, self-aware individuals. Children must be encouraged to trust their knowledge of themselves, combined with corrective feedback from reliable sources, to move toward independence.

Making Connections . . .

Imagine that tomorrow you will take a position as a teacher in a primary-grade classroom. What are some of the first things you would do to create a classroom learning environment based on the three principles of learning and teaching just presented? Explain why you feel your decisions are important for young children.

🍎 A FRAMEWORK FOR LITERACY TEACHING AND LEARNING

In 2000 the National Reading Panel (NRP) identified important areas of reading that are supported by research and should be included in early reading instruction:

- 🍎 alphabetics (which includes phonemic awareness and phonics),
- 🍎 fluency, and
- 🍎 text comprehension (which includes vocabulary). (National Institute of Child Health and Human Development, 2000).

Components of the Framework

No Child Left Behind (2001), the federal legislation that requires all schools to document that all children are able to achieve adequate yearly academic progress, adopted the findings of the NRP and advocates that early literacy instruction should focus on phonemic awareness, phonics, vocabulary, fluency, and comprehension. Each of these five essential skills is defined as follows:

- 🍎 *Phonemic awareness* is the ability to hear, identify, and manipulate the sounds within words. The sounds of a spoken language work together to form words; thus knowledge of sounds in spoken language is an aid to reading and spelling words.
- 🍎 *Phonics* is the awareness that there is a predictable relationship between phonemes (units of sound) and graphemes (letter and

spellings that represent those sounds in written language). Knowledge of letter-sound relationships is essential to both reading and spelling.

🍎 *Vocabulary* is development of stored information about the meaning and pronunciation of words in spoken and written language. Vocabulary is essential in comprehending spoken and written language.

🍎 *Fluency* is the ability to read text accurately and quickly with expression. It requires the automatic recognition of most words in a text. Fluency is believed to be an aid to comprehension.

🍎 *Comprehension* is an active cognitive process that requires intentional and thoughtful interactions between a reader and a written text in which the reader constructs meaning from the text.

Though specific skills in writing were not addressed in these federal policy reports, writing is a reciprocal process of reading and thus shares the need for the development of the same linguistic skills. To effectively learn and utilize these skills, young children should receive guided instruction within the context of authentic literacy situations.

To learn more about the elements of reading identified by the National Reading Panel and Reading First, visit *http:// www.nationalreadingpanel. org* and *http://www.nifl. gov/partnershipforreading/ publications/ reading_first1.html.*

Instructional Strategies in the Framework

As a teacher, it is important to be knowledgeable about the development of literacy skills and organize classroom literacy programs around a defensible and informed framework for instruction. In this text, a framework for early literacy instruction is developed around strategies that, when taken together, provide a balanced and integrated approach to reading and writing for young children (see Figure 1.1). The literacy framework of this text is based on theories of how children learn and advocates explicit guidance from the teacher, with systematic release of control to children as they are able to monitor and regulate their own reading and writing behaviors.

Simply put, a balanced approach to literacy provides teaching and learning opportunities in reading and writing *to, with,* and *by* children (Mooney, 1990). To accomplish this, teachers utilize a variety of strategies that provide teacher

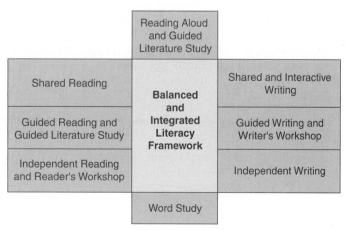

FIGURE 1.1
A balanced and integrated literacy framework.

guidance as needed, with the gradual release of control to children in order for them to develop skills in monitoring and regulating their own literacy learning.

The instructional strategies presented in this text are:

- 🍎 Reading to children (*to/with children*)
- 🍎 Shared/Interactive reading and writing (*with children*)
- 🍎 Guided reading and writing (*with children*)
- 🍎 Independent reading and writing (*by children*)
- 🍎 Word study (*with children*)

At the beginning of this chapter you were introduced to the children in Carmen's first-grade classroom. Let's revisit her classroom as an introduction to a balanced and integrated literacy framework in action:

🍎 *Reading to children*

Carmen reads aloud to the children several times a day. She finds several versions of the "Old MacDonald" song that have been published as books and shares them with the children through reading aloud. She reads aloud both fiction and nonfiction books about farms and farm animals.

Her purposes are to introduce children to the sounds of written language, model fluent reading for children's enjoyment, build their language and background knowledge for this theme unit, and teach the thinking skills required for comprehension of a text.

🍎 *Reading with children*

When the children know the words to the song, Carmen introduces a large chart with the basic frame of the song, and blanks in the appropriate place for an animal.

> *Old MacDonald had a farm*
>
> *E-i-e-i-o*
>
> *And on this farm he had a _____*
>
> *E-i-e-i-o*

She models the fluent reading of the text, placing a picture of an animal in the appropriate blank spaces for children to "read." Children are encouraged to share the reading as soon as they feel comfortable predicting the print based on their knowledge of the song. During repeated reading, individual children, such as Jeremy, lead the shared experience.

Carmen has used the song as a text for shared reading, in which she models what readers do, supports children's efforts to use phonemic awareness and phonics to build word recognition skills, and provides opportunities to develop skill in fluent reading.

When the words of the song are very familiar to children, the song is made into individual books for each child. Carmen guides daily small-group reading, listening carefully to the control that individual readers have over the text.

Guided reading provides an opportunity for Carmen to observe what knowledge, skills, and strategies for word recognition and text comprehension children are using from whole-class literacy experiences. Guided reading of familiar text also provides practice in fluency. Carmen meets small groups of children each day for guided reading experiences, using books that slightly challenge the children.

🍎 ***Reading by children***

Carmen gathers a variety of books about farms and farm animals and places them in the library corner. Many of the books are familiar from read-aloud and guided-reading experiences. She provides time each day for children to explore the books and read independently.

Frequently she listens to children's independent reading to better understand the skills and strategies over which they are gaining control.

Carmen understands that independent reading provides daily opportunities to practice fluency, as well as other important reading skills and strategies, such as word recognition and comprehension.

🍎 ***Writing with children***

At another time, the class composes a new verse for the song, sharing ideas about the writing. At various times during the writing, Carmen shares the marking pen with individual children as they write words and phrases to complete the composition. The class works together to assist the writer in figuring out the conventions of language and spellings for the new verse.

On other days, Carmen assists individual children as they write their own versions of animal songs and stories.

Carmen uses shared/interactive writing experiences to model how ideas can be written and to introduce new letter-sound relationships and writing conventions to the children. When she shares the pen with the children, their writing shows whether they are gaining an understanding of phonemic awareness, phonics, and vocabulary. Rereading and discussion of the text also demonstrates their skills in fluency and comprehension.

Guided writing of children's own stories enables Carmen to observe the level of control that children are developing over the production of written language. She is available to help children think about their composition and to help them as they wrestle with spelling and other conventions of written language.

🍎 ***Writing by children***

In the writing center, Carmen places a variety of writing materials such as colored and plain paper, farm-related pictures, blank books shaped like animals, scissors, tape, a stapler, and writing implements for children to compose stories during the daily "choice time."

Carmen understands that independent writing provides time to practice fluency in their writing skills and helps develop a sense of control over written language. Independent writing also encourages and supports children's personal interests as writers.

The framework that guides Carmen's literacy program engages her children in a range of literacy activities that vary in the amount of assistance she provides. Each day she engages all students in literacy activities that integrate oral and written language and provide opportunities for students to demonstrate their growing knowledge of how to use language effectively. She provides balance between reading and writing, between learning new skills and practicing old ones, and between reading for pleasure and reading for information. Carmen's classroom is one example of the way that teachers draw upon a variety of strategies to create a balanced and integrated framework for literacy learning.

The remaining chapters of this text will provide theory and application for each strategy. You will learn *what* each strategy is, as well as *how* and *when* to engage children in the strategy.

Making Connections . . .

Take a moment to reflect on your decision to become a teacher. What images do you see when you imagine yourself in a classroom teaching children to read and write? You bring more than 13,000 hours of watching someone else do what you will soon do. All of that experience can be both an asset and a challenge! You bring both conscious and unconscious attitudes and beliefs to the act of teaching. This is an important time in your preparation to become aware of the full range of those attitudes and beliefs. Begin to think deeply about your decision to teach and its potential impact on the children who will be in your classroom.

C H A P T E R

2

Learning about Words I: Making the Transition to Print

Beginning to develop our literacy framework . . .

	Reading Aloud and Guided Literature Study	
Shared Reading	**Balanced and Integrated Literacy Framework**	Shared and Interactive Writing
Guided Reading and Guided Literature Study		Guided Writing and Writer's Workshop
Independent Reading and Reader's Workshop		Independent Writing
	Word Study	

In this chapter, we learn about . . .

- The emergent stage of development
- Developing a schema for written language
- Concepts about print
- Principles of written language
- Foundations for decoding print

Looking into Classrooms . . .

The children in Elena's kindergarten class gather on the alphabet carpet for their morning opening. Though everything that the children do during the half-day kindergarten relates to literacy and language in some way, Elena plans the morning opening to emphasize awareness of sounds in language, encouraging children to be playful with language. As part of a study of healthy foods, Elena teaches the children a traditional song, Apples and Bananas, that provides opportunities for changing the vowel sounds of syllables in familiar words. The children sing:

I like to eat, eat, eat ee-ples and bee-nee-nees.

I like to ate, ate, ate ay-ples and bay-nay-nays.

I like to oat, oat, oat o-ples and bo-no-nos. . . .

They laugh as they sing the "funny" words. After the song Elena asks children to be sound detectives, stretching the words from the song and listening to the sounds they hear. She asks, "What sound do you hear at the beginning of "_ee-ples?_" The children all respond, "e." Crystal comes to the white board and points to the letter e on the alphabet chart. The children show their agreement with the letter she points to by giving the "thumbs up." The children write the letter e with a finger in the air, then on the carpet. Elena guides them as they talk about the sounds at the beginning of other words in the song—_ay_-ples, _o_-ples, and so on. Scenes like this take place each day in Elena's kindergarten as she helps children develop their awareness of sounds in words.

BUILDING A THEORY BASE . . .

Children's concepts about oral and written language are formed from their earliest years by observing and interacting with others as well as through their own attempts to read and write (Sulzby & Teale, 1991a). Over time qualitative differences in children's literacy behaviors can be observed (Adams, 1990; Biemiller, 1970; Bissex, 1980; Chall, 1967, 1983; Clay, 1967; Ehri, 1991, 1998; Juel, 1991; Mason, 1984; Snow, Burns, & Griffin, 1998; Sulzby & Teale, 1991a). These developmental changes are gradual, but occur for most children in a predictable manner.

In this text, these developmental differences will be identified as:

- emergent (kindergarten through early-first-grade reading level),
- developing (early/middle first grade through early third grade), and
- transitional (early-third-grade through sixth-grade reading level)

This chapter describes the foundation for learning about words to support children in the emergent stage as they make the transition from oral language to print. Chapter 3 continues the focus on learning about words in the developing and transitional stages.

AN OVERVIEW OF THE EMERGENT STAGE

Read here to find a definition of *emergent literacy*.

The term *emergent literacy* was first used by Marie Clay (1966) as she studied the acquisition of literacy by young children. Clay used the term to describe the stage at which children begin to receive formal reading and writing instruction in a school setting, the point at which children are expected to begin to demonstrate an understanding of print. Today the term is used to describe the gradual development of literacy behaviors in children, typically from birth to about age 5 (Sulzby & Teale, 1991a). This initial phase of development has also been characterized as the "learning about print" stage (Brown, 1999/2000).

Children in the emergent stage of development are just making a start with print (see Figure 2.1). Learning in this stage is dominated by a growing awareness of sounds in language and the awareness that those sounds can be represented by letters of the alphabet. Children's initial interactions with print are guided predominately by the illustrations in texts and recollections of books read aloud to them, rather than by the print itself.

> While emergent readers and writers already have some knowledge of *phonemes,* the individual sound units in words, through their oral language ability, they are not consciously aware that spoken language has a structure. Knowledge of oral language is so automated that conscious control is not necessary. To learn to read and write an alphabetic script, such as English, children must learn to pay attention to the very sounds (phonemes) to which they have learned not to attend. (Adams, 1994, p. 3)

They must also become keenly aware that sounds can be manipulated in language to form many varied words. Even with extensive language support and storybook experiences at home, many kindergarten and first-grade children lack

FIGURE 2.1
Characteristics of emergent readers and writers.

During the emergent stage children begin to:

- Internalize purposes of print and understand that print is used to communicate and make meaning.
- Develop knowledge about and appreciation of different types of text through repeated exposures.
- Show increasing interest in reading and writing independently.
- Develop concepts about print, including book-handling skills and an understanding of the permanence and directionality of print.
- Develop concepts about words including distinguishing letter shapes, letter names, and the sounds represented.
- Develop basic levels of phonological awareness (sounds in language), including the concept that words are composed of strings of sounds that can be manipulated to make other words.
- Make meaning from simple books but rely heavily on memory of familiar words, illustrations, story context, and selected letter cues.
- Recognize that printed English moves from left to right and top to bottom on a page.
- Recognize that the same letter shapes reoccur from word to word and can appear in different places within words.
- Recognize that a particular ordering of letters stands for a particular object and is called a word.
- Recognize that there is a relationship between the sounds in words and the letters that we use to represent those sounds.
- Recognize that words in writing are shown by making spaces between groupings of letters.

the awareness that spoken words are streams of sounds that can be disentangled, and that sounds can be assembled to produce words (e.g., see Adams, 1990; Pennington, Grossier, & Welsh, 1993; Pressley, 1998; Stanovich, 1986).

Emergent writers demonstrate a rudimentary understanding of writing (Clay, 1975). Early in this stage children learn that meaning can be transferred from the head to the page, taking shape through the movement of a pen on paper or fingers on a keyboard. Writing in the emergent stage begins with scribbles and forms that begin to resemble letters and numbers. With added print experience, writing becomes strings of letters that usually have little or no relationship to sound and frequently no spaces to acknowledge the beginning and end of words. Finally, letters are used to represent sounds in words. One letter, typically the first sound in the word, may stand for an entire word, as in *b* for *bed*. By the time that children make the transition to the developing stage, beginning and ending consonant sounds in words are being consistently represented. Middle vowel sounds are beginning to be represented, though often not accurately.

During children's earliest formal experiences in learning to read and write, teachers must be interested in the variability that can exist in children and how they change over time (Clay, 2004). In a typical class, 80% of children will be able to benefit from the instruction we offer. As many as 20%, however, cannot take what we offer and use it to extend their own learning (Clay, 2004). It is with these children that we must intervene in deliberate ways that relate their past learning experiences to the new literacy concepts and skills required for early reading and writing. A teacher's responsibility is to focus on the individual variability of each child and to take those differences into account as you plan and teach literacy experiences, focusing especially on the children who do not construct literacy understandings at the pace of others in the class (Clay, 2004).

Making Connections . . .

This would be a good time to observe young children interacting in a rich literacy environment, especially a kindergarten. What emergent literacy behaviors do you notice? Listen to children's talk when they are engaged in their "work." Ask them to tell you about what they are doing. What do their actions and words suggest about their developing understandings about language, reading, and writing?

🍎 DEVELOPING A SCHEMA FOR WORDS AND PRINT

Read here to find a definition of *schema*.

All human beings possess categorical "rules," or schemata (plural for *schema*), that they use to interpret the world. *Schema* is defined as "a mental condification of experience that includes a particular organized way of perceiving cognitively and responding to a complex situation or set of stimuli" (Merriam-Webster, 2003, p. 1110). A well-formed schema for written language helps children mentally organize personal experiences into networks of concepts and procedures that allows for access of knowledge and ideas in different contexts to make sense of new experiences (Adams & Collins, 1985; Schank & Abelson, 1975; Shanklin, 1982). A schema can be used not only to interpret but also to predict situations that occur in the environment.

Think, for example, of a situation in which you were able to finish another person's thoughts. Schema theorists suggest that you used your schema for the topic of conversation to predict what your conversation partner was going to say. Information that does not fit into our schema for a particular experience may not be comprehended, or may not be comprehended correctly. This is the reason why, for example, readers may have a difficult time comprehending text on a subject with which they are not familiar. Schemata are context specific, they are dependent on experiences with and exposure to particular subject matter, rather than simply on "raw intelligence" (Driscoll, 1994).

Over time children add new information about reading to their "reading" schema by "filing" the new information with similar concepts and/or procedures within their existing framework. If a child's schema for reading does not include an appropriate place to "file" the new information, the brain must create a new

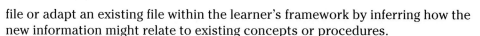

file or adapt an existing file within the learner's framework by inferring how the new information might relate to existing concepts or procedures.

As learners, we can add to, change, or create a new schema. When confronted with new information:

- We may assimilate it into our existing schema without making any changes to the overall schema.
- We may realize that our existing schema is inadequate for the new knowledge and modify our existing schema accordingly.
- We may create a new schema to address the inconsistencies between an old schema and the newly acquired information.

Children's various schemata for oral and written language continually change over time. As teachers plan learning experiences, the schemata children have for particular topics, events, and so on must be considered in order to engage them in comprehensible activities. This is particularly important for children who are learning English or lack extensive experiences with print outside of school.

A major change for children as they transition from oral to written language is developing an understanding of concepts about print and how words are learned. What concepts about print do readers and writers need to understand? The next section will answer this important question.

CONCEPTS ABOUT PRINT

Children's concepts about written language develop slowly as they begin to realize that the print around them has meaning. From the many meaningful interactions young children have with more knowledgeable readers and writers, their interest in language and print emerges. With assistance, children begin to internalize meanings for print, just as they internalized speech. They begin to notice that funny-shaped symbols reoccur in their name, in their favorite cereal, and on billboards that advertise favorite places or foods. Children's interest in print provides wonderful opportunities for knowledgeable adults to help them begin to connect sounds and symbols and understand that there is a relationship between speech and print.

Basic to all reading and writing is an understanding about the rules of print. To play a game like soccer we must know and understand the rules of the game. Without this knowledge we would have difficulty being a successful player, even if we observe others playing the game. Print also has rules that readers must understand to be successful participants (Clay, 1979). The rules or conventions of print that are most essential for beginning readers include:

- permanence of print,
- directionality of print,
- concept of word, and
- language to talk about print.

Permanence of Print

My son, Steve, taught me about permanence of print when he took a favorite book to his babysitter's house. Steve was surprised that Nancy, his babysitter, read the book just as I read it. Before that episode, I had not realized that Steve might think print in books could change from reading to reading. If print could move inside of books as it does on television or on the computer screen, children might come to the conclusion that stories and words could change from reading to reading. Young children who do not expect that print in books is permanent may not be able to use their remembrance of past readings to predict words or events in the text. Expecting stories and words in books to remain the same from reading to reading allows print to become predictable. Children begin to notice details and patterns that aid in distinguishing letters and words from one another.

To emphasize the permanence of print, children must notice that rereading familiar texts yields the same story or text with each reading. We can also emphasize permanence through rereadings of children's dictations that they have watched being recorded. Such instructional techniques will be examined in Chapter 8 when we explore shared and interactive writing.

Directionality of Print

Concepts about directionality of print are essential to success in reading and writing, but they develop slowly, through many experiences with print (Clay, 1979). When children observe us tracking print, when we slide our finger or a pointer along under words as we read, the left-to-right direction of reading English can be observed. The same directional movement can also be observed when children watch us write.

Concepts about directionality of print include the following:

- Books have fronts and backs; we read a book from front to back.
- We read print, not pictures.
- There is a right-side-up to print.
- We read the left page before the right page when text is on both pages.
- We read left to right, top to bottom on a page.
- When we finish one line of print we make a return sweep, returning to the left side of the page and dropping down one line to continue reading.
- Words in a sentence must be arranged in a certain left-to-right order, or syntax, to make sense in the English language (e.g., "here is a cat" and "cat is here a" do not communicate the same ideas).

Through many demonstrations of page turning, tracking of print, and watching spoken language be written by more knowledgeable others, children begin to understand that our written language does have rules.

Through children's desire to be understood, they have already internalized many rules for meaningful use of oral language. Interactions with print, especially in school, need to provide similar meaningful experiences to focus children's attention on learning the rules of written language. To be effective

Active involvement with others is the basis for learning, both in and out of school.

teachers of young children, then, we must understand the processes by which we can guide them to connect their knowledge of oral language with written language.

Language to Talk about Print

There is a language that teachers use to talk about reading and writing with children. To understand the importance of this language we must think back to our discussion of principles for learning and teaching in Chapter 1. As more knowledgeable readers or writers help children learn by demonstrating reading or writing, they use language to clarify their demonstrations and call attention to certain behaviors that might not be noticed. For example, when my daughter, Heather (age 3), and I read bedtime stories I would say, "Let's start at the *front* of the book so we can read the whole story," as I would turn the book to the front and point to the front cover. I did this because she had a tendency to begin at the back of a new book, working right to left instead of left to right through the book.

In addition to *front,* what other words or phrases might be used when we talk about print? When reading a book with a young child we might use words such as *front, back, title, author, page, beginning, end, top, bottom, left, right, line, sentence, word(s), letters(s), capital letter, period, question mark, quotation marks,* or *exclamation point.* Understanding this language will be essential to a child's future success in literacy. It is particularly important that children for whom English is not their first language receive instruction to develop an understanding of this academic language to support their academic success (Cummins, 1981). The development of everyday conversational language may not support children's learning of these concepts.

Children's schema for print will be limited by their prior literacy experiences. The print language that children know will have developed through experiences in which a reader or writer talked about print and demonstrated the meaning of the "print" language. Vygotsky (1962) suggests that competence in oral language enables us to control our thinking. If we apply his ideas to print we might say that knowing the language to talk about print can help children gain control over their thinking about print. The English language learners in your classroom will be doubly challenged by the need to learn English words as well as the specialized meanings of those words when you use them to talk about print.

To understand the language of print, children require more knowledgeable readers and writers to demonstrate to them the use of print language in the context of meaningful reading and writing activities. Children, in turn, need to be encouraged to demonstrate their understandings of print language, especially English language learners, so that we can understand when misconceptions occur.

Making Connections . . .

Find out what a young child knows about books and print. Administer a Concept about Print (CAP) assessment found in the assessment section near the end of this chapter.

🍎 PRINCIPLES OF WRITTEN LANGUAGE

Read here to find a definition of *metalinguistic awareness.*

"There are uniform rules governing the relationship between sounds and symbols, between different kinds of words, and between ideas in a paragraph. While children may form some rudimentary ideas about the structure of language as they acquire meta-linguistic awareness, these ideas become crystallized as the child learns to read and write" (Bedrova & Leong, 1996, p. 103). *Metalinguistic awareness* means the ability to reflect on and think about the language being used. For example, a child may have a vague understanding that words make up sentences, but when that child participates in creating sentences that are written, the idea of "word" becomes clearer.

Through extensive experiences with written language, emerging writers demonstrate a developing understanding of principles that govern print (Clay, 1975). Over time, their writing shows a growing awareness of the details of print, as shown in Figure 2.2, through the following principles:

- 🍎 recurring principle,
- 🍎 generative principle,
- 🍎 sign concept,
- 🍎 flexibility principle, and
- 🍎 directionality.

Recurring Principle

Children begin to notice that the same shapes occur repeatedly in English words. They demonstrate their awareness of these recurring shapes by using one or two shapes (perhaps a hump, loop, or cross) over and over again to fill pages of paper.

FIGURE 2.2
Examples of principles of written language.

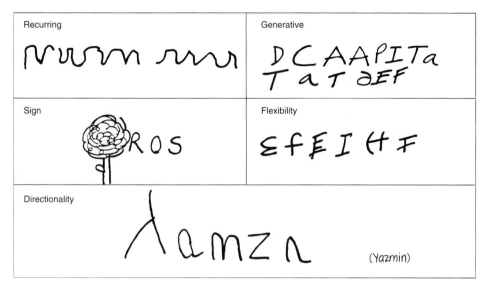

Generative Principle

As children notice more of the detail of writing, they use several letters repeatedly (often letters in their name), but vary the patterns or combinations. Children's repeated use of some letters suggests their observation of the variety of arrangements of letters that can be used to generate words.

Sign Concept

Children must come to understand the arbitrary nature of signs in written language, in contrast to graphic representations, which are not arbitrary. To facilitate communication, people who use a particular language agree to use the same word to label a particular object or idea. For example, we agree that in English, the letters *r-o-s-e* will stand for a particular type of flower that is quite fragrant, but also has thorns. The choice of the letters *r-o-s-e* is arbitrary. The choice is not necessarily related to the object itself (rose), but speakers of English agree to let the letters *r-o-s-e* represent this particular flower, just as a picture of a rose represents the flower.

Flexibility Principle

As children's familiarity with print grows, they begin to notice that letters share similar lines and shapes. For example, upon discovering that some letters can be made by arrangements of horizontal and vertical lines, children will experiment. A capital *I* can be made by adding a horizontal line at the bottom of a *T*. A capital *E* can be made by adding a horizontal line to the bottom of an *F*. As they begin to discover flexibility in print, they will experiment with various symbols to see which are allowable in English, such as adding lines to *H* or *L* to see if they can make other letters. Another aspect of the flexibility principle is children's recognition that letters have an upper- and lowercase form, can be written in manuscript or cursive, and can be made in different sizes and fonts.

Directionality

English writing is linear. It is laid out from left to right and top to bottom on a page. The orientation of letters to one another is important. Letters must face in a particular direction on a page. In addition, letters must be in a particular order to make words. In the natural world an object can change its orientation and still be that object. For example, a cup can be turned upside down, but it is still a cup. However, if the letter *b* is turned upside down it becomes a *p*.

Making Connections . . .

Collect several samples of young children's writing (preschool through early first grade). What do you notice? Compare the samples to the descriptions discussed in this "Principles of Written Language" section. Can you see evidence of children's experimentation with any of the five principles (similar to Figure 2.2)? What does children's writing suggest to you about their current understandings about print?

FOUNDATIONS FOR DECODING PRINT

Read here to find a definition of *decoding*.

Good readers are good decoders. In reading materials that are appropriate, *decoding* is the ability to accurately pronounce words, regular and irregular, in ways that are consistent with the conventions of written English. For skilled readers, decoding is so automatic that it requires virtually no conscious effort, so the reader can devote full attention to the task of comprehending text. Children in the emergent stage are not yet decoders, but they should be guided to begin developing the skills that lead to fluid decoding.

Fluid decoding involves the orchestration of:

- the automatic recognition of *sight words* both regular and irregular, that appear frequently in text;
- the use of *context,* relating background knowledge and language to the contextual clues provided by a text; and
- the application of *phonics* and *morphemic analysis,* using the sounds of letters and groups of letters (chunks) to pronounce words that are not recognized automatically.

High-Frequency Sight Words

Many words in English appear quite frequently in texts, so it is best for readers to recognize these words automatically, rather than having to take time to figure out each word. These words are commonly referred to as *high-frequency sight words.* Some high-frequency words are not easily decoded because they do not sound like their spellings might suggest (Cunningham, 2005). Therefore, it is best for readers to recognize them automatically.

A large storehouse of sight words is necessary for the development of fluent reading (Holdaway, 1980; National Institute of Child Health and Human Development, 2000). Reviews of research suggest that sight words are stored in memory by linking distinctive spelling features to the phonological (speech sound) structure of words in memory (Ehri, 1991). As a word takes on meaning for a reader and the reader notices enough detail in the word to distinguish it from other words, the reader is able to store the word in memory for later use.

Meaningful words are easier for readers to remember. Familiar words from children's home environment are often the first words they are able to recall automatically, such as their own name, *mom, love,* and the like. Reading environmental print is possible because children have connected the distinguishing contexts of such words, such as McDonald's golden arches®, with personal experience. Words become familiar and recognized automatically through repeated exposure and the efforts of children to make meaning from their experience.

Automatic recognition of irregular words becomes especially important because they are not decoded as their letter patterns indicate they should sound. For example:

- *Said* is pronounced with a short *e* sound like *sed,* not a long sound like *sade.*
- *Have* is pronounced with a short *a* sound like *hav,* not a long a sound like *have.*
- *Of* is pronounced with a short *u* and consonant *v* sound like *uv,* not short *o* and consonant *f* sound like *off.*

Until children have a firm concept of word and knowledge of letter-sound patterns, they will recognize few words automatically.

The first words that beginning readers recognize automatically are usually supported by strong emotional context. Sylvia Ashton-Warner (1963) capitalized on strong emotional context for learning words when she used "key word vocabulary" to teach non-English-speaking children in New Zealand to read. Children selected favorite words they wanted to learn to read to have as their key words. The words were printed on cards and used as the primary source of reading material in literacy activities. Ashton-Warner found that key words served as a base for building an initial bank of sight words. Sight words can then serve as an anchor for developing knowledge of letter-sound patterns in words.

Two widely used lists of high-frequency sight words are the Dolch 220 list and Fry's Instant Words. The Dolch 220 list was developed by Edward William Dolch, Ph.D. in his book, *Problems in Reading* (1948). The words he identified as high usage have held up over time. A more extensive list of 1,000 high-use words, known as Fry's Instant Words (Fry, Kress, & Fountoukidis, 2000), is also available. The words on Fry's list are separated into levels of difficulty. The words, along with numerous teaching activities, can be easily found by searching the Internet with the term "sight words."

Read here to find a definition of *high-frequency sight words.*

For more information about sight words, visit http://www.eduplace.com/rdg/res/frequent.html, http://www.createdbyteachers.com/sightfreemain.html, http://www14.brinkster.com/readwrite/sightwords2.htm, and http://www.literacyconnections.com/SightWordPractice.html.

Context

Read here to find a definition of *context*.

Context is information that is available to us in our surroundings from which we can make meaning. An everyday example of the use of context might be opening the door to leave your house in the morning, only to see dark clouds on the distant horizon. Familiarity with the significance of dark clouds suggests that an umbrella might be needed. The decision to take an umbrella results from meaning derived from context clues.

Young children already know how to use the context of oral language as a check for meaning. Literacy instruction must help them learn that context can also be used in written text as a means of confirming the meaning of unfamiliar words. Young readers find the use of context especially helpful when they have only partial knowledge of the phonics or morphemic patterns within an unfamiliar word. They are able to use that partial knowledge to predict a word that fits the current context and confirm it through clues from meaning and language.

Context is used most effectively in conjunction with phonics and/or morphemic analysis. As young children begin to read, teachers should always combine prompts to "sound out words" with asking children, "What word could have these letters and make sense here?" This is a "context + something else" strategy that can be used successfully by children at all developmental stages (Holdaway, 1980). Over time, as children learn more about words, their use of the strategy becomes more complex. For example:

- An emergent reader may use an illustration (context) + beginning sound to predict and confirm an unfamiliar word.
- An early developing reader may use context + beginning, middle, and ending sounds to predict and confirm an unfamiliar word.
- A later developing reader may use context + chunks of letters to decode and confirm an unfamiliar word.

In each case, context provides a means of cross-checking for meaning following the use of various visual cues within an unfamiliar word.

Emergent readers are capable of using meaningful contexts to help them understand words. While listening to texts read aloud by a teacher or parent, children are able to use their knowledge of oral language to identify the meaning of

Read here to find a definition of *aural context*.

many words. *Aural context,* the meaningful context of spoken language, is used to predict and understand words. This ability to think and arrive at meaning within a particular context is the foundation for cross-checking decoding when children begin to read.

As we will learn in Chapter 4, reading aloud to children provides a guided aural context that helps them learn to make meaning with written language. Beginning readers should be encouraged to use familiar words and ideas to make meaning. As we read aloud and pause at appropriate points in a text, children should be encouraged to supply a predictable word.

Read here to find a definition of *decoding*.

Fostering contextual thinking should eventually lead children to read independently with an eye for words that make sense in context. To learn to *decode* print in English, thinking in context must include learning to use visual cues (phonics, morphemes, sight words), cross-checked by meaning and knowledge of language (context). Because emergent readers are just learning to decode individual letters and associate those letters with representative sounds, they are not usually ready to decode whole words in a text. They can, however, isolate the first sound in words and make predictions about what might start with a particular letter and make sense in the text. Rereading familiar text and confirming distinctive words in a familiar context also helps beginning readers begin to understand what it means to decode a word.

Phonics and Morphemic Analysis

As children begin to read, they learn to recognize that letters of the alphabet represent sounds in spoken words. To become proficient readers and writers they must learn to "map" letters to the sounds they represent. Mapping letters and chunks of letters to sounds enables children to begin to decipher unfamiliar words.

Phonics

The term *phonics* actually refers to connecting an individual sound in speech (phoneme) to the letter or combination of letters (graphemes) that represent that sound. When readers encounter an unfamiliar word, they need an efficient way to determine a possible pronunciation of the word to match against words they know. Knowledge of the possibilities of consonant and vowel patterns in English is an aid to decoding, or determining how to pronounce a given word. This knowledge is also an aid to developing skill in conventional spelling of words.

> **Read here to find a definition of *phonics*.**

Understanding that words are composed of a stream of sounds, or phonemes, serves as an anchor for connecting sounds with letters of the alphabet. This knowledge is referred to as *phonological awareness*. Developing phonological awareness is a main focus of the emergent stage. Extensive and intensive exposures to language, both oral and written, provide opportunities for children to refine their phonological awareness and make connections to recurring visual patterns in the English language.

> **Read here to find a definition of *phonological awareness*.**

Researchers have been able to identify levels of awareness, with the more complex levels having a strong relationship to the developing understanding of letter-sound relationships and learning to spell (Griffith, 1991; Juel, Griffith, & Gough, 1986), as well as a strong relationship to skilled reading (Adams, 1990; Slocum, O'Connor, & Jenkins, 1993; Stahl & Murray, 1994; Wagner, Torgensen, Laughon, Simmons, & Rashotti, 1993; Yopp, 1988; Yopp & Yopp, 2000). It is the ability to manipulate the phonemes within words, however, that appears to have the strongest relationship to developing skilled reading and writing abilities (Morris, Bloodgood, & Perney, 2003). This ability is referred to as *phonemic awareness*.

> **Read here to find a definition of *phonemic awareness*.**

The difficulty with phonics for many children is that letters or combinations of letters in English can represent more than one sound. At best, teaching children to use visual cues, such as familiar letter-sound patterns, to decode unfamiliar words provides a means for making a prediction that is confirmed by other language cues such as the meaning of words and the structure of phrases and sentences in English.

> Example: The letters *ea* can represent more than one sound, as in m*ea*t (long *e*), br*ea*d (short *e*), and st*ea*k (long *a*). A reader must know the sounds that are possible to select the correct pronunciation that fits the meaning of the sentence.

Example: Consider the word *bow* — *The bow was made of purple ribbon*. The letters *ow* can be decoded in two ways—as "ow" and "oh." The pronunciation of this word cannot be determined without considering the context in which it is used.

Knowledge of the possibilities of letter-sound patterns is very important, especially to early reading and writing, but phonics knowledge is only part of the knowledge children need to be competent readers and writers.

Morphemic Analysis

Recognition of the *morphemes,* or meaning units, of a word—base word, root, prefix, suffix — can be helpful in determining the overall meaning of an unfamiliar word. Many words in the English language are composed of two or more morphemes that have meaning. Using knowledge of morphemes to decode an unfamiliar word is referred to as *morphemic analysis.*

Read here to find definitions of *morphemes* and *morphemic analysis.*

Example: *Doghouse* is a compound word composed of two base words (dog + house); when combined each unit contributes to the overall meaning of the new word—a house for a dog.

Example: *Overdrawn* is also a compound word composed of two base words (over + drawn), but when the units are combined a new meaning emerges. Determining the meaning of *overdrawn* requires knowledge beyond merely decoding the two base words.

Effective use of morphemic analysis relies on a reader's ability to see meaning units within a larger word, draw upon phonics knowledge to determine the pronunciation of each unit, then blend the units into a pronounceable word and use context to confirm its meaning.

Skill in morphemic analysis becomes increasingly important as children begin to encounter more complex words. Readers begin using morphemic knowledge as early as first grade when they encounter words like *jumping, butterfly,* and *can't.* As words with morphemes begin to appear in children's reading materials with greater frequency, teachers must help children develop strategies to independently recognize and understand word meanings.

DECODING IN THE EMERGENT STAGE

As children begin to read, they recognize that letters of the alphabet represent the sounds of spoken words. Children "map" these letters to the sounds they represent. This mapping enables children to begin to decipher whole words. By breaking up words into their component sounds, or phonemes, children can "sound out" words. For example, the child sees the letters *d-o-g* and thinks of the three phonemes (/d/, /o/, /g/) that make up the word. For children who decode easily, the brain automatically separates sounds into distinct phonemes. With practice, decoding becomes automatic for the normally progressing reader. Children see words and read them without struggling, even if they don't know the meaning of every word. Decoding is a foundation that children need to read quickly and fluently.

During the emergent stage, when children are forming concepts about words in print, they should also explore the sounds of language and learn the names of letters of the alphabet. The focus on letter-sound relationships in this stage is through:

- phonemic awareness,
- naming and recognizing letters of the alphabet, and
- associating alphabet letters with the most prevalent phonemes they represent.

Children need fairly extensive experienes with print to understand how they should attend to the meaning units of language within words, such as base words and word endings (jump + ing). Morphemic analysis takes on greater importance in later stages of development.

Skill in phonemic awareness, the foundation for breaking the code of written language, begins with children's awareness of spoken words, then syllables, then parts of syllables, and finally individual phonemes within words. It is this ability to deal with any size unit of sound that becomes crucial at later stages of development.

Research in emergent reading and writing suggests that developing skill in phonemic awareness can be broken into levels of knowledge and/or skill (Beach, 1990; Fox & Routh, 1984; Griffith & Klesius, 1990; Maclean, Bryant, & Bradley, 1987; Yopp, 1988; Yopp & Yopp, 2000). Emergent readers should focus on these aspects of sounds in words:

- rhyming words,
- syllable units,
- onsets and rimes, and
- phonemes.

Phonological skills begin at an auditory level, but become the basis for connecting speech to print as readers learn to decode written symbols that are used to form words in print. Such knowledge in reading and writing lies more in training than in age or maturation (Adams, 1990). The ability to relate phonemes and print in kindergarten is a predictor of success in reading in the primary grades (Morris, Bloodgood, & Perney, 2003)

Rhyming

According to Adams (1990), the most primitive level of phonological awareness is simply having enough of an ear for sound to remember rhyming words more easily than nonrhyming words. At this level, an emerging reader would be able to recall some rhyming portions of familiar nursery rhymes, songs, or chants more easily than a child without this level of phonemic awareness (Maclean et al., 1987).

A child who is developing phonological awareness can recall portions of a rhyme.

Humpty Dumpty sat on a wall,
Humpty Dumpty had a great fall.

In addition to remembering rhymes, children should also be able to discriminate words that do not rhyme, or sound the same. At this level of awareness, an emergent reader should be able to sense that a word does not sound like other words in a group.

cat   *rat*   <u>*sock*</u>   *mat*

A child should be able to identify *sock* as sounding different from the other words that rhyme. The child may not be able to articulate what is different, but should intuitively recognize a difference.

Syllable Units

Young children already have some experience with hearing words that have been segmented into syllables. Chants and songs from early childhood are filled with rhythms based on syllables.

Twink-le twink-le lit-tle star,

how I won-der what you are.

Clapping or counting syllables begins to sensitize the ear to sound. Attending to the syllable within words is actually attending to the rhythm in words. Teachers help children learn to listen for larger sound parts, syllables, before they ask children to listen for individual phonemes within a syllable.

Teacher asks, "What parts do you hear in *twinkle?*"

Children say, "Twink-le."

Notice that the teacher did not use the term *syllables* with the children. That terminology is not necessary at this stage of their development.

As children work with syllables, they should learn to segment, blend, match, isolate, and change syllable units in words. This flexibility with language will make future learning easier.

Blending syllables means that children listen to a word "stretched out like a rubber band" into syllables, then push the syllables back together to form a word.

Teacher says *"dog _____ house"*

Children say "doghouse."

Teacher asks, "What is the first part you hear in this word?

Children say, "dog."

Matching syllables in words requires children to segment a word into syllables then compare two syllables.

Teacher asks, "Do these words start the same? *starfish—starlight*"

Children say, "Yes."

Teacher asks, "What part do you hear first in *starfish?*"

Children say, "star."

Teacher asks, "What part do you hear first in *starlight?*"

Children say, "star."

When children answer "star," they demonstrate the ability to isolate a syllable in a word.

After isolating a syllable, it is possible for children to change the syllable to create a new word.

Teacher asks, "What part do you hear first in *starlight?*"

Children say, "star."

Teacher asks, "What word can we make if we change *star* to *sun?*"

Children say, "sunlight."

Begin manipulating syllables with compound words so that children's segmenting, blending, matching, or changing is meaningful. This is easier than a syllable that represents sound, but no meaning, such as *ta-ble.* When children can play with compound words, they become more successful at manipulating other syllables.

Teacher asks, "What part do you hear first in *noodle?*"

Children say, "noo."

Teacher asks, "What word can we make if we change *noo* to *doo?*"

Children say, "doodle."

When children are able to segment syllables within longer words, they are ready to try splitting the syllable itself to make an onset and a rime.

Onset and Rime

Syllables typically are made of an *onset* (beginning consonant sound) and a *rime* (the remainder of the syllable beginning with the vowel, followed by one or more consonants).

Read here to find definitions of *onset* and *rime*.

man = m- *(onset)* -an *(rime)*

ship = sh- *(onset)* -ip *(rime)*

Syllables that begin with a vowel sound (such as *at, in, up*) do not have an onset, only a rime. Splitting a syllable into an onset and a rime is a skill that precedes being able to break a syllable into individual phonemes. Children can be taught to split, or segment, syllables by first listening for the onset in a word.

Teacher says, "bag."

Children say, "b."

Isolating the sound of the onset, /b/, is a first step toward work with initial consonants. Later, children learn to connect the sound, /b/, to the letter shape and name, *b.* This skill, being able to identify the beginning sound of a word (checked by the context of the text), is a key decoding strategy for beginning readers.

Splitting a syllable and isolating the rime makes it possible for children to begin to identify medial vowels.

Teacher says, "bag."

Children say, "-ag."

In a rime, vowel sounds are usually stable and predictable. Hearing and repeating the rime portion of a syllable enables students to build skills that will eventually support learning about vowel patterns and making new words by exchanging onsets, or initial, consonant sounds. The vowel sound is easier for children to discriminate when it is heard at the beginning of a rime, as in *-ag.* Learning to listen for chunks of words—chunks that contain a manageable number of sounds—provides an essential piece of becoming a good speller.

After children are successful in splitting a syllable into an onset and a rime, sorting or categorizing activities are appropriate. To sort or categorize by beginning sound is a two-step process requiring syllable splitting, then sound matching. A child must separate the onset from the rime within a syllable and decide which phoneme is similar to the onset.

Looking at three pictures—bird, girl, and ball—the child thinks, b-bird, g-girl, b-ball, then compares the beginning consonants to find the two that sound the same and feel the same way in the mouth.

This thinking strategy is essential for making generalizations about the sounds that letters represent. Changing beginning and ending sounds to make new words is a natural extension of children's play with language. For example, children often play with each other's names by changing phonemes, such as Heather Feather or Silly Billy. Changing phonemes begins as an oral word-play activity and later becomes a decoding or spelling activity as children make associations with letters of the alphabet. Changing the beginning sound or onset in the word can make *man, ran, fan, tan,* and *van.* The skill of changing phonemes gives children flexibility to decode or encode many words that have related letter-sound patterns.

Phonemes

Ultimately, children should be able to show the sounds they hear in words by clapping or tapping an appropriate number of times. Discriminating the vowel in the middle of a syllable presents the greatest challenge.

Teacher says /m/-/a/-/n/.
Children clap three times (once for each phoneme).

Hearing the number of sounds in a word helps children stretch words for themselves, hear phonemes, and begin to match sound to symbols in order to write words.

Teacher stretches "man" so children hear each phoneme.
Children say, "/m/_____/a/_____/n/."
Teacher reverses the process and says "/m/_____/a/_____/n/," emphasizing each phoneme.
Children blend the phonemes and say "man."

Changing phonemes in a word helps children hear how words can be related to each other by sharing particular letter patterns or sounds.

Teacher asks, "What do you hear at the beginning of *bell?*"
Children say, "/b/."
Teacher asks, "What word can we make if we change */b/* to */sm/?*"
Children say, "smell."

Changing the ending sound of the rime in the word can make *cat, cab, cap, calf,* and *cast.*

Teacher asks, "What do you hear at the end of cat?*"*
Children say, "/t/."

Teacher asks, "What word can we make if we change /t/ to /p/?"
Children say, "cap."

When children progress to the developing stage, where they are "glued to print," they may decode words as individual phonemes, saying each phoneme aloud just as the teacher did in our example. Children who are able to decode and blend sounds are then able to hear the recognizable word.

To read and write competently, children must be able to blend, split, or change syllables in print. Consequently, as children are developing phonological awareness they also should be learning about the printed symbols that represent sounds.

RECOGNIZING LETTERS OF THE ALPHABET

As children become aware of sounds in words they also begin to notice print in the world around them. Children who are learning to speak English must come to understand that:

> all twenty-six of these strange little symbols that comprise the alphabet are worth learning and discriminating one from the other because [they stand] for . . . the sounds that occur in spoken words. (Adams, 1990, p. 245)

With exposure to print, children typically begin to show an interest in what the print represents. When that occurs, it is appropriate to help them focus on the symbols used to create words, the letters of the alphabet.

Reviews of research suggest that instruction in letters of the alphabet be sequenced in the following manner:

- Learn to say letter names, such as the ABC song, and recognize those sounds as names of letters of the alphabet.
- Match letter names to their corresponding shapes.
- Match letter names and shapes with corresponding sounds. (Adams, 1990)

Letter Names

Knowing letter names is a good predictor of reading achievement and seems to transfer to an interest in learning letter-sound relationships. Prior to coming to school, most English-speaking children are introduced to the names of letters by learning to sing "The Alphabet Song." It is often sung to the tune of "Twinkle, Twinkle Little Star." A popular version goes like this:

> *A, B, C, D, E, F, G*
> *H, I, J, K, L, M, N, O, P*
> *Q, R, S, and T, U, V*
> *W, X, Y, and Z*
> *Now I sing my ABCs*
> *Next time won't you sing with me?*

Similar alphabet songs, chants, and rhymes help children develop an ear for the sound of letter names when spoken. The sound of letter names becomes an anchor in children's concepts about words and print to which letter shapes and eventually letter sounds can be attached. Having a name for letter shapes hastens children's ability to generalize similiarites about letters across various print experiences.

Letter Shapes

Matching names of letters with shapes can be challenging for children. The shapes of letters are not graphically memorable; that is, the shape of a letter has very little to do with the name it was arbitrarily given. Instruction must help children learn to attend to distinctive features of print as they make associations between names and shapes.

It is important to remember that there are actually four sets of letter shapes that children must learn over time:

- 🍎 manuscript lowercase,
- 🍎 manuscript uppercase or capitals,
- 🍎 cursive lowercase, and
- 🍎 cursive uppercase or capitals.

Before entering school, children typically know the most about uppercase manuscript letters. Knowledge of lowercase manuscript letters, however, is most important for learning to read.

For children with limited print experience, it is best to avoid introducing both upper- and lowercase letters at the same time. Being faced with two distinctly different shapes that bear the same name may be confusing. If a choice must be made, Adams (1990) suggests that instruction in kindergarten should emphasize uppercase letters and instruction in first grade should emphasize lowercase letters.

Instruction in the formation of letters that focuses on the contrasts between letters hastens children's ability to recognize and distinguish letter shapes. Discriminating letter shapes requires children to attend to the visual features of letters. Many children do not naturally notice the subtle differences in the lines and curves used to form letters.

The difference between making a C and a G is a short horizontal line at the opening of the G.

Becoming sensitive to the differences among letter shapes develops over time, through many varied print experiences. It is best to separate instruction about confusable forms of letters, such as *b* and *d,* until at least one of the forms is known well.

Children must also understand that it is the position of a letter in relation to other letters that enables us to know the name of a letter shape.

b turned upside-down becomes *p*

b reversed becomes *d*

p reversed becomes *q*

n reversed and turned upside-down becomes *u*

In the real world, a pencil remains a pencil regardless of its position or orientation to other objects. In contrast, children must learn that the position or orientation of a particular letter shape can change the name we give it.

Varied experiences with print should lead children to realize that letters can be found in many different types and sizes of fonts. Children's experiences with print in their neighborhood environment have already shown them some possibilities that they may not yet understand.

The letter g may appear in many forms, such as

G g G g G g G g

To become independent readers, children must be able to genralize their knowledge about letters to new forms. When letter shapes are highly familiar and able to be discriminated, introducing letter sounds to children will be more successful.

CONNECTING LETTERS TO SOUNDS

To unlock the sounds of unfamiliar words, children must be able to connect letter names and shapes to the sounds they represent. For instruction in letter sounds to make sense to children, they must have developed some phonemic awareness and the concept that letters make up words in print. Without an awareness of sound within words, children will find little purpose in letter-sound activities.

Children who know the names of letters find it easier to make connections to their associated sounds. Eighteen letters of the alphabet have sounds that consistently resemble the letter's name. Knowing the names of the letters, then, becomes an anchor for some letter sounds.

The letters A, E, I, O, and U name long-vowel sounds.
The letters B, D, F, J, K, L, M, N, P, R, S, T, V, and Z name consonant sounds.

To aid associations between letter names and shapes with their corresponding sounds, letter shapes can be introduced through pictures that integrate the shape of a familiar object with the shape of the letter (Ehri, Duffner, & Wilce, 1984). The name of the object should begin with the corresponding letter sound, and the pictorial representation should include the letter shape.

Lowercase *b* is presented as a baseball bat and ball.
Lowercase *h* is presented as a house with a chimney.
Uppercase *M* is presented as a mountain.
Uppercase *V* is presented as a vase of flowers.

Pictorial mnemonics, such as those shown in Figure 2.3, are remembered by very young children (Pressley, 1997) and can increase the rate at which they learn letter-sound associations (Ehri et al., 1984). Early consonant instruction that focuses on letter names and sounds that are similar is most effective.

When we say the name of the letter *b,* we also make the sound, /b/, that represents the sound of the consonant in words, such as *bell* and *rib.*

FIGURE 2.3
Pictorial mnemonics for
alphabet letters.

We refer to letters, such as *b,* as letter-name consonants because the letter name is a clue to the consonant sound. There are 13 single consonants that have letter names that consistently represent the consonant sound in the initial position in a syllable. Because of utility and ease of learning, these consonants should be taught before other, less consistent consonants. The letter-name consonants are identified in Figure 2.4. Notice that though all of the consonants name their sound, some do it at the beginning of the name and others at the end.

The letters *h* and *q* are consistent in the sound they represent, but the letter names do not identify their consonant sound. These consonants challenge children's early understanding about the sounds that consonants represent. Emergent readers and writers may overgeneralize the use of letter-name clues, trying to make all consonants fit the letter-name strategy.

The letter name *h,* pronounced "aaa-ch," represents the sound "huh." It is frequently confused with the sound for /ch/. The single consonant *h* typically appears at the beginning of a syllable.

The letter name *q,* pronounced "ku," represents the sound "kwuh." *Q* is always followed by the vowel u and found only at the beginning of syllables. An awareness of vowels is helpful in decoding qu.

Finally, the letters *c, g, s, w, x,* and *y* represent variable sounds, depending upon their placement within the syllables of words and the letters that follow them.

Example: *c* like k (hard c) — cat, coat, cut
c like s (soft c) — cent, city

g (hard g) — gate, goat, gum
g like j (soft g) — gem, giant

s at the beginning — saw, sugar
s at the end — his, dress

w at the beginning — want
w at the end — saw, bow

y at the beginning — yes, yellow
y at the end — fly, baby

Sound at Beginning of Name			Sound at End of Name		
Shape	**Name**	**Sound**	**Shape**	**Name**	**Sound**
b	"bee"	"bbb"	f	"eff"	"fff"
d	"dee"	"ddd"	l	"ell"	"lll"
j	"jay"	"jjj"	m	"emm"	"mmm"
k	"kay"	"kkk"	n	"enn"	"nnn"
p	"pee"	"ppp"	r	"arr"	"rrr"
t	"tee"	"ttt"	s	"ess"	"sss"
v	"vee"	"vvv"			
z	"zee"	"zzz"			

FIGURE 2.4
Letter names that correspond to consonant sounds.

As we help children associate a letter name with a symbol and a particular sound, we must remain keenly aware that the application of this knowledge to the decoding of words will become dependent upon the arrangement of letters within words.

WRITING ALPHABET LETTERS

Handwriting instruction in school typically focuses on either a traditional "ball and stick" method of forming letters or an italicized form of manuscript that reflects the cursive forms of each letter. Traditional handwriting methods have a long history of instruction in elementary schools, dating back to the 1890s. Italicized methods became popular in the 1960s.

Research suggests that the handwriting method selected for instruction should:

> For additional information on styles of letter formation, see *http://www.ericfacility.net/ericdigests/ed272923.html*, *http://www.zanerbloser.com*, and *http://66.113.195.73/*.

- 🍎 Provide opportunities for children to verbalize the rules of letter formation and to evaluate their own success. Talking aloud as they write helps the brain to bind the visual, motor, and phonological images of the letter together (Adams, 1990).
- 🍎 Combine verbal and visual feedback, such as teacher explanation and demonstration, with rewriting or reinforcement (Furner, 1985).

Regardless of the program, copying letters leads to better results than just tracing, but only for letters that are familiar. When verbal instructions are added, such as rules for correct letter formation, children's performance improves (Peck, Askov, & Fairchild, 1980). Verbal instructions by the teacher that students are encouraged to repeat can become a "script in the head" for children to draw upon as a verbal reminder that supports the physical act of letter formation.

Regardless of the method chosen, handwriting instruction should provide consistent and patient guidance to develop an understanding of the directions in which letters are formed in order to achieve fluid and legible handwriting. Instruction should occur in small increments and on a daily basis until the fluid and legible production of letters is mastered. Handwriting should be taught daily, with about 10 minutes of teacher-guided instruction and an additional 5 minutes of individual practice time. Letters should be organized in groups with similar strokes and frequency of use. Instruction periods should end well before children show signs of frustration.

In the early stages of writing letters of the alphabet, children will not necessarily have accurate mental images of letters. They should be taught to write a letter and check its formation against a model. As they write, they should be encouraged to talk aloud about:

- 🍎 the name of the letter,
- 🍎 the directions they move the pencil while forming the letter, and
- 🍎 the sound the letter can represent.

Talking aloud as they write helps the brain to bind the visual, motor, and phonological images of the letter together (Adams, 1990). Helping children make connections between letter names, shapes, and sounds is accomplished best in the context of real reading and writing activities. Remember that handwriting is developmental. Size, quantity, position, and spacing of letters improve with age and experience (Tan-Lin, 1981). Typical students in the latter half of kindergarten have the foundation skills needed to begin formal handwriting instruction (Marr, Widsor, & Chermak, 2001).

To find ideas to help with issues regarding handwriting instruction, see *http://www.hwtears.com/solutions2.htm.*

Making Connections . . .

Take time to interview a kindergarten and a first-grade teacher about the ways that they help young children become aware of the features of print. How do they approach the learning of letters of the alphabet and the sounds they represent? How do they introduce children to books? How do they help children learn about the relationship between talking and writing? Share your findings with your peers.

PUTTING THEORY INTO PRACTICE . . .

Developing concepts about words for emergent readers and writers is best organized around word play through music, chants, and rhymes; reading aloud and storytelling (Adams & Bruck, 1995; Beck & Juel, 1995; Yopp & Yopp, 2000); and shared/interactive writing and reading (see Chapter 8). In this portion of the chapter, we explore socially stimulating ways to engage young children in language-rich environments. Though we consider playful and engaging experiences as best for young children, we must always remember that our instruction should be deliberate and purposeful. Word study, especially the development of phonological awareness, is only one part of a balanced and integrated literacy

Emergent Readers and Writers . . .	In this stage children learn . . .
Function from preschool to early first-grade reading level.	• print has meaning, such as environmental print
They read — words in meaningful contexts and some high-frequency sight words	• print has rules
	• letters have names
	• words are made up of sounds
They write — words that range from letter strings, to initial and final consonants, to short-vowel words, to long-vowel words without long-vowel markers	• letters represent sounds in words
	• all sounds in a word can be represented by letters
	• letter names can be a clue to letter sounds
	• to discriminate initial and final single consonants
	• to acknowledge vowels in words

FIGURE 2.5
Overview of instruction in the emergent stage.

program and must be placed in the context of real reading and writing experiences (Griffith & Olson, 1992).

Figure 2.5 summarizes the focus of instruction in the emergent stage. Notice how our instructional focus is centered on helping children understand the fundamentals of print and its relationship to spoken language. We will explore ways to organize learning experiences to best serve the needs of children in this stage of development. Uses of music, oral word play, sound boxes, and sorting activities are among the activities suggested for developing awareness of sound and relationships between sounds, letter names, and letter shapes. These activities are frequently integrated with other components of balanced literacy instruction to provide extended practice for children.

USING MUSIC TO FOCUS ON SOUNDS

Rhyming

To encourage attention to sound, children must first be able to detect rhyming patterns. Songs such as "The Ants Go Marching," provide excellent opportunities for children to play with language and attend to rhyme. The main portion of the verse is:

> *The ants go marching one by one,*
> *The little one stops to have some fun,*
> *And they all go down in the ground,*
> *To get out of the sun.*

With each verse, the number of ants changes and consequently the rhyming words change (e.g., two—tie her shoe, three—scratch her knee).

Blending Syllables

The song "Clap, Clap, Clap Your Hands" provides a pattern that is useful to play with joining the syllables of two-syllable words. The pattern of the verse is:

Clap, clap, clap your hands,
Clap your hands together,
Clap, clap, clap your hands,
Clap your hands together.

Yopp and Yopp (2000) suggest the following verse to encourage the blending of syllables:

Say, say, these parts,
Say these parts together,
Say, say, say these parts,
Say these parts together.

The teacher, then, says the two syllables, and children blend the syllables together.

Teacher says, "rab" (pause) "bit."
Children say, "rabbit"
Teacher says, "farm" (pause) "er."
Children say, "farmer."

We want to select a variety of types of words, for example:

compound words (doghouse)
words with inflected suffixes (jumping, horses)
words with independent prefixes (untie)
two-syllable base words (rabbit, river, market)

Blending Phonemes

To provide practice in blending phonemes in words, you can use the tune of "If You're Happy and You Know It" (Yopp, 1992):

If you think you know this word, say it now
/m/-/oo/-/n/
If you think you know this word, say it now
/m/-/oo/-/n/
If you think you know this word,
Then tell me what you've heard,
If you think you know this word, say it now.

This activity is used with one-syllable words. Children can also be encouraged to provide segmented words for others to blend.

Splitting Syllables

To encourage identifying the onset, or beginning, consonant sound for a syllable, use a familiar tune, "Old MacDonald Had a Farm" (Yopp, 1992). The song frame would be:

> *What's the sound that starts these words:*
> *moon, man, mask?*
> */m/ is the sound that starts these words:*
> *moon, man, mask.*
> *With an/m/, /m/ here, and an/m, /m/ there,*
> *Here an/m/, there an/m/,*
> *Everywhere an/m/, /m/.*
> */m/ is the sound that starts these words:*
> *moon, man, mask.*

Onset and Rime

The song "Old MacDonald" provides an opportunity to segment onsets and rimes, depending upon the words chosen.

Segment the onset only:

> *Old MacDonald had a farm*
> *E-I-E-I-O*
> *And on his farm he had some sheep*
> *E-I-E-I-O*
> *With a sh- sh- (onset) here*
> *And a sh- sh- there*
> *Here a sh-, there a sh-*
> *Everywhere a sh- sh- . . .*

Segment onset from the rime:

> *Old MacDonald had a farm*
> *E-I-E-I-O*
> *And on his farm he had some sheep*
> *E-I-E-I-O*
> *With a sh- (onset) -eep (rime) here*
> *And a sh- -eep there*
> *Here a sh-, there an -eep*
> *Everywhere a sh- -eep . . .*

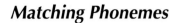

Matching Phonemes

Practice in phoneme matching helps children select a phoneme that is the same as another. Using the tune of "Jimmy Cracked Corn and I Don't Care" you might sing (Yopp, 1992):

> *Who has an /m/ (phoneme) word to share with us?*
> *Who has an /m/ word to share with use?*
> *Who has an /m/ word to share with us?*
> *It must start with the /m/ sound!*

In reply, a word is suggested and the class sings together:

> *Moon is a word that starts with /m/.*
> *Moon is a word that starts with /m/.*
> *Moon is a word that starts with /m/.*
> *Moon starts with the /m/ sound.*

Changing Phonemes

Practice adding or substituting sounds in words encourages flexibility in making new words. Yopp (1992) suggests using a part of "I've Been Working on the Railroad" that begins with "Someone's in the kitchen with Dinah."

> *I have a song that we can sing*
> *I have a song that we can sing*
> *I have a song that we can sing*
> *It goes something like this:*
> *Fe-fi-fiddly-i-o*
> *Fe-fi-fiddly-i-oooo*
> *Fe-fi-fiddly-i-o*
> *Now try it with the /m/ sound*
> *Me-Mi-Middly-i-o*
> *Me-Mi-Middly-i-oooo . . .*

Initial consonants, blends/clusters, and consonant digraphs can be used to make new words. For example:

ch-digraph — che-chi-chiddly-i-o
gr-blend — gre-gri-griddly-i-o

When children demonstrate ease of blending phonemes, splitting syllables to segment the initial phoneme, and matching phonemes, consider connecting oral activities to print. For some children, visual cues are a necessary anchor for sounds.

GAMES

Many game formats lend themselves to attention to words and sound units. Yopp and Yopp (2000) suggest "Mother, May I?". In this game children line up and ask the "mother" for permission to move a specified number of steps. Children can be asked to attend to the number of syllables (beats or chunks) in a word to determine the number of steps they may move.

> Teacher says, "Happy"
>
> Children say, "Hap-py!" (children hop twice)

The words used should vary in number of syllables, depending on children's ability to pronounce words correctly and count syllables. After learning to play the game, children can serve as the "mother." Children who play can check each other for correct syllable count. See Yopp and Yopp (2000) for numerous suggestions.

For more songs to aid in teaching phonological awareness, see *http://www. songsforteaching. homestead.com/PA.html.*

SORTING ACTIVITIES 🍎

Sorting Phonemes

In the emergent stage, children are developing their ability to discriminate initial and final consonant sounds. They do not yet recognize many words out of familiar contexts. They can, however, demonstrate their ability to focus on particular phonemes and match phonemes at the beginning and end of words by sorting small picture cards. Sorting pictures, and eventually words, provides individual and guided group opportunities to refine phonemic awareness.

When teachers ask children to distinguish between sounds, they begin with phonemes of high contrast, phonemes that sound dramatically different and are formed in different places in the mouth (e.g., b/s, m/d). They do not begin with phonemes that are low contrast, especially those formed in a similar place in the mouth (e.g., f/v, b/p, d/t). These sounds are more difficult for a young sensory learner to discriminate.

Children can sort pictures in at least two ways:

🍎 They can form their own groupings of picture cards, clustering cards they believe share the same beginning (and eventually ending) sounds (open sort).

🍎 Teachers can also guide the sorting by asking children to cluster pictures that share a particular sound (closed sort).

Sample picture cards for sorting activities can be found in Appendix B.

When children choose how to group the items for sorting, their groupings show relationships they see among the pictures. Using an open sort is a good way to assess the general level of students' understanding about a particular grouping of objects. When the teacher guides children to focus on particular groupings of items, the categories, such as making a group of all pictures that begin like *ball* and another category of pictures that do not, focuses children's attention on particular phonemes. Closed sorts enable us to assess students' understanding of specific phonetic elements.

Early sorting activities should use pictures of objects that begin with a single consonant, such as *ball*. Words that begin with more than one consonant, such as *bread* or *ship,* should not be used at this time. At this stage of development, discriminating a single consonant may be challenging enough. Two consonants, such as *br,* are difficult to separate from each other. Two consonants that represent one new sound, such as *sh,* do not represent any one consonant letter. Single consonants should be the initial focus.

An open picture sort (see Figure 2.6) could be set up in the following manner:

- Provide a group of 10 to 15 pictures that represent particular consonants for each child or pair of children.
- Children spread out their pictures and orally name each one (a child cannot sort a picture accurately that is named incorrectly).
- Children listen for the phoneme at the beginning of the word.
- They isolate and say the phoneme, such as "/b/- /b/ -/b/."
- Children place the pictures together that they think begin (or end) with the same sound.

FIGURE 2.6
Sample open picture sort.

A closed sort (see Figure 2.7) can be set up in the following manner:

🍎 Provide a group of 10 to 15 pictures that represent particular consonants for each child or pair of children.

🍎 Children spread out their pictures and orally name each one.

🍎 Direct children to select one or more example pictures to guide the forming of categories.

🍎 One picture at a time, children name the picture and listen for the phoneme at the beginning of the name.

🍎 When they are able to isolate and say the phoneme, children compare the phoneme to the example picture/sound chosen by the teacher.

🍎 Children place pictures under the appropriate example card or, if they believe a picture does not match, the card is placed in an "other" pile (discard pile).

To encourage children to isolate consonant sounds, care must be taken not to distort the pronunciation of consonants. Pronouncing a consonant in isolation usually adds a short *u* sound ("uh") after it, making /b/ sound like "buh." As much as possible, try to keep the phoneme in the context of a word, such as *b*ed or ca*b,* so children can use their knowledge of segmenting phonemes to isolate the sound.

FIGURE 2.7
Sample closed picture sort.

In early letter-sound instruction, it is important to carefully select consonants that are predictable. Consonants in which the letter names the phoneme are easier for children, because the letter names are already familiar. Letters that do not name their sound present some challenge for children in the emergent stage and should not be the focus of early phonics instruction.

To guide the sorting of initial consonants (closed sort), follow a basic progression to compare several consonant sounds:

2-level sort	initial b, other (not b)
	initial f, other (not f)
3-level sort	initial b, initial f, other
2-level sort	initial m, other (not m)
4-level sort	initial m, initial b, initial f, other

- 🍎 Begin with a 2-level sort by sorting one consonant with an "other" pile to be sure that children can segment that sound. Segmenting the consonant requires children to segment the onset (consonant) from the rime (remaining vowel and consonants).
- 🍎 When children demonstrate that they are able to segment two consonants, those consonants can be compared, which creates a 3-level sort.
- 🍎 Then introduce a third consonant and return to a 2-level sort to be sure that children can segment its sound.
- 🍎 Finally, compare all three consonants, creating a 4-level sort. Always keep an "other" pile.

The basic progressions to follow with final consonants are:

2-level sort	initial b, final b
	initial f, final f
3-level sort	final b, final f, neither
5-level sort	initial b, final b, initial f, final f, other

The first consonants selected for study should be consonants that represent the same sound in both the initial and final positions. Over time, guide children to generalize which consonants tend not to change their sound when the position of the letter changes within a syllable.

As children demonstrate comfort with discriminating consonant sounds and are beginning to recognize those particular letters of the alphabet, replace the example picture with a letter card. Now guide children to sort for pictures that begin with that particular letter. For example, replace the picture of a ball with a card for the letter *b* as the example of the sound for which children are listening.

Sorting by Letters

Children need varied experiences to associate letter names with their corresponding shapes and sounds:

❦ *Sort words according to length*

With familiar words on individual cards, children sort all words with one letter into the same group, two letters in the same group, and so forth (Cunningham, 1995). Children's names are excellent to use in the beginning.

Sorting the Number of Letters in a Child's Name:

1	2	3	4	5	6
	Al	Ben	Anna	Jorge	Yazmin
		Sam	Rosa	Emily	Roberto
			Yuen	Jason	Hannah

Sorting the Number of Letters in Sight Words:

1	2	3	4	5	6
I	go	and	make	funny	little
A	me	big	come	three	yellow
	no	can	down		
		for	jump		

❦ *Sort words according to letters*

Each child has a word on a card, beginning with their name. Focusing on one letter at a time, children search their word for that letter. When the letter is found, children show that letter to a partner or the class, then the class makes a tally of the number of times each letter was found (Cunningham, 1995).

The letter t is found in words such as it,

little, the, three, to, two, at, and eat.

❦ *Sorting words according to placement of a letter*

Using familiar one-syllable words, the class sorts words according to the position of a particular letter (beginning, middle, or end of the word). We sort in this manner to help children begin to generalize where particular letters are most likely to occur.

Sorting for the Letter *b*:

beginning	middle	end
big		cab
blue		tub
be		
brown		

Sorting for the Letter *a*:

beginning	middle	end
a	ball	
and	can	
are	make	
at	what	

As children acquire words that are known in isolation, typically as developing readers, sorting activities begin to include the sorting of words to study visual patterns needed for decoding unfamiliar words in text.

 USING SOUND BOXES

Say-It-and-Move-It

In Say-It-and-Move-It (Blachman, 1991) each child is given three flat buttons or chips and a sheet of paper with several connected boxes drawn side by side, as shown in Figure 2.8. The number of boxes corresponds to the number of phonemes in the selected words. It is best to begin with words that have three phonemes, such as *hat*.

One button or chip is moved into a box to show each phoneme that is heard in a one-syllable word. Before the lesson prepare a set of boxes with buttons for each child, as well as a set for modeling on an overhead projector. In addition, prepare a list of one-syllable words with three phonemes, such as:

> bag, ball, bed, bug, cup, dig, dog, duck,
> fan, fish, gum, hen, hop, jet, jug, leg,
> man, mud, net, pig, pop, red, run, sun,
> ten, top, van, web, yes, and zip.

Select words that contain phonemes that are familiar to the children. For emergent readers and writers, select only words that have single consonants.

Begin the activity:

- 🍎 Let children practice with the manipulative before the activity begins by pushing each button up into a box as the teacher counts, "1 - 2 - 3."
- 🍎 Say a word aloud, stretching the word enough to segment the phonemes, such as *b-a-t*.

FIGURE 2.8
Sound boxes for Say-It-and-Move-It.

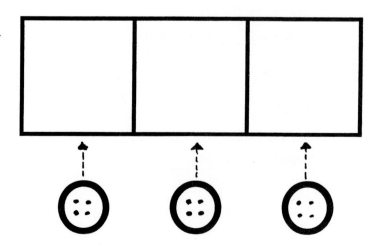

- Ask the children to repeat the word, stretching the word and listening for each phoneme. They know by the boxes that there are three phonemes.
- Repeat the word and model on the overhead projector how to move a button as we say each phoneme. At the end of saying a word, each of the three buttons have been pushed up into a box.
- The children repeat the word and push one button into a box for each phoneme.
- Then, together, touch each button and isolate that phoneme and the corresponding letter name for that sound.
- Then try another word.

Say-It-and-Write-It

As children acquire knowledge of letter names and shapes, letter shapes can be written in each box to represent each sound that is heard. In this activity, a sheet of paper with rows of connected boxes is prepared (see Figure 2.9). Continue to use the buttons, pushing a button into a box for each phoneme, then writing the letter that represents the sound that is heard. Later, discontinue the use of buttons. Instead, have children point to the appropriate box, then write the letter.

Begin the activity:

- Say a word with three phonemes, such as *b-a-t,* stretching the phonemes for children to hear. Point to one box for each phoneme.
- The children repeat the word, also stretching it to hear the phonemes, pointing to one box for each phoneme they hear.
- Ask, "What sounds do you hear?" or "What sound did you hear first?".
- Children reply with the phonemes they hear.

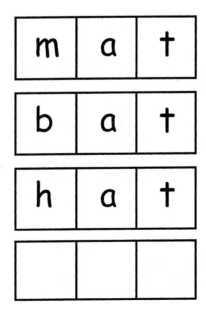

FIGURE 2.9
Sound boxes for Say-It-and-Write-It.

Note: Some children will remember best the last sound they heard. As children supply sounds, repeat the word, emphasizing that phoneme, and encourage children to point to the appropriate box. Confirm by pointing to the appropriate box on the overhead projector.

- Ask, "What letter makes that sound?" Children reply.
- Say, "Write that letter in the box" (to which children are pointing). Confirm by writing in the box on the overhead projector.
- In the same manner, elicit other sounds that are heard.

Until children are aware of short-vowel sounds, the teacher may choose to supply the vowel. As children gain confidence with segmenting sounds within a syllable, the pace of the activity picks up, working toward more fluent writing of the sounds within a word.

 # USING ENVIRONMENTAL PRINT TO FOCUS ON LETTERS AND SOUNDS

Environmental print has a context of its own, which children "read." Through instruction we help children consider how they use the context of environmental print to read words. While children watch:

- separate environmental print from its familiar packaging,
- compare the separated print with the print on an uncut package, and
- discuss how the context of the packaging helped in reading the words.

Environmental Print Books

Collect multiple copies of logos and labels of environmental print that focus on a particular category, such as favorite foods.

- Children use one label to cut out the key word(s), such as cutting just the word "McDonald's" from a container that holds fried potatoes.
- On each page for the book, children glue a full logo and, underneath, the isolated word.
- Children can write or dictate the name of the product or a sentence about the label or logo. A highly predictable sentence structure, such as "This is _____," should be chosen.
- The pages are stapled into a book for individual, partner, and group reading.

Environmental Word Wall

Words on the wall (Cunningham, Moore, Cunningham, & Moore, 2003) made of environmental print, in and out of context, can be read by the class and referred to often. Children can also look for print around the school to add to the wall, such as the school name on the front of the building, labels on restrooms and offices, or labels on food in the cafeteria that can be read because they are in context.

USING CHILDREN'S LITERATURE TO FOCUS ON SOUNDS AND LETTERS

Alphabet Books

Alphabet books provide a rich source of exposure to the names of letters, both upper- and lowercase, and letter sounds. As books are read aloud, we take time to call attention to letter shapes, encourage children to provide letter names, and talk about the words that represent the sound of the letter. Rereading of alphabet books provides practice in hearing letter names and sounds, and seeing letter shapes in a meaningful context.

Chicka Chicka Boom Boom (Martin & Archambault, 1989) uses a rhyming pattern to name the letters of the alphabet. Letters in the illustrations are shown in lowercase, while letters in the text are shown in uppercase.

> A told B, and B told C,
> "I'll meet you at the top
> Of the coconut tree."

On *Market Street* (Lobel, 1981) identifies objects that begin with each letter, one letter per page.

> A apples (shows a person dressed in apples),
> B books, . . .

A My Name Is Alice (Bayer, 1984) uses words that begin with a specific letter to make rhythmical patterns with names of people, places, and objects.

> A—my name is Alice and my husband's name is Alex.
> We come from Alaska and we sell ants.

An Edward Lear Alphabet (Newsom, 1983) provides opportunities for word play with each letter, changing to onset to make rhyming words.

> A a A was once an apple-pie,
> Pidy, Widy, Tidy, Pidy,
> Nice insidy,
> Apple-pie!

Familiar alphabet books can also be enlarged to provide shared reading experiences (see Chapter 5). Children can participate in making a class version of a favorite alphabet book, supplying the illustrations for the text. Transparencies of pages from a favorite alphabet shown on the overhead projector also become a "big book" for shared reading. Figure 2.10 provides suggestions for other alphabet books that children will enjoy.

FIGURE 2.10
A sampling of alphabet books.

Ainsworth, L. (2000). *Creepy Crawlies from A–Z.* New York: Scholastic.
Baker, A. (1999). *Black and White Rabbit's ABC.* Boston: Houghton Mifflin.
Bayer, J. (1987). *A My Name is Alice.* New York: Puffin.
Cousins, L. (1993). *Maisie's ABC.* Cambridge, MA: Candlewick Press.
Dragonwagon, C. (1992). *Alligators Arrived with Apples.* New York: Simon & Schuster.
Ehlert, L. (1993). *Eating the Alphabet.* New York: Harcourt Brace.
Feelings, M., & Feelings, T. (1981). *Jambo Means Hellow: Swahili Alphabet Book.* New York: Puffin.
Jay, A. (2003). *ABC: A Child's First Alphabet Book.* New York: Dutton Juvenile.
Johnson, S. T., (1999). *Alphabet City.* New York: Puffin.
Kirk, D. (2003). *Miss Spider's ABC.* New York: Scholastic.
Lionni, L. (2004). *The Alphabet Tree.* New York: Random House.
Lobel, A. (1989). *On Market Street.* New York: William Morrow.
Martin, B. (1989). *Chicka Chicka Boom Boom.* New York: Aladdin Paperbacks.
Miller, J. (1981). *Farm Alphabet Book.* New York: Scholastic.
Murray, M. (2003). *The Alphabet Keeper.* New York: Random House Children's.
Rey, H. A. (1972). *Curious George Learns the Alphabet.* Boston: Houghton Mifflin.
Rey, M., & Rey, H. A. (1998). *Curious George's ABCs.* Boston: Houghton Mifflin.
Sendak, M. (1990). *Alligators All Around: An Alphabet.* New York: HarperCollins.
Seuss, Dr. (1996). *Dr. Seuss's ABC: An Amazing Alphabet Book.* New York: Random House.
Shannon, G. (1999). *Tomorrow's Alphabet.* New York: William Morrow

Feed the Hungry Thing

The children's books *The Hungry Thing* (Slepian & Seidler, 1967) and *The Hungry Thing Returns* (Slepian & Seidler, 1990) provide excellent opportunities to encourage language play and changing onsets to create new, rhyming words. In the texts, the Hungry Thing points to a sign around his neck that reads, "Feed me." The townspeople try to figure out what it means when he says that he wants some "hookies" (cookies) or "shmancakes" (pancakes).

Children experiment with changing the initial phoneme, or onset, as they feed the Hungry Thing:

- Read *The Hungry Thing* aloud so that children hear the nonsense words introduced in the text.
- Reread, hesitating after nonsense words for children to fill in the real words.

  "I think," said the little boy, "it's all very clear. Tickles . . . sound like Sickles . . . sounds like . . . P _____ to me." (hesitate for children to complete)
- Encourage children to say the nonsense words and real words aloud to hear the sounds. Discuss how the beginning sound was changed to make a new word.
- From a large paper bag create a "Hungry Thing," such as the example shown in Figure 2.11.

FIGURE 2.11
Feed the Hungry Thing.

The first time, the game is played as follows:

- Teacher provides 10 to 15 pictures of familiar foods, displayed so that children can see them.
- Teacher says, "The Hungry Thing wants some 'schmandy.' What does he want?"
- Children look at the pictures and identify "candy."

Discuss how beginning sounds were changed. Make up other words that can also be candy, such as "dandy" or "jandy."

Try another version of the game:

- Provide plain paper for children to draw their favorite foods or magazines from which they may cut pictures of foods and paste the pictures on pieces of paper.
- Children take turns feeding the Hungry Thing by changing the phoneme at the beginning of their food, making it a nonsense word as in the text.
- The class tries to guess the real name of the food.

Following the whole-class activities, place the Hungry Thing in an activity center, along with food cards drawn by the class or pictures cut from magazines. Encourage children to continue their practice of changing beginning sounds. *Note:* As children build background knowledge of letter names and sounds, encourage children to state the letter name for the sound that was changed and write the letter that represents the sound. This should be done first in whole group, then in activity centers or independently. It is best to begin with single consonant changes, such as *dandy* for *candy,* stating that *dandy* begins with the letter *d*, /d/-/d/-/d/.

Making Connections . . .

Begin a collection of teaching ideas for developing phonological awareness, including:

- songs that can be adapted to rhyme, segment, and blend words;
- games and sorting activities that can be adapted to focus on sounds within words;
- environmental print; and
- literature that emphasizes sounds, such as ABC books.

ASSESSMENT: MONITORING EARLY CONCEPTS OF SOUNDS AND LETTERS

To collect evidence of children's growing knowledge about print, make observations of daily literacy experiences. In addition, meet individually with children, focusing their attention on particular aspects of literacy to learn more about what they know, are beginning to attend to, and have not yet begun to notice about language and print. Research suggests that two types of assessments can be particularly helpful to us in predicting children's future success in reading: alphabet recognition and spelling with beginning and ending consonants (Morris, Bloodgood, & Perney, 2003).

Phonological Skills

Using the same types of activities described in this chapter, interview individual children to determine the level of their developing phonological awareness. The interviews should be informal and focus on rhyming, syllable splitting, onset-rime splitting, as well as hearing and segmenting phonemes as each is appropriate for the child's development. Be sure to make careful records of children's responses, including the date and specific observations.

Sample Phonological Awareness Assessment

Rhyming

Teacher says, "Make a rhyme.

      I see a *cat*

      Sitting on a _____."

Child supplies a word that rhymes with *cat.*

Teacher says, "Which word does not rhyme with the others? *Bee, dog, me, see.*"

Child says, "Dog."

Syllables

Teacher says, "What is this word—snow_____man?"

Child says, "Snowman."

Teacher says, "What part do you hear first in *snowman?*"

Child says, "Snow."

Teacher says, "What is this word—twink_____le?"

Child says, "Twinkle."

Teacher says, "What part do you hear first in *twinkle?*"

Child says, "Twink."

Onset/rime

Teacher says, "What is the first sound you hear in the word *jet?*"

Child says, "/j/."

Teacher says, "What is the other part of *jet?*"

Child says, "et."

(Try several one-syllable words that begin with single consonants, blends, and digraphs.)

Phonemes

Teacher says, "Stretch and say all of the sounds in *moon.*"

Child says, "/m/-/oo/-/n/."

(Try several one-syllable words with different consonant and vowel sounds.)

While children are in the emergent stage, phonological assessments should be frequent. A baseline assessment conducted at the beginning of the school year for rhyming, syllable-splitting, onset and rime, as well as hearing and manipulating phonemes, provides a means of comparison for seeing growth. Following the baseline assessment, ongoing monthly assessments will provide valuable information for planning phonological activities that will be most useful in both whole-class and small-group settings.

Alphabet Recognition

Until children demonstrate knowledge of all upper- and lowercase manuscript letters, assessment of the alphabet should occur frequently. This assessment may occur in the midst of whole-class, small-group, or individual activities. It may occur during observation of children writing their name, while they are looking at a familiar text, or using familiar print in the classroom such as labels. This assessment also may be formalized by having a set of cards, with one letter on each card, that are flashed for rapid recognition of letters in random order.

Teachers typically create a chart on which to record student responses and progress. The chart can contain the names of all children in the class, or it may be an individual chart with space for recordings over time. A class chart would typically be a grid with the children's names down the left-hand side and the letters of the alphabet across the top. An individual chart might have letters down

FIGURE 2.12
Recording progress in learning letters of the alphabet.

Letter Recognition							Name _____ Grade _____							
Date Tested(/) **Date Mastered (*)**							**Date Tested(/)** **Date Mastered (*)**							**Comments**	
A							a								
B							b								
C							c								
D							d								
E							e								
F							f								
G							g								
H							h								
I							i								
J							j								
K							k								
L							l								
M							m								
N							n								
O							o								
P							p								
Q							q								
R							r								
S							s								
T							t								
U							u								
V							v								
W							w								
X							x								
Y							y								
Z							z								

the left-hand side with columns for recording assessments at different times of the year (see Figure 2.12).

Letter-Sound Relationships

To understand the connection that a child is making between speech and print, teachers can ask children to:

- make the sound of a phoneme that is cued by a particular letter of the alphabet, and
- write the letter that represents a particular phoneme.

By asking a child to associate the symbol with the sound (decoding = reading) and associate the sound with the symbol (encoding = writing) to demonstrate their knowledge, a teacher has a more complete picture of the child's developing skills.

> Example: Decoding:
> Teacher shows the child the letter *m*.
> Child says "/m/".
>
> Encoding:
> Teacher makes the sound, "/m/".
> Child says the letter name, *m,* and writes the letter.

It is appropriate to assess consonant and vowel sounds that have been introduced to the child. Try not to distort the sound of consonants in isolation, such as "buh" for *b*.

As children develop skill with words it is appropriate to assess their ability to hear phonemes within words and their memory for words. See the assessment section of Chapter 3, Learning about Words II, for additional ways to identify a child's developing understanding of letter-sound relationships.

Concepts about Print (CAP)

Concepts about print are assessed most effectively in the context of real print sources, such as books. Both commercial and teacher-made instruments can effectively measure concepts about print. Marie Clay (2002) has developed an assessment that enables teachers to observe children's print knowledge as a text is read to the children and the children participate in applying print knowledge (see Clay, 2002, *The Observation Survey,* 2nd edition). Her assessment uses specially constructed texts. Clay's books have been altered so that on some pages print and illustrations have been turned upside down. In addition, line order, word order, and letter order within some high-frequency words have been altered.

The examiner reads the text aloud and asks the child what he or she notices about the text. Children can demonstrate their knowledge that print carries the message by noticing a discrepancy between what is read aloud and what is on the page. The items on the assessment have been validated for children ages 5 to 7 years. Directions for administration and scoring are available in *Early Detection of Reading Difficulties* (Clay, 1985) and *The Observation Survey* (Clay, 2002).

A teacher-made assessment can simulate Clay's CAP assessment, as shown in Figure 2.13. Although a published children's book does not have altered pages, children's concepts about book handling and print can still be observed. As in Clay's assessment, the text is read aloud to the child. As the text is read aloud during the assessment, the child is asked to demonstrate concepts about book orientation and handling, directionality, and print language.

To assess a child's concepts about books and print, select a book that is not familiar to the child. Be sure there is a title on the front cover and that the first page of printed text also has an illustration. There should also be text on two facing pages somewhere in the book. To document growth, this assessment should

FIGURE 2.13
Concepts about books and print assessment.

Do:	Say:	See:
Hand child a book, spine first, ask #1, 2, 3.	1. Show me the front of the book.	1. Child points to front cover.
	2. Show me the title of the book.	2. Child points to any words in title.
	3. Show me where I should start to read the story.	3. Child turns to first page of text.
On first pages of story, ask #4.	4. Where should I start to read?	4. Child points to print, not illustration.
Read first facing pages of text, then ask #5. After child turns page, ask #6, 7, 8. Then, read facing pages of text. Turn page. Read several more pages.	5. I finished reading this page, now what do I do?	5. Child turns to next page of text.
	6. Where should I start to read on this page?	6. Child points to first word, top left side.
	7. Which way should I go when I read?	7. Child moves finger to right end of line.
	8. Which way should I go after that?	8. Child does return sweep, moves left to right on another line of text.
On two facing pages with print on both sides, ask #9.	9. Where should I start to read?	9. Child points to left-hand page, first word on top left.
Turn page, ask #10, 11.	10. Show me the first word on this page.	10. Child points to first word on top left.
	11. Show me the last word on this page.	11. Child points to last word on bottom right.
Read last facing pages of text. Then give child two small cards (1" × 2"). Show how to move cards, to close and open like a window. Use for #12, 13, 14.	12. Show me one letter. Show me two letters.	12. Child slides cards apart to show any single letter, any two letters together.
	13. Show me one word. Show me two words.	13. Child slides cards apart to show one word, two words together.
	14. Show me a capital letter.	14. Child points to any capital letter.
Close the book. Ask #15, 16.	15. Show me the beginning of the story.	15. Child shows title page or first page of text in book.
	16. Show me the end of the story.	16. Child shows last page of text in book.

Item/Concept	Score	Comments
Concepts about Books and Print Assessment	Name _____	
	Date _____ Age ____ yrs. ____mo.	
1. Front of book		
2. Title of book		
3. Begin to read book on first page of text		
4. Read print, not picture		
5. Turn page when finished reading		
6. Begin to read page on top left, first word		
7. Read line of text left to right		
8. Return sweep		
9. Read left page before right page		
10. First word on page		
11. Last word on page		
12. One letter, two letters		
13. One word, two words		
14. Capital letter		
15. Beginning of story		
16. End of story		
Total	/16	

Overall Observations:

FIGURE 2.14
Assessment record form.

be completed with all emergent readers and selectively with developing readers early in the school year and intermittently throughout the year. For comparison, also conduct this assessment with a book that is very familiar to the child. A child who scores better with a familiar text may be demonstrating the potential for instruction in print concepts with familiar texts. A record-keeping form (see Figure 2.14) is provided.

Over time, emergent and early developing readers show increasing understanding of print and how readers respond to print. Begin administering the CAP assessment early in kindergarten and continue periodic assessments until children demonstrate knowledge of all items. Knowledge of print is essential for children to make accurate predictions about print in their reading.

As this assessment is administered, observe all students in the class to make decisions about the skills and strategies to emphasize in classroom reading experiences. For example, early in kindergarten children may not demonstrate knowledge of return sweep (i.e., when we get to the end of a line of text we return to the left side of a page and drop down one line). If several children have not yet developed that concept, model that skill in shared reading and ask children to demonstrate that skill by reading sentences that are longer than one line of text.

Keeping Records of Children's Development

It is important to keep accurate records of observations of children's reading and writing development. Record-keeping forms, such as Figures 2.15 and 2.16, can be made to reflect the knowledge and strategies expected at a particular stage of development. Such forms should be combined with other assessments to serve as a more complete picture of development.

Making Connections . . .

It might be beneficial to spend time with a child in the emergent stage to explore what he or she is coming to understand about the names and shapes of letters and the sounds they represent. Develop a short phonological awareness assessment such as the one described earlier in the assessment section. Also show the child cards with individual letters for letter recognition. For a kindergarten child, begin with the letters in the child's name. Finally, find out a little about letters the child can write—name, other favorite words, or individual letters.

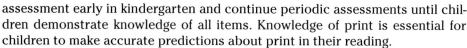

RESPECTING DIVERSITY IN DEVELOPMENT OF WORD KNOWLEDGE

Learning about words and print is very important in the processes of reading and writing. Confidence in one's own ability to read and write words can greatly influence daily reading and writing performance. If children are to be successful in learning words, we must consider their experiences with print, their knowledge of how to monitor their own reading and writing, language we use for instruction. In addition, we should provide a variety of opportunities for children to make sense of reading and writing words.

FIGURE 2.15
Development of letter-sound knowledge: Emergent stage.

Recognizes Letters of the Alphabet:

	Reads	Writes		Reads	Writes		Reads	Writes		Reads	Writes
A			a			N			n		
B			b			O			o		
C			c			P			p		
D			d			Q			q		
E			e			R			r		
F			f			S			s		
G			g			T			t		
H			h			U			u		
I			i			V			v		
J			j			W			w		
K			k			X			x		
L			l			Y			y		
M			m			Z			z		

Distinguishes Initial Consonants:

	Reads	Writes		Reads	Writes		Reads	Writes		Reads	Writes
b			h			n			t		
c			j			p			v		
d			k			q			w		
f			l			r			y		
g			m			s			z		

Distinguishes Final Consonants:

	Reads	Writes		Reads	Writes		Reads	Writes		Reads	Writes
b			g			n			t		
d			l			p			z		
f			m			r					

FIGURE 2.16
Development of word
knowledge: Emergent stage.

Context:	Usually	Sometimes	Rarely
Uses aural context to figure out unfamiliar words during read-aloud			
Recognizes print in familiar environmental contexts			
Sight Vocabulary:			
Recognizes some familiar words in isolation			
Phonics:			
Is developing phonemic awareness			
-remembers rhymes & rhyming words			
-can split words into syllables			
-blends syllables to make a word			
-can split syllable into onset & rime			
-can segment one-syllable word into phonemes			
-can categorize phonemes			
Self-Monitoring Strategy:			
Searches for information in illustrations to make meaning			
Is beginning to use context + first sound to identify words in familiar text			
Observations/Comments:			

Experience Sets Children Apart

As we engage children in activities to learn about words and print, we should keep in mind that it is often experience that sets children apart from one another (Allington, 1994). As we plan for learning about words and print, we except children's differences in experience to enrich daily talk about words. Children will make sense of their word-study experiences in different ways and will, if given the opportunity, teach each other what they understand about reading and writing words.

Teaching according to children's developmental levels also acknowledges difference in experience with words. Adopting one level of a spelling or phonics program for all children in a classroom does not acknowledge or respect the diversity that experience brings. One level of instruction may reach children in the middle but provide little challenge to children with extensive print experiences and will certainly fail to help children with limited print or English language experiences connect their prior experience to new academic knowledge.

Language of Instruction

For children whose first language is not English, the language we use for instruction can be a mystery. Who else will they hear talk about long and short vowels or base words? Teachers have a special language they use in school with children. Consider how well children will know that special language. It is our responsibility to teach the meaning of the language of instruction to all children, so that everyone has a more equal opportunity to benefit from word-study instruction.

Making Connections . . .

What have you added to your understanding of the development of children's literacy from this chapter? Make a notation in a personal reflective journal. Compare your thinking to notations that you made at the end of Chapter 1. Is your thinking changing? If so, in what ways? What is your understanding of children at the emergent stage of development?

C H A P T E R

3

Learning about Words II: Phonics and Morphemic Analysis

Adding to our literacy framework . . .

	Reading Aloud and Guided Literature Study	
Shared Reading	**Balanced and Integrated Literacy Framework**	Shared and Interactive Writing
Guided Reading and Guided Literature Study		Guided Writing and Writer's Workshop
Independent Reading and Reader's Workshop		Independent Writing
	Word Study	

In this chapter, we learn about . . .

- The importance of learning about words
- What children need to know about phonics and morphemes
- Debates about phonics instruction

- Suggested sequences of instruction
- Learning about words through building words
- Learning about words through sorting words
- A variety of ways to assess word knowledge

Looking into Classrooms . . .

"Look at all of the words we can make with the letters in prince," *exclaim the children in Nikki and Mary's second-grade, team-teaching classroom. The class has been studying different versions of* The Frog Prince *story, so Nikki and Mary decide to use the word* prince *for a whole-class activity. Using all of the letters in the word* prince, *the children are able to build the words* in, pin, rip, pen, ice, rice, nice, ripe, pine, cried, price, *and* prince. *The children each have cards for the letters in the word* prince—p, r, i, n, c, e. *Nikki and Mary begin with two-letter words and work up to using all of the letters to spell* prince. *Together the class builds a word, then talks about sounds in the word and how parts of words they build are similar. The variety of words that can be built from the letters in* prince *provides opportunities for every child to find some familiar words and some challenging words. These developing readers and writers find building words to be very engaging.*

DOWN THE HALL . . .

It is time for daily word study in David's third-grade classroom. The children move to the place in the room where their word study group meets. For the 20 children in David's classroom, there are four levels of developmental word study: single long vowels (early-middle developing stage), double vowels (later developing stage), inflected endings with no change to the base word (early transitional stage), and multisyllable patterns (middle transitional). It is Tuesday, so the children know that this day's activity involves closed word sorts and examining patterns within their words for the week. David sits with the syllabication group because they are struggling to understand how their phonics knowledge can help them with words that are more than one syllable. He understands that children frequently experience some confusion over using phonics knowledge with the longer, more complex words they find in their reading materials. As he talks with the children, David discovers that they are not aware of how to look into multisyllable words to see the phonics patterns they already know. David decides to restructure the next several weeks of word study lessons to help children first consider two-syllable patterns that focus on familiar words that have only one consonant between two vowels. He chose this pattern because he knows that the first syllable in these words can decode as either a long-vowel (mu-sic, ta-ble) or a short-vowel syllable (riv-er, stud-y). Children in this group know both long- and short-vowel patterns in one-syllable words. David will guide them to apply their knowledge in new ways.

BUILDING A THEORY BASE . . .

In Chapter 2 we learned about the foundations of developing concepts about words during the emergent stage, typically kindergarten to early-first-grade reading level. In this chapter we add to that knowledge with a focus on supporting developing and transitional readers and writers as they refine their concepts about print and learn to decode and spell more complex words.

WHO ARE THE DEVELOPING READERS AND WRITERS?

Developing readers typically function somewhere between early/mid-first-grade and early-third-grade reading level. Early in this stage, children are described as learning to break the code (Brown, 1999/2000), being glued to print (Chall, 1979, 1983), and engaged in word-to-word matching (Holdaway, 1980) because they are intent upon generalizing their concepts about words in print and letter-sound patterns to the words that dominate their reading texts. Unfamiliar words with more than one syllable present much challenge early in this stage, but by the end of the stage students are becoming quite proficient at reading two- and some three-syllable words. Through extensive reading in easy or familiar text, they develop a large sight vocabulary.

   As writers, these students are gaining control over the conventional spelling of one-syllable words, particularly predictable vowel patterns. They are also gaining some skill in accurately representing the second and third syllable in longer words. In the early part of this stage the vowel in the second or third syllable, however, is frequently absent. For example, a child in the developing stage might write the word *beaches* as *bechz, beechs,* or *beachs.*

Throughout the developing stage, children must be guided to refine their understandings about how words are formed in English. They should have extensive experiences with print to make generalizations about letter patterns that are likely to occur in English. They will need to develop the knowledge that phonics generalizations enable them to make predictions about the pronunciation of unfamiliar words. The accuracy of their predictions must then be checked against their knowledge of English words (language cues) and the appropriateness of the context in which the words appear (meaning cues). Knowledge of letter-sound possibilities by themselves does not lead to meaning.

WHO ARE THE TRANSITIONAL READERS AND WRITERS?

Transitional readers, children who typically function between early-third-grade and sixth-grade reading level, have the ability to be quite fluent. They are ready to be challenged as they think about written language. They have made the transition from picture books to chapter books, or novels, and are able to sink into periods of silent reading for 30 minutes or more. Because of such behaviors, this stage has also been characterized as the "going for fluency" stage (Brown, 1999/2000).

Children come to the transitional stage with a strong concept of words in print and a foundation in letter-sound patterns. Teachers build on this knowledge to help children acquire increased proficiency in reading and writing multisyllable words. With multisyllable words, children must be flexible in applying both phonetic and structural knowledge about words.

To become fluent readers and writers, children must be able to effectively and efficiently break the code of written language with complex words. Using knowledge of the visual cues of phonics and morphemic analysis is one means to achieving fluency. The daily study of words, in meaningful contexts and in isolation, provides much needed practice in the continued development of concepts about words and print that leads to spellings that are more and more conventional.

THE IMPORTANCE OF LEARNING ABOUT WORDS

Literacy research suggests that knowledge of words and print are major predictors of future success in reading and writing:

- Differences in word knowledge consistently account for variations in performance among readers and writers (e.g., Biemiller, 1977/1978; Gough & Tunmer, 1986; Perfetti, 1985; Rack, Snowling, & Olson, 1992; Stanovich, 1982; Stanovich, Cunningham, & West, 1981).
- Children who do not develop effective code-breaking strategies early in their reading histories are likely to experience reading difficulties as

they progress through the school grades (Byrne, Freebody, & Gates, 1992; Clay, 1991).

🍎 Developing power with words depends on children's ability to automatically recognize or produce words, combined with their ability to think with those words (Holdaway, 1980).

🍎 For knowledge of words, both speed and effortlessness are integral to competent reading (Adams & Osborn, 1990).

🍎 Linking meaningful units within words helps children enlarge their vocabulary by seeing how words are related to one another through word parts or chunks (Beck, Perfetti, & McKeown, 1982).

Children in the primary grades need many opportunities to focus their attention on the distinctive features of words in order to develop a rich meaning vocabulary, an extensive sight vocabulary, and skill in using familiar letter-sound patterns to decode unfamiliar words (Ehri, 1991). Through the daily study of words, teachers guide children to understand and use letter-sound and meaning patterns in the words they read and write. It is through the fluid decoding of print that readers are able to devote sufficient cognitive attention to the comprehension of text.

HOW DO CHILDREN LEARN ABOUT WORDS?

In the primary grades, the study of words should occur throughout the school day. Children learn about words when they:

🍎 Participate in teacher-guided whole-class and/or small-group activities such as building words, sorting words, hunting words, and other word games to understand and apply phonic and morphemic generalizations (discussed later in this chapter);

🍎 Participate in an interactive read-aloud, with teacher guidance to appreciate the sounds of the language that authors use and learn meanings of new words (see Chapter 4);

🍎 Engage in shared reading of a text, with teacher guidance to compare features of words and their patterns (see Chapter 5);

🍎 Examine unfamiliar words in guided reading texts, with teacher guidance to learn new patterns and make comparisons to familiar chunks or words (see Chapter 6);

🍎 Read independently or with partner, using familiar contexts and letter-sound knowledge to figure out unfamiliar words or phrases (see Chapter 7);

🍎 Write, with the teacher support, a thank-you letter to the principal using letter patterns in familiar words to figure out the spellings of some unfamiliar words (see Chapter 8).

🍎 Revise and edit their writing to communicate their ideas more clearly (see Chapter 9);

🍎 Engage in a variety of activities in a basal reading series that draw upon the instructional strategies identified earlier in this list (see Chapter 10); and

Engage in integrated units of study that focus on concepts in science, social studies, and/or mathematics to develop their knowledge of the specialized vocabulary of the topic, applying that knowledge through personal reading and writing (see Chapter 11).

The study of words permeates this text. Each instructional strategy that is highlighted includes aspects of word study.

Because students' needs for learning are different, no singular approach to word study will be effective for all students in a classroom. Teachers must carefully observe children's strategies and target instruction to the needs that children demonstrate (Hauerwas & Walker, 2004).

PHONICS IN THE DEVELOPING AND TRANSITIONAL STAGES

We know that phonics is the knowledge and use of letter-sound patterns to decode, or accurately pronounce, words. English words are created with recurring combinations of consonants and vowels. Some patterns occur more consistently than other patterns. Phonics instruction should help children recognize frequently occurring patterns and skillfully generalize those patterns to read and write unfamiliar words. Instruction in phonics begins with patterns in one-syllable words then applies those patterns to multisyllable words. Figures 3.1 and 3.2 provide a detailed overview of the content of phonics instruction. Through teacher guidance children should develop an understanding of the possibilities of what consonants and vowels can do in the English language.

Consonants

In general, consonants are letters whose sounds are produced with the aid of a physical part of the mouth, such as the lips, tongue, or teeth. Consonants can appear at the beginning and end of syllables, they can be sounded or silent, and they can appear by themselves or combined with other consonants. The following are terms used to describe consonants:

 Initial consonant—A consonant that appears at the beginning of a syllable (*s* in *sun*).

 Final consonant—consonant that appears at the end of a syllable (*n* in *sun*).

 Consonant blend—two or three consonants that frequently appear together in either the initial or final position of a syllable. Each consonant in the pattern is sounded (*dr* in *drop*), but the individual sounds are blended.

 Consonant digraph—two or three consonants that frequently appear together in either the initial or final position of a syllable. The combined consonants result in only one sound—the sound of one of the consonants (*ghost, sign*) or a new sound that is not represented by the letters in the digraph (*chip, fudge*).

FIGURE 3.1
Overview of consonant patterns.

Single Consonants		Consonant Teams	
Consistent Sound	**Variant Sound**	**2 Consonants—2 Sounds**	**2 Consonants—1 Sound**

letter names sound
b   bat, cab
d   dot, mad
f   fan, leaf
j   jam, —
k   kid, peek
l   lid, pail
m   man, ham
n   nut, bun
p   pin, map
r   rug, car
t   tag, cat
v   van, —
z   zoo, quiz
 	
letter does NOT name sound
h   hat, —
qu   queen, —
	varies by vowel that follows
	c (hard c=/k/)
	    cage
	    cone
	    cut
	c (soft c=/s/)
	    cent, face
	    city
	    cycle
	
	g (hard g = /g/)
	    gate, bag
	    girl
	    gone
	    gum
	
	g (soft g = /j/)
	    gem, cage
	    giant
	    gym
	
	varies by position
	s sand, bus
	    sure, —
	    —, his
	
	w win, saw
	
	x x-ray, fox
	    xylophone
	
	y yes my
	          baby
	          say
		initial blends
		r family
		br break cr crown
		dr drop fr frog
		gr grapes pr prize
		tr tree
		
		l family
		bl blue cl clown
		fl flag gl glass
		pl play
		
		s family
		sc scarf sk skip
		sl slide sm smile
		sn snap sp spoon
		st stop sw swim
		scr scrap
		
		spl split spr spray
		squ squirt
		str street
		
		w family
		dw dwell sw swim
		tw twin
		
		final blends
		lb bulb ld hold
		lf golf lk milk
		lt belt
		
		mp lamp
		
		nd hand ng bang
		nk pink nt went
		
		sk mask sp crisp
		st fast
			h digraphs
			ch chip, each
			    chef, —
			    school, —
			gh —, laugh
			ph phone, graph
			sh ship, dish
			th this, breathe
			    thin, breath
			
			double-letter digraph
			bb rabbit
			dd add
			ff cuff
			gg egg
			ll ball
			nn inn
			ss dress
			zz fuzz
			
			silent letter digraph
			gh ghost, —
			gn gnat, sign
			kn knock, —
			wh what, —
			    who, —
			wr write, —
			
			ck —, duck
			dge —, fudge
			mb —, lamb
			tch —, match

Vowels

In general, vowels (*a, e, i, o, u,* sometimes *w* and *y*) are letters whose sounds are not obstructed by the physical parts of the mouth. Vowels, like consonants, can be sounded or silent and they can appear by themselves or combined with another vowel. In contrast to consonants, vowels can appear at the beginning, in

FIGURE 3.2
Overview of vowel patterns.

Single Vowels					Vowel Teams				
Short		**Long**		**Neither Long nor Short**	**Long— Consistent**		**Long—Short Variable**		**Neither Long nor Short**
vc **cvc**		**cv** **vce**		**r-controlled**	**vowel** **digraph**		**vowel** **digraph**		**diphthong**
a - at	bag	a- —	cake	ar car	ai	rain	ea	meat	au haul
e - egg	bed	e- me	——	er her	ay	may		bread	aw saw
i - in	hit	i- —	hide	ir bird	ee	feet		great	
o - on	log	o- go	rope	or for	igh	night			oi oil
u - up	sun	u- —	cute	ur fur	oa	boat	ei	seize	oy boy
			rude					vein	
				are care					oo boot
		y- fly	——	ere here			ey	key	foot
		—	baby	there				they	
				ire fire					ou through
				ore more			ie	pie	round
				ure sure				chief	
									ow grow
							ou	soul	cow
								young	
									ui fruit
									ue blue
									ew flew
									r-controlled
									air fair
									ear hear
									bear
									learn
									eer peer
									ier pier
									oar roar

the middle, and at the end of syllables. The following terms are used to describe vowels:

- *Single long vowel*—the sound of a vowel that resembles the letter's name (*ate*), and takes longer to form in the mouth than a short vowel.
- *Short vowel*—the sound of a vowel that is shorter in duration and does not name the letter it represents (*at*).
- R-*controlled vowel*—vowel patterns combined with the consonant *r*, in which the sound of the vowel blends with the sound of the consonant /r/ (*car, care, fair*).

🍎 *Vowel digraph*—two vowels, or a vowel and silent consonant(s), that appear together in a syllable and represent one sound, usually either a long-vowel or short-vowel sound, usually represented by one of the letters in the vowel team (*b<u>oa</u>t, gr<u>ea</u>t, l<u>igh</u>t*).

🍎 *Diphthong*—two vowels that represent a blending of both vowels, beginning near the position of the first vowel and moving toward the position of the second vowel. The sound produced does not typically represent either the long- or the short-vowel sound of the letters in the team (*<u>oi</u>l, c<u>ow</u>, s<u>aw</u>, f<u>oo</u>d*).

 # WHAT DO CHILDREN NEED TO LEARN ABOUT PHONICS?

For children to become competent readers and writers during the primary grades, they must develop an understanding that:

🍎 Letters must be written in a particular left-to-right order to make specific words; therefore, a particular word is always spelled the same way.

Example: The letters *a, s,* and *w* can be arranged to spell both *was* and *saw*. To make the word *saw*, the letters must always be arranged left-to-right as *s-a-w*.

🍎 The position of letters within a word influence the sound represented.

Example: The letter *s* typically represents the /s/ sound at the beginning of a syllable, as in *sun*, but can also represent the /z/ sound at the end of a syllable, as in *his*.

🍎 Each sound in a word can be represented by a letter or letters.

Example: /ch/-/i/-/n/ is written as *chin*.

/f/-/o/-/ks/ is written as *fox*.

🍎 Just as letters can represent sounds in words, some letters in particular positions can represent silence.

Example: *bike, e* is silent

light, gh is silent

write, w is silent

🍎 The sound of a phoneme can be influenced by a letter or letters that immediately follow.

Example: In *mad, a* is pronounced as short *a*.

In *maid*, with the addition of *i, a* is pronounced as long *a*.

Example: In *sin, i* is pronounced as short *i*.

In *sign*, with the addition of *g, i* is pronouncd as long *i*.

🍎 The sound of a phoneme can be influenced by one or more nonadjacent letters.

Example: In *kit, i* is pronounced as short *i*.

In *kite*, with the addition of *e, i* is pronounced as long *i*.

🍎 The sound of a phoneme can be influenced by the division of syllables.

Example: In *mu-si<u>c</u>, c* is pronounced as /k/.

In *mu-si-cian, ci* is pronounced as /sh/.

- Some spelling patterns can represent the same sounds in different words.

  Example: The pattern *-eal* can be found in *m<u>eal</u>*, *st<u>eal</u>*, *conc<u>eal</u>*, and *app<u>eal</u>ing*.

- Some spelling patterns can have more than one pronunciation.

  Example: *ou* can be pronounced as:

  > long *o* (*soul*)
  >
  > short *u* (*young*)
  >
  > *oo* (*through*)
  >
  > *aw* (*ought*)
  >
  > *ow* (*cloud*)

- Some letter patterns are never found in certain positions within a syllable.

  Example: The consonant blend *nt* never begins a syllable. It is always found at the end of a syllable, as in *we<u>nt</u>*.

- Certain letter patterns are characteristic of English words, but other patterns are not.

  Example: Whereas *gh* can be found in *<u>gh</u>ost* and *laug<u>h</u>*, *hg* will not be not found in English spellings.

> For more information about the number of phonemes and spelling patterns, see *http://www.sedl.org/reading/topics/phonicsrules.html*).

The 26 letters of the English alphabet decode as 44 or 45 different phonemes (the exact number is debated by linguists) that can be spelled in as many as 350 different ways. Therefore, a teacher's goal is not to teach each separate word in a language, but rather to help children make generalizations about the possibilities of phonetic elements or morphemes that might appear in words they have yet to encounter. Understanding the predictable possibilities of English makes it easier for a child to make a reasoned prediction when meeting unfamiliar words in print or while trying to spell words that are seen infrequently.

Making Connections . . .

Begin to challenge your understanding of phonics patterns. Collect other words that fit the generalizations just described. You must see those patterns in words for yourself before you can guide children to see them.

WHAT ARE MORPHEMES?

Multisyllable words dominate the English language and are typically composed of meaningful units called *morphemes* (base words or roots and affixes). Children begin to encounter words composed of morphemes in reading as early as the latter part of first grade; words that contain a familiar word plus "something more," such as *jump + ing*. That "something more" is an affix, a prefix or suffix added to the base word to alter the meaning or use for a particular context. As morphemic words begin to appear in reading materials, the study of multisyllable words should begin. An overview of basic elements of multisyllable words is shown in Figure 3.3.

FIGURE 3.3
Structural patterns.

Base + Base		Base + Affix(es)	
Compound Words	**Contractions**	**Prefixes**	**Suffixes**

literal meaning
dog+house
bed+room
gold+fish
play+ground
after+noon
play+time
eye+sight
wild+life
	***not* family**
	are+not = aren't
	can+not = can't
	have+not = haven't
	do+not = don't
	will+not = won't
	would+not = wouldn't
	could+not = couldn't
	should+not = shouldn't
		independent—not bound to base
		dis disobey
		en enjoy
		for forgive
		fore foretold
		im impure
		in inactive
		inter interview
		mis mislead
		non nonstop
		pre preview
		re repay
		un undo
			inflectional nouns
			s dog+s
			es dish+es
			   horse+es
			's one boy's
			   two boys'

implied/accepted meaning
every+one
out+side
run+away
over+drawn
fall+out
soft+ware
butter+fly
	***are* family**
	you+are = you're
	they+are = they're
	we+are = we're
			verbs
			s jump+s
			ed jump+ed
			   bat+t+ed
			   bake+ed
			ing jump+ing
			   hit+t+ing
			   bake+ing

	***will* family**
	I+will = I'll
	you+will = you'll
	we+will = we'll
	they+will = they'll
		dependent—bound to base/root
		com combine
		con concern
		de decide
		dis disturb
		ex excuse
		pre prefer
		pro process
			adjective
			er tall+er
			   big+g+er
			   pretty+er
			   nice+er
			est tall+est
			   big+g+est
			   pretty+est
			   nice+est

two words fly paper ironing board steam engine wagon wheel	***is* family** he+is = he's she+is = she's it+is = it's I+am = I'm		
hyphenated cut-off part-time play-offs tongue-tied	***have* family** I+have = I've you+have = you've we+have = we've they+have = they've		**derivational** able comfortable ance allowance ess princess ful careful ify classify ion addition division ish foolish ism criticism ist finalist ity ability ive productive ize organize less painless ly friendly ment payment ness kindness

Free and Bound Morphemes

Morphemes can be either free from or bound to other morphemes.

- *Free morphemes* function as words without needing to be attached to other morphemes.
- *Bound morphemes* must be attached to at least one other morpheme to make a recognizable word. Most multisyllable words are created from combinations of free and bound morphemes.

  Example: crosswalk = cross (free) + walk (free)

  repaint = re (bound) + paint (free)

  richest = rich (free) + est (bound)

  inspection = in(bound) + spec(bound) + tion(bound)

It is often easier to determine the meaning of longer words that are made from free morphemes than those that are made from bound morphemes, particularly words that contain a root.

Base Words and Roots

Many multisyllable words contain at least one base word or root. The essential meaning of longer words can be found by identifying the meaning of either the base word or the root. Some educators define base words and roots as synonymous, as the meaningful core of words. In this text we make a distinction that focuses on utility for the types of words that primary-grade children encounter.

- Base word—A base word is a free morpheme and can function as a word by itself or have affixes added to create related words. Children often know the meaning of a base word from their early language experiences. This knowledge is useful in determining the meaning of other words that contain the same base.

  Example: *joy*

  joyful

  enjoyment

  The base word, *joy,* can stand by itself as a word. It has meaning as a word. When it is found within a longer word, the meaning of the base word is used to help determine the related meaning.

- Root—A root can also serve as the meaningful core of a word, but a root is typically a morpheme that must be bound to an affix to be recognized as a meaningful word. Typically, the meaning of a root is not as familiar to children as the meaning of a base word.

  Example: *graph* (to write or record)

  autograph (auto = self or same)

  photography (photo = light)

  Through experiences in school, children may think of *graph* as a chart for recording data in mathematics. They should also relate its broader meaning, "to write or record," to other words that contain the root *graph*.

Children can dramatically expand their knowledge of words if they use meanings of word parts in known words to figure out meanings of unfamiliar words. Flexibility with language is an important part of expanding reading and writing vocabulary beyond one-syllable words. Children must understand that a morpheme can appear in multiple words, but will carry its meaning with it in some way. Words with roots are typically studied in the transitional stage, when children reach third-grade reading level and beyond.

Affixes

An affix is a bound morpheme that can modify or change the meaning of a base word or root. There are two types of affixes, prefix and suffix. A prefix is a morpheme that is added before a base word or root, and a suffix is a morpheme that follows a base word or root. Neither prefixes nor suffixes can stand alone as words. They must be combined with at least one base word or root.

Types of Prefixes

A prefix modifies the meaning of the base word or root to which it is added. The modified meaning is easier to determine if the prefix is attached to a base word, a free morpheme, rather than a root.

> Example: *rejoin* (*re* = again, *join* = bring together)
> *revive* (*re* = again, *vive* = live, from *vivere*)

The morpheme *join* is a base word, whereas *vive* is a root. Using the meaning of the word parts, we can collude that the overall meaning of a base word + affix is easier to determine than the meaning of a root + affix.

- *Independent prefix*—A prefix is considered to be independent if it is attached to a base word that can function without the prefix.
  Example: *rejoin* = *re* (independent prefix) + *join* (base)
- *Dependent prefix*—A prefix is dependent if it must be attached to a root to create a meaningful word.
  Example: *revive* = *re* (dependent prefix) + *vive* (root)
  Children typically know the meaning of words with a dependent prefix by considering the word as a whole in a meaningful context, and not the meaning of its parts.

Types of Suffixes

There are two types of suffixes that can be attached to the end of a base word or root: inflectional suffixes and derivational suffixes.

- *Inflectional suffix*—Inflectional suffixes are added to a base word and include the endings *s, 's, es, ed, ing, er,* and *est.* These suffixes affect the number or possession of nouns, the tense of verbs, or the comparison or degree of adjectives.
  Example: dog + s — singular to plural noun
  jump + ed — present to past verb tense
  small + er — comparative adjective

Adding an inflectional suffix typically does not change the part of speech or usage of the base word, except in the case of + *ing* (*build* to *building*). Determining the meaning of the new word with an inflected suffix is relatively easy.

Derivational suffix—In comparison, derivational suffixes do affect the meaning and usage of base and root words, and add greatly to the richness of language. Adding a derivational suffix usually changes the part of speech of a base word, thereby changing the way that the word may be used.

Example:

pain (noun)	+	*less*	=	*painless* (adjective)
assign (verb)	+	*ment*	=	*assignment* (noun)
week (noun)	+	*ly*	=	*weekly* (adverb)

Focusing on the meaningful units in words provides the opportunity to help children combine their knowledge about phonics patterns within syllables with a growing knowledge of the units within more complex words. This knowledge will become the foundation for mature reading.

WHAT DO CHILDREN NEED TO LEARN ABOUT MORPHEMES?

As children encounter greater numbers of multisyllable words, they must learn to integrate their knowledge of phonics generalizations for one-syllable words with the meaningful syllables found in longer words. The relevant generalizations children need to understand and use are:

- Syllables in multisyllable words contain some of the same patterns that are known from smaller, one-syllable, words.

  Example: Compound words, such as *upstairs,* often contain two one-syllable base words that are already known.

  Example: In the two-syllable word *after,* the first syllable, *af,* is like the one-syllable word *at* and the second syllable, *ter,* is like the one-syllable word *her.*

- Multisyllable words can be composed of parts, or chunks, that contribute to the overall meaning of the word.

  Example: *untie* = *un* (not) + *tie* (to fasten or join), means to loosen or undo.

  Example: *childish* = *child* + *ish* (like, adjective forming), means like a child.

- Joining syllables to make multisyllable words can cause changes in the sounds or spelling of individual syllables.

  Example: The *o* in *sec-ond* does not receive vocal emphasis or stress and is pronounced like the *u* in *up.*

  Example: Joining *run* + *ing* to make *running* requires the addition of another *n* to preserve the short *u* sound.

🍎 Multisyllable words can be made of sound chunks, meaning chunks, or both.

Example: sound chunks (*dam-age, fiz-zle*), meaning chunks (*club-house, treat-ment*), or both meaning and sound chunks (*mar-ket/a-ble*).

Making Connections . . .

Begin to challenge your understanding of morphemic patterns. Collect other words that fit the generalizations just described that children need to learn. You must see those patterns in words before you can guide children to see them.

INSTRUCTION IN THE DEVELOPING AND TRANSITIONAL STAGES

Learning words, a critical skill for proficient reading and writing, develops slowly over time. In this text we discuss children's development in broad stages: emergent, developing, and transitional. The emergent stage, when children make the transition from oral to written language, is given special attention in Chapter 2. In this chapter we focus on instruction during the developing and transitional stages.

Children's development at the beginning of a stage can look quite different from development at the middle and end of the stage. It takes varying amounts of time and experiences for children to construct new understandings about words. Even after multiple opportunities to learn a new concept (direct instruction by the teacher, guided practice in reading groups, completing focused activities), many children may still be inconsistent in their ability to apply the new concept independently.

For example, as children first learn that an adjacent letter (*i* in *rai̱n*) and a nonadjacent letter (*e* in *mad̲e̲*) can influence the sound of another letter (*a* in *ra̱n* / *ra̱in*, *ma̱d* / *ma̱de*), they are likely to be inconsistent in their ability to use that knowledge independently.

When meeting unfamiliar long-vowel words in reading they will sometimes decode the word as a short vowel, as if the second vowel was not present in the word.

In writing, they are likely to write long-vowel words without the vowel marker (*bot* for *boat*, *chas* for *chase*), or they may include the the vowel marker but place it in an incorrect position (*rian* for *rain*, *ried* for *ride*).

When teachers carefully observe the progressions in children's learning they are able to provide the appropriate types and amount of support for children to become independent in their use of decoding knowledge. It is important to remember that children may not construct the same understandings from their learning experiences (Hauerwas & Walker, 2004). As children attend to the details in the words they read and write, they begin to be more conventional with some but not all words in a particular pattern. The more that children talk about patterns with teachers who provide guidance and support as children refine and revise their concepts about words, the greater the likelihood children will become fluent decoders.

Instruction in the Developing Stage (Early/Mid-First-Grade to Early-Third-Grade Reading Level)

The major focus of instruction during the developing stage is using phonics generalizations to decode one-syllable then multisyllable words. During this stage it is important to teach phonics as generalizations, rather than rules. Rarely does a phonetic pattern hold true in all situations. Instead, children should learn to generalize their knowledge to the most predictable situations. Figure 3.4 provides an overview of suggested progressions during the developing stage. As with all developmental theories, it is important to fit phonics instruction to the particular needs of the students. The suggested sequence is meant to be adapted to the needs of students.

Instruction in the Transitional Stage (Third- through Sixth-Grade Reading Level)

The major focus during the early part of the transitional stage is to refine phonetic concepts and help children integrate phonics and morphemic understandings. Figure 3.5 provides an overview of the beginning of this stage and a suggested progression for decoding instruction. Third- and fourth-grade-level reading materials will begin to introduce a wider range of multisyllable words. There will be a good variety of vocabulary words to use for word study. As always, the progression followed should have high utility in children's reading and writing.

For teachers to make appropriate decisions about what children will learn about words in the developing and transitional stages, it is important to note the general order of content identified in Figures 3.4 and 3.5.

Phonics—In general, children should study:

- Single-letter patterns (consonant *b*) before multiple-letter patterns (consonant blend *bl*);
- Consistent patterns (*rope, boat*) before variable patterns (*rough, though*);
- Initial position (*sun*) before final position (*his, dress*); and
- Sounded letters (*me*) before silent letters (*make*).

Morphemes—In general, children should study:

- Words with a base (*played*) before words with a root (*decide*);
- Words with inflectional suffixes (*painting*) before derivational suffixes (*slowly*); and
- Words with a free prefix (*untie*) before words with a bound prefix (*concern*).

FIGURE 3.4
Word knowledge and instruction in the developing stage.

Early in Developing Stage:
Mid-First-Grade Reading Level

- "glued to print"
- finger pointing to track text
- some sight words, mostly one-syllable, some two-syllable, words
- partial decoding of one-syllable words, using initial consonants and context (illustration and print)
- spell one-syllable words with beginning and ending consonants; sometimes spaces between words are absent
- Decoding more advanced than spelling

Middle of Developing Stage:
Late-First/Early-Second-Grade Reading Level

- oral reading becoming more fluent with a larger store of sight words
- decoding many one-syllable words with short, and some long, vowels
- beginning to decode base + inflected suffix with familiar base
- developing monitoring skills with familiar letter patterns and context and/or language.
- one-syllable spellings becoming more conventional
- represent sounds in second and third syllables of words
- writing becoming more fluid as sight words are written automatically
- decoding more advanced than spelling

Later in the Developing Stage:
Mid-Second/Early-Third-Grade Reading Level

- fluent oral reading in appropriate-level text
- large store of sight words
- able to decode multisyllable words that have familiar chunks
- able to decode by analogy, use familiar chunks to figure out new words
- decoding more advanced than spelling

Early in the Stage:
Sequence of Decoding Instruction

- initial consonants (consistent)
- final consonants (consistent)
- introduce short vowels (a, o)
- initial and final digraphs (sh, th, ch)
- continue short vowels (u, e, i)
- initial blends (l, r, and s families) as they appear in text
- introduce long vowels (a, e, etc.)

Middle of the Stage:
Sequence of Decoding Instruction

- continue long vowels, contrast with short vowels
- continue initial blends
- base + inflected suffix, no change to base (apples, jumping)
- r-controlled (ar, or, er/ir/ur)
- contractions (as they appear in text)
- variant consonants as they begin to appear in text (soft c, g, s)
- continue long vowels (consistent double vowels, ai, oa, ee)
- base + base, familiar base words, literal meanings (snowman, doghouse)

Later in the Stage:
Sequence of Decoding Instruction

- continue long vowels, variant
- continue contractions (as they appear in text)
- continue r-controlled (are, ere, ire, ore, ure; air, oar, eer, ear)
- base + inflected suffix, base changes (running, babies)
- final blends (nt, lk, etc.)
- base word + derivational suffix (careful)
- diphthongs (oi, oo, au/aw, ou)
- base + base, less familiar base words, literal meaning (wildlife, eyesight)
- consonant digraphs with silent letters (wr, kn, etc.)
- syllable patterns in phonetic words (ta-ble, riv-er, mar-ket)

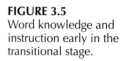

FIGURE 3.5
Word knowledge and instruction early in the transitional stage.

Early in the Transitional Stage:
Early Third/Fourth-Grade Reading Level

- read multisyllable words, phonetic and morphemic
- solidify fluid silent reading with a large store of sight words
- become more flexible in the use of strategies required by different texts
- multisyllable words written more conventionally, phonetic and morphemic
- decoding still more advanced than spelling

Early in the Transitional Stage:
Sequence of Decoding Instruction

- base + base, implied/accepted meanings and hyphenated forms *(overdrawn, play-off)*
- continue syllable patterns with more complex words, integrate phonics and morphemic analysis *(tri-an-gle, u-su-al-ly)*
- independent prefix + base *(pre+view)*
- continue base + derivational suffix as they appear in text *(classify)*
- affixes that change pronunciation *(music/musician, divide/division)*
- complex words with multiple affixes *(fool+ish+ness)*

Making Connections . . .

Survey the sequence of decoding activities in a basal reading series at the first- and second-grade levels. Make a list of the basic phonic and morphemic patterns in the suggested order of instruction. How do the expectations for decoding skills compare with the expectations of the developing and early transitional stages of word knowledge presented in this chapter? Can you explain any differences that exist?

GUIDING PRINCIPLES FOR INSTRUCTION

Regardless of children's stage of word knowledge development, the following principles should guide the planning of meaningful instruction for learning words. The daily study of words should:

- Be systematic, that is, organized, sequential, and deliberate;
- Be explicit, making useful knowledge about words evident to children;
- Be developmentally appropriate, focused on individual children's needs;
- Build on children's concepts about print and phonological awareness;
- Provide multiple opportunities to apply skills and strategies in the context of meaningful reading and writing;

🍎 Develop independent word-recognition strategies in reading, promoting fluency and enabling children to devote their full attention to building meaning; and

🍎 Develop conventional spellings of frequently used words in writing, promoting fluency and communication of ideas.

Systematic Instruction

Read here to find a definition of *systematic instruction.*

Systematic instruction involves teaching a planned sequence of phonetic elements rather than incidentally highlighting phonetic and morphemic elements as they may appear in children's reading materials. The report of the National Reading Panel (see Chapter 1) concluded that systematic instruction in phonics makes a larger contribution to children's growth in reading than nonsystematic instruction.

Systematic, however, does not mean a rigid sequence of instruction. Teachers who provide systematic instruction for children follow a general sequence of instruction that is responsive to children's needs. They are deliberate in their decisions about what and how best to help children become fluent decoders of text. Research in developmental stages demonstrates that children generally move through similar, but not exact, progressions in their learning (Henderson & Beers, 1980; Piaget & Inhelder, 1969). Adopting a rigid sequence for instruction is not likely to meet the needs of a classroom of diverse readers and writers.

Explicit Instruction

Read here to find a definition of *explicit instruction.*

Explicit instruction utilizes direct instruction on specific phonetic and morphemic elements and the application of those elements in words. The sequence of instruction in such programs is predetermined and frequently delivered to the class as a whole. Explicit instruction typically takes a *synthetic approach,* which teaches students to convert letters (graphemes) into sounds (phonemes) and then to blend the sounds to form recognizable words. The analysis and blending of larger chunks of words (onsets, rimes, phonograms, spelling patterns) are also taught through direct instruction.

For more information about explicit phonics, see *http://www.reading.org/adv ocacy/nrp/chapter2.html.*

Proponents of explicit instruction advocate the use of decodable texts . . . texts specifically written with a controlled vocabulary using words that follow particular phonetic or morphemic patterns. Decodable texts provide opportunities for children to practice decoding the phonetic patterns that were taught through direct instruction. Because vocabulary in decodable texts is controlled, the language often seems stilted and contrived. Practice in reading decodable texts is typically guided by the teacher then becomes partner and independent rereadings. Explicit instruction typically utilizes decoding exercises in the form of workbook-type pages that attempt to focus children's attention on specific letter-sound patterns.

Example of an explicit phonics lesson:

> To teach short *i* (*did, hid, hit, kit, sip, tip,* etc.), the teacher guides children in using knowledge of consonants and short *i* to pronounce each sound in a word, then blend the sounds together to pronounce the word. The teacher leads the children in saying, "/d/-/i/-/d/—*did*" as she

points to each letter in the word, then runs her hand from left to right under the word as children repeat it.

After segmenting and blending sounds for a variety of short *i* words, children practice using their knowledge of short *i* by completing independent exercises such as:

- identifying pictures of objects that have the short *i* sound,
- matching pictures with decodable short *i* words, and
- selecting the appropriate word to complete a simple sentence.

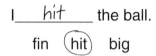

I ___*hit*___ the ball.

fin (hit) big

Embedded Instruction

In contrast to explicit instruction, *embedded instruction* focuses on application of phonetic or morphemic elements as they naturally occur in the texts children read. Because children in a classroom read at different levels, the sequence of instruction may be similar for all children, but children may not be studying the same elements at the same time. Embedded instruction does not attempt to control the vocabulary of the texts that children read. Proponents of embedded instruction prefer to use children's literature for reading, literature that uses natural language, and address phonetic elements as needed to enable children to decode words that are important to comprehension of text.

Read here to find a definition of *embedded instruction*.

Example of an embedded phonics lesson:

Children are reading *The Chick and the Duckling* in their guided reading group. Before the reading begins the teacher introduces the text and asks if children can read the title. The teacher and children together read the title aloud. The teacher writes the word *chick* on a small dry-erase board, and says, "Let's stretch this word and listen for all of the sounds we can hear." Together the teacher and children say, "/ch/-/i/-/k/—*chick.*" Then the teacher asks "What sound do we hear for the letter *i* in *chick*?" The children answer, "/i/." The teacher asks, "If we did not know this word, what might make us think that the letter *i* would make the /i/ sound?" The children say, "Because it's the only vowel." "Because it's in the middle." Then she introduces other short *i* words that appear in the text (*swim, swimming, digging*), one at a time, guiding the decoding of each word, reinforcing the short *i* sound, and noting the reason why the children should expect that sound by looking at the pattern of letters in each word. As the children begin to read the text, the teacher listens for the accuracy of children's decoding, especially the short *i* words. Following the reading the teacher returns to the dry-erase board and asks children to read the short *i* words that were in the text. Then she adds a few new words that have the same short *i* pattern, but were not in the text. She encourages children to apply their knowledge to new words. To follow up this lesson, the teacher asks the children to make a list of other short *i* words they find in the books they are reading independently. The teacher will reinforce the day's lesson using words that children gather from their independent reading.

Children learn in different ways and at different rates. To enhance the opportunity for all children to become fluent readers it is best to use a combination of explicit and embedded instruction. The strength of explicit instruction is the direct introduction to phonetic elements that the teacher provides by modeling and supporting children's practice of segmenting and blending. The strength of embedded instruction is its emphasis on the application of decoding strategies in instructional-level text that is well written and comprehensible for students.

As with other aspects of literacy instruction, balanced instruction in phonics and morphemic analysis should be both explicit and embedded. There will be times when children will need to be taught phonics or morphemes directly, then encouraged to apply their knowledge. At other times, children should be guided to use their knowledge to make associations between the known and the new.

Making Connections . . .

Imagine that you have just been hired as a new first- or second-grade teacher and you are about to hold your first parent meeting to explain your stance toward phonics and phonics instruction in the primary grades. What would you tell the parents? What is your professional stance at this time? Explain why you hold that view. It is important to be aware of your professional position on topics that are highly debated in the field of education.

PUTTING THEORY INTO PRACTICE . . .

To develop an effective word study program for children at any stage of development, consider:

- a variety of ways to organize learning experiences for learning words as a class and in small groups,
- systematic instruction in the analysis and blending of phonemes and morphemes, and
- ways to assess children's development of word knowledge.

We begin with two primary ways to organize the focused study of words: building words and sorting words.

BUILDING WORDS—A WHOLE-CLASS APPROACH TO WORD STUDY

With the diversity of knowledge about words that is likely to exist among any group of children, building words (Cunningham & Hall, 1994) is an excellent way to approach word study with the whole class or a small group. In building words, letter by letter, children are guided to use their skills in phonemic awareness to segment sounds in words and chunks of words, connect each sound to the appropriate letter, then place letter cards in the appropriate sequence, from left to right, on the desk or table in front of them.

Building words provides children the opportunity to experience firsthand that changing just one letter or the sequence of the letters within a word changes that word (Cunningham & Cunningham, 1992). This concept is essential to children's developing concepts about words, especially words in the English language.

Selecting a Focus for Building Words

There are at least two ways to organize for building words:

- Work with a particular phoneme or morpheme

  Example: phonics element, short *a:*

  > *can, map, sad, fat, bag, ham, flat, bath, match, black, stamp, crash.*

  Example: base word, *care-:*

  > *cares, cared, careful, carefully, caring, uncaring, careless, carelessness*

  Example: inflected suffix, *-ing:*

  > *barking, jumping, sleeping, playing, thinking, flying, raking, hitting, running, using, making, hopping, hoping*

  Advantage—repetition of pattern within one lesson, especially when a pattern is new, with some control of the amount of challenge by the element that is chosen.

- Select a longer word, usually six to eight letters, from which a variety of words can be constructed (Cunningham & Hall, 1994).

  Example: Select the letters for the word *spring* to make words such as *in, pin, pig, rig, rip, rips, nips, spin, snip, pins, ping, sing, ring, rings,* and *spring.*

  Example: Select the letters for the word *breaking* to make words such as *be, beg, bag, rag, bar, bare, bake, bike, bang, bank, bark, bear, brag, baker, brake, bring, break, brain, being, began, begin, biker, baking, banker, braking, barking, bearing,* and *breaking.*

  Advantage—reinforcement of patterns previously introduced and the ability to challenge differing levels of children's development by using words of varying length and complexity.

Preparing Materials

To make words, children need a set of letter cards that can be manipulated. Individual letters will need to be duplicated, cut apart, and placed in a small plastic bag or envelope, one container for each letter of the alphabet. When a letter "a" is needed, give one card to each child from the "a" envelope. It is helpful to have the cards that contain different elements (vowels, affixes) printed on contrasting colors of paper to call attention to their position within words.

At the beginning of a building words session, children assist with passing out copies of the particular letters that are needed that day.

> Templates for building a variety of words are available at *http://www.k111.k12.il.us/lafayette/fourblocks/making_words_templates.htm.*

Example: To make words with short *a,* children will need one card for the letter *a,* then individual cards for each consonant needed to make the selected words.

Example: To make words with the base word *care,* children will need a card for each chunk—*care, s, ed, ing, ful, ly, less, ness,* and *un.*

Example: To make words from the word *spring,* children will need the letter cards *s, p, r, i, n,* and *g.*

In addition, teachers need a set of large cards with the same letters or chunks to display the correct spelling of each word in a pocket chart. Large cards for each word will also be needed for sorting. The word cards should be arranged in the order in which children will make the words. Helping children see relationships between words is an important feature of any building words lesson (*spring* can be made by adding *sp-* to *ring*).

Basic Procedures for Building Words

To begin a building words session, children arrange their letter cards (or chunks) on the desk, leaving a space immediately in front of them for arranging letters (or chunks) as words are made, one at a time. Building words might include the following steps:

- Teacher holds up each letter (or chunk), one at a time, and names the letter (or chunk). Children do the same.
- The teacher states the number of letters (or chunks) in the word, such as "Let's make the two-letter word *at*" or "Let's make the two-chunk word *careful.*" The teacher then observes to see that children make the correct word.
- One child who made the word correctly then comes to the front and places the large letters (chunks) for the word in the pocket chart for all to see.
- The teacher helps children check their spelling of the word, letter by letter (chunk by chunk), against the model in the pocket chart.
- The teacher guides the children in building of one word at a time.
- After building the words for the day, the teacher uses large word cards to help children sort words in the pocket chart that have similar spelling patterns and to consider the meaning of particular words. At their tables, children are given a set of small word cards to participate in the sorting of words to reinforce patterns.
- To apply patterns from the lesson, the teacher asks children to speculate on how to spell a new word, a word that uses knowledge from a word in the lesson.
- Encouraging children to record words in a word study notebook is also a valuable activity. It may be most beneficial to record the results of the application and sorting activities.

It may take several days to complete the activities for building words with a particular set of words in order to provide ample opportunity for all children to participate, ask questions, spell, sort, and write words. If building words occurs in a small group, the steps involving the use of large letter and word cards may not be necessary. The teacher is able to see and reinforce the words children make in the small group.

Building Phonetic Words

In the opening vignette, we visited a second-grade classroom where children were building words from the letters used to spell *prince*. The following words can be made using the letters in *prince: in, rip, pin, ice, pen, rice, nice, ripe, pine, ripen, cried, price, prince.*

There are a variety of spelling patterns. Because the teacher carefully guides the lesson, all of the students have success with several words and are supported to spell the words that are challenging.

Example: The word *prince* provides the opportunity to practice:

short e	short i	long i	soft c	blend	suffix
pen	in	ice	ice	price	cried
	rip	rice	rice	prince	ripen
	pin	nice	nice	cried	
		ripe	price		
		pine	prince		
		price			

Building many words from one longer word provides a variety of opportunities to revisit letter-sound patterns that have been introduced before.

For the word *prince,* children can practice:

- rimes (*-in, -ip, -ice, -ine, -ipe*) that form sound chunks within words,
- the effect of silent *e* (*pin, pine; rip, ripe*),
- how the sound of *c* can be softened by the vowel that follows, and
- the different sounds of single consonants and consonant blends (*rice, price*).

For developing readers and writers who are refining their consonant knowledge and learning a great deal about vowels, the letters in the word *prince* are automatically set up for attention to long and short *i.* In addition, it is possible to review the initial blends *pr-* and *cr-*. The letters *c* and *e* provide an opportunity to focus on how *c* represents the *s* sound when followed by *e.*

For transitional readers and writers, children who function between third- and sixth-grade reading levels, the teachers might decide that the words *cried* (*cry + ed*) and *ripen* (*ripe + en*) are appropriate because of the change to the base word when the suffix is added.

To encourage children to apply their new knowledge, consider several new words for children to spell that guide them to apply their knowledge to a new pattern, such as *strip* and *princes.*

Example: Teacher asks:

"To write the word *strip,* which word in the list will help?" (*rip*). "What letters need to be added to rip?" (*st-,* at the beginning).

"Which word can help to spell *princes*?" (*prince*).

"What letters need to be added? Where?"

(-*s,* at the end).

The children thus use analogy to spell new words, using what they know about a group of letters in a familiar word to spell a less familiar word that has the same group of letters. Teaching this strategy reinforces the relationships between many English words.

Building Morphemic Words

Imagine that during a unit of study about fire safety, the children notice that the words *careful* and *carefully* contain the base word *care*. The teacher decides to use this opportunity to focus on how affixes enable us to create many related words in English. The following words contain the base word *care* and familiar suffixes.

Example: *car<u>es</u>*   *care<u>ful</u>*   *care<u>fully</u>*
              care<u>fulness</u>   *care<u>less</u>*   *care<u>lessness</u>*
              car<u>ed</u>   *car<u>ing</u>*   *<u>un</u>car<u>ing</u>*

To make these words children need a word card containing the base word, *care*. They also need a prefix card that contains *un-* and suffix cards for *-s, -ed, -ing, -ful, -ly, -less,* and *-ness* as shown in Figure 3.6.

It is good to make the base word, prefix, and suffix cards each a different color to call attention to their placement in words (for example, base word = black, prefix = red, suffix = green).

Notice that the *-are* vowel pattern is in the word *care*. Also note that in the previous list of words, three words have a change to the base word when the suffix is added:

care + ed = cared (e dropped)
care + ing = caring (e dropped)
un + care + ing = uncaring (e dropped)

FIGURE 3.6
Building words with the base word *Care.*

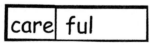

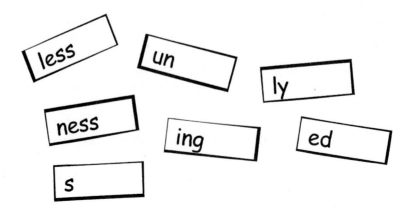

As children make these words, the teacher should observe how they deal with the silent *e* at the end of *care.* Begin the lesson with the most familiar or least complex words. The order for building words depends upon children's experience with base words, especially words that involve change. If children have had some experience, use this lesson to observe which students understand such changes and which need further instruction.

To make the word *caring,* children must lay the suffix *-ing* over the end of the base word *care,* covering the final *e.* This demonstrates understanding that when a base word ends with a silent vowel and has a suffix added that begins with a vowel, there will usually be a change to the base word by dropping the silent *e* in the base word.

After all words in the lesson have been made, use word cards and a pocket chart to help children sort words by the patterns they observe. Children can also have cards for each word to participate in sorting words before the teacher guides sorting. What patterns might they notice?

🍎 Visual patterns:

Base Changes	No Change to Base	
cared	cares	careful
caring	careless	carefully
uncaring	carelessness	carefulness

Because of the attention given to the change to the base word care, children can sort words into those with a change to the base words and those with no change.

🍎 Meaning patterns: *Change in part of speech*

care (verb)	I don't *care* if it rains.
careless (adjective)	Please don't be *careless* with my car.
carefully (adverb)	She cut the vegetables *carefully.*
carelessness (noun)	This accident is because of your *carelessness.*

Because the words have the same base word, they have meanings that are related, but not exact. Derivational suffixes change the part of speech and thus make changes to the overall meaning of the word.

To focus children's attention on the power of a prefix or suffix, make words using only that particular affix.

Example: *-ing: barking, painting, sleeping, thinking, flying, building, raking, hitting, running, using, making, hopping*

To build these morphemic words, select a variety of base words to which *-ing* can be added. Adding *-ing* to *bark* changes the verb *bark* from present tense to a participle that can be used to describe past (*was barking*), present (*is barking*), or future (*will be barking*) action. Consider *paint* and *painting. Paint* can be both a noun and a verb; adding *-ing* maintains both the noun (object) and the verb form (action).

Adding *-ing* changes the spelling of some base words. Do you notice the pattern?

🍎 Words that end in silent *e* drop that e.
🍎 Words that end in a single consonant have the consonant doubled before adding *-ing.*

This relates to preserving the vowel sound in the base word. To make these words children will need a card for each base word, the suffix *-ing,* and single consonants cards for the consonants that are doubled, *t-, n-,* and *p-.*

As in building words with the base word *care,* make each word, discuss potential changes in meaning or word usage, and note spelling changes that occur. After building words, children can sort for patterns. What patterns might they notice?

🍎 Visual patterns:

Drop e	Double Consonant	No Change to Base
raking	hitting	painting
using	hopping	thinking
making	running	building
		sleeping
		flying

🍎 Meaning patterns:

Verb	Verb or Adjective	Verb or Noun
raking	sleeping	building
hopping	flying	painting
using		
running		
making		
hitting		

A sample for building words is shown in Figure 3.7. Sentences can be made with the words to note potential changes in meaning when the suffix *-ing* is added. With a number of words, the possible contexts in which words can be found must be considered.

Example: The new apartment *building* had three floors. (noun)
The workers are *building* some new apartments. (verb)
The geese are *flying* in a V-shaped formation. (verb)
A *flying* fish can glide in the air for a short distance. (adjective)

Challenge the children to hunt for similar words in their reading materials to help them solidify their understandings about morphemic patterns.

Selecting multisyllable words for study should be guided by the words that are showing up in children's reading materials or words that children are trying to use in their writing. Utility is important. Children must be able to apply new knowledge to print in some manner fairly soon after word study lessons.

When children are sorting morphemic patterns, the words are typically categorized according to meaning and visual patterns as in the previous examples. Because morphemic units are also meaning units, be sure to emphasize meaning at some point in the sorting process.

During word study lessons, children can be encouraged to write the words they make. Writing is an excellent reinforcement for phonics and morphemic patterns. A word study notebook, described in an upcoming section, can be quite useful in word building lessons.

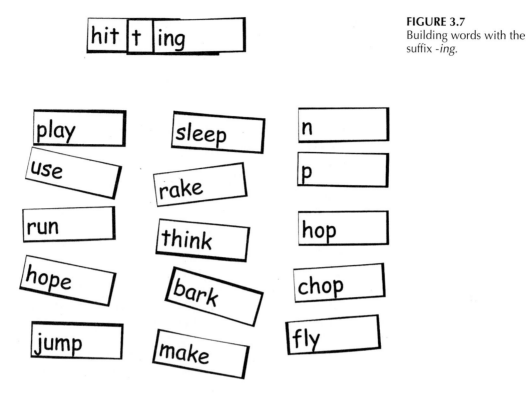

FIGURE 3.7
Building words with the suffix *-ing*.

Lengthening the amount of time focused on one set of words can increase learning for many children in the class. Experiences with building words such as those presented can occur each day in primary-grade classrooms. Building words provides opportunities for children to hear spoken words, then use letters to construct those words. Children also have opportunities to participate in sorting words by patterns and spelling by analogy. Children can extend their vocabulary knowledge through discussion of the relationship among words.

Lessons in building words can be adapted to small developmental groups, with similar procedures as whole-class word study. It is more challenging, however, to find ample time to devote to daily small-group word building when teacher guidance is required. An alternative is small-group instruction that focuses on sorting, building, and hunting for words with patterns that are at children's developmental level.

SORTING WORDS—A SMALL-GROUP APPROACH TO WORD STUDY

In developmental word study, children who are at approximately the same level of word knowledge are grouped together for small-group word study. Within one class there will probably be at least three to four different developmental levels for word study. In addition to sorting words, small-group study can also include building words and hunting for words in instructional- and independent-level reading materials.

Organizing developmental word study involves:

- Lists of 10 to 15 words that follow a pattern(s) and are developmentally appropriate for each small group;
- Blank word cards on which children write words or preprinted word cards that can be sorted and categorized;
- A word study notebook in which children record their thinking about words;
- Discussion with a partner/group and teacher about the patterns that evolve from sorting to either confirm or redirect children's thinking about words; and
- Guidance by the teacher to enhance children's understanding of spelling patterns.

In small-group word study, children participate in a week-long study of particular patterns. This study takes the place of traditional spelling instruction. Approximately 20 minutes per day is given to small-group word study activities. This time can be in addition to other whole-class word study activities.

All children meet in their small groups at the same time so that the teacher is able to interact with children and closely monitor their progress. Children can move to a particular place in the room to meet their "word study group." Figure 3.8 provides an overview of activities in a week of word study.

FIGURE 3.8
Sample activities for a week of small-group word study.

Monday	Tuesday	Wednesday	Thursday	Friday
Provide new list of appropriate words.	Review word cards individually or with partner.	Individually review word cards.	Individually review word cards.	Take posttest with two to three new words that fit the pattern to test ability to generalize pattern.
Children check to be sure they can read each word.	Complete a closed word sort for sound, visual, or meaning patterns.	Participate in word building or word hunting activities.	Participate in word building or word hunting activities.	
Add the list of words to the word study notebook.	Write the results in the word study notebook.	Write results in the word study notebook.	Write new words in word study notebook.	Discuss comfort/confidence with patterns following test.
Make word cards (about 1" × 3") for sorting activities.	Discuss patterns observed with a partner.	Discuss results with partner.	Compare new words and word list, note similarities and differences in notebook.	Plan for next week of word study.
Take a spelling pretest with a partner.	Discuss patterns observed in sorts in a word study group.	Discuss patterns in a word study group.	Discuss results with partner.	
			Discuss patterns in word study group.	

Many children need our support to hear sounds in words and related those sounds to letters.

The purpose of a weekly pretest is to help children identify understandings and misconceptions related to the focus words. Partners within each group can learn to administer the pretest to each other. Through whole-class modeling and guided self-correction, children can learn how to check their spellings, letter by letter. The outcome of the pretest should guide teacher-student and student-student interactions during the week of study. Children want to improve their spelling, but they need to know how to correct their thinking when it interferes with spelling patterns.

The posttest can be administered in the same manner. If the purpose of word study is personal improvement, then it is best for children to learn to correct their own work. Focusing on personal growth, rather than class competition, may reduce the anxiety some children have about being "right." Learning must become its own reward.

Guiding Small-Group Word Study

For small-group word study to be effective, teachers should:

- Become knowledgeable about the stages of word knowledge development and the content of phonics and morphemic analysis.
- Develop lists of words that fit patterns in each stage of development, such as the lists in Appendix C. Word lists are also drawn from words that appear in instructional and independent reading materials.
- Determine each child's stage of word knowledge and make functional word study groups that will allow children to study words that are known words and within reach for learning to spell conventionally (see Assessment section later in this chapter).
- Create manageable word study groups of children with similar word knowledge and instructional need.

- 🍎 Prepare weekly charts listing the words for each group and provide sheets of blank word cards for the children to use when preparing words for sorting.
- 🍎 Take time to teach the routines for weekly word study. This may take several weeks at the beginning of the school year.
- 🍎 Circulate while children are working on word study activities and plan for group meetings to discuss what patterns children have noticed. Mediate between what children already know and what they might need to clarify to make sense of the patterns being studied (Vygotsky, 1962).
- 🍎 Use assessment information to continually monitor groups for appropriate placement of all children and to guide the focus of instruction.

To implement a word study program, help children:

- 🍎 Understand the purpose for each part of the weekly study.
- 🍎 Learn to be good partners, assisting and supporting the efforts of another to learn words.
- 🍎 Learn to record the results of their picture and/or word sorts, as well as their thinking about their sorts, in their word study notebooks.

Forming Developmental Groups for Word Study

For word study to be most beneficial, children should focus on patterns that they are beginning to notice but may not fully understand. If children are asked to attend to patterns in words that are above their own reading level, they will not be able to make full use of instruction.

To have a sense of what children are noticing about language, look at the spellings that appear in their writing. As children are learning about letter-sound relationships, they will invent spellings to stand for patterns they have not yet internalized (Temple, Temple, & Burris, 1993). Invented, or temporary, spellings are children's best attempts to represent words that are beyond their independent level of performance.

Examining children's writing is one of the best ways to see what they know about written language. Children's writing shows what they:

- 🍎 have gained control over and consistently use,
- 🍎 are just beginning to figure out and use inconsistently or incorrectly, and
- 🍎 have yet to notice or understand because it is absent from their writing.

For example, Figure 3.9 shows a sample of writing from Beatrice journal in December of second grade. Her first language is Spanish. Beatrice might benefit from a closer look at digraphs that contain a silent letter, such as -ck in *chicken* and *stick*. It is helpful to recall that in Spanish, the /k/ sound is represented by only one letter. She might also benefit from examination of the inflected suffix, -es, and the sounds that are possible when -es forms its own syllable. To determine the types of patterns that will be most helpful to Beatrice, evaluate this and other samples of her writing.

To identify children's stage of word knowledge development, analyze a sample of words of varying difficulty that children attempt to spell on their own. This inventory is constructed of words that represent a particular level of knowledge,

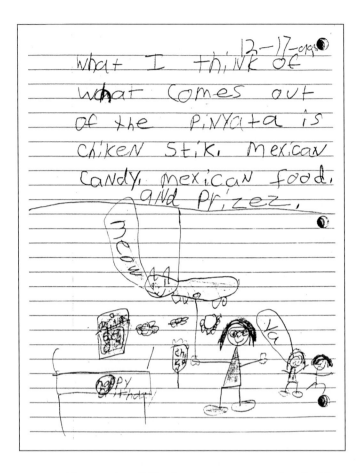

FIGURE 3.9
Beatrice's journal entry
from second grade.

or are of increasing difficulty to determine a level of knowledge. Some example words are provided in the Assessment section of this chapter. Children write the example words as they are dictated. It is important to observe children during the writing for signs of their level of confidence in spelling each word. Assessing and evaluating children's stage of word knowledge is discussed again in the Assessment section of this chapter.

SELECTING WORDS FOR STUDY

Select words for study based upon children's stage of development and knowledge of phonics and/or morphemic analysis. Gather words that appear in children's reading materials and familiar words that pose challenges in children's writing.

Words Have Multiple Possibilities

Individual words contain elements for the study of a number of phonic or morphemic patterns.

> Example: *map* can be included in the study of:
>> initial consonant /m/,
>> final consonant /p/,

short *a*, and
rime/word family *-ap*.

Example: *careless* can be included in the study of:
words with a base,
meaning of words with *care* as the base word,
words with a derivational suffix that changes meaning, and
meaning of words with *less*.

Patterns Have Levels of Complexity

Select words for a particular phonetic or morphemic element that have different levels of complexity to accommodate the varying levels of readers and writers in the classroom.

Example: short *a* with single consonants:
bag, can, ham, map, sad.
short *a* with blends and digraphs:
black, bath, crash, match, stamp.
short *a* in multisyllable words:
apple, happy, magnet, capsule, hatchet.

Sample lists of words by pattern can also be found in Appendix C.

Making Connections . . .

Begin to collect sets of words that reflect children's knowledge in the developing stage. Do the same task for the early part of the transitional stage. Explain how each word reflects knowledge that is developed in this stage.

 TYPES OF SORTS

Children can demonstrate their understandings of phonemes, phoneme patterns, and morphemes with either pictures or words. Until children have acquired a sight vocabulary of words that can be studied (most emergent readers), pictures can be used to focus attention on particular phonemes. Pictures should be clear and easily recognized. Children must be able to verbally name pictures in a picture sort (picture sorts were introduced in Chapter 2).

When children have a sight vocabulary of at least 100 words, they are usually ready to begin sorting words. As with picture sorts, word sorts can either be open or closed. To see what children already recognize about pattern(s) in the words, have children first complete an open sort, during which they determine the categories by either sound or meaning patterns they recognize within a group of words. A closed sort is used to determine children's ability to identify particular elements within words.

Sorting activities may be either open or closed:

- An *open sort* allows children to determine categories for the cards (either pictures or words) by selecting the patterns they notice independently. Some focus can be given to the sort without stipulating categories by asking children to sort for either sound or meaning patterns.
- A *closed sort* directs children to attend to specific, predetermined characteristics, showing their depth of understanding about particular letter-sound patterns or word structures.

To learn about the depth of children's understandings of a particular pattern(s) guide their attention by selecting categories for a closed sort. In a closed sort children are given the exemplars for categories. Imagine that children are sorting the following words:

ship	chop	shot	chin
and	was	chip	she
shop	chat	said	

They have exemplar pictures of a shell and a chick as representations of the sounds for which they will listen. The teacher asks the children to place those pictures at the top of the sorting area at their desk or table. There is also an "other" card for all of the pictures that children think do not belong in the other piles. Notice that words that do not fit either pattern are included (*said, was, and*).

To sort, the child should:

- say the name of each word aloud,
- listen for the onset at the beginning of the word,
- segment the onset (*sh-* or *ch-*) and say it aloud,
- compare the onset with *shell* and *chick,*
- place the words that begin like *shell* under the shell picture, and place the words that begin like *chick* under that picture, and
- place all other pictures in the "other" pile.

A sample closed word sort is provided in Figure 3.10. The complexity of word sorts can vary from two categories to four or more categories. Examples of a variety of word sorts can be seen in Figures 3.11 through 3.14. Figure 3.15 shows other possible patterns for two-, three-, and four-level sorts.

In most sorting activities, it is informative to include a discard, or "other," pile to indicate children's uncertainty or confusion about words or patterns. Without a discard pile, children may feel forced to place words in a category even if they are not certain about the characteristics of the word or picture. Talking with children about the placement of the words reveals the clarity of their thinking.

FIGURE 3.10
Sample closed word sort—
digraphs *ch-* and *sh-*.

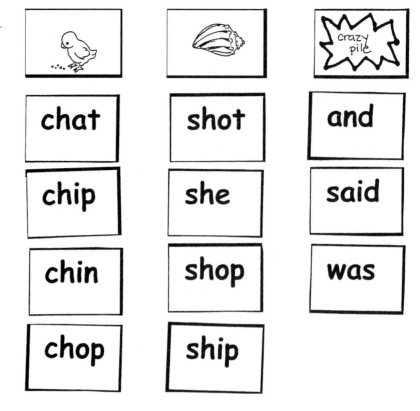

🍎 USING A WORD STUDY NOTEBOOK

A word study notebook is an excellent record-keeping device. Each child should have a notebook or folder for recording words that are studied each week. Pages can be duplicated with a particular format that aids children's recording of weekly activities. The pages should be secured in the notebook and there should be a sufficient number of pages to record several weeks of study. Children should be able to refer to past lists and sorts to remind themselves about patterns they have studied. The notebook also enables children to see growth in their knowledge of words. Examples of ways to use a notebook for a week of word study are shown in Figure 3.16.

The word study notebook is a functional writing experience for children. Even children who are completing picture sorts rather than word sorts can record the results of sorting by drawing or gluing pictures and recording sounds they hear. Children should be asked to use what is recorded in the notebook on a daily basis for discussions about words. If not, they may feel that the recording is not valued. Children should be asked to refer to their notebooks during word study discussions.

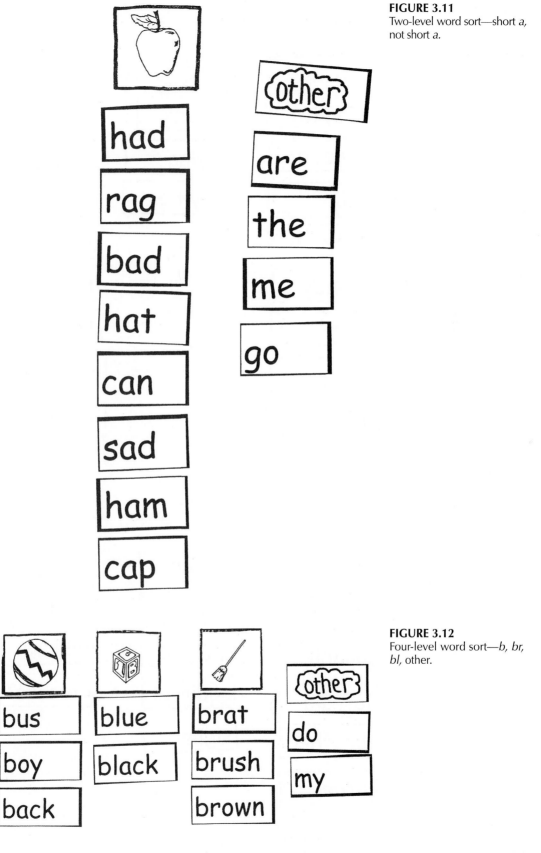

FIGURE 3.11
Two-level word sort—short *a*,
not short *a*.

other

had	are
rag	the
bad	me
hat	go
can	
sad	
ham	
cap	

FIGURE 3.12
Four-level word sort—*b*, *br*,
bl, other.

other

bus	blue	brat	do
boy	black	brush	my
back		brown	

FIGURE 3.13
Three-level word sort—
base + suffix.

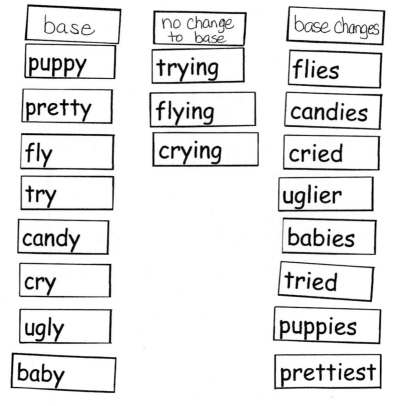

base	no change to base	base changes
puppy	trying	flies
pretty	flying	candies
fly	crying	cried
try		uglier
candy		babies
cry		tried
ugly		puppies
baby		prettiest

FIGURE 3.14
Sorting words with a schwa
vowel sound—three-level
sort with the schwa vowel
sound.

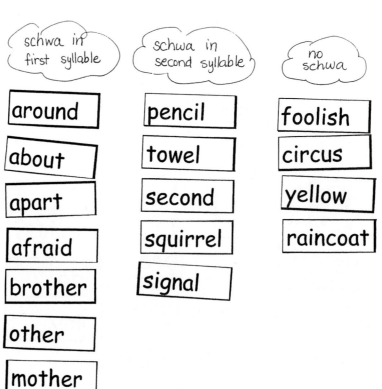

schwa in first syllable	schwa in second syllable	no schwa
around	pencil	foolish
about	towel	circus
apart	second	yellow
afraid	squirrel	raincoat
brother	signal	
other		
mother		

FIGURE 3.15
Examples of sorts.

Examples of two-level sorts

1	2
initial *m* (mop)	other (not initial *m*)
short *a* (*cap*)	other (not short *a*)
compound word	other (not compound word)
has a prefix	other (no prefix)

Examples of three-level sorts

1	2	3
initial *b* (*boy*)	final *b* (*cab*)	other
short *a* (*bat*)	long *a* (*cake*)	other
base + inflected suffix (no change to base)	base + inflected suffix (base changes)	other
two-syllable words, first vowel long (ta/ble)	two-syllable words, first vowel short (riv/er)	other other

Examples of four-level sorts

1	2	3	4
long *a* (cake)	long *a* (rain)	short *a* (cab)	other
initial *b* (bat)	*br* blends (*brown*)	*bl* blends (*blue*)	other

FIGURE 3.16
Entries for a word study notebook.

Possible Word Study Notebook Entries	
Monday	List of words for the week Open sort Pretest
Tuesday	Closed sort Explain of patterns
Wednesday	Words from word building or word hunting Explanation of patterns
Thursday	Words from word building or word hunting Explanation of patterns
Friday	Posttest

FIGURE 3.17
A week of word study.

My Word Study Notebook

1/16 new words

fish	she	dish
shake	wish	flash
ship	his	stop
sad	shop	

1/17 word sort

begins with sh	ends with sh	crazy pile
she	dish	his
shake	fish	sad
ship	wish	stop
shop	flash	

dish, wish, and fish have -ish.

1/18 building words
sh, i, a, o, f, l, k, e, w, d,

fish	ship	she	flash
dish	shop	shake	
wish			

new words–dash
                    wishes

1/19 word hunt

fishing	wishes
milkshake	shopping
sheep	

sh can be in bigger words too.

A sample of children's entries for 1 week are shown in Figures 3.17 and 3.18. This notebook shows words being studied by a developing reader early in second grade. At this stage, children are able to tell more about patterns verbally than they can in writing. The word study notebook can also be used to record whole-class word building lessons as described earlier in this chapter.

🍎 ASSESSMENT: MONITORING GROWTH IN WORD KNOWLEDGE

"Kidwatching" (Goodman, 1985), carefully observing children's reading and writing behaviors, is an essential first step in the assessment of their development. Observations should be guided by asking questions that focus attention on the integration of decoding skills into daily literacy activities.

For students who are in the *early part of the developing stage,* teachers should collect data to answer the following questions:

🍎 What strategies does the child appear to use in developing sight vocabulary?

🍎 How much instructional and independent reading seems to be necessary for the child to learn new words?

FIGURE 3.18
Word study notebook—
V/CV and VC/V patterns.

Word Study Notebook

4/1 Word List

cider	radish	open
linen	rocket	lizard
later	diner	ticket
travel	music	pilot

4/3 Word Building—Syllables

V/CV	VC/V
ci-der	rad-ish
o-pen	rock-et
pi-lot	trav-el
di-ner	tick-et
la-ter	liz-ard
mu-sic	lin-en

4/2 Closed word sort—listen for the first vowel sound to be long or short.

secret	river
cider	radish
open	linen
later	rocket
diner	lizard
music	ticket
pilot	travel

Words like <u>secret</u> have a long vowel first.

Words like <u>river</u> have a short vowel first.

4/4 Word Hunting in <u>Chocolate Fever</u>

V/CV	VC/V
be-lieve	com-ical
be-cause	choc-olate
u-sual	prob-ably
u-sually	im-agine
co-coa	ev-ery
	sep-arate
	ex-act

Our group looked for words that have a VCV pattern at the beginning. Then we tried long- and short-vowel sounds to see what made sense.

🍎 How consistently does the child use the "context +" strategy with beginning consonants? Final consonants?

🍎 Is the child actively searching to represent most phonemes when writing one- or two-syllable words?

🍎 Is the child becoming more accurate in representing short-vowel phonemes in one-syllable words?

🍎 Is the child beginning to notice that some words have parts (base + inflected suffix)?

For children who are in the *later part of the developing stage,* teachers should collect data to answer the following questions:

- Does the child's sight vocabulary show a marked increase over the early part of this stage?
- Does the child's reading and writing reflect a growing knowledge of single- and double-vowel patterns? What behaviors suggest that the child understands that some letters in English will be silent and may serve as markers for a vowel in the same syllable?
- How consistently does the child use the "context +" strategy with consonants? With vowels? With morphemes?
- How consistently is the child able to find base words within multisyllable words in which the base does not change?

For children who are in the *early part of the transitional stage,* teachers should collect data to answer the following questions:

- Does the child have a large enough sight vocabulary to read fluently in appropriate text?
- Is the child able to use morphemic knowledge with words in which the base has been changed by the joining of syllables?
- Is the child beginning to integrate phonics and morphemic patterns to decode unfamiliar multisyllable words? How consistently is the child able to use the "context +" strategy to decode multisyllable words?
- What behaviors suggest that the child is nearly ready to break into flexible, more mature reading?

Gathering data to address these questions guides the learning experiences we plan for reading and writing. Conferring with children about their reading and writing and collecting samples of reading and writing over time is essential for planning effective instruction. Observations of children's reading and writing direct us to the types of words they may need to study more closely in order to generalize patterns to other English words.

To assess and evaluate word knowledge development, teachers collect data concerning:

- Children's use of decoding knowledge and strategies during reading, both in context and isolation, and
- Children's spelling development, as shown in samples of writing.

Making Connections . . .

Begin to collect words that will be appropriate for building words and word sorts. Challenge yourself to categorize the words according to sequences suggested in this chapter. Compare your lists with those suggested in Appendix C.

Also, begin a file of other suggested activities to develop word knowledge in phonics and morphemic analysis. Organize the activities according to the phonetic and morphemic elements that are being emphasized. Clearly identify the purpose and possibilities of each activity that you collect.

ASSESSING WORD KNOWLEDGE IN READING

Miscues in Oral Reading

As children progress through the primary grades, we should notice marked differences in their ability to accurately decode words, moving from one-syllable to multisyllable words. When children read orally they often miscue, or give an oral response to print that is different from what might have been expected. Miscues provide a "window" into a reader's thinking in response to print (Goodman & Burke, 1970). As children read orally, listen for the types of miscues they make. For example, consider the following miscues made in the context of a story:

Text: The white and brown horse trotted along.
Child 1 reads: The white and brown *house* trotted along.
Child 2 reads: The white and *black* horse *totted* along.
Child 3 reads: The white and brown horse *galloped* along.

Child 1 and child 2 attend to visual patterns (*horse-house, brown-black, trotted-totted*) but may be missing some essential consonant and vowel patterns. In addition, they do not monitor or cross-check for meaning. Child 3 does not attend to letter-sound patterns (*trotted-galloped*), but instead appears to use context and/or known language patterns to make sense. Making records in the context of children's reading, such as in this example, reveals knowledge and strategies that are used effectively, as well as knowledge that is not yet well-developed. Making records of children's reading is discussed extensively in the context of guided reading in Chapter 6.

Decoding words in context should be compared to children's ability to decode similar words in isolation. Automatic recognition of high-frequency sight words and decoding of words with various phonic and morphemic patterns are two assessments that are frequently used in the primary grades.

High-Frequency Sight Words

Monitor children's progress toward developing a large store of words known automatically by using lists of words such as the Dolch 220 and Fry Instant Words. A baseline assessment should establish a child's present level at the beginning of a school year. Then periodic assessments should occur, more frequently for developing readers, throughout the school year.

> Find more about high-frequency words at *http://www.createdbyteach ers.com/sightfreemain.html* and *http://www14.brinkster. com/readwrite/ sightwords2.htm.*

The most efficient assessments are lists of about 20 to 25 words grouped by utility and presented in an easy-to-read format, such as:

the	of	he	can
and	in	for	on
to	a	are	as
is	you	with	his
that	it	they	me

Keep a record of children's progress, including the dates of assessment and words correctly identified. The focus should be on automatic recognition, so allow only about 3 seconds for each word. Note any miscues above the word, such as:

Miscue —   *has*
            —————
Actual Word —   his

Phoneme and Word Recognition

In addition to knowing how children decode words in meaningful contexts such as stories, it is important to be aware of the accuracy of decoding words without the aid of context and language cues. Words can be grouped by patterns, assessing only those patterns that are appropriate for the child at that time. A sample assessment is provided (Figure 3.19), including directions for administering the assessment (Figure 3.20).

A clean copy of the recording form can be given to the student. Following the directions for administration, the teacher asks the student to either reproduce sounds or decode words, one section at a time. This assessment provides a quick assessment of a student's overall knowledge of letter-sound relationships in isolation. A student's performance should be compared to reading in context to determine how effectively the student is able to apply that knowledge.

ASSESSING WORD KNOWLEDGE IN WRITING

To identify and monitor children's growth in word knowledge, analyze their writing at the beginning of the school year and at least two or three other times during the year. Collect and analyze writing samples for evidence of word knowledge, both focused and unfocused.

Unfocused Writing Sample

Examine Enrique's writing about magnets as shown in Figure 3.21. This sample came from his independent journal and was written near the end of the second-grade year. The word *magnet* probably came from the word wall that grew out of the class study about magnets. Also be aware that Enrique's first language is Spanish, which may account for the omission of the letter *s* on the word *magnet* as a plural marker. What does Enrique know about words that appear frequently in reading materials? As a developing reader/writer, Enrique is expected to be nearing mastery of writing most single-syllable short- and long-vowel words.

- Notice the conventional spelling of the high-frequency words *and, can, to,* and *not,* as well as the decodable word *clips.*
- Notice also the correct spelling of a two-syllable word, *paper.*
- Notice the absence of *ck* in *stick.* In his acquisition of a new language, Enrique may not understand that English words that have a short-

---

Name _____   Date _____

Grade _____   **Instructional Reading Level** _____

---

1. Consonants in Isolation:

f	b	r	n	k	m	p	s	t	w	x
z	l	v	c	j	y	g	d	h	q	

2. Digraphs and Blends in Isolation:

sh	bl	th	gr	ch	st
pr	sm	fl	wr	ph	kn

3. Vowels in Isolation:

e	o	i	a	u	y

4. Using Consonants and Short Vowels in Words:

sun	wig	map	hen	shop
step	cob	chin	bag	doll
fin	jug	bath	plug	keg

5. Short Vowel to Long Vowel (Silent E) in Words:

mad	hid	not	tub
made	hide	note	tube

6. Using Consonants and Vowel Digraphs in Words:

weep	rail	toast	weak
maid	beam	wheel	boat

7. Using Consonants and R-Controlled Vowels in Words:

jar	bird	fur	here	more
ear	hair	care	roar	fire

8. Using Consonants and Diphthongs in Words:

toy	hook	shout	now
food	raw	coin	haul

9. Using phonics Multisyllable Words:

mailman	review	we're	inhabit
dangerous	wonder	spectacle	city
musician	overdrawn	giant	shouldn't
dislocate	tricycle	spinning	aren't

FIGURE 3.19
Word recognition assessment—recording form.

---

vowel sound and end with -*k* will usually spell that sound with the digraph -*ck*. In English, -*ck* has a silent letter and represents one sound, /-k/ (see Helman, 2004).

 Notice the spelling of *pencils* (*pensels*) and *quarters* (*calrs*). Both words contain phonetic elements that are beyond his knowledge at the time— soft *c*, schwa (*cil* sound like *sul*, etc.). His pronunciation of *quarters* may not be accurate, thus the difficulty in more accurately representing *qu* and the *r*-controlled vowels *ar* and *er* that appear in both syllables.

By studying several samples of Enrique's independent writing, we would begin to see patterns helpful in making decisions about appropriate words for him to study.

FIGURE 3.20
Directions for administering the word recognition assessment.

1. **Consonants in Isolation:**
   Point at the letter *f* and say, "Tell me the sound this letter can make." After the child responds, begin pointing at each letter across the row, prompting the child for the sound it represents. Some children may say the sounds for both hard and soft c/g. Record incorrect responses exactly as spoken.

2. **Digraphs and Blends in Isolation:**
   Point at the letters *sh* and say, "Tell me the sound these letters can make." After the child responds, begin pointing at each group of letters, prompting the child for the sound it represents. Record incorrect responses exactly as spoken.

3. **Vowels in Isolation:**
   Point at each vowel and say, "Tell me the sounds this letter can make." If the child gives only one sound for the vowel (long or short) prompt for the other sound. For example, if the child says "e-e-e-e-," say, "Can *e* make any other sounds?" Record incorrect responses exactly as spoken.

4. **Using Consonants and Short Vowels in Words:**
   Point at the word *sun* and say, "What is this word?" After a response begin pointing at each word, moving across each row, allowing 3–5 seconds for response. Record incorrect responses exactly as spoken.

5. **Short Vowel to Long Vowel (Silent E) in Words:**
   Point at the word *mad* and say, "What is this word?" After a response, point to the word below it, *made,* and ask, "What is this word?" Proceed with each set of words, allowing 3–5 seconds for a response to each word. Record incorrect responses exactly as spoken.

6. **Using Consonants and Vowel Digraphs in Words:**
   Point to the word *weep* and ask, "What is this word?" After a response, proceed across each row, point at a word, and allow 3–5 seconds for response. Record incorrect responses exactly as spoken.

7. **Using Consonants and R-Controlled Vowels in Words:**
   Point to the word *jar* and ask, "What is this word?" After a response proceed across each row, point at a word, and allow 3–5 seconds for response. Record incorrect responses exactly as spoken.

8. **Using Consonants and Diphthongs in Words:**
   Point to the word *toy* and ask, "What is this word?" After a response, proceed across each row, point at a word, and allow 3–5 seconds for response. Record incorrect responses exactly as spoken.

9. **Using Phonics in Multisyllable Words:**
   Point to the word *mailman* and ask, "What is this word?" After a response, proceed across each row, point at a word, and allow 3–5 seconds for response. Record incorrect responses exactly as spoken.

Focused Writing Sample

The words that appear in children's independent writing may not show some of the phonetic elements we are interested in understanding. In that case, it is appropriate to develop an assessment that focuses children's writing on particular elements. In the middle of the first-grade year, Leslie's teacher asked her to write

FIGURE 3.21
Enrique's journal entry—
second crade.

a sentence that the teacher dictated. The sentence contained many high-frequency words.

Words in Context

The teacher dictates a sentence to the child. The child is encouraged to write what he or she hears in the words of the sentence. The sentence is repeated as needed so that the child is aware of all of the words in the sentence. The teacher isn't looking so much at conventional spelling, but rather at the number of phonemes that are heard within the words, and the sound-symbol relationships the child knows or uses to represent those phonemes. Other aspects of writing, such as capitalization, spacing, punctuation, and left-to-right recording, are also noted.

The sentence chosen for the dictation should contain familiar one- and two-syllable words with a variety of consonant and vowel patterns, including some high-frequency words. The sound of each phoneme that is represented accurately is counted. Vowels are counted as correct if the letter used to represent the sound in a plausible selection, such as *to* for *Tue*sday (as Brenda wrote in May of kindergarten). Letter reversals are not counted.

FIGURE 3.22
Brenda's dictations over time.

Note: Letters in bold are correct representations.

May of kindergarten:

I have **a** big **d**o**g** at **h**ome. **T**uesday I **am**
going to take **h**im to **s**chool.

October of first grade:

I **can** see the **red** bo**at** that **we are**
going to ha**ve a** ride in.

January of first grade:

I **have a** big **d**og at **home**. T**uesday** I **am**
going to take **him** to **school**.

May of first grade:

I **can** see the **red** bo**at** that **we are**
going to have a ride in.

Figure 3.22 shows four examples that Brenda wrote over the course of 12 months—at the end of kindergarten, early in first grade, the middle of first grade, and at the end of first grade. Notice that Brenda, an English language learner, began by representing some words with only one letter. Also, she did not acknowledge word boundaries by leaving spaces between words. Within 1 year Brenda progressed to clearly showing word boundaries and representing most phonemes within the dictated words.

Making Connections . . .

Collect samples of focused and unfocused writing from several children in the developing stage and make some general determinations about what they know about words. Based on the writing samples, what types of word knowledge activities might be planned that would be developmentally appropriate?

Words in Isolation

Another type of focused assessment is to select a list of words that represent particular spelling patterns. In Figure 3.23, we can see five samples of Leslie's word knowledge taken over a 3-year period, beginning in first grade. The words in this focused assessment are drawn from a sample of words used for assessing children's stage of word knowledge (Bear & Barone, 1989).

By using the same words, Leslie's teachers are able to observe growth in Leslie's knowledge over a number of years. What do you notice? In second grade, she continues to struggle with how long-vowel sounds are shown in English. Leslie is not yet consistent with long vowels. By third grade, Leslie is ready to focus on hearing those same sounds within multisyllable words. She represents each syllable, but does not yet relate the chunks in longer words to what she already knows, except for familiar inflected suffixes.

A focused spelling assessment can be designed for any level of word knowledge. Children write groupings of words that represent particular phonics and morphemic knowledge along the continuum of word knowledge.

Example: To assess a child early in the developing stage, select single-syllable words with a variety of short vowels and single consonants, such as:

rag	*jet*	*kid*	*log*	*tub*
fan	*men*	*win*	*hop*	*sun*

FIGURE 3.23
Focused spelling assessment for Leslie, grades 1–3.

Focus Words	Beginning 1st Grade	Beginning 2nd Grade	End 2nd Grade	Beginning 3rd Grade	End 3rd Grade
bed	be	bed	bed	bed	bed
ship	hep	ship	ship	ship	ship
drive	r	driv	drive	drive	drive
bump	bup	bup	bump	bump	bump
when	wen	when	when	when	when
train		trene	train	train	train
closet		closet	closit	closet	closet
chase		chaes	chas	chas	chase
float		flowt	flowt	flot	flote
beaches		beches	beaches	beaches	beaches
preparing			preparing	preparing	preparing
popping			poping	poping	poping
cattle			catol	cattle	catel
caught			cote	cote	cot
inspection					inspection
puncture					punksher
cellar					seller
pleasure					plesher
squirrel					squirle
fortunate					forchynet

Focused Spelling Assessment   Name – Leslie

These 10 words provide two opportunities to spell each short vowel, as well as a variety of single consonants.

Focused assessments are most useful when administered individually. It is important to watch as a child writes each word. For example, Leslie's assessment in third grade could have stopped after the 15th word, *inspection*. Her responses show that these multisyllable words were not yet appropriate and the spellings of the last group of words did not add to our knowledge of Leslie's development.

Samples of focused and unfocused writing and records of miscues during reading (see reading records in the Assessment section of Chapter 6) should be primary sources of information about phonics and morphemic knowledge that children can use independently. Emerging knowledge can also become the focus of instruction for reading and writing.

Making Connections . . .

Develop sets of words for a focused assessment that represent the morphemic units and syllabication generalizations that are the focus of the transitional stage. For example, which words would you select to assess children's understanding of base + suffix words? You should be able to explain how each word in the set reflects knowledge that is developed in this stage.

KEEPING RECORDS OF WORD KNOWLEDGE DEVELOPMENT

Each time that a child's reading or writing is evaluated for evidence of word knowledge, it will be helpful to record observations. Record-keeping forms, such as those provided in Figures 3.24 through 3.27 can be made to reflect the knowledge and strategies that are the focus of instruction at each stage. Such forms are combined with other assessment data to build a more complete picture of children's development.

 RESPECTING DIVERSITY IN LEARNING WORDS

As we have discussed in previous chapters, children learn at different paces and in different ways. The understanding and needs of children in the developing stage are different from children in the transitional stage. In any classroom of second-grade children, for example, we can expect a range in what children understand about words. Therefore, learning experiences provided by the teacher must continue to help children move forward in their understanding, while also recognizing the individual needs of children.

Assessment of individual development is critical to making informed decisions about instruction. When children's development is understood, provisions must be made for meeting individual needs with various types of grouping at appropriate times. Whole-class instruction, as well as flexible small groups, will be needed to be sure that the focus of instruction is aimed at what children are ready to learn.

In addition, the ways in which we engage children must consider their preferred styles of learning. Some children will learn best in the company of others, conversing informally about what and how they know, while other children may need time alone to practice new skills they have acquired. The instructional decisions that teachers make must consider the ways in which particular children best receive and use new information in order to accommodate that information into their schema about words.

Making Connections . . .

What have you added to your understanding of the development of children's literacy from this chapter? Make a notation in a personal reflective journal. Compare your thinking to notations that you made at the end of Chapters 1 and 2. Is your thinking changing? If so, in what ways? Pay special attention to your understanding of the differences in word knowledge between emergent, developing, and transitional readers and writers. How do these differences influence the way you think about designing learning experiences for children at different stages?

FIGURE 3.24
Development of word knowledge: Developing stage.

	Usually	Sometimes	Rarely
Context:			
Uses written context to determine unfamiliar words and word meanings.			
Sight Vocabulary:			
Adds meaningful words to sight vocabulary.			
Frequently reads low-challenge text.			
Increases amount of independent reading time.			
Reads widely.			
Returns to familiar texts for rereadings.			
Phonics Patterns:			
Uses familiar sound chunks to read unfamiliar words.			
Uses familiar sound chunks to write unfamiliar words.			
Morphemic Patterns:			
Recognizes familiar words with added inflectional suffix (jump + ing).			
Recognizes compound words as familiar base + base.			
Recognizes/uses contractions -are family (*'re*) -not family (*n't*) -will family (*'ll*) -is/am family (*'s, 'm*)			
Recognizes/uses independent suffix + base.			
Recognizes/uses base + derivational suffix.			
Self-Monitoring Strategy:			
Uses context + beginning letters strategy, checked by sense and remaining letters to decode one-syllable words.			
Uses context + beginning letters strategy, checked by sense and remaining letters to decode two- or three-syllable words.			
Self-monitors for meaning, searching for clues and cross checking sources of information when meaning breaks down.			
Is moving toward silent reading in easy text. Oral reading reappears in difficult text.			
Oral reading is very fluent in familiar text, and somewhat fluent in unfamiliar text.			

FIGURE 3.25
Phonics knowledge—
consonants.

Consonants:
blends/clusters—initial

Reads	br-	cr-	dr-	fr-	gr-	pr-	tr-		
Writes	br-	cr-	dr-	fr-	gr-	pr-	tr-		
Reads	bl-	cl-	fl-	gl-	pl-				
Writes	bl-	cl-	fl-	gl-	pl-				
Reads	sc-	sk-	sl-	sm-	sn-	sp-	st-	scr-	spr-	str-
Writes	sc-	sk-	sl-	sm-	sn-	sp-	st-	scr-	spr-	str-

h digraphs—initial

Reads	sh-	th-	ch-
Writes	sh-	th-	ch-

h digraphs—final

Reads	_sh	_th	_ch		Writes	_sh	_th	_ch

single variant consonants

Reads	c-	g-	s-	x-		Writes	c-	g-	s-	x-

double consonants (2 letters, 1 sound)

Reads	_bb	_dd	_ff	_gg	_ll	_ss	_tt	_zz
Writes	_bb	_dd	_ff	_gg	_ll	_ss	_tt	_zz

silent letter consonant digraphs—initial

Reads	gh_	gn_	kn_	wh_	wr_
Writes	gh_	gn_	kn_	wh_	wr_

silent letter consonant digraphs—final

Reads	_ck	_gn	_dge	_tch
Writes	_ck	_gn	_dge	_tch

FIGURE 3.26
Phonics knowledge—
vowels.

Vowels:
short vowels:

Hears phoneme	a	e	i	o	u	y		
Reads words	a	e	i	o	u	y		
Writes words	a	e	i	o	u	y		

single long vowels (CVCe, CV)

Reads	a_e	_e	i_e	_o, o_e	u_e	_y
Writes	a_e	_e	i_e	_o, o_e	u_e	_y

vowel digraphs (long, consistent)

Reads	ai_	_ay	ee_	_igh	oa_
Writes	ai_	_ay	ee_	_igh	oa_

vowel digraphs (short & long)

Reads	ea_	ei_	_ey	ie_	ou_
Writes	ea_	ei_	_ey	ie_	ou_

diphthongs—look same, sound different

Reads	oo	ou	ow
Writes	oo	ou	ow

look different, sound same

Reads	au	aw	oi	oy	eu	ew	ui
Writes	au	aw	oi	oy	eu	ew	ui

r-controlled—single vowel + r

Reads	_ar	_or	_er	_ir	_ur
Writes	_ar	_or	_er	_ir	_ur

long-vowel marker + r

Reads	_are	_ere	_ire	_ore	_ure
Writes	_are	_ere	_ire	_ore	_ure

vowel digraphs + r

Reads	_air	_ear	_eer	_oar
Writes	_air	_ear	_eer	_oar

125

FIGURE 3.27
Development of word knowledge: Transitional stage.

Context:	Usually	Sometimes	Rarely
Uses written context to determine unfamiliar words and word meanings.			
Sight Vocabulary:			
Adds meaningful words to sight vocabulary.			
Reads widely.			
Frequently reads low-challenge text.			
Increases amount of independent reading time.			
Phonics Patterns:			
Continues to refine ability to use sound chunks to decode unfamiliar multisyllable words.			
Recognizes/uses syllabication generalizations in reading. V/CV or VC/V VC/CV C+le			
Recognizes/uses syllabication generalizations in writing. V/CV or VC/V VC/CV C+le			
Morphemic Patterns:			
Recognizes/uses base words with inflectional suffixes that change the base word. drop silent *e* double final single consonant change *y* to *i*, add suffix			
Reads/writes independent prefix + base word.			
Reads/writes base + derivational suffix.			
Begins to read/write dependent prefix + root.			
Integrates use of structure + phonics as needed in multisyllable words.			
Self-Monitoring Strategy:			
Uses context + beginning syllable strategy, checked by sense and other syllables.			
Oral reading is fluent in low-challenge materials.			
Silent reading is rapid in low-challenge text.			
Decoding is becoming fairly automatic.			

C H A P T E R

4

Reading Aloud to Children: Foundations for Comprehension of Text

Adding to our literacy framework . . .

	Reading Aloud and Guided Literature Study	
Shared Reading	**Balanced and Integrated Literacy Framework**	Shared and Interactive Writing
Guided Reading and Guided Literature Study		Guided Writing and Writer's Workshop
Independent Reading and Reader's Workshop		Independent Writing
	Word Study	

In this chapter, we learn about . . .

- The role of comprehension of text in literacy development
- How to use read-aloud to develop comprehension skills
- How to lead a whole-class study of quality literature

128

Focus Literature:

- *A Chair for My Mother* by Vera B. Williams
- *Trains* by Gail Gibbons
- *The Snowy Day* by Ezra Jack Keats
- *Chocolate Fever* by Robert Kimmel Smith

Looking into Classrooms . . .

The kindergarten children in Sheila's classroom are just completing their morning calendar routine. Sheila moves to a chair at the corner of the carpet area and prepares for the daily read-aloud time. Without being directed to do so, the children move away from the calendar and settle themselves in front of Sheila.

Sheila always begins the read-aloud with an old favorite. Today she holds up several books from past readings and asks the children which they prefer. A show of hands indicates that Amazing Grace *by Mary Hoffman and Caroline Binch is the "old favorite" for today.*

The children know this story well and love the way that the main character, Grace, pretends to be all kinds of different characters and earns the lead in a school play as Peter Pan. The children are quick to say, "Grace can be anything she wants, if she puts her mind to it," just like Grace's Nana says.

As Sheila turns each page, the children respond in chorus with the different characters that Grace pretends to be. The children are completely engrossed in the story. Story time spills over into activity time as several children play dress-up and are overheard to say, "I'm just like Grace. Guess what I am."

DOWN THE HALL . . .

Gabriel, a third-grade teacher, uses read-aloud to begin the study of a chapter book with his students. He settles the children on the carpet area and begins to read aloud from Chocolate Fever *by Robert Kimmel Smith. Pairs of children follow along in copies of the text as Gabriel reads aloud. There is occasional laughter and commentary that pauses the reading. At the completion of the reading of that chapter the children break up into small groups to talk in more depth about their responses. After about 10 to 15 minutes, the class gathers again on the carpet area to share ideas generated in the small groups. Each day the children gather to read and talk about a chapter or two of* Chocolate Fever. *Gabriel uses read-aloud as a way to introduce all of the children in his class to guided literature study.*

BUILDING A THEORY BASE . . .

Read here to find a definition of *comprehension* of text.

A central purpose of learning to read is to be able to comprehend the variety of texts that are encountered in daily life. *Comprehension* is defined as the act of mentally grasping the nature, significance, or meaning of ideas (Merriam-Webster, 2003, p. 522). Wren (2004) states that:

> The ultimate goal in reading is, of course, to make meaning from text. That is, to comprehend the information that is conveyed in the text. What that means is that, at the least, the reader should gain some understanding of the message that is being conveyed by the author. Moreover, however, comprehension should go beyond simply understanding the explicit message that is being conveyed by the author. To truly comprehend text is to make connections between the information in the text and the information in the reader's head, to draw inferences about the author's meaning, to evaluate the quality of the message, and possibly even to connect aspects of the text with other works of literature.

The meaning that children are able to construct from a written text depends in whole or part on:

- 🍎 the child's understanding of a topic or particular type of text,
- 🍎 the context in which the text is being read,
- 🍎 the child's understanding of the purpose of the reading,
- 🍎 the level of attention or motivation the child has for making the text meaningful, and
- 🍎 the match between the child's language and the level of difficulty of the language of the text.

Comprehension of text is a complex task for a reader, one that requires the orchestration of numerous skills. In this chapter we explore a variety of ways that reading quality literature to children becomes an instructional tool for developing the thinking skills required to comprehend text.

WHY READ AND STUDY QUALITY LITERATURE?

What does participation in read-aloud experiences contribute to children's schema for reading? As a more knowledgeable reader reads to and guides children through books, children are exposed to the language structures that distinguish written language from spoken language (Elster, 1998). Such linguistic knowledge is the foundation of children's emergent reading behaviors.

Why should we engage children in listening to and reading children's literature?

- Meaningful experiences with literature develop knowledge and strategies typically taught in reading programs, and teach children strategies for processing literary texts (Walmsley, 1992).
- Quality literature enables children to draw analogies between stories and their lives, encouraging reflection on life and experiences with the lives of others they might not otherwise know (Cullinan, 1989).
- Quality literature has been shown to have a powerful impact on children's language development (Britton, 1970; Rosen & Rosen, 1973) and the way they talk about books (Eeds & Wells, 1989; Raphael & McMahon, 1994).
- Experiences with quality literature encourage children to become fluent readers (Durkin, 1966; Wells, 1986) and provide a stimulus for critical reading and writing (Blackburn, 1985; DeFord, 1981; Graves, 1983, 1994; Hansen, 1987).

Research documents that all types of students successfully learn to read in programs that use children's literature as the primary instructional material (Tunnell & Jacobs, 1989). Teachers who are committed to teaching reading with children's literature share the belief that children are makers of meaning and deserve quality literature with rich language that is likely to evoke a strong response.

To learn more about children's literature, visit sites such as *http://www.cbcbooks.org* and *http://www.acs.ucalgary.ca/~dkbrown/*.

LITERATURE COMES IN A VARIETY OF GENRES

Experiences with the different genres of printed materials help children develop schemata for the various forms of written language, including technological forms. In this context *genre* is defined as "a category of literary composition characterized by a particular style, form, or content" (Merriam-Webster, 2003, p. 522). To build background and expectations for print, children in primary-grade classrooms should have extensive experiences with a range of literature:

Read here to find a definition of *genre*.

- Contemporary realistic fiction
- Information/Nonfiction
- Fantasy
- Poetry
- Folk literature/Traditional literature
- Biography and autobiography
- Historical fiction

For additional background information on literary genre, see Appendix A.

Children's knowledge and reading behaviors are influenced by the types of books read to them (Elster, 1998). The different types of books we choose to read to children can be particularly helpful to emergent readers as they rely first on pictures for meaning, then on story language, and finally on the print (Sulzby, 1985) to comprehend. Reading books from a variety of genres provides effective scaffolds for emergent readers, who, like older readers, form concepts using visual information with memorable story language (Elster, 1994, 1995).

When reading or listening to a book that belongs to a particular literary genre, readers frequently have expectations based on knowledge of other books in the genre. For example, *Mufaro's Beautiful Daughters* (Steptoe, 1987), an African Cinderella tale, begins, "A long time ago . . . ." Experience with other picture books that begin similarly leads a reader to expect a fairy-tale-like story.

In contrast, the book *Chicka Chicka Boom Boom* (Martin & Archambault, 1989) begins:

> *A told B,*
> *And B told C,*
> *I'll meet you at the top*
> *Of the coconut tree.*

Experience with texts that use rhythm and rhyme to convey a message leads the reader to realize that this text is actually a poem. The author uses poetry to tell a story about letters of the alphabet that are trying to race each other up a tree. Experiences with poetic forms lead the reader to different expectations for this book than for *Mufaro's Beautiful Daughters*.

In yet another book, *How Is a Crayon Made?* (Charles, 1990), the text begins:

> It's hard to imagine a world without crayons.
> If all the regular size crayons made
> in the United States last year were laid
> end-to-end around the equator, they
> would circle the globe four and a half times!

From these first two sentences the reader is aware that this text is different from the previous two books and will probably provide factual information about crayons, rather than a fairy-tale or a poem.

Prior experiences with various genres help readers realize that poetry, the Internet, fairy tales, realistic fiction, and information books do not have the same characteristics or purposes, so readers must deal with each type of text in different ways. To help children develop comprehension skills through read-aloud, teachers must help children learn to use their knowledge of various genres to respond and make meaning (Duke & Purcell-Gates, 2003).

Multicultural Literature

Within the abundant pieces of literature published yearly for children are texts that describe the contributions, lifestyles, and values of diverse individuals and groups. Reading literature with characters who reflect the demograpics of the classroom helps children have a better understanding of who they are and what contributions they can make to their communities (Martinez & Nash, 1990). If used thoughtfully, literature can play an important role in helping children learn about themselves, as well as about new ideas, new worlds, and different ways of doing things, which benefits them as human beings (Rasinski & Padak, 1990).

In selecting multicultural literature for the classroom, Reimer (1992) cautions teachers to guard against using literature that presents characters who appear as "cultural conglomerates," one individual who seem to represent all people of a particular group. For example, the term *Hispanic* refers to Spanish-speaking children, but does not acknowledge the specific contributions of particular groups such as Mexican Americans or Puerto Ricans. Authentic multicultural literature, literature that is "culturally conscious" (Sims, 1983), can help teachers become more familiar with some of the cultural contexts of diverse groups. Such books may focus on heritage, everyday experiences, battles against racism and discrimination, urban living, friendship, family relationships, and growing up. Authenticity is enhanced with texts that are written by people who are members of the culture they write about, providing more of an insider's view of the culture.

To learn more about quality multicultural children's literature, see *http://www.ncrel.org/sdrs/ areas/issues/educatrs/ presrvce/pe31k28.htm* or *http://www.leeandlow.com/ search/advsearch.html.*

Making Connections . . .

At this point in our discussion, how do you define reading comprehension? What factors do you think have an impact a reader's comprehension of text? It is important that you identify your own beliefs because they will influence not only the ways that you teach children but also how you respond to the content of this text.

COMPREHENSION OF TEXT—LEARNING TO THINK LIKE A READER

As children gain experience thinking about an author's ideas during read-aloud, teachers have many opportunities to guide children as they learn to comprehend text. Comprehension of text is influenced by a number of factors. We begin our discussion with the influence of both the reader's and author's intentions.

A Reader's Intentions

Part of thinking like a reader is realizing that readers have intentions when they read. Intentions influence how readers approach print, expectations for print, and willingness to think about the print to make it meaningful. If print seems to offer something personally meaningful, readers are more likely to be motivated to spend time thinking about the ideas that authors express and relate the author's ideas to their own. If readers don't want to be involved with the print, they are less likely to work to make sense of the ideas, especially if the text is difficult. Interests, needs, and desires as human beings influence the types of texts readers find meaningful. Past experiences with text, positive and negative, may also influence readers' intentions.

An Author's Intentions

Authors have intentions when they write, intentions that guide how they communicate with their potential readers. An author's intentions will, in large part, determine the choice of form the text takes. The more we are aware of and consider an author's possible intentions, the closer we may come to meaningfully interacting with that author's ideas. Our ability to make inferences about a text is affected, in part, by the ways in which an author attempts to communicate with the reader.

COMPREHENSION OF TEXT—WAYS OF THINKING ABOUT WRITTEN LANGUAGE

Through interactions with others, young children have already learned to think about and make meaning with oral language. As children begin to interact with written language, they must learn to use various ways of thinking about texts to make meaning. To effectively comprehend the variety of texts they will encounter as readers, children must be able to think in different ways depending upon the nature of the text and their purposes for reading. They must know when to use the following strategies:

- Literal comprehension,
- Inferential comprehension, and
- Personal and/or critical comprehension.

Literal Comprehension—Text-Explicit Thinking

Explicit understanding of an author's words depends in part on knowing the words in a text and knowing about the topic. In *A Chair for My Mother* (Williams, 1982), a young girl begins telling her story with:

> My mother works as a waitress in the Blue Tile Diner. After school sometimes I go to meet her there. Then her boss Josephine gives me a job too.

If, after hearing the story, children are asked to recall what type of work the mother does, the children should state, "waitress." To prove that fact, they can return to the text and find that word in the first sentence. Children's level of understanding of explicitly stated information, however, relies on background knowledge of the topic. Such background is influenced by cultural experiences.

Inferential Comprehension—Text-Implicit Thinking

Making appropriate inferences from text is one of the most challenging types of comprehension expected of young children as they learn to read. Authors do not always explicitly tell readers what they need to know. It would be impossible for an author to anticipate everything that every reader might need to know about a topic. The author must assume that the reader knows some things about the topic and that the reader will "work" to make sense by filling in or linking ideas during the reading.

The act of filling in or linking ideas is referred to as *implicit thinking.* Anderson and Pearson (1984) identify four types of implicit thinking that readers will draw upon to make inferences about an author's ideas in text. When there is an "empty slot" in the text, or information that seems to be missing or has not been explicitly stated by the author:

- The reader may have a schema for the topic that is sufficient to accurately complete the idea without clues from the author.

or

- The reader may need to link specific pieces of information at various places in the text to "fill the empty slot."

or

- The reader may need to link clues from the author with knowledge the reader has to "fill the empty slot."

or

- Because the reader lacks sufficient schema, the reader fills the "empty slot" with erroneous information based on what seems to be logical reasoning, but without appropriate clues or support from the text.

The first three types of implicit thinking can lead to appropriate conclusions through varying combinations of a reader's schemata (plural for *schema*) and ideas in a text. The fourth type, however, can be problematic if a reader's line of reasoning leads to misconceptions about the author's ideas.

Making inferences about a text can be very challenging for English language learners. Students who are learning English may lack the specific schema, assumed present by the author, to comprehend certain ideas in the text. English language learners may also have limited experiences with the language the author uses to cue understanding in the reader. For example, on the second page of *A Chair for My Mother,* the young girl who is narrating the story tells us that:

> My mama empties all her change from tips out of her purse for me to count. Then we push all the coins into the jar.

From the first page of the story the reader learns that the mother is a waitress. If the reader knows about that type of work, then the reader might know that customers give tips, or extra money, for good service. Using the schema for what waitresses do and clue words in the text to link ideas from one page to another, the reader "fills the empty slot" to complete the idea. Competent readers have learned to think their way through text and operate as if text should make sense, filling in missing pieces of information to make sense. To become competent readers, teachers must help young children learn to accurately "fill empty slots."

Personal and/or Critical Comprehension— Scriptal Thinking about Text

Readers' experiences in the world and understanding of reading processes influence the "script" from which ideas are drawn to respond to text. Scriptal thinking typically leaves the page of the text and is influenced more by a reader's

For further discussion of comprehension, visit a Reading First website such as *http://www.nifl.gov/partnershipforreading/publications/PFRbooklet.pdf.*

ways of thinking about and responding to the world. Those responses may be personal and they may be critical. Thinking becomes scriptal in nature when the questions teachers ask about text are not answered by the author's words.

A personal and/or critical response to a character, for example, takes place when readers go beyond the author's ideas and let personal ideas and emotions take over. Although initially readers may be influenced by the author, readers soon realize that their responses do not require consideration of the author's ideas. A personal response may occur as readers feel a certain connection to a character or situation. Readers may also make judgments about the value or merit of the author's ideas based on a set of personal criteria. In contrast, a critical response requires that readers use background knowledge accurately and approach reading as a thinking process.

The author of *A Chair for My Mother* crafts a story that values disciplining oneself to save money for personal wants, as well as the importance of helping others in times of need. Readers may respond and/or reflect on these issues both personally and critically. As readers listen to the young girl in *A Chair for My Mother* narrate the story of her family, they may or may not empathize with the family's situation. They may admire the commitment that the family members have to each other. In contrast, they may critique the desire for what appears to be a lavish piece of furniture when the family has so little else. In this case, the scriptal meanings that readers make derive from impressions created in personal response to the text, but not directly by the author's ideas.

Assessing Children's Comprehension of Text

How effectively students comprehend text is a national concern. In Chapter 1 we learned that the National Assessment of Educational Progress (NAEP) is "the nation's only ongoing, comparable, and representative assessment of student achievement" (Mullis, Campbell, & Farstrup, 1993, p. 1). We also learned that students in the United States are not demonstrating the levels of achievement in literacy that are expected.

What types of comprehension of text does NAEP assess? In the reading sections of the NAEP, students are expected to:

- 🍎 demonstrate an initial understanding of text (explicit),
- 🍎 develop an interpretation (inferential),
- 🍎 articulate a personal reflection and response (personal), and
- 🍎 demonstrate a critical stance (critical).

In 2003, fourth-grade students were able to provide accurate responses to multiple-choice questions about explicitly stated information 94% of the time and were able to make inferences 76% of the time. The most challenging questions required students to construct a response that supported or made interpretations about information from a text (both narrative and expository texts). Forty-two percent of fourth-grade students could construct a response that gave essential information or support, but only 12% could construct a response that gave extensive information or support.

To improve reading achievement in the United States, teachers must help children learn how to make text meaningful in different ways and how to judge the types of thinking that a particular text demands of them. In addition, teachers must help students learn to communicate their thinking in response to text, explaining what they think and providing appropriate support. The scores for the NAEP assessment suggest that teachers must continually engage children in talking and writing in response to ideas presented in the texts children read.

When children come to school they are already experienced language learners (Clay, 2004). How do we build on children's existing language knowledge to enhance their expectations of print, motivation to read, and knowledge of book language? Reading aloud to/with children can begin to develop skills and strategies that lead to the comprehension of text required of competent readers and writers. The remaining sections of this chapter focus on applications that help teachers apply theories about reading processes to reading to or with children using children's literature.

To see the types of texts and questions used by NAEP to assess students' comprehension in fourth grade, visit *http://www.nces.ed.gov/ nationsreportcard/itmlrs.*

Making Connections . . .

As you examine your own responses to text, how do you feel about your ability to effectively comprehend text? Are there times when you are uncertain? If so, what factors might contribute to your uncertainty about your comprehension skills? How might these factors relate to the ways that students feel about their own ability, or lack of ability, to comprehend text, especially when they are expected to get the "right" answer to a teacher's questions? How could your teachers have better helped you to develop skills and confidence in your ability to effectively comprehend the texts you were expected to read in school?

PUTTING THEORY INTO PRACTICE . . .

The single most important thing we can do to help children build knowledge about reading and the language of books is to read to them (Anderson, Hiebert, Scott, & Wilkinson, 1985). Think of that! Reading to children is our "most direct way of communicating the special qualities of written language to children" (Holdaway, 1980, p. 17). With such potential, reading aloud should be "the centerpiece of the curriculum from which all else flows" (Kristo, 1993, p. 54).

What does participation in read-aloud experiences contribute to a child's schema for reading? As a more knowledgeable reader reads to and guides children through books, they are exposed to the language structures that distinguish written language from spoken language (Elster, 1998). Such linguistic knowledge is the foundation of children's emergent reading behaviors.

Through reading aloud to children:

- adults model fluent skillful reading as they bring the words in books to life and show children that reading is both pleasurable and worthwhile,
- adults share the sounds and rhythms of language in print,
- adults engage in rich discussions and animated conversations with children about the images of the world as presented in books,
- both adult and child work out the meaning of a text, and
- the child learns to think like a reader and to navigate through the ideas in books without needing to be the decoder.

READING TO/WITH CHILDREN—AN INVITATION INTO LITERATURE

When teachers read to/with children they invite them into books, creating opportunities for children to become more receptive to written language. Inviting children into literature should:

- take place in a comfortable environment,
- expose children to new books,
- provide time to revisit old favorites,
- encourage children to share their responses,
- help children interpret and/or appreciate literature,
- encourage children to give direction to read-aloud discussions, and
- happen more than once per day.

Create a Comfortable Environment

Gather children close around for reading to re-create the warmth of bedtime story reading. Make an inviting place in the classroom for the reading to happen. This says to children that reading is important and deserves a special place. Think about where to sit in relation to the children. Sit in a comfortable chair and have the children gather on the floor nearby. Sitting near or in the classroom library corner is another good choice because it is usually a comfortable area where children feel welcome.

Expose Children to New Literature

Use read-aloud time to expose children to new books, new ideas, new authors, and new illustrators. When a new book is read, make a special introduction. Tell

What literacy knowledge and skills are we able to model as we read aloud to children?

children where the book was found and what led to selecting it to share with them. If the author or illustrator is new, share information about that person to help children understand that real people write the books they love. Interesting pieces of information about authors and illustrators can be found on the inside flaps of a book jacket and in *Something About the Author* (Telgen, 1986), *Children's Literature Review* (Senick, 1990), and other similar resources. For example, children delight in knowing that Tomie dePaola really took dancing lessons as a boy just like Oliver in *Oliver Buttons Is a Sissy* (1979) or that Gail Gibbons, author and illustrator of such books as *Trains* and *Weather Words,* puts people and places she knows in the information books that she writes.

Provide Time to Revisit Old Favorites

Children of all ages need opportunities to realize that the worth of a book is not used up after one reading (Beaver, 1982). By dedicating part (at least 25%) of the read-aloud time each week to rereading old favorites, children see that their enjoyment, understanding, and confidence are increased by listening again to familiar stories. Revisiting an old favorite enables emergent readers to realize that texts remain the same from reading to reading, thus reinforcing the concept of permanence of print.

Encourage Responses to Literature

Watch children during a read-aloud and notice the variety of responses they have to literature. The types and frequency of children's responses will vary depending on the ways that response is encouraged, the connection between the book and children's background knowledge, and children's familiarity with the book. Children's responses may be nonverbal, responsive, or evaluative, among others (Kristo, 1993). Observe children's nonverbal responses as they smile, grimace, lean forward, squirm, and hold their breath in anticipation. This body language shows their involvement with the story. Acknowledge these responses, because children may not yet be ready to make public verbal responses.

Children also show their response when they repeat words or ask about words in a text. Sometimes the words will catch children's attention, such as in *The Snowy Day* (Keats, 1962):

> *Down fell the snow—*
> *plop!*
> *—on top of Peter's head.*

Children might repeat "plop" because it has an interesting sound and creates pleasing sensations in the mouth when it is repeated; or they may ask about a "heaping mountain of snow," wondering what that means.

Children respond when they make connections between pieces of literature. For example, Tony reads *Hattie and the Fox* (Fox, 1986), a cumulative predictable story about a fox that is stalking a hen, to his first-grade children. One child comments that the repetition of the animals' talking reminds him of *The Little Red Hen* (Galdone, 1973). There are comments about the repetitions and how the children delight in knowing what comes next. Tony values the children's thinking and uses their responses to direct the discussion of books.

Children also make evaluative statements or ask evaluative questions about books. Children reveal their thinking when they make statements such as:

"I don't like that mean sister."

"He looks like my grandpa."

"Why did they tease him? That hurts."

The more experience children have with stories, especially in conversational settings, the more likely they are to share their responses to books. Young children form opinions and feelings about books and they should be encouraged to share and explore those opinions and feelings to validate their thinking as readers.

Help Children Interpret and Appreciate Literature

When teachers read aloud to and with children, they are doing more than just making the print come alive; they also have the opportunity to help children make connections between themselves and books. During read-aloud teachers serve as a guide who helps children begin to focus on what the author has to share. Teachers should model their own responses to the author's choice of words, the mood set by the illustrator, an important theme in the text, or a character's motives. Figure 4.1 provides a reminder of tips to consider in planning read-aloud experiences for children.

Making Connections . . .

As you consider your own style as a teacher, select a favorite children's book and read the book aloud to a small group of children. Do not rehearse the book. The purpose of this activity is for you to hear your natural style of engaging children with good books. Tape record the read-aloud so you can listen to yourself. Notice your natural strengths, but also make note of ways you can improve your read-aloud style. Be conscious of and practice those aspects you need to improve.

 GUIDING CHILDREN'S COMPREHENSION OF TEXT

When teachers read aloud to or with children, they serve as the decoder of text. Teachers also help young children learn how to listen to and appreciate good literature, to make meaning with book language, and to think like a reader. Because it is important for teachers to support and extend children's interactions with text, teachers' techniques must be fluid and responsive to children. It is important to assist children as they learn to make meaning with text through an instructional technique called *mediated read-aloud.* Mediated read-aloud is a highly interactive learning activity.

Through mediated read-aloud teachers assist children in developing skills and strategies for thinking about and making meaning with written language. Reading aloud that is interactive can help children focus their thinking about a text before, during, and after the reading and extend their understanding of

The following tips are suggestions from authors (Freeman, 1992; Trelease, 2001) and teachers who bring books to life for children.

- *Pick books that you like or are your old favorites.*
  When you "love" a book, you are more likely to share that book with genuine enthusiasm.

- *Preview the book.*
  Read a new book to become acquainted with its language and ideas before presenting it to class.

- *Allow ample time.*
  Do not start a read-aloud session unless you have time to do justice to the text.

- *Children need to see illustrations.*
  Be sure that children sit close enough to see details because much of the plot, characters, and setting are told through the illustrations. Be aware of how you are holding the text.

- *Connect with your audience.*
  To let your listeners know they are involved in the reading with you, make frequent eye contact with the children as you read.

- *Read with expression and in your own style.*
  Try to maintain good pitch, volume, and expression while you read. Practice reading aloud by tape recording yourself to hear your expression and pacing. If you are comfortable with your style, you will be more likely to relax and enjoy the experience with your children.

- *Adjust your pace as you read.*
  Slow the pace of reading for sections that are more complex and require concentrated mental processing. Don't be afraid to reread sections as children's responses may indicate.

- *Do not read above a child's emotional level.*
  Consider children's emotional maturity and background knowledge when selecting books. Children may not always be ready for the emotional demands of specific events or themes such as death.

- *It is okay to abandon a book.*
  Sometimes, even when we preview and thoughtfully select books, we find the choice of a book may be a poor match for a particular group of children. This can be especially true with chapter books. In such cases, abandoning the book may be the best solution.

- *Make read-aloud books available to children.*
  As you finish a read-aloud, give the book a place of honor in your library area. Some children will want to revisit the book during independent reading time.

- *Award winners are no guarantee.*
  Just because a book has won an award does not guarantee it to be a good read-aloud for your children. Be sure to preview the book with an ear for the way that the story sounds when read aloud and an eye to the appropriateness for your children.

FIGURE 4.1
Tips for a quality read-aloud.

that text. With the assistance of a more knowledgeable reader, children begin to internalize the strategies for thinking about text. Internalization enables children to begin to independently use skills and strategies in new reading situations.

Helping children focus their attention on salient aspects of literature is not new. Techniques such as a Directed Listening–Thinking Activity (Stauffer, 1959), in which a teacher directs children to listen or read to obtain certain outcomes, has been shown to improve children's comprehension of stories (Morrow, 1985). Considering current views of how children learn (e.g., Vygotsky's theories of development), it may be more appropriate to view the teacher as a mediator rather than director. A mediator adjusts the amount of support or assistance provided during instruction, gradually reducing that assistance as children are able to accomplish a task independently.

🍎 COMPREHENSION OF NARRATIVE AND EXPOSITORY TEXTS

To prepare a read-aloud that assists children in making meaning with text, teachers should:

- 🍎 think about the purpose(s) for engaging children with a particular book;
- 🍎 plan the strategies that are needed to support children and assist as they make meaning before, during, and after the reading of a book; and
- 🍎 reflect on interactions with children before, during, and after the reading as indications of where assistance is needed in order to make meaning with a text.

The steps of purpose, strategy, and reflection provide a cycle of planning for mediated learning (Dixon-Kraus and Powell, 1995) that teachers repeat throughout the reading of a particular text. As teachers engage children in a read-aloud, they adjust the level of assistance they provide as feedback from children indicates ability to be independent, self-regulated learners.

Planning for read-aloud should focus on helping children think about the text before, during, and after the reading (Powell, 1993). In each segment a teacher considers the purpose for using the selected book, the strategies that will be used to support children's learning from the text, and how reflecting on children's interactions might be used to adjust instruction. An overview of what a teacher and children might do during a mediated read-aloud is shown in Figure 4.2. Please review the figure before reading further.

The following sample of a mediated read-aloud shows how a teacher assists or supports children's thinking in a narrative, or fictional, text. *A Chair for My Mother* by Vera B. Williams (1982) is used as an example of how a teacher can support children's comprehension in a narrative text. An additional sample is provided for informational text in order to compare and contrast the use of both fiction and nonfiction in the classroom.

FIGURE 4.2
Mediated read-aloud.

Before the reading:

The teacher should

- plan clear purpose(s) for reading a particular text
- identify strategies for meeting that purpose
- consider how support can be adjusted during the reading to help children move toward independent thinking

With children, the teacher should

- encourage children to anticipate reading using text and background knowledge
- focus children's attention on the reading for identified purposes

In response, the children are assisted as they

- predict what might come next in the reading using available information
- connect the prediction to current background knowledge
- prepare for meeting the purpose(s) of the reading

During the reading:

The teacher should

- read aloud in a fluid and lively manner
- stop the reading at appropriate places to assist children in making meaning and meeting reading purposes
- encourage children's use of identified strategies
- encourage children's responses, listening thoughtfully to what they say
- provide assistance and adjust support according to need reflected in children's responses

In response, the children are assisted as they

- use listening–thinking strategies to meet reading purpose(s)
- participate, giving feedback to teacher about thinking during the reading
- receive support, adjusted to level of need, to meet purpose(s) of reading
- receive support with essential vocabulary as needed

After the reading:

The teacher should

- encourage response through open-ended questions such as "Well, what did you think of that story?"
- elicit retelling, first unaided through open-ended questions, then aided by probing for specific points
- based on response, determine which essential words may warrant further discussion
- reaffirm strategies used to meet reading purposes
- depending on purposes and children's responses, determine whether repeated readings are warranted or desirable

In response, children are assisted as they

- share responses to the reading (creative/personal meanings)
- retell most important points (explicit/implicit meaning)
- recall essential vocabulary (explicit/implicit meaning)
- discuss important meanings of text as a whole (implicit/critical meaning)

GUIDING COMPREHNSION OF NARRATIVE TEXT—A CHAIR FOR MY MOTHER BY VERA B. WILLIAMS

A Chair for My Mother is the story of the members of a hardworking family (mother, young daughter, and grandmother) who have lived through a fire in their house and are working to rebuild their lives. The story is told through the voice of the young girl, who often goes to her mother's place of work after school to help out. The mother is a waitress at the Blue Tile Diner. The family is saving coins in a large glass jar to buy a special armchair to relax in after a long day. The story features a flashback in the middle that fills in information about the fire and helps the reader understand the strong desire to save for the special chair.

Before the reading of *A Chair for My Mother*, the teacher thoughtfully considers the purpose(s) in selecting and reading this text to children. Purposes for reading *A Chair for My Mother* might include helping children understand that:

🍎 The use of *I, me,* and *my* in the story means that the little girl is telling the story (first person is one point of view authors can use to tell stories).

🍎 This story teaches the satisfaction of working hard for something that is important and the value of people helping each other in times of need (theme(s) of a plot can help with understanding life lessons).

As teachers support children's comprehension of text, these two purposes are kept in mind.

Planning for reading aloud helps a teacher determine how best to guide children's attention to particular ideas or information in a text. Open-ended questions encourage children to use what they already know and to be curious about what they might find. Each time a question is asked, the teacher pauses to give children time to think, then listens carefully to their responses as evidence of their thinking.

To prepare children for the reading of *A Chair for My Mother,* a teacher might:

🍎 Point to the title of the book on the front cover and say, "The title of this book is *A Chair for My Mother* and it is written by Vera B. Williams."

🍎 Point to the illustration on the front cover and ask, "What do you think this blue shape might be? What do you see as you look through the windows?" Pointing to the back of the girl and the mother in the doorway ask, "Who do you think the people in the picture might be? What do you think this story might be about?"

🍎 Begin the reading of the text by saying, "Let's read and see what we learn."

Remember, if children are unfamiliar with the story, then the preview of the text is intended to get them thinking about possibilities, not "right" answers. Children's responses should be treated as possibilities that can be confirmed or revised throughout the reading. Notice that prediction questions use the word *might* rather than a more definitive word such as *is*. Remember, also, that the purpose for encouraging children to make predictions at this point is to prepare for comprehending the text by anticipating outcomes.

As children are guided through this book, assistance is focused on helping children understand each of the three parts to this story:

Part 1: Introduction to the family and how they are saving money to buy a special armchair for the mother (pages 1–8)
Part 2: A flashback to a fire in their house and how neighbors helped (pages 9–16)
Part 3: A description of getting the new armchair (pages 17–28)

In the first reading of this text, the flashback in part two might not be specifically addressed. It is more suitable to focus on the purpose and use of a flashback during the rereading of the book when children have some familiarity with the story. There is further discussion of the use of flashback later in the chapter during our discussion of text rereadings.

Children's understanding of essential vocabulary is revealed through discussion during and after the reading. Most texts contain vocabulary that needs explanation or emphasis to assist children's understanding and enjoyment of the story. To decide how to handle essential vocabulary, consider the following questions:

- Is the word likely to be in the listening vocabulary of the children?
- Is the word used in a context that helps children figure out the meaning?
- Is the word essential to understanding the story during the first reading?

Give children the opportunity to figure out the meaning of a new word if the answers are yes to the three questions above. If the answers are no to one or more of these questions, introduction to the vocabulary will be needed. Be careful, however, not to overnurture children, reducing their drive for independence as readers (Speigel, 1985). Check for understanding of the vocabulary during discussion. Provide additional assistance during the reading if children's background experience or the context is insufficient to make meaning.

Sample Mediated Read-Aloud with Narrative Text—*A Chair for My Mother*:

Prereading

make predictions — Ask the children, "What do you see in the illustration on the cover of this book?"

Point to the title on the front cover and say: "The title of this book is *A Chair for my Mother*. What do you think this story might be about?"

PART 1
Pages 1–2

initial engagement — Point to the illustration on page 1 and say: "This is the Blue Tile Diner. What is a diner? Why do you think the girl is going into the diner? What makes you think that?"

clarify point of view — Read the text on page 2, then ask: "Who do you think is saying the words 'My mother works as a waitress . . . '?" Wait for children to respond. Confirm their understanding that the little girl is telling this story about her mother.

Continued

Sample Mediated Read-Aloud with Narrative Text—*A Chair for My Mother (continued):*

Pages 1–2
(continued)

clarify vocabulary	"The mother is a waitress. What does a waitress do?"
recall details	"What does the little girl do to help her mother at the diner?"
clarify reference	"The last sentence says, 'And every time, I put half of my money into the *jar.*' What jar do you think they are talking about?" Pause for children to respond.

Pages 3–4

confirm reference from page 2	Point to the illustration of the jar on page 3, then ask: "Do you think this is the jar?" (from page 2)
	After reading the text on page 4, ask: "What do we know about the jar now? What do you think this jar might be for?"
clarify vocabulary	"What are the 'tips' that the mother puts into the jar?"
make and confirm an inference	"Why do you think the little girl says that her mother looks worried? What makes you think that?"

Pages 5–6

interpret illustration	Looking at the illustration on page 5, ask: "Who do you see in the picture?"
clarify vocabulary	After reading page 6, ask: "How does Grandma get money for the jar?" (It may be necessary to reread and explain the sentence, "Whenever she gets a bargain on tomatoes or bananas or something she buys, she *puts by* the savings and they go into the jar.")
make connection to previous information	"Look at the jar here (page 3) and now here (page 5), and what do you notice?"

Pages 7–8 (end part 1)

draw conclusion	Read page 8, then ask: "What do we know about the money in the jar now?"
recall details	"What happened to their other chairs?"
recall details	"What kind of chair are they dreaming about?"

PART 2 Pages 9–12

make and confirm an inference	Read pages 10 and 12, then ask: "What do you think happened to their house? What makes you think that?"
make an inference	Ask "What do you think the little girl meant when she said, 'But everything else in our whole house was spoiled'?"

Pages 13–14

Read page 14, then ask:

confirm inference from previous page   "Now what do you know about how the fire 'spoiled' everything?" (charcoal and ashes)

recall details   "What did the little girl, her mother, and her grandmother do after the fire?"

Pages 15–16

recall details   Read pages 15 and 16, then ask: "After the fire, what did their friends and family do to help?"

draw a conclusion   "How do you think Grandma felt about that? How do we know?" (Reread her words, "You are all the kindest people," she said, "and we thank you very, very much . . . ")

PART 3
Pages 17–18

make and confirm an inference   Point to the illustration on page 17 and say: "Look at the jar now! How do you think it got so full?"

make and confirm an inference   "Why do you think they have such a big jar?" What makes you think that?

Pages 19–20

activate background knowledge   Point to the illustration on page 19 and ask:
"What is this place? Where do you think the mother and daughter are now? (a bank) What do people do at a bank?"

recall details   Read page 20, then ask:
"What did they do with the money?"

make an inference by connecting to previous information   "What kind of chair do you think they will buy? What kind of chair did they say they wanted in the beginning of the story?" (Recall pages 7 and 8.)

Pages 21–26

recall details   Read pages 21 to 26, then ask:
"What did they do as they shopped for a new chair?"

make and confirm an inference   "Did they find the right chair? What makes you think so?"

make and confirm an inference   "What do you think will happen after they get the chair home? Why do you think so?"

Continued

Sample Mediated Read-Aloud with Narrative Text—*A Chair for My Mother* (continued):

Pages 27–28

make and confirm an inference	Read page 28, then ask: "Where did they put the chair? Why do you think they put it there?"
draw a conclusion	"How do we know that the chair is a big chair?"

AFTER THE READING

respond to text	"What did you think of this story?"
recall plot and character actions	"Let's see if we can remember all of the important things that happened in the story." (Based on their retelling, determine which essential words/ideas may warrant further discussion.)
confirm point of view	"How do we know that the little girl is telling the story?"
respond to theme	"What do you think about working hard for something you want? About helping others? Can you think of a time that you helped someone or you worked hard to save for something you wanted? How did you feel?"

Depending on children's responses and the purposes for the first reading of the story, determine whether repeated readings of this book are warranted or desirable. How does supporting children in read-aloud with narrative texts compare with what may be needed for information texts?

🍎 GUIDING COMPREHENSION OF EXPOSITORY TEXT— <u>TRAINS</u> BY GAIL GIBBONS

For additional discussion of using expository text with young children, visit *http://www.stanford. edu/~mkamil/nrc97b.htm*.

Expository text, also called nonfiction or informational text, is written in a different style than narrative text. In expository texts the literary elements of narrative text (plot, setting, characters, theme, etc.) are no longer present. To make meaning readers learn to focus on understanding main ideas and important details about a real-world topic. Knowledge of the world is used to make meaning. Understanding essential vocabulary—the technical vocabulary of the topic—is also crucial to understanding the text.

Most texts read by adults are expository. In school, children find that expository texts become increasingly more prominent in the curriculum as they progress from grade to grade. To prepare children for learning from expository texts, teachers help them develop an ear (and an eye) for the differences between narrative and expository texts. This requires both extensive and intensive experiences with expository texts, the same types of experiences we provide with narrative texts.

Many children begin hearing narrative texts read aloud as toddlers, long before they are expected to read such texts for themselves. Expository texts are not typically introduced in the same manner, unless children demand it because of their personal interests. If expository texts are read aloud as frequently as narrative texts, children may be better prepared for reading expository texts for themselves. How does reading aloud from expository text compare with narrative?

Sample Mediated Read-Aloud with Expository Text— Trains *by Gail Gibbons*

Trains by Gail Gibbons (1987) provides a description of different types of engines and the fuels that are used to power each, information about passenger and freight trains, and information about types of train cars. Specialized vocabulary to talk about trains is introduced and supported by descriptions and illustrations. In general, each page typically has one detailed sentence supported by the illustration.

Before the reading of *Trains,* consider the purpose(s) in selecting and reading this text to children. The purposes for reading *Trains* might be to expose children to:

- information about types and purposes of trains,
- specialized vocabulary pertaining to trains, and
- using illustrations to comprehend specialized vocabulary.

To prepare children for the read-aloud, guide their attention to particular information in preparation for what might come. Ask open-ended questions to encourage them to use what they already know and to be curious about what they might find. When asking a question, pause to give children time to think, and listen carefully to their responses as evidence of their thinking.

While reading aloud, adjust the support to children based on what they say in response to the reading and discussion. The organization of information in a text also guides the amount of support we provide. For example, *Trains* has three distinct sections:

Part 1:   A little history of trains (pages 1–9)
Part 2:   The two main types of trains (pages 10–17)
Part 3:   The types of cars found on a train (pages 18–27)

Each section will require differing amounts of support based on children's prior experiences with the particular information.

The first reading of the text will focus more on parts 1 and 2, which contain main ideas that are attainable without extensive background knowledge. The amount of detail in part 3, the types of train cars, will be challenging for most children to comprehend and will require rereadings and closer study.

Before the reading, try to anticipate the essential vocabulary needed to engage children during the first reading. Some vocabulary will require rereadings and additional background to be understood and retained by children.

- First reading—Vocabulary that might require attention during the first reading includes locomotive, steam, diesel, subway, freight, couplers, and cargo.
- Rereading—Vocabulary that might require additional attention includes the types of train cars identified in illustrations in part 3 (flatcars, refrigerator cars, hopper cars, piggyback cars, box cars, tank cars, gondola cars, three-level rack cars, and caboose).

The author uses both illustrations and explanation to describe the characteristics and function of each car. This amount of detail, however, should not be expected during the first reading. Rereadings will be needed to provide support for attending to and retaining this specialized vocabulary. Because of the format of the text, it will be helpful to teach children how to use the illustrations to help them predict word meanings.

Sample Mediated Read-Aloud for Expository Text—*Trains*:

Prereading		
	make and confirm a prediction	To prepare children for the reading of *Trains*:
		Point to the illustration of the train engine on the front cover and ask, "What do you think this book might be about?" Confirm children's thinking by reading aloud the title and the author's name (Gibbons is also the illustrator).
	activate background knowledge	Then ask, "What do you already know about trains?" Somewhere in children's background will be ideas about trains. As children comment, listen for their ideas about types of engines and trains and the types of cars found on a train.
PART 1, Pages 1–3		
	interpret illustrations	Point to the illustrations on page 1, then pages 2 and 3 (extension of page 1), and ask: "What do you see in the illustrations?" (different kinds of trains)
		"Let's read to see what we can find out about trains."
	clarify vocabulary	Read the text on pages 1 to 3, then ask: "*Locomotive.* What is a locomotive?" "Where is a locomotive in this illustration (pages 2 to 3)?"
Pages 4–5		
	context clues	Point to the illustrations on pages 4 and 5 and ask: "Do these locomotives look new or old? Listen to what the words say."
	build background knowledge	Read the text on pages 4 and 5. Children find out that trains have been around for a long time, and used to be powered by wood and coal. Briefly discuss coal and how it can be used for heat.
Pages 6–9		
	make a prediction	Look at illustrations on pages 6 to 8, and ask: "What types of locomotives do you think these might be? Let's read to find out."
	confirm prediction	Read pages 6 to 8, and ask:
	recall details	"We know that wood and coal were used to make steam to run a train. What other kinds of power did we find out about?"
	interpret illustration	Read page 9, and ask: "Look at the illustration that shows how a train sits on the track. Do you see how the wheels of the train fit on the track?"

recall important details	"What do we know about trains so far?" (Retell the most important ideas up to this point, end of part 1. Look back at illustrations to support retelling. It is important to help children begin to connect the details they are hearing about.)

PART 2,
Pages 10–13

make a prediction	Look at illustration on pages 10 and 11 and ask: "In this part we are going to learn about the two main types of trains, passenger and freight. What type of train do you think this might be?" Call attention to the many people in the illustrations (passenger train). Say, "Let's read to find out."
make and confirm a prediction	Read pages 10 to 13, then ask: "What did we find out about passenger trains?" Help children notice the labels on parts of the train (e.g., berth, dining car) to support what they know.

Pages 14–17

interpret illustration	Look at the illustrations on pages 14 and 15, then ask: "Does this look like a passenger train? What kind of train could this be? Let's read to find out."
recall details	Read pages 14 to 17, then ask: "What did we find out about this train?" (discuss freight trains and their functions)
recall details	Review part 2, using illustrations to support. "What two types of trains have we learned about? What is a passenger train for? What is a freight train for? How can we tell if a train is a passenger train or a freight train?"
anticipate text	"We know that a freight train can have many kinds of train cars. Let's see what we can find out about the different kinds of train cars."

PART 3,
Pages 18–25

interpret illustrations and recall details	For each two facing pages, read the text, calling attention to the illustrations for clues about the types of train cars. After reading, point to illustrations on each page and ask, "What kind of train car is this? What does it carry?"

Pages 26–27 and
AFTER THE READING

	Read the last two pages.
respond to text	After reading *Trains,* help children reflect on the story by asking: "Would you like to be a passenger on a train? What would you do if you were a passenger?"
recall main ideas and important details	"What other type of train is very important today? What are some of the kinds of train cars that can be on a freight train? Which train cars do you like the best? Why?" "How do trains get their power to go?"

FIGURE 4.3
Comparison of narrative and expository texts.

A Chair for My Mother	*Trains*
Organization	**Organization**
Use characters' actions and interactions to tell a life story. Characters' actions and reactions create a plot sequence that the reader is able to follow because it simulates familiar life experiences.	Explain/teach new ideas about trains, using specialized vocabulary. Text describes trains. Descriptive writing does not have a particular sequence. The reader must know enough about trains to connect relevant ideas.
Comprehension of Text	**Comprehension of Text**
To comprehend the text readers must link ideas in the text to familiar life experiences. In addition, readers must use what they know about how stories are told. Inferences about characters' motivations are required for deeper understanding of the plot and themes.	To comprehend the text readers must activate background knowledge about trains and link it with new information in the text. A lack of previous experiences with trains will impact the depth of comprehension.

Depending on the purposes for selecting this text and children's responses, determine the extent to which rereadings of this book are warranted or desired.

Are there differences between reading aloud a narrative text and reading aloud an informational text? Reflect on the two samples provided. What do you notice? Figure 4.3 provides a brief comparison of the texts used as examples in this section. Sensitivity to the types of texts and how readers relate to, or make sense of, those texts should guide the level of assistance provided before, during, and after the reading. Expository texts will typically require increased support before, during, and especially after the reading to help children develop their schema about the world that is forming and refining with each learning experience. Revisiting texts enables all children to continue to build and refine their life and world knowledge.

Making Connections . . .

This would be an appropriate time for you to select a text that you believe would be an engaging read-aloud for primary-grade children. Prepare a mediated read-aloud experience similar to those shown as examples in this chapter. How would you prepare children for the read-aloud, guide them through the text, and help them reflect on the reading afterward? When you have completed your plans for the read-aloud, take time to compare your plan with the way that you naturally read to children (response to a previous **Making Connections** . . .). It is important to understand how your natural style compares to the planned ways that you engage children when comprehension of text is your goal.

EXTENDING COMPREHENSION OF TEXT— REREADING AND REVISITING TEXTS

All children do not learn at the same rate or in the same way, nor do they bring the same background experiences to school. It stands to reason, then, that children with varied backgrounds will need to have varied experiences with books that are read aloud in order to build comprehension skills. Supporting children in books for a second, third, or fourth reading can provide the extended experience that many children need (Beaver, 1982). Texts that are reread frequently become old favorites and are requested again and again, just as children request rereading of bedtime stories.

Children come to a rereading with a version of that story or text already in their heads. They remember portions of the previous reading of the text, which become a schema or background knowledge to use as they revisit the text. During a rereading, help children use their knowledge of the text to derive greater pleasure and understanding.

Figure 4.4 notes how the first reading of a text might compare with a rereading of the same text. During a rereading, children receive support as they use their knowledge of the text to:

- expand vocabulary and book language,
- achieve a deeper appreciation and understanding of the text, and
- focus on a specific aspect of the text, such as the author's style of writing, use of a literary device, or strategies for understanding the text.

First Reading	Rereading
Before you read, we think: • What is this about? • What do I already know?	**Before you read, we think:** • What do I remember about this from before? • What did I like about this?
While reading, we think: • How does this fit with what came before? • How does this fit with what I already know? • What will happen next? • Do I need to change what I was thinking?	**While reading, we think:** • I think I know what's coming, let's see if I'm right! • That's what I thought it would be! or That's different than I remembered. • Oh, I didn't see that before. That's new.
After you read, we think: • How do I feel about this? • What do I want to remember about this?	**After you read, we think:** • I really know this book! • It feels good to know what is coming.

FIGURE 4.4
Thinking about a text—first reading versus rereading.

Developing Vocabulary and Book Language

Rereading text provides additional exposure to new vocabulary and book language. Children's familiarity with book language is important to their future success as readers and writers. Revisiting text enables children to focus on essential words and expand on their understanding of other interesting language presented by an author. Rereading texts develops vocabulary and book language in a variety of ways:

- 🍎 Reread texts to help children add new words that are used in unique contexts, especially specialized vocabulary for a topic.
- 🍎 Reread texts to expose children to new phrases or ways of saying things, such as how Grandma "*puts by* the savings" as a way of talking about the money she adds to the jar.
- 🍎 Reread texts to provide repeated exposure to language used to create vivid descriptions.
- 🍎 Reread expository texts to support children's developing understanding of content and build background knowledge.
- 🍎 Reread parts of texts to focus children's attention on specific information/descriptions the author/illustrator provides.

During a rereading, children have a familiarity with a text that enables them to focus on more details in the story. Encourage them to be more actively involved, recalling and confirming what they already know. Knowing the text and interacting more during the reading brings increased satisfaction for more reluctant readers. Support helps children feel affirmed for what they already know.

Enhancing Understanding and Appreciation of Text

In the first reading of a text, support children as they think about new ideas before, during, and after the text is read aloud. Mediate between children and texts so that children will successfully follow the gist of the plot and character's actions or the main ideas. In a rereading, help children become more familiar with the general language of the book and the ways this particular author expresses ideas. In addition, rereading provides needed repetition to add new vocabulary introduced by the author. Children find great pleasure in knowing that they already "know" a story and are able to join in the telling.

Rereading also can develop deeper understanding of the themes of a text, such as children's appreciation of how people, sometimes with the help of friends and neighbors, work hard to make a new life after something as devastating as a fire destroys all of their belongings. Rereading helps children gain a greater appreciation for themes in texts, such as how long and hard people must work to save money to buy something they dream about.

Another reason for rereading text is to help children learn strategies that they can use to increase their understanding and enjoyment of text. Some texts are challenging and require the reader to notice particular details to gain a fuller understanding; however, noticing such details requires a familiarity with the text. For this reason a rereading can be useful in guiding children to think about such details. Be sure that children have a general understanding of the text before attempting to examine specific details, such as the specific types of train cars introduced in *Trains* by Gail Gibbons.

Children's development as readers should guide the selection of which ideas or details seem to be most important to revisit during rereading. There are usually more possibilities in a text than time will allow. *A Chair for My Mother* might be revisited to help children understand the author's use of flashback to tell about how the fire destroyed all of the characters' belongings. A flashback is a literary device an author uses to fill in details that are needed to better understand the story. Try reading this book by skipping the flashback (pages 9–16). Is the significance of saving for the chair affected? In a rereading, the flashback might be read first to make the time sequence of the story more concrete.

BUILDING COMPREHENSION THROUGH RETELLING

Telling and retelling stories was an oral tradition long before it became a written tradition. Children can use the retelling of favorite stories as a way to solidify their understanding of plot sequence and character traits (Morrow, 1985). Retelling requires tellers to identify, clarify, and organize their thinking, thus building a base of literal and implied meaning for both narrative and expository text.

Children need to verbalize their retelling to enhance their language knowledge, especially expressive language. There is a "linguistic spillover" as children practice retelling a text. As children retell a plot or main ideas of a text, they borrow particular linguistic forms, structures, concepts, and conventions from that author (Brown & Cambourne, 1987). Retelling provides practice with language models that are crucial to children's success in reading and writing.

Retelling with Text Illustrations

Young children attend to illustrations before they attend to print. Using illustrations to guide a retelling builds on their visual strengths.

- After reading the text aloud, return to the beginning of the text and encourage children to retell important story events as cued by the illustrations. Seeing the illustrations in sequence as we turn the pages of the text helps children remember the story events in correct order.
- Invite children to participate in shared retellings. The safety of the group may let some children be willing to risk in their retellings. Wordless or nearly wordless books are excellent for this form of retelling, such as *Do You Want to Be My Friend?* (Carle, 1971) or *Rosie's Walk* (Hutchins, 1968).
- Verbal retellings can be captured on a tape recorder for children to hear and appreciate their own comprehension of text.

FIGURE 4.5
Simple story map—
beginning, middle, end.

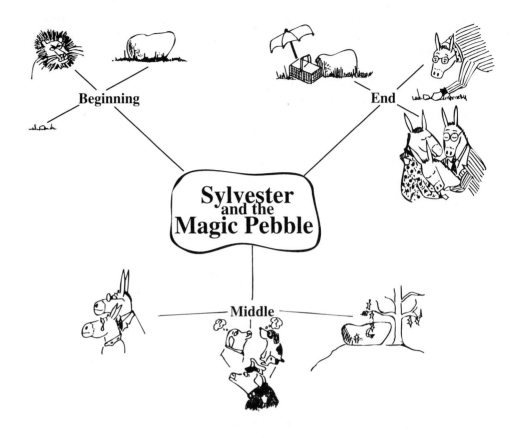

Retelling with a Story Map

A story map shows the main parts of a story and the relationships among the parts.

- A story map can be organized either by
  - the beginning, middle, and end of the story (see Figure 4.5), or
  - the problem, events, and resolution of the story (see Figure 4.6).
- A story map may be written in words or drawn with pictures. A picture story map is most appropriate for emergent and developing readers.

Retelling with Drawings

Retelling through drawings allows children time to recall details and organize ideas about a story.

- As children are drawing, either individually or in groups, they can write or dictate their retelling. Folding under the bottom two or three inches of the drawing paper provides ample space for children's written responses or dictations.
- Illustrations should be shared through verbal explanation then displayed around the room, along an inside hallway, or as a class or individual retelling book.

Sylvester and the Magic Pebble	
Problem:	Sylvester becomes a rock.
Events:	• Sylvester is scared by a lion. • He makes a wish. • He becomes a rock. • Mother and father look everywhere. • Time passes. • Mother and father go for a picnic. • Father finds a magic pebble. • He wishes for Sylvester.
Resolution:	Sylvester changes back to a donkey.

FIGURE 4.6
Simple story map—
problem, events, and
resolution.

Retelling with a Flannel Board

A large display surface covered in flannel or felt becomes the backdrop for introducing and manipulating pictures of the most important characters and scenes in a story.

- A flannel board is especially good for sensory learners. Manipulating the props for a flannel board story provides a sensory stimulus for children's recollections of story sequence and details.
- Flannel board pieces can be made from copies of illustrations of a favorite children's book. Select the illustrations that are essential to the retelling of the text; individually mount them on heavy paper, laminate each picture, then glue flannel or felt to the back so they will adhere to the board.
- If a commercially made flannel board is not available, an old game board, a thin piece of wood, or extra heavy cardboard can be covered with flannel or felt.
- An individual student flannel board is made by lining the inside top of a box. Pictures for the retelling can be stored neatly inside the box.
- A flannel board is also good for activity centers. Many teachers like to set up places around the classroom where children can make work choices and continue activities that the class has begun together.

Retelling through Writing

The time required to form letters and words on paper provides additional time for children to process their thoughts about a text.

- A written retelling can be individual or group. Groups of children can share the task by each writing one part of the story.
- Emergent writers may dictate their retelling to a more knowledgeable writer.
- Children can share their written retelling with a peer or class.

See Figure 4.7 for a sample written retelling.

FIGURE 4.7
Written story retelling.

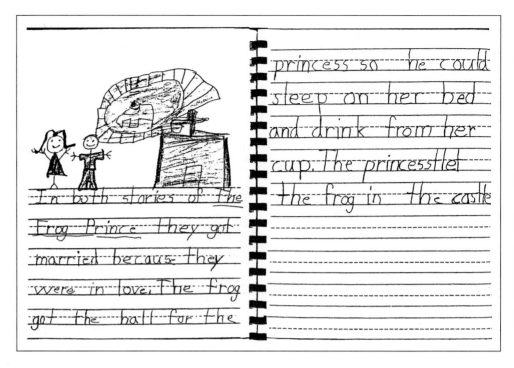

In both stories of the Frog Prince they got married becaus they were in love. The frog got the ball for the princess so he could sleep on her bed and drink from her cup. The princess let the frog in the castle

Retelling through Drama

Bringing physical movement into retelling aids children's sensory learning. Retelling may be easier for some children if they are allowed to pretend to be the character and to play act.

 The use of props from the story, such as the chairs and bowls of porridge from Goldilocks and the Three Bears, supports children's recollections of details and sequence.

🍎 Early dramatic versions of a story may have very little narration or speaking as a part. Some children will need the security of movement to help them remember story events and the language they can use for the retelling. As children gain confidence, encourage more narration or explanation along with the movement.

In this section, we have explored a number of ways to help children gain experience in retelling stories that are read aloud. Retelling helps children notice detail in story events and helps children assign value or importance to story events and order. Retelling activities are helpful in supporting children's comprehension of text.

🍎 BUILDING COMPREHENSION THROUGH RESPONSE

Readers return to books because of the way they feel about the reading. Responding to literature enables children to think in explicit, inferential, personal, and critical ways. Value children's opinions about literature and help them find the words to talk about their interpretations of books. Support and extend their re-

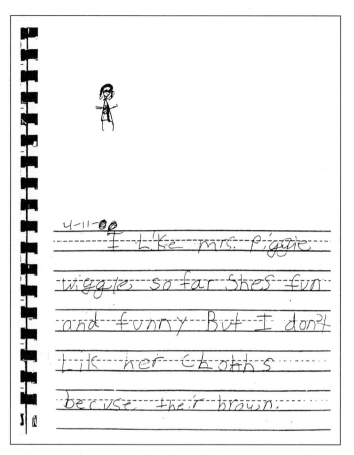

FIGURE 4.8
Written response to
Mrs. Piggle Wiggle.

sponses to literature through discussion. Response can also be enhanced through the use of response journals, chants and rhythms, creative movement, and art.

Response in Journals

- From the very first days of school, encourage children to explore and share their responses to literature read-aloud, even if that response is scribble, letter strings, or initial attempts at spelling (see Figure 4.8).

- Response journals do not have to be a daily routine. They can be a special activity that follows the readings of favorite texts.

- A response journal can contain written and illustrated interpretations to text, including dictations or shared child–teacher writing. For example, Figure 4.9 shows a first-grade response to an old favorite, *The Three Little Pigs,* with teacher support for some letter-sound patterns.

- Response journals can be simply made using stapled paper, lined or unlined. If children are illustrating and writing, we might alternate lined and unlined paper as needed.

- Consider varying the size and shape of the journal. A journal for *A Chair for My Mother* might be shaped like the Blue Tile Diner or a big, overstuffed armchair. Journals for *Trains* might be shaped like a locomotive or a particular train car.

FIGURE 4.9
First-grader's response to
The Three Little Pigs.

🍎 Journal responses can be used to focus on particular types of entries (illustrate/describe favorite parts, explore feelings toward characters).

🍎 Journal responses can also explore understandings of the significance of story events, themes, and character's actions.

🍎 Nonfiction text responses can focus on understanding of key concepts and technical vocabulary.

🍎 Responses to literature should be discussed and shared.

Response with Chants and Rhythms

🍎 Chants, or rhythmic poems without music, provide an opportunity for a class to create a shared response to literature.

🍎 Begin with a simple rhythmic pattern and fill in with story events. Example—*A Chair for My Mother:*

> *We are saving, saving, saving,*
> *Every nickel, Every dime,*
> *We are saving, saving, saving,*
> *And soon it will be time—*
> *To buy a special chair.*

or

> *My mother wants a chair,*
> *A soft, soft chair,*
> *A velvet chair,*
> *A beautiful chair,*
> *My mother wants a chair.*

- 🍎 Chants can be combined with creative movement to let children express their response to the rhythms of language.
- 🍎 When chants are well known, the words can be written on large charts and used as a text for shared reading.

Response with Creative Movement

- 🍎 Young children find it satisfying to express feelings through movement.
- 🍎 Invite them to "become" a character and show their interpretation of their favorite thing about that character.
- 🍎 To support reluctant children, involve the whole class in this activity, with everyone becoming a character.
- 🍎 After learning to recite a chant, children can find "their" space, reciting the chant as they move about the room. Encourage children to add movements and use their voice intonation to emphasize the mood of the chant.
- 🍎 Props such as scarves, hats, and masks can be used to enhance creative movement. Props can help children lose themselves in the movement and feel less self-conscious.

Response with Art

- 🍎 Art is an excellent vehicle for children to use to respond to literature.
- 🍎 Children may enjoy emulating an illustrator's style (Madura, 1995). Caldecott Award winners, best-illustrated children's books, are an excellent starting point
- 🍎 Having a wide variety of media available in the classroom helps children explore their feelings about a literary experience. (Bold tempera colors suggest very different feelings than do gentle watercolors. Collage combines textures, patterns, and colors to suggest complex feelings; crayon resists with a black tempera wash might suggest hidden or mysterious feelings.

For information about the Caldecott Award for the best illustrated children's book, see *http://www.ala.org/ala/alsc/ awardsscholarships/ literaryawds/caldecottmedal/ caldecottmedal.htm.*

- 🍎 A class mural is always a favorite. Children enjoy contributing ideas to a class project. Each child can create a small part of a text that, when combined, provides an illustration of the theme or main idea of a text.

Helping children develop the ability to express their responses to literature enhances their enjoyment of it and their reading experiences (and ours, too!). Children who enjoy literature are more likely to spend time reading.

Making Connections . . .

Which types of retelling and responding activities are more appealing to you as a teacher? Why do you think certain activities appeal to you more than others? Consider which types of activities might be most useful with different ages and developmental levels of children. Think of one or two books that you have read aloud to children. What types of retelling and responding activities would be most effective for those particular books? Why did you select those activities? At this stage of your development as a teacher, it is important to become aware of the types of activities that naturally appeal to you. You want to be sure that your preferences do not limit the opportunities for some of your students.

READ-ALOUD LITERATURE STUDY

There is never enough time in the school day for all that teachers want and need to do with children. One way to maximize time devoted to reading to/with children is to also use the daily read-aloud to study literature as a class. Read-aloud literature study may simply be the study of one text, but it can also include a focused unit of study across multiple texts that provide time and opportunity for deeper examination of an author, topic, genre, or literary element. Depending upon the needs and interests of the children, literature study can focus on picture books, fiction or nonfiction, as well as chapter books. Figure 4.10 provides an overview for organizing whole-class guided literature study. Mediated read-aloud is the focal point of the literature study; however, small groups and independent work are also possible.

FIGURE 4.10
Organizing time for whole-class literature study.

Whole Class:
60% of time
	• Teaching points—mini-lessons
	  Procedures
	  Literary knowledge
	  Reading skills and strategies
	• Mediated read-aloud and
	  whole-class and/or
	  small-group discussions
	• Planning for the day

Work Time:
30% of time
	• Small-group discussions (optional)
	• Response activities
	  Literature log
	  Art
	  Related reading
	  Drama

Whole Class: 10% of time	• Sharing/closure discussion • Planning for next day

Guided literature study can also focus on the reading of expository texts. Reading expository texts to/or with children provides added opportunities to engage in developing familiarity with the technical language of a topic or concept. Expository texts also provide the much needed opportunity for children to develop an ear for the structure of such texts—description, sequenced events or ideas, compare/contrast, cause/effect, and problems/solutions (Carter & Abrahamson, 1998; Meyer, 1985). Children have had many more years to listen to fiction to begin to internalize the structure of plot that is created by characters actions and reactions. They begin to build equivalent experiences for expository text through many opportunities to listen and respond.

Reading aloud chapter books provides support to children who are making the transition into more challenging literature. Initially, the study of chapter books should focus on a unique feature of chapter books—the need to mentally link chapters from reading to reading. Provide support to children as they learn to think about connecting the ideas presented in each chapter into a whole over the course of reading a text.

A class set of books allows literature study to move from read-aloud to a shared read-along. Many schools have purchased class sets to support the study of literature. Chapter books are most effective when children have access to the text while it is read aloud. If children can read along, call attention to specific passages they can both hear and see.

For children at the transitional stage, discussion skills should be emphasized, with the ultimate goal of literature study being student-led small groups (see Chapter 6), also called Book Clubs or Literature Circles. To work toward greater student participation in literature study, students should have the opportunity to meet in small groups to discuss text that has been read aloud.

Focusing Literature Study

Linking learning experiences can enhance children's enjoyment and achievement. The books selected for a unit of study may:

- 🍎 cluster around a topic,
- 🍎 be written by the same author and/or illustrator,
- 🍎 represent the same genre, or
- 🍎 provide opportunity to study a particular literary element, such as character.

Selecting books that are related can make planning and instruction more coherent and effective. Related texts can also provide opportunities for children to develop deeper understanding.

Focus on a Topic or Theme

Integrated units drawn from science or social studies provide an excellent opportunity for literature study. Both narrative and informational literature are appropriate. Some example topics might include:

- animals
- insects
- families
- friendship
- problem solving
- school
- weather
- famous Americans
- holidays

For author information, visit *http://www2. scholastic.com/teachers/ authorsandbooks/authorstu dies/authorstudies.jhtml.*

- human body
- plants
- cultures
- community
- environments/habitats
- motion

A to Zoo (Lima & Lima, 2002), a subject guide to picture books, is an excellent resource for locating potential books for a unit of study.

Focus on an Author or Illustrator

One way for children to become committed readers is to help them become personally involved with the writers and illustrators of the books they read. Indepth study of an author enables children to become interpreters of an author's style. A good way for teachers to introduce author studies is to begin with an author who is a personal favorite. Another way to find good candidates for an author study is to watch children's responses during read-aloud activities. Authors of books who get a favorable response from children are worth investigating.

Focus on a Particular Genre

Reading several pieces of literature from a particular genre, such as fairy tales, helps children understand how ideas in that genre are organized and presented. Understanding a genre helps children become more critical readers of that genre. Examining the characteristics of a particular genre provides opportunities to encourage critical thinking, such as comparing and contrasting texts and ideas. Being familiar with various genres can widen horizons, making children more aware of the variety of literature that is available. Appendix A provides a discussion of the various genres that are appropriate to study in the primary grades.

Focus on a Literary Element

As children discuss books, their talk naturally moves to issues of:

- characters,
- plot,
- setting,
- theme, and
- point of view.

To help children deepen their understanding of how authors use literary elements to develop narratives, it is appropriate to focus attention on texts in which authors use literary elements skillfully. Appendix A provides an overview of the development of literary elements in children's books.

READ-ALOUD LITERATURE STUDY—PICTURE BOOKS

For 1 week a class might study books by Ezra Jack Keats. The language of his texts is simple yet descriptive and is supported by the illustrations. This sample week of study might focus on children's responses to Keats's characters, especially Peter in *The Snowy Day*. Figure 4.11 provides an overview of how a teacher might organize this whole-class study of literature. Mediated read-aloud is the focal point of the literature study. Small groups provide close study of *The Snowy Day* throughout the week. Children's engagement with Keats's texts occurs during both whole-class and small-group work time. If teachers organize around only one of Keats' books, such as *The Snowy Day,* the following might be considered:

DAY 1: READ-ALOUD

Before the reading:

- Discuss favorite things to do in snow
- Make a cluster of children's ideas
- Preview illustrations in The Snowy Day and make predictions

Read-aloud and response:

- How did our favorite things about snow compare with Peter's?
- Focus on Keats's use of language:
  - crunch, crunch, crunch
  - dragged his feet s-l-o-w-l-y
  - smacking a snow-covered tree
  - a great big tall heaping mountain of snow

DAYS 2–5: REREADING

Teaching points:

- Descriptive language
- Plot structure—beginning, middle, and end
- Using illustrations as context to predict words in text
- Using context clues to predict words in text

Possibilities for retelling and response:

- Illustrate and describe what you would do if you were Peter
- Try to use interesting words like Keats does
- Draw a story map to retell the story
- Illustrate/describe a favorite part of the text
- Create own "Snowy Day" story.

Possibilities for word study:

- Make a cluster of descriptive snow words
- Make a cluster of personal experiences with snow

A literature log becomes a record of each child's participation in read-along literature study (see Chapter 9 for more information on journals and logs). Retelling, response, and word study activities can be placed in the literature log and used for discussion. Entries for several picture books can be combined, especially for related books.

FIGURE 4.11
One-week literature unit—author study of Ezra Jack Keats.

Explanation of Activities	Monday	Tuesday
Whole class • Shared reading • Mediate read-aloud • Rereadings • Shared writing	Shared writing—snow cluster What do we know about snow? Mediated read-aloud—*The Snowy Day* Introduce Keats as author/illustrator Second mediated read-aloud—*Peter's Chair*	Shared reading of snow cluster—review and add new ideas Compare with *The Snowy Day* Rereading of *The Snowy Day* Mediated read-aloud—*Whistle for Willie* Begin shared writing—We Like Ezra Jack Keats!
Small groups • Guided reading and rereadings Independent writing in literature response log Extension activities	Guided reading—*The Snowy Day* (multiple copies) Literature log • Copy and expand snow cluster • Response to *The Snowy Day* • Vocabulary—choose three favorite words from *The Snowy Day* Extensions • Tape recorder—Keats's stories taped, choice of texts • Art—collage in Keats's style • Independent reading—Keats's books	Guided reading—choral reading of *The Snowy Day* Literature log • Add to personal snow cluster • What I Know about Snow • Vocabulary—illustrate and describe three favorite words Extensions • Tape recorder—Keats's stories • Art—continue making collage • Independent reading—Keats's books
Community Closure	Share favorite words written in literature response log Plan for tomorrow	Share collages, make comparisons with Keats's artistic style as shown in his books Plan for tomorrow

 READ-ALOUD LITERATURE STUDY—CHAPTER BOOK

Chocolate Fever *by Robert Kimmel Smith*

Chocolate Fever by Robert Kimmel Smith (1972) serves as an example of a read-aloud literature study of a chapter book. *Chocolate Fever* is humorous, presents little challenge, and is an easy transition into chapter books. The story is a fantasy about Henry Green, who loved chocolate so much that he made medical history with the only cure for *Chocolate Fever*. The book has 12 short chapters, which can be easily read over one week by reading two to three chapters per day. Small-group and independent extension activities provide additional engagement with the text. The literature response log becomes an integral part of a child's response to each chapter in the book. Extensions emphasize independent reading and writing over elaborate teacher-made or commercial materials.

Wednesday	Thursday	Friday
Shared reading—weather poem	Shared rereading—weather poem	Mediated read-aloud—*Maggie and the Pirates*
Listen for "noisy" words	Mediated read-aloud—*Louie*	
Mediated read-aloud—*Goggles*	Reread—a Keats favorite	Reread—a Keats favorite
Reread—a Keats favorite	Shared writing—reread, add, revise, prepare to make a big book	Shared writing—make final revisions for class big book
Shared writing—reread and add to We Like Ezra Jack Keats!		
Guided reading—choral reading of *The Snowy Day*, compare with language in weather poem	Guided reading—partner reading of *The Snowy Day*, share favorite part with group members	Guided reading—class big book, divide shared writing into pages for a big book
Literature log • Write "noisy" words you like • Respond to favorite Keats character	Literature log • Sentence building using favorite Keats words, "noisy" words • Begin What I Like about Ezra Jack Keats (continue on Friday)	Guided reading of What I Like about Ezra Jack Keats Literature log— • Continue What I Like about Ezra Jack Keats
Extensions • Tape recorder—Keats's stories • Art—continue collage • Independent reading—Keats's books	Extensions • Tape recorder—Keats's stories • Art—decide how to use collages in big book and Keats bulletin board. • Library corner—Keats's books	Extensions • Tape recorder—Keats stories • Art—add collages to complete big book • Library corner—Keats's books
Share logs of favorite Keats characters Plan for tomorrow	Share logs of What I Like about Ezra Jack Keats Plan for completion of class big book	Share class big book

Procedures for organizing read-aloud literature study with chapter books:

DAY 1: READ-ALOUD

Before the reading:

- Introduce the story *Chocolate Fever* and the author Robert Kimmel Smith.
- Preview text cover, table of contents, and limited illustrations and make predictions.

Read-aloud and response:

- Chapters 1 and 2 (pages 1–23)
  - Encourage continued predictions, including revising predictions based on new information.

- Discussion centers on:
  - What do we know about Henry?
  - How did we find out?

Teaching point:

- Reality versus fantasy:
  - How do we know this is a fantasy?
  - What are the clues?

DAYS 2–5: CONTINUE READ-ALOUD

- Day 2: Chapters 3–5, pages 24–40
- Day 3: Chapters 6–7, pages 41–55
- Day 4: Chapters 8–9, pages 57–71
- Day 5: Chapters 10–12, pages 72–93

Before each reading:

- Retell previous chapters.
- Help children link chapters to have a sense of the whole.
- Make inferences about motivations for characters' actions.
- Follow the plot and clearly identify problem and events that lead to resolution of the problem.

Daily small-group discussions:

- Provide a discussion guide to help children learn to guide their own discussions (see discussion and samples in next section).

Possibilities for retelling and response:

- Make a chart of all the chocolate things Henry ate.
- Henry discovered brown freckles on his skin. What are freckles? Make a prediction, then research the topic.
- Could freckles just appear on Henry's skin? Why or why not?
- Make a prediction—Henry said he was "feeling funny," then he discovered brown freckles. What do you think might happen next?

The length and complexity of chapter books offer more possibilities for study than picture books. Care must be taken to select a few essential elements that allow children to focus their attention while reading. The study of other chapter books during the school year provides additional opportunities for skill and strategy development. The selection of skills and strategies for instruction depends upon other daily reading and writing activities that are occurring.

With chapter books, the literature response log becomes the collection place for a variety of written retellings, responses, and word study activities. Extended study in chapter books provides many opportunities for a literature response log to become an integral part of the classroom literature study.

Literature response logs and extension activities can be shared in a community session that ends the literature study period each day.

Developing Discussion Skills

Children in the later primary grades enjoy discussing books with their peers and can gain new perspectives through discussion (Peterson & Eeds, 1990). Discussion takes on greater importance in literature study as children transition from picture books to chapter books. Read-aloud literature study can provide focused experiences with discussion. Small-group discussions can be an effective follow-up to the whole-class reading, to learn and practice discussion skills. The small groups all meet at the same time, so the teacher is not typically a member of any one group. Instead, the teacher circulates among the groups while the children have the opportunity to independently think and talk about the book.

To begin a focus on discussion skills, the class talks about what makes a good discussion and the skills needed for discussion. This discussion occurs before children move into their small groups. Initially, children need assistance to think about what discussion is and how it compares with past experiences in reading groups. Most children may have participated in groups that are actually teacher-guided question-answer sessions, but not in discussions in which they initiate the talk. Learning how to actively listen and take turns talking are two important parts of discussion that must be practiced.

Children learn to be independent if given time and proper support. During preschool years, children learn to be quite independent because an adult is not always around to take care of things. Successful literature study also promotes independence as a part of growing as a reader and thinker.

To focus on developing discussion skills, prepare a daily discussion guide that children use in small groups to focus their student-led discussion (see upcoming section). Encourage discussion skills at all levels of thinking by designing questions for the discussion guides that encourage children to think in different ways. Focus on verbal, rather than written, responses to provide more talking time in the small groups.

During the small-group discussions, the teacher circulates among the small groups, listening to the tone and direction of the talk. It is important to listen and notice what children are thinking and talking about. Children need time to learn to make decisions for themselves. They will seek affirmation that they are doing the "right things." It is best to respond with "What do you think about . . . ?"

At first, children's responses may be primarily focused on only answering the questions on the discussion guide and not much more. Don't be disappointed. This is what they know how to do! Slowly begin to make the questions more general and open-ended to facilitate children's willingness to direct the discussion. They took several years to learn to answer teacher's questions in reading groups, now they need time to learn to pose and answer their own questions.

After about 10 to 15 minutes, gather children back together for a sharing session. Provide opportunity for each group to contribute ideas from their discussion. During this time help groups focus on the factors that promoted good discussion within the group. Slowly, children begin to have confidence in their abilities to guide book discussions.

Preparing a Discussion Guide

To make a discussion guide, consider the reading that will take place during one day and create a few questions to help children focus their attention on the major issues being revealed in the text. Select questions that will help children focus on the main themes of the text and clarify vocabulary. A sample discussion guide for *Chocolate Fever* is shown in Figure 4.12.

Over the course of the 12 chapters in *Chocolate Fever,* the questions become more general and more open-ended. Note how questions change from Chapter 1 to Chapter 5. After reading about two thirds the text, begin inviting children to pose personal questions. To model the forming of questions, invite children to brainstorm questions during the read-aloud that can be answered in the small groups.

During the next book that the children study, the questions on the discussion guide can be half teacher-made and half child-made. Teachers guide discussion during whole-class meetings; small-group meetings are children's opportunity to learn independence in discussion.

FIGURE 4.12
Sample discussion guide for a chapter book, *Chocolate Fever.*

Discussion Guide—Day 1

Chapter 1

Daddy Green said that Henry liked his chocolate "bitter, sweet, light, dark, and daily" (page 18).
What do you think he meant by that?
How can you tell that Henry really loves chocolate?

Chapter 2

What do you think is happening to Henry?
What clues did you find in the text?

Discussion Guide—Day 2

Chapter 3

On page 25, what do you think the word *phenomenon* means? What clues helped you figure it out?
What are freckles? Do you think Henry's spots are really freckles?
How do you think Henry feels at the end of Chapter 3?

Chapter 4

On page 30 it says that Nurse Farthing looked at Henry through her *spectacles.*
What are spectacles? What clues helped you figure it out?
What is happening to Henry at the end of chapter 4?

Chapter 5

What did you think when the doctors discovered that Henry's spots were pure chocolate?
How would you feel if you were Henry right now? What would you do?

ASSESSMENT: MONITORING COMPREHENSION DURING READ-ALOUD

Read-aloud provides information about children's attitudes toward reading and their ability to make meaning with text they hear. Careful observation of responses during read-aloud activities gives some indication of children's developing attitudes about reading, as well as foundations of making meaning. Making anecdotal records, or notes about informal observations, can document specific behaviors and growth over time. Figure 4.13 provides an example of a sample record-keeping form to make notations of observations during read-aloud. It is important to notice the skills that different children are demonstrating, as well as those skills that appear to be challenging to the majority of the class.

Whole-class read-aloud should be followed up by informal discussions with individual children as a way to confirm or disconfirm observations. Children's individual responses about a particular text can reveal whether they are gaining literal, inferential, personal, and/or critical understandings of text.

Evaluating children's responses to retelling and response activities is also an excellent way to better understand their comprehension of text. Activities can be structured to focus children's responses to particular portions of a text. For example, after reading *Trains* by Gail Gibbons, children might be asked to draw their favorite type of train car. As children share their drawings they will provide additional details about their comprehension of the text, particularly train vocabulary.

Assessment of children's comprehension of text should include the evaluation of experiences in which text is read aloud, discussed, and responded to. Reading aloud to children is the foundation for the development of comprehension skills in which decoding text does not inhibit children's opportunities to demonstrate their capacity to think as readers.

RESPECTING DIVERSITY DURING READ-ALOUD

Children bring a richness of experience to the classroom that should be acknowledged, supported, and enhanced through read-aloud. It is important to be keenly aware of children's interests, world knowledge, cultural experiences, and experience with book language. Children should be involved in the selection of some texts for read-aloud. Their selections reflect their interests in books. Sensitivity to their interests can increase children's motivation to interact with print.

Children's knowledge and interests are the starting point for sharing print in the classroom. Balancing narrative and informational texts provides opportunity for children with specialized knowledge to share what they know. In this way, children's lived experiences are validated. If uniqueness is to be an asset in the classroom, teachers must draw upon children's knowledge and interests as one basis of the curriculum. Encouraging interaction, especially during read-aloud, enables children to share what they know about the world.

Historically, people of different cultures have shared their values, beliefs, and experiences with others through story. Using quality multicultural literature

FIGURE 4.13
Demonstrating reading behaviors.

Demonstrating Reading Behaviors			Name	
Response to Read-Aloud	**Usually**	**Sometimes**	**Rarely**	**Comments**
Shows positive physical and/or verbal responses during read-aloud.				
Participates in read-aloud discussions.				
Thinking Like a Reader	**Usually**	**Sometimes**	**Rarely**	**Comments**
Uses background knowledge to predict/confirm meaning during read-aloud.				
Is developing a well-formed sense of story, follows sequence, can retell stories.				
Uses knowledge of story elements in response to read-aloud (plot, character traits, setting, theme).				
Uses background knowledge to understand main ideas and details presented in nonfiction.				
Uses oral context to make meaning for unfamiliar words.				
Remembers past stories, relates knowledge to new stories.				
Shows greater depth of understanding through repeated readings.				

for read-aloud can show children that people with whom they identify are worthy of being central characters in books. Each of us needs cultural models that validate our worth as human beings (see Figure 4.14).

The language of books is a different way of thinking and talking for all children. The difference for individuals is really a matter of degree of experience with books. Sensitivity to making the transition from oral to written language for all children should be apparent in the books that are selected for read-aloud. The

Ada, A. F. (2003). *My Name Is Maria Isabel*. NY: Atheneum.
Altman, L. J., & Sanchez, E. O. (1995). *Amelia's Road*. NY: Lee & Low.
Andrews-Goebel, N. (2002). *The Pot That Juan Built*. NY: Lee & Low.
Braine, S. (1995). *Drumbeat . . . Heartbeat: A Celebration of the Powwow*. NY: Lerner.
Bunting, E. (1997). *A Day's Work*. Boston: Houghton Miffling.
Cheng, A. (2000). *Grandfather Counts*. NY: Lee & Low.
Choi, S. N. (1993). *Halmoni and the Picnic*. Boston: Houghton Mifflin.
Cisneros, S. (1994). *Hairs/Pelitos*. NY: Knopf.
Dooley, N., & Thornton, P. (1992). *Everybody Cooks Rice*. NY: Lerner.
Dorros, A. (1991). *Abuela*. NY: Dutton.
Falwell, C. (2004). *Butterflies for Kiri*. NY: Lee & Low.
Greenfield, E. (1978). *Honey, I Love, and Other Poems*. NY: Dillon.
Hamanaka, S. (1999). *All the Colors of the Earth*. NY: HarperCollins.
Hamilton, V. (1985). *The People Could Fly: American Black Folktales*. NY: Knopf.
Harjo, J. (2000). *The Good Luck Cat*. NY: Harcourt.
Heo, Y. (1994). *One Afternoon*. Fremont, CA: Orchard.
Levine, E., & Bjorkman, S. (1995). *I Hate English*. NY: Scholastic.
McKissack, P. (1988). *Mirandy and Brother Wind*. NY: Knopf.
Mochizuki, K. (1993). *Baseball Saved Us*. NY: Lee & Low.
Ortiz, S. (1988). *The People Shall Continue*. San Francisco: Children's Book Press.
Polacco, P. (1994). *Mrs. Katz and Tush*. NY: Bantam Doubleday Dell.
Polacco, P. (1998). *Chicken Sunday*. NY: Putnam Juvenile.
Reiser, L. (1993). *Margaret and Margarita*. NY: Greenwillow.
Ringgold, F. (1991). *Tar Beach*. NY: Crown.
Soto, G. (1996). *Too Many Tamales*. New York: Putnam Juvenile.
Soto, G. (1997). *Chato's Kitchen*. New York: Putnam Juvenile.
Steptoe, J. (1988). *Baby Says*. NY: Lothrop.
Steptoe, J. (2004). *The Jones Family Express*. NY: Lee & Low.
Tarpley, N. A. (1998). *I Love My Hair*. New York: Little Brown.
Te Ata. (1989). *Baby Rattlesnake*. Children's Book Press.
Thomas, J. C. (1999). *You Are My Perfect Baby*. NY: Harper Collins.
Thong, R. (2000). *Round Is a Mooncake: A Book of Shapes*. NY: Chronicle.
Vaughn, M. (2004). *Up the Learning Tree*. NY: Lee & Low.
Waboose, J. B. (1998). *Morning on the Lake*. Tonawanda, NY: Kids Can Press.
Weatherford, C. B. (2004). *Jazz Baby*. NY: Lee & Low.
Weiss, G. D., & Thiele, B. (1995). *What a Wonderful World*. NY: Atheneum.
Wolf, B. (2004). *Coming to America*. NY: Lee & Low.
Wong, J. S. (2002). *Apple Pie 4th of July*. San Diego: Harcourt.

FIGURE 4.14
Suggestions for multicultural literature.

fewer experiences children have had with the formality of written language, the more conscious teachers must be in providing repeated exposure to books. Rereading of stories provides practice for children in this new language—the language of print. Teachers are the "language bridge" between children and texts.

Reading aloud is one part of a balanced literacy framework. Reading aloud to children provides wonderful experiences with book language and the world of ideas, but it is not enough to prepare them for independence as competent readers and writers. Even though we share many books with children through read-aloud experiences and we talk extensively with them, we need to do much more to help them develop an understanding of the relationships between oral and written language. We need many other techniques to help them learn how readers decode, or break the code of written language, to make meaning and how writers encode, or create the code of written language, to communicate.

Making Connections . . .

As you reflect on the content of this chapter, what ideas do you have about helping children to build a foundation for comprehension of text? What strategies will you use to help all children in your classroom, regardless of their prior literacy experiences, understand and appreciate the variety of texts they encounter? How will you help your students learn to think like readers? Record your thinking in a reflective journal. Share your thinking with your peers. It is important for you to notice your level of understanding about ways to engage students with texts that build comprehension skills.

C H A P T E R

5

Shared Reading: Participating in a Community of Readers

Adding to our literacy framework . . .

	Reading Aloud and Guided Literature Study	
Shared Reading	Balanced and Integrated Literacy Framework	Shared and Interactive Writing
Guided Reading and Guided Literature Study		Guided Writing and Writer's Workshop
Independent Reading and Reader's Workshop		Independent Writing
	Word Study	

In this chapter, we learn about . . .

- The value of shared reading experiences
- Planning and organizing shared reading experiences
- Developing literacy skills and strategies through shared reading experiences
- Integrating shared reading into a balanced literacy program
- Assessing a child's concepts about words and print in books

Focus Literature:

- *The Chick and the Duckling* by Mirra Ginsburg
- *Down Comes the Rain* by Franklyn M. Branley
- *Third-Grade Detectives #1: The Clue of the Left-Handed Envelope* by George E. Stanley

Looking into Classrooms . . .

Antonio gathers the first-grade children on the floor near his chair. On the easel is an oversized book with print and illustrations large enough for all of the children to see. He uses a pointer to draw children's attention to the front cover as he says,

What do you see on the front cover of this book? The title of this book is The Chick and the Duckling *and it was written by Mirra Ginsberg (pointing to the words on the cover). What do you think we might find out as we read this book?*

Antonio opens the book and walks the children through the pictures in the text as a preview of its content—each bird hatching from an egg, and the Chick trying to imitate each action of the Duckling. During this "picture walk" Antonio checks to be sure that the children can accurately interpret the illustrations as an aid to predicting what the words on each page say.

Now the reading begins. Pointing to each word as he reads aloud, Antonio leads the children in this first reading of the text, encouraging them to join in the reading whenever they wish. The dialogue between the Chick and the Duckling is quite repetitive and the children soon join in the reading, especially each time the Chick says, "Me too."

Over the course of the week Antonio and the children will read, reread, and explore various aspects of this big book together as a class, in small groups, with partners, and independently. Antonio is guiding the children in the shared reading of a text.

DOWN THE HALL . . .

As part of their study of weather, Edith and her third-grade students have just completed a mediated read aloud, Down Comes the Rain by Franklyn Branley, which provides explanation of the water cycle. To determine how well her students comprehend the vocabulary and concepts introduced in the text, Edith guides the children through a shared writing of how water evaporates from earth in the form of water vapor and eventually forms clouds from which water in the form of drops can fall to the earth. Edith believes that it is important to make the content of a text such as this, with its technical vocabulary, comprehensible for all students, especially English language learners.

After the shared writing, Edith leads the children in a shared reading of the text. The text is already somewhat familiar because children participated in its composition. Edith begins to read aloud while pointing to the words and encourages children to join in. As they do she listens intently to children's reading of the technical vocabulary (such as evaporate, water vapor, droplets). Over the next few days the class will once again join in a shared rereading of the text, focusing on the sequence of the water cycle and comparing the meanings of related words:

vapor
evaporate
evaporation

Edith believes that it is important for children to become aware of the ways that meaningful chunks in words can be clues to word meaning and spelling. It takes time for children to acquire new vocabulary. During a unit of study in which new concepts are introduced, the shared reading of text is only one of many literacy activities that Edith uses to support children's learning.

BUILDING A THEORY BASE . . .

Shared reading, which Antonio and Edith model in the opening vignette, is a group reading experience that simulates the best aspects of a bedtime reading experience and provides whole-class or small-group instruction in reading skills and strategies. Shared reading was originally called *shared book experience* by Don Holdaway (1979), a New Zealand educator. He studied children's experiences during bedtime story situations to discover how this type of interaction between parent and child was related to children who became successful young readers. Holdaway advocated the re-creating of bedtime stories in school with the use of "big books," or texts that had been substantially enlarged so that all children can share in class reading experiences.

Reading aloud to children, as we explored in Chapter 4, can provide *extensive* experiences with a variety of literature and enables children to enjoy and think about a text that is read by someone else, whereas shared reading engages children in *intensive* reading experiences through repeated readings and close study of a text over several days. Such close inspection of print is necessary if children are to develop the competencies needed to decode and understand print in a fluent and accurate manner.

Children teach us about the power of intensive experiences. In their play, children often continue at the same game or activity, day after day, until they get it "just right." They ask for the same bedtime story again and again, until they know it so well they confidently join in and even lead the reading, or telling, of the story. Through such intensive, repeated exposures, children become comfortable with a text or a task and gain confidence in their abilities to perform it. Children involved in the shared re-reading of text often make statements such as:

- "Now it's easy."
- "I know all of the words."
- "I can read it by myself."
- "I can read it to my mom."

TEXTS FOR SHARED READING

Enlarged print can be made available to children through a variety of sources, including:

- Big books, both commercially produced and class-made;
- Using an overhead projector to enlarge a small text;
- Songs, poems, and chants written on large charts;
- Shared writings or language experience charts;
- Using a pocket chart to build and manipulate a text;
- Scripts for reader's theater; and
- Multiple copies of a text.

Big Books

Enlarged versions of children's books turn a read-aloud experience into a shared reading experience, making print accessible for children to join in the reading. Quality big books are readily available from publishers such as Scholastic (see Figure 5.1), Wright Group, and Rigby. In addition to commercial big books, teachers and children can also make big books. Gail Heald-Taylor (1987) suggests that class-made big books can:

- be replicas of original books,
- have new illustrations decided by the children, or
- be a new version written jointly by teacher and children during shared writing.

Enlarge a Book Using an Overhead Projector

If a particular book is not available in an enlarged version, the overhead projector can be used to enlarge the pages of the text. Overhead transparencies of desired pages can project text onto a screen, enlarging the print and making it accessible to a group of children. As the text is shared together, transparency by

FIGURE 5.1
A sample of texts available as big books.

Apples and Pumpkins by Ane Rockwell
A Chair for My Mother by Vera Williams
Chicka Chicka Boom Boom by Bill Martin, Jr.
Chicken Soup with Rice by Maurice Sendak
Cookie's Week by Cindy Ward and Tomie dePaola
Does a Kangaroo Have a Mother too? by Eric Carle
The Doorbell Rang by Pat Hutchins
Each Peach, Pear, Plum by Allan Ahlberg
Families Are Different by Nina Pellegrini
Five Little Ducks by Pamela Paprone
If You Give a Mouse a Cookie by Laura Joffe Numeroff
Pumpkin, Pumpkin by Jeanne Titherington
Red Leaf, Yellow Leaf by Lois Ehlert
The Snowy Day by Ezra Jack Keats
This Is the Way We Go to School by Edith Baer
The Very Hungry Caterpillar by Eric Carle
What Will the Weather Be Like Today? By Paul Rogers

transparency, teachers guide the reading by pointing to the text on the transparency. Children are able to participate in the reading just as they do with a big book.

Charts: Songs, Poems, Chants, Letters, and Recipes

Large charts of text, visible to all of the children in the group, offer a myriad of possibilities for shared reading. Songs, poems, and chants are usually rhythmical, rhyming, and repetitious. Children's prior knowledge becomes a "text in the head" and can be drawn upon to match against the text printed on a chart. Songs, poems, and chants work best for shared reading when the language has

Re-reading a big book with the help of a partner provides important practice for young readers.

strong rhythm and the vocabulary contains both predictable and decodable words. Friendly letters and simple recipes offer another type of "everyday" text from which children can learn. Letters and recipes should demonstrate the appropriate format and use language that is accessible to the children.

Songs

It is not uncommon for children to sing a song as they "read" the song on a chart, drawing upon the form in which they know the text best. Class songbooks and anthologies can be made to preserve favorite pieces in a class big book that grows over time. In the vignettes of Carmen's first-grade classroom from Chapter 1 we have seen how a song such as "Old MacDonald" can be used for shared reading.

Poems/Chants

Teachers and children can create a chant or poem in response to a favorite piece of children's literature, such as this one for *Sylvester and the Magic Pebble* (Steig, 1969):

> Sylvester found a pebble,
> a magic pebble.
> Sylvester saw a lion,
> a hungry lion.
> Sylvester made a wish,
> a foolish wish,
> Now Sylvester is a rock,
> a donkey rock!

A list of sample childrens poetry books is given in Figure 5.2. Moving from a verbal chant to a shared reading text enables a teacher to focus children's attention on decoding strategies for relevant vocabulary from a text.

Dakos, K. (1995). *If You're Not Here, Please Raise Your Hand: Poems About School.* New York: Aladdin.

Dakos, K. (1998). *Don't Read This, Whatever You Do: More Poems About School.* New York: Aladdin.

Ferris, H. (1957). *Favorite Poems Old and New.* New York: Doubleday.

Katz, B. (2004). *Pocket Poems.* New York: Dutton.

Little, J. (1990). *Hey World, Here I Am.* New York: HarperTrophy.

Prelutsky, J. (1986). *Read Aloud Rhymes for the Very Young.* New York: Knopf.

Prelutsky, J. (1999). *20th Century Children's Poetry Treasure.* New York: Knopf.

Prelutsky, J. (2000). *Random House Book of Poetry.* New York: Random House.

Rossetti, C. G. (1969). *Sing Song: A Nursery Rhyme Book.* New York: Dover.

Silverstein, S. (1981). *A Light in the Attic.* New York: HarperCollins.

Silverstein, S. (2004). *Where the Sidewalk Ends* (30th Anniversary Edition). New York: HarperCollins.

Steinberg, D. (2004). *Grasshopper Pie and Other Poems.* New York: Grosset and Dunlap.

Viorst, J. (1981). *If I Were in Charge of the World and Other Worries: Poems for Children and Their Parents.* New York: Aladdin.

Viorst, J. (2000). *Sad Underwear and Other Complications: More Poems for Children and Their Parents.* New York: Aladdin.

FIGURE 5.2
Sample of children's poetry books.

Shared Writing or Language Experience Charts

Teachers and children can create texts together from shared classroom experiences. Such charts are also referred to as *language experience* charts (Hall, 1981; Nessel & Jones, 1981; Stauffer, 1975; Van Allen, 1974) and have been successfully used for reading instruction for quite some time. Children who participate in the composition of a shared writing (see Chapter 8) or language experience chart know its content. Rereading provides opportunities to focus on details of the text.

A *morning message* is a particular type of experience chart. It can be written by the teacher to the students, written interactively with students, or written independently by students. A morning message usually focuses on things that are happening in the classroom. An example of a morning message is:

> Today is Monday, March 19.
>
> Today Is Raul's birthday.
>
> We will make tortillas after lunch.
>
> Raul's grandmother will help us.

Dear Boys and Girls,

Please help me find the missing letters. The caterpillars are h_r_. We will m_k_ a h_m_ for them. We will f_d the caterpillars and watch them gr_.

Your teacher,

Mr. Chen

The language in experience charts can be sheltered, or made more accessible, to support emergent readers and children who are learning English. Language is *sheltered* when unfamiliar content is represented through language that is carefully selected to make it comprehensible to the learner (Cummins, 1981). The most meaningful words are placed in simple sentence patterns. The teacher works with the children to construct the language of a sheltered text with attention to how ideas are presented and linked together. The sheltered text then becomes a text for shared reading.

An example of a sheltered text was highlighted in the opening scenario with Edith's third-grade students. The text was composed as a shared writing after several readings (mediated read-aloud) of *Down Comes the Rain*. The teacher guided the composition to include several key vocabulary words in sentence structures that were not too complex.

The Water Cycle
Water evaporates from rivers, lakes, and oceans.
Water evaporates from plants, animals, and people.
Water that evaporates becomes a gas called water vapor.
You can not see water vapor in the air.
Air moves the water vapor up and away from the earth.

> When water vapor cools it changes to water droplets.
> Millions of water droplets join together to make a water drop.
> Then millions of water drops join together to make a cloud.
> Rain is water drops that fall from clouds.

Notice that from sentence to sentence the ideas are related and key vocabulary is explained and repeated. To make this text for shared reading, the teacher must guide children's content knowledge toward sentence structures that are accessible to all of the children. For further information about shared writing, see Chapter 8.

Using a Pocket Chart

A pocket chart is a large chart, usually about $3' \times 4'$, that displays sentence strips, word cards, or picture cards (see Figure 5.3). Text can be arranged in a pocket chart before or during a lesson. The text can also be rearranged in the midst of a lesson to demonstrate a new idea. Engaging children in manipulating text provides opportunity to assess children's understanding of language and/or print. Pocket charts are available through school supply companies or can be teacher-made. Individual pocket charts ($12'' \times 18''$) can be made from posterboard and masking tape, and used with appropriately sized sentence strips and word cards.

Scripts for Reader's Theater

Reader's theater is "the oral interpretation of literature presented by readers who bring forth the full expression of the literature through their oral reading" (Kelleher, 1997, p. 6). It is an instructional strategy that focuses on fluent oral reading to enhance comprehension and encourages students to read for pleasure. Performance reading "can allow students to see that reading aloud can be more than simply reading from their textbooks" (Person, 1990, p. 428). In addition, the rereading of material encourages better retention of vocabulary and key concepts.

Many different types of texts can be made into scripts for reader's theater. The dialogue from a favorite big book can be developed into a script by teacher and children through shared writing. A poem or chant can be divided among a number of speakers. Sheltered texts from content-area studies can become scripts for performance. For example, a group of second-grade students studying weather might turn some of the text of *Hurricane* by David Wiesner (1990) into a reader's theater to perform for the class. In the story, two brothers experience a hurricane, then turn its aftermath into a fanciful experience. The following conversation is adapted from one episode in the text, during the hurricane, and is suitable for reader's theater:

Younger brother:	Could the hurricane wind really be strong enough to blow our cat away?
Older brother:	The radio said that we could expect sustained winds of fifty miles per hour, gusting to ninety.
Younger brother:	Look at the leaves. They look like a green blizzard.

FIGURE 5.3
Pocket chart.

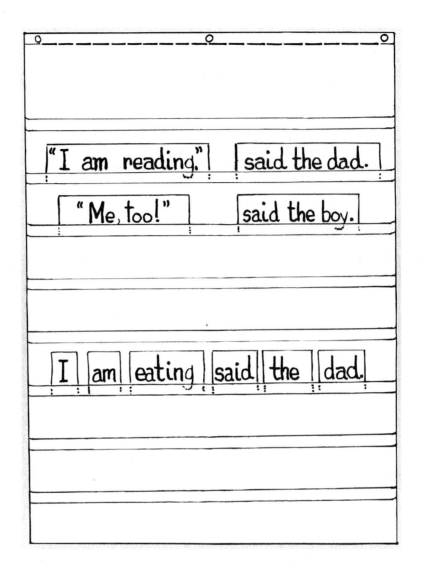

| **Older brother:** | I'd like to fly in one of those weather planes that goes into the eye of a hurricane where the winds are calm. |
| **Younger brother:** | Do you think anything awful has happened outside? |

This conversation continues as the brothers talk about the effects of the hurricane. Preparing a text for performance invites students to listen to and enjoy the written word, as well as provides an opportunity for readers at varying developmental levels to work together.

Multiple Copies of a Text

Children reading at second-grade level and above can benefit in teacher and children sharing the reading of a text, particularly in their transition to chapter books. Shared reading in individual texts provides opportunity for children to focus on their own text while the teacher initially takes the lead in the reading.

This reading can be with the whole class or a small group. As in all shared reading, the children are encouraged to join in as soon as they are comfortable. The reading should be lively and expressive, just as with a big book or a chart with a song or poem. The focus of the reading should be on helping children refine their ability to navigate print in a fluent manner.

CRITERIA FOR SELECTING QUALITY TEXTS

Teachers can use commercially produced materials with large print, such as big books, for shared reading. The following traits should be considered for *narrative texts:*

- A strong story line in which something actually happens,
- Characters and situations with which children strongly identify,
- Attractive illustrations that support and enhance the text,
- Humor and warmth, and
- Rich and memorable language features that ensure predictability such as rhythm, rhyme, and repetition. (Butler, 1987, p. 5)

If *expository* text is the focus, consider the following qualities:

- Clear photographs that build vicarious background and are supported by text
- Accurate information presented in a clear and concise manner
- Background information provided to enhance reader understanding

Finally, regardless of whether a text is fiction, nonfiction, poetry, or the like, we must consider the size and amount of text on each page so that we can adequately engage all children in the shared experience.

Quality of Illustrations

Young children are influenced by the illustrations on the pages of text (Sulzby, 1985). Illustrations are a representation of the world and are often better understood by emergent readers than the abstractness of print. Select books for emergent readers and English language learners, especially, in which the illustrations are simple and clear and have a strong link to the content of the text on that page. Guide children's eyes to carefully examine illustrations or photographs before the text is shared so their knowledge of the illustration or photograph allows them to anticipate the content of the text.

Size and Amount of Print

It is important that the print of a shared text be clearly visible to all children in the group. If size prohibits all children from being able to distinguish details in the print, then shared reading will be no different than a typical read-aloud. The amount of print should fit our instructional purpose and children's level of functioning. If the purpose is to help children think about written language and directionality, then the amount of print is not as important as children's familiarity with its content. If, however, the purpose is for children to learn to independently read the text, children's reading levels should guide the amount and type of print.

Structure or Predictability of Text

Text that allows the reader to use patterns or background knowledge to anticipate upcoming text is considered predictable (Barrett, 1982; Holdaway, 1979; Rhodes, 1981). Bridge, Winograd, and Haley (1983) report that children who participated in repeated reading of predictable books learned more sight words than comparable children who were placed in a basal reading series. Texts become more predictable for young readers when there is:

- 🍎 repetition of vocabulary or story structure,
- 🍎 a cumulative sequence,
- 🍎 rhythmic or rhyming language patterns,
- 🍎 familiar sequences or content, or
- 🍎 rereading of familiar text.

Repetitive Pattern

A repetitive pattern uses repetition of words, phrases, or sentences throughout a text. The fewer words that are changed in the pattern, the more predictable the text. Illustrations that clearly support word changes further increase predictability. Consider the pattern in *Ten in the Bed* (Rees, 1988):

> *There were ten in the bed*
> *and the little one said,*
> *"Roll over, roll over."*
> *So they all rolled over*
> *and one fell out.*
>
> *There were nine in the bed*
> *and the little one said, . . .*

Once readers know the pattern, they can expect it to be repeated and can anticipate the words that are coming. The illustrations show the actual number of children in the bed. The only word that changes in the pattern is the number of children in the bed. Children who know how to count backward from 10 are able to anticipate the appropriate number word for the pattern.

Cumulative Pattern

A cumulative pattern adds one new element, then repeats all previous elements. A cumulative sequence builds to a climax, then either ends or reverses the cumulative order, for example:

> *There is a house,*
> *a napping house,*
> *where everyone is sleeping.*
>
> *And in that house*
> *there is a bed,*
> *a cozy bed,*

> *In a napping house,*
> *where everyone is sleeping . . .*

The pattern in *The Napping House* (Wood, 1984) continues to add and repeat, accumulating a snoring granny, a dreaming child, a dozing dog, a snoozing cat, a slumbering mouse, and a wakeful flea that awakens everyone and reverses the order of the sequence. Children who recognize the pattern are able to join in the repetition of the cumulative sequence. Illustrations cue the reader about each new element.

Rhythmic and Rhyming Pattern

Rhythmic patterns can help readers anticipate the rhythm of specific language that could possibly fill the pattern. Rhyming patterns help readers narrow the choice of possible words that could fit a particular pattern, considering sound and meaning, as in *Chicka Chicka Boom Boom:*

> *A told B, and B told C,*
> *"I'll meet you at the top of the coconut tree."*
> *"Whee!" said D to E, F, G . . .*

The rhythm of the language in *Chicka Chicka Boom Boom* (Martin & Archambault, 1989) combined with repetition and rhyme makes this text predictable. The authors also draw on children's knowledge of the sequence of the letters of the alphabet to add to predictability, as discussed next.

Familiar Sequences and Content

Familiar sequences such as the days of the week, months of the year, numbers, and letters of the alphabet increase the predictability of text, such as:

> *On Monday he ate through one apple.*
> *But he was still hungry.*
> *On Tuesday. . . .*

Children's knowledge of days of the week and counting increases the predictability of text in *The Very Hungry Caterpillar* (Carle, 1969).

Being familiar with the content of a text helps a reader predict the type of vocabulary and the relationships among ideas that might be included. Firsthand experiences with the content are the most powerful. Shared reading that grows out of shared content experiences provides excellent predictability, especially for English language learners.

Shared Rereading

Another way that text becomes familiar and, consequently, predictable is through repeated readings. Once children have heard a text read aloud, they have a version of the text in their heads that they can draw upon in subsequent interactions with that text. Though the "text in the head" may not be complete or totally accurate, it serves as background knowledge that enables children to anticipate content and thus gain control over text (Rhodes, 1981). Children's ability to anticipate parts of classic stories such as *The Three Pigs, Jack and the Beanstalk,* and *The Three Billy Goats Gruff* often comes through repeated exposure. A list of other suggested predictable books can be found in Figure 5.4.

FIGURE 5.4
Suggested predictable
books.

Repetitive Pattern

Carle, E. (1987). *Have You Seen My Cat?* New York: Scholastic.
Eastman, P. D. (1960). *Are You My Mother?* New York: Random House.
Flack, M. (1932). *Ask Mr. Bear.* New York: Simon & Schuster.
Fox, M. (1987). *Hattie and the Fox.* New York: Simon & Schuster.
Galdone, P. (1974). *The Little Red Hen.* New York: Scholastic.
Ginsburg, M. (1972). *The Chick and the Duckling.* New York: Simon & Schuster.
Keats, E. J. (1971). *Over in the Meadow.* New York: Scholastic.
Langstaff, J. (1974). *Oh A-Hunting We Will Go.* New York: Atheneum.
Martin, B. (1967). *Brown Bear, Brown Bear, What Do You See?* New York: Holt,
    Rinehart & Winston.
Raffi. (1988). *The Wheels on the Bus.* New York: Crown.
Rees, M. (1988). *Ten in a Bed.* Boston: Little, Brown.
Shaw, C. G. (1947). *It Looked Like Spilt Milk.* New York: Harper & Row.

Cumulative Pattern

Fox, M. (1987). *Hattie and the Fox.* New York: Simon & Schuster.
Kalan, R. (1981). *Jump, Frog, Jump.* New York: Scholastic.
Mayer, M. (1975). *What Do You Do with a Kangaroo?* New York: Scholastic.
McGovern, A. (1967). *Too Much Noise.* Boston: Houghton Mifflin.
Scott, Foresman Reading Systems, level 2, book A. (1971). *The Bus Ride.*
Shulevitz, U. (1967). *One Monday Morning.* New York: Scribner's.
Tolstoy, A. (1968). *The Great Big Enormous Turnip.* New York: Franklin Watts.
Wood, A. (1984). *The Napping House.* New York: Harcourt Brace Jovanovich.

Rhythm and Rhyme

Ahlberg, J. A. (1978). *Each Peach Pear Plum.* New York: Viking.
Hoberman, M. A. (1978). *A House Is a House for Me.* New York: Viking.
Kraus, R. (1948). *Bears.* New York: Scholastic.
Kraus, R. (1970). *Whose Mouse Are You?* New York: Simon & Schuster.
Martin, B. (1970). *Fire! Fire! Said Mrs. McGuire.* New York: Holt, Rinehart & Winston.
Martin, B., & Archambault, J. (1989). *Chicka Chicka Boom Boom.* New York: Holt,
    Rinehart & Winston.

Familiar Sequences

Carle, E. (1969). *The Very Hungry Caterpillar.* New York: Putnam.
Hutchins, P. (1968). *Rosie's Walk.* New York: Simon & Schuster.
Martin, B. (1970). *Monday, Monday, I Like Monday.* New York: Holt, Rinehart &
    Winston.
Martin, B., & Archambault, J. (1989). *Chicka Chicka Boom Boom.* New York: Holt,
    Rinehart & Winston.
Raffi. (1988). *Five Little Ducks.* New York: Crown.
Rees, M. (1988). *Ten in a Bed.* Boston: Little, Brown.
Shulevitz, U. (1967). *One Monday Morning.* New York: Scribner's.

Repeated Readings of Familiar Stories—Predictable Plot

Adams, P. (1974). *This Old Man.* New York: Grossett & Dunlap.
Brown, M. (1957). *The Three Billy Goats Gruff.* New York: Harcourt Brace Jovanovich.
Galdone, P. (1970). *The Three Little Pigs.* New York: Seabury.
Galdone, P. (1972). *The Three Bears.* New York: Scholastic.
Nodset, J. (1963). *Who Took the Farmer's Hat?* New York: Scholastic.
Sendak, M. (1963). *Where the Wild Things Are.* New York: Scholastic.

Making Connections . . .

Develop a list of your favorite books that are simple, repetitive, and/or predictable and will lend themselves to shared reading. Find out if they are available as big books. If not, consider an appropriate way to enlarge the text for possible shared readings. This might also be a good time to begin a collection of favorite songs, poems, and chants that would make exciting shared readings.

WHY DO SHARED READING?

Shared reading, as a part of a balanced and integrated literacy framework, enables teachers to provide whole-class guided learning experiences that develop and refine:

- confidence and a sense of control,
- concepts about print,
- decoding skills,
- vocabulary,
- comprehension of text, and
- fluency.

Confidence and a Sense of Control

Repetition in learning experiences enables children to feel a sense of control (Rhodes, 1981), which encourages confidence in their ability to participate in the shared reading and rereading of texts. Repetition in opportunities to learn essential reading skills also develops a child's sense of self as reader.

Confidence is supported by shared rereadings in which children's developing skills and strategies are supported by the teacher and membership in the group. Repetition of experiences with a text over time will deepen children's understanding of text (Yaden, 1988), a necessary knowledge base for proficient reading. Keep in mind, however, that by the fourth rereading of a text most of the benefits in word recognition accuracy and speed will have been gained (O'Shea, Sindelar, & O'Shea, 1985; Taylor, Wade, & Yekovich, 1985).

Concepts about Print

Teacher guidance during shared reading helps children deepen their understanding of print. Children who are still forming their understandings about how language can be displayed in print, especially emergent readers and English language learners, need to be shown that the words spoken by the reader are coming from the print in the text, and not from the illustrations (Holdaway, 1979). In addition, children who have not participated in the reading of many bedtime stories need the interactions with a more knowledgeable reader to expand their concepts about print . . . . and expectations for what text can contain. Shared reading is an instructional component that exemplifies the importance of the role of a responsive adult in scaffolding children's print experiences.

Decoding Skills

Children's ability to learn words is closely tied to their proficiency as readers (Adams, 1990; Chall, 1983; Ehri, 1998). In shared reading, children first become familiar with the text as a whole. Then, through repeated exposures, they begin to see the details that comprise the whole—details they usually do not notice during their initial interactions (Kawakami, 1985). Rereading of texts can help young readers attend to letter patterns and word formation. Children's learning often moves from whole to part, which means that new details may not be recognized initially. It is easier to distinguish particular features when the parts are familiar. As children strengthen their schema for the whole, they are able to recognize how new parts may fit within the whole. Intensive experiences such as shared rereading provide time and opportunity to build the schema needed for learning about words and making meaning with particular texts (Johnston, 1998). In addition, children who participate in shared reading learn more about phonics than in round-robin reading, in which children take turns reading out loud (Eldredge, Ruetzel, & Hollingsworth, 1996).

Developing Vocabulary

There is positive evidence that children do readily acquire vocabulary when provided with explanations as novel words are encountered in context (Beck & McKeown, 1990; Beck, Perfetti, & McKeown, 1982; Whitehurst et al., 1988), especially over an extended period of time. The theories of learning discussed in Chapter 1 remind us that learning something new, such as the vocabulary related to a new concept, is enhanced by opportunities to use that knowledge, especially in different contexts. Shared reading provides repeated exposure to vocabulary, which aids word learning. It is important to select of a variety of texts that contain the types of words children are ready to learn.

Comprehension of Text

Comprehension of text is an active mental problem-solving process of making meaning from a text. Good readers draw upon meaning (semantics), language (syntax), and visual (graphophonic) cues as they process the meaning of text. Good readers consistently monitor their understanding of text and have strategies to "fix up" problems when they occur. During shared reading experiences, especially shared rereading, teachers should model effective comprehension strategies and encourage children to actively monitor their understanding of text by answering and generating questions, recognizing patterns in text, and summarizing ideas in text. Children should be encouraged to talk about the strategies they use in particular situations.

Fluency

Read here to find a definition of *fluency.*

Fluency is the ability to read a text accurately, quickly, and with expression, and it develops slowly over time. Fluent readers recognize words automatically, grouping words into meaningful phrases as they make connections among the ideas in the text and between the text and their background knowledge. Fluent readers also read with expression. Fluent reading is a sign that a reader is making the bridge between word recognition and comprehension. (Armbruster, Lehr, & Osborn, 2001). Readers who have not yet developed fluency read slowly, word by word. Their oral reading is often choppy and plodding. Their comprehension is likely to be effected by their slow and/or inaccurate rate of processing text. Fluency is not a state of being, however. Even skilled readers are not equally fluent in all types of texts. A reader's knowledge of the content, vocabulary, and structure of the text can impact fluency.

Shared reading experiences are built upon repeated readings of texts, which have been shown to affect fluency (Dowhower, 1987; Herman, 1985; National Institute of Child Health and Human Development (NICHD), 2000; Rasinski, 1990; Samuels, 1979). Practicing fluent oral reading helps children realize that reading is a natural part of life and that it is a language process related to writing and speaking (Kozub, 2000; Opitz & Rasinski, 1998).

Making Connections...

Think back to some of your earliest experiences with reading. Did you participate in round-robin reading, in which you took your turn reading orally? If so, how did you feel about reading by yourself, in front of your classmates? How might such individual experiences contrast with the support provided during a shared reading experience? What value do you see in shared reading experiences to help students learn new skills and strategies?

PUTTING THEORY INTO PRACTICE...

As we begin to consider how to plan shared reading experiences for children, let's return to Antonio's first-grade grade classroom and Edith's third-grade classroom to listen to the way these teachers engage children in shared reading.

PLANNING SHARED READING EXPERIENCES

How do teachers make decisions about engaging children in a shared reading?

- 🍎 Be clear about instructional goals/purposes,
- 🍎 Analyze the demands of the selected text, and
- 🍎 Consider what is observed in children in relation to the selected text and instructional purposes (Powell, 1993).

Clear Goals/Purpose(s) for Instruction

In Antonio's and Edith's school district, academic standards have been adopted for language arts. The standards for reading in the primary grades focus mainly on developing:

- 🍎 word knowledge, including phonics; and
- 🍎 skills and strategies related to comprehending both narrative and expository texts, including self-monitoring skills.

Antonio and Edith consult the standards for their respective grade levels, but they know that not all of the children are the same stage of development, that children have different understandings of any text that is shared as a whole class. These teachers select skills and strategies currently needed by a majority of children, as well as skills and strategies that introduce some children to new ideas for future development.

Analyzing the Demands of Text

After selecting goals for student learning, planning involves analyzing the demands of the text chosen for instruction.

Antonio's First Grade

In The Chick and the Duckling, *there are two obvious patterns that can aid comprehension of the text:*

🍎 *One pattern is an exact repetition cued by the illustration.*

   "Me too," said the Chick,

🍎 *One pattern is cued by the illustration and relates to the actions of the duckling.*

   "I am _____ing," said the Duckling.

Antonio's students need support in learning to use knowledge of letter-sound relationships when they meet unfamiliar words in text. The first-grade children should focus on:

🍎 *Using context + beginning letter of a word to predict what the word might be, then confirming or disconfirming the prediction.*
🍎 *Developing sight recognition of a number of high-frequency words that are used continuously throughout the text.*

Each reading and rereading provides instruction and support to develop the skills and strategies needed to fluently read and comprehend this text.

Edith's Third Grade

To comprehend the sheltered text that Edith composed with her children after rereading Down Comes the Rain, *children must:*

🍎 *Understand specialized vocabulary such as* evaporates, water vapor, *and* water droplet; *and*
🍎 *Follow the sequence of changes that result in the formation of a cloud.*

By third grade, informational text takes on greater importance. Edith helps children develop strategies to fluently read and comprehend expository text.

Observing What Children Know

Antonio's First Grade

Before beginning instruction with The Chick and the Duckling, *Antonio observes the children's interaction with other predictable texts, paying special attention to their ability to:*

🍎 *detect and use pattern in text to support their reading,*

🍎 *utilize their natural inclination to look at the illustrations for support during reading, and*

🍎 *use the beginning letter of a word to predict an appropriate word for the context.*

Based on observations, Antonio decides how much guidance and support to give during his teacher-led activities. Observations also help him decide which extension activities will be most helpful to engage the children in using illustration, pattern, and letter-sound relationships in their reading. He listens carefully to what they say before, during, and after the reading of a text. He also considers what children might understand about reading based on those interactions.

Edith's Third Grade

As she engages children in a mediated read-aloud with Down Comes the Rain, *as well as other books in the weather unit, Edith watches and listens for signs that children are developing the specialized vocabulary needed to comprehend concepts about weather. Her observations guide the content of the sheltered text that she composes with the children. Edith thinks about the sequence of ideas to understand how clouds form. She also considers how to make the sheltered text comprehensible to the English language learners in her class.*

ORGANIZING SHARED READING EXPERIENCES

Shared reading is intended to introduce and practice the reading of text within the safety and support of a group. Shared reading combines:

🍎 shared reading or rereading,

🍎 time to focus on developing skills and strategies, and

🍎 activities to extend children's engagement with text.

The new text is read, reread, and explored over several days to give all children time for the "new" to become "familiar."

First Shared Reading

The purpose of the first reading is to make public the content/storyline, patterns, and vocabulary of the text, which will allow children to join in the reading. During the first reading:

🍎 introduce text, encouraging children's anticipation;

🍎 take a "picture walk" through the text if there are illustrations, to help children become familiar with text features they can use to make meaning while reading;

🍎 read the text in a fluent manner, stopping briefly to help children focus their attention on the salient features needed to comprehend text;

encourage children to join in the reading;

 ask for responses after the reading to check for general understanding; and

 reread the text at least one time during that sitting.

Shared Rereadings

During shared rereading of a text:

 Reread the text in a fluent manner with children joining in the reading.

 Focus each rereading on a salient feature of the text that will support children's ability to read the text independently.

 Provide opportunities to use meaning-making and language skills and strategies to comprehend text.

 Provide opportunities to use visual and phonological skills to notice letter-sound patterns and decode unfamiliar words.

 SAMPLE SHARED READING: BIG BOOK

In the example that follows, notice how Antonio guides and supports children's learning throughout the shared reading of *The Chick and the Duckling*.

Before the first reading

Antonio uses a pointer to point to the cover of the big book and says,

> *"What do you see on the front cover of this book?"*

He takes responses.

> *"What do you think this book might be about?"*

Again, Antonio takes responses, then points to the words as he says,

> *"The title of this book is* The Chick and the Duckling. *It was written by Mirra Ginsburg. Jose Aruego and Ariane Dewey drew the pictures. Does the title give you any other ideas about this story?"*

He takes responses, then opens the big book to the inside title page and asks,

> *"Do you see the words of the title again? Let's read the title together,* The Chick and the Duckling,"

He points to the words as he reads.

Opening to the first page of text, Antonio says,

> *"Let's look at the illustrations and see what we can learn about this story before we start to read it."*

Antonio begins turning the pages of the text and guides children to examine key elements in each illustration that will be useful in predicting new words in the repetitive text.

> *"Look at what is happening to the egg.*
> *A duckling is hatching.*
> *It breaks out of the shell."*

Turning to the next page, he points and says,

> *"Look, another animal is hatching.*
> *What is this? Yes, it's a chick.*
> *Do you remember the title of this book?*
> Yes, The Chick and the Duckling."

Antonio turns the page and asks,

> *"What is the duckling doing? Yes, it's walking.*
> *What is the chick doing? Yes, it's walking too."*

He continues in this same manner, moving briskly through the text to help the children see that as the duckling dug a hole, found a worm, caught a butterfly, and went for a swim, the chick did the same thing. In the end, the duckling must save the chick from drowning and the chick realizes it cannot swim like the duckling.

During the first reading

After the picture walk, Antonio returns to the front of the book and begins reading the text, pointing to each word as he reads aloud. He moves fluidly through the text during this first reading to help children develop a sense of the whole text. In this first reading, Antonio's main focus is to help children use the illustrations showing the chick to anticipate and join in the reading of the repetitive sentence, "Me too!" said the Chick."

The words on the first two pages of text are:

> *A Duckling came out*
> *of the shell.*
> *"I am out!" he said.*

Antonio turns to the next two pages of text and reads aloud to reveal the repetitive pattern:

> *"Me too," said the Chick.*

On each page with the duckling, Antonio calls attention to the illustration and reads the text aloud. Then he turns the page, calls attention to the chick, and reads,

> *"Me too"' said the Chick.*

He encourages children to join in the reading. After several sets of actions, the children begin to join in, showing that they recognize a pattern and can predict the words on the pages where the chick appears.

After the first reading

Antonio invites children to respond to the text. He asks,

> *"What do you think about that story?"*

He takes most all the personal responses that children offer.
Then he asks,

> *"What is your favorite part?"*

The children agree that the best part is when the duckling saves the chick from drowning.

Rereading the text

During this first rereading Antonio wants to know which children are able to use illustrations and language structure to make meaning with this simple text. As he reads aloud and points to the appropriate text, several children join in by finishing the word. For example, on the next duckling page, Antonio hesitates before the word walk. He thinks that children will be able to use their knowledge of language and the illustration to fill in words:

> *"I am taking a w_____," said the duckling.?*

He continues in this manner, using cloze procedure (Taylor, 1953), hesitating before the most obvious words that are cued by illustration and language structure and encouraging children to supply the word. Cloze procedure draws upon a reader's understanding and use of cues in the context of a text.
After the rereading, Antonio asks,

> *"How did the illustrations help us read this story?" Children offer their ideas about how the illustrations help them remember that part of the story.*

He continues with,

> *"What did you notice about the words that the chick said?" Repetition helps the children anticipate the words on the page.*

Then Antonio asks,

> *"How did you know what words would fit in the places where I stopped reading? How did you know that the word walk would fit in the sentence, 'I am taking a w_____, said the Duckling.'?"*

A few children suggest that they just remember the text, others say,

> *"That's how we talk."*

Few children think of using visual cues such as a word that might start with /w/.

To emphasize the use of context plus the beginning sound as a strategy for early decoding, Antonio asks,

> *"Look at this word. Get your mouth ready to say this word. What could start with the letter* w *and make sense here?"*

To further reinforce using the "context + letter-sounds" strategy to predict and confirm words in the text, Antonio guides children toward using visual cues as an important word-getting strategy. He reads,

> *"A Duckling came out of a sh_____."*

He hesitates at the beginning of *shell* and asks the children,

> *"When we look at this word (shell) how can we know it is* shell *and not* egg?"

He encourages children to cross-check meaning with the visual cues of the text.

In subsequent rereadings of this text, Antonio will continue to build on the same reading strategies as an aid for guiding children as they learn to decode and cross-check for meaning.

SAMPLE SHARED READING: EXPERIENCE CHART

In the text that follows, notice how Edith guides and supports children's learning throughout the shared reading of the sheltered text *The Water Cycle* based on *Down Comes the Rain,* discussed earlier.

Before the reading
Edith gathers the children on the carpet in front of the chart they composed together the day before. She asks,

> *"What did we write about yesterday?"*

The children provide a range of responses based on their recollections of listening to Edith read *Down Comes the Rain* and the shared writing of the chart.

During the reading
Edith directs children's attention to the chart and says,

> *"Help me read the words."*

She points to each word in the text as she models fluent oral reading. As she reads she also listens carefully to the children's reading, especially when they come to the words *evaporates, water vapor,* and *water droplets.*

Then Edith invites a child to come to the front of the group and lead the rereading of the text. Like his teacher, Wade takes the pointer, points to the first word of the text, turns to his classmates, and says,

> *"Help me read the words."*

While Wade leads the reading Edith watches the match between the words that he says and where he points in the text. She also listens to the children's reading for clues as to which words might need closer examination. Prior to the reading she had decided to focus on three terms—*evaporates, water vapor,* and *water droplets*—but she realizes there may be other trouble spots in the text that she did not anticipate.

After the first reading
When Wade is finished leading the rereading, Edith asks,

> *"What do we know about how clouds are made?"*

The children describe what they have been learning about the water cycle, especially where the water comes from that forms a cloud. Edith listens for the words children choose to describe that process and where they are beginning to accurately use some of the specialized vocabulary. She is also concerned about children's understanding of the sequence of the water cycle so she listens for the order in which children relate the information. Sequence will be a focus with the next rereading.

Then, Edith turns children's attention to the chart. In the first line of the text she points to the word *evaporates.*

> Water <u>evaporates</u> from rivers, lakes, and oceans.

She asks,

> *"What is this word?"*

As a group, the children answer,

> *"Evaporates."*

Edith asks,

> *"What does* evaporate *mean?"*

Various children respond,

> *"Disappear . . . all gone . . . vanish . . . goes away."*

She asks,

> *"How do we know this word is* evaporates?"*

At first the children seem puzzled. One child says,

> *"It begins with* e."

Another child says,

> *"It ends with* ate."

Edith writes the word *evaporate* on the whiteboard, just to the left of the chart. Under *evaporate* she writes the words *even* and *ever*. She asks the children to read each word and think about the sound of the first letter, *e*. The class discusses how the letter *e* can have a long sound when it is alone in a syllable (*e-ven*) or a short sound when a consonant is in the same syllable (*ev-er*). Edith says,

> *"Let's try an either/or strategy. We know that a vowel usually (but not always) has either a long or a short sound. When we come to a big word that we don't know, let's try a long-vowel sound first. If that doesn't make a word that sounds right, then we'll try a short-vowel sound. Let's try our either/or strategy with the word* evaporate."

The children begin to try the strategy and are able to pronounce the first two syllables, *e-vap*. They talk about how they see two familiar chunks, *-or* and *-ate*. When the children pronounce the word using the either/or strategy and the familiar chunks, they say *e-vap-or-ate*. (Note: The dictionary pronunciation is actually *e-vap-o-rate*, with the *o* pronounced as a *schwa*, or short *u*, but the either/or strategy works well enough to get a close pronunciation that children can confirm by the context and their background knowledge.)

Edith confirms their use of the either/or strategy. Next she writes the word *vapor* on the whiteboard and asks the children to try their either/or strategy. The class discusses how vapor is pronounced *va-por*, not *vap-or*. Then a child notices the word *vapor* in *evaporate*, so Edith writes the words in a column to compare.

vapor

evaporate

The children notice that the pronunciation is different and Edith explains that many English words have a change in pronunciation when suffixes are added. She gives the children a more familiar example and asks them what they notice.

music

musician

The children notice how the first syllable of both words is the same, but the sound of the consonant *c* at the end of music changes from a *hard c* to a *soft c* in musi<u>c</u>ian. Edith explains that knowing that *musician* comes from *music* helps to determine its meaning, but not the sound of all of its letters. In *musician*, the consonant *c* begins a new syllable, *cian*, rather than ending a syllable, *ic*. She then returns to the terms *vapor* and *evaporate* and asks,

> *"If we know that evaporate means to disappear, how does that help us figure out the meaning of* vapor?"

The class discusses the related meanings. They also have a similar discussion relating the terms *water droplets* and *water drops.*

The next rereadings will focus on the sequence of the water cycle. Along with rereading the chart and retelling the sequence, Edith will also place each sentence of the experience chart on a piece of sentence strip paper for use in a pocket chart. The sentence strips will be placed on the floor so that children can order the sentences in the chart to retell the water cycle. Edith will lead a discussion of the strategies children use to determine the order of the text. Are there words in the text that provide clues? Do the children draw on their developing knowledge of the water cycle to determine sequence?

FIGURE 5.5
Sample plan—extending shared reading.

Explanation of Activities	Monday	Tuesday
Whole-Class Opening: • warm up with song, poem, chant, rereading of "old favorite" • introduce and guide reading/rereading of new text • plan/organize for work time, explain activity choices	**Whole-Class Opening:** • sing "Five Little Ducks," use hand motions • reread "old favorite" (children's choice) • introduce/read new book, *The Chick and the Duckling* • encourage response after reading • explain activity choices	**Whole-Class Opening:** • read "old favorite" • recall first reading of *The Chick and the Duckling* • reread, discuss each page, illustrations • make activity choice
Work Time: Teacher-Led Small Group • shared rereading • retelling of text • responding to text • word knowledge skills • reading strategies	**Work Time: Small Group** • reread in small group • encourage response	**Work Time: Small Group** • reread big book, notice patterns 　(1) use illustrations to support duckling's actions, 　(2) notice how chick repeats what duckling says • attend to individual responses
Text Extensions • taped books • art • retelling • responding • word knowledge • reading corner • writing center	**Text Extensions** • tape recording of *The Chick and the Duckling* • art center, response to text • reading corner, old favorites • writing center, shape book of chick or duckling, topic open	**Text Extensions** • tape recording of *The Chick and the Duckling* • painting: something chick and duckling could do together • writing center, books shaped like chick or duckling • reading corner
Whole-Class Closure: • share small-group/independent activities • plan for upcoming activities	**Whole-Class Closure:** • share art or writing • discuss new activity choices for tomorrow	**Whole-Class Closure:** • share paintings or shape books • plan for puppets tomorrow

EXTENDING SHARED READING EXPERIENCES

The longer children are engaged with one particular text, the greater the likelihood they will learn from that text (Beaver, 1982; Yaden, 1988). Extending experiences for children can take place both in small groups with an adult and independently in activity centers. Figure 5.5 illustrates 1 week of related activities for *The Chick and the Duckling* in which shared reading and rereading are prominent:

- Each day opens with whole-class activities, which include singing or shared poems, shared reading and rereading of the focus text, and response.
- Following the opening activities, children break into small groups for shared rereading, as well as activity choices that support the shared

Wednesday	Thursday	Friday
Whole-Group Opening: • sing "Old McDonald" • reread text, children join in • record memorable words, phrases • read together • discuss paintings of things chick and duck can do together • encourage others to go to painting • introduce stick puppet activity	**Whole-Group Opening:** • sing/read *Five Little Ducks,* use Raffi book • recall what duckling did to prepare for reread • reread, use oral cloze to anticipate key words, encourage "reread, read on" strategy • reread using puppets to take parts of chick and duckling • introduce new activities	**Whole-Group Opening:** • read "old favorite," children's choice • reread big book, use oral cloze, predictable actions and character names
Work Time: Small Group • reread big book, encourage use of illustrations to cue words about duckling • introduce flannel board retelling of big book	**Work Time: Small Group** • reread big book, take parts, use puppets • return to words/phrases children remember, place in pocket chart	**Work Time: Small Group** • select sentences for written cloze, place in pocket chart • reread, with few key words covered, predict, uncover, discuss
Text Extensions • tape-recorded book • art, painting • make stick puppets of chick and duckling • reading corner • writing center, shape books	**Text Extensions** • tape recording of book, add response sheet • flannel board retelling • reading corner • writing center: (1) shape books (2) draw/write "Things I Can Do" (put on bulletin board)	**Text Extensions** • tape recording, encourage children to take part, use puppets • flannel board retelling • reading center • writing center (continue from Thursday)
Whole-Group Closure: • share puppets, writing, painting • plan for using puppets during whole-group opening tomorrow	**Whole-Group Closure:** • pairs of children use puppets and role-play chick and duckling • help children plan for a center they have not worked at yet	**Whole-Group Closure:** • share pictures for bulletin board, reread others

reading. Small-group shared reading can also serve as guided reading, even though the text is already familiar (see Chapter 6 for more information on guided reading). The level of text will present challenge to some children.

🍎 Choices for extension activities are related to the content of the text, the knowledge of language patterns needed to successfully read it, and the level of independence of the children.

To have access to print, many children will need extended exposure to that print. Shared reading and rereading, combined with extension activities, maintain children's interest in reading and writing.

Additional possibilities for extending children's engagement with *The Chick and the Duckling* might include:

🍎 using enlarged text to create wall stories,

🍎 creating floor puzzles, and

🍎 preparing a reader's theater.

Retelling and Responding to a Shared Reading

As we discussed in Chapter 4 with reading aloud, retelling and responding activities offer many choices for extending children's shared reading experiences. We can engage children in a variety of retelling and responding modes: discussion; support of text illustrations, story map, or flannel board; drama, chants, and creative movement; and children's art and writing. Retelling focuses children's attention on recalling the author's text in an appropriate order. Responding provides opportunity for children to focus on their personal response to a text. Retelling and responding require readers to think in different ways about a text. Both ways of thinking are needed for effective literacy development.

In the sample weekly plan that focuses on extending shared reading, the following retelling and responding activities are highlighted:

🍎 puppets in a dramatic retelling,

🍎 felt board retelling,

🍎 an artistic response through painting, and

🍎 drawn and written response: "Things I Can Do!"

The weekly plan emphasizes retelling and response, as we learned in Chapter 4, because children should be guided to notice the characters' actions, which leads to noticing patterns in the text. Other extensions to consider are wall stories and floor puzzles.

Using Enlarged Text to Create Wall Stories

Wall stories enable children to "read the room" during activity periods by using a pointer while reading the text with a partner.

🍎 Copies of book illustrations and text are cut apart.

🍎 The illustrations are placed on a wall or in a hallway in proper order.

🍎 The text, which was separated from the illustrations, is available for matching.

🍎 Children can also retell the story by using illustrations, then match with the text.

🍎 Matching text to illustration reinforces interpretation of illustrations and provides practice in reading sentences without the support of illustrations.

🍎 Wall stories can also be made from children's illustrations and teacher-written text.

🍎 Children can also innovate on a text by composing their own version through shared/interactive writing.

Creating Floor Puzzles

🍎 Copy the pages of a text.

🍎 Mount each page on a sturdy piece of paper, then create puzzle pieces by making distinct cuts between picture and text so that related pieces will match.

🍎 When all pages are mounted and separated, the puzzle pieces are spread out on the floor.

🍎 Children help each other read the text and match the pieces to make each page.

🍎 As matches are made the pages can be placed in proper order to tell the story.

🍎 The pieces can be stored in a large, self-closing plastic bag or box.

Preparing for Reader's Theater

A text, such as *The Chick and the Duckling,* may become a simple script for reader's theater in one of three ways:

Children develop the script—

🍎 Choose an appropriate text that will result in a script that will be about 3 to 5 minutes long.

🍎 Make a copy of the text for each participant.

🍎 Decide which characters and narrators are needed and assign a marker color to each.

🍎 Highlight all dialogue with the appropriate color.

🍎 The text that is left is for the narrator(s).

or

Teacher and children develop the script together—

🍎 Select an appropriate text that is familiar.

🍎 Teacher engages children in retelling section of text.

- Teacher guides children to determine characters and narrator.
- Teacher records children's dictations for each character's lines on a chart.
- Teacher makes a copy for each participant to practice.

or

Teacher develops the script—

- Teacher selects section of familiar text.
- Teacher develops script and makes a copy for each participant to practice.

A script for *The Chick and the Duckling* has two characters, the Chick and the Duckling, and a narrator.

Narrator:	A Duckling came out of the shell.
Duckling:	I am out!
Chick:	Me too!
Duckling:	I am taking a walk.
Chick:	Me too!

The dialogue continues in the same fashion until the final scene, the swimming scene, when the Chick realizes that it can't swim.

Narrator:	The Duckling pulled the Chick out.
Duckling:	I'm going for another swim.
Chick:	Not me.

Then the practice begins to prepare for a fluent and lively performance of the story.

SHARED READING OF CHALLENGING TEXT

The shared reading of text, when all children participate in the oral reading, is preferred over round-robin or popcorn reading, when only one child at a time reads out loud (Eldredge, Reutzel, & Hollingsworth, 1996). Teachers who must use a basal reading series that provides one level of text for a class of children can use shared reading to provide support to readers who find the text challenging. After introducing the text to the class, children are guided through a shared reading of the text in which each child has a copy of the text. After discussing the text as a whole, children participate in the shared rereading of the selected sections of the text. The shared rereading can be as a class or in small groups.

Shared reading in multiple copies of a text is most beneficial in content-area textbooks, such as science or social studies. The teacher previews the text with the children, noting cues that help to activate prior knowledge and encouraging children to anticipate what might be learned during the reading. The children are led to consider how to use headings and subheadings, photos and drawings, captions, and highlighted words to anticipate the content of the section. The teacher then begins reading aloud a particular section of the text, encouraging children to join in. The section is then reread, with attention to decoding strategies and discussion of the most important ideas. Sections of text for close study may also be put on an overhead transparency for shared reading and rereading.

Transition chapter books, such as *Third-Grade Detectives #1: The Clue of the Left-Handed Envelop* by George E. Stanley (2000), are excellent for shared readings. Each of the 10 chapters in this text contains about 600 words and can be read in one sitting. Shared reading of a chapter provides support for children who are not yet confident of themselves reading longer texts. Shared rereading of specific portions of text can be used to clarify comprehension and new vocabulary or to emphasize the appropriate use of a particular reading strategy. Over the course of 2 weeks students are able to complete the reading of a chapter book with support.

To scaffold support to children, the shared reading of the first chapter can be presented on an overhead projector to provide additional teacher guidance until children are comfortable with the format of the text. The plot of this text is developed through description by the narrator and dialogue between characters. Shared reading of the text on the overhead projector enables the teacher to guide children as they distinguish dialogue from description. Children may also come to the overhead to highlight dialogue to distinguish it from the narrator's description (see the example in Figure 5.6).

FIGURE 5.6
Sample of text with highlighted dialogue.

Chapter One

It was the first day of the third grade, and Noelle Trocoderro was late.

She ran down the sidewalk outside the school building.

All summer long, Noelle had been looking forward to starting school again.

Mrs. Trumble would be her teacher this year.

Everyone loved Mrs. Trumble.

She was the nicest teacher in the whole school.

Finally, Noelle reached Mrs. Trumble's third-grade classroom.

She stopped at the door.

There was a *man* writing on the chalkboard.

Something's wrong here, Noelle thought.

1

She looked around.

Her friend Todd Sloan was waving to her.

Todd lived across the street from Noelle.

They did a lot of things together.

Noelle thought Todd was more interesting than most of the girls in her class.

She hurried over and sat down in the empty seat next to him.

"Who's that man?" Noelle whispered.

"Mr. Merlin," Todd replied. "He's our new teacher."

"What happened to Mrs. Trumble?" Noelle asked.

"She moved," Todd said. He leaned closer to Noelle. "Amber Lee Johnson said Mr. Merlin used to be a spy."

Noelle blinked. "How did she find out?"

Todd shrugged.

Noelle looked at Mr. Merlin again.

She liked spy shows on television.

Maybe she wouldn't miss Mrs. Trumble after all.

Mr. Merlin stopped writing on the chalk-board.

He turned around and faced the class.

2

To guide children's eyes as they track the text, the teacher can mask, or cover, the text with a full sheet of paper, sliding the paper down one line at a time to reveal the text on which children should focus. With some groups of children it may be necessary to guide the shared reading on the overhead projector for more than one chapter. Masking text will be discussed again in an upcoming section (see Figure 5.7).

🍎 DEVELOPING WORD KNOWLEDGE THROUGH SHARED READING

In the primary grades, children must develop many concepts about the generalizations that govern words in the English language. Shared reading of tests provides many opportunities for adults to scaffold children's word knowledge in the following areas:

- 🍎 concepts about print,
- 🍎 high-frequency sight words,
- 🍎 using context clues, and
- 🍎 letter-sound patterns.

Concepts about Print

Early reading success relies on children's understanding about print and the "rules" that govern how words are displayed in print (Clay, 1991). Bedtime stories and environmental print provide an excellent introduction to how written language can be displayed. What can children learn about print as they participate in shared reading?

- 🍎 *Purposes of print*—Print is meaningful and carries messages. We read print, not pictures; however, children's early retellings/rereadings of a text are guided by illustrations and recollections of the text before they understand that it is the print that carries the message.
- 🍎 *Permanence of print*—When we make print on paper, the letters remain where we put them. When a book is closed, letters and words do not move around. With rereading, children begin to notice that the text is the same from reading to reading. We guide them to notice that words are in the same place on a page as they were during the previous reading.
- 🍎 *Directional concepts*—We read left to right, and top to bottom on a page. To move through a text we use "return sweep," returning to the left side of a page and droppoing down one line of text, to move through text.
- 🍎 *Concepts about words*—Empty space defines the beginning and end of a word. We match speech to print to help us read words. We need to know letter names, shapes, and sounds that letters represent to read many words. Letters are sequenced from left to right to form a word.

🍎 *The language of print*—We use words in particular ways to talk about print and books, such as *front, back, left, right, top, bottom, letter, word, line,* and *sentence.*

Shared reading with enlarged text, in either whole-class or small-group settings, can be used to reinforce print concepts for children. During shared reading, especially rereading of text:

🍎 We model how proficient readers use an understanding of print to read.

🍎 We ask children to demonstrate their understandings of print concepts.

🍎 Children "show what they know" when they point to the text to guide the class through a rereading, or when they find the word said on each page and notice that it is always spelled with the same sequence of letters.

High-Frequency Sight Words

Many words that young readers encounter appear frequently in texts. Readers become fluent when they remember these frequently occurring words. Fluent readers notice certain distinguishing features of these words and commit them to memory after a few meaningful exposures. When they encounter the words in future readings they are often able to instantly recall them. Extension activities should provide opportunities for children to notice the features of words that appear with great frequency and think about how to remember those words for future use. Amazingly, young readers often remember longer, distinctive words such as *dinosaur* and *elephant.* Such words are typically nouns that have high meaning for children and are remembered as whole words.

> Also see Chapter 3 for more discussion of high-frequency sight words.

A *word bank,* a child's personal bank of words that are known in isolation, is useful for children who are just beginning to read.

> Read here to find a definition of *word bank.*

🍎 Children can build a word bank by selecting their favorite words from a familiar text.

🍎 The selected words are placed on word cards for the child to keep.

🍎 These words can be kept in a small box or other container and used for small-group and individual word-building and word-sorting activities.

🍎 As the word bank grows, dividers can be used so that words are easier for children to find and use.

🍎 Words can be placed in alphabetical order, but Trachtenburg and Ferruggia (1989) suggest the following categories: words that describe (adjectives), people and animal words (nouns), action words (verbs), and words that tell how, when, and where (adverbs).

Using Context Clues

As children gain skill and confidence in using initial consonants, we encourage them to use their "context +" strategy. During shared reading:

🍎 Cover all but the beginning letter(s) of a predictable word.

🍎 Ask children to orally predict what would make sense in the context and begin like the letter(s) shown.

🍎 Help children check their thinking by discussing appropriateness for meaning and sound and eliminating unreasonable choices that do not have the same beginning sounds.

🍎 Reveal the word and check for meaning by considering beginning and ending sounds of the word.

Written cloze is one way to prepare children for decoding unfamiliar words.

Masking text is effective for pacing children's reading and focusing their attention on particular words or word parts (Holdaway, 1979). Masking also enables us to encourage children to use their knowledge of context and beginning sounds, with their "reread, read on" strategy, to anticipate words in text. The type and amount of text that we mask depends on children's level of development as readers. Masking text can also be used with older students who are still in emergent or developing reader stages. Examples of masking devices are shown in Figure 5.7.

🍎 *Big books*—Mask words or portions of words with a "magic window"—a sturdy cardboard rectangle with a small rectangle cut out of the center that allows words in the enlarged text to be singled out for sight-word development (Trachtenburg & Ferruggia, 1989). A masking device with a sliding opening can direct children to attend to detail within words (Cooper, 1993). We can also mask individual words with small pieces of paper that can be removed after their prediction.

FIGURE 5.7
Masking text.

🍎 *Pocket chart*—Mask words or parts of words by placing blank cards in front of text, covering all or portions of words for attention. After predictions, the blank card is removed to enable children to confirm their thinking.

🍎 *Overhead projector*—Text is reproduced on a transparency, then desired portions can be masked. Strips of heavy paper are laid over each line of text. The strips can be moved, one at a time, to reveal text. Individual words, or portions of words, are masked with small pieces of paper to focus attention on particular decoding elements or strategies.

🍎 *Charts*—On a chart containing a poem or song for shared reading or a text jointly composed through shared writing, portions of words are masked. As children participate in the shared reading or rereading of the text, they are encouraged to use beginning letters plus context to predict the masked words. Words are then unmasked to confirm the accuracy of children's predictions.

Decoding Words

Children should be guided to use visual cues to generalize their knowledge about words as they examine patterns in both familiar and unfamiliar words.

🍎 A pointer, a locater device (such as a fly swatter with the center cut out), or Wikki Sticks™ (wax-covered yarn) can be used to isolate letters and groups of letters that occur frequently in words that children are ready to learn to decode.

🍎 Word cards for the pocket chart provide opportunities to sort and compare patterns and sounds in words.

🍎 A whiteboard is excellent for calling attention to a word in a text, examining it in isolation on the whiteboard, then returning to the text to use context to confirm the decoding process.

🍎 Finally, extension activities such as copies of text that can be cut apart and reconstructed, especially words used to construct sentences, reinforce accurate decoding of words.

INTEGRATING WRITING WITH SHARED READING

Emergent readers and writers are working to develop their concepts about print, learning letters and associated sounds, and just beginning to consider who they are as authors. Writing should be integrated with shared reading experiences to help children retain, recollect, and represent their ideas about a text (see guided writing in Chapter 9).

In the sample weekly plan (see Figure 5.5) for *The Chick and the Duckling,* a variety of writing opportunities are included:

🍎 *Annotated drawings*—Throughout the book, the duckling is telling the chick the things he can do. The children draw a picture of something they can do, and they write a statement about what they are doing in their pictures. These drawings are arranged as a bulletin board entitled,

"Things We Can Do!" The bulletin board can also become a shared reading activity.

🍎 *Shape books*—Construction paper that can be cut into meaningful shapes, filled with blank paper, and stapled as a book is placed in the writing center. Posterboard templates can also be placed in the writing center for children to make their own blank books in various shapes. Even first-grade children are able to trace around a template for the cover of the book, staple a few sheets of blank paper between the covers, and cut out the book along the template lines. (Good scissors are needed.) For *The Chick and the Duckling,* use the shapes of both a chick and a duck. Children can write their own stories or respond to the text. This open-ended task enables all children to be successful.

Functional writing can be used to support and extend the shared reading, depending upon our purposes for instruction and the children's background as writers, in the following ways:

🍎 *Idea clusters*—Children can draw a cluster of ideas or list "Things ducks can do" and "Things chicks can do." They can then use intersecting circles, as in a Venn diagram, to identify what is common to both chicks and ducks, as well as what is different (shown in the intersection of the two circles).

🍎 *Journals*—In a journal or learning log, children can record a variety of responses or ideas about the text. They can respond to their favorite part of the story, write their favorite words, or describe what they would have done if they were the duckling or the chick.

🍎 *Innovation on a text*—Use the pattern from the story to create a predictable text. In *The Chick and the Duckling,* the pattern to innovate on might be:

"I am (action)-ing," said the _____

"Me too," said the _____

If this text is being read in October, the class might innovate on the pattern by using two Halloween characters.

"I am flying," said the ghost.

"Me too," said the witch.

In a unit on families the class might use a parent and child for the two characters.

"I am reading a book," said the dad.

"Me too," said the boy.

By innovating on a pattern, the children extend their practice with patterns and also sight words. When appropriate, the pattern can be copied for children to fill in with a personal innovation. Multiple pages can allow children to make a small book.

The innovation can also be made into a class big book. Individuals or pairs can contribute pages. The innovated book is then enjoyed as a shared reading experience by the whole class or a small group. The completed big book is placed in the library corner for independent rereading. The innovation can also become a script for a reader's theater, created by the children.

Making Connections . . .

Prepare a plan for a shared reading:

- Select an appropriate text.
- Analyze the text for predictable pattern and illustrations.
- Make decisions about possible skill/strategy instruction.
- Outline a 5-day plan that includes the following:
  - Introduction of the text,
  - Whole-group reading and rereading,
  - Attention to print concepts and word knowledge,
  - Small-group study of the text with individual copies for the children,
  - Possible text extensions that encourage children to revisit and respond to the text,
  - Independent reading of the text, and
  - Independent writing/drawing as response or retelling.

ASSESSMENT: MONITORING DEVELOPMENT IN SHARED READING

In shared reading, children refine their concepts about print, especially how words appear in print. We can observe their word-to-word matching when they point to text as they read the text aloud. Because shared reading is a familiar text "in the head," children show their concepts about words as they match each word in their head with the words on the page. This is the basis of the concept of word assessment.

Concept of Word (COW)

Concept of words in print is the ability to match speech to print, integrating knowledge about what words are and how they are formed. Concept of word is essential to the development of word knowledge and to success in early reading (Morris, Bloodgood, & Perney, 2003). Emergent readers and English language learners are formulating and consolidating their concept of words in print. For children who seem confused by reading or are having difficulty learning words, assessment of concept of word may provide some insight into the child's understandings about print.

To assess concept of word, a short piece of patterned text is needed that the child can verbally repeat, but cannot yet read independently. For example, the song "Twinkle, Twinkle, Little Star" might be used. Children may know how to sing the song, but not necessarily how to read the song when it is printed. Other familiar songs such as "Mary Had a Little Lamb" can be used.

In the selected text, be sure that there are several words with more than one syllable, as well as repeated words, so that children can be asked to find more than one instance of a word. Print or type the text clearly on a page, leaving some space between lines, with five to six words per line. Be sure to have one copy of the text for the child to read and one copy on which to record the child's responses.

As the child reads, place a mark over each syllable (not word) above the place in the text to show how the text was read. For example, a child with a strong concept of word would read:

//   //   //   /

Twinkle   twinkle   little   star

This child realizes that words are delineated by the white spaces around them and that the spoken word *twinkle* is not two separate words even though it has two parts, or syllables.

A child who is still formulating a concept of word will not match the oral and written text word to word, especially when words have more than one syllable. Syllables will be treated as words, so we would mark the text as:

/(twink)   /(le)   /(twink)   /(le)

Twinkle   twinkle   little   star

A child who is just beginning to formulate a concept of word may treat each letter as if it is a word. The child might touch one letter while saying a word. This child may only be at the end of the first line of text by the time the oral rendition of the song is finished

///////   ///////   //////   ////

Twinkle   twinkle   little   star

Procedure for assessing concept of words in print:

- 🍎 Rehearse the rhyme/song orally with the child several times to be sure it is in memory. The rhyme/song may also be taught to the entire class in anticipation of assessing each child's concept of word. This will save time with individual assessments.
- 🍎 Present the written text and tell the child this is the same song, poem, or chant that was just said together.
- 🍎 Tell the child that you will read the text first and the child should carefully watch as you read and point. Then the child will read and point.
- 🍎 Read at a normal pace, clearly pointing once to each word as you read the text. Use the eraser end of a pencil so the child can clearly see how you point to each word.
- 🍎 Ask the child to read the text and point to the words he or she is reading.

🍎 Use a second copy of the text to show the exact match between the child's reading and the text.

🍎 After the reading, ask the child to locate several words in the text:

🍎 Find a word that is repeated,

🍎 Find high-frequency sight words,

🍎 Find a common word with the same beginning sound as another word in the passage, and

🍎 Find a longer word that is distinctive.

In "Twinkle Twinkle Little Star," a child could be asked to find:

🍎 a word that is repeated (*twinkle*),

🍎 high-frequency sight words (*I, you, up, the, in*),

🍎 a common word that begins like other words in the text (*sky, star*), and

🍎 a longer word that appears only once (*diamond*).

Watch to see how the children locate each word—do they go directly to the word, hesitate at first, and then locate the word, or go back to the beginning to the text and reread/point again to find the word in the text? Note your observations.

A concept of word assessment should be administered early in the school year and periodically throughout to show how each child is formulating his or her concept of words in print.

Making Connections . . .

Take time to find out about a young child's understanding of print by administering a concept of word (COW) assessment that appears in the assessment section of this chapter. The first few times that you do this, it is good to do it with a partner. Rehearse the procedure you will use, including what you will say to the child as you give directions. Together, plan the words you will ask the child to find after the reading. One of you can prompt the child and the other can record the child's responses. Then discuss your observations and describe what you think the child demonstrated about his or her concept of words. Make only those interpretations that the child actually demonstrated.

RESPECTING DIVERSITY THROUGH SHARED READING

Using enlarged print for reading makes text more accessible to children. However, their background experience as readers and with the English language may not allow them full access to meaning. Your thoughtful use of shared reading experiences can provide:

🍎 support and safety within a group,

🍎 support through modeling and guided participation,

🍎 language support through predictability, and

🍎 extended reading experiences through sheltered text.

Safety and Support of a Group

Within the group during a shared reading experience, children are able to participate at different levels without calling attention to their individual performance. Everyone is absorbed in the activity, whether they are reading every word with the teacher or observing the illustrations and listening. Shared reading allows children at all levels of development to take from the reading what they desire. Shared reading also allows all children to participate at a level in which they are comfortable and confident.

Support through Modeling and Guided Participation

As a shared reading begins, you assume the responsibility of showing children what they need to do as readers by modeling. Through extended experiences with the same text, the level of your support for children is adjusted depending on what the children show you they need. Your role as model and guide provides opportunity for children to feel successful at their level of performance within the group.

Language Support through Predictability

Having a sense of pattern and anticipating what will come enables children at all levels of experience to find success in shared reading. Predictable text supports children's efforts to figure out the rules of written language. Combined with your modeling and guidance, predictability will enable children who are learning English to find success in early reading experiences.

Extending Learning through Sheltered Text

Children who are learning English and/or have limited experience with print will find success when text is made more accessible. You can enhance children's feelings of success when you are sensitive to the demands that texts make on less experienced readers. When your analysis of text suggests that it lacks the support of predictability, you should provide sheltered text experiences. Bringing sheltered text to shared reading experiences can be beneficial for all children.

Making Connections . . .

As you reflect on the content of this chapter, what ideas do you have about helping children to build a foundation for concepts about print and fluent reading of text? How will you help all children in your classroom, regardless of their prior literacy experiences, develop their skills in recognizing words and pacing their reading in a fluent manner? Record your thinking in a reflective journal. Share your thinking with your peers.

C H A P T E R

6

Guided Reading:
Scaffolding Children's Reading

Adding to our literacy framework . . .

	Reading Aloud and Guided Literature Study	
Shared Reading	**Balanced and Integrated Literacy Framework**	Shared and Interactive Writing
Guided Reading and Guided Literature Study		Guided Writing and Writer's Workshop
Independent Reading and Reader's Workshop		Independent Writing
	Word Study	

In this chapter, we learn about . . .

- Organizing guided reading experiences with small groups of children with similar needs as readers
- Selecting texts for guided reading, including quality children's literature and selections from a basal reading series
- Developing reading skills and strategies to improve children's reading achievement

Focus Literature:

- *Three Little Ducks* (created for this text)
- *Sylvester & the Magic Pebble* by William Steig
- *Too Many Tamales* by Gray Soto and Ed Martinez
- *Stone Fox* by John Gardiner

Looking into Classrooms . . .

Katarina and four of her first-grade children are sitting at a small table along the side of the classroom. The other children in the class are engaged in independent rereading of familiar books and in literacy activity centers that contain tasks the children can complete independently. Guiding reading groups such as this last about 20 minutes.

Katarina selects a text she thinks is appropriate for the skill and strategy level of these four children. After introducing the book in an engaging manner, she assists the children in previewing the book in preparation for guided reading. Then, each child begins to read the book orally while Katarina listens in on each child's reading. These first-grade children still read orally as they read to themselves. She notices that several words are a struggle for the children, so she carefully observes which word recognition strategies the children seem to be able to use by themselves. She assists only when a child seems unable to use his or her own skills and strategies successfully.

After the reading there is a short response time, followed by a focus on a teaching point, which today is the decoding and meaning of the contraction I'm, and the suffixed word yelled. During these teaching points Katarina will emphasize how children can monitor their own decoding of such words.

DOWN THE HALL . . .

At the beginning of the school year Greg listened to each of his third- and fourth-grade students read a number of different texts, until he could determine each child's instructional level, the level that was best for helping them learn new skills and strategies in reading. Then Greg formed flexible groups for guided literature study. He rechecks students at various times throughout the year to determine if their instructional reading level is changing. With this information, Greg chooses a variety of texts to meet the needs and interests of his students.

At the present time, Greg's students are studying the literary element of character and how authors develop interesting characters. There are four groups of about six students each in Greg's class. Each group is reading a book that is at their instructional level. For this character study Greg selected Stone Fox *by John Gardiner (the most challenging text),* Beans on the Roof *by Betsy Byars,* Staying Nine *by Pam Conrad, and* The Poppy Seeds *by Clyde Robert Bulla (least challenging text). Each book has a strong central character.*

Greg meets with each group, on a rotating basis, to guide the discussion after the children have read portions of the text either independently or with a partner. Because these children are sinking into silent reading, the first reading of new text is a silent, rather than an oral, reading. Then he meets with his students to discuss the portion of the text they have just read and to reread portions that help to clarify understanding. In the small group Greg is able to guide students to examine text more closely and discuss how to use certain strategies to figure out new words or make inferences about a particular part of a text. Sometimes a group meets without him to have discussion, especially when they are well into a text. While Greg is meeting with a particular group, the other children are reading and writing to prepare for their book discussions or completing other extension activities related to the character study.

BUILDING A THEORY BASE . . .

Although reading aloud and shared reading are important parts of a balanced and integrated literacy program, it is through guided reading that teachers truly come to know children as readers. During guided reading children can provide a window into their thinking as readers.

WHAT IS GUIDED READING?

In contrast to shared reading (see Chapter 5), which usually involves the whole class, guided reading occurs in small groups with the support of the teacher:

Read here to find a definition of *guided reading.*

Guided reading is a context in which a teacher supports each reader's development of effective strategies for processing novel texts at increasingly challenging levels of difficulty. The teacher works with a small group of children who use similar reading processes and are able to read similar levels of text with support. (Fountas & Pinnell, 1996, p. 2)

During guided reading the teacher becomes a bridge between child and text for a small group of children, carefully observing each child's interactions with and response to the text. After preparation by the teacher, emergent and developing readers read through a selected portion of text, often at their own pace, as the teacher carefully listens and assists, prompting individual children as needed to link from what they known to what is new. The teacher reduces support to children as they demonstrate the ability to guide their own reading processes. Children in the transitional stage frequently read text silently, then participate in discussion and rereading of text as needed.

Guided reading is a key component in a balanced literacy program. Fountas and Pinnell (1996) remind us, "It is through guided reading, however, that teachers can show children how to read and can support children as they read. Guided reading leads to the independent reading that builds the process; it is the heart of a balanced literacy program" (p. 1). It is through guided reading that teachers come to truly understand children as individual readers and how to mediate, or support them, as they move toward independence.

MATCHING CHILDREN AND TEXTS

It is imperative that children experience success in their reading, especially during the first year of formal reading instruction. Therefore, it is important to consider the varying levels of text difficulty that are possible when finding suitable materials for children to read. Texts that are available for children to read in a school literacy program vary in difficulty, but it is the match between a child and a text that is most important for a teacher to consider. In guided reading, texts should not be too challenging for a child so that they may learn and practice new skills.

Levels of challenge of reading texts are described as follows:

- *Reading potential*
    - highest level at which a listener can hear and make adequate meaning from a text read a loud to them

- *Frustration level*
    - reading text that is highly challenging
    - may be too difficult for making meaning without high motivation from the reader

- *Instructional level*
    - reading text with some challenge
    - some support may be needed to make adequate meaning

- *Independent level*
    - reading text with little challenge
    - can be understood without additional support

These levels describe the relationship between a reader and a text, not the readability level of the text itself. As we select texts for children to read, one child may be able to read a text independently that is at the frustration level for another child. Children's prior knowledge and experiences influence their comprehension of text.

Reading Potential

A child's reading potential is described as the highest level of text in which he or she is able to listen and comprehend at least 75% or more of the text, accurately and without assistance. Theoretically, a child's reading potential shows the level at which a child might read if decoding and comprehension skills functioned fully, without any inhibiting factors. Children's reading potential is what teachers must consider when selecting texts for read-aloud.

Frustration Level

In contrast to reading potential, frustration level is a level of text that becomes too difficult for a child to read with or without support. Frustration may come from an inability to decode a sufficient amount of the text and/or difficulty linking the essential ideas for comprehension. In general, a text is considered to be at a child's frustration level if less than 90% of the words are read accurately with less than 75% comprehension. Even with support, children may not be able to achieve enough understanding of such text to make reading worthwhile. Repeated exposures to text that is initially frustration level can often reduce the level of difficulty and allow a child to achieve success in the text. This often occurs in shared reading (see Chapter 5).

Great effort is required to sustain one's self in a text in which many ideas are only partially understood. If we select frustration-level text for guided reading, children's motivation to deal with the text may not be high enough to avoid harmful effects such as loss of confidence. Self-monitoring strategies are difficult to develop in this level of text; in fact, self-monitoring strategies may actually be thwarted.

Instructional Level

Instructional level is the ideal level of text for guided reading, text that is "just right." In general, a text is considered at a child's instructional level if 90% to 97% of the words are read accurately and 75% to 90% of the ideas in the text are comprehended without teacher assistance. Through teacher guidance in instructional text, children are able to learn from the text and become more accurate in their reading, approaching a level of independence.

When children have support as they work with a text, they can tolerate a margin of error or inaccuracy and still learn from the text. With support of a more able reader, children will be able to use what they know to fill in missing ideas from the text and with rereading reach an independent level of functioning in the text. Developmentally, we typically think of the instructional level as having sufficient challenge to motivate learning, without being either too easy or too difficult.

Independent Level

When children read text that is at their independent level, their comprehension and word knowledge is almost completely accurate. Word recognition in independent-level text is 98% to 100% and comprehension is 90% or higher, without assistance. Children reading at their independent level know enough to fill in missing understandings on their own. Extensive reading at this level builds confidence, habituates decoding, and moves many competencies to an automatic level. Extensive experience with independent-level text encourages fluency and the control of reading strategies.

Reading in this level of text should take place during independent reading time in the classroom, when the purpose is fluency and enjoyment. It is essential that teachers guide children's selection of texts for independent reading.

Comparing Levels of Text

Different levels of text serve different purposes for readers and require different levels of motivation for successful use. The match between readers and texts can be summarized as shown in Figure 6.1. Throughout the school day children should have extensive opportunities to read texts that are either at their instructional or independent reading level. Reading text that is either easy or "just right" provides opportunities for the application of new skills and strategies to become more automatic.

Stages of Development and Levels of Difficulty

Emergent readers are making the transition from oral to written language and read with support from a more knowledgeable other. Children in this stage should read texts with words that are highly predictable, which may begin as frustration level in shared reading but become instructional and then independent through repeated readings that are supported by the teacher. Shared and interactive writings, which children compose with the teacher, are quite familiar and offer ease for practice. Texts for guided reading should fall within the

Text Level	Purpose	Challenge	Word Recognition	Comprehension
Listening	Potential as a reader	Medium	not applicable	75–100%
Frustration	Stretch, challenge	High	less than 90%	less than 75%
Instructional	Learn with guidance	Moderate	90–97%	75–90%
Independent	Practice, confidence	Low	98–100%	90–100%

FIGURE 6.1
The match between readers and text.

instructional range, offering some challenge that is supported by assistance from the teacher. Assisted rereading of these texts allows them to become independent for children. During some quiet reading times, emergent readers may challenge themselves by selecting frustration-level library books, which they may have heard read aloud.

Developing readers, children who are becoming more independent as readers, need some instructional-level challenge, with the remainder of the school day spent in independent-level materials. A developing reader typically has an instructional reading level between middle-first-grade to late-second-grade level. Developing readers are working to gain control over print and need confidence with text to be willing to persevere. The most appropriate texts for developing readers contain many words that are decodable, that is, words that have predictable letter-sound patterns (*cap, sing, rope*) that are familiar to children. Then they practice their decoding skills as they read. Frustration-level text may sometimes be self-selected during quiet reading times, but will not be very helpful in gaining control over reading processes.

Transitional readers know quite a lot about print and are ready to sustain more challenge with guidance or with self-selected materials they are highly motivated to read. A transitional reader typically has an instructional reading level of late-second-grade level or beyond. To help them solidify silent reading, be sure children spend much of their day with instructional and independent materials that offer "controlled challenge." Transitional-level children have established effective strategies for making meaning. They are able to teach themselves new skills and refine old ones when the amount of challenge is monitored.

Making Connections . . .

It is important to begin to note the match between children and the texts they choose to read or are asked to read by a teacher. Can you hear differences in the ways that a child reads various texts? How can you describe those differences? Focus on one child and make notes about what you hear as the child reads various texts aloud. Describe what you notice. How well is that child able to talk about different texts? Is there any relationship between the difficulty of the text and the way that the child reads each text? Try to relate your observations to the descriptions of independent-, instructional-, and frustration-level text in the previous section.

 SELECTING APPROPRIATE TEXTS

Fountas and Pinnell (1996) suggest that the following factors be considered in selecting guided reading materials:

- 🍎 length of text,
- 🍎 size and layout of print,
- 🍎 illustration support,
- 🍎 vocabulary and concepts,

🍎 text structure and genre,

🍎 language structure, and

🍎 predictability and pattern of language.

For a guide to leveling texts by difficulty, visit *http://www. harcourtcanada.com/pdf/ Rigby-Levelling/pdf.*

Texts may be selected from a variety of sources: children's literature, selections from a basal reading series (see Chapter 10), leveled books from publishers such as Wright Group and Rigby, as well as shared writings developed by teacher and children.

Length of the Text

Emergent readers should begin with short, simple texts, typically one sentence per page. Developing and transitional readers slowly progress to longer and more challenging books. Varying the length of texts that are of similar difficulty can help children learn to sustain their own reading. Length of text is also dependent upon the amount of text on a page. When selecting a text, consider how well children are able to sustain themselves at any one sitting. Teachers can also adjust longer texts for children by breaking the reading into appropriate lengths over several days.

Size of the Print and Layout on the Page

The size of print and amount on a page should match children's visual acuity and ability to process print. For emergent readers, the placement of print on the page should be predictable, such as print appearing on each page below the illustration. As children gain experience with print, it is possible to select books in which print appears in various placements from page to page. Children who understand the rules about the placement of English print on pages of text learn to handle greater variation in print placement, particularly novel formats such as cartoon style.

Illustration Support

Illustrations, including photographs, not only add interest to a text, but can also provide clues to the meaning of the print on the page. Illustrations that cue the key words in a predictable manner provide excellent support to emergent readers and English language learners. It is important to select texts for novice readers that are clear and enhance the contents. Illustrations may also support children's development of new understandings, especially in informational texts. As the complexity of text increases, illustrations begin to be replaced by descriptive language. Transitional readers learn to understand and use description in place of illustration.

Genre and Text Structure

Children should be exposed to a variety of texts so they learn to appreciate various types of writing and expand their knowledge of what is possible in books.

Some genres, such as informational text, may be more challenging for children because their knowledge of a topic or organization of the ideas is unfamiliar. Regardless of genre, texts should be "information-rich texts" (Clay, 1991, p. 262), enhancing children's ability to make meaning.

Language Structures and Concepts

The closer the match between a child's knowledge of language and the language structures of a particular text, the easier it is for the child to understand the ideas and concepts presented by the author. Sentence structures that are uncommon in a child's language background will present challenge, which at times may be too much to overcome, especially for English language learners. For example, texts that are written for children in New Zealand typically contain vocabulary and phrases that are not widely used in the United States. Be sensitive to children's language and world knowledge and select texts for which they have sufficient background to connect to new ideas they will encounter. This makes a text more comprehensible, especially for English language learners (Cummins, 1981).

Predictability and Pattern

Repeated patterns of language, along with rhythm and rhyme, make text more predictable to support emergent readers and English language learners. Predictable patterns from page to page help children make predictions about the text. As text loses strong patterns, children must rely more and more on their own ability to decode text and make connections with an author's ideas. Pattern and predictability support emergent readers and English language learners while they are learning to use more than context plus the beginning sound to decode words.

Linking Learning Experiences

To learn more about readability and readability formulas, investigate web sites such as *http://www. school.discovery.com/ schrockguide/fry/fry.html.*

The more that learning experiences are linked together for the study, of a particular topic, genre, or author, the more that children are able to bring experiences to the reading. Texts that are related in some way provide natural links for children's thinking. Related vocabulary appears in more than one text. Children have background knowledge and experience to connect to the ideas in a text. Providing opportunities to hear about ideas in read-aloud, write about those ideas in shared writing, and read about similar ideas in guided and independent reading can dramatically increase a child's opportunities to learn.

Many publishers provide a readability rating for a text as an indication of level of difficulty. A readability rating, such as 2.0 or beginning second-grade level, is an attempt at an objective prediction of text difficulty. A readability formula may simply compare length of sentences with the number of complex words in the text. It is difficult for a readability formula to consider the structure of sentences, the match between text and illustration, or the reader's background knowledge about a topic. Only the teacher who selects a text for guided reading can do that!

Making Connections . . .

To prepare for selecting appropriate texts for guided and independent reading, become familiar with the various levels of text that children might read during the primary-grade years. Survey a range of texts that children might read (picture books, leveled readers, selections from a basal reader). Pay special attention to changes in the amount and positioning of text on each page and the complexity of the language from level to level. Challenge yourself to place several books in an approximate order of difficulty. Describe and defend your thinking with a peer.

THE NEED FOR FLEXIBLE GROUPING

Read-aloud and shared reading are typically whole-class contexts for learning. Guided reading, however, requires a small-group setting for careful observation of children. What factors should be considered in forming small groups for guided reading instruction? Does it matter how children are grouped?

As teachers come to know their children as readers, they are able to form small groups for guided reading. These groups consist of children who, at that point in time, are at a similar level of reading development and will benefit from a guided reading experience in the same text. These small groups serve a particular purpose and complement the mixed-ability groupings of read-aloud, shared reading, shared or interactive writing, and other literature experiences discussed in this text.

For small groups to enhance children's literacy development, teachers must carefully monitor those groupings. Ample evidence suggests that low-ability groupings that are static can affect children's opportunities to learn (e.g., Allington, 1977; Allington & McGill-Franzen, 1989) and damage self-confidence and self-esteem (e.g., Filby, Barnett, & Bossart, 1982). Children's needs are best served through flexible groupings, including a combination of whole-group instruction and needs-based smaller groups.

How do teachers achieve flexible, dynamic groupings? Continuous assessment is the key. Observations of children's behaviors during a variety of reading contexts helps determine the span of a child's zone of performance in a variety of reading situations—the range from independent to instructional to frustration. Making continuous records of the accuracy of children reading is a must (see the Assessment section later in this chapter). As children demonstrate new skills and strategies, groupings are adjusted. Groups should always reflect children's current level of functioning.

If children are to become independent readers who find pleasure and satisfaction in reading and are able to monitor their own performance as readers, guided reading instruction must be appropriate. Children who are motivated to read stand a good chance of becoming lifelong readers. To support children's reading of text, consider the strategies readers use to make meaning with text and how the level of difficulty of a text may affect the reader.

DEVELOPING STRATEGIES FOR SELF-MONITORING

Reading involves the patterning of complex behaviors (Clay, 1979), learning to use "in-the-head" operations that "allow a learner to use, apply, transform, relate, interpret, reproduce, and re-form information for communication" (Fountas & Pinnell, 1996, p. 149). Over time, and with proper guidance and support, readers establish inner control over reading processes, monitoring their own reading by using knowledge of language and reading processes deliberately, yet flexibly, at appropriate times and under a variety of conditions (Paris, Wasik, & Turner, 1991).

It is the integrated use of meaning, language, and visual language cues that enables readers to make meaning (Clay, 1991). The ability to monitor one's reading requires the integration of these language cues.

Meaning Cues

Read here to find a definition of *semantics.*

Meaning cues, or *semantics,* enable readers to use the general sense or meaning of written or spoken language to determine either the meaning of an unknown word or the overall meaning of a piece of text. Meaning cues draw upon a reader's prior knowledge and sense of story.

> Example: Sherlock Holmes, a famous detective, could crack criminal cases better than anyone else.

Readers use knowledge of what detectives do to determine that *crack,* in this context, probably means to solve.

Language Cues

Read here to find a definition of *syntax.*

Language cues, or *syntax,* draw upon our knowledge of the structure, rules, and patterns of a language to aid in identifying an unknown word or word part by the way it is used in a text. To use language cues readers draw on perception of grammatical patterns and knowledge of English.

> Example: John r__ so fast that when he reach__ the store, he stop__ at the door to catch his breath.

Knowledge of word forms that are used to express time help us supply and confirm words and word parts. The use of language cues to monitor reading is especially challenging for English language learners.

Visual Cues

Read here to find a definition of *graphophonics.*

Visual cues, or *graphophonics,* draw upon our knowledge of letters and letter patterns and the possible sounds they may represent. Readers use their knowledge of print conventions and generalizations about sounds and symbols.

> Example: The police o_____ stopped to help.

Visual cues enable a reader to self-correct police "man" to "officer" by comparing letter-sound patterns and length of word against the reader's original decoding of an unfamiliar word.

The cue or cues a reader uses at any one time depend upon the type of text being read, the reader's purpose for reading that text, and the reader's knowledge of reading processes.

Becoming a Strategic Reader

Selecting the most appropriate cues to make meaning at the appropriate time is called *strategic reading* and requires the use of "in the head" strategies such as:

Read here to find a definition of *strategic reading.*

- 🍎 detecting and correcting miscues or errors in the reading,
- 🍎 adjusting the rate of reading to the type of text and to purposes for the reading,
- 🍎 drawing upon what a reader knows about a topic from various sources of information.
- 🍎 using meaning, language, and visual cues together to cross-check.
- 🍎 when meaning breaks down, a reader searches for sources of information that may have been overlooked and may help to repair meaning.

Strategies must be explicitly taught and reinforced through guided reading experiences.

What do teachers say to encourage children to use strategies to figure out unfamiliar words and to monitor their reading?

- 🍎 To encourage the use of meaning cues, a teacher might say:

    - 🍎 Does that make sense?
    - 🍎 Does the picture help you?
    - 🍎 What do you know about that topic that can help you?
    - 🍎 Does rereading help you?

- 🍎 To encourage the use of language cues a teacher might say:

    - 🍎 Does that sound right?
    - 🍎 Is that the way we say it in English?
    - 🍎 Does rereading help you?

- 🍎 To encourage the use of visual cues a teacher might say:

    - 🍎 Does that look right?
    - 🍎 What letter does that start (or end) with?
    - 🍎 Can you get your mouth ready to say the first sound?
    - 🍎 Can you point?
    - 🍎 Can you match your voice and the words?
    - 🍎 Can you find that word?

Guided reading experiences must help young children develop these "in-the-head" processes. Teaching should model, encourage, and support the use of strategies for meaningful reading. Observing children's reading behaviors and the miscues they make during reading is a window into their thinking about reading (Goodman & Burke, 1970).

Making Connections . . .

Listen to children read orally. Notice their miscues, or words that do not match the text. Do miscues make sense in the sentence? (Child is guided by meaning cues.) Do miscues sound like English? (Child is guided by language cues.) Do miscues look like the word on the page? (Child is guided by visual cues.) Do some miscues seem to be a combination? (E.g., the word makes sense and sounds right, but does not look right.) Developing an ear for the types of miscues children might make in reading will begin to prepare you for the skilled assessment of children's reading presented later in this chapter.

PUTTING THEORY INTO PRACTICE . . .

The remainder of this chapter focuses on planning and implementing guided reading experiences in the classroom. What factors must be considered to plan successfully for children? How do teachers organize for guided reading? How might guided reading change across the grades as children acquire knowledge as readers?

 PLANNING FOR GUIDED READING

What steps do teachers go through to prepare guided reading lessons for primary-grade children? Teachers:

- 🍎 set up flexible groups,
- 🍎 select appropriate texts,
- 🍎 guide the reading and rereading of the text, and
- 🍎 provide instruction, or teaching points, that focus on skills needed in the text.

To begin, we will consider what a first-grade teacher like Katarina (the teacher from the opening vignette) might do.

Setting Up Flexible Groups

Initial Assessment
At the beginning of the school year Katarina assesses the literacy development of each child:

- 🍎 She evaluates what they know about letters of the alphabet and the sounds that letters can represent.
- 🍎 She individually assesses children's concepts about words in print and book-handling skills (see Chapter 5 for concepts about print [CAP] assessment and concept of word [COW]).
- 🍎 Based upon the concepts that children are able to demonstrate, she forms tentative groups of four to five children who demonstrate similar levels of development.

Katarina adjusts these groups as warranted by her frequent assessment (see the Assessment section later in this chapter).

Continuous Monitoring

Every few weeks in the early part of first grade, Katarina makes a record of reading for each child to monitor development of reading skills and strategies. The reading record shows how accurately the child reads a particular text and what strategies the child employs while trying to make sense of the text. Results of reading records, and observations during guided reading and other literacy activities, provide assessment information that supports moving children between groups to better meet their needs. Reading records are discussed in the Assessment section at the end of this chapter.

Selecting Texts for Guided Reading

Katarina selects instructional-level texts for guided reading. She knows that the text should require children to use skills and strategies that are for the most part familiar. The text should also have a few challenges that will provide opportunity for children to learn new skills or strategies. The type of challenge presented by the text should be within reach for the children in the group. This level of text is referred to as instructional-level text. To select a text that is instructional level, Katarina asks herself questions about:

- 🍎 text content,
- 🍎 organizational features, and
- 🍎 relation to the curriculum.

Text content:

- 🍎 Do children have adequate background knowledge to understand the main concepts and ideas in the text?
- 🍎 Is there essential vocabulary the children may not know, but will need to make meaning? Do children currently have the decoding skills to figure out the new words?
- 🍎 Are illustrations clear? Will children be able to use the illustrations to support comprehension?
- 🍎 Do illustrations provide additional information and support for understanding the text?

Organizational features:

- 🍎 Are children familiar with the manner in which text is laid out on the pages?
- 🍎 Are sentence structures familiar? Will children be able to use their existing knowledge of language to understand the language of the text?

Relation to the curriculum:

- 🍎 How does the text fit in with, or relate to, the many stories, poems, and picture books used with the class?
- 🍎 Does this text provide an opportunity to link children's learning to other literacy experiences?

Based on answers to these questions, Katarina decides whether she is able to provide appropriate support to help children use their current knowledge, skills, and strategies to successfully read the text. Her observations of the first reading confirms whether her selection is appropriate and the amount of rereading that may be necessary for children to achieve a more independent level of reading of the text.

Guiding the Reading of a Text

Books selected for guided reading should be at the instructional level of the children in the small group. Though children are able to figure out much of what is in the text, children should be guided to anticipate and make sense of what is new. Before and perhaps during the reading, teachers provide clues for children to draw upon as they apply existing knowledge, skills, and/or strategies to make meaning from new vocabulary, sentence structure, text format, or literary device used by the author of a text. Teachers anticipate children's need for guidance and support and provide assistance in anticipation of what children will do with a text.

Guiding Less Complex Texts

The goal for guided reading should be to introduce a new book in a way that leads to a successful reading. In guided reading with emergent and early developing readers, all children read individually at their own pace. In guided reading, Katarina observes, prompts, and provides only the essential support that children need to read independently. In these early stages especially, one of the teacher's main functions is to listen to portions of the reading by each child. This opportunity is used to assess children's strengths and needs, provide guidance as needed, and evaluate each child's ability to use the instruction provided.

Following the reading of texts that have simple plots and little or no character development, Katarina engages children in personal response and retellings. Simple stories are primarily plot, with little attention to the development of other literary elements. As stories begin to include more complex use of literary elements to tell the story, the nature of the guided reading time begins to change. Simple nonfiction texts are primarily descriptive writing about ideas around a topic. The variety of retelling and response activities discussed in Chapter 4 can be useful to extend children's engagement with a guided reading text.

Guiding More Complex Texts

The pace of the reading and discussion of a text is structured according to the way that ideas are organized in the text, similar to the ways that children are guided during a mediated read-aloud (see Chapter 4). Some texts are read in their entirety during the first reading, while other texts are broken into more manageable chunks to help children develop strategies for linking ideas from reading to reading. As children are able, the initial reading moves from oral to silent, except when the text needs to be heard to support discussion. For children who are able to read silently, oral reading becomes oral rereading of selected portions of the text in preparation for discussion.

Interactions between adult and child should support and extend children's thinking. Questions and comments should "agitate" children's thinking by asking them to explain their thoughts and supply supporting evidence, which may include citing, locating, and orally rereading particular portions of a text. At significant points in the text, children may need support to connect new ideas to what they already know in order to construct a fuller understanding. Children become active readers by using their background knowledge and what they read in a text to think ahead, anticipating where the text might be going. As children read, they should be encouraged to pause to reflect on what they think they know, and on where they got their ideas.

ENGAGING CHILDREN IN GUIDED READING EXPERIENCES

To understand some of the dynamics of guided reading instruction, we return to Katarina's first-grade classroom while she is working with a small group of children who are preparing to read a short text, *Three Little Ducks* (created by the author for demonstration, see Figure 6.2). This small book has 12 pages of text,

FIGURE 6.2
Sample text for guided reading, *Three Little Ducks.*

Once upon a time, there were three little ducks. They liked to swim, and swim, and swim all day.	"Time to eat," said Mother Duck. So the three little ducks went home to eat supper. They were very hungry.
The first little duck said, "I'm sleepy." The second little duck said, "I'm sleepy." The third little duck said, "Me, too!" So they all went to sleep.	In the morning Mother Duck said, "Time to get up." The three little ducks could not get out of bed. All of their feet were stuck together.
"Where are my feet?" asked the first little duck. "Where are my feet?" asked the second little duck. "Where are my feet?" asked the third little duck.	"I need help," said the first little duck. "I need help, too," said the second little duck. "Help!" yelled the third little duck.
"I can help you," said Mother Duck. She took a big feather from her tail. "I will tickle your feet with the feather," said Mother Duck.	Tickle, tickle, tickle! The first little duck laughed. "Here are your feet," said Mother Duck.
Tickle, tickle, tickle! The second little duck laughed. "Here are your feet," said Mother Duck.	Tickle, tickle, tickle! The third little duck laughed. "Here are your feet," said Mother Duck.
"Thank you, mother," said the first little duck. "Thank you, mother," said the second little duck. "Oh, thank you, mother," said the third little duck.	"You are welcome," said Mother Duck. Then they all went for a swim.

each with an illustration, and two to three lines of text. In the story, three little ducks have a funny thing happen while they are sleeping. There is an ordinal pattern throughout the book with the first, second, and third duckling responding to a situation, such as being sleepy or needing help.

A SAMPLE GUIDED READING LESSON: FIRST GRADE

The guided reading lesson Katarina prepares for one group of first-grade students includes the following steps:

> *Before Reading*—Teacher and children preview the text to notice unique features. Teacher encourages use of strategies.
>
> *During Reading*—Children individually read the text at their own pace while the teacher listens to each child.
>
> *After Reading*—Teacher engages children in a follow-up discussion and selected teaching points.

Before the reading:

Katarina prepares the children to preview the text, or take a book/picture walk through the text. She shows the front cover of a small book and says,

> *"The title of this book is* Three Little Ducks.*"*

Katarina opens the book and begins to turn the pages, inviting children to observe the illustrations and comment on ideas they have about the story. The story line of this book is quite predictable, with repetition of the actions of the first, second, and third duck. The class has worked with ordinal numbers (first, second, third, etc.) in math, but Katarina wonders if the children will pick up on those words in this text.

For one illustration, she points to the first duck and asks,

> *"What is the first duck doing? And the second? And the third?" (Katarina will listen during the reading to see if this is helpful to the children's decoding of ordinal number words.)*

Katarina is also wondering if the children will be able to decode a new word, *tickle,* that is critical to the humor of the story and also the resolution of the story's problem. When she turns to the page where the word *tickle* is first introduced, Katarina calls attention to the fact that one character, the mother duck, has a large feather. She says,

> *"This is Mother Duck. What do you think she might do with this feather?"*

The children are unsure, so she turns the page to reveal an illustration that causes the children, in chorus, to say,

> *"Tickle their (the three ducks) feet."*

Katarina holds her copy of the book closer to the children and asks them to identify a word they think might be the word tickle. The children identify the first three words on the page that each say tickle, but one begins with a capital T. Katarina wants to be sure that the children are aware that whether written with capital or lowercase letters, the letters t-i-c-k-l-e, spell the word tickle.

Katarina asks the children, "What can you do when you come to a word you do not know?" There is a brief discussion of the strategies that are familiar to the children—looking at the illustration; rereading the text; asking if that makes sense, sounds right, or looks right. Katarina encourages children to use their strategies to help themselves during the reading.

During the reading:

Katarina now provides individual copies of the book for each child, encourages them to reread the title, then to proceed at their own pace through the first reading of the text. As the children begin to orally read, she listens in for a while to each child's fluency and use of strategies.

Today Katarina asks Christina to sit beside her, to listen more carefully to Christina's reading and make a written record (see reading records in the Assessment section later in the chapter). Ben finishes the story before the other children, so Katarina encourages him to enjoy rereading the story while the others finish.

During the reading, Katarina notices that several of the children have difficulty with the contraction *I'm* (e.g., *I'm sleepy*). They read *I'm* as *I am*. She had anticipated this difficulty, so she will make that a teaching point for the day. She believes that the children know contractions in oral language, but are not as familiar with the way that contractions appear in print.

After the reading:

Following the reading of the text, the children share their enjoyment of the story—how silly it is that the three little ducks got their feet tangled together. The children also think it is funny that Mother Duck pulls a feather from her tail to tickle the little ducks' feet.

In the after-reading discussion, Katarina encourages the children to retell the story, to see how well the children followed the sequence of the story. Frequently she engages children as a group in retelling, then encourages individual children to retell the story on their own. Retelling builds a framework for story structures. Katarina finds that verbal retellings provide support for written retellings of stories and the composing of children's personal stories. Experiences with retelling stories are especially important to the comprehension of English language learners in the group.

Teaching Point 1: The Contraction I'm

Next Katarina turns the children's attention to using their knowledge of print to figure out unfamiliar words in a story. Returning to page 3 in the text, Katarina calls children's attention to the first sentence on the page,

"I'm sleepy," said the little duck.

Once again the children struggle with *I'm* or read it as "I am" because their sense of language tells them that "I am" sounds right. Katarina uses magnetic letters on a metal baking sheet to spell the words "I am." She asks if children can read the two words. Then she replaces the letter *a* with an apostrophe, then pushes the letters together to form the contraction *I'm*. Again she asks the children to read the word, moving her finger from left to right under the word. Then, Katarina gives each child four small cards *(I, a, m, ')*.

- With Katarina's support, each child builds the words *I am*.
- Then the children remove the letter *a* and replace it with an apostrophe.
- Next the children push the letters together to spell the contraction *I'm*.

Katarina asks each child to read the contraction, moving a finger under the word from left to right. The children mix up the letters and repeat the exercise. Katarina explains to the children that when they speak, they often use contractions, but do not always recognize the same contractions in writing. She helps the group think about other common contractions *(I'll, can't)*. Katarina writes those contractions on a small white board that she keeps at the reading table. In upcoming texts, Katarina will watch for other contracted forms of words to gradually introduce children to this contraction, a base + base configuration. After the word building, Katarina asks the children to begin on page 1 and scan the text for the contraction *I'm*. The children find two examples on page 3.

Teaching point 2: Base word + inflectional suffix, yelled

As Katarina planned this guided reading lesson she predicted that the children might experience some difficulty with the word *yelled* on page 5 of the text and she was right. The sentence in the text says:

> *"Help!" yelled the third little duck.*

Katrina guides the children in building words.

ell	With magnetic letters Katarina builds the word chunk (rime) *-ell*. She reminds the children that they have seen this chunk in other words and encourages them to decode the chunk.
bell	Then she places the consonant letter *b* in front of the chunk to make the word bell. Katarina asks, "What word do we have now?" The children respond with "bell." They have encountered this word before.
tell	Katarina exchanges the letter *b* with the letter *t* and asks, "Now what word is this?" The children respond with *"tell."*
yell	Next, Katarina exchanges the letter *t* with the letter *y* to make *yell*. The children know the consonant sound that *y* can represent, and respond with *"yell."*

yelled   Finally, Katarina asks, "What if I put the suffix *-ed* on the end of *yell.* What word do we have now?" Two of the children are quite confident that the new word is pronounced as *"yeld,"* while one child, an English language learner, thinks it might be pronounced *"yell-ed,"* making a second syllable, *-ed.*

Katarina asks the children to return to page 5 in the text and encourages the children to consider how they can use their knowledge of language to decide the right pronunciation for yelled. She asks, "Which word sounds right in the sentence?"

> *"Help!" yelled the third little duck.*
>
>   *or*
>
> *"Help!" yell-ed the third little duck.*

The children decide that "yelled," not "yell-ed," sounds right. The children think that yelled (not yell-ed) sounds like the way they talk in English. Most of the children say that *yelled* is a word they have heard before. The English language learner in the group often pronounces *-ed* as a separate syllable. She has not yet acquired a complete understanding of past tense in English, as compared to Spanish. Katarina will continue to provide support while the acquisition process continues.

Katarina encourages self-monitoring as she reminds the children that sometimes they can figure out which way to pronounce a word they are unsure about by asking themselves if the word looks right, sounds right, and makes sense when compared with the text.

For 2 days Katarina engages the children in reading and rereading *Three Little Ducks.* The children have the chance to explore other aspects of the text, such as using quotation marks to show the words that someone speaks, then the book is placed in the group's book box (also called book tub) for independent reading practice. In addition to guided reading each day, the children also spend at least 20 minutes each day rereading familiar books in their group's book box to build fluency and confidence as developing readers.

Guided Reading of More Challenging Text

As children progress in the development of reading skills and strategies, what do teachers do to plan for guided reading? Do guided reading procedures change? Teachers who work with children reading in second-grade-level text and higher:

- 🍎 think about the purpose(s) for engaging children in reading a particular book,
- 🍎 plan specific strategies to assist children as they make meaning before, during, and after the reading, and
- 🍎 reflect on how teacher support should be adjusted to children's levels as indicated by interactions during discussion.

These steps form a purpose-strategy-reflection cycle for mediated learning (Dixon-Krauss & Powell, 1995) that is repeated throughout the guided reading. The cycle is similar to the cycle used during a mediated read-aloud (Chapter 4). Teachers should adjust the level of assistance as children show what they know and understand. The goal of guided reading is to help children learn strategies to become independent, self-regulated readers and thinkers.

As support is provided for children's reading and thinking in a text, guided reading of more complex text becomes a cycle of predict-read-explain-connect. The cycles occur because teachers pose open-end questions and statements that continue to nudge children's reading and thinking. In response to questions and comments:

- 🍎 children read text,
- 🍎 explain and provide support for their thinking,
- 🍎 make connections to what they already know, and
- 🍎 think ahead about where the text seems to be going.

As children mature in their reading, teachers promote more independent reading and thinking during mediated reading by broadening questions and offering children more opportunity to set directions during the reading.

Similar to the guided reading of simple texts such as *The Three Ducks* presented earlier, guided readings of more complex texts are also planned in three segments:

- 🍎 before the reading,
- 🍎 during the reading, and
- 🍎 after the reading.

In planning each segment, consider the purpose for using the selected text, the strategies that will support children's reading, and how children's feedback will be used to adjust instruction.

An example of the guided reading of a more complex text, *Sylvester and the Magic Pebble* (Steig, 1969), follows. The teacher asks open-ended questions that encourage children to use a predict-read-explain-connect cycle. A careful analysis of the text guides decisions about which events and story elements to emphasize.

Sylvester and the Magic Pebble consists of three episodes:

- 🍎 *Episode 1 (pp. 1–9).* Sylvester finds the magic pebble, then becomes a rock on Strawberry Hill. Sylvester, the main character is introduced, along with the problem of the story—Sylvester being magically turned into a rock.
- 🍎 *Episode 2 (pp. 11–17).* A series of events are described in which Mr. and Mrs. Duncan, Sylvester's parents, try to find him.
- 🍎 *Episode 3 (pp. 18–30).* Time passes. Mr. and Mrs. Duncan picnic on Strawberry Hill, discover Sylvester, and bring him back to life. Resolution of problem.

The reading of more complex texts can be broken into sittings that correspond with the episodes in the plot.

The predict-read-explain-connect cycle is used throughout the guided reading to focus children's attention on aspects of the text and to promote comprehension. Notice in the example that each predict-read-explain-connect cycle focuses on a small section of the text. The teacher guides the children through each cycle to help them monitor the comprehension of the text. The guided reading of Sylvester and the Magic Pebble may take 2 or 3 days to complete the first reading of the three episodes presented in the text.

SAMPLE GUIDED READING LESSON: THIRD GRADE

Text:	*Sylvester and the Magic Pebble* (Steig, 1969).
Purpose:	Appreciate use of magic to develop the fantasy. Notice author's use of problem-events-resolution plot structure.
Strategy:	Use illustration and language clues to signal reader.
Vocabulary:	*CEASED, stone-dumb.*

Before the first reading:

Read:	"Look at the cover of this book and think about the title."
Explain:	"What ideas do you have about this book? What leads you to think that?"

During the first reading:
Episode 1, Pages 1–2

Predict:	"What do you think might happen? Let's read and find out."
Read:	(*begin Episode 1*) Begin mediated reading by reading aloud pages 1–2 to introduce characters and Sylvester's interest in pebbles. Children follow along in their copies.
Explain:	"What do you know about Sylvester so far? What makes you think that?"
Connect:	"What do we know about the 'magic pebble,' the one that we thought about in the title of the book?" (*nothing yet from the text*)

Pages 3–5

Predict:	"What do you think might happen with the shiny red pebble?"
Read:	Read pages 3–5 silently and see what you find out.
Explain:	"What does Sylvester know about the pebble? What makes you think so? (*notice the use of language to describe the pebble and its power*) What do you think

CEASED means (p. 3)? Why do you think the author printed the word in capital letters?"

Pages 6–9

Predict: "What do you think Sylvester will do now?"

Read: "Read pages 6–9 silently, to the end of Episode 1, and introduction of problem, to find out."

Explain: "What do you think about Sylvester now? What parts of the story give you those ideas?"

Connect: "What do we know so far?" (*problem is established, preparation for beginning of Episode 2*)

Episode 2, Pages 10–15

Predict: Turn to page 10, notice the change of setting shown in the illustration, read aloud "Meanwhile back at home, . . . " (*pause*). Ask, "What do you think might happen 'back at home'?"

Read: "Read pages 10–15 silently and see what you find."

Explain: "What do you think about Mr. and Mrs. Duncan's efforts to find Sylvester? What makes you think that?"

Pages 16–17

Predict: "How do you think Mr. and Mrs. Duncan might be feeling after all of their searching?"

Read: "Read pages 16–17." (*silently*)

Explain: "What did you find out about Mr. and Mrs. Duncan? What makes you think that?"

Connect: "Turn to page 18 (*beginning of Episode 3—resolution*)." Ask, "What does the illustration suggest to you? What do you think has been happening on Strawberry Hill?"

Episode 3, Pages 18–23

Predict: "What do you think might happen now?"

Read: "Read pages 18–23 silently to find out."

Explain: "What do you think about Sylvester's problem now? What makes you think that?"

Pages 24–27

Predict: "Now that spring has come to Strawberry Hill, what do you think might happen?"

Read: "Read pages 24–27 silently to find out what happens next."

Explain: "What do you think about the picnic? What makes you think that? What does it mean to be *stone-dumb?*"

Connect: "What do we know about the pebble's magic?"

Pages 28–29

Predict: "What do you think might happen, now that the red pebble is resting on the big rock?"

Read: "Read pages 28–29 silently to see what happens."

Explain: "What do you think about the picnic now?"

Page 30

Predict: "What do you think happened in the 'scene that followed' (p. 29)? How do you think the story will end?"

Read: Read page 30 aloud.

Explain: "What do you think about the way the story ended? What makes you think that?"

After the reading:

Connect: (*personal responses*) "What do you think about this story that William Steig told us?"

Explain: If responses do not lead to a retelling of major events, ask "What did we find out about that magic pebble in the title of the book? What made us think that?"

Reread: Encourage children to support retelling by returning to the text and rereading aloud parts of text that help to explain their thinking and responses.

Connect: "Has there ever been a time that you felt like Sylvester?"

SELECTING TEACHING POINTS FOR GUIDED READING

A teaching point is a particular skill or strategy that is appropriate to the selected text. The teaching point(s) emphasized with a particular book depends on:

🍎 the academic standards expected by the school district,

🍎 the needs of the children in the guided reading group, and

🍎 the demands of the text to be read.

Teachers use knowledge of children's strengths and needs as readers to predict and confirm the areas in which children need instruction. Decisions about a teaching point may be revised after initial observations of children's interactions with a text.

General teaching points for *emergent readers:*

🍎 Track words left to right on the page.

🍎 Read left page before right page.

🍎 Match words read orally one-to-one.

🍎 Use illustrations to confirm meaning.

- Use illustrations + beginning letters to read unfamiliar words.
- Reread to confirm meaning, language, or visual cues.

General teaching points for *developing readers:*

- Use familiar chunks to decode unfamiliar words.
- Add more to a base word (inflected suffix) to make new words.
- Predict a word using context + beginning (and ending) letters, checked by meaning and/or language.
- Decode regular one-syllable and some two-syllable words.
- Connect events in the sequence of a plot, either beginning-middle-end or problem-events-resolution sequence.
- Identify main ideas and important details in a text.
- Self-monitor for meaning.
- Cross-check visual cues with meaning and language.

General teaching points for *transitional readers:*

- Use context + word chunks to decode unfamiliar multisyllable words.
- Connect important sequences in plots.
- Understand relationships between plot sequences and character actions.
- Identify and infer character traits.
- Identify and infer theme.
- Identify main ideas and supporting details.
- Draw conclusions and predict outcomes.
- Self-monitor for meaning.
- Cross-check visual cues (phonics and morphemic analysis) with meaning and language.

Many of these teaching points are introduced during whole-class read-aloud and shared reading, then reinforced during guided reading in instructional-level texts.

GUIDED LITERATURE STUDY IN SMALL GROUPS

At different times during the school year, the time devoted for daily guided reading may be used for guided literature study of picture books or chapter books that support a unit of study. In contrast to whole-class literature study in which the class studies a text during read-aloud time (Chapter 4), a major benefit to guided literature study in small groups is the selection of instructional-level texts that are related by topic, genre, use of literary element, or author.

Each day's guided literature study period can begin with whole-class instruction through a mini-lesson. The books under study are usually related in some way, enabling the teacher to identify particular procedures, skills, or strategies that are helpful to all groups. The majority of guided literature study is "work time" for group meetings and extension activities. The activities se-

Whole-Class:
10% of time
	• Teaching points—Mini-lessons,
	      procedures for literature study,
	      literary elements/text structure,
	      reading skills and strategies
	• Planning for the day

Work Time:
80% of time
	• Guided literature groups—
	      guided reading and rereading,
	      teacher-led and/or student-led discussions,
	      application of teaching points
	• Independent/partner reading
	• Extension activities
	      Literature log
	      Art
	      Related reading
	      Drama/reader's theater
	      Research on topic

Whole-Class: 10% of time	• Sharing/closure discussion • Planning for next day

FIGURE 6.3
Organizing time for guided literature study.

lected can be similar across books to provide for rich whole-class discussions at the close of each guided literature study period. Figure 6.3 provides an overview of guided literature study.

Guided Literature Study: Picture Books

To enhance a unit of study, such as "Families Are Alike and Different," in second grade, teachers can combine guided reading and literature study. For a unit that is about 3 weeks long, multiple copies of several selected fiction and nonfiction books or selections from a basal reading series will be needed. An example of texts for a families unit is shown in Figure 6.4. The texts represent a range of reading levels and will accommodate the guided reading levels of the children in the class.

Analyze the Texts
The focus of this unit of study is families, the importance of home culture, and the roles of individuals within families. Consequently, three aspects of the texts selected for this unit will be very important for study:

Plot
The ability to identify the problem presented in the text is at the heart of understanding the family and the importance of family roles that are presented.

FIGURE 6.4
Guided reading texts for
the unit "Families Are Alike
and Different."

Week 1
A Chair for My Mother by Vera Williams
Dad Told Me Not To by Susan Talanda
Now One Foot, Now the Other by Tomie dePaola
Too Many Tamales by Gary Soto and Ed Martinez

Week 2
How My Family Lives in America by Susan Kuklin
Going Home, Coming Home by Truong Tran and Ann Phong
La Familia/The Family by Clare Beaton
Coming to America: A Muslim Family's Story by Bernard Wolf

Week 3
Dim Sum for Everyone by Grace Lin
Black Is Brown Is Tan by Arnold Adoff
Grandma Maxine Remembers: A Native American Family Story by Ann
Morris and Peter Linenthal
Grandma Esther Remembers by Ann Morris and Peter Linenthal

Character
The understanding of characters' actions is essential to understanding the importance of individual's roles within a family and how individuals contribute to a family.

Theme
The enduring values portrayed by the author through the characters and their actions help us understand what is important to families.

The focus of the unit thus structures thinking about guided discussions of texts, selection of possible teaching points for mini-lessons, and the use of the literature response log and other extension activities. Literature response logs can be used to help children focus their attention on retelling, responding, and word study.

Figure 6.5 provides an example of a text analysis for *Too Many Tamales,* a text used during week 1 of the Families Unit. Complete an analysis such as this for each book to determine what might be emphasized during the study of each text. Given the unit of study on families, a teacher might choose to focus on the theme of the text and develop an understanding of the theme through a study of the characters and their actions.

Possible Extension Activities
After analyzing the content of each text, brainstorm a variety of ways to extend children's engagement with each text. Some activities will be useful with all texts in the unit of study.

Literature log possibilities for *Too Many Tamales:*

- Make a story map of major events to retell the plot.
- Illustrate a favorite part of the story and tell why.

- Plot — Chronological set of events from problem to resolution (Maria tried on her mother's diamond ring while making tamales and thinks it is now somewhere in one of the tamales she made. Maria admits her actions to her mother, who still has the ring, relatives are supportive of Maria's honesty.)
- Setting — Backdrop to the action, not essential for understanding plot or character's actions.
- Point of View — Narrator provides information about all key characters, especially Maria, the main character.
- Characters — Maria shows the curiosity of a child, the dilemma of trying to solve a problem without adults finding out, but honesty in the end to admit her mistake. Adults in the story are empathetic.
- Theme — Inferred through character's actions and dialogue: It is good to admit a mistake, adults can be understanding.
- Style — Descriptions are clear and simple. Dialogue is used to reveal nuances of the plot.
- Vocabulary — *tamale* (meat wrapped in masa and a corn husk, traditional Mexican food), *masa* (corn flour).

FIGURE 6.5
Sample text analysis: *Too Many Tamales.*

🍎 Develop a character chart for Maria to understand her character.

🍎 Describe how family members responded to mistakes or showed understanding.

🍎 Respond to what Maria did to solve her problem.

🍎 Tell about a time when you made a mistake and what you did to try to correct it.

Word study possibilities for *Too Many Tamales:*

🍎 Children select new words/phrases from the text to illustrate, such as *a batch of tamales, a bowl of masa, delicious-smelling curls of steam, tagging along after them,* and *corn husks littered the floor.*

🍎 Build words with the letters in the word *tamales.*

Organizing for Guided Picture Book Study

The small groups can be rotated so that the teacher is able to meet with each group on a regular basis. Figure 6.6 provides suggestions for meeting with four small groups. Notice that the rotations are staggered so that only two groups are beginning a new text on the same day. Each group studies a text for 4 days, meeting with the teacher for guided reading on 2 of those days.

Guided Literature Study: Chapter Books

Guided literature study of chapter books requires multiple copies of chapter books. For example, to study a literary element such as character in third grade, we might select books that vary in their complexity and level of difficulty, from early-second-grade reading level to fourth-grade level.

FIGURE 6.6
Possible group rotation in guided literature study of picture books.

Group	Day 1 BEGIN NEW TEXT	Day 2	Day 3	Day 4	Day 5 BEGIN NEW TEXT
A & B	**Guided Reading:** Preview text Guided reading of Part I Discussion Predictions for Part II **Extensions** Literature log— Story map of Part I, identify problem, main events Word study— illustrate/describe vocabulary such as *tamales, masa*	**Independent/ Partner Reading:** Retell Part I Read Part II Make predictions for reminder **Extensions:** Literature log— continue story map for Part II, add to main events Word study— choose word or phrase to illustrate/describe	**Guided Reading:** Retell Part II Guided reading of remainder of text Discussion Word study **Extensions:** Literature log— continue story map, add to main events, identify resolution	**Independent/ Partner Reading:** Reread complete text **Extensions:** Literature log— respond to favorite parts, illustrate	
C & D	**COMPLETE PREVIOUS TEXT** **Independent/ Partner Reading:** Reread complete text **Extensions:** Literature log	**BEGIN NEW TEXT** **Guided Reading:** Preview text Guided reading of Part I Discussion Predictions for Part II **Extensions** Literature log— story map of Part I, identify problem, main events Word study— illustrate/describe vocabulary such as *tamales, masa*	**Independent/ Partner Reading:** Retell Part I Read Part II Make predictions for remainder **Extensions:** Literature log— continue story map for Part II, add to main events Word study— choose word or phrase to illustrate/describe	**Guided Reading:** Retell Part II Guided reading of remainder Discussion Word study **Extensions:** Literature log— continue story map, add to main events, identify resolution	**Independent/ Partner Reading:** Reread complete text **Extensions:** Literature log— respond to favorite parts, illustrate

Book A: *Stone Fox* by John Gardiner (most challenging)
Book B: *Beans on the Roof* by Betsy Byars
Book C: *Staying Nine* by Pam Conrad
Book D: *The Poppy Seeds* by Clyde Robert Bulla (least challenging)

Analyze the Texts

As with picture books, planning begins with the reading and analysis of each text, considering children's background knowledge and experience as readers of chapter books. For this literature study, analysis of the development of literary elements in each book is needed to determine the focus of the study. Vocabulary and writing styles should also be considered. Figure 6.7 provides a sample text analysis for *Stone Fox*.

Possible Extension Activities

After analyzing the content of each text, brainstorm a variety of ways to extend children's engagement with each text. Some activities will be useful with all texts in the unit of study.

Plot	Provides a quick-paced, progressive, exciting climax. Open-ended resolution allows reader to know Little Willy (main character) wins the race but not what happens afterward to Willy and Grandfather. Leaves reader to speculate on resolution, provides a good focus for discussion and follow-up activity.
Setting	Jackson, Wyoming, a highly integral setting, serves as an antagonist to show us Willy's courage and highlights his relationship with Searchlight, his dog. Children may need help understanding that authors sometimes use setting as if it is a character in the story.
Characters	Pay special attention not only to understanding the main character, but also to understanding how the other characters and the setting contribute to the reader's response to Little Willy. • Little Willy is round and dynamic; in our comparison with the other flat characters we are able to learn about him. • Searchlight, the dog, is flat and static, reflecting Willy's growth. • *Stone Fox* is flat but dynamic, changing at the end to accentuate the climax. • Grandfather and Doc Smith act as foils, pushing Willy in certain directions that the reader needs to see.
Point of View	A limited-omniscient narrator outside of the characters tells the story. The narrator lets readers know what Willy is thinking about and helps them understand Willy's drive to win the race.
Theme	This book is about perseverance, personal strength, and finding courage in the face of defeat. The theme can be seen through the characters.
Style	There is a good balance between description and dialogue: Descriptions are clear, language is simple and straightforward.

FIGURE 6.7
Sample text analysis: *Stone Fox.*

Literature log possibilities for *Stone Fox:*

🍎 Open response to group discussions that can provide a glimpse of how children are dealing with the text.

🍎 Double-entry journal responses for independent reading days. A double-entry journal consists of a quote from the text on the left side of the page in the literature log and the reader's personal response to the quote on the right side of the page. Other ways to use the double-entry journal are suggested in Chapter 9. A sample entry is shown in Figure 6.8.

Word study possibilities for *Stone Fox:*

🍎 Identify interesting/challenging words that warrant attention or study in the log and discuss during group meetings. Encourage children to determine meanings.

🍎 Collect descriptive words for each of the main characters.

Character sketches for *Stone Fox:*

🍎 Keep notes on different characters, what is being learned about each, and how it is being learned.

🍎 Add to sketches with each reading; use in group for discussion of the characters.

Discussion guides for *Stone Fox:*

If children are new to student-led literature study, teachers can develop a discussion guide for each chapter to nudge their thinking (see Discussion Guides in Chapter 4). Over the period of study, the questions could become more open-ended.

Organizing for Guided Chapter Book Study

Organizing for Teacher-Led Groups
Children who are new to guided literature study may need to be in teacher-led groups, whereas children with some experience with guided literature study

FIGURE 6.8
Sample double-entry journal for *Stone Fox*.

Stone Fox

Quote from text: p. 12

"A ten-year-old boy cannot run a farm. But you can't tell a ten-year-old boy that. Especially a boy like little Willy."

Response:

I'd be scared to try to do what Willy did. He was brave. His grandfather taught him to work hard. I don't have to work so hard at my house. Maybe if I did I'd be more like Willy.

may begin to move toward child-led groups. The teacher's intention determines the way that groups will meet and use their time together. Figure 6.9 provides an example of how to organize teacher-led literature groups with a chapter book, *Stone Fox*. The procedure the groups follow is very similar to the guided reading of complex texts presented in an earlier section of this chapter.

When the focus is on teacher-led groups, it is best to stagger the reading plans for the four chapter books, just as we did for the four picture books (Figure 6.6), seeing two groups each day while the other two groups read independently. For example, children reading *Stone Fox* could meet as a group on days 1, 3, and 5 of the first week. One other book group would follow a similar schedule.

When deciding how to stagger the groups, consider having the readers of the least challenging books begin with independent reading after the introductory meeting. Readers of the most challenging books begin with guided reading before reading independently.

Organizing for Child-Led Groups

Child-led literature groups are typically referred to as *book clubs* (McMahon, 1991) or *literature circles* (Daniels, 2002). There are at least two important distinctions between the procedures to use for teacher-led and child-led groups:

🍎 how to use time during literature study, and
🍎 the roles of teacher and child.

In child-led literature study, all reading and writing that is done to prepare for group meetings can take place at the beginning of the literature study period. Children are then reading and writing ideas or questions for that day's discussion at the same time, so the teacher can provide support to the children who

Day 1	Teacher guides the reading of chapter 1 (9 pages) to begin the book study. Discuss plans for reading and how children will get independent/partner reading completed; begin a group character chart of major characters.
Day 2	Independendent/partner reading, chapters 2 and 3 (18 pages); no group meeting but children work on log and extension activities.
Day 3	Group meets, reads chapter 4 in group (8 pages) and discusses, shares literature log entries from day 2; add to group character chart; make new log entry as response to group discussion of character.
Day 4	Independent/partner reading, chapters 5 and 6 (18 pages); no group meeting, log entry, extension work.
Day 5	Group meets, reads chapter 7 (8 pages) and discusses, adds to character sketches, shares log entries, makes new entries after group.
Day 6	Independent/partner reading chapters 8 and 9 (15 pages); no group meeting, literature log, extension work.
Day 7	Group meets, reads chapter 10 (6 pages) and discusses open resolution and personal impact, makes log entry after group.
Day 8	Children are involved in independent follow-up activities, extensions.
Day 9/10	Group meets and shares work, revisits character sketches, engages in overall responses to book.

FIGURE 6.9
Example of teacher-led literature groups: *Stone Fox*.

Independent reading time provides opportunities for children to practice skills and strategies learned during guided literature study.

are most in need of it. Following such preparation, all groups can meet for discussions at the same time because their group meetings do not require our attendance. Attend one group meeting each day, listening, observing, and participating as needed to support children's growing discussion skills. Following group meetings, all children can participate in extension activities, which the teacher oversees.

Observation of group interactions and individual participation in literature activities provides information about instruction that may be needed for either the class as a whole or for groups of children within the class. For example, after the groups meet for discussion on day 1, the teacher might provide instruction in how to develop a character chart for each text. After instruction, each group identifies the characters that were introduced in chapter 1 and places names in the appropriate place on a character chart. The group brainstorms characteristics that have been introduced in the text and places them on the chart.

Additional instruction might come in the form of mini-lessons that focus children's attention on how they might infer character traits from dialogue and descriptions in text, using examples from the four different texts. Make daily suggestions to the class and/or groups for literature response log entries that children complete following small-group discussions. On appropriate days after the groups meet, we bring the class together to discuss ideas that have been entered into the literature response logs. Children bring their logs to this discussion and may even read aloud from their entries as a way of sharing their ideas about the literature. Figure 6.10 provides an example of organizing for child-led literature groups.

Guided literature study provides a variety of opportunities to engage children in quality literature, enhancing their understanding of the potential that literature has for telling stories about life and the motivation to read those stories.

Day 1	Teacher meets with each group to help children develop a reading plan for the 2-week period, children then independent/partner read chapter 1 (9 pages).
Days 2–8	Children will independent/partner read one chapter each day (7–9 pages), make literature log entries in preparation for discussion, and the group will meet daily for discussion. Continue literature log and extension activities as time permits.
Day 9	Independent/partner read chapters 9 and 10 (13 pages), make literature log entries in preparation for discussion, group meets for discussion, continue literature log and extension activities as time permits.
Day 10	Whole-class meeting/sharing of work, revisit character sketches, engage in overall response to book.

FIGURE 6.10
Example of child-led literature groups: *Stone Fox.*

TEACHING SKILLS/STRATEGIES THROUGH MINI-LESSONS

Mini-lessons and flexible skill/strategy groups are two ways to support children's development as readers and thinkers in guided literature study. Mini-lessons lay the foundation for further development in small groups.

Mini-lessons (Five, 1988; Hagerty, 1992) are short, whole-class lessons, lasting 5 to 15 minutes, in which children focus on an essential aspect of reading or on how to use a particular skill or strategy in their reading. Analysis of the books to be used in literature study and observation of children's interactions with those books provide information to select teaching points for mini-lessons. In a mini-lesson, teachers demonstrate a skill or strategy that is useful and think aloud to share the internal decision making that readers go through as they decide how to best use a skill or strategy. Examples are usually drawn from the book being studied or books that are familiar to all of the children.

Teachers who "think aloud" during a mini-lesson help children learn how readers make the decisions that they do, what information gets considered, and why some possibilities get discarded (Davey, 1983). Remember, reading is a thinking process that often involves an emotional response. Because thinking cannot be observed, it must be shared verbally. Figures 6.11 and 6.12 provide example scripts of mini-lessons that focus on using knowledge of the literary element of character and using context clues to confirm word meanings.

Preparing and presenting mini-lessons during guided literature study provides opportunity to teach skills and strategies that are integral to the reading process and common to different types of literature. The suggestions in this section can also be used for the study of literature during reader's workshop (see Chapter 7).

The possibilities for mini-lesson topics are limitless. The literature selected for study and the needs of the children as readers determine the selection of topics for mini-lessons. To decide on appropriate mini-lessons teachers answer the question, "What do the books in this guided literature study require of the

FIGURE 6.11
Sample mini-lesson:
Learning about a character.

The teacher might say:
"Each time I read a new book, I'm introduced to a new character. I've noticed there are different ways that an author helps me get to know the character. In *A Chair for My Mother* (a picture book the class read), the main character is a girl and she tells the story. To get to know her, I have to listen to how she tells the story and what she says about herself and others. I know that I'll have to look at the story through her eyes. There's not much dialogue for me to listen to, mostly description of people, places, and events.

"In *Stone Fox* (a chapter book we are in the process of reading), the story is told by a narrator who is not part of the story. The narrator tells me everything that's happening and what everyone says. Then I can decide for myself about the characters. In this type of story, I have to listen to what people say about a character, what the character says, and how the narrator describes what goes on. I think about characters talking just like I think about my friends and me talking. I learn about what my friends are like by listening and watching them. That's how I learn about characters in *Stone Fox*.

"When you are reading today, try to notice how your author lets you learn about what your characters are like. Perhaps some of you might like to share what you find in our closing group time."

Notice how we end this mini-lesson with a suggestion of what children might do. Then we observe to see how useful this particular suggestion was for children.

reader?" For example, the group of picture books described earlier on families provides opportunities for whole-class mini-lessons for:

- How to use personal background knowledge about families to understand a text, and
- What to do when personal knowledge about families differs from the book.

In contrast, the chapter books selected for a character study provide opportunities to examine:

- How an author introduces and develops a character, and
- How to make inferences about a character's actions and motivations.

Figures 6.13, 6.14, and 6.15 provide lists of possible topics for mini-lessons.

ASSESSMENT: MONITORING GROWTH IN GUIDED READING

How do teachers know that children are making progress in reading? Teachers listen intently to children read orally and talk about what they read. Samples of children's reading serve as documentation of their growth as readers. During

The teacher might say:

"When I'm reading, sometimes I come to a word that I think I know, but the way it's used in the story doesn't seem to fit what I am thinking. Then I remember that in English some words can have more than one meaning. So I have to look carefully at how the author used the word.

"Yesterday we started reading *Chocolate Fever* by Robert Kimmel Smith. When we got to page 16, we came across the word *stunt* and several of you asked me if it meant something about doing tricks. Let's look at that part of the text again.

"Remember, we were reading about how much Henry loved chocolate and how chocolate even seemed to love him." (We place a copy of that page of text on the overhead with this sentence highlighted:

> It didn't stunt his growth. (He was just about average height, perhaps even a little taller for his age.)

"In this sentence, *tricks* doesn't make sense. Then I look past that sentence, because I know that clues can come after a word, as well as before a word. I see that the author put something in parentheses. Maybe he wanted me to pay attention to those words, like he was giving me a hint. So I think if Henry is average height or taller he must be growing; he didn't stop growing. Maybe *stop* fits, so let's try it in the sentence:

> It didn't *stop* his growth.

"That makes sense to me and fits with the other sentences. *Stunt* is one of those words that can have more than one meaning. Sometimes I can find out what meaning the author is using if I look at the other words around it for clues.

"In our reading today, if we come to a word where the meaning you are thinking of doesn't fit with the way the author is using it, let's stop and see if we can figure it out by looking at the other words around it."

After the mini-lesson, the class continues the reading of *Chocolate Fever*. The teacher follows up the reading with questions such as, "How did you figure out what a 'light dusting of cocoa' meant in the story?"

FIGURE 6.12
A sample mini-lesson to teach the use of context.

- What to do during independent work time
- Recording and responding in a literature log
- Deciding what type of response to make
- Choosing words to put in the response log
- Learning how to participate in discussions
- What to do when I have finished my reading
- How to get ready for a teacher conference
- What to do during a community sharing session
- Responding to other reader's ideas

FIGURE 6.13
Mini-lessons: Procedures of literature-study.

FIGURE 6.14
Mini-lessons: Genre and literary elements.

Learning about Plot
- Stories have beginnings, middles, and ends
- Plots can go forward
- Plots can sometimes go backward
- When conflict is a good thing
- Does there have to be a problem?
- Different ways that authors end stories

Learning about Character
- Different types of characters
- What purpose an antagonist serves
- Why does an author use a foil character?

Learning about Setting
- There are different types of settings
- A setting can be a character

Learning about Point of View
- Who is telling the story?
- What difference does point of view make?

Learning about Genre
- Characteristics of a particular genre
- How genres make different kinds of stories
- Recognizing the difference between narrative and informational writing

FIGURE 6.15
Mini-lessons: Reading skills and strategies.

Word Knowledge
- How to tell when a book is easy, just right, or too hard
- How to figure out unfamiliar words
- When to use context (words and/or illustrations)
- When to use structural patterns
- When to use particular phonics patterns
- Can I skip words I don't know?
- How to use my "checking system"
- Asking myself, "Is this making sense to me?"
- Tips for fluent, expressive audience reading

Comprehension of Text
- Recognizing main ideas
- Recognizing important details
- Retelling stories
- Making a story map
- Storytelling the story
- Sequencing important events
- Summarizing what I read
- Drawing conclusions
- Making inferences
- Distinguishing fact and fiction/opinion
- Distinguishing reality and fantasy

each day of guided reading, teachers observe children read. Records of those observations should be made on a continuous basis, recording what children actually say while reading, then analyzing any miscues, or words that differ from those in the actual text. Analysis of children's reading should then help to make more appropriate decisions to support children's growth as readers.

The study of children's oral reading has a long history as an indicator of performance (Betts, 1946; Durrell, 1937; Gates, 1935; Gilmore & Gilmore, 1951; Gray, 1915; Spache, 1963). Over the past several decades this procedure of making records of children's oral reading behaviors has been referred to by different terms: *running records* (Clay, 1979), *miscues analysis* (Goodman & Burke, 1970), and *informal reading inventories* (Beldin, 1970). Because there is a lack of agreement about terms, in this text we simply refer to such records as *reading records,* which is what they are. A record of children's oral reading reflects the strategies they use to monitor for meaning while they read.

Reading records may be made with both familiar and unfamiliar text. When text is familiar we should expect fewer miscues and, consequently, more fluent reading. When text is unfamiliar, we have our best opportunity to see and hear the self-monitoring strategies over which students have gained control and use most accurately and automatically.

Reading records can either be scripted or unscripted:

- 🍎 A *scripted reading record* uses a duplicate copy of the same text the child reads aloud. The teacher marks directly on a copy of text to show how the child actually read the text.

- 🍎 An *unscripted reading record* is made on a blank sheet of paper or recording form. The teacher makes check marks to indicate each correct word in a line of text and also note children's miscues.

Read here to find definitions of *scripted* and *unscripted reading records.*

When we make a reading record the teacher sits side by side with the child, but slightly behind so that the recording is less distracting. As the child reads, the teacher makes a record of the reading. When first learning to make reading records, it is a good idea to tape record the reading to confirm that an accurate record was made. The tape recording may also be used during parent-teacher conferences to help parents hear a child's strengths and/or need for support as a reader.

Scripted Reading Record

Scripted reading records can be used early in the school year as a way of learning about children's self-monitoring strategies. It is best to examine a child's reading level in a variety of texts—independent, instructional, and frustration. Making a record of reading is an excellent way for a teacher to check the instructional decisions being made, to know that children are placed in appropriate levels of text for guided reading.

Every few days Katarina (the teacher from our earlier vignette) selects one child to be the focus child and checks the child's progress by making a reading record during the guided reading group. On the day before she makes a scripted reading record in a guided reading group, Katarina selects and copies an appropriate passage. The next day, she listens carefully for the accuracy of that child's reading. Katarina records the reading by marking her copy of the text with the codes shown in Figure 6.16. Katarina records all miscues, but does not count all

FIGURE 6.16
Marking a scripted running
record.

Miscues that are counted:

Substitution—Child reads a word differently than the printed text. Multiple substitutions of same word throughout text are counted only once.

three
Once upon a time, there were three little ducks.

Omission—Child leaves out a word printed in the text.

Once upon a time, there were three (little) ducks.

Insertion—Child adds a word or words that are not in the printed text.

the
Once upon a time there were ˄three little ducks.

Teacher Tells—Child appeals to the teacher for help, teacher first responds, "Try it," child is unable to respond after 2-3 seconds, then teacher tells.

T
Once upon a time there were three little ducks.

Try That Again—Child becomes completely lost in a section of text, teacher brackets problem section and says, "Try that again." The whole passage is coded as TTA and counted as one miscue. Any additional miscues that are made in the rereading are marked with the usual codes. Miscues from the first reading are ignored.

TTA
                        sc
        the   tree   was   the
[Once (upon a)time there were three little
duck
ducks.   ⌐

Miscues that are NOT counted:

Repetition—Child repeats a word or phrase. This usually indicates that they have lost the meaning or they are using rereading as a strategy to figure out an unknown word. One line over or under the text is used for each repetition.

R
Once upon a time there were three little ducks.

Self-Correction—Child corrects own miscue *without* assistance. The original miscue is recorded but does not count.

sc
three
Once upon a time there were three little ducks.

Teacher Encourages—Child stops reading at point of unknown word, may or may not appeal for help, teacher encourages but does not tell, saying "try it," *E* (encourage) is recorded. Child's response is recorded.

E
Once upon a time there were three little ducks.

FIGURE 6.17
Sample scripted reading record.

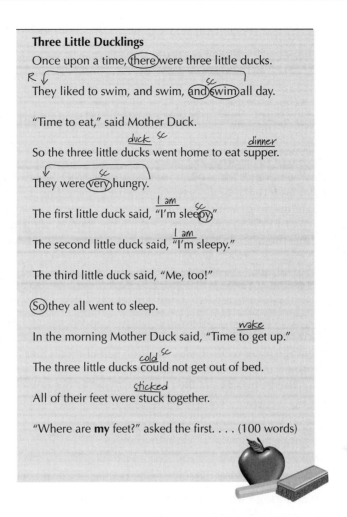

Three Little Ducklings

Once upon a time, ⟨there⟩ were three little ducks.

R ✓
They liked to swim, and swim, ⟨and⟩ ⟨swim⟩ all day.

"Time to eat," said Mother Duck.

duck ˢᶜ   dinner
So the three little ducks went home to eat supper.

✓   ˢᶜ
They were ⟨very⟩ hungry.

I am   ˢᶜ
The first little duck said, "I'm sleepy."

I am
The second little duck said, "I'm sleepy."

The third little duck said, "Me, too!"

⟨So⟩ they all went to sleep.

wake
In the morning Mother Duck said, "Time to get up."

cold ˢᶜ
The three little ducks could not get out of bed.

sticked
All of their feet were stuck together.

"Where are **my** feet?" asked the first. . . . (100 words)

miscues when she determines oral reading accuracy. She counts only miscues that may interfere with meaning and are not self-corrected.

Imagine that Katarina listens to Christina read *Three Little Ducks* during guided reading. Using a copy of the text, Katarina makes the scripted reading record shown in Figure 6.17. There are 100 words in this passage. Which errors should by counted? Look at Figure 6.15 for help in deciding.

How accurately does Christina read? Is this text appropriate for her? Why or why not? (Remember that instructional level text is 90% to 97% accuracy of word recognition.)

Miscues that are counted: 6

Miscues that are not counted: 6

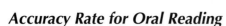

Accuracy Rate for Oral Reading

Calculate Christina's accuracy rate:

$$\text{Total words} - \text{counted errors} = \text{words correct}$$
$$100 - 6 = 94$$

$$\text{Words correct/total} = \text{accuracy rate}$$
$$94/100 = 94\%$$

Self-Correction Rate

How well does Christina monitor and correct her own reading? How might you calculate that? Self-corrections and repetitions are signs of self-monitoring. Christina frequently uses repetition to check her thinking. If she did not self-correct her miscues, there would have been 6 additional miscues, for a total of 12 miscues. To calculate her rate of self-correction, we must consider all possible miscues compared with the number of miscues that were corrected.

$$\text{Self-correction ratio} = \text{total miscues: self-corrections}$$
$$\text{Christina's self-correction rate} = 12{:}6 \text{ or } 2{:}1$$

The ratio means that for approximately every two miscues, Christina self-corrects one—a good rate of self-correction. She is learning to monitor her own reading quite well. If she did not self-correct, her accuracy rate would have dropped to 88%, or frustration level.

When Christina makes a miscue that is not self-corrected, what type of miscue(s) does she make? To what type of cues should she have paid attention? It is appropriate here to consider the three types of cues that influence our reading:

meaning: makes sense in this context
language: sounds right according to English structure/syntax
visual: looks right according to the word pronounced

Considering Christina's miscues, which cues seem to be influencing her reading of the text? See Figure 6.18.

From analyzing responses on the reading record, what might be inferred about Christina's reading? When she makes a miscue, she seems to be thinking about what makes sense and sounds right in the sentence. She does not always seem to check the word she pronounces against the actual word in the text. From her miscues, she appears to make meaning through repetition, self-correction, and miscues that preserve structure and meaning. Katarina uses a form like the one shown in Figure 6.19 to analyze cues used for each miscue and self-correction.

Calculate Christina's fluency rate:

Total words correct—94

Time—1.5 minutes

Words correct per minute (WCM) = 63

Christina's fluency rate is quite adequate for a child in first grade. The time that Katarina devotes to shared rereadings, assisted reading during guided reading groups, and independent/partner reading has supported Christina's fluency development.

Errors/Miscues:	Information that appears to influence error:			Information that appears to influence self-correction:		
	Meaning	Structure/Language	Visual	Meaning	Structure/Language	Visual
omission (there)	X	X				
omission (and)	X	X				X
omission (swim)	X	X				X
duck (ducks)	X	X			X	X
dinner (supper)	X	X				
omission (very)	X	X				X
I am (I'm)	X	X				
Sleep (sleepy)			X	X	X	
omission (so)	X	X				
wake (get)	X	X				
cold (could)			X	X	X	
sticked (stuck)	X	X				

FIGURE 6.18
Information that appears to influence errors and self-corrections.

Unscripted Reading Record

When Katarina wants to assess a child's oral reading without prior planning, she takes an unscripted reading record. She uses a blank form that does not have a copy of the text. While looking at the text the child is reading, she uses check marks to show the child's accuracy (see Figure 6.20). The advantage of an unscripted reading record is the ability to make a record at any time, without advance notice.

If Katarina is listening to a focus child read during independent reading (see Chapter 7), she does not need to make a copy of the text ahead of time. An unscripted record of Christina's reading might resemble that shown in Figure 6.21. The reading record is scored and analyzed in the same manner as a scripted reading record.

Keeping accurate records of children's progress in reading is important for planning appropriate instruction and for communicating with parents. Reading records should be made routinely for all children, but especially for emergent and early developing readers. Two reading records per month are the absolute minimum for children at these levels. Frequent records help us to adjust the

FIGURE 6.19
Form for recording reading record showing cueing strategies.

Reading Record

Name _____ Date _____

Title of Text _____ Level _____

# Words: _____	**Fluency Rate**	**Accuracy Rate**	**Comprehension/Retelling**
# Errors: _____	Words correct: _____	_____ Independent (98–100%)	_____ Complete, unaided
# Self-corrections: _____	Time: _____	_____ Instructional (90–97%)	_____ Complete, but aided
Self-Correction Rate _____:_____	Words correct/ minute: _____ Expression: _____	_____ Frustration (less than 90%)	_____ Partially complete
			_____ Incomplete

Analysis of Errors   **Information Used:**   M = Meaning   S/L = Structure/Language   V = Visual

Error/Original Word	Information Used			Self-Corrected	Information Used		
	M	S/L	V		M	S/L	V

Miscues that are counted:

Substitution—Child reads a word differently than the printed text.

✓ ✓ ✓ ✓ three/there ✓ ✓ ✓ ✓

Omission—Child leaves out a word printed in the text.

✓ ✓ ✓ ✓ ✓ ✓ ✓ (little) ✓

Insertion—Child adds a word or words that are not in the printed text.

✓ ✓ ✓ ✓ ✓ ✓ the/∧ ✓ ✓ ✓

Teacher Tells—Child appeals to the teacher for help, teacher first responds, "Try it," child is unable to respond, then teacher tells.

✓ T/upon ✓ ✓ ✓ ✓ ✓ ✓ ✓

Try That Again—Child becomes completely lost in a section of text, teacher brackets passage that has caused the problem and says, "Try that again." The whole passage is coded as TTA and counted as one miscue. Any additional miscues that are made in the rereading are marked with the usual codes. Miscues from the first reading are ignored.

TTA
[✓ upon ② the/time tree/there sc was/were the/three ✓ duck/ducks]

Miscues that are NOT counted:

Repetition—Child repeats a word or phrase. This usually indicates that they have lost the meaning or they are using rereading as a strategy to figure out an unknown word. One over or under the text line is used for each repetition.

R ✓ ✓ ✓ ✓ ✓ ✓ ✓ ✓ ✓

Self-Correction—Child corrects own miscue *without* assistance. The original miscue is recorded but does not count.

✓ ✓ ✓ ✓ three/there sc ✓ ✓ ✓ ✓

Teacher Encourages—Child stops reading at point of unknown word, may or may not appeal for help, teacher encourages but does not tell, saying "try it," E (encourage) is recorded, child response is recorded.

✓ E/upon ✓ ✓ ✓ ✓ ✓ ✓ ✓

FIGURE 6.20
Marking an unscripted running record.

FIGURE 6.21
Sample form for unscripted reading record.

Reading Record

Name _____   Date _____

Title of Text _____   Level _____

| # Words: _____

 # Errors: _____

 # Self-corrections: _____

 Self-Correction Rate
 _____ : _____ | **Fluency Rate**

 Words correct: _____

 Time: _____

 Words correct/
   minute: _____

 Expression: _____ | **Accuracy Rate**

 _____ Independent
   (98–100%)

 _____ Instructional
   (90–97%)

 _____ Frustration (less
   than 90%) | **Comprehension/Retelling**

 _____ Complete,
   unaided

 _____ Complete,
   but aided

 _____ Partially
   complete

 _____ Incomplete |

Analysis of Errors   E = Errors   SC = Self-Corrections

                Information Used: M = Meaning S/L = Structure/Language V = Visual

Page	Title:	E	SC	Analyze Errors			Analyze Self-Correction		
				M	S/L	V	M	S/L	V

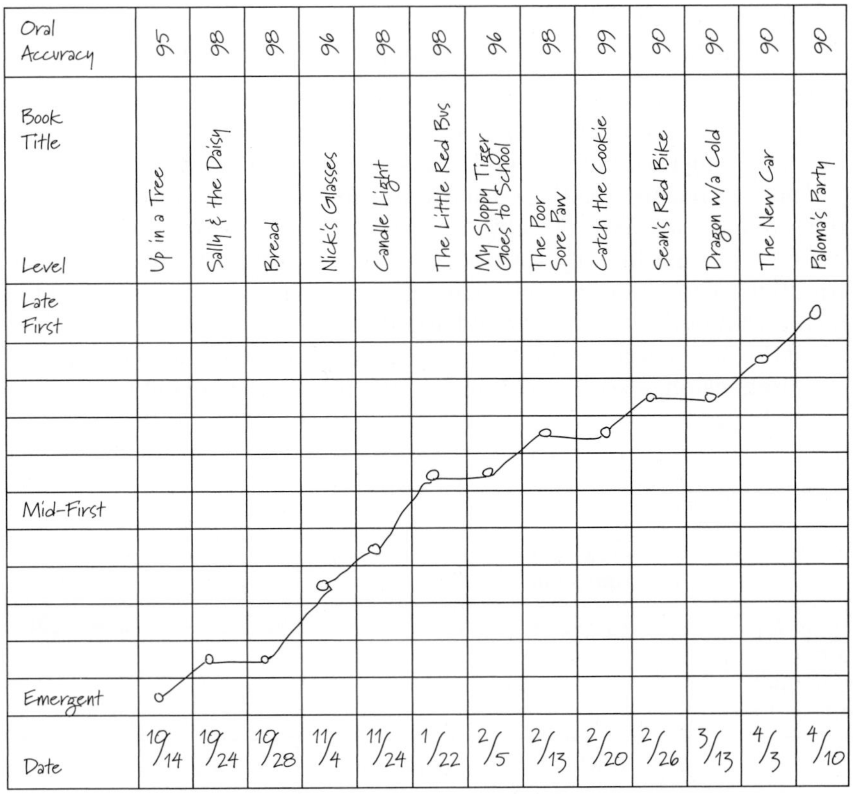

	Up in a Tree	Sally & the Daisy	Bread	Nick's Glasses	Candle Light	The Little Red Bus	My Sloppy Tiger Goes to School	The Poor Sore Paw	Catch the Cookie	Sean's Red Bike	Dragon w/a Cold	The New Car	Paloma's Party
Oral Accuracy	95	98	98	96	98	98	96	98	99	90	90	90	90
Book Title / **Level**													
Late First													
Mid-First													
Emergent													
Date	10/14	10/24	10/28	11/4	11/24	1/22	2/5	2/13	2/20	2/26	3/13	4/3	4/10

FIGURE 6.22 A year-at-a-glance reading record.

composition of guided reading groups, as well as the level of texts we select for guided reading, and ultimately independent reading.

Charting changes in children's reading levels helps us see the ways in which children are and are not making progress. The chart should show the date of the reading record, the level of the text, and the oral accuracy rate of the child's reading. A sample for a child in first grade is shown in Figure 6.22. The reading levels are adjusted to reflect the appropriate levels for the individual child.

Assessing Fluency

Fluency is likely to occur when reading functions are fairly automatic. The indicators of fluency are the ability to read an unfamiliar text orally with:

- 🍎 Accuracy (98% or better word recognition),
- 🍎 Speed (depends on grade level, see Figure 6.20),
- 🍎 Expression (natural intonation as when speaking), and
- 🍎 Comprehension (75% or better as indicated by a sufficient retelling, unaided and aided).

Appropriate fluency rates to work toward by the end of each grade are:

- 🍎 first grade, 30–60 words/minute;
- 🍎 second grade, 70–100 words/minute;

🍎 third grade, 80–110 words/minute;

🍎 fourth grade, 100–140 words/minute. (Rasinski, 2004)

In addition to fluency rate, it is also appropriate to evaluate the quality of a child's fluent reading. Pinnell et al. (1995) developed a scale that is quite useful for evaluating the quality of children's fluency (see Figure 6.23).

Successive oral readings of a text are an excellent way to identify the factors that are most influencing a child's fluency. A tape recording of each reading can help the teacher identify specific aspects of a child's reading that may be contributing to nonfluent reading. The tape recordings can also be used to communicate with both parent and child about progress in fluency.

If the first reading is not fluent considering accuracy, speed, expression, and comprehension, a second reading should follow immediately. The child should

FIGURE 6.23
Rubric to evaluate the quality of a reader's fluency.

	Phrasing	Expression	Pacing
Level 1	• reads word-by-word • Occasional two- or three-phrasing, but may not preserve meaningful syntax	• lacks expressive interpretation	• reads excessively slow
Level 2	• two-word phrase groups with some three- and four-word groupings • word groupings may seem awkward and unrelated to context	• small portion is read with expressive interpretation	• reads significant sections of text excessively slow or fast
Level 3	• reads primarily in three- and four-word phrase groups • some smaller groupings may be present • majority of phrasings are appropriate and preserve the syntax of the author	• little or no expressive interpretation • attempts to read expressively • some text is read with expression	• generally reads at appropriate pace
Level 4	• reads primarily larger, meaningful phrase groups • some regressions, repetitions, and deviations from the text may be present, but do not detract from the overall structure of the text • preserves author's syntax	• some or most of text is read with expressive interpretation	• reads at an appropriate pace

be asked to reread the text to see if he or she can improve fluency. In this reading it is important to observe the relationship between fluency indicators for the two readings. Up to two more rereadings may be warranted to determine which factors may be providing the greatest hindrance to the child's fluency. Observations made during these rereadings enable the teacher to make informed decisions concerning the instructional strategies that would be most beneficial for the child.

Keeping Accurate Records

Records of observations of children's performance in reading also help to focus attention on areas of support that we should provide to individual children. Notes remind teachers of specific behaviors on which to focus. Notes are also helpful for conferencing with parents about a child's progress. Figure 6.24 provides a sample record for noting growth in reading behaviors during guided and independent reading.

RESPECTING DIVERSITY THROUGH GUIDED READING

Children Vary in Their Reading Interests

The school will need an extensive collection of sets of books, as well as various levels of basal reading materials from which to select guided reading texts. Motivation to read is an important factor in a child's willingness to learn from text. The interests of the group must be considered. Linking guided reading to class study of a topic, literary element, or author can enhance interest in reading particular texts.

Children Vary in Reading Ability

Regardless of socioeconomic levels and background experiences, children vary in their ability to deal with print. The diversity that exists in children's ability to decode and process print in guided reading groups must be considered when selecting a text that is appropriate for a specific group of children. Remember that instructional-level text provides some, but not too much, challenge for students, enabling them to learn from their experiences in the guided reading group. Making records of children reading within a group provide added information about particular children's use of skills and strategies.

Text Can Influence Comprehension

The structure and format of texts can affect the comprehension of struggling readers and English language learners. As teachers consider the diversity of our students, especially their facility and confidence in using English for learning, it is important to carefully examine the texts selected for guided reading. For all students to be successful in reading at their true instructional level, teachers

FIGURE 6.24
Record of reading
behaviors.

Observations of Growth in Reading Behaviors

Name _____

Date _____ Grade _____

Attitudes   Notes:

- demonstrates interest/response
- participates in discussions
- chooses to read

Thinks at different levels: Notes:

- recalls explicit information
- makes inferences
- thinks critically, makes judgments
- thinks creatively/responds personally

Uses Literary Knowledge: Notes:

- follows the plot
- understands characters
- describes setting
- identifies point of view
- infers theme
- uses knowledge of genre

Uses Knowledge of Information Text: Notes:

- identifies relevant details
- identifies main idea
- follows sequence
- understands compare/contrast
- understands cause/effect

Use Strategies to Make Meaning: Notes:

- anticipates/predicts before reading
- uses illustrations to make meaning
- anticipates/predicts during reading
- reads with a purpose in mind
- monitors/changes thinking while reading
- can locate important ideas in text

Repairs Breakdown in Meaning: Notes:

- notices when reading does not make sense
- makes an attempt to repair meaning
  - searches illustration
  - rereads/reads on text
  - uses visual cues to check meaning

Shows Signs of Independence: Notes:

- selects appropriate texts
- reads fluently
- sustains own reading
- reads silently

must evaluate the ways in which authors use words and the ways that publishers format texts to communicate with the reader, and how those characteristics interact with each particular child's knowledge and skill in using English for learning.

Making Connections . . .

As you reflect on the content of this chapter, what ideas do you have about helping children to refine their skills and strategies for decoding words, comprehending text, and continuing to develop fluency? What do you think will be most important for you to consider as you prepare to teach guided reading groups? Record your thinking in a reflective journal. Share your thinking with your peers.

C H A P T E R

7

Independent Reading and Reader's Workshop: Encouraging Independence

Adding to our literacy framework . . .

	Reading Aloud and Guided Literature Study	
Shared Reading	**Balanced and Integrated Literacy Framework**	Shared and Interactive Writing
Guided Reading and Guided Literature Study		Guided Writing and Writer's Workshop
Independent Reading and Reader's Workshop		Independent Writing
	Word Study	

In this chapter, we learn about . . .

- Setting up a reading environment that supports and encourages effective independent reading
- Organizing and maintaining a reader's workshop that enhances children's independence as readers

Looking into Classrooms . . .

Lon knows that the independent reading levels of his second-grade students span from first grade to fourth grade. How did Lon identify the level at which each child could function independently in text? During the first few weeks of school Lon listened to each child read a variety of texts at various levels. He made careful records of each child's reading, which was a difficult task. Lon had to use precious minutes when the majority of children were at recess or structured work times, when children were occupied and he could evaluate a student or two. Slowly over several weeks, Lon came to have a general idea of where each of his children was functioning.

All of the children in Lon's second-grade classroom read independently for 20 to 30 minutes every day. He takes great care to help children learn how to select books that are "just right" for them, books that present a little challenge but not too much. Lon continually builds the classroom library and guided reading group book tubs (plastic tubs filled with familiar books and unfamiliar books of similar levels) to have ample materials from which children can select independent reading material.

Over the course of the school year, Lon teaches short lessons about selecting books that fit independent reading—books that allow children to read fluently and enjoy the chosen text. A number of children still read orally, whereas some children have begun to read silently, so SSR (sustained silent reading) isn't exactly silent. During daily independent reading, Lon moves around the room, sitting briefly by a number of focus children, and listens in on what is being read. He uses this time to assess the match between child and text and observe each child's independent fluency.

DOWN THE HALL . . .

The children in Karen's third/fourth-grade classroom are just beginning the day's reader's workshop. Karen teaches a short mini-lesson about how readers often have to adjust the pace of what they read to the difficulty of the text. The class is engaged in individual reading of books related to a science unit about animal groups (e.g., mammals, birds, fish, reptiles). After the mini-lesson, a period of quiet reading begins. Karen also reads during this time.

After about 10 minutes, she begins to meet with individual readers in conferences to catch up on where they are in their progress as readers of expository text. During the conferences Karen learns a great deal about children's individual preferences in reading, the level of engagement they have with their books, their effective use of reading strategies, and their ability to express their thoughts in literature logs. Today Karen will meet with four students for about 5 to 8 minutes each.

After the conferences Karen will mingle with the children as they read, make literature log entries, and work on personal projects, all the time observing carefully as they complete "work time" that is associated with the reader's workshop. To end the 60-minute period the class comes together to share what is happening in their books and plan for the next day.

BUILDING A THEORY BASE . . .

Time for independent reading in school should not be considered a frill! Research clearly demonstrates that wide reading in meaningful connected text improves reading achievement (Taylor, Frye, & Maruyama, 1990). The amount of time children spend reading (Anderson, Wilson, & Fielding, 1992) and the availability of books (Morrow & Weinstein, 1986) are excellent predictors of their reading achievement.

WHAT IS INDEPENDENT READING?

Independent reading occurs when children are provided blocks of uninterrupted time to immerse themselves in texts of their own choosing as well as texts selected by their teacher. In a primary-grade classroom, independent reading time often follows guided reading and provides opportunity for rereading of guided reading or other familiar texts. Independent reading also occurs when children are individually engaged with text that is easily read without the assistance of the teacher and presents little challenge in word recognition and comprehension.

Independent reading has been included in school reading programs for well over 40 years. It was first called *uninterrupted sustained silent reading* by Lyman Hunt in the 1960s, but is now known by other acronyms such as:

- sustained silent reading (SSR),
- drop everything and read (DEAR),
- daily independent reading time (DIRT),

- sustained quiet uninterrupted reading time (SQUIRT), and
- positive outcomes while enjoying reading (POWER).

It is based on the premise that reading is a skill that requires extensive practice. Independent reading can be the component of the reading program that gives children the opportunity to transfer and apply isolated skills in a pleasurable, independent experience (Gambrell, 1978).

The amount of time students are engaged in silent reading in school may be more important than time spent reading outside of school (Taylor et al., 1990). Research suggests that the amount of independent silent reading that children do in school is significantly related to gains in reading achievement (Anderson, Hiebert, Scott, & Wilkinson, 1985). However, these researchers go on to note that most students spend very little school time engaged in silent reading—an average of only about 7 minutes a day in the primary grades and about 15 minutes in the intermediate grades. Students who do read more typically attain higher achievement scores on standardized reading tests such as the National Asessment of Educational Progress (NAEP: Donahue, Voelkl, Campbell, & Mazzeo, 1999).

It is during daily independent reading that teachers have their best opportunity to evaluate children's reading development. What children demonstrate during independent reading, without teacher assistance, are the skills and strategies that are truly their own and under their control. Independent reading is when children can teach us a great deal about who they are as readers. It is also through independent reading that teachers can evaluate the effectiveness of their instruction.

Don Holdaway (1984) states: "Traditional practice assumes that independence is a step to be reached after learning to read rather than an integral process within early learning" (p. 5). Instead, we view independent reading as an integral part of a balanced literacy program right from the start. Children must be provided daily blocks of time to practice reading skills and strategies they are learning, as well as time to peruse books to learn about what they like most as readers.

A quality independent reading program requires a classroom library that is diverse and appealing. In addition, teachers must help children learn to select appropriate texts. Finally, independent reading requires scheduled blocks of time in the day that help children learn how to sustain themselves in their reading.

WHAT IS READER'S WORKSHOP?

Independent reading can also be used as the center of a balanced literacy program. Historically, this type of reading program has been referred to as individualized or personalized reading (Veatch, 1959). Currently, the term *reader's workshop* (Hagerty, 1992; Routman, 1991) or *reading workshop* (Orehovec & Alley, 2004) is used. In this text we use the term *reader's workshop*.

Drawing upon the ideas of those who advocate the study of quality children's literature (Atwell, 1998; Five, 1988; Hagerty, 1992; Hansen, 1987; Raphael & McMahon, 1994), a reading workshop might include the following components:

- time,
- choice,

🍎 response,

🍎 community, and

🍎 structure.

Time

For reader's workshop to be successful teachers must commit blocks of time for reading, particularly silent reading, because of the belief that children learn to read by reading (Holdaway, 1980). When time for daily independent reading is predictable, children realize that they will not be hurried and can read in a more natural way, just like adults who enjoy pleasure reading (Hagerty, 1992). Ample time for browsing and selecting books must also be provided. Time for personal reflection is also an important part of the time devoted to reader's workshop.

Choice

Advocates of reader's workshop recognize the role of personal motivation to read in the process of making meaning (Holdaway, 1980). Learning to make good personal choices for reading requires practice and knowledge of the possibilities in literature. In reader's workshop, choice is a joint responsibility between child and teacher.

Children must come to know themselves as readers, as well as their personal preferences in reading. Teachers must learn about children's interests and provide quality literature and numerous reading opportunities for them to discover the wide range of possibilities. Unlike guided reading selections at a student's instructional reading level, reader's workshop selections are often at a student's independent reading level.

Response

Reader's workshop encourages readers to explore and extend their personal responses to literature as a part of becoming independent readers. Reader-response theory (Rosenblatt, 1978) suggests that it is a reader's personal response to literature that encourages that reader to return to literature experiences. Response comes from the reader; personal response can be encouraged. . . but not controlled. . . by an outside force.

Community

Interaction and collaboration are important in learning (Johnson, 1981; Slavin, Madden, Karweit, Dolan, & Wasik 1991; Vygotsky, 1962). Sharing sessions and encouraging cooperation during work time provide opportunities for children to learn to depend on each other and to learn from each other. The teacher is a model for how to listen to and respect the ideas of others. A sense of community in a classroom creates the feeling that everyone in the room is a teacher and a learner with knowledge to share (Hagerty, 1992). Much of what individuals know they teach themselves or learn by observing and interacting informally with more knowledgeable others. In reader's workshop, children teach each other what they know if given the opportunity and an environment that supports risk-taking.

Structure

Reader's workshop requires a well-planned organization and consistent management that children can count on (Hagerty, 1992). The teacher's role is one of guide and facilitator, anticipating the types and degree of support children will need to become independent readers. Some teacher-guided instruction is provided to the whole class, as well as small groups. Individual conferences with children are used to monitor and evaluate their progress.

Individualized reading programs, such as reader's workshop, use independent reading of literature as the primary focus with group work as the supplement. Because children are on their own much of the time, individualized reading is more appropriate for children who are moving into the transitional reader stage.

MOVING TOWARD INDEPENDENCE

Teachers support children's strategy development in order for them to become independent readers. Next to being read to, independent reading is the most important way that children can spend their time if they are to become fluent, competent readers (Center for the Study of Reading, 1990). Regardless of the organization of one's literacy program, independent reading should be a daily occurrence in the classroom.

What are the benefits of independent reading?

- 🍎 *Fluency*—Reading performance improves when students read and reread substantial amounts of text (Allington, 1977, 1984; Dowhower, 1987; Herman, 1985).
- 🍎 *Vocabulary*—One third or more of vocabulary growth can be accounted for by independent reading (Center for the Study of Reading, 1990; Nagy, Herman, & Anderson, 1985).
- 🍎 *Background Knowledge*—Reading widely exposes children to many new ideas and helps to build schema about the world (Anderson & Pearson, 1984; Bartlett, 1932).
- 🍎 *Motivation*—A child's attitude toward reading also improves through self-selected independent reading (Tunnell & Jacobs, 1989).

It is fluent independent reading that typically becomes the motivator for the development of personal reading. Holdaway (1980) tells us that in the acquisition of independent skills, children become their own monitors and critics. They practice repeatedly to gain control over the task and find pleasure and satisfaction in being able to perform it. Their practice is usually at a level that provides little challenge so skills can become automatic. Children must have some control over reading tasks to let their natural desire to monitor and critique their own performance be developed.

Making Connections . . .

Make an attempt to observe a period of independent reading in a primary-grade classroom. What do you observe? Are all children engaged? If not, what do you think prevents them from being fully engaged? Interview the classroom teacher to better understand if/how the teacher prepares students for independent reading.

PUTTING THEORY INTO PRACTICE . . .

 ## PROMOTE A READING ATMOSPHERE

A "reading atmosphere" should permeate everything that is done in the classroom, from the area devoted to a classroom library to the way that independent reading time is treated. The classroom library should invite children to want to read. It does not have to be a large area, but it must be inviting. Throughout the school year, children can help to decide how to make the library area an attractive place where they want to spend time. Involving children in the planning increases their sense of ownership in the classroom.

Consider locating the library near a wall area or bulletin board so that a display of books can be set up about a featured author, a special day such as Earth Day, or other topic of study. Something from the display can be highlighted each day, inviting children to share what they are discovering about the books. Reading aloud from the selected books also increases children's interest in exploring the books independently or with a partner. Books can also be featured in other areas of the classroom, such as next to the science inquiry center or near the theme study area.

Book talks are a good way to introduce new texts that are being placed in the library. Just because great books are displayed in the classroom does not mean that children will automatically become independent readers. Children's interest in books can be encouraged by giving book talks, special introductions for new books. As a part of each read-aloud time, plan to give a short book talk about a new book. Tell a few highlights from a book, give a brief summary, or pose an interesting situation that could be explored by reading the book. For chapter books, read part of an exciting event aloud as an enticement. Acquaint children with books, then make then available. Children also enjoy giving book talks about their favorite books. Suggested guidelines for book talks are provided in Figure 7.1.

A reading atmosphere includes physical conditions for reading. Most adults prefer a comfortable, relaxed atmosphere for reading. Children are no different. When they are reading independently, consider allowing children to go anywhere in the room that is comfortable for them, within reason. It may take a while for them to become committed to independent reading, but it will come— with much patience and support.

Tips for Effective Book Talks
- Talk about books that you like or your students would like.
- Write your main points on a sticky note for a reminder.
- Be informal and relaxed.
- Be brief, about 2 to 3 minutes for the book talk.
- Show the book and some illustrations if applicable.
- Tell something interesting about the author and/or illustrator.
- Tell something interesting about the book, but do not summarize the book or give away the ending.
- Read aloud an engaging part that makes the reader want to know more.
- Make comparisons to other books that students might already know.

FIGURE 7.1
Tips for effective book talks.

Book Boxes or Tubs

To facilitate independent reading with emergent and developing readers, we can create book boxes or tubs for each guided reading group. As a group completes the guided reading of a book in Katarina's first-grade classroom, for example, she places copies of that book in the group's designated book box or tub. Everyone in that guided reading group is familiar with all of the books in the box. Children know they can independently read any of the books. Following daily guided reading, Katarina asks children to independently reread books from the box for 15 to 20 minutes. Rereading these familiar books builds fluency and confidence.

As new books are added to the book boxes, the oldest books are typically removed. It is important to keep enough variety of titles to accommodate the range of interests of children in each group. Book boxes or tubs can be stored near the classroom library for easy access during the daily independent reading block. Books of a similar level can also be added to "freshen" the choices that children have.

Teach Children How to Select Books

Many children need help to learn how to self-select books for independent reading that are at an appropriate reading level. One day after returning from a trip to the school library to check out individual books, I encouraged my first-grade children to talk about how and why they selected a particular book. What a surprise I had when Tracy said, "I always pick blue books, because blue is my favorite color." Then I realized that I had not done enough to help Tracy know how to select a book that was "right" for her.

Two primary issues involved with selecting books are interest and difficulty. For interest, work with the librarian and plan with children before a library visit. Knowing children's interests, teachers can guide children to areas of the library where particular books are housed. It may be helpful to make a list of children's interests for the librarian, asking that a variety of books be highlighted during the library visit. Before leaving the classroom, get children into the habit of planning for that library visit. Discuss the type of books they might like to look for that week. Beginning to plan before the visit to the library can make the short library period more productive for selecting books of interest.

The Five-Finger Test	The Finger Guide
1. Choose a book you think you would like to read.	1 — This book is OK
2. Find a page of text somewhere in the middle of the book. Find a page with lots of words and few or no pictures.	2 — Still OK
3. Read the page aloud or in a whisper so you can hear the places where you have difficulty.	3 — Could be a bit hard to understand
4. Each time you come to a word you don't know, hold up one finger.	4 — Probably too difficult to read and understand
	5 — Choose another book

Difficulty level of books is another issue in selection. When children select a book they think they would like to read, encourage them to try it out first to see how it suits them. Teach children to use the *five-finger test* (see Figure 7.2). If children are highly motivated to read a particular book, even if the book might be difficult, they should be allowed to try. Children cannot become independent if adults always select their books or try to control their choices.

It can be worthwhile to have discussions with the children about reading books that are easy, medium, and hard. The term "just right" might have more meaning for children. As in the story of Goldilocks and the Three Bears, teachers want children to feel that their books are "just right." Teachers can also tell children how books are selected for guided reading and book boxes, and why it is good to have a lot of practice in books that are "just right." Books that are just right are books from which children can learn.

Children should be encouraged to share their book choices and how they make the choice. It is helpful for the children to hear their classmates' views about the pleasure derived from selecting books that are just right. Place a chart on the wall of the classroom (see Figure 7.3) with questions that will help children check themselves to see if a book is just right. Discuss the idea of "too easy," "just right," and "too hard" throughout the school year so that children will see how a book that is too hard at the beginning of the year may be just right at a later time.

Ensure Adequate Reading Time

Acquiring skill involves practice over time. How much practice time do children need to develop independence in reading? The amount will vary. Some children will practice more reading outside of school. Some children will not require as much reading practice as others. Some children may slow their own progress because they continue to select books that are actually too challenging, such as when they want to read books at the same level as a friend.

How can teachers respond to children's varying needs for reading time?

🍎 Set a time each day for everyone to read independently.

🍎 Provide flexible time for choosing independent reading during work periods.

Too Easy Books	Just Right Books	Too Hard Books
1. Have I read this book many times before? 2. Do I understand the story very well without much effort? 3. Do I know and understand almost every word? 4. Can I read it smoothly and fluently without much practice or effort?	1. Is this book new to me? 2. Do I understand most of the book? 3. Are there a few words on each page that I don't recognize or know the meaning of instantly? 4. Can someone help me with the book if I hit a tough spot?	1. Are there more than a few words on a page that I don't recognize or know the meaning of? 2. Am I confused about what is happening in most of the book? 3. Am I struggling with the words when I read and does it sound choppy? 4. Is everyone busy and unable to help me if I hit a tough spot?

FIGURE 7.3
The Goldilocks test.

As early as kindergarten, time should be set aside each day for children to be engaged independently with books and other forms of print.

- 🍎 Emergent readers will probably begin with 5 minutes and slowly progress to 10 to 15 minutes of independent reading at a time.
- 🍎 Developing readers may also begin with 5 minutes, but should work toward 15 to 30 minutes of sustained reading at a time.
- 🍎 Transitional readers may begin with 10 minutes of sustained reading and work up to as much as 30 to 45 minutes at a time.

Sustained independent reading requires children to build stamina for reading. Children who have not had the opportunity for sustained reading will need patient guidance to learn how readers sustain their own reading. Build independent reading time into the school day by making it a regular activity choice during instructional blocks such as reading/language arts or theme activities.

Devoting instructional time to independent reading allows children who either want or need more practice time to have it. Children can read at their desks, in the library area, or at other designated places in the classroom. Remember that in the hustle and bustle of the school day it is easy to let independent reading time slip away. To begin to equalize differences between children's background experiences with books, provide time for children to read in school.

Making Connections . . .

Make a point of visiting several primary-grade classrooms to see how teachers arrange for independent reading. Are library corners inviting and organized? Are books given prominent places? Do children have opportunities to talk about selecting new books? What is the teacher's view of the place of independent reading in the curriculum?

PLAN FOR INDEPENDENT READING

Make a Predictable Time to Read

Lon, for example, chooses to have an independent reading block each day when all children are reading independently. Because independent reading time occurs every day in Lon's classroom, children anticipate having time to read books of their choosing and they settle into the routine fairly quickly, During this time he frees himself from other instructional activities so that he can move about the room, observing children and listening in on the reading of several "focus" children.

Time for independent reading in the primary grades can be provided in a variety of ways during the school day:

- A block of time (20 to 30 minutes) for sustained independent reading when the entire class is reading self-selected books,
- A choice during independent or small-group work time,
- A period of time for book boxes or tubs for rereading of guided reading texts, or
- Reader's workshop, or individualized reading, that involves self-selected reading as the center of instruction.

Meet the Range of Reading Levels and Interests

Most children in Lon's classroom have between first-grade and fourth-grade independent reading levels, so Lon must be concerned with having a variety of appropriate-level materials. Children in his classroom who read at second-grade level and above are typically engaged over a period of several days in a chapter book or information books.

Lon is most concerned that children who read below second-grade level have books that are truly independent for them. He urges these children to reread familiar books to build fluency and confidence, especially books introduced in guided reading. In addition, he helps children identify unfamiliar books that are at approximately the same level as the familiar texts. These texts will provide some new challenges for children but still allow them to draw upon familiar strategies to make meaning and check their understanding and ability to decode less familiar words.

Build an Inviting Classroom Library

If children are to value their independent reading time, a wide and diverse collection of books must be available to them. Children bring a variety of interests into the classroom. Will they find books to feed those interests there and/or in the school library? Children come with varied reading abilities. Will they find appropriate materials to fit their independent reading level?

Ten books per child is a good start for a classroom library. More books are preferable. To develop the classroom library, we can check out books from both the school and public libraries. These books can usually be kept in the classroom for about a month.

For children who are reading picture books primarily, books will need to be circulated more frequently than for children reading primarily chapter books. When it is time for new books, involve the children in deciding which books should be renewed and which should be changed for new texts.

Reasonably priced paperback books are also available from mail-order book clubs such as Scholastic and Trumpet. One suggestion to implement at the beginning of the school year is to ask parents if they are willing to buy and donate a few books to the classroom library from book club orders during the year. Most parents are very willing, especially because the books are relatively inexpensive when compared with bookstore prices.

For information about mail-order book clubs, visit *http://www.scholastic.com* or *http://www. trumpetclub.com.*

Making Connections . . .

Gather information about school book clubs and other ways to acquire books in your community. Find out what types of budgets teachers and schools have for building classroom and school libraries.

Observe Children's Progress

Each day Lon focuses on the literacy development of several of his children, making notes about their progress in reading and writing. Today, he particularly watches Darren and Inez, his "focus children" for the day, noting how they settle into this independent time. While he hears several children read aloud from self-selected books, Lon spends a little added time with Darren and Inez, making a record of their independent reading (see Reading Records in Chapter 6).

When Lon sits beside a particular child, that child knows to begin reading orally wherever he or she may be in the text. As he listens to a child read aloud he makes notes about miscues—reading that does not match the text. He notes the correct words from the text and the child's mistaken responses. He estimates the number of correct words and then compares the number of correct words with the number of miscues to determine an approximate difficulty level of the text. Lon wants independent reading to be in texts in which children accurately read 98% to 100% of the words and understand most all of the ideas.

After listening to a portion of text, Lon asks open-ended questions to elicit the child's general response to the text, how the child comprehends the text, what the child predicts might happen next, and the like. Listening to children read aloud in their chosen texts helps Lon know whether children are selecting texts that are truly independent for them and whether children independently apply the skills and strategies he has taught them.

If independence is to thrive in the classroom, teachers must plan for independent reading just as they plan other instruction in literacy programs. Children know by the way that independent reading is treated whether it is really important.

READER'S WORKSHOP: INDEPENDENT READING AS THE CENTERPIECE

In a reader's workshop children spend extensive amounts of time reading independently, keeping records and responses for their reading in a response log, and conferencing individually with a teacher. Figure 7.4 provides an overview of reader's workshop. Teachers who use reader's workshop as a focal point of their literacy program face a number of issues:

- helping children select literature at an independent reading level,
- providing ample time for silent reading,
- carefully monitoring children's growth through teacher-child conferences,
- encouraging exploration of literature through response activities, and
- providing whole-class and small-group skill/strategy instruction.

Help Children Select Literature

In reader's workshop, children must learn to select books that are appropriate for their interests and reading level. Karen (one of the teachers in the opening

FIGURE 7.4
Organizing time for independent literature study.

Whole Class: 10%–15% of time	• Teaching Points—Mini-lessons Procedures Literary knowledge Reading skills & strategies • Book talks • Planning for the day
Work Time: 70% of time Silent reading (30%) Other activities (40%)	• Silent reading period • Individual conferences • Response activities Literature log Art Related reading Drama • Individual help/questions • Flexible skill groups • Making new selections
Whole Class: 15%–20% of time	• Sharing • Planning for next day

vignette) helps her third-grade children learn to effectively select books in a variety of ways:

- Reading aloud from a wide assortment of books provides children with knowledge of the topics and styles of writing in different genres. Children also become acquainted with the work of various authors and the possibilities that books offer.

- Book talks, given by teachers or other children, can provide just enough information about a book to motivate a child to read. Librarians can also give book talks during routine library visits to inform children about new books that have recently been acquired. Book talks should give an overview of a book without giving the plot away.

- Author studies provide opportunity to focus on the work of one author and can link a child to a series of books for extended reading. A few of an author's books can be read aloud, with others displayed in a prominent place in the room. Sharing information about the author's life, especially how that life was reflected in the author's work, can be of particular interest to children. Becoming aware of an author's work also helps children learn where to look for books in a library. Information about children's authors and illustrators can be obtained from a variety of Web sites.

Visit *http://www.cbcbooks.org/html/aboutauthors.htm* or *http://www.ucalgary.ca/~dkbrown/authors.html* for author and illustrator information.

Sharing personal responses to books along with personal projects completed during independent work time can interest other children in reading a particular book. Karen, for example, knows that when a sense of community has been developed in a classroom, children will place importance on the views of their peers and will allow those views to influence selection of new books for reading. Children who happen to read the same book can also form small sharing groups during the work time to talk about their responses.

Karen understands that making a commitment to a book is also a part of the selection process. In their reading log, children should make a dated record of the title of each selection they make. This list serves as a chronicle of a child's progress through books. If a child abandons a book, he or she should explain why in the log. Making such a record encourages children to view selection as an important part of reading.

Promote Silent Reading

To become independent, a reader must develop "the ability to persevere at a personal pace that makes efficient use of current skills" (Holdaway, 1980, p. 34). Perseverance requires sustained practice. In this way, independent reading becomes a reflection of reading proficiency (Fielding, Wilson, & Anderson, 1984).

Karen, for example, plans block of time each day in which only silent reading is permitted, to enable children to settle into their reading. Independent reading can extend beyond the "quiet time" if children so choose, because independent reading is also self-paced reading. The time that had been devoted to sustained silent reading (SSR) can become a part of the reader's workshop. Combining SSR time with independent literature study helps to extend the amount of time available for sustained reading.

Conference with Children

Karen meets with four to five children each day for individual conferences to monitor children's progress. Conferences are short meetings, about 5 to 10 minutes, between teacher and child that provide time for open dialogue about a book the child is reading or has just completed. Conferences are intended to give children an opportunity to share their personal responses to their reading. In addition, conferences are intended to give us an opportunity to personally monitor a child's progress, provide guidance where needed, diagnose difficulties, and encourage the use of particular skills or strategies (Hagerty; 1992; Holdaway, 1980). Karen knows that conferences are not the time for instruction. Mini-lessons and skill groups are better suited to that purpose (see later section for discussion of mini-lessons). Karen uses conferences to learn about how children are handling the books they have chosen.

Conferences may begin during the quiet reading period at the beginning of a reader's workshop and extend into the activity period. For example, Karen schedules conferences on a regular basis, as well as when children request a conference after completing a book. She plans to see three or four scheduled children per day with one or two open slots each day for other children. It is appropriate to spend 30 to 45 minutes each day in conferences because they are central to independent literature study.

What Happens in a Conference?

🍎 The child shares personal responses.

🍎 The teacher probes those responses.

🍎 The child reads the selected passage orally.

🍎 The teacher and child review the literature log.

🍎 The teacher encourages and guides the child's efforts as a reader based on conference dialogue.

🍎 The teacher makes records to monitor the child's progress.

Conferencing with children is an excellent way to learn about them as readers. What can we do to encourage children to share themselves as readers?

Children Share Personal Responses

Karen, for example, opens a conference by asking the child about his or her response to the book. She is accepting of responses. She knows that children's responses are an indication of their level of involvement with the book. She listens carefully not only to *what* the child says, but also to *how* the child talks about the book.

Possible response questions might be:

- How is your book going?
- What is your book about?
- What do you think about your book so far?

Teachers Probe Responses

Based on a child's response to a book, Karen asks thought-provoking questions. She is sensitive to the direction the child sets in the conference because the goal is reader independence. She knows that the teacher's major role during conferences is to help each child take the next step in thinking about the book.

Possible probing questions include:

- What makes you think that?
- Based on what you have told me, what do you think might happen next?
- Why did you choose this book?

Children Read Orally

Once children know how conferences work, they will come prepared to share a part of their book. How to select a part to read can be the topic of a procedural mini-lesson. Children should read aloud a sufficient amount of text that allows them to get in their stride as readers and to show word recognition abilities and fluency. At least once per grading period (four to six times per year), Karen tape-records children's oral reading as a record of their growth. She listens carefully during the reading for miscues, intonation, fluency, and strategies the child is using successfully.

Karen compliments the child on the productive use of strategies during oral reading, saying such things as:

- "I noticed the way that you went back and corrected that word, once you realized it didn't make sense. That's what good readers do."
- "When you read the dialogue, it sounded just like people talking to each other. That is the way that good readers make their reading interesting to others."
- "I noticed the way you emphasized some words. I could tell that you thought they were important and wanted to be sure I heard them."

Then, she probes one aspect that is relevant to the child's selection of a favorite part:

- "Tell me a little about your favorite part."
- "Tell me what you think about . . .
    that character,
    what the character did,
    the conflicts the character is having,
    the impact of who is telling the story."

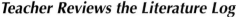

Teacher Reviews the Literature Log

Children should bring their literature response log to each conference sharing so that entries that have been made since the last conference can be reviewed. Children should feel accountable for their entries. Karen, for example, asks children who are scheduled for a conference on a particular day to turn in their log the day before. She reviews their entries so that she can prepare to use the content of the entries during the conference.

Possible questions about the response log entries include:

- How is your response log going?
- What kinds of things do you like to put in your response log?
- How do you choose what to write in your response log?
- Can you tell me a little more about this entry?

Teacher Encourages and Guides

At the end of the conference, Karen makes a suggestion for each child based on observations and impressions of their progress. She focuses on one skill or strategy. The conference is not the only opportunity to make suggestions. Karen tries to remember that the conference is not an instructional time; it is a relaxed time to let children teach about who they are as readers.

Comments to encourage and guide further growth that Karen might say are:

- "As you continue on in this book,
    - you might think about . . .
    - you might try to . . . "
- "As you make entries in your log,
    - you might think about . . .
    - you might try to . . . "
- "When you come to words that you are not sure about,
    - you might think about . . .
    - you might try to . . . "
- "As you choose another book,
    - you might think about . . .
    - you might try to . . . "

When Karen is not conferencing with children, she circulates among the children, providing support and encouragement for their individual endeavors. This is an opportunity to build upon suggestions made in the conferences. This is also a time to continue learning about children as individuals and as readers. Karen makes notes about observations and adds the notes to conference records (see Figure 7.5). She finds it helpful to carry a clipboard for note-making. Some teachers prefer to transfer their notes to the conference record, whereas others prefer to use sheets of computer labels, with 20 to 30 labels on a sheet. If sheets of computer labels are used, write a child's name on each label. When a child's label is filled, peel off the label and place it on the inside flap of a child's reading folder. Each label should be dated. Labels that do not fill as quickly as others can signal that some children are not being watched closely.

FIGURE 7.5
Example of recording observations during work time.

Terra:	Jango:	William:	Ivy:	Chi Chi:
11/12-read all of work time 11/15-helped Ivy with project	11/12-spent 30 minutes selecting book	11/13-book may be too difficult, asking about many words	11/15- sought help, big step!	11/14- sustained reading for 15 minutes, that's good progress

Date	Book Title	Comments
November 17	Stone Fox	fluency increasing, good intonation, improving on multisyllable words, challenging level but more appropriate than last selection

FIGURE 7.6
Example of an open conference entry.

Teacher Makes a Record of Conference

Teachers should keep careful records of conferences. A conference notebook should have space set aside for each child (see Figures 7.6 and 7.7). Immediately following each conference, Karen makes notes about children's behaviors, including:

- 🍎 fluency,
- 🍎 word recognition and self-monitoring,
- 🍎 level of response and comprehension,
- 🍎 ability to select appropriately,
- 🍎 self-pacing, and
- 🍎 self-evaluation.

Independent literature study provides a number of challenges for meeting the needs of each child. At least some portion of the school year, however, should be devoted to having children select their own reading materials. Children can thrive when their personal interests in reading are being met.

FIGURE 7.7
A focused conference entry with prearranged categories for comment.

Date Book Title	Comments
November 17 *Stone Fox*	Response/understanding: _____ _____ _____ Fluency/intonation: _____ _____ _____ Word recognition/self-monitoring: _____ _____ _____ Pacing: _____ _____ Other: _____ _____

 INSTRUCTION IN READER'S WORKSHOP

Instruction is provided through mini-lessons and flexible small groups.

Mini-Lessons

In a mini-lesson, Karen demonstrates the use of a skill or strategy, especially combined with thinking aloud about mental processes. She thinks aloud as an instructional tool to help children learn how readers make the decisions that they do, what information gets considered, and why some possibilities get discarded (Davey, 1983). Examples for mini-lessons are usually drawn from the texts being studied or books that are familiar to all of the children.

At the beginning of using reader's workshop in the classroom, procedures will need to be taught, including book selection, sustaining silent reading, participating in an individual conference, responding to literature, and effective ways to use strategies to extend one's reading skills.

As children gain background experience in reading literature, mini-lessons can become more interactive. Karen, for example, invites children to share their thinking about how to use a skill or strategy. She encourages children to provide support for their thinking. When she opens the mini-lesson for interactions it takes more time to complete the desired task.

Sample Mini-Lesson: Getting Ready for a Reading Conference

Karen might say,

> "We've been having reading conferences for several weeks now and I've noticed that you've been remembering to bring your book and literature log to the conference. That's part of getting ready for a conference.
>
> "Another part of getting ready takes place in your head. When I'm going to conference with you, I think back to our last conference. I think about the things you told me about your book; I look at the notes I made about our conference and I think about the book you were reading. I also think about what I've seen you doing in reading since that last conference and the mini-lessons we've had that might help you enjoy reading your books more. Then I anticipate what you might say to me when we meet. That's what I do in my head.
>
> "When you get ready for a conference with me, you should also spend some time thinking about what will happen in the conference. You'll think about what you want to tell me about your book. Because you know that our conference is also to help you be a better reader, you might think about something I can do to help you enjoy your book the most.
>
> "Tomorrow I will be conferencing with Chi Chi, William, Terra, and Rhonda. Each of you might spend some of your work time today getting your head ready for our conference tomorrow."

As children gain background experience in reading literature, mini-lessons can become more interactive. Karen invites children to share their thinking about how to use a skill or strategy. She encourages children to provide support for their thinking. One caution: When you open the mini-lesson for interactions, make plans for a slightly longer mini-lesson time.

For independent literature study, mini-lessons grow out of our observations during conferences and during children's work time. Karen looks for trends across children by reviewing the notes from observations. Based on her observations she may design either whole-class or small-group instruction. She selects whole-class instruction when the majority of children demonstrate a need for specific support.

Flexible Groups

Flexible groups can extend the ideas that are emphasized in whole-class mini-lessons and provide practice that may be needed by some but not all children. Skills groups serve a limited purpose—to develop a particular skill or knowledge—and then are disbanded. Karen, for example, presents ideas first to the whole class in mini-lessons. When she notices that a number of children are still not using specific literary knowledge or particular reading skills and/or strategies, more extensive small-group work is warranted. Skills groups can fill this need.

Topics for skills groups may be drawn from the lists of suggested mini-lesson in this text, from knowledge of reading processes and children's literature, from the school district's curriculum standards, or from a basal reading series that is in use. Skills group instruction is teacher-led and may resemble small groups used in other patterns of reading instruction. Holdaway (1980) suggests that skills groups should be by invitation, letting children attend if they want help in that particular area.

Example of a Flexible Group: Decoding Multisyllable Words

Imagine that Karen notices a number of children who are experiencing some difficulty with multisyllable words now that they have moved almost exclusively into chapter books. Over a period of several weeks she offers small-group work in strategies for decoding multisyllable words, cross-checking for sources of information to help with decoding and self-monitoring for meaning. She offers these groups only for the children who demonstrate need. Examples for instruction are drawn from what she notices during observations and from books that children are currently reading. Following instruction she observes children to see whether their decoding of multisyllable words shows improvement. Additional instruction is provided for children who continue to demonstrate a need.

Skill/strategy groups are an effective tool for reaching children within their zone of proximal development. Karen focuses her teaching points and observes how children use the instruction she provides.

EXTENDING ENGAGEMENT WITH BOOKS IN READER'S WORKSHOP

Using Literature Response Logs

Each day of literature study, Karen asks children to make some type of entry in their literature response logs. In the early stages of literature study, focus children's entries; later, allow more opportunities for children's choices.

A Literature Response Log May Be:

- a daily reading record that includes date, book title, and pages read,
- a page(s) devoted to words that are of interest or are unfamiliar, and/or
- responses to reading (open, focused, double-entry journals, story frames, dialogue letters, story map, and so on).

Keep a Daily Log of Reading:

- This record can be useful in helping children evaluate the pace of their reading and their ability to persevere with a book (see Figure 7.8).

FIGURE 7.8
Sample daily record log.

Date	Book Title	Pages Read
Nov. 12	Stone Fox	Ch 1, 3–11 in group
Nov. 13		Ch 2 & 3, 12–21 Home– 22–29
Nov. 14		

Interesting Words	Words I Need to Study
Stone Fox	p. 4 explanation
p. 7 harmonica	p. 9 examination
p. 16 hand-and -finger code	p. 16 inspected

FIGURE 7.9
Sample personal word lists.

Make a List of Words from Reading:

🍎 Independence in word recognition means helping children become aware of their ability to work with new words. Word lists can be reviewed in whole-class discussions, in small groups of children who are at similar stages of development of word knowledge, and in individual conferences. Recording page numbers makes it possible to refer to the use of a word in the text (see Figure 7.9).

Responses to Reading:

🍎 The types of entries children make and the time when entries will be made are things the teacher needs to decide. For the most part, focus on retellings, responses, and word study.

Possible Responses Might Include:

🍎 Illustrated retelling,
🍎 Written retelling,
🍎 Story maps,
🍎 Personal responses to content, theme, characters, etc., and
🍎 Illustrated response.

Focus on Words Might Include:

🍎 "Favorite words,"
🍎 "Words I want to learn,"
🍎 "Words I am not sure about," and
🍎 "Phrases I like."

The literature response log is an excellent place to collect words and demonstrate knowledge of individual words. A page in the log can be devoted to words that children want to discuss with others. Entries in the response log can also illustrate children's comfort with using the vocabulary of a specific text:

Example: On page 28 of *Stone Fox,* as Willy and Searchlight practiced for the sled race, Searchlight "forged ahead with such speed . . . "

Independent Book Extensions

Over the period of time that a book is being studied, children should engage in meaningful activities that help them continue to think about a book, for example, the literary element of character. Karen keeps the activities simple. As children become more comfortable with chapter book study, she invites them to make suggestions for extensions. The following list is only a beginning.

- Tape-recorded books for repeated reading and fluency—Tape recordings can be made as teachers read books in preparation for the literature study. Tape-recorded books provide support to less experienced readers.
- Art—Karen provides opportunities for children to share and/or create displays of artistic responses using painting, drawing, collage, crayon resist, or dioramas as a medium for responding to the book or extending into personal experience.
- Drama—When appropriate, Karen encourages children to re-create and respond to books through reader's theater, role-playing, playlets (scenes), puppets, or reader's theater. For chapter books, the dialogue is a natural for making a reader's theater. Karen makes copies of text for children to highlight their spoken parts and decides if a narrator is needed.
- Writing—Children can create personal and/or creative stories or poems as spin-offs from the books they have read. Books made in a variety of shapes evoke interest and should be made available for independent writing.

 ## ASSESSMENT: MONITORING CHILDREN'S GROWTH IN INDEPENDENT READING

Reading Records

As we learned in the assessment section of Chapter 6, making a record of children's reading is an excellent way to monitor children's development of skills and strategies. When children sign up for a reading conference, ask them to identify the text they will share orally during the conference. Make a copy of those pages prior to the conference. Use the copies of text as a scripted reading record to document the accuracy and strategies students use during oral reading of familiar text. Of course, an unscripted reading record is also an option for teachers who feel comfortable with this form. The scripted reading record, however, preserves the context for reviewing patterns of miscues for a particular child.

Periodically, about every 6 to 8 weeks, Karen and Lon make records of students' reading in unfamiliar, independent-level text to document progress in the effective use of skills and strategies. They compare reading records in familiar and unfamiliar text and typically see some differences in word recognition, comprehension, and fluency; but scores for accuracy are still within the instructional range (98% to 100% word recognition, 90% or better comprehension, and appropriate fluency).

Focus Students

Teachers can determine the true impact of instruction by listening to students read during daily independent reading time. Lon focuses on two students each day. During independent reading time he sits down beside a focus child and asks him or her to begin reading orally in the text. If possible, Lon listens to approximately 100 words of text. He is prepared to make an unscripted reading record (see Chapter 6) or he simply records the number and types of miscues (original word/miscue). At an appropriate point in the reading, Lon asks the child how the reading is going, what he or she likes about the text, to make a prediction about what might happen next, or similar questions to get a sense of the level of engagement between the child and the text.

By focusing on two students each day, every child in the class is heard during each month. These records are added to other assessments to provide a more comprehensive picture of where a child actually functions.

Conferences

Records of reading conferences also serve as an excellent assessment of children's progress. During a reading conference Karen probes for children's personal responses to text, as well as general comprehension of text. During a conference children share their responses, read favorite passages orally, share entries in their literature logs, and plan for experiences that will stretch them as readers. Karen keeps careful records of these one-on-one assessment sessions to document children's growth.

Samples of Student Work

Because of the individualized nature of a reader's workshop, it is essential that teachers keep careful records of student's development, including the work that students produce related to the texts they read. Karen has the children keep a "working portfolio" with samples of all work completed related to a particular text. When a text is completed, Karen and the child select examples of "best work" to place in a Literacy Assessment Portfolio that documents student growth in literacy. Entries from the literature log and extension activities enable Karen and the children to see the level of a student's engagement with a text. Samples of work combined with Karen's conference notes provide compelling evidence of a student's growth. Maintaining samples of student work is a form of accountability that Karen believes is essential in an individualized reading program.

RESPECTING DIVERSITY DURING INDEPENDENT READING AND READER'S WORKSHOP

Pursuing Personal Reading Interests

Independent reading provides opportunity for children to pursue personal reading interests in the literature of their choice. Of the different organizational patterns explored in this text, independent reading is the most responsive to children's needs and desires as readers. Pursuing personal interests requires access to a wide range of books, particularly those that reflect the cultural background of the children in the class. Providing for independent choices tells children that a teacher values them as individuals and trusts their judgment. Just as adults come to know their own taste in literature, so can children. Sometimes poor choices will be made, but it is difficult to learn about poor choices if there are few opportunities to practice decision making.

Learning about Oneself as a Reader

Independent reading allows children to learn to pace their own reading. Teachers provide large blocks of time for reading so that through self-pacing, children can find their rhythms as readers. Learning to select one's own books helps individual readers learn to effectively monitor their own reading and to recognize levels of comfort with different types of reading material.

The Continuing Need for Self-Monitoring

Strategic readers develop through many opportunities to monitor their own reading. It is not enough to know what a skill is and how to do it. The real test comes when the reader realizes that now is the time to use a particular skill and knows how to activate and use that skill in a strategic manner. Self-selection of reading material can support the development of self-monitoring. Self-monitoring one's own reading provides opportunity to evaluate personal performance. Independent reading can provide opportunities for children to develop trust in their own judgment and ability to evaluate reading performance.

The Need to Be a Kid-Watcher

When teachers organize whole-class mini-lessons and small-group instruction they should become particularly sensitive to interactions with children. Whole-class instruction makes it more difficult to be keenly aware of what each child is doing or thinking. Developing skill as a "kid-watcher" (Pappas, Kiefer, & Levstik, 1999) becomes vitally necessary. Teachers should challenge themselves to make anecdotal records of interactions with children, and to be especially sensitive to children who are being watched too much because of behavior and others who are not being noticed at all.

In this chapter we have explored a range of ways to engage children in the independent reading of texts, another form of literature study. Literature study has as its goal the appreciation of quality literature. It goes beyond the teaching of reading and writing to engage children in the thoughtful examination of other people's lives. The individualized study of literature is a complement to other components of a balanced and integrated literacy program.

Making Connections . . .

As you reflect on the content of this chapter, what ideas do you have about helping children become independent readers, select appropriate texts, and sustain themselves in meaningful independent reading? What do you think will be the most important things for you to consider as you prepare to set up a classroom library and organize time in the school day for independent reading? Record your thinking in a reflective journal. Share your thinking with your peers.

C H A P T E R

8

Shared and Interactive Writing: Participating in a Community of Writers

Adding to our literacy framework . . .

	Reading Aloud and Guided Literature Study	
Shared Reading	**Balanced and Integrated Literacy Framework**	Shared and Interactive Writing
Guided Reading and Guided Literature Study		Guided Writing and Writer's Workshop
Independent Reading and Reader's Workshop		Independent Writing
	Word Study	

In this chapter, we learn about . . .

- 🍎 Engaging children in the act of shared compositions that model writing processes

- 🍎 Examining the process of developing a shared composition, as well as extending children's interactions with the text

Oo Pp Qq Rr Ss Tt Uu Vv Ww Xx Yy Zz

Looking into Classrooms . . .

One morning Kelli brings a frog into her first-grade classroom. The class is studying about different ways that animals move and Kelli thinks this is a wonderful opportunity for the children to explore the movement of frogs. She places the frog in an aquarium with a screen cover and asks the children to spend time observing the frog during their morning activities. All during the morning children gather around the aquarium in small groups, watching the frog and talking with each other.

After lunch Kelli gathers the children in a circle on the carpet and asks them what they noticed about the frog. At first, the children talk about the frog's smooth skin, bulging eyes, the long back legs, the markings on the frog's back, and its wide mouth. Then the talk begins to center on how the frog jumps. Kelli removes the frog from the aquarium and places it in the center of the circle. At first the frog sits very still. Then with some prodding, it jumps across the circle, changes directions, and jumps several more times. Each time it jumps, Kelli asks the children to notice what the frog does when it jumps. Talk continues as the children explore words that help to describe what they observe in the frog's movement.

Kelli puts the frog away and asks the children to pretend they are frogs. The children crouch down, with legs bent and arms out front to steady themselves. She asks them to jump once like a frog and notice what they have to do to get off the floor. Then the children sit again, whereever they are in the circle, and talk about what they noticed about their own jumping. Kelli encourages the talking until she feels that the children are comfortable with the language they need to describe the experience.

To begin the shared writing, Kelli asks the children, "How do frogs jump?" Several children volunteer ideas. Kelli then asks for the children's thoughts on the best way to start the writing, and the class begins to compose. Kelli serves as the scribe for the children as she guides the composition. As each sentence is written it is also read aloud to check for meaning. After each sentence Kelli asks what idea should come next. She raises questions about which ideas are most important to include, and the order that makes the most sense. Throughout the writing Kelli helps children clarify their thoughts as they dictate what they are thinking about frogs. She also asks questions about the use of conventions like capital letters and ending punctuation.

The shared writing that the class composes together is:

How Do Frogs Jump?

Frogs can jump a long way.
Frogs jump with their back legs.
The back legs stretch out.
Front legs are not for jumping.
We jumped like frogs.
We pushed with our legs.

Kelli uses similar shared writing experiences to model the purposes and processes of writing. At appropriate times the writing becomes interactive, and Kelli shares the pen and the children do the writing. She invites children to write familiar words or familiar sounds within words. Kelli provides daily shared and interactive writing experiences because she knows that learning to write occurs over time. It is through many experiences with making print that children form concepts about what purposes print serves and how people use print.

DOWN THE HALL . . .

The third graders in William's class are studying ways to care for the environment. After seeing how much paper and food is thrown away at lunch each day in the school cafeteria, the children become very curious about where all the garbage goes. So William invites several people from a waste management company in town to come and talk with the children about how the city manages everyone's garbage. William also gathers books that address how to reduce, reuse, and recycle materials to have less garbage. After the guests leave the children talk about the new things they learned—that there is a large landfill outside of town and that recyclable items are collected from people's houses twice a month and taken to recycling centers.

To help the children process what they are learning William leads the class in creating an interactive writing chart about the good and bad aspects of garbage (see Figure 8.13 later in this chapter). The children share the pen and throughout the discussion write most of the words and phrases on the chart. There are discussions about the meaning and spelling of words like disease, poison, pollutes, *and* incineration. *The chart is one of many shared and interactive writings the children participate in during this unit of study. William finds that discussion and recording of ideas as a class provides a model for ways that writers can think about and organize their ideas.*

BUILDING A THEORY BASE . . .

From previous chapters, we know that shared activity provides a meaningful social context for learning. Children are motivated to interact with others socially. Learning experiences that are grounded in shared activity provide appropriate social contexts for the acquisition of literacy skills. Shared and interactive writing, as demonstrated by Kelli and William in the opening vignettes, are powerful instructional tools for teachers.

Lucy Calkins (1994), who has much experience writing with young children, tells us:

> The powerful thing about writing with words is that we are really working with thoughts. Writing allows us to put our thoughts on the page and in our pockets; writing allows us to pull back and ask questions of our thoughts. It is this dynamic of creation and criticism, of pulling in to put thoughts on the page and pulling back to question, wonder, remember more, organize and rethink that makes writing such a powerful tool for learning. (p. 222)

Shared and interactive writing provide excellent opportunities to explore writing collaboratively with children.

WHAT IS SHARED WRITING?

Shared writing is the use of children's language and thinking as a foundation for developing a written text. Moira McKenzie (1985) was one of the first to use this term to describe the assistance that teachers can provide to model writing processes and support young writers. Children's knowledge, personal experience, and language are used to create written texts that show children the relationship between written language and their already familiar oral language (McCarrier, Pinnell, & Fountas, 2000).

Read here to find a definition of *shared writing.*

Using children's language to create written texts is a method used by many primary-grade teachers to teach beginning reading. Formerly known as language experience approach, or LEA (Nessel & Jones, 1981; Stauffer & Hammond, 1967), the joint creation of text by teacher and children has been viewed as an effective way to engage children in early print experiences. LEA, however, was primarily used as a personalized approach to reading instruction, during which children read texts created with their own words. Shared writings begin as compositions drawn from children's experiences, then become shared and individual reading materials.

In the language experience approach, the teacher does not attempt to shape the content of the text. The children's grammar is recorded just as it is spoken. In contrast, shared writing is a joint composition between children and teacher, with content and form guided by the teacher. In a shared writing, children's language and the teacher's knowledge of writing are used to construct a joint text. The teacher serves as the scribe, using knowledge of writing to nudge children's thinking in certain directions. In doing so, the teacher raises questions, as if thinking aloud, about the writing. Shared writing provides a model of how writers think while they are writing. Talking about the writing, its content and organization, serves as a verbal composition in preparation for the written composition.

Shared writing is assisted writing. Teachers must work thoughtfully with children's responses, however, so that children retain ownership of the writing. Interactions with children should not impose the teacher's ideas on the composition, but rather bring to a level of consciousness children's understanding of possibilities in the writing. For the writing to be shared, teachers must work from what children know, such as the shared writing about frogs produced by Kelli's first-grade children in the opening vignette.

Shared writing can be adapted to different groups of children or learners for a variety of purposes, for example, to:

- 🍎 assist children and adults who are learning to read and write,
- 🍎 model writing processes through shared experience,
- 🍎 assist children whose first language is not English,
- 🍎 support handwriting instruction,
- 🍎 supplement other methods of teaching reading and writing such as basal reading series and literature-based reading,
- 🍎 supplement language arts and content-area instruction at all grade levels, and
- 🍎 provide a tutorial device for students with special needs.

Shared writing engages children in different types of thinking. Writing, in general, enables the writer to retain and recollect what is known. In addition, group writing experiences that deal with vicarious experiences and secondhand information can support children as they learn to reconstruct new ideas. Many of the types of writing that children are asked to do in school require them to reconstruct their thinking, or combine ideas from several different sources in a new way. With assistance, children become aware of the forms or structures of different types of writing, such as the differences between narrative and informational texts. Through assistance, teachers are able to model how writers compose various types of texts.

Shared writing becomes interactive writing when we share the pen with children. What can they learn about writing by participating in such an activity?

WHEN DOES SHARED WRITING BECOME INTERACTIVE WRITING?

As Kelli and William develop various forms of writing as a class, they often "share the pen," inviting children to share in the actual writing of letters, words, phrases, and sentences. When shared writing becomes *interactive writing,* the act of composing adds new dimensions for children's thinking—the appropriate use of symbols, letter-sound relationships, and language conventions. During interactive writing, children are able to demonstrate to themselves and others what they understand about the formation of letters, the order of letters to form words, the function of punctuation and capital letters, and so on. Figure 8.1 illustrates how interactive writing can help children process their learning in all subject areas, including mathematics; second-grade students recalled a previous experience that included sorting, measuring, and counting pumpkins.

Read here to find a definition of *interactive writing.*

Interactive writing, a term first used in 1991 by faculty members at Ohio State University (McCarrier et al., 2000), continues to focus children's attention on the message of the text, but provides more attention to the principles of written language (Clay, 1975). For example, Kelli and William consider each child's level of literacy development when they invite them to write parts of a composition. Which children are invited to write depends on their developing

FIGURE 8.1
Second-grade interactive writing.

knowledge about print. As one child writes, Kelli invites the other children to activate their knowledge about letters, sounds, and other language conventions as a way of learning through the experience of others. She often uses a small dry-erase board to write in responses to children's thinking about what is being written on the class chart. When William invites a child to write he asks the child to repeat the words/phrase/sentence that is to be written, then asks the class to be thinking about the conventions that will be needed (such as spelling, punctuation).

Interactive writing can also be used with individual children. This is especially effective in kindergarten as young children are gaining confidence in their independence as writers. Figure 8.2 shows one of Roseanne's journal entries. This entry was written interactively with her kindergarten teacher. After drawing a picture of herself, Roseanne told the teacher that she was thinking about her first day at school (2 months earlier). Roseanne and the teacher shared the writing of the sentence,

This is My First Day Of School.

The letters in bold are those that Roseanne was able to hear and write as her teacher helped her stretch words and listen for the phonemes that she could distinguish. Notice that even early in the kindergarten year, interactive writing enabled Roseanne to write the first letter of five words.

FIGURE 8.2
Personal interactive
writing—kindergarten.

WHY USE SHARED/INTERACTIVE WRITING?

When a more knowledgeable other assists a child in communicating through writing, the probability is high that the child will realize the communicative value of writing. "As children see their spoken thoughts put into written form, they can grasp the concept that communication is the purpose" (Hall, 1981, p. 2). Children are already aware that oral language serves communication purposes. Shared and interactive writing extend that understanding to include the communication purposes of written language as a part of learning to read and write. Engaging in verbal composition prior to written composition helps children develop understanding of essential vocabulary and practice appropriate sentence structures.

In shared and interactive writing, instruction in listening, speaking, and writing are integrated with reading. Children think, talk, look, and listen. Teachers write children's spoken thoughts, then read the written thoughts aloud. Children read their thoughts as recorded by either the teacher or the children and talk about the meanings that the words create. Stauffer (1975) supports this interrelatedness of language when he states, "The processes that children have developed for oral communication must be used to full advantage in a similar way by having written words trigger the same concepts" (p. 170).

Just as in LEA, shared writings become excellent texts for shared and guided reading instruction. Children are highly motivated to read jointly composed texts. Learning to read is easiest and most enjoyable when the language of instructional materials matches the language of the reader (McCarrier et al., 2000; Nessel & Jones, 1981). As a main approach to beginning reading instruction, research suggests that jointly constructed texts can be as effective in helping children learn the skills of reading as using a basal reading series (Bond & Dykstra, 1967; Dykstra, 1968; Stahl & Miller, 1989; Stauffer & Hammond, 1967), and may even have some advantages over basal approaches (Hall, 1978; Stahl & Miller, 1989).

As children actively participate in constructing meaningful texts, they are able to see a relationship between school learning activities and learning to read and write. Children see writing as functional when it involves such activities as documenting the birth and growth of the class's baby mice or constructing a letter of appreciation to a grandmother who taught the class about making tortillas. Shared and interactive writing is purposeful for children because learning to read and write is integrally linked to personal interests and learning experiences in general.

Making Connections . . .

In your experiences with primary-grade classrooms, have you observed teachers using shared or interactive writing? If so, what procedures did you observe? What do you think the teacher's intentions were for engaging the children in shared or interactive writing? Compare shared/interactive writing to the ways teachers use chalkboards/whiteboards to record ideas throughout the school day. What parallels can you make? Share your thinking with a peer.

THINKING ABOUT WRITTEN LANGUAGE

The learning environment in the classroom should support children as they think about and shape meaning with written language. D'Arcy (1989), working from Frank Smith's ideas about how the "learning brain" functions, identifies several ways that writing supports and enhances our thinking. Engaging in writing enables us to:

- *retain* memories of experiences with the world,
- *re-collect* memories/experiences,
- *re-create* memories from firsthand knowledge,
- *re-construct* ideas by arriving at new perceptions of experiences with secondhand knowledge, and
- *re-present* in some way what is known now that was not known before.

D'Arcy deliberately hyphenates the terms to call attention to the fact that as we arrive at new knowledge and new understandings, we draw upon what has already been collected, constructed, or created by our brains.

Teachers ask children to write by drawing upon their experiences and their knowledge of language. To do this, children need support and encouragement as they learn to value their own thinking. A writing program that encourages and supports thinking focuses on what children have already retained from their life experiences, then enables them, in D'Arcy's terms, to re-collect, re-construct, re-create, and re-present their thinking.

Retaining Experience

Through our senses we constantly take in new experiences, or *memories* as D'Arcy (1989) refers to them. For young children, processing through their senses is a natural way of learning (Piaget & Inhelder, 1969). Our senses influence how we interpret the experiences in which we find ourselves. D'Arcy's use of *retaining* is similar to our previous discussions about schema. We could say that as children retain new experiences they are building schema about their world.

One marvelous aspect of thinking, and perhaps the most problematic, is that the retaining that children do is virtually effortless. Children are often unaware that they are retaining memories or experiences and do not realize all that they know. When we ask children to write about what they know, they may respond in dismay because they do not think they know much about the world. Experiences that are retained, especially without conscious effort, may not be readily available to children. To draw upon their experiences in school writing activities, children will need help in organizing their thinking and learning to recognize and use what they know.

Re-Collecting Experience

"None of us are in a position to 'know what we know' until we are given opportunity to re-collect what we have retained" (D'Arcy, 1989, p. 4). Re-collecting provides opportunities with each new encounter we have to connect back to past experiences that have begun to take shape. In connecting back, we are able to revisit and also reshape what has been retained. The ease of using what we know is related to the frequency of re-collecting those retained experiences.

When children write, teachers should encourage them to write from what they know. Planning activities that enable children to re-collect retained experiences is an essential step for successful and satisfying writing. Demonstrating how to re-collect experiences can be accomplished through the recording of children's shared and personal experiences, as Kelli did with her first-grade children in the opening scenario. Children can also re-collect their ideas in many forms of functional, or everyday, writing such as the chart of ideas that William and his third-grade children constructed about garbage.

Re-Creating Experience

Our firsthand experiences with the world are usually easier for us to recall than vicarious, or secondhand, experiences. When we sift through the incredible amount of detail we have retained from personal experiences, certain memories stand out as significant to us. We re-create those experiences in our mind, perhaps highlighting some part of the experience differently than we had on previous occasions.

It is also possible that we re-create responses to literature that we experience. When we identify with the triumphs and struggles of characters, we use literature as a mirror reflecting back on ourselves. In that reflection, we use our own life experience, combined with our literary experience, to look closely at some particularly relevant life event.

Writing should enable children to re-create their lived experience and write about what they know best. Children who struggle with what to write about may be the ones who do not value their lived experience. Carefully selecting literature for the reading program that connects with children's lives can provide opportunities for re-creating experiences through writing.

Re-Constructing Experience

Clarifying our thinking is valuable to better understand what we know. With each new experience, we gather re-collections of past experiences to understand the proper connections to make with the new. Through re-constructing previously held ideas, we adjust our ideas in light of what we know. In other words, we build or revise a particular schema. Much of the knowledge we gain is through secondhand experience, which can be more difficult to manipulate or reshape than knowledge gained through firsthand experience. Almost daily we ask children to re-construct their previous knowledge in light of new information. We introduce new concepts for which children often lack firsthand experience. To enable children to use this new knowledge effectively we should help them first re-collect what they already know. Writing is instrumental in helping children see what they know in preparation for re-constructing their knowledge.

Re-Presenting Experience

To reinforce and value children's sense of what they know, they need many opportunities to move thinking and learning outside of themselves. Re-presenting
their thinking in writing, using words to stand for what they know, enables children to see their thinking. It is especially important for children to realize when
they have learned and when they know something new.

If in our classrooms we treat writing as an active process, children will have
numerous opportunities to re-present their thinking. During the process of developing a piece of writing to completion, children may see a change in their ability to clearly re-present their thinking. By re-presenting their thinking in writing
at different points in their learning, children can focus on what they know that
was not known before. Seeing their own growth can lead to self-satisfaction with
themselves as writers and learners.

Making Connections . . .

Consider your own processes for writing. In what ways do you retain, re-collect, re-
create, re-construct, or re-present your life experiences? Do you re-collect your experience through writing, retelling the day's events to friends and family through
emails? Do you re-create experiences, reliving them in whole or part as you describe them? Do you re-construct experience as you try to explain the process you
are going through as you learn something new, such as yoga or piano? Do you represent your experience when you press the "send" button for that email? Reflect
on the impact of these types writing on your own thoughts as you think about engaging children in exploring their experiences through writing. Share your thinking
with a peer.

 # HOW IS WRITING USED IN CLASSROOMS?

How do the thousands of hours we spend as students shape our views about
writing and of ourselves as writers? Children learn about writing by the ways
that writing is used in the classroom and by the things that we emphasize about
writing. Children may learn that writing is:

- 🍎 a symbolic *code* that must be mastered,
- 🍎 a *medium* through which they may communicate,
- 🍎 an end *product* to be achieved,
- 🍎 an active *process* or activity, or
- 🍎 a *combination* of all of these.

D'Arcy (1989) suggests that the writing teachers require from students and responses they receive will influence the students' expectations and consequently
their approach to and performance in writing, possibly for life. Lucy Calkins
(1994) also comments, "What our students do as writers will largely depend on
what we expect them to do and on what they've done in the past" (p. 113).

Writing as a Code

If we view writing as a code, then we give attention to the correct use of language symbols. In our own experience as writers, we probably had many teachers who viewed writing as a code. We spent endless hours completing exercises that focused on grammar, sentence structure, spelling, and so forth. (That practice continues today as daily oral language (DOL), in which children correct sentences presented by the teacher that are isolated from real writing.) We received feedback on our writing in the form of red marks on compositions. We were given specific formats in which to fit our ideas about a topic. Although these practices were intended to focus our attention on the details of written language, we also learned that there was a "right" way to write.

Research in writing (Calkins, 1986, 1994; Clay, 1975; Graves, 1983, 1994) helps us realize that overemphasis on code, at the expense of meaning, can lead children to see writing as a tedious task and themselves as inadequate writers. As young children make the transition from oral to written language, they must learn a new symbol system. Such attention to detail requires an extensive background with print that will be acquired over many years. We know that concepts about written language are best acquired in the context of meaningful activity.

Writing as a Medium

Writing is a medium when words are viewed as "verbal play dough" (D'Arcy, 1989) out of which something useful can be made. Just as an artist uses a medium as a vehicle of expression, writers use words; just as an artist experiments with a medium to see what it can do, a writer experiments with language without being quite sure where it will lead. An artist knows that though the medium is visible, its meaning lies within its creator and the individuals who observe it. So, too, the meaning of writing lies within its creator and observers.

By the ways that teachers engage children with written language children can come to see language as a flexible and responsive medium, able to be manipulated or reshaped to meet different intentions. Children's experiences with written language influence their views about the possibilities of language.

Writing as a Product

The completion of projects or tasks is important to our sense of self-satisfaction in our work and our lives. It is one way that personal success is measured. However, when completion becomes more important than the tasks themselves, work can become personally meaningless and unsatisfactory. In writing, children need to experience the self-satisfaction of finished products. They should be encouraged to move their writing in certain directions, but what will ultimately be most important is the direction that children think their work should take. Producing a written product should never become more important than the meaning it holds for the writer.

Writing as an Active Process

Research in writing documents that writing is an active, not passive, process. Writing is full of activity, mental and physical, that enables us to move our thinking out of our heads, down our arms, and out our fingers by way of a pen or keyboard. In the process of writing, thoughts and feelings become visible. Mental images can also become visible. Thinking of writing as an active process is tied to viewing writing as a medium that is responsive and flexible. For children to recognize the existence of this process, we must help them become aware of their thinking through talk, drawing, and physical actions, then show them how that thinking can be captured with words to represent the talk, drawing, and actions. Many and varied writing experiences help children see that writing serves different purposes, takes different forms, and can be directed to different audiences.

Calkins (1994) pushes our thoughts of writing as a process even further. Her experiences with writing have taught her that "[w]riting does not begin with deskwork but with lifework" (p. 3). Calkins shares comments by Cynthia Rylant, a children's book author, who described her writing process as " . . . being an artist every single day of one's life" (cited in Calkins, p. 3). Calkins believes the process of writing begins in living with a sense of awareness of what is happening around and inside of us.

Making Connections . . .

Take a moment to reflect on your experiences with the purposes of writing. What messages did you infer from your teachers about writing? Did you experience writing as a process, evolving over a period of time as you manipulated the words to shape your message in a particular way? Did you experience writing as a finished product in correct form, but were not sure how you were supposed to know how to get it in that correct form? Your experiences as a writer can influence the ways in which you approach writing with children. What models of writing will you present to your students? Share your reflections with a peer.

 ## THE VALUE OF FUNCTIONAL WRITING

Composing paragraphs and other more fully developed pieces of writing are not the only types of writing from which students can learn. In everyday life adults use functional writing much more than composition—writing notes/emails to others, making notes/reminders for ourselves, taking phone messages, making shopping or to-do lists, sketching and labeling directions to someone's house, and completing a variety of forms. These are all examples of writing that serve a specific function, thus the term *functional writing*.

Formal writing, pieces of thinking that get fully developed, are not always feasible or the most desirable types of writing to accomplish a goal (Calkins, 1994). In today's busy classrooms, functional writings are very useful. Teachers can easily integrate writing instruction into any subject area using functional writing. Shared and interactive writing is an effective way to model the use of functional writing as a way to help children retain, re-collect, re-create, and re-construct their experiences as a support for learning.

Functional writing can take on many forms, such as:

🍎 lists,
🍎 annotated drawings,

🍎 graphs,

🍎 descriptions,

🍎 records of events,

🍎 clusters,

🍎 charts,

🍎 labels,

🍎 notes, and

🍎 explanations.

Lists

Class-made lists, such as words-on-the-wall (Cunningham, 1995), demonstrate the making of lists and their potential use for retaining ideas. Children can learn to use lists to retain information for later use or to re-collect ideas (e.g., books I have read, the lunch menu, special words we are using in our rocks and minerals unit, names of people who will bring items for a party, or the sequence of steps used to make a paper maché project). At a more complex level, descriptive writing can begin with a list of what is known about the topic.

Ordered Lists

Lists can be expanded to become a record of events, or an orderly list, that shows sequence and important details. When it is important to recall in an orderly fashion, making a record of events would be a helpful form of informal writing (e.g., a class field trip, a science experiment, life events in preparation for writing an autobiography, or re-collecting the events of a playground disturbance to prepare for problem solving). Figure 8.3 shows an ordered list that became the basis for the interactive writing shown in Figure 8.1.

Descriptions

Relationships among ideas can also be shown with words. Descriptions can use words to build images of objects, people, places, and events we know, just as with illustrations. In descriptions, we re-collect ideas we have retained or re-create a

Pumpkins

1. sorted by size

2. measured stems

3. counted by twos

4. made sets of 15¢

FIGURE 8.3
Ordered list.

FIGURE 8.4
Sample list that becomes description—third grade.

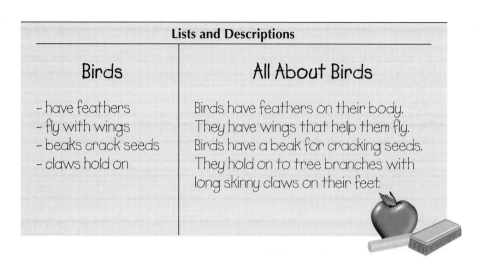

Lists and Descriptions

Birds	All About Birds
- have feathers - fly with wings - beaks crack seeds - claws hold on	Birds have feathers on their body. They have wings that help them fly. Birds have a beak for cracking seeds. They hold on to tree branches with long skinny claws on their feet.

FIGURE 8.5
Sample clusters.

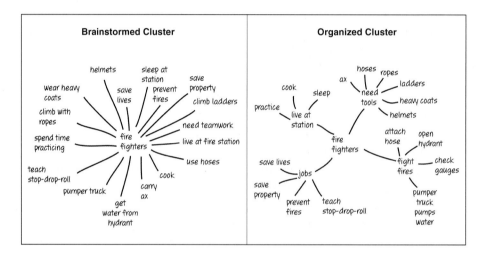

portion of an experience we have had. Figure 8.4 shows an example of description that began as a list of characteristics about birds in third grade.

Clusters

Visual arrangements of ideas are a way to show ideas and perhaps how the ideas are related. Clusters can be thought of as lists that are organized into a visual display that is a helpful tool for retaining and re-collecting specific ideas. Initially, a brainstormed cluster may not be organized to show relationships. Re-collecting the ideas to show relationships can make the ideas more usable. Figure 8.5 shows an example of a cluster that is merely a collection of ideas, as well as a sample cluster in which the ideas have been organized to support further writing in a second-grade unit about community helpers. Figure 8.6 shows a spider cluster used to re-collect information about spiders during a third-grade unit of study.

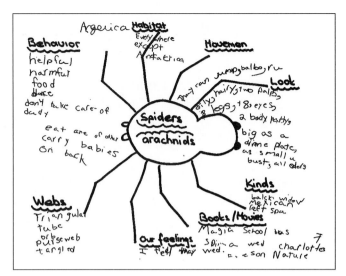

FIGURE 8.6
Organized cluster for spiders.

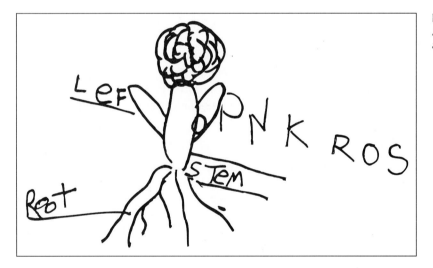

FIGURE 8.7
Annotated drawing of a plant.

Annotated Drawings

Writing can elaborate on ideas that are drawn or vice versa. The annotation may be labels, descriptions, or explanations that comment on or clarify the illustration. Annotated drawings help children develop the technical language for a topic, the language required for academic success. Figure 8.7 shows an example of a plant with parts identified.

Charts

Sometimes ideas are more helpful if they are arranged in an orderly manner. Charts show ideas arranged so that the relationship of the ideas is clear. Charts can help children to re-construct ideas, sometimes into new relationships. Figure 8.8 shows an example of a simple chart that supports what a child in second grade knows about the topic of living and nonliving things.

Sample chart and graph.

Chart	Graph
Living **Not Living** people rocks snail cup bird pencil flower car grass watch	When Do We Go to Bed? (graph of X marks over times 8:00, 8:30, 9:00, 10:00) Bedtime

Graphs

Ideas can be represented in a symbolic form. Graphs use lines, bars, portions of circles, and symbols to represent relationships. Words help to identify the type of data, define categories, and determine the type of relationship among the data. Figure 8.8 shows an example of a class-made graph about bedtimes in kindergarten.

Explanations

When events require elaboration, an explanation is useful. An explanation asks the writer to tell more than the mere ideas or events by providing a rationale or support for one's thinking (e.g., steps in solving a math problem, response to a book or character, hypothesizing in a science experiment, or selecting a particular form for a piece of process writing). Figure 8.9 shows an example of a first-grader's explanation of states of matter in a science lesson.

Making Connections . . .

What types of functional writing do you use in your everyday life? What purpose(s) does functional writing serve for you? How might functional writing serve as a bridge for children into more complex forms of writing such as letters, paragraphs, and stories? Make a list of learning experiences you have observed in primary-grade classrooms and the types of functional writing that might have been modeled to build children's understanding of using written language to organize and communicate ideas.

PUTTING THEORY INTO PRACTICE . . .

Anything that teachers and children think and talk about in the classroom provides possibilities for shared/interactive writing. It is a matter of what we want to show children about how and why we put ideas on paper.

FIGURE 8.9
Explanation of states of
matter—first grade.

POSSIBILITIES FOR SHARED AND INTERACTIVE WRITING

In the opening vignette, Kelli uses shared writing to help children express their observations of a frog in the classroom. She shows how a teacher can guide and extend children's thinking. The writing that results from this guidance is a good example of descriptive thinking that is written down. William engages children in the interactive construction of an information chart that will be used in future writing experiences. What other options might teachers have for using shared/interactive writing? Can children express what is being learned or explore their ideas through shared/interactive writing? Can teachers use shared/interactive writing to help children organize their thinking about what they are learning?

Composing as Expressions of Learning

Shared and interactive writing can serve as an expression of learning. Consider the following possibilities provided for each grade level.

Kindergarten

🍎 Kindergarten children express what they have learned about farm animals as they create a farm mural with animal names and the sounds each animal makes (see Figure 8.10).

🍎 Kindergarten children explain facts they have gathered about wolves and bears as they look and listen during read-aloud.

First Grade

🍎 First-grade children describe the results of collecting data and graphing their favorite ice cream flavors (see Figure 8.11).

🍎 First-grade students compose a thank-you letter to a local business after a field trip.

FIGURE 8.10
Kindergarten interactive
writing—a portion of a
farm animal mural.

FIGURE 8.11
First-grade explanation of
favorite ice cream graph.

Our Favorite Ice Cream

We asked every one in our class,

"What is your favorite ice cream?"

Here is what we said.

2 like vanilla the best.
2 like strawberry the best.
1 likes peppermint the best.
2 like rocky road the best.
9 like chocolate the best.

Chocolate is our favorite ice cream.

Second Grade

🍎 Second-grade students state names and definitions of solid geomtric
shapes being studied to create a classroom display.

🍎 Second-grade students record details about lightning (see Figure 8.12).

Third/Fourth Grade

🍎 Third-grade students create their own legend about why the owl is
awake at night as a model for personal legends that each child will
write as the culmination of a unit about nocturnal animals.

🍎 Third-grade students begin a class list of ideas they already know (K)
and what (W) they want to learn (the beginning of a K-W-L Chart) as
they begin a study about their community. Later they will state what
they learned (L) (Ogle, 1986).

Composing as Organization of Thinking

The process of creating a shared or interactive experience can serve as an excellent model for ways to organize thinking. Consider the following examples for
each grade level.

Lightning

Lightning is electric. It can be very dangerous. Lightning goes zig zag. It hits tall things first. Sometimes lightning strikes trees and starts a fire.

FIGURE 8.12
Second-grade shared/interactive writing—what we know about lightning.

Farm Animal	Sound
cow	moo
pig	oink
sheep	baa
chicken	cluck
duck	quack

FIGURE 8.13
List of farm animals—kindergarten.

Kindergarten

- Kindergarten children make a list of farm animals and the sound that each can make, adding to the list with each book that is read aloud during a farm unit (see Figure 8.13).
- Kindergarten children retell the tale of *The Three Little Pigs* as practice for a class play.

FIGURE 8.14
Third-grade interactive writing.

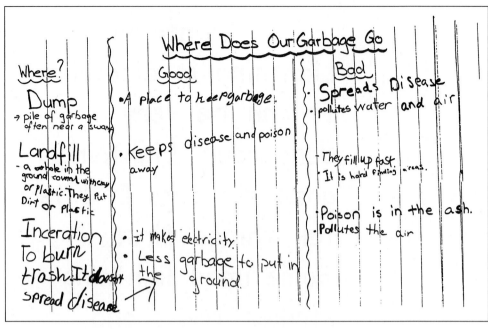

First Grade

🍎 First-grade students collect important details from a read-aloud spanning several days, organizing details into a story summary.

🍎 First-grade students develop accurate retellings of the scientific method followed in a class experiment.

Second Grade

🍎 Second-grade students use a Venn diagram to compare and contrast the attributes of frogs and toads during a unit about amphibians (see Chapter 11, Figure 11.25).

🍎 Second-grade students develop a chart to compare the use of literary elements (plot, characters, setting) in several versions of a favorite fairy tale.

🍎 Second-grade students participate in the labeling of a frog drawing prepared by their teacher to "see" what they know and what they still need to learn about frogs (see Chapter 11, Figure 11.8).

Third/Fourth Grade

🍎 Third-grade students develop a chart to organize such questions as "Where Does Our Garbage Go?" in preparation for beginning personal research (see Figure 8.14).

🍎 Third-grade students develop a chart to connect ideas about a text, *The King of the Beasts,* in preparation for writing an essay stating and supporting a personal opinion in response to the text (see Figure 8.15).

In each case, the teacher makes a decision about the importance of the thinking to be done by the children and the need to share in the actual writing.

Text:	King of the Beast
Introductory Statement	Our favorite character is the elephant.
Appearance & Characteristics	His nose looks like a trumpet. He is fast and strong. He is fat and huge.
Opinion	We like the elephant because he is rough and tough.
Evidence	In the story, he stomped on the ground and picked up the lion and spun him around and threw him away.
Concluding Statement	We think the real king of the beasts is the elephant.

FIGURE 8.15
Third-grade shared/interactive writing—organizing ideas for literature response.

When one goal of the writing is for children to write independently, teachers tend to engage children to "share the pen." From the previous lists, it is apparent that anything that teachers can think about and talk about with children can become a shared or interactive writing experience. Each of the resulting products is then displayed somewhere in the classroom. The text is revisited by the class and by individual children as they "read the room."

If we want to engage children in such assisted writing experiences, how do we develop meaningful experiences from which children can learn about print?

GROUPING FOR SHARED AND INTERACTIVE WRITING

Shared and interactive writing can be used with a whole class, small groups, or individuals. In Kelli's classroom, the composition about the frog comes from the whole class because Kelli believes that the experience is best suited to whole-group interaction. At times, Kelli provides a whole-group experience and discussion, but saves the composition and follow-up for small groups in which she can better observe the children.

Early in the school year, emerging and developing readers benefit from the safety and security of whole-group situations. They also benefit from the attention they are able to receive in smaller groups.

Whole-class, small-group, and individual compositions provide a variety of benefits, which are noted in the following lists.

Whole-class compositions:

 are excellent for introducing children to shared writing and reading,

 make efficient use of time,

 can be followed up in small groups as needed,

 are excellent when writing is being used as to supplement other reading/writing activities,

 give children equal access to learning,

 allow children to hear many other ideas and compare their ideas with those of others, but

 do not allow for all children to contribute to the dictation.

Small-group compositions:

 provide more personalized attention,

 can be with mixed-ability or similar-ability group,

 can be compared between groups that compose about the same topic,

 allow teachers to observe student interactions more closely, and

 allow more children to contribute to a dictation.

Individual compositions:

 provide for individualized participation in the dictation process,

 are most effective for beginning writers, including English-language learners who are just beginning to learn English,

 require more time than whole-class or small-group compositions, but

 do not provide the benefit of joint thinking between children.

The grouping we select depends on our purposes for instruction, the needs of our children, and the demands of the shared texts we are using.

PROCEDURES FOR SHARED/INTERACTIVE WRITING

Shared/interactive writing weaves life experience and oral language together with modeled writing to provide reading materials that are personal and meaningful for children. To use shared/interactive writing effectively, some basic steps are important to include in instruction. For example, think back to the vignettes of Kelli's first-grade and William's third-grade classrooms at the opening of this chapter. During the shared/interactive writing experience, these teachers provide opportunities for:

 a meaningful shared experience,

 talk about the experience to organize thinking and prepare for writing,

 shared composition between teacher and children,

 writing modeled by a more knowledgeable other,

 writing by children, assisted by the teacher to focus on language principles,

 shared reading, discussion, and rereading of a text, and

 follow-up activity to extend the learner's interaction with text.

Meaningful Shared Experiences

Rich experiences such as observation of the frog and classroom visits by knowledgeable guests are easily retained and motivate children to develop understanding. Units of study—drawn from the school curriculum, academic standards, and children's experiences—serve as a base for developing children's understandings about the world. William and Kelli plan connected learning experiences, such as integrated or thematic units, to provide multiple experiences for exploration. In-depth learning experiences enable all her children to build or broaden background knowledge.

Talking about Experiences and Ideas

Kelli and William believe that talking through experiences with their children develops language for a particular concept or topic. If children can easily talk about a concept, they are more likely to be able to read and write about that concept. William and Kelli encourage much talk prior to writing because they believe that focused talk serves as a verbal composing process. Through verbal composition, children rehearse the ideas they might write. Rehearsal with a teacher's assistance provides children with practice in regulating their thinking about the ideas that will be written.

Shared Composition and Modeled/Interactive Writing

By the end of first grade, Kelli hopes that children are able to compose simple descriptive or expository texts about familiar topics, personal narratives, or simply a friendly note. To encourage such compositions, she must model how to think about and organize ideas. While the class talks about and Kelli begins to record ideas, she talks aloud about ways that writers think and what writers might need to know about various forms of writing. Kelli must also support children's developing concepts about language principles such as how we write words, how letters are formed, sounds that letters represent, and predictable patterns that we can expect in English.

When the writing begins for the frog composition, Kelli models how to use print to express ideas. As Kelli records the children's ideas, typically she:

- solicits ideas from the children about what to write,
- repeats the sentence that was suggested and confirms its accuracy with the children,
- thinks aloud to nudge children's thinking about the composition,
- says each word aloud before she writes it,
- names letters as she writes each word, thinks aloud about sound patterns that are heard, or invites children to offer information about known letter-sound patterns,
- reads the complete sentence and asks children to check the accuracy of its content, then
- rereads the complete sentence encouraging children to join the reading, then
- begins the process again for the next idea.

When appropriate, Kelli moves beyond shared writing to an interactive experience. She invites children to provide the letters that represent known sounds, leaving space for sounds that are unfamiliar (th___r), and fills in letters for sounds that are unfamiliar to the children (th<u>ei</u>r).

Shared Reading, Discussion, and Rereading of Text

Shared/interactive writings become shared readings and rereadings. For example, after the initial composition is completed, Kelli rereads the entire text. She asks children to listen carefully and watch as she points to the words that are read aloud to be sure that the ideas expressed are what the class intended. Asking children to give such attention to the accuracy of recording acknowledges the importance of the text's meaning to the learner. It also models how to monitor one's own writing. Once a text is read in its entirety, several rereadings follow with children joining the reading as Kelli points at each word in the text. Composing the text and participating in several rereadings makes the text familiar and predictable to the children.

Over the next several days, Kelli invites children to participate in shared rereadings of the text that was created the first day. As individual children read, Kelli adjusts the level of her support to the needs of each child:

- Some children still need Kelli to lead the reading by pointing to each word and softly reading aloud with the child close behind.
- Other children are ready to take the lead and the pointer, pointing to words and reading aloud with the rest of the group joining in.
- Still other children read aloud as Kelli points to the text, needing her support only on occasional words.

To support comprehension development, Kelli guides children to predict, read, and prove (Stauffer, 1975) their thinking just as they do with other pieces of literature.

Extending Interaction with Text

Over the remainder of a week Kelli brings children back to a text they have written to provide repetition that is needed to increase children's knowledge of fundamental reading processes. Kelli chooses follow-up activities that fit her purpose(s) of instruction, are appropriate for the shared composition, and support the level of children's development as readers.

Kelli provides several duplicate copies of the shared writing. The copies are used at various times to:

- read and illustrate the main idea or favorite parts,
- cut apart sentences to reconstruct the text (see Figure 8.16),
- underline known words in the text, then place particular known words on small cards that become part of a child's personal bank of words, and
- be added to individual folders of past shared/interactive writings.

In addition, Kelli also provides extension activities that utilize art, handwriting, and games (see extension activities later in this chapter).

We pushed with our legs.
Frogs jump with their back legs.
The back legs stretch out.
How Do Frogs Jump?
We jumped like frogs.
Front legs are not for jumping.
Frogs can jump a long way.

FIGURE 8.16
Sentences for reconstructing text.

EXPLORING COMPOSITION PROCESSES

In previous sections of this chapter we observed how Kelli provides her first-grade children with the opportunity to explore their ideas about frogs through shared and interactive writing. Kelli engages the children as writers learning to organize and express ideas. Shared writing in particular is a useful tool for teaching children about writing in specific narrative genre or information structure.

In this section we visit Brad's second-grade classroom to observe how he supports children's developing understanding of the composing process. The children have just finished reading and rereading a version of *The Ugly Duckling* by Hans Christian Andersen in their basal reader. The class has been discussing characteristics of fairy tales and how the authors of retold versions sometimes make changes in the story.

The children are interested in writing their own retold version of a fairy tale. Brad wants to nudge the children to consider the characteristics of fairy tales so that their retold versions will have appropriate characteristics of the genre. He decides to use shared writing to model thinking about fairy tale characteristics and support children's attempts to retell the story of *The Ugly Duckling*. The dialogue from the children is a composite of many children's ideas.

Brad:	Before you write your own a fairy tale, maybe we should write one together. Hmmm. We're going to write a fairy tale, but what makes a good fairy tale? When I'm reading a fairy tale, I feel like I know the characters.
Children:	You can tell real easy who is good and who is bad.
Children:	Yeah, and people act just like you think they will.
Brad:	That's good thinking. I'll write your ideas here so we can use them later on. (Brad writes both statements off to the side of the chart.) I think when people act just like I think they will, I'm not really surprised by the ending of the story.
Children:	Yeah. The good characters usually win. (Brad records off to side of chart.)

Brad:	Yes, that's what I think too. Is that what happened in *The Ugly Duckling?* Were we surprised by the ending?
Children:	No. (Brad records to side of chart that the ending is not a surprise.)
Brad:	If we are making our own version of *The Ugly Duckling,* what are the things we want to remember to put in our story so we are sure it is a fairy tale? Think about the ideas that have been suggested. (He points to notes on side of board.)
Children:	Our ugly duckling has to be really good and the other ducks need to be bad!
Brad:	Yes, usually in a fairy tale we care about the good character. We don't want anything bad to happen to that character. Do you feel that way about a character in *The Ugly Duckling?*
Children:	Yes, the ugly duckling. (Brad records to side of chart that children care about the duck character.)
Brad:	So, at the beginning, do we want to let everyone know who the good and bad characters are? How can we do that? How should we write that part?
Children:	We could write, "Once there was a mother duck who was waiting for her eggs to hatch."
Brad:	(Repeats child's statement.) Is that what you want me to write? Does that sound like the beginning of a fairy tale?
Children:	Yeah, or we could say "once upon a time"—fairy tales can start like that too.
Brad:	(Class settles on the second suggestion and Brad records, then reads back to group to confirm.) What else do we need in our beginning to make it sound like a fairy tale?
Children:	"Out came five yellow ducks and a big ugly gray duck."
Brad:	How does that fit with our first sentence?
Children:	Good. . . . Write that next. (Brad writes and reads aloud.)
Brad:	Remember what we are trying to show (points to side notes), that we need good and bad characters.
Children:	We could write, "The other ducks picked on the gray duck. He felt ugly so he ran away."
Brad:	(Repeats children's statements.) Does that help our fairy tale? (Based on responses, Brad records both statements, then reads back all that has been written so far.) Okay. Do we have good and bad characters yet?
Children:	The ducks are bad.
Brad:	(to the class) Do you agree? And do we have a good character?
Children:	The ugly duckling.
Brad:	How will other people know that the ugly duckling is our good character?
Children:	Because the one who gets picked on isn't bad. The ugly duckling didn't do anything to the other ducks.

Brad:	Hmmm. When I read fairy tales, there is usually a character that I am rooting for, one that I want to win. For me, it is the ugly duckling. I feel bad that he is picked on and I want things to be better for him. What do you think?
Children:	(Responses generally concur.)
Brad:	Then we will need to be sure that we help our good character be the winner in the end. What are some other things we want to have happen in our fairy tale? . . .

The conversation and writing continue over several days as the teacher and children complete the introduction of the characters, develop the events in the middle of the plot, and bring the fairy tale to a close with the triumph of the ugly duckling becoming the most beautiful swan on the lake.

The class continues to work out their ideas and Brad records what the class decides to write. When the fairy tale is complete, the class reads and rereads it. Brad types the fairy tale, creating a book for each student and leaving space for illustrations. The children enjoy reading the class book in guided reading and rereading it during independent reading time.

The composition process serves as a model experience for the children in writing fairy tales. Later Brad uses the shared composition to compare it with the version in the basal reader. He models strategies for saving ideas by writing notes to the side of the chart.

EXPLORING VARIOUS FORMS OF WRITING

Brad used shared writing to model the organization of a literary genre, fairy tales. Kelli engaged her children in writing a description of frog movements. William constructed an information chart to help his students begin to organize their developing understanding about garbage. Teachers can model composing processes for literary genres, informational text structures, and the functional types of writing presented earlier in this chapter. Shared/interactive writing can be used to model how authors develop particular literary elements within a composition. The variety of writing that can be modeled through shared or interactive writing is endless.

We expose children to a great deal of literature, predominantly narrative forms. We know, however, that expository, or informational, text is structured differently than narrative and is filled with details and concepts that are often new to children. Using shared writing to explore informational text structures, and functional writing which also tends to be informational, can help children retain, re-collect, and re-construct what they know in disciplines such as science (Daniel, Fehrenbach, & Greer, 1986) and mathematics (Ferguson & Fairburn, 1985). The possibilities that may be modeled and/or processed through shared/interactive writing include, but are not limited to, the following examples.

Literary Genre

- 🍎 Fantasy (fairy tales, folk tales, fables)
- 🍎 Realistic stories (people, animals, humorous, mysteries)
- 🍎 True stories (autobiography and biography)
- 🍎 Poetry

Literary Elements

🍎 Creating a plot with a beginning, middle, and end
🍎 Introducing the problem of the plot
🍎 Building progressively to a climax
🍎 Resolving the problem of a plot
🍎 Introducing a main character

Informational Text Structures

🍎 Description
🍎 Order/Sequence
🍎 Compare/Contrast
🍎 Cause/Effect
🍎 Problem/Solution
🍎 Question/Answer
🍎 Explanations

Functional Writing

🍎 Lists, including ordered lists
🍎 Clusters
🍎 Annotated drawings
🍎 Charts and graphs
🍎 Explanations
🍎 Descriptions

See Appendix A for a detailed discussion of literary genre, literary elements, and informational text structures. A more detailed discussion of functional writing appears in an upcoming section of this chapter.

Making Connections . . .

Imagine that you are in a primary-grade classroom where children are learning about insects. What types of shared and interactive writing might you create with the children? Brainstorm ideas with a peer. Which topics would be best as shared writing? As interactive writing? As a combination?

🍎 EXTENDING INTERACTION WITH SHARED/ INTERACTIVE COMPOSITIONS

Shared/interactive writing can also be used to prepare and support children's learning in other literacy activities, as explained in the following subsections.

Building Background before Reading

🍎 Experiences to build background knowledge and particularly specialized vocabulary required for fluent reading can be recorded through shared writing as children re-collect and re-construct their knowledge in preparation for reading.

🍎 Reading the shared text, which is familiar, rehearses vocabulary and concepts needed in the basal text.

Making Predictions before Reading

🍎 Prediction is encouraged to help children mentally prepare themselves for reading.

🍎 After previewing the text, record and read back children's predictions.

🍎 Return to the shared writing to confirm or prove predictions during and after the reading.

Responding to the Text

🍎 While children are acquiring fluency as writers, you can encourage response to text by using shared writing to record children's general and specific responses to reading.

🍎 Typically responses are discussed.

🍎 Recording responses preserves children's thinking for use on subsequent days.

Retelling the Text

🍎 Retelling enhances children's comprehension of stories (Morrow, 2005).

🍎 Verbal retellings are excellent for helping children rethink a story and decide about the most important elements.

🍎 Shared/interactive writing is an excellent way to preserve the retelling, which can reinforce concepts of plot, provide a copy for comparison to the plots of other stories, and provide a model for independent written retellings.

Innovating with the Text

🍎 Make children's versions of predictable books by using children's language to complete the author's pattern.

🍎 For example, in *It Looked Like Spilt Milk* (Shaw, 1947) the pattern is:

> Sometimes it looked like a _____,
>
> But it wasn't a _____.

🍎 Shared innovation provides a model for individual innovations during guided and independent writing.

Group Literature Log

🍎 A big book that simulates an individual literature log can be kept in the early stages of literature study.

🍎 Model the possibilities of literature logs, such as responses to literature and collecting words that are of interest to the group.

Mini-Lessons

🍎 Children's literature provides excellent examples of the variety of options open to writers.

🍎 Provide short, focused lessons for children, often called mini-lessons, to teach children about specific aspects of literature, reading, and writing.

🍎 Samples of mini-lessons can be found in Chapters 4 and 6, which focus on using children's literature for reading instruction.

🍎 Shared/interactive writing, on charts and on overhead projectors, becomes an essential tool for helping children process their thinking about the content of the literature mini-lesson.

Making Strategy Use Explicit

🍎 To support children's developing understanding of the strategies that they use to read more effectively, teachers must do more than discuss these strategies with children.

🍎 After discussion of how children used a particular strategy, record children's definition of the strategy, when it should be used, and how it helps a reader to use the strategy.

🍎 Display charts in a visible area to help reinforce children's use of reading strategies.

K-W-L Charts

🍎 K-W-L (Ogle, 1986) is a strategy to help children prepare for and focus their attention for learning from informational text. Space is provided on a chart to record:

K = What I think I *know* about this topic,

W = What I *want* to know about this topic,

L = What I *learned* by reading.

🍎 Children complete the "K" and "W" sections of the chart before reading, and the "L" portion of the chart after reading/learning the material.

🍎 After reading the text and learning the material, children go back to the "K" column and see if any of their prior knowledge was not accurate. They put a check mark next to statements that are not accurate, according to the text, and correct those statements. Then they go to the "W" column and put a check mark beside each question that the text did not answer. These questions should be discussed in the group.

- The teacher makes a large class chart and records children's dictations in the appropriate area.
- Reading and rereading occur as children use the chart throughout the unit of study.

Adapting Difficult Informational Texts

- Informational books are often too difficult for children to read independently. Shared/interactive writing can be used to create informational texts that are within reach for primary-grade children (also see discussion of sheltered text in Chapter 5).
- Read and discuss informational books that provide facts that children are interested in knowing.
- Begin to record their ideas about the relevant content and add new information to the shared/interactive chart over a number of days as reading and discussions continue.
- Read and reread charts as new information is added.
- Make individual shared/interactive charts or individual books that can be read by the children. Books made from shared/interactive compositions by small groups and individuals can be sources of new information with a familiar vocabulary.
- When a unit of study is completed, shared/interactive books can be placed in the class library for checkout and at-home reading.

This approach has been used successfully in first grade (Siera & Combs, 1990).

Developing Labeled Drawings

- The day before the discussion of information about a topic is to begin, lightly sketch an outline of our subject, such as salamander, on a large piece of chart paper and have notes written around the edge of the chart or on sticky notes as reminders about the facts to discuss with the children.
- Engage children to talk about the subject, such as salamanders, and begin to "fill in" the sketch with a marker.
- Encourage the children to talk about what they know and, as they do, add the information to the drawing.
- Children should help decide where and what information should be recorded.
- The completion of the drawing involves the re-collecting and re-presenting of what is known about a topic.
- With the completion of a composition, teachers must then consider how to best use that composition to extend children's interactions with print, as well as reading and writing processes.

Making Connections . . .

Return to the second-grade composition about pumpkins. Imagine that it is late October. If you invite children to write portions of this text interactively, to share the pen and write words on the chart paper, which words might be most appropriate for second-grade children to attempt to spell? Which words might be sight words by this time of the school year? Which words might have beginnings and endings that children will know? Which words have letter patterns that some children might know? Provide support for your thinking.

Extending interactions with shared/interactive texts provides opportunities for all children to add to their knowledge about reading and writing. Kelli extends interactions through rereading and guided and independent activities with both the original and duplicated copies of the text. William uses interactive writing as prewriting or the "getting started" phase in which children prepare for writing. How might teachers make decisions about the ways to extend children's interactions with texts? Shared compositions become shared readings (see Chapter 5), and include all of the various types of text extensions that are possible with a text.

 EXTENDING INTERACTIONS WITH THE ORIGINAL TEXT

Once the composition is complete, the following activities are appropriate to use with the rereading of the text in a teacher-guided group.

Editing Text

🍎 To promote comprehension of text, children have the opportunity to edit the text with the teacher.

🍎 As children carefully reread, they are asked—sentence by sentence—if there is anything about the text they want to change.

🍎 Editing emphasizes both meaning and correctness. Reasoning for a change or no change is discussed.

Concept of Word in Print

🍎 A child points to text while other children read aloud, matching spoken words with text.

🍎 The teacher notes the accuracy of the match.

🍎 When asked to find a word that should be familiar, the child should be able to pick out the word.

🍎 The teacher notes whether the child is developing sight recognition of the word and can find the word without rereading from the beginning of the text.

Guided Rereading

🍎 The teacher guides reading by asking children to predict, read, and prove their predictions in the text (see Chapter 6 for procedures).

🍎 Even though the text is familiar, attention to thinking and making meaning should be stressed.

Use Context, Written Cloze

🍎 The teacher blocks or masks a word, exposing only the beginning sound(s); children supply the word and tell how they know.

🍎 A sentence can also be taken out of context and written on the chalkboard,

We pushed with our l_____.

🍎 Children discuss the reasoning to support their prediction.

Reinforcing Sight Words

🍎 Children use a "magic window" (heavy paper rectangle with a word-size window in the middle) to read words in isolation as sight words (see Figure 8.17).

🍎 A locating device such as plastic fly swatter with a hole cut in the middle may also be used to highlight text.

Reinforcing Alphabet Recognition

🍎 Children find multiple examples of a letter in a chart to reinforce letter recognition (see Figure 8.18).

FIGURE 8.17
Magic window for sight word practice.

Frogs

Frogs can jump a long way.

Frogs jump with their back

legs. The back le[g]

stretched out. The[ ] legs

are not for jumpin[g]

jumped like frogs. We pushed

with our legs.

FIGURE 8.18
Finding letters in text.

Find "f"

Frogs

Frogs can jump a long way. Frogs jump with their back legs. The back legs get all stretched out. The front legs are not for jumping. We jumped like frogs. We pushed with our legs.

 The teacher writes words on the chalkboard and the children circle the target letter(s) in each word and also identify capital and lowercase forms of letters that appear in the text.

Reinforcing Phonics Patterns

 Depending upon children's word knowledge, the text can be used to identify particular letter-sound patterns (such as *fr* or short *a*).

 The teacher writes the words on the chalkboard/whiteboard, and:

 children read in isolation,

 listen for the sound pattern,

 look for visual patterns, and

 reread in context.

Reinforcing Morphemic Patterns

 Depending upon children's word knowledge, use the text to identify appropriate morphemic patterns. For example, in the frog story, the base word *jump* appears with different inflectional suffixes (*jumped, jumping*).

 Group activities should be selected based on children's background experiences with print and their familiarity with the text.

EXTENDING INTERACTIONS WITH DUPLICATED TEXT

After the text is composed and read on the first day, individual copies of text should be made for the children. For future reference, be sure to date each text. These copies may be typed or handwritten in manuscript. The text should be written in the same format as the original text. Duplicate copies can be used for the following activities.

Rereading Text

- Practice reading as a group, with a partner, or individually.
- Make a personal collection of cumulative shared texts for each child.
- Make a class booklet of shared texts to place in the library corner for independent reading.

Reconstructing Text

- Cut up and match sentences, phrases, or words to an intact copy.
- Cut up and reconstruct the original text or revise in a form that makes sense.

Class-made Big Book

- After a text has been composed, read, and discussed, it can be written on separate pages for children to illustrate the next day.
- The big book can be read by small groups or the whole group, then placed in the library corner for all to enjoy.

Individual Books

- Illustrate the text by leaving space at the top of the copy or make a personal booklet from the shared text by cutting apart text and gluing it on separate pages to create a book that may also be illustrated.
- Individual books of shared readings are great for at-home reading, along with commercially published texts.
- Using shared reading as little books validates children as authors.

Sentence Building

- With words from the text, children build meaningful phrases and sentences to practice with sight words and reinforce their knowledge of the syntax of our language.
- Stauffer (1975) suggests giving children a word-card holder made of flannel-covered cardboard, on which to arrange word cards. Desktop size (9″ × 12″) is sufficient. The felt will help to keep the cards in place as children construct phrases and sentences (see Figure 8.19).

Frogs	jump	can	a	long
way	with	their	back	legs
We	jumped	our	like	pushed

FIGURE 8.19
Sentence building—build sentences from the text or create new ones.

FIGURE 8.20
Word building—*frog, frogs, jump, jumps, jumped, jumping.*

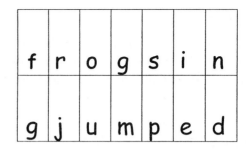

Word Building

🍎 Use letter cards to build words from the text. Focus on letter-sound or structural patterns when possible.

🍎 Example—Build a rime (*-og*), then add the onset (*fr-*) to complete the word.

🍎 Example—Build a base word (*frog*), then add a suffix (*-s*) to make a related word (*frogs*). See Figure 8.20.

Word Sorts

🍎 Both open and closed words sorts (see Chapters 2 and 3 for numerous examples) may be done with words that have been accumulated from shared texts. Children determine categories in open sorts, and teachers determine categories in a closed sort.

🍎 Word sorts may use meaning sorts or characteristics of words, such as phonics or morphemic patterns. Hall (1981) suggests a variety of meaning sorts, such as:

descriptive words	foods
compound words	naming words
colors	feelings
action words	people
sports	interesting words
animals	science words

Word Bank Books

🍎 Small books can be made out of blank paper, folded and stapled, with a child-decorated cover.

🍎 Children write one word bank word or a meaningful phrase or sentence on each page. The phrases/sentences may be constructed during the sentence-making activity.

🍎 Each page is then illustrated and taken home to read.

🍎 Books with a theme can also be made following sorting activities.

Magic Window Words

- Use an index card with a word-size window cut out of the center to isolate and read words in the duplicate shared text.
- Children can test themselves or a partner on sight words.

Word Hunts

- Children enjoy finding their words in other published materials such as newspapers, magazines, and children's literature.
- Words found during the hunting activity can be recorded in a list or cut out for sharing.

Word Posters

- Stauffer (1975) suggests that word posters have a focus or theme, such as words for colors, words for people, *-ing* words, or words that begin like *frog* (*fr*).
- Words can be cut out of newspapers and magazines and used to make word posters.
- Word posters can be individual or group. Individual posters can be kept in children's shared writing folders until they are filled. Group posters can be prominently displayed in the classroom so that children can add to the posters as words are found.

Picture Dictionary

- To stimulate an interest in words, children can keep personal dictionaries where they collect words they want to learn to read and/or spell.
- A folder of 26 pages of blank or lined paper, one for each letter of the alphabet, can become a picture dictionary.
- When a word is added, children may make a small illustration to remind them of the word.

Word Wall

- A word wall can be thought of as a group word bank. Words that are common to most individual word banks or commonly needed for writing activities can be drawn from shared texts, placed on large cards, and added to a word wall.
- It is helpful for the words to be related in some way such as theme (frogs), type of word (verbs), or spelling pattern (_____og words).

Games

- Many common and commercial game formats can be used to extend children's work with words. Lotto (like Bingo), Go Fish, Concentration, and jigsaw puzzles can be made into extension activities.

Art

🍎 At the art center, children can paint pictures. The bottom of the painting paper is folded under. After the painting is completed, unfold the paper and record children's ideas about their painting.

🍎 The paintings are displayed around the room. Children are encouraged to read each other's dictations and to find words they know in the dictations.

🍎 To help the children who need practice with their handwriting, duplicate sentences from the shared writing and provide space for children to practice writing the words, leaving spaces between words.

Once students have been introduced to cutting/reconstructing text and checking self-knowledge of known words in a shared text, these activities can be completed independently with follow-up by the teacher. These are but a few of the possibilities for extending shared/interactive texts and children's interest in words. Children will be successful in extension activities if there has been adequate practice in appropriate-level activities.

From the ideas and activities discussed in this chapter it is clear that shared/interactive writing is an engaging way to model writing processes and develop accessible reading materials for all students. Composition may be made with the whole class, in small groups, or with individual children. Any topic in our knowledge is a topic about which we can write. The important consideration is that the topic is meaningful to the children and one that is worth preserving for future rereading and rethinking.

Making Connections . . .

Return to one of the shared or interactive compositions presented in this chapter. Imagine that you are going to develop this composition with a class of students. Describe the procedure you might use. After the composition is complete, how might you extend children's interactions with the text? What activities might you do with the original chart? What activities might you do with duplicated copies of the text? Can you explain the rationale for your choices? Share your thinking with a peer.

ASSESSMENT: MONITORING CHILDREN'S DEVELOPMENT IN SHARED/INTERACTIVE WRITING

Shared/interactive writing provides opportunities for teachers to observe children's development of:

🍎 knowledge of ways to organize writing,

🍎 ways to include appropriate ideas and content in writing,

🍎 use of conventions in writing,

🍎 showing voice in writing,

🍎 ability to reread for meaning, and

🍎 ability to attend to details and patterns in words.

Shared/interactive compositions serve as a model for writing. During composition with children, teachers should carefully observe the level of their engagement, their thinking that is evidenced by personal contributions, and their interactions with text during rereading and extension activities.

Shared/interactive writing is integrally linked to shared, and possibly guided and independent, reading. Children demonstrate their learning from shared writings through shared readings and rereadings.

Shared writing will model composing processes for children. Interactive writing will directly engage children in the composing process. To observe the full effect of such modeling and engagement, teachers should observe children during guided and independent writing, as discussed in Chapter 9. Look for evidence of children's developing knowledge of the composing process, of the traits embodied in good writing (e.g., organization, ideas/content, voice conventional use of language). A discussion of the traits to look for in children's writing can be found in Chapter 9.

Writing development occurs slowly over time. Consequently, observations of children must also be made over time, keeping in mind the changes observed and making records to accurately recall those changes. A sample form for recording such observations is provided in Figure 8.21. Such record-keeping forms should be developed to fit the particular behaviors that a teacher desires to help children develop and the curriculum standards adopted at a particular grade level.

RESPECTING DIVERSITY WITH SHARED/ INTERACTIVE WRITING

In shared/interactive writing, the text comes from the children. The content of the text relates to children's interest and knowledge of a topic. These factors make shared/interactive compositions an excellent approach for reading and writing instruction in a diverse classroom. The flexibility of grouping, the nature of the content, and the length and complexity of the text are easily adjusted to the needs of the learners.

Respecting the Language of the Learner

Seeing one's own words in print is affirming. English language learners understand material that is culturally and/or experientially familiar to them better than they understand unfamiliar content (Barnitz, 1986; Rigg, 1986). The personalized nature of shared/interactive writing provides the opportunity to develop reading materials that are familiar to children who are English language learners. Sharing stories from children's culture provides excellent content for shared writings (Rigg, 1989). The oral language used during shared compositions represents the language patterns and content over which English language learners have control. Compositions should affirm children's ability to communicate their thinking.

FIGURE 8.21

Record keeping for shared/interactive writing.

Name				Shared/Interactive Writing
Shared Compositions	**Usually**	**Sometimes**	**Rarely**	**Comments:**
Contributes ideas/content to composition.				
Contributes ideas for organization to composition.				
Demonstrates knowledge of composing processes.				
Demonstrates knowledge of voice by expressing ideas in personally unique ways.				
Attends to the recording of ideas.				

Interactive Compositions	**Usually**	**Sometimes**	**Rarely**	**Comments:**
Contributes ideas/content to composition.				
Contributes ideas for organization to composition.				
Demonstrates knowledge of conventions—letter-sound knowledge to write words.				
Demonstrates knowledge of conventions—capital letters and punctuation.				
Attends to the recording of ideas.				

Read/Reread Text	**Usually**	**Sometimes**	**Rarely**	**Comments:**
Rereads composition, using knowledge of composing process.				
Tracks text while rereading.				
Demonstrates concept of word in rereading.				
Uses familiar context to predict words in text.				
Finds details in text.				
Reconstructs text from sentences, words.				

Developing Word Knowledge	**Usually**	**Sometimes**	**Rarely**	**Comments:**
Adds sight words to writing vocabulary.				
Adds sight words to reading vocabulary.				
Demonstrates knowledge of letter-sound patterns in words.				
Demonstrates knowledge of structure units in words.				

Shared writing is appropriate for use with English language learners, with a few modifications. For example, children can illustrate words that are being added to their word bank. Encourage children to draw a small picture on the back of each word-bank card to provide an association with the word. Content words, words that can be pictured, will be most useful in early reading instruction.

Encourage retellings of well-known stories and information. After reading a text that children enjoy, encourage children to retell the most important parts. The language of the retelling will be simplified when compared with the text. Record the retelling and use it for instruction, especially if the original text was not a repetitive, patterned text. Sheltering the English of a text and using a simplified version for instruction can be successful with English language learners (Treadway, 1993).

Respecting Special Learning Needs

The personalized nature of shared/interactive writing is an excellent approach for working with children who have special learning needs (Bowyer, 1988; Ewoldt & Hammermeister, 1986). For learners who have special needs, emphasis might be placed on individual compositions. Shared writing results in personalized reading materials. Individual compositions can provide reading material that is appropriate to the needs and interests of the learner. Careful observation during rereading helps us identify strategies that individual readers use successfully and those strategies that are absent or misused. Comprehension is supported by the child's firsthand knowledge of the text. Learners who experience difficulty with decoding text are also supported by familiar content as decoding skills are practiced.

Respecting the Thinking of the Learner

Recording children's language also shows them that their ideas are important and valid. Small-group and individual dictations are especially important in this respect. The smaller the group, the greater the likelihood that individual children will find their ideas reflected in print. They will hear their ideas read aloud by others.

Respecting Experiential Background

Shared texts grow out of classroom experiences and the interests of the children. The flexibility of shared compositions enables the teacher to engage children in writing and reading about experiences that are shared by the class, as well as those that are known and valued by individuals.

Making Connections . . .

As you reflect on the content of this chapter, what ideas do you have about modeling writing processes for children and guiding their thinking about how writers compose their thoughts on paper? What do you think will be the most important things for you to consider as you plan for shared and interactive writing experiences? How will you integrate your knowledge of children's development of word knowledge from Chapters 2 and 3 to help you make decisions about the appropriate circumstances to "share the pen" with your students during interactive writing? Record your thinking in a reflective journal. Share your thinking with your peers.

C H A P T E R

9

Guided and Independent Writing

Scaffolding Children's Writing

Adding to our literacy framework . . .

	Reading Aloud and Guided Literature Study	
Shared Reading	**Balanced and Integrated Literacy Framework**	Shared and Interactive Writing
Guided Reading and Guided Literature Study		Guided Writing and Writer's Workshop
Independent Reading and Reader's Workshop		Independent Writing
	Word Study	

In this chapter, we learn about . . .

- Examining writing both as a process and as a functional task
- Exploring how to extend composing processes that began in shared writing to support children in their move toward independence as writers
- Planning for a variety of types of writing that occur in primary-grade classrooms

Looking into Classrooms . . .

One day in January, Renee begins guided writing, also known as writer's workshop, with her first-grade children gathered on the floor for a read-aloud. The book is about a boy who uses his imagination, pretending he is an astronaut that discovers a new planet. As she finishes the story, Renee begins a mini-lesson about using imagination in writing: "I have noticed that several of you are using your imagination in your writing just like the author of this book." Renee encourages children to share about their imaginative writing and she comments on the writing of two other children. The workshop does not always begin with a read-aloud, but there is usually some "tip" for authors that comes from Renee, the children, or another author such as Tomie dePaola or Ezra Jack Keats.

As their writing folders are passed out, Renee asks the children to turn to their neighbor and tell what they will be doing today during the writing time. Doug asks if Renee will help him brainstorm ideas, because he's "stuck." When everyone has their writing folder, the children are free to find a comfortable place to go and begin a period of sustained writing and talking about their writing.

Four girls settle together on the floor near a bookshelf that has a display of alphabet books. Each of them is making an alphabet book, and occasionally they refer to alphabet books by other authors for ideas. William settles at a table and begins to reread aloud what he wrote the day before about a tornado that came near his house. Sarah, who just returned from a 3-week absence, has some difficulty settling in. She approaches Renee, who is sitting with Doug, helping him brainstorm topics for his writing. Renee encourages Sarah to "ask someone else, because there are lots of other teachers in the room" who can help her. Sarah leaves and finds Bonita at a table in the corner. The girls begin to talk and write, side by side.

When Renee leaves Doug to write on his own, she sees that Sarah has begun to write so she stops and glances around the room. Justin approaches her to tell "facts" he knows about tornadoes. Renee suggests that he share his ideas with William, who might find the facts helpful for his story on tornadoes.

335

From across the room Marty motions to Renee. She kneels down beside him at the reading table as Marty reads aloud his piece about the cold night when his lambs were born. He has signed up for the author's chair today and he appears a little nervous about the questions the other children might ask about his piece. Forty-five minutes have passed and Renee calls the children back to the carpet for the author's chair. Three children have signed up to share their writing. Marty is first. After he reads his piece aloud, William compliments him by saying, "I really liked your story." Then William asks, "Did the baby sheep really die?" Quickly, Justin echoes, "The cutest one? The one I saw?" Questions arise about the red light that Marty mentioned but didn't explain in his piece. When the questions and comments cease, the children clap and Marty leaves the author's chair for the next author to share. And so goes a day of guided writing during writer's workshop in this first-grade classroom.

DOWN THE HALL . . .

Peggy and her second-grade children are in the computer lab putting the polishing touches on their latest compositions. Peggy has shown the children how they can breathe life into their words by using different font sizes and types, as well as color, to accentuate particular words in their compositions (see Figure 9.1). The class has been discussing the importance of word choice in getting a message across to others. The children type intently in their best "hunt and peck" method. Occasionally they solicit assistance from a neighbor or from Peggy. There is excitement in the lab as the words they emphasize in their compositions seem to jump off the page with interesting shapes and colors. Peggy sees how creating a finished product, like the published writings that children read each day, motivates the children to want to communicate their ideas and be heard. She witnesses their growth in confidence as they begin to believe in their own power as writers.

FIGURE 9.1
Visual writing—second grade.

> The Seagull Life
> by *Francisco*
>
> If I could be anything, just for today, I would be a seagull. I would be big and have long wings. I would be brown with **BLACK** on the tips of my wing. I would fly HIGH over the ocean. I would eat fish. I would be HAPPY.

BUILDING A THEORY BASE . . .

To support children's development as writers, teachers move from shared writing to guided and independent writing as children's actions demonstrate their ability to monitor and guide themselves as writers. In Chapter 8 we explored the potential of shared and interactive writing to model writing processes and scaffold children's thinking about producing written communication. Now we turn our attention to guided and independent writing opportunities, in which children learn more about their own strengths as writers.

All journeys take time, and when the going is tough some travelers will take longer than others. It is possible on a journey to have a rest along the way—several rests, if the journey is an extended trek over unfamiliar ground. It is possible to look back over ground already covered and to look forward at least as far as the next bend. It is useful to be able to call on help if you get stuck, and it can be reassuring to have company, at least from time to time, as the journey progresses (D'Arcy, 1989, pp. 27–28).

WRITING—GUIDING CHILDREN'S JOURNEY IN THINKING

Writing is like a journey, developed over time through a recursive, or flexible, process (D'Arcy, 1989; Calkins, 1986, 1994; Graves, 1983, 1994). The process of exploring, developing, or examining one's ideas through written language is considered to be a recursive process because writers move between phases of writing as it suits the writer's need. Once children have developed a good sense of letter-sound relationships, are combining words into sentences, and have a beginning understanding of the use of punctuation and capitalization, teachers should provide scaffolding that moves them toward developing and evaluating their own pieces of writing. This is a fragile process and very dependent on carefully observing children's readiness (Soderman, Gregory, & O'Neill, 1999).

When teachers encourage children to approach their writing as a process, children learn that writing is indeed a process, a medium, a code, and a product, as we discussed in Chapter 8:

- *Writing as process* is a perspective that undergirds the writing from start to finish.
- *Writing as a medium* comes into play as students consider their options for shaping ideas.
- Knowledge of *writing as a code* is vital for meaning and clarity during both composing and editing.
- *Writing as a product* is realized during the publishing/re-presenting phase.

To develop an idea fully, writers go through different phases with their thinking and writing. The phases of writing serve different purposes. In this text we use labels that are descriptive of each phase:

- Getting started
- Finding a focus

- Composing
- Editing for meaning and correctness
- Re-presentation

Getting Started

Getting started with writing is also referred to as prewriting or rehearsal. The term *prewriting* may be misleading for young children, whereas *rehearsal* may be too abstract. Children often describe themselves as "getting started," hence the choice of the term. During this phase children will do such things as:

- conside their purpose for writing,
- consider what they know about topics,
- use a variety of strategies to explore their thinking, and
- consider who the writing might be for, or the audience.

Children may start their writing in a variety of ways. Some children need to read and think, some need to draw, some need to brainstorm or make a cluster of their ideas, and some appear to daydream but are really "writing in their heads" (Murray, 1985). Because writers use different strategies as they get started, teachers should not dictate one strategy, such as clustering, for all children. Learning only one strategy may limit some children who plan through means other than the one chosen. Experiences with informal types of writing—such as making lists, writing notes, or writing an explanation of an idea—help children see the many different forms that their thinking can take as they prepare to develop a piece of writing.

Teachers should not hurry children through this phase. If so, children may struggle with a piece that never really takes shape and, consequently, is not self-satisfying. Exploring ideas during this phase is essential if children are to find a focus.

Finding a Focus

At some point during the getting started phase, children are ready to clarify their topic and direction. This is when response from someone else may be very helpful. Having another listen to our ideas can affirm or help clarify our thinking. Children can learn to become responsive listeners. Teachers must model what responsive listening looks and sounds like, then coach partners as they practice responsive listening. Teachers become responsive listeners as they conference with children about the focus of the writing. This is the point when, as D'Arcy (1989) suggests, teachers must look *through* children's writing, rather than at the writing itself. Once children find their focus, sustained writing will usually follow.

Composing

Sustained writing is the goal of this stage. When children have a clear sense of where they are trying to go with a piece of writing, sustaining their effort is not so difficult. Children who continue to struggle with their writing during this phase usually have not really found their focus. A teacher's role during the composing phase is to "get out of children's way." As long as they are sustaining the writing, let them go. Children can use this phase to build stamina as writers. The composing phase may be the first time for many children that writing continues beyond short bursts.

Composing is the phase when the recursive nature of writing can be observed. Some children will move back to strategies from the getting started phase, especially when they find the need to question or clarify what they know about their topic. Some children will, on occasion, move ahead into editing. For some writers, moving back and forth between composing and editing is a natural activity for checking their thinking. One reason to step back when children are composing is to let them begin to discover their own style as writers. Children cannot learn about their own style if teachers continuously intrude when they are in a sustained effort with their writing.

Figure 9.2 shows an example of a composition by a second-grade student, Ramon, in response to a folktale read aloud by his teacher. During the composing process his teacher and classmates were available for guidance and response, but Ramon had a great deal of freedom to organize and develop his composition in ways that pleased him.

Editing for Meaning and Correctness

The phase of the writing process called editing for meaning and correctness is frequently referred to as two separate phases, revising and editing. Revising typically refers to making changes for meaning, whereas editing usually refers to making changes for language conventions or correctness. In this text we simply use the term *editing*. Children understand that editing means "making changes," both changes for meaning and changes for correctness.

Editing for meaning requires a writer to become a reader, and read for meaning. Making meaning may involve more than just changing words. Children may need to restructure sentences or rearrange words to communicate their ideas more clearly. Minor changes also may be made, such as adding punctuation to clarify the meaning. The more teachers are able to help children view language as a medium of communication, the easier it is to get them to mold their words, just as they mold clay. A pinch here, and extra piece there, improves the form of a clay sculpture. Teachers can help children see their words as clay that can be molded into more meaningful and satisfying text.

Editing for correctness requires a writer to become a reader and read for surface details, so that the writing looks the way other readers expect English to look. Writers want other readers to understand the message, so it must follow the rules of English. This phase usually focuses on conventions of writing such as capitalization and spelling. How well children are able to edit for conventions in their writing depends on their stage of word knowledge and spelling development.

Teachers must use what they know about children during this phase so that expectations for children's use of correct spelling remain realistic. For example, if we know that a child is just beginning to spell short-vowel words such as *cap* and *hot,* we should not expect to see most other complex words spelled correctly.

FIGURE 9.2
Ramon's retelling of *Maui and the Sun.*

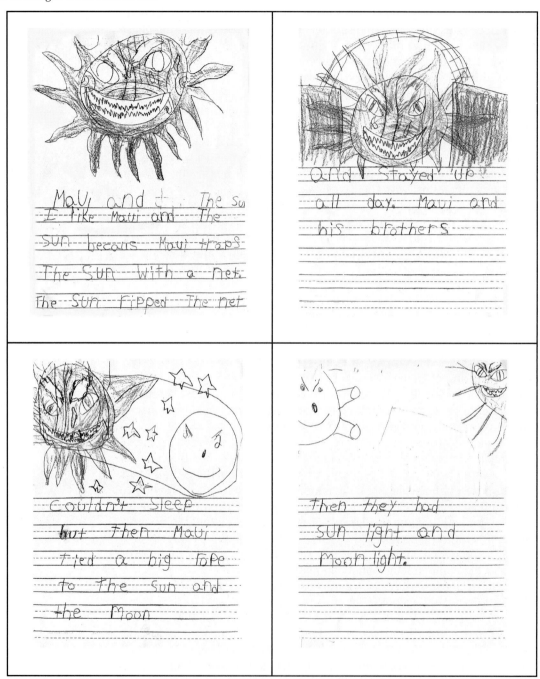

Forming editing groups can assist children with achieving a satisfactory level of correctness in their writing. Here again, teachers must model for children how to read someone's writing and help them find details that might need attention. During the modeling, emphasize that attention to the code is done in order to communicate with others. For example, words are spelled in certain ways because speakers of English have agreed to use the same spellings in order to understand one another. If each of us chose our own spellings for a word, or our own grammatical structures, we would probably need others to interpret their writing for us.

Re-Presenting the Writing

During the re-presenting phase, children should have opportunities for public sharing of their writing. In an author's chair (Graves, 1983, 1994), a child reads aloud a piece of writing to which other children respond and question. Writing should also be prominently displayed in the classroom or published in books that are available for all to read. Children learn about writing through sharing in the writing of their classmates. As children journey as writers, we must provide appropriate assistance, guiding their writing as needed, to help them achieve satisfaction with their ability to communicate with others through print.

MOVING TOWARD INDEPENDENCE AS WRITERS

As teachers participate with children in many varied writing experiences, such as shared writing and writer's workshop, they scaffold children's understanding of ways in which individuals can use written language to communicate with others. Teachers serve as models of fluent writing, support children's developing understanding of concepts about print, collaborate in the act of composition, think aloud as authors, and share things they have learned about writing.

Children who are fortunate to live with other responsive adults have seen similar models during their preschool years. Slowly, as children become more aware of print and its possibilities, they attempt to produce their own print, making their

Children become each other's teachers as they talk about and share what they know about writing.

FIGURE 9.3
Alex's kindergarten composition.

own messages to self and others. Teachers, as more experienced writers, also encourage children to venture out on their own. During independent writing, children have the opportunity to work alone and use their current knowledge of the writing process to compose and construct their own texts (McCarrier, Pinnell, & Fountas, 2000). Their independent writings enable children to orchestrate on their own all that they have observed and participated in as writers. Independent writings enable teachers to observe and value children's personal development as writers. For example, Figure 9.3 shows an independent writing opportunity that allowed Alex to express his sense of satisfaction with himself as he writes, "I like me." In this kindergarten classroom, children have daily opportunites to demonstrate their ability to use written language to express ideas and communicate with others.

To encourage independence teachers can provide daily opportunities for writing in a writer's workshop and throughout the school day. Personal journals in which topic, focus, length, and format are controlled by the children can be encouraged (Soderman et al., 1999). Teachers can also integrate many shorter writing opportunities into the day, functional writings that will not receive the extended focus of a writer's workshop. Functional writings, examined in Chapter 8 as a part of shared and interactive writing, allow children to experiment with many varied formats for a range of purposes. These writings may take the form

of annotated drawings, lists, responses, and explanations. The key is daily time to write in meaningful ways.

Making Connections . . .

What experiences have you had as a writer? How have others supported you to become a better writer, providing guidance as you seek to understand the processes writers can use to communicate their thinking? How have others thwarted your progress as a writer? It is important to understand your own growth as a writer, your own journey toward communicating your sense of yourself in the world, and your sense of yourself in relation to others. Understanding your own journey as a writer is the foundation for preparing to support children in their journey.

PUTTING THEORY INTO PRACTICE . . .

An excellent way to put the writing process to work in the classroom is through a writer's workshop. A workshop is a very flexible format for organizing learning experiences that can meet the diversity of children's learning styles and preferences (Five, 1988; Hansen, 1987). A workshop format moves from whole-group activity, to a work time for individuals and/or small groups, then back to whole group during a specified time period that can vary from 30 to 90 minutes depending on the activities planned. To maximize children's development as writers, a writer's workshop should occur daily for 40 to 60 minutes (Calkins, 1994; Graves; 1994).

GETTING STARTED IN WRITER'S WORKSHOP— A VISIT TO PEGGY'S CLASSROOM

We begin considering classroom practices in writing with Peggy, a second-grade teacher who shares how and why she approaches helping her students learn the potential for writing through guided writing. Peggy's school is located in a lower-socioeconomic neighborhood that is somewhat diverse.

Peggy narrates:
My students come to second grade with a limited understanding of writing. My initial goal is to have students be able to complete a cohesive, organized piece of writing that communicates their response to personal experiences. It is also important that they learn to use the basic conventions of English (capital letters, punctuation, spelling, and complete sentences). During the year we focus on both fictional and informational writing. It is important to me that children's writing is personally meaningful and that the process seems purposeful to them. I provide varying levels of support to help their writing become fluid. I don't want these developing writers to be overwhelmed or discouraged by the process.

Writing fiction:

I listen to their thoughts during calendar/sharing activities. To encourage fictional writing I focus on what's interesting to them. I try to use their language and thoughts so they can see/hear themselves telling stories. For example, one morning I start calendar activities as normal but, after business is taken care of, launch into a personal story about seeing the neighbor come home and then a big, striped cat jumping up on the hood of his car. I begin to talk about wishing I could have been that cat—just for one day. I begin to tell a story, like I'm making it up on the spot. I describe myself (big, fluffy gray cat with green eyes—because I like green eyes). I talk about hopping the fences and spying on the neighbors, about sneaking food from neighbor cats, about hiding in the bushes near the mailbox and leaping out to scare the mailman, and finally sneaking into the house to lie down by the heater vent to go to sleep. I describe the neighborhood and house like those that surround the school so the students can connect familiar elements to the storytelling. I tell them, in the end, that I'd only want to be the cat for a day because I really like being who I am. They all laugh and tell me it's a good story.

Some children ask me to retell certain parts. I stumble a bit so they will direct me through the retelling. That's when I pull out a piece of chart paper, fold it into four rectangles (2 × 2), and say, "We better write down these ideas so we won't forget." Then, interactively, we fill in simple details. In the center, we make a circle and write "big, fluffy gray cat with green eyes." Then, in each square we write one thing that the cat would do (spy on the neighbors, eat other cat's food, scare the mailman, sneak in the house and go to sleep). I ask the children as if I don't remember why I even told this story. (This approach is adapted from the *Four-Square Writing Method,* Gould & Gould, 2002).

Eventually someone says, "Because you said you wished you were a cat for just today." Then I say, "That could be a beginning sentence, if I ever wanted to write this story down," and I have students write the sentence interactively at the top of the paper. Finally, I ask, "What would be a good ending to this little story about the cat?" Someone repeats what I said, that it was the best day of my life. Again, we interactively write that at the bottom of the paper and leave the activity for the day.

The next day, after calendar, we revisit the story. This time I get the chart paper out and ask the students to retell the story. They usually correct others in the group when they don't retell it in order or leave out details. I say, "I guess I could draw a couple of pictures above my words so I remember the way I meant it," and I draw a few things. Usually I have to retell my story one more time because they like to hear it. Then I suggest that we all could write a story like this. First, they think about something they would like to be for just one day. We explore animals, like horses, dogs, monkeys, and birds, and how their day might turn out, in their natural habitat or in the neighborhood. Then, I tell them that is doesn't have to be a real animal. What about a dragon or a unicorn? They all chatter about that. What about being a changed human—like being able to fly or being invisible or having an identical twin? What if you were tiny? Lots of chatter and thoughts emerge as the children consider different ideas.

Then I ask the children to pick one animal or change and think about four things they could do if they were transformed. We think back to our in-

teractive writing and how the cat began his day. I ask, "How do you begin
your day? What would you do during the afternoon? When I was the cat, I
scared the mailman during the afternoon. How would your day end? Think
about these things and then write what you have changed into in the middle of your paper. Fold the paper into fours and write the things you'd do
during the day in the four boxes. The easy part will be the sentences."

At the top of my paper, I write, "Just for one day, I wish I were a cat." I
ask, "What will you write on the top of your paper?" At the bottom I write,
"This was the best day of my life." I ask, "What will you write?"

After our work together, I send them out to plan for their writing. They will
create a four-square story map just as we did together. I circulate the room to
support, praise, show astonishment, and encourage. Once I see everyone coming up with an idea, I mention that some people might want to make small drawings in their boxes after they write their ideas so they can remember exactly
what they meant. Austin imagines that he is a ghost (see Figure 9.4). At the end
of that writing time the children put their papers in their writing folders.

FIGURE 9.4
Organizing ideas—second grade.

The next day we revisit and retell the cat story and, using the folded chart paper, we write the story interactively. During the interactive activity, I remind students about all the conventions we need in the story and why. We talk about how easy it is when you have this little story map to help remind you about what you want to say. Then, time permitting, the children go to their desks and use the story maps to start writing their own stories. I remind them to look at the one we just did together for any unknown spelling words and as a reminder about periods, capital letters, and complete sentences. This writing may take 2 or 3 days to complete.

We (my team-teaching partner and I) do the editing individually, having a short meeting with each student to have them read their story and help them with words that they read aloud but are not on the paper or ideas from their story map that don't make it to the paper. Finally, we have mini-word study talks as we correct spelling. Their final step is to rewrite the story with corrections. This is their least favorite part, so I always tell them how great their story is and that I want a really nice copy to put on the wall, use in the computer lab to type, add with an art piece, send home, and so on. Austin presents his ideas for sharing with the class (see Figure 9.5).

FIGURE 9.5
Final copy—second grade.

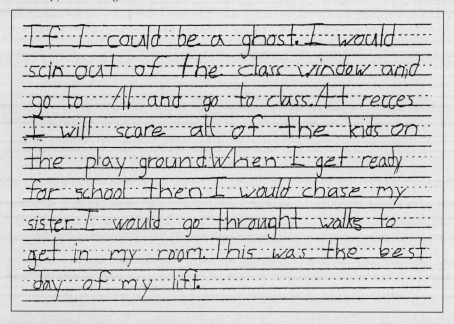

If I could be a ghost. I would scin out of the class window and go to All and go to class. At recces I will scare all of the kids on the play ground. When I get ready for school then I would chase my sister. I would go throught walks to get in my room. This was the best day of my lift.

Writing nonfiction:
The writing standards for second grade in my school district require me to focus on descriptive and informational writing. I think this works best when we focus on something accessible that my children may overlook but can be brought to life. I use a story as an entrance into writing about the real world. One afternoon, I read Byrd Baylor's *Everybody Needs a Rock.*

The next day, after calendar, I tell the students about a trip my family made to the beach. I tell them everything: the fight that happened between my 5- and 7-year-old sons in the front room while Grandma and I were making the picnic lunch; that my sister wouldn't eat mayonnaise and how we had to make special sandwiches for her; how we put sun lotion on everyone because we hate sunburns; how we saw seals in the water and, at first we were watching them but later we caught them watching us; how Liam found a big crab and he thought it was dead and he brought it over to show us and it moved and scared him so much that it flew out of his hands and landed in the sand; how our hands were sandy, and, no matter how we tried, we kept getting sand in the sandwiches; and how the bathroom at the beach was kind of stinky and had no toilet paper. Then I told them that we took a walk on the beach and that's when we realized that the seals were watching us. I tell them I found this rock (I show them my beach rock), and since that day, I have always kept it.

I talk aloud about why I keep a rock. They share thoughts about how the rock helped me remember the whole funny story about the beach. Then I ask them to see if they can find a special rock to bring to school. I remind them of what Byrd Baylor said—that it has to fit into your pocket (I've had boulders show up without this comment) and that it can be special for a lot of reasons. It could come from a special place, like your grandma's house or the park, or the place where you like to hide and no one knows where to look. It could just look interesting to you. It could remind you of something special, like a birthday party or a trip, or when you learned to ride a two-wheeler or of a special person. We collect rocks for 2 weeks (it takes that long) and bag and label them as they come in. We share the rocks each day to remind the others to bring one in.

The process of writing about a rock is like our fiction writing. I retell my beach story and then show my rock. We use a piece of chart paper folded into four squares and interactively write about my rock. This time, I tell them that we have all sorts of rocks and I wonder if we could describe my rock clearly enough that, if someone read our paper, they would know which rock was mine. I begin with an opening sentence to put at the top of the paper: "My special rock came from . . . " in my case, Half Moon Bay. During the 2 weeks of waiting for rocks to show up at school, we've done some rock activities for science. We talked about physical traits, like color, shape, pattern, and texture. We use these descriptors for each of the four squares on the chart paper. Interactively, we write "shape" and then decide how to describe the shape of my rock—oval. In the next square we write "color" and then decide my rock is three colors: white, tan, and brown. In the next square we write "pattern" and that my rock has swirls on it. Finally, in the last square we write "texture" and decide the best word is *smooth*. For a closing sentence we write that my rock is special because it reminds me of the fun day I had with my family and Grandma at Half Moon Bay (see Figure 9.6).

The next day we review my "rock map" and brainstorm some other words for each category. They suggest colors, shapes, and so on that we write down on separate pieces of chart paper for spelling purposes. I post

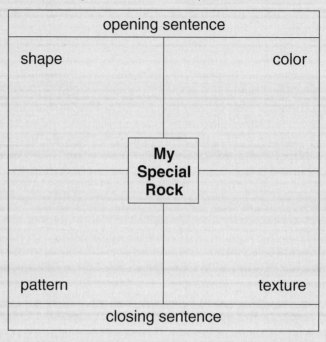

FIGURE 9.6
Four-square organization for "rock maps."

opening sentence	
shape	color
pattern	texture
closing sentence	

(center: **My Special Rock**)

these in the front of the room along with my "rock map" and hand out paper and each student's rock as their reference. My students sit in mixed-ability groups of six, so I encourage them to share their rock and map with others at the table when they're done to see if their tablemates agree with their descriptions (see Austin's rock map in Figure 9.7). We do the same thing for the writing process as we did with the fiction. They do the final piece in their best printing to use in the computer lab to type about their rocks (see Austin's final draft in Figure 9.8).

For a culminating experience and publication of their writing, we put six writings on the bulletin board (without names) and six rocks in a shallow box with a grid on the bottom. The rocks are labeled A through F and the writings are labeled 1 through 6. As a literacy center, the students have to match the rock to the writing. For each grouping I select rocks that have variations. At the end of each week, we read the six writings and ask which rock the writer is describing. During this discussion, lots of dialogue goes on about what made one easy to guess and how another was a bit confusing. Through this, the students see the importance of descriptive writing.

I frequently read student work to the class just as I read published books. In the process, the group will say, "That's Julian's work" or "That's Vanessa's story." I'll ask them how they know and they'll tell me "It's because that's the way Julian (or Vanessa) talks." From these discussions, we'll talk about voice and how much better it is to write the way you say it and not the way someone else does. We also talk about different kinds of stories, how some are strong stories of tough dogs and others are silly, like

FIGURE 9.7
Organizing ideas—second grade.

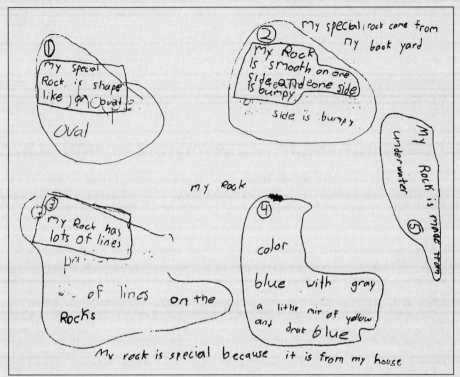

FIGURE 9.8
Final copy—second grade.

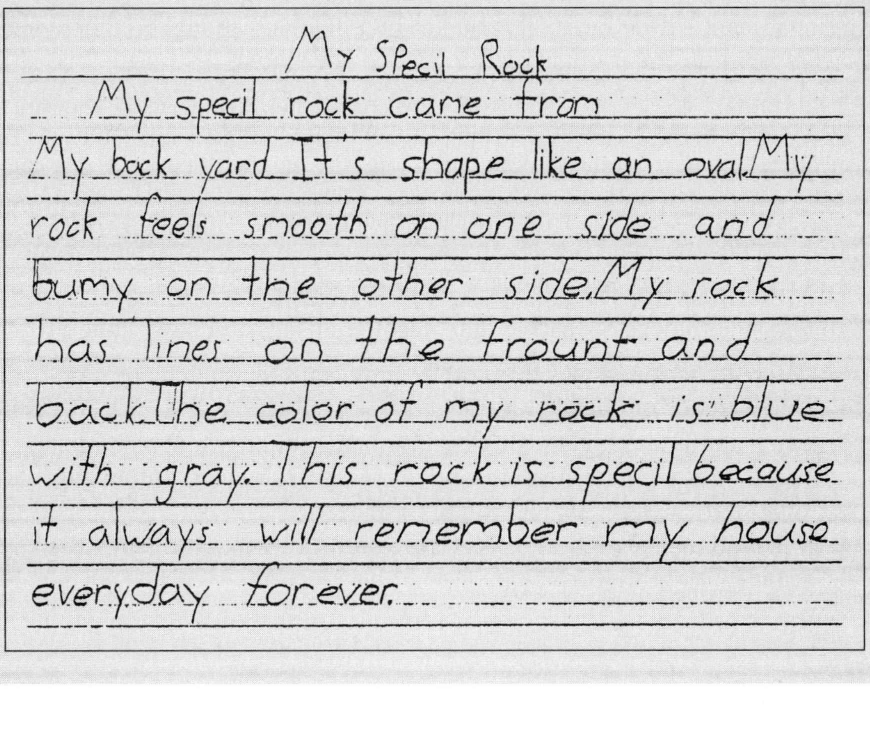

My SPecil Rock
My specil rock came from
My back yard It's shape like an oval.My
rock feels smooth on one side and
bumy on the other side.My rock
has lines on the frount and
back.The color of my rock is blue
with gray. This rock is specil because
it always will remember my house
everyday forever.

the boy who was a squirrel, and how others were sneaky, like one about a little mouse. I can't have these discussions without real, uninhibited writing as examples from my students. They don't seem to hear or value voice in the same way from a published text. They feel it's more attainable or feasible if they hear it from their own classmates.

ORGANIZING A WRITER'S WORKSHOP

A writer's workshop maintains a predictable structure that everyone in the classroom knows. Children have blocks of time for writing, have a choice of certain topics, receive response to their writing, have opportunity to see writing demonstrated, and participate in the evaluation of their writing. The phases of a writer's workshop and the components in each phase are shown in Figure 9.9. Each phase and component is discussed in this chapter.

If children are to become writers, they must have predictable time for writing every day (Calkins, 1994). When the time is predictable and children know when it will happen, they anticipate what they will do with their writing time that day. Calkins tells the story of a child who gets her ideas for writing just as she is about to fall asleep, so she keeps paper and a pencil near her bed to write down ideas as they come to her, saving the ideas for her next opportunity to write. For this young girl writing has become an expectation, something she plans for. This type of response to writing is not likely to happen unless your classroom makes a real commitment to time for daily writing.

Time for writing should also be a sustained block. The work of a writer requires time to settle in and to get in one's stride. Graves (1994) suggests a minimum of 35 to 40 minutes, 4 days per week, beginning in first grade. Calkins (1994) suggests at least 1 hour a day. She makes no apologies about the time commitment that is required for quality writing when she states:

> If students are going to become deeply invested in their writing, and if they are going to live toward a piece of writing and let their ideas grow and gather momentum, if they are going to draft and revise, sharing their texts with one another as they write, they need the luxury of time. For students to have the chance to do their best and, then, to make their best even better, they need long blocks of time. Sustained effort and craftsmanship are essential in writing well, yet they run contrary to the modern American way. (p. 186)

To find such blocks of writing time, teachers use writer's workshop to:

🍎 complete writing tasks from other subject areas, such as report writing from science or social studies;

🍎 teach and practice handwriting, grammar, punctuation, and spelling as a part of editing for meaning and correctness, instead of teaching each separately at some other time of the day; or

🍎 join reading instruction or literature studies with writing into a reader's/writer's workshop.

Whole-Class Opening Meeting (10–15 minutes)	Demonstration of writing mini-lesson or shared/interactive writing
	Plans for the day
Writing Time: (20–40 minutes)	Individual writing
	Writing conferences
	Response partners/groups
	Editing partners/groups
Whole-Class Closing Meeting (10–15 minutes)	Author's chair
	Closure for the day

FIGURE 9.9
Organizing a writer's workshop.

WHOLE-CLASS OPENING MEETING

Writer's workshop begins with some type of demonstration of writing that provides group instruction in the form of a mini-lesson or shared/interactive writing. The class also discusses what different individuals in the class will be doing that day.

Demonstrations of Writing: Mini-Lessons

Just like reading, writing involves ways of thinking about language that cannot be observed. Children need to see writing modeled and hear various writers think aloud about the content and process of their writing. Mini-lessons and shared writing experiences provide explicit demonstrations of workshop procedures, writing processes, forms of writing, and conventional uses of language.

From discussion of reader's workshop (Chapter 7) we know that mini-lessons are short, focused lessons, usually lasting no more than 5 to 10 minutes. They are intended to address knowledge, skills, and strategies that are helpful for children to know at a particular time or that children are "using but confusing." Mini-lessons serve as a "forum for planning a day's work, a time to call writers together . . . for raising a concern, exploring an issue, modeling a technique, reinforcing a strategy" (Calkins, 1994, p. 193).

Mini-lessons are intended to "put the idea in the room" as Calkins (1986) suggests, so that children can explore the idea if it is helpful to them or share the idea with each other. Mini-lessons plant seeds of ideas or extend upon what children already have demonstrated an awareness of. Mini-lessons should extend what children have begun to learn through informal writing.

Procedural Mini-Lessons

In the beginning stages of writing workshop, various mini-lessons offer help for learning workshop procedures and routines, such as:

- How to Sustain My Writing
- It's Okay to Abandon a Piece of Writing
- Rereading to Check for Meaning
- Making Changes in My Writing
- How to Conference with Another Writer
- How to Conference with Myself
- When Am I Ready for Author's Chair?

Topics for procedural mini-lessons come from the way that teachers set up a writer's workshop and from observations of the children's response to the workshop.

Content Mini-Lessons

To develop mini-lessons that draw upon the content of the writing, consider what is known about various genres, literary elements, and text structures. Primary-grade children can benefit from mini-lessons about the following:

- sequence of a plot,
- using character dialogue to tell the story,
- getting a story started,
- who's telling the story,
- how to write persuasively,
- comparing and contrasting two things, and
- making descriptions come alive.

As children's writing develops, mini-lessons become specific to writing in a particular genre, such as mysteries. For such mini-lessons, examples from literature and children's writing can be used to illustrate:

- how to get a mystery started,
- how authors use clues to build suspense, and
- how authors resolve their mysteries.

Strategy Mini-Lessons

With procedures and content underway, children can benefit from support in thinking about the personal strategies they use as writers. Mini-lessons can focus on such topics as:

- different ways to get started with writing,
- checking for ending punctuation,
- how to use the word wall to check for spelling,
- rereading to check for meaning, or
- using a rubric to evaluate writing.

Sample Mini-Lesson in Kindergarten. An important strategy lesson for emergent writers, children who are just getting started in writing process, is to demonstrate that young children "write" in a variety of ways. In an early mini-lesson Elena demonstrates on a chart in front of the children that there are a variety of ways that kindergarten children might write a "story." Elena writes:

- 🍎 Pictures that stand for words,
- 🍎 Loops and other shapes that resemble letters,
- 🍎 Strings of letters that might be familiar to a child but are not linked to particular sounds,
- 🍎 One or two letters to stand for words, such as the letter *b* to stand for *bed,* and
- 🍎 Some familiar words such as *mon, love,* and her name with conventional spellings.

Each time she writes in one of the ways just identified, she "reads" what she has written to let the children know that authors always know what they write. Elena wants her kindergarten children to know that these are all valid ways to write during a writer's workshop. Acknowledging the range of possibilities for writing that might be seen lets children know that their attempts during writer's workshop are valued.

Sample Mini-Lesson in First Grade. Observe an example of a mini-lesson at the beginning of writer's workshop in Kelli's first-grade classroom. She has noticed that a number of her children always write in one particular form—personal narratives using "I" or informative pieces about a familiar topic. Kelli wants children to realize that as authors, they have many choices about how to tell their "story."

In her mini-lesson, Kelli uses several familiar books as illustrations to call children's attention to the way authors use point of view or "who is telling the story." She returns to a familiar book, *The Pain and the Great One* by Judy Blume, to remind the children about the impact of a first-person point of view. She guides the children in contrasting the point of view of The Pain (younger brother) and The Great One (the older sister). As each character tells his or her view of the story the children are reminded that each character told their version of the same events.

To contrast a first-person telling of a story with a third-person/narrator telling, Kelli uses *Where the Wild Things Are,* by Maurice Sendak. She helps the children notice that this fantasy is told by someone who is not a character in the story (the narrator) and that someone seems to know all that Max, the main character, says and does. Kelli asks the children how the story might be different if Max was telling the story.

Comparing these two books and the difference that point of view can make for the telling of the story serves as an example of choices that authors have in the way they develop their writing. Kelli encourages children to think about all the literature they read as a potential source of ideas about how people write.

After this mini-lesson, Kelli notices that several children use the ideas and explore writing "I" stories. These children announce such things to Kelli as, "I'm writing like *The Pain and the Great One*." Kelli also observes that some children do not find the mini-lesson helpful until several months later when they begin to experiment with point of view. As Calkins (1986) says, the "idea is in the room," and individual children are able to use it when their understanding of writing develops to the place that point of view is useful to them. Other examples of mini-lessons that draw ideas from literature can be found in Chapters 4 and 6.

Making Connections . . .

Practice developing the dialogue for several mini-lessons that you might present at the beginning of a writer's workshop to support children's development in guided and independent writing. Work with a peer to help each other think about how to state your ideas and the most appropriate examples to use. Suggestions include:

- Focus one mini-lesson on teaching a writer's workshop procedure, such as how to be a helpful response partner.
- Focus one mini-lesson on a content strategy, such as using character dialogue to tell a story.
- Focus one mini-lesson on a writing strategy, such as how to reread your own writing as a first step in editing for meaning or conventions.

Demonstrations of Writing: Shared/Interactive Writing

Through shared/interactive writing, teachers and children collaborate in the development of a piece of writing, recording the shared thinking on a large chart or overhead transparency (see Chapter 5). The focus of what is written depends on the particular writing strategies that children need to see modeled. Shared writing lessons are typically more in-depth than mini-lessons and allow for both demonstration and discussion. On the days when shared writing occurs, the initial whole-group time is extended and individual writing time or author's chair is shortened.

Illustrating the Use of Imagination—First Grade

Like mini-lessons, shared writing helps children explore writing in different genres or using literary elements in new ways. Writing strategies, especially editing for meaning and correctness, are also modeled through shared writing. As an example, instead of using a mini-lesson about imaginative writing (in the opening first-grade scenario), Renee could engage the children in shared writing to demonstrate how writers think while writing imaginative style, Renee chooses to use their sharing during a mini-lesson as her first step, then wait and see if other children use the idea.

Illustrating the Need for Punctuation—Second Grade

Coral notices that the children in her second-grade classroom are using "and" in place of punctuation. She wants to remind them that listening to the sound of language can help point to where punctuation might belong. At the beginning of a writer's workshop, Coral invites children to think about what the class is learning in their weather unit. She uses this discussion as both a warm-up for writing ideas and a demonstration about rereading to check punctuation. Children talk about a variety of ideas they might use that day for writing. For the composition, Coral focuses on one of the most frequent suggestions, how weather influences the way people dress. On the easel she writes the children's dictation:

> We wear jackets when it is cold
> and tank tops when it is hot and
> we wear raincoats when it rains
> and boots when it snows.

During this shared writing, Coral does not question the children's use of "and." She simply says,

"This is a very long sentence. Is this really only one sentence? Maybe we have more than one sentence and just forgot to put in a period. Let's reread this story to see if we can hear where we might need a period to show the end of a sentence."

Coral leads the children in rereading the text, encouraging them to listen for places where their voices suggest the end of a sentence. The children decide that a period is really needed after "hot." Coral asks if they still need the word "and." The children decide they don't need "and," but now they will need a capital *W* for *We*.

> We wear jackets when it is cold
> and tank tops when it is **hot.**
> **We** wear raincoats when it rains
> and boots when it snows.

They discuss how the word "and" is good for connecting ideas, but also how they need to be careful about how many ideas to put together. As children prepare to return to their desks to begin writing, Coral encourages them to reread their own writing, listening for places where they might be using the word "and" instead of punctuation.

Making Plans for the Day

As the whole-group meeting comes to an end and children are moving on to their writing time, some teachers use this time to ask children about their writing plans for that day. Asking children about their writing plans each day sends the message that it is the children who are taking charge of their writing and are expected to be thinking about their writing and themselves as writers.

In the opening vignette of Renee's first-grade classroom, she encourages planning by asking children to tell their partners what they will be doing that day during writing time. When planning is a regular part of the way we begin a workshop, it moves very quickly because children know what is expected. After the discussion of weather and clothing in Coral's second-grade classroom, she asks children to share with the class an idea for their writing that day. One by one as children share an idea, Coral allows them to return to their desks to begin writing.

Atwell (1998) encourages teachers of older students to conduct a "status check" each day. She quickly checks each child, asking what they are planning to do that day. Will they be getting started with a new piece, meeting with a partner to find a focus, composing, conferencing, getting response to their draft writing, working with an editing group, or practicing for author's chair? Beginning in second or third grade, children who are consistently involved in writer's workshops can report their status during group meetings. Status checks encourage children to be aware of, and perhaps more accountable for, their own writing process. To keep a record, we might use a sheet of paper marked off into boxes with students' names down the left-hand side and days of the week across the top. We can develop a simple code to indicate what students report they are doing. Then we record their response each day as we do our status check. Students come to expect the status check and are prepared to report. Expecting the status check encourages children to plan their work time. Our records show us patterns in ways that children progress through the writing process.

WRITING TIME

As children move from the whole-class meeting to individual writing time, teachers should observe how children settle themselves and make the transition to this sustained time. When Renee's children leave the whole group, she sits with Doug to brainstorm ideas, but looks around the room to see what the other children are doing. If children have difficulty getting settled, Renee leaves Doug for a few moments to oversee the transition and troubleshoot if needed. It is Renee's belief, however, that children learn to direct themselves if given the opportunity. In the opening vignette, notice how Renee acted on her belief by the way she responded to Sarah's need for help, saying that there were many other teachers in the room who could help Sarah. Renee reminded Sarah about how their classroom works and gave Sarah the opportunity to be more independent.

Individual Writing

The Need for Choice

Professional writers select their own topics for writing. In an effective writer's workshop, children should have some freedom to choose their topics. Research suggests that children even as young as first grade are quite capable of selecting their own topics for writing (Douglas, 1988; Graves, 1973). For young writers whose handwriting is still a slow, laborious process, it is all the more important that they choose subjects for which they have an experiential, chronological base, because slow speed hampers access to information as well as the sense of where the word or sentence under construction fits in with the overall idea of the paper (Graves, 1994, p. 252).

At times teachers might provide a broad focus for the writing, such as exploring how to write a fairy tale or writing in response to part of a unit on moths and butterflies. Within these broad areas children still have many choices for the specific content and form they prefer.

Learning to Sustain Writing

Calkins (1994) suggests that teachers should not underestimate children's ability to sustain their writing by stopping the writing time as soon as children become restless and say they are "done." From the beginning of the school year, 40 to 60 minutes should be planned for the workshop. When children indicate that they are having difficulty sustaining their writing, attention should shift to nudging their independence by suggesting that they reread their writing to themselves or a partner and begin to ask the self-conferencing questions suggested in the next section. Observations of children's writing behavior should also suggest mini-lessons that can help children learn self-sustaining behaviors.

Providing opportunity for children to select their own topics requires that teachers take their choices seriously and respond based upon what each child is trying to accomplish in the writing. Children need the response of others to their writing, "to discover what they do and do not understand" (Graves, 1994, p. 108) about their topic, the writing process, and their desire to be understood by others.

Writing Conferences

Meeting one-to-one enables teachers to become more personally involved with children as writers and to become more sensitive to their individual needs for in-

As often as we can, we should meet with children to talk about their writing. What can we learn as we listen to them talk about their writing and themselves as writers?

struction. Children can conference at different points in their writing—getting a focus, refocusing a piece, questioning a choice of form, thinking about getting started on a new piece, and so forth. There is no need to save conferencing until pieces are near completion. Conferences can be formal or informal. Informal conferences happen as teachers circulate among children and a conversation begins, initiated by either the child or the teacher. In the opening vignette, Renee and Doug have an informal conference about finding topics for writing. After the conference with Doug, Renee moves about the room, responding to children who need assistance.

Children can sign up for formal conferences ahead of time if there is a posted sign-up sheet somewhere in the room. By allowing 5 to 10 minutes per conference, there is time to see several children each day during the independent writing time. When children sign up for the conference, ask them to indicate their purpose or need for the conference. When a child comes to a conference to talk about his or her writing, support is most helpful if it is directed toward the child's concerns or what the child is trying to do with the writing. Conferencing is not a time to teach everything that the child needs to know. Support the child's concern first, then provide instruction at a more appropriate time through flexible groups that include other children with similar needs.

Although it can be very helpful to conference with children about their writing, it may be more important for them to learn to conference with themselves as writers. Smith (1982) notes: "Writing separates our ideas from ourselves in a way that it is easiest for us to examine, explore, and develop them" (p. 15). Early on in writing, teachers must help children learn why and how to step back from their writing to see themselves in their words. Teachers need to promote self-monitoring of children's writing, just as they support self-monitoring in reading.

What questions do writers ask of themselves to monitor their own writing? Calkins (1994) suggests the following:

- What have I said so far? What am I trying to say?
- How do I like it? How does it sound? How does it look?
- What will my readers think when they read/hear this? What questions will they ask?

🍎 What will they notice? Feel? Think?

🍎 What is good here that I can build on? What is not so good that I can fix?

🍎 What am I going to do next? (pp. 222–223)

Children can learn to ask these questions by participating in conferences with teachers who ask the same questions. Mini-lessons can also teach self-monitoring behavior.

Calkins (1994) suggests that it is important for conferences to focus on children's writing processes, not just the content of the writing. She learned this from Donald Murray, a writing teacher in her graduate program, who focused on her processes as a writer. The art of focusing on process lives on beyond a piece of writing and becomes instructive for future pieces.

Making Connections . . .

Ask a child whom you know to share a piece of writing with you and talk with you about it. Remember to focus more on finding out about the processes the child used to develop the piece rather than on the content of the piece. After the conference, reflect on your response to talking with this child about his or her writing. What do you think you did well? If you could repeat the conference, what might you do differently?

Response Partners/Groups

Response from others helps a writer. Children also need response to their writing that goes beyond conferencing with a teacher. Helping children learn how to respond to one another's writing strengthens writing in the classroom, allowing everyone to become a teacher. Topics for mini-lessons that support responding to others might include:

🍎 How to respond to the writing of another, and

🍎 How to ask for the type of response that will help your writing.

In the vignette of Renee's first-grade classroom, Sarah has difficulty getting settled, but once she does, she writes about her recent trip to Arizona. Then Sarah talks with Bonita, who listens to Sarah's draft and asks questions, just as Renee models in her conferences with children. As the workshop draws to a close Sarah tells Renee that Bonita helped her think about her story.

In the early stages of implementing a writer's workshop, teachers can use mini-lessons to teach response. Children also learn responding from the models provided in conferences, during shared writing, and in other interactions that involve writing. It will take time for children to learn to respond in ways that will help them as writers. Teachers must be patient and supportive of children's efforts, and compliment the instances when their responses are sensitive and of help to others. The success of response in the classroom is related to the fostering of an overall climate of support and respect.

Finding a response partner can be either formal or informal. A sign-up sheet can be provided on which children can indicate their need for response and select their own response partners. The procedure used to enable children to get response to their writing depends on how the classroom functions. In some classrooms, small groups can work effectively to respond to a child's writing. This typically happens at the upper end of the primary grades. Careful observation of children indicates whether partners or groups are most effective.

Editing Partners/Groups

At times, children need assistance from a more able writer to notice details in their writing that need attention. Children can be very helpful to each other, teaching strategies for checking spelling and other conventions. As children are matched with others to assist, consider their respective stages of development as readers and spellers. Editing with others is an excellent topic for a mini-lesson. Pieces of writing can be used to illustrate editing strategies for meaning and correctness. Children's writing is used as an example only with their permission.

Editing for meaning should take precedence over correctness. Editing for meaning can be modeled during shared writing through think-aloud strategies. Children should be encouraged to read their writing aloud to check for meaning. They should be able to edit for meaning at their level of independent reading, where they have enough control over the words to think about the meaning of what is written.

The most common form of editing for meaning that we see in kindergarten and first grade is adding on to a piece. Adding ideas to other parts of a written piece may begin in second and third grade. Learning how to insert words into sentences will be necessary. Cutting apart a draft and taping or stapling more paper in key places can encourage the process of making changes. Some children will cut apart their writing so that its order can be more easily changed. Teachers must take care with the strategies suggested to young children because they often take adults literally and may think that the same strategy must be used each time they write.

Editing for correctness is encouraged after editing for meaning. It is important to remember that children are not usually able to successfully edit the spelling of words that are beyond their level of word knowledge. Teaching children to read their work aloud helps them to discover places where punctuation belongs. Punctuation is needed by readers to interpret an author's ideas, so that the reader will read the piece as the author intended. Working with punctuation is another excellent mini-lesson, as well as knowledge that should be modeled in shared writing.

Whether editing for meaning or correctness, children must learn to see that the knowledge they have as readers can also help them as writers. This should be stressed as editing skills are modeled throughout daily writing activities.

WHOLE-CLASS CLOSING MEETING

A writer's workshop ends with the sharing, or re-presenting, of children's writing in the author's chair. It is also important to take stock of the day, children's successes and struggles, and use that information to make suggestions for what might need to take place during the next day's writer's workshop.

The Author's Chair

In an author's chair activity, a group of children become the audience for a child to read a piece aloud and receive response. The purpose of an author's chair is to celebrate and receive response to a piece of completed writing. The author usually sits on a chair in front of the group, introduces the piece, then reads the piece aloud.

After the reading, the audience learns how to offer *remembers, reminders,* and *questions* (Graves, 1994):

- 🍎 *Remembers* encourages active listening as children are encouraged to tell the author what they heard in the piece.
- 🍎 *Reminders* occur as children make connections between the piece and their own lives, sharing something they are reminded about by the piece.
- 🍎 *Questions* also indicate the listeners' connections with a piece, as questions are asked to clarify meaning in what was heard. Questions also provide impetus for further editing on some pieces in which authors are heavily invested and wish to publish.

When children learn to listen to and appreciate another's writing, they are also learning more about how to listen to their own writing.

In the opening vignette of Renee's classroom, Marty shared his writing in the author's chair. He rehearsed for the sharing by reading his piece aloud to himself, then to Renee. He anticipated the questions that children would ask, because he has participated in author's chairs several times over the 5 months that he has been in first grade. The children in Renee's classroom remembered many details from Marty's story and asked many sincere questions. They really wanted to know more about Marty's sheep and what had caused one of them to die.

Author's chair in Renee's classroom evolved over time. Early in the school year, Renee coaxed retellings, connections, and questions from the children and modeled telling the author what she heard in the piece. She also modeled asking questions about the writing, but questions seemed to come more naturally to the children. They wanted to know more about their classmates' experiences. Learning to respond to the writing of another in response groups carries over to the group experience of author's chair.

Closure for the Day

When a significant block of time is devoted to instruction such as writer's workshop, it is important to help children realize what has transpired during that time and what they have learned that day. After the author's chair, the teacher leads a brief discussion that recounts major happenings that day, inviting children to share successes and struggles. This knowledge helps the teacher and the children anticipate what might need to take place during the next writer's workshop.

Making Connections . . .

Plan to interview several primary-grade teachers to learn about the components of the writing program in their classrooms. Develop a form to record notes from the interviews so that you can compare and contrast responses of different teachers. Be sure to ask about essential components for writing: predictable time to write, demonstrations of writing, blocks of guided/individual writing time, choice, opportunities to have response to writing, and opportunities to self-evaluate. Also be sure to ask the teachers to explain their rationale for the decisions they have made about writing. consider other important ideas you might like to know about each writing program. What conclusions did you reach as a result of your interviews?

MOVING TOWARD INDEPENDENCE AS WRITERS

During each day there should be time for children to write on their own, especially without teacher guidance. This is a teacher's best opportunity to observe the impact of instruction on children's knowledge of writing. Journals and learning logs are excellent vehicles for independent writing.

Trying out a Variety of Journals

Many people make written records of the everyday events in their lives in some form of *journal.* Though the form of the records may differ, the intent is similar— to capture feelings and experiences for personal, not public, purposes. In school, however, teachers often use journals to provide an outlet for children's personal thoughts and as a daily independent writing opportunity. Journals may also become a dialogue between teacher and child.

> **Read here to find definitions for** *journal.*

Some journals are called *working journals,* because writers record observations and other information that will be used for another purpose (Tompkins, 2000). Many professions require the observation, collection, and use of data. These professionals keep a type of working journal as they observe and record progress or outcomes, consider or make predictions about next steps, chart data to consider its meaning or patterns, and consider what data should be shared and in what manner. In this text, working journals are referred to as *learning logs,* to differentiate their intended use from journals (see next section).

Personal Journals
Topics for personal journals are usually the choice of the writer. The contents of a personal journal typically focus on events in the writer's life and personal concerns. The personal journal serves as an outlet and is made public only by the choice of the writer. For emerging writers, personal journals may also be annotated drawings. Teachers often write responses to children's entries to stimulate children's writing and model elements of language. Figures 9.10 and 9.11 show journal entries by two first-grade children, José and Angie, who use their journals to respond to life experiences.

Dialogue Journals
Personal journals become dialogue journals when the writer addresses the writing to another, who is expected to respond. This exchange is a conversation through writing (Bode, 1989; Gambrell, 1985; Staton, 1987). The children set the direction for the conversation. The teacher's role is to encourage, support, and nudge or stretch children's thinking. The goal should be for children to become the question askers (Tompkins, 2000). Dialogue journals can be of great value in

FIGURE 9.10
Personal journal entry—first grade.

I like My dog wen He Hawls at the fol Moon

FIGURE 9.11
Personal journal entry—first grade.

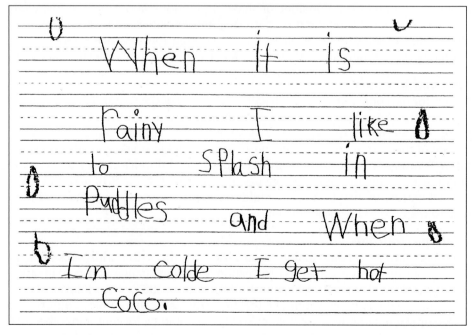

When it is rainy I like to splash in puddles and when I'm colde I get hot coco.

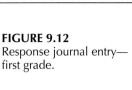
FIGURE 9.12
Response journal entry—
first grade.

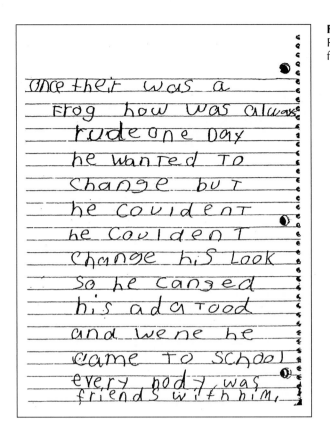

bridging the gap between talking and writing (Kreeft, 1984), helping children work out nonacademic school problems (Staton, 1980), and supporting children as they learn to talk about books (Barone, 1990).

Response Journals
As part of a literacy program, children may be asked to write their responses to books they are reading or their responses to experiences of a class read-aloud or literature study, such as Ursala's response to a fantasy about a frog (see Figure 9.12). Tompkins's (2000) review of research reveals that children's responses may include the following:

- Retellings and summaries,
- Questions related to understanding the text,
- Interaction or empathy with characters,
- Predictions of what will happen and validation after reading,
- Personal experiences, feelings, and opinions related to the reading,
- Simple and elaborated evaluations, and/or
- Philosophical reflections. (pp. 90–91)

Response journals also serve as an excellent assessment of children's responses to and understanding of class learning experiences. When substantial amounts of new informational text are included in the curriculum, it is important

FIGURE 9.13
Enrique's response to
magnets—second grade.

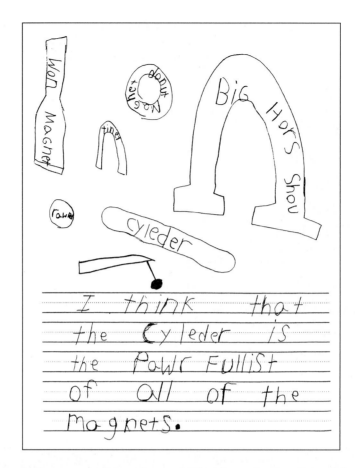

to know something about children's understanding of those new ideas and concepts. Inviting children to comment on their learning provides insight for teachers. For example, Enrique's second-grade class has been reading about and experimenting with magnets. He uses his journal writing time to comment on his ideas about magnets (see Figure 9.13).

Double-Entry Journals

Children respond to the authors they read. A double-entry journal (Barone, 1990) combines a quote from a text with the child's response. The journal page is divided into two columns with a quote from the text (noting chapter/page for future reference) on the left and the child's response on the right. Because the quote is provided, double-entry responses are focused and interpretable. Other variations of the double-entry journal can be to place

- 🍎 "Reading Notes" on the left, and response or
- 🍎 "Discussion Notes" on the right; or
- 🍎 "Predictions" on the left, and validation or
- 🍎 "What Happened" on the right. (Tompkins, 2000, p. 92)

Figure 9.14 shows sample double-entry journals from third-grade children. The first example uses a quote from the narrative text *Amazing Grace* as the focus of the response. The second double-entry journal begins with notes from an informational text about making crayons, then the child adds a response to the in-

Double-Entry Journal	***Amazing Grace,*** **by Mary Hoffman and Caroline Binch**
Text Quote— "And she always gave herself the most exciting part."	Response— I like to pretend too. I pretend I am in Beauty and the Beast. I think the Beast is the most exciting part.

Double-Entry Journal	***How Is a Crayon Made?*** **by Oz Charles**
Reading Notes from the Text— Crayons are made from clear wax and a colored powder. The hot wax is put in a special mold like a muffin tin.	Discussion Notes— I wondered how crayons got shaped like a pencil. A muffin pan to make crayons is a funny idea.

FIGURE 9.14
Sample double-entry journals.

formation. Double-entry journals are useful for focusing children's responses to a variety of texts.

Learning Logs

Learning logs are intended to be a vehicle for helping children use writing as a functional tool for learning, particularly in content areas such as science, social studies, and mathematics. Learning logs can be used to help children record and react to their learning in mathematics, science, and social studies (Fulwiler, 1985), and this benefit can also be expanded to include literature study.

Read here to find a definition of *learning log.*

An example of a learning log that might be used during a whole-class literature study of *Owl Moon,* by Jane Yolen, might include:

- Writing response to the text using a particular journal style,
- Drawing and labeling different kinds of owls,
- Clustering what they know about owls and adding to the cluster as they gain new knowledge,
- Making a list of interesting words in the text and adding other related words that could be used to describe the setting or the owling experience,
- Writing a description of a familiar setting, and
- Description of a time when children had to be very quiet and still.

Another example of learning log entries that might be used in a unit of study about the seasons and seasonal change might include:

- Drawing pictures of changes that occur during each season and identifying those changes with labels,
- Writing brief descriptions of what they do during each season,

- Adding to a chart that compares the four seasons according to average temperatures, amount of daily sunlight, weather, what happens to plants, and what happens to animals,
- Clustering or brainstorming ideas on what children know about each season,
- Answering questions posed by the teacher,
- Responding to literature read during the unit,
- Adding to shared writings developed by the class, and
- Making a list of season words, adding to the list as they find new and interesting words.

Learning logs provide great versatility. In practice, learning logs can combine the formats and intentions of the journals described earlier, as well as a variety of informal and formal writing formats. Learning logs can stimulate writing through the use of a variety of formats, meeting the needs and preferences of individual children. Experiences with writing help writers decide what thoughts need to be re-collected and what form would be best to re-present thinking. A variety of informal writing may help children see that writing is beneficial and within reach.

Making Connections . . .

Begin to make a collection of topics that might be appropriate for journals and learning logs at different grade levels. Consider the development of children in that grade level. What needs and interests of the children might be important to consider, especially in personal journal entries?

TRYING ON DIFFERENT FORMS OF WRITING

When writing is taught as a way of exploring and organizing thinking, children have opportunities to "try on" different types of writing. These writing experiences grow out of learning experiences that might be a part of the literacy program using basal readers, authentic literature, or content-area materials. Studies of the topics children write about in self-selected writing programs reveal that boys and girls have different interests (Douglas, 1988; Graves, 1973). Boys often write about the world outside of themselves, with a focus on informational writing. Girls often write with a focus toward "I" and personal narratives. Knowing this, teachers can encourage different forms of writing to enhance the writing opportunities for all children.

Extending Personal Narratives

Children's writing often begins with pieces that grow out of their own experience. Early on, the narrative lies mostly in children's drawings, with writing to comment on the drawing. To push children's written narratives, whole-class shared writing can demonstrate how to use words to elaborate on what is shown in the drawing with the intention of replacing illustration with written description and to break an experience into "episodes" to encourage more elaboration.

Going Beyond the Illustration

Young children put a great deal of energy and detail into their drawings, often because writing is slow and tedious compared with drawing. The "story" they have to tell takes shape as the drawing takes shape and is frequently unplanned. The following activities can extend children's engagement with illustrations:

- Make an overhead transparency with an illustration similar to what children are doing in their writing.
- With the children, discuss what the drawing shows and read the written comments on the drawing.
- Brainstorm ideas that are related to the experience but may not be shown in the illustration.
- Taking one idea at a time from the brainstorming, have children compose other things the author could have written, then use interactive writing to record.

Be sure to discuss how the combination of illustration and "new" writing enhances the total composition. Then encourage children to try extending their own illustrated narratives. In the weeks that follow, observe the impact of the interactive writing lesson.

Extend Writing by Making Episodes

Children's illustrations often describe an experience that actually has several parts.

- To encourage more elaboration for each part or episode of the experience, demonstrate how writers can break their stories into parts. The illustrations in favorite picture books may be used as examples. Show children how an author elaborates on the illustration that appears on two facing pages to tell a story.
- Using an experience that is familiar to children (with a sample one-page illustration), brainstorm the parts or episodes that are part of the experience. Use one piece of paper for each episode. Use shared or interactive writing to help children consider what might be written about each part and what the illustration might show.
- Show children how the parts can be assembled to make a book. Compare the expanded narrative to the one-page illustration of the experience.
- Encourage children to try breaking their experiences into parts, telling about each piece so the reader will know more.

Words in Place of Illustration

As children acquire more proficiency with handwriting and word knowledge, extended writing becomes more possible (usually by second grade). At this point, demonstrating the use of writing to stand in place of drawings can be helpful:

- With the children's help, brainstorm descriptions that can stand in place of the drawing.

🍎 Using the brainstormed ideas, have children verbally compose sentences that when taken together will "show" what is illustrated.

🍎 Take away the illustration and read the description. Encourage children to build a mental image in place of the illustration.

🍎 At the same time, for classroom writing experiences, substitute paper that has all lines instead of paper that provides a blank space for illustration. Ask children to "show" their narrative with words before drawing.

In these examples, brainstorm and record children's ideas, and model the use of functional writing for children (see discussion of functional writing in Chapter 8). Many types of writing can begin with clusters of ideas or lists that are moved into phrases, sentences, and descriptive paragraphs. Help children see that functional writing can be very useful to them as they write independently.

Experimenting with Fiction

To try on different forms of fictional writing, children must first have opportunities to listen to literature for the writer's style—to listen like a writer. Instead of listening just for the storyline, children listen more for what the author did to create the story. As the teacher reads aloud, encourage children to listen for such things as:

🍎 words that create mental pictures,

🍎 how characters are introduced,

🍎 places in the story where the tension builds, where we say to ourselves, "Something's going to happen,"

🍎 how we come to know about a character, or

🍎 how the author helps us see the setting in our minds.

When the reading is finished ask, "What did you notice?" and the discussion begins. Learning to listen like a writer can change what children notice about other people's writing. This knowledge begins to inform their understanding of different types of writing. Children will discover some forms of writing, but other forms may be best developed with our guidance. As a reminder about literary elements and genre, see the information provided in Appendix A.

Developing a Plot

For primary-grade children, plot is an important literary element. The picture books they read are dominated by plot development. To help children enhance their fiction writing, conduct shared writing activities that guide children to think of plot as:

🍎 beginning-middle-end (inexperienced writers; see Figure 9.15), or

🍎 problem-events-resolution (more experienced writers; see Figure 9.16.

A story map is an excellent planning tool for narrative writing. A story map is a word or picture diagram that shows the main events in a story and the relationship of those events (see the illustrated story map for *Sylvester and the Magic*

Beginning-Middle-End Story Map
Sylvester and the Magic Pebble (Steig, 1969)

Beginning:
- Sylvester finds a magic pebble and makes the rain stop and start.
- Sylvester is scared by a lion and wishes to be a rock.

Middle:
- Mr. and Mrs. Duncan look for Sylvester.
- They ask neighbors, children, police, and dogs.
- Fall and spring pass and Sylvester is still a rock.

End:
- In spring, Mr. and Mrs. Duncan go to Strawberry Hill for a picnic.
- Mr. Duncan finds a pebble and puts it on a rock that is really Sylvester.
- Sylvester wishes he is himself again.
- They all go home together.

FIGURE 9.15
Story map—beginning-middle-end.

Problem-Events-Resolution Story Map
Sylvester and the Magic Pebble (Steig, 1969)

Problem:
- Sylvester becomes a rock on Strawberry Hill and he cannot move.

Events:
- Sylvester finds a magic pebble and makes the rain stop and start.
- He is scared by a lion and wishes to be a rock.
- Mr. and Mrs. Duncan look everywhere for Sylvester.
- They ask neighbors, children, police, and dogs.
- Fall and winter pass.
- In spring, Mr. and Mrs. Duncan go to Strawberry Hill for a picnic.
- Mr. Duncan finds magic pebble and places it on a large rock (Sylvester).

Resolution:
- Sylvester wishes he is himself again and the wish comes true.
- They all go home together.

FIGURE 9.16
Story map—problem-events-resolution.

Pebble in Figure 4.5). Mapping a story can help children identify the detail and sequence they want to use in their plot. A story map can be used to check a child's understandings as a reader or to plan a story as a writer.

To help children plan their own writing, study how other authors organize their plots. Originating from the literature that is studied in the classroom, the first step is to develop a story map to examine how a plot can be structured.

After developing a story map for a familiar book with the children, help them see how the story map retells the plot of the book. A class book can be made from the story map using one sheet of paper for each major event, which will help children elaborate their ideas. Shared or interactive writing can be used. Spread out the events on separate pages to emphasize the structure of the plot, as shown in Figure 9.17. Guide the children to reread and check for the flow of the story as ideas are recorded. For children with little experience in writing narratives, leave space for their illustrations on each page because when they begin to write their own stories, both text and illustrations will be used to tell the story.

After the class has worked together making story maps of familiar books and turning the maps back into stories, children will be ready to write an original group story. As a group, select an idea to develop, brainstorm the plot, and make a map. Use shared writing for a retelling of the story similar to the one used for *Sylvester and the Magic Pebble.*

After group writing, children should be ready to try to apply their experiences to developing a plot in their personal writing. As a strategy for getting started, encourage children to develop a map for the story they are thinking

FIGURE 9.17
From story map to story writing.

Beginning . . . Sylvester found a magic pebble. He made the rain stop and start.	On his way home he got scared by a lion and wished to be a rock. Then he couldn't go home.	Middle . . . Mr. and Mrs. Duncan looked everywhere for Sylvester. They asked the neighbors, children, and police. They were very sad.
Fall and winter passed. Sylvester was still a rock on Strawberry Hill.	End . . . Spring came. Mr. and Mrs. Duncan went to Strawberry Hill. They had a picnic on a big rock. Mr. Duncan found a red pebble and put it on the big rock.	Sylvester wished he was a donkey again and he was! Then they all went home.

about, then have a classmate respond to their ideas. In the writing center provide small sheets of paper that children can use to write their story, spreading out the events as modeled for them. Spreading out the events makes it much easier to change the story. Ideas can be added or ordered differently by simply changing the pages.

Helping children write well-developed plots is only one element of telling a story that can be modeled in shared writing. Using a process similar to the one just described, children can explore:

🍎 introducing a character in a story,

🍎 letting characters talk to tell part of the story,

🍎 making a story out of one main event, and

🍎 telling stories from different points of view.

Exploring Poetry

Poetry is using language to communicate feelings, experiences, ideas, reactions, and so on. There is no need to wait until National Poetry Month (April) for an excuse to read and write poetry. The foundation for engaging children in writing poetry is in engaging them in the shared reading of poetry. *The Random House Book of Poetry for Children* (selected by Jack Prelutsky and illustrated by Arnold Lobel) is a great place to start—Jack Prelutsky's humor is very engaging. More sources for poetry are suggested in the chapter on Shared Reading (Chapter 5). The Internet is also a wonderful source of information about children's poetry.

> Web sites for writing poetry with children include *http://teacher.scholastic.com/writewit/poetry/* and *http://www.kn.pacbell.com/wired/fil/pages/listpoetrymr14.html.*

The variety of types of poems is so great that there is probably a type of poetry for almost everyone. It's not just about rhyming words! Young children seem to naturally gravitate to word play. The following subsections describe a few possibilities.

Acrostic Poem

A form of short verse constructed so that the initial letters of each line taken consecutively, from top to bottom, form one or more words. Aidan, in second grade, composed a poem about fall:

> **F**all is fun
> **A**fter we rake
> **L**eaves into piles we
> **L**eap into them.

BioPoem

A BioPoem is a type of autobiography in verse. The number of topics to include and the order of the lines is up to the author:

> *Line 1 — Your first name*
> *Line 2 — Four adjectives that describe you*
> *Line 3 — Brother or sister of . . . (or son/daughter of)*
> *Line 4 — Who loves . . . (3 items/ideas)*
> *Line 5 — Who feels . . . (3 items/ideas)*
> *Line 6 — Who needs . . . (3 items/ideas)*
> *Line 7 — Who gives . . . (3 items/ideas)*

Line 8 — *Who fears . . . (3 items/ideas)*
Line 9 — *Who enjoys . . . (3 items/ideas)*
Line 10 — *Who would like to see . . . (3 items/ideas)*
Line 11 — *Who shares . . . (3 items/ideas)*
Line 12 — *Your last name only*

Chant

Chants do not have a particular form, but usually have one or more lines that are repeated. A chant is meant to be read or said aloud. In Chapter 4, several chants created with children were introduced as response to books read aloud. In addition, the following chants were inspired by children's books:

In *The Snowy Day* (Keats, 1962), Peter explores in the snow:

> *Peter went walking in the snow, snow, snow.*
> *Peter went crunching in the snow, snow, snow.*
> *Peter made angels in the snow, snow, snow.*
> *Peter had fun in the snow, snow, snow.*

In *Sylvester and the Magic Pebble* (Steig, 1969), Sylvester, a donkey, becomes a rock:

> *Sylvester found a pebble,*
> *a magic pebble.*
> *Sylvester saw a lion,*
> *a hungry lion.*
> *Sylvester made a wish,*
> *a foolish wish,*
> *Now Sylvester is a rock,*
> *a donkey rock!*

Concrete Poem

A concrete poem forms a picture of the topic or follows the contours of a shape that is suggested by the topic. The language is descriptive of the object. Concrete poems can be used effectively in science or social studies, with shapes such as a tornado, a lightbulb, a flag, or a state/country (see Figure 9.18).

Diamonte

A diamonte is a seven-line unrhymed poem that appears in a diamond shape. This form uses grammatical elements to build the poem. The subject of the poem begins with one noun and in the middle of the poem begins to change to its opposite. This form of poetry is best for later in the primary grades when children have been introduced to the different parts of speech.

> *One noun (subject of the poem)*
> *Two adjectives (describe the noun in line 1)*
> *Three verbs (-ing, -ed, -s words that relate to the subject)*
> *Four nouns (two nouns relate to line 1, two nouns relate to line 7)*
> *Three verbs (-ing, -ed, -s words that relate to the subject)*
> *Two adjectives (describe the noun in line 7)*
> *One noun (contrasting/opposite of the noun in line 1)*

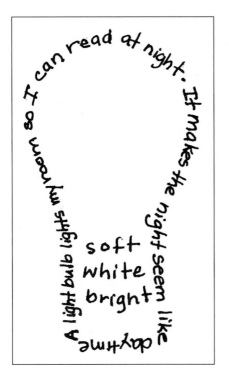

FIGURE 9.18
Concrete poem—third grade.

Five Senses Poem

A five senses poem is a variation of a list poem (see next section) in which each of the senses is used. There are several possible formats. The order in which the senses are used is up to the author.

Describe various objects:	Describe one object:
I see _____	(object) looks _____
I hear _____	(object) feels _____
I smell _____	(object) tastes _____
I taste _____	(object) sounds _____
I touch _____	(object) smells _____

Describe one object:	Julian, Third Grade:
object	**Snow**
touch word(s)/phrase	cold, wet
sight word(s)/phrase	white mountains
sound word(s)/phrase	crunchy
smell word(s)/phrase	clean, fresh
taste word(s)/phrase	frosty, delicious
object	snow

List Poem

A list poem, also called a *catalog poem,* consists of a list of things or events with some elaboration. Emily, in second grade, makes a list of things she is thankful for:

> I am thankful for...
> my mom
> because she loves me so much,
> school
> because you learn a lot,
> my house
> because it keeps us safe,
> my friends
> because they are so kind to me,
> food
> because we would starve to death if we did not have food,
> my grandpa
> because he spoils me a lot.

Song Frame

The tune of any familiar song can become the frame for a poem. Teachers frequently model how to innovate on a song by developing texts for shared reading.

Edwardo, in first grade, wrote this poem during a unit on the five senses. It is set to the tune of "Farmer in the Dell."

> I use my tongue to taste.
> I use my tongue to taste.
> I love to taste burritos and corn.
> I use my tongue to taste.

Edwardo's teacher suggested the song to use. All of the children in the class were able to write at least one verse of their own using the song as a frame.

Jenny and Marsha, in third grade, wrote a poem about starting a new school year to the tune of "Three Blind Mice."

> We love school.
> We love school.
> We get to make new friends.
> We get to make new friends.
> We'll have fun and play four square.
> We'll comb and braid each other's hair.
> We'll be good friends and always share.
> We love school.

Sound Poem

A sound poem calls attention to the sounds around us and how we react to the sounds. The poem answers several questions:

- Can you describe the sound?
- What does the sound make you think of?
- How do you feel when you hear the sound?

Carson, in third grade, writes about thunder:

Thunder

Crack, pop

Crack, crack, pop

Scary thunder will not stop

Shaking everything in my house

Makes me wish I was a little mouse.

Writing poetry with children has a myriad of possibilities to explore and can expand children's interest in language.

Exploring Informational Writing

Informational writing is organized differently than narratives. Whereas narrative seeks to tell a story, informational writing:

- describes,
- makes order or sequence clear,
- shows comparison,
- explains cause and effect,
- describes problems and solutions,
- poses questions with answers, or
- attempts to persuade.

Additional discussion of each text form can be found in Appendix A, which provides explanations of literary genre and elements. As teachers begin to explore informational writing, it is helpful to use visual representations, when possible, to help children think about arranging their ideas.

Use writer's workshop to model specific types of informational writing that relate to unit concepts and provide opportunities for children to explore with our support. Taking one type of structure at a time, develop shared or interactive writings with the children that model possible ways to organize ideas in that structure. Then encourage children to develop their own ideas during independent writing time.

Description

Ideas for description can be illustrated like the spokes of a wheel, relating to a central topic but not necessarily to each other in any particular order. To demonstrate description, work with children to build a cluster of ideas/details about a single topic. Select a topic that is familiar to children, then help them examine the cluster for relationships among the ideas.

Through shared or interactive writing, develop sentences with the related ideas. Write these ideas on sentence strips and place them in a pocket chart,

FIGURE 9.19
Brainstorm cluster becomes a descriptive paragraph—third grade.

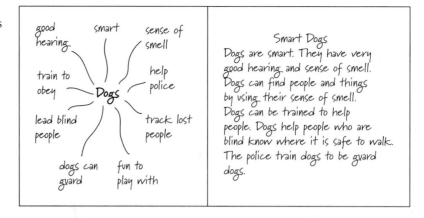

FIGURE 9.20
Ordered or sequential writing—first grade.

An Alphabet of Favorite Books			
A is for... Amazing Grace by Mary Hoffman and Caroline Binch	B is for... Blueberries for Sal by Robert McCloskey	C is for... Chicken Sunday by Patricia Polacco	D is for... Doctor DeSoto by William Steig

then rearrange the ideas until the organization provides a satisfactory description. Figure 9.19 shows a third-grade example of descriptive writing about dogs. Notice how ideas from the cluster become sentences in the paragraph.

Order or Sequence

Describing a sequence of steps involves order, such as giving directions or retelling the steps in a science experiment. Children can retell the steps used to plant seeds and chart the plants' growth during science. An autobiography is also a form of ordered writing that children can try. For time sequences, a timeline makes a good "getting started" tool. Alphabet and counting books are also good examples of ordered writing for the primary grades. Examine various types of ABC or number books to show children possibilities for presenting their ideas. The topic of the ABC or counting book can be tied to literature the class is reading or a unit of study. Figure 9.20 shows an example of a class or individual book that is sequenced in ABC order.

Making Comparisons

Introduce comparison by intertwining a description of one topic with a related topic. Cluster the first topic and identify main ideas. Then introduce and cluster the second topic according to the main points established for the first topic.

FIGURE 9.21
Steps in compare/contrast writing—second grade.

Step 1: Details for Winter–Summer Compare/Contrast

Weather		Clothing		Things We Do	
winter	summer	winter	summer	winter	summer
cold	hot	coats	shorts	snow ski	water ski
snow	dry	hats	hats	play inside	play outside
sunny	sunny	gloves	swimsuit	ride stationary	ride bike
		boots	sandals	bike	
			no shoes		

Step 2: Develop Compare/Contrast Statements

Weather	Clothing	Things We Do
Winter is cold but the summer is hot. or Winter is cold and snowy, but summer is hot and dry.	In the summer we wear shorts and swimsuits but in the winter we have to wear coats, gloves, and boots.	We can ski in the summer and winter. In summer we ski on water but in winter we ski on snow.
Days are sunny in summer and winter.	We wear hats in winter and summer.	In the summer we can play outside, but in the winter we play inside a lot. We ride our bikes in the summer and winter.

Identify details that are similar and those that are different. For similarities, develop "and" statements, and for differences develop "but" statements.

For example, to compare/contrast the topics of winter and summer, the following might be the main ideas:

- Weather
- Clothing
- Things We Do

Record details for one topic, then compare/contrast those ideas to the second topic. From the details, write "and" (comparisons) and "but" (contrasts) statements. Figure 9.21 shows an example of the development of compare/contrast writing with second-grade children.

As a group, decide how to:

🍎 introduce the piece so that the purpose is clear,
🍎 introduce each part,
🍎 make a transition between parts, and
🍎 conclude the piece.

Thinking About Cause and Effect

Thinking through cause/effect relationships requires the use of background experience with the topic to recognize how a particular cause and effect are related. Cause/effect relationships also rely on language to give clues about the existence of the relationship, using words and phrases such as *because, as a result, makes,* or *leads to.*

Cause and effect writing is often seen in social studies and science texts. For example, in a unit that focuses on understanding weather and its impact on land and people, the concept of rainfall may lead to discussion of cause/effect relationships:

> Cause—too much rainfall (*causes, makes, leads to*) floods
> Effect—floods happen (*because of*) too much rainfall
>
> Cause—too little rainfall (*causes, makes, leads to*) droughts
> Effect—droughts happen (*because of*) too little rainfall
>
> Too much rainfall (*causes, makes, leads to*) a flood.

Cause/effect can be illustrated to emphasize the relationship by filling in the essential language.

After the class develops cause/effect statements, help children brainstorm ideas that elaborate on and explain the relationship. As children gain experience and confidence as writers, begin to explore cause/effect relationships that have multiple causes and/or multiple effects.

Problem/Solution or Question/Answer

Another structure that can be found in informational writing is the identification of a problem and its solution(s). This relationship can also appear as a question with an answer(s). In informational writing, the author may introduce the piece using the problem or a question, then develop the piece by presenting and discussing solutions or answering the question. This type of writing may be most useful as a way to structure the study of a topic, especially using question/answer. Question/answer relationships can be a beginning format for independent research in a unit of study.

🍎 The first step may be to generate one problem or question as a group, then brainstorm and write about possible solutions or answers.
🍎 The second step is exploring the use of this structure to organize a number of problems or questions as a way of studying a topic.
🍎 After a brainstorm session to generate problems or questions about a topic, place each problem or question on a separate chart so that everyone can see it.

🍎 As children search for information, the charts serve as a means of organizing ideas. Children write important words or phrases on the relevant charts—problem or question.

🍎 After enough ideas are gathered, hold another shared writing session to discuss how to organize each solution or answer.

🍎 Then, as a group, decide how to place the problems or questions in a coherent order. On the overhead or another large chart, lead a shared writing activity that shows children how to organize the problem/solutions or questions/answers into a "report."

🍎 Follow up this exercise by providing an opportunity for children to develop their own "report," using cards for each problem or question rather than large charts.

🍎 Small groups can also successfully write in this format, assuming you have already been working with small-group writing tasks.

Persuasion

Children are already well aware of persuasion. They attempt it daily with parents, teachers, and friends! When appropriate, provide support for children to begin to use persuasion in their writing. Persuasive writing depends on presentation of facts in a carefully crafted order. Persuasion also requires careful attention to the selection of words that will persuade. The voice of the writer also becomes important. The reader is more likely to be persuaded if the tone is sincere and the argument seems well supported.

🍎 Persuasive writing begins with reading aloud particular examples, then modeling how to think about persuading someone else through the shared writing of persuasive pieces, and

🍎 finally, providing opportunities for children to attempt their own persuasive pieces.

Letters are an excellent form to begin persuasive writing in the primary grades. See the example of a persuasive letter from Raymond in Figure 9.22. After his third-grade science project with the mealworm is completed, he wants permission from his mother to bring it home.

Other forms of writing that can be introduced through shared writing and then developed during guided writing include letter writing, biographies and autobiographies, and various types of poetry. For other examples of forms of writing, see Gail Tompkins's (2000) *Teaching Writing: Balancing Process and Product.*

To extend children's interest in writing, provide opportunities for exploration with writing through activity centers in the classroom. Time provided for making choices in activity centers can be highly motivating.

Making Connections . . .

Collect ideas for a variety of forms of writing. Consider academic standards and the topics that are typical in the curriculum at each grade level, K–3. Also consider writing that you have observed in primary classrooms. What various forms of writing might support and encourage development of children's understanding of the purposes and possibilities for writing?

FIGURE 9.22
Persuasive letter from Raymond—third grade.

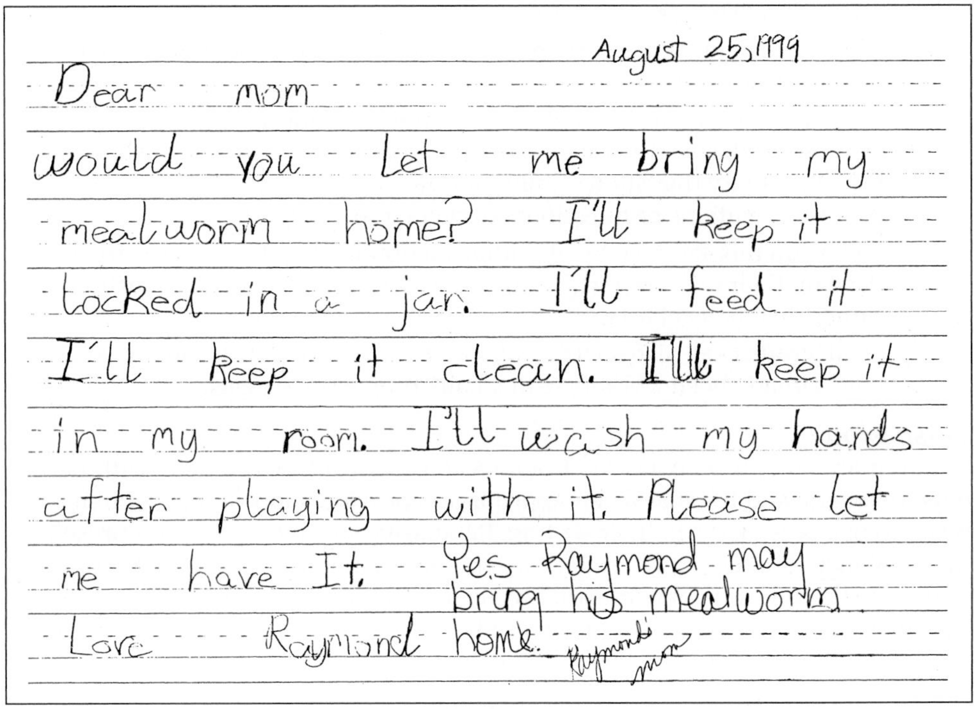

> August 25, 1999
>
> Dear mom
>
> would you let me bring my mealworm home? I'll keep it locked in a jar. I'll feed it I'll keep it clean. I'll keep it in my room. I'll wash my hands after playing with it. Please let me have It.
>
> Yes Raymond may bring his mealworm home.
>
> Love Raymond
>
> Raymond's mom

🍎 INDEPENDENT WRITING IN ACTIVITY CENTERS

Many teachers in the primary grades use activity centers as extensions of work time or for enrichment. The possibilities for centers seem endless, but may include the following:

- 🍎 Quiet reading or library corner,
- 🍎 Language arts center,
- 🍎 Writing center,
- 🍎 Math center,
- 🍎 Theme/unit center,
- 🍎 Listening center,
- 🍎 Home center (includes dress-up/pretend materials),
- 🍎 Construction/block centers, and
- 🍎 Sand/water/exploration areas.

Set up centers to extend children's work time or for enrichment. Consider examples of the natural uses of writing that might fit the various centers:

- 🍎 A home center might become a restaurant with menus, order tablets, and so forth.

- The language center might provide materials for children to respond to books they have completed on their own or as extensions of class lessons.
- The writing center might include all types of writing implements and interesting colors and shapes of paper for writing. Materials and ideas for making books are also a must. Additional ideas for making books are provided in an upcoming section. In addition, personal mailboxes can be provided to encourage communication.
- In a math center, children might indicate their preference for breakfast cereals on a class graph and record the reason for their selection on a group response sheet.
- Theme or unit centers offer extensive possibilities for writing, including:
  - blank booklets in different shapes related to the theme,
  - group response sheets for different theme-related issues such as "My favorite type of weather . . . ,"
  - records of experiments that are tried, or
  - displays of children's drawings, clusters, records, and so on, related to the theme.

Additional ideas for using reading and writing in integrated units can be found in Chapter 11.

EXTENDING WRITING THROUGH BOOKMAKING

Throughout this text we have discussed a variety of ways to engage children in class-made books. Making individual books is highly motivating for children, especially when the topic is their choice. A variety of formats are possible. Materials can be provided in a writing center for independent bookmaking or during writer's workshop as children complete drafts, edit for meaning and convention, then prepare to re-present their ideas. Figure 9.23 provides a variety of sample book formats that can be adapted to any topic of study or a child's personal interests.

Accordion Books

Accordion books are made from folded paper and lend themselves to a variety of shapes. These books work well for both narrative and informational writing.

Fan-Page Books

Fan-page books are made from layers of paper, each page slightly larger than the one before, allowing labels or headings for each page to show. Topics that have distinct sections, such as informative reports, work well.

FIGURE 9.23
Sample designs for bookmaking.

Accordion Books:
1. Fold paper lengthwise and crease. Folded edge will be top of book.
2. Fold strip in half and crease center.
3. Fold each edge back toward the center fold and crease. The strip should be in the shape of a W.
4. On one side (front) number each panel, 1–4. If more pages are desired, number back panel, 5–8. Panel 8 will be the title page.
5. Write text on separate paper cut slightly smaller than book panels.
6. Glue text on appropriate panels.

Option:
1. Shapes—holding closed book, cut shape leaving some part of fold on sides uncut to keep the book together.
2. Make tagboard books by placing tape along edges of pages like a hinge.

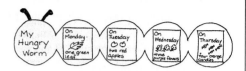

Fan Page Books:
1. Decide on the number of pages for the book.
2. Largest page will be the back cover of the book.
3. Cut 1" off right-hand side for next to last page.
4. For each preceding page cut off an additional 1" strip so that each page is 1" smaller than the next.
5. Assemble pages in order of size and staple.

Hint:
1. Using 8½" × 11" paper = max. of 7–8 pages
   Using 11" × 14" paper = max. of 10–11 pages

Pocket Books:
1. Make books with paper pages, stapled on the spine. Pages should be large enough to accommodate a small envelope.
2. Glue an envelope to the lower half of each right-hand page with the flap side accessible.
3. On left-hand page, children place a question or riddle.
4. A small card with the answer is placed in the envelope.

Variation: Flap Books
1. Instead of an envelope, place a paper flap on the lower part of the right-hand page. Glue only the top ½" of the flap to the page.
2. Write the answer under the flap.

Shape Books:
1. Provide tagboard templates in different shapes to trace for books.
2. Trace shape on paper that will be front cover and cut out.
3. Stack front cover, several sheets of writing paper, and paper for a back cover.
4. Staple on left-hand side for spine.
5. Holding carefully, cut around edge of front cover, being sure to cut through all pages at the same time.

Hint:
Simple shapes work best. Consider the actual writing surface that will be left after cutting the paper.

FIGURE 9.23
Continued.

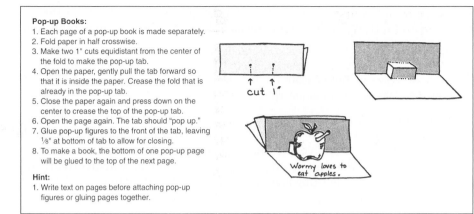

Pop-up Books:
1. Each page of a pop-up book is made separately.
2. Fold paper in half crosswise.
3. Make two 1" cuts equidistant from the center of the fold to make the pop-up tab.
4. Open the paper, gently pull the tab forward so that it is inside the paper. Crease the fold that is already in the pop-up tab.
5. Close the paper again and press down on the center to crease the top of the pop-up tab.
6. Open the page again. The tab should "pop up."
7. Glue pop-up figures to the front of the tab, leaving ⅛" at bottom of tab to allow for closing.
8. To make a book, the bottom of one pop-up page will be glued to the top of the next page.

Hint:
1. Write text on pages before attaching pop-up figures or gluing pages together.

Pocket Books

Pocket books have envelopes glued to pages in a book, with small cards placed in the envelopes that are just right for answers to questions (such as riddles), solutions to problems, or cause/effect situations.

For more information on bookmaking, see *http://www.makingbooks. com/projects.html*

Pop-up Books

Pop-up books let children represent ideas in three dimensions. Any topic that can be illustrated makes a good pop-up book.

Sequence Books

Sequence books have panels that show sequence of an activity or process. These are excellent for both informational texts and developing plot in fiction.

Shape Books

Shape books have paper covers cut in various shapes with writing paper inside. Any person, place, or thing can become a fun shape book.

These are but a few ideas for making books. We are only limited by our imagination!

HELPING CHILDREN DEVELOP LEGIBLE HANDWRITING

The goal of handwriting instruction is to develop fluent and legible handwriting. As emergent readers and writers are developing knowledge about print and learning the letters of the alphabet (phonemic stage), it can also be useful to help them develop enough control over the muscles in the hand and arm to form legible letters and become fluent writers.

For additional information on styles of letter formation, see *http://www.ericfacility.net/ ericdigests/ed272923.html* and *http://www. zanerbloser.com*, and *http://66.113.195.73/*.

One caution: Never let handwriting become more important than the expression of ideas. Graves (1994) reminds us to keep handwriting in perspective:

> Handwriting is the vehicle carrying information on its way to a destination. If it is illegible the journey may not be completed. Handwriting, like skin, shows the outside of a person. But beneath the skin beats the living organism, the life's blood, the ideas, the information. (p. 241)

Young children often interpret a teacher's instructional suggestions literally, so care must be taken to help children balance their attention to legible handwriting with the effort they give to composing. Overemphasizing the surface aspects of their writing, the way writing looks on the paper, may inadvertently be telling children that handwriting is more important than thinking.

Purposes in handwriting instruction should be twofold:

- To provide instruction in patterns of formation that will allow handwriting to become fluid and eventually unconscious, and
- To help children see the purpose of legibility as a vehicle to clear communication.

The elements of fluent handwriting are letter formation, size and proportion, spacing, slant, alignment, and line quality (Barbe, Wasylyk, Hackney, & Braun, 1984). If the formation of letters is tedious for children, they will soon tire in their attempts to communicate. Handwriting instruction should help children see that some methods of letter formation are less tiring for their hands. Learning to be consistent in letter formation, moving top to bottom and left to right, will generally lead children toward fluid hand motions. To this end, some directed handwriting instruction and practice is warranted, especially when a pattern is first introduced (Farris, 1991). Instruction and practice should be supervised so that children can received feedback from a more knowledgeable other about the progressions they follow to make letters.

Fluency in the formation of letters becomes a factor when young children are composing. Observation of young writers suggests that as they are composing, words are produced at a rate of 1.5 letters per minute, or 9 minutes for a six-word sentence (Graves, 1994). Graves states:

> If the familiar motor pathways are not built up through regular writing about topics the writer knows, then slowness can hamper the expression of content. The writing goes down on the page so slowly that the writer pokes along word-by-word on the page. That is, each word takes so long to write down that the next word, or even the rest of the sentence, cannot be contemplated at the same time as the one under construction. (p. 251)

The manner in which children hold a pencil, marker, or crayon can also be a positive or negative factor in the physical exertion of writing. Some children have taught themselves to hold a pen or pencil in what appears to be an awkward position. Before attempting to change a child's grip, observe the child during writing to see if the grip is functional and whether the child's hand tires easily.

The real purpose of writing is for communication. Therefore, handwriting's true purpose is a vehicle for communication. Handwriting instruction, then, must reflect this purpose or the message communication will be lost. The most appropriate place to reinforce this idea is in the midst of writing experiences that are shared with others. When children gather together in response pairs or editing groups, it becomes apparent when someone cannot respond because the writing is illegible. The more children are engaged in sharing their writing, the more functional opportunities teachers have to reinforce real reasons for legibility. When children care about communicating, they will care about legibility.

ASSESSMENT: MONITORING CHILDREN'S DEVELOPMENT AS WRITERS

Children develop as writers through both functional and writing process experiences. Understanding the quality of thinking and the processes each child uses to produce meaningful print requires the collection of data that demonstrates:

🍎 What a child understands about writing as a code, a medium, a product, and a process;

🍎 how a child uses writing as a form of thinking to re-collect, re-create, or re-construct ideas;

🍎 how a child uses various forms of functional writing to communicate; and

🍎 how a child uses the phases of the writing process to explore and develop understandings of a topic and/or to communicate that topic to others.

In many respects, monitoring growth in writing is somewhat easier than in reading, because the results of writing are more visible. However, it is still important to go beyond the product to understand children's thinking processes and response to writing as a means of communication.

Observing Writers at Work

When teachers watch children writing, what can be observed? In a room full of writers, there will be different styles, different levels of understanding about how and why one writes, and different levels of confidence and experience as writers. While observing children write, teachers should ask, "What do I know about each child as a writer and how did I gain that knowledge?" To answer this question, teachers return to their instructional purposes of writing, the writing activities that have grown out of those purposes, and observations of each child. Were children observed based on knowledge of their development and the teacher's instructional goals? Were accurate records of that development kept?

In a writing process classroom there is a great deal of activity. Conscious effort must be made to watch children in a systematic manner. As with independent reading, each day teachers should make careful notes about the writing behaviors of one or two children so that over the course of a month every child is observed. Systematic observation provides opportunity for all children to be seen.

What behaviors might teachers look for as children are observed while writing?

- 🍎 How children respond to mini-lessons and shared writing activities,
- 🍎 How they settle into their writing each day,
- 🍎 How they give and receive help during response and editing activities,
- 🍎 How their attitudes reflect their own writing and the writing of others, and
- 🍎 How they sustain themselves during independent writing and how they choose writing strategies.

Observation notes should be reviewed routinely, reflecting on each child's progress. A scarcity of information for some children should be a signal that more frequent and focused observations are needed.

Evaluating Writing Traits

For more information on writing traits, see *http://www.nwrel.org/assessment.*

Many states are now using writing traits to evaluate children's writing. Samples of children's writing serve as a starting point for assessment and evaluation. What can samples of writing reveal? Over time, samples can be compared for growth in the following writing traits:

- 🍎 organization,
- 🍎 ideas and content,
- 🍎 voice,
- 🍎 use of language, and
- 🍎 use of conventions.

Although evaluating traits of a child's writing may allow for a more detailed discussion of writing, we need to remember that an analysis of writing traits may not reveal aspects of the "child as writer" that ought to be known. The traits show writing as a code, a medium, and a product. Writing traits are usually analyzed in writing that has had the opportunity to be taken through the writing process, including editing for meaning and correctness.

Instruction in writing should provide children with experiences in selecting ideas and content for writing, ways to organize their writing, how to bring their own voice to their writing, and how they use language. The use of conventions is always an issue, and is usually emphasized in school. Through reading aloud from quality literature, we show children how other authors use writing traits to tell their stories or share their ideas. Then through shared writing we model the use of particular writing traits as they are appropriate to various forms of writing. Through writer's workshop, we guide children to evaluate the traits of their own writing. Figure 9.24 provides a sample form for the ways that we might begin to help children think about the traits of their own writing. It is best to focus on one trait at a time, typically beginning with ideas and content. Organization is one of the most difficult traits for children and develops slowly over many writing experiences.

FIGURE 9.24
Rubric to help children
evaluate writing traits.

Evaluating My Writing

Writing Trait	1	3	5
Ideas & Content	When someone else reads my paper, it is hard for that person to understand what I mean or what it is all about.	The reader usually knows what I mean. Some parts will be better when I tell just a little more about what is important.	I know a lot about my topic, my ideas are interesting, the main point of my paper is clear, and my topic is not too big.
Organization	The ideas and details in my paper are sort of jumbled and confused. I don't really have a good beginning, middle, and end.	The details and order of my paper make sense most of the time. I have a beginning but it may not really grab the reader. I have a conclusion but it seems to sum up my paper in just an OK way.	My beginning gets the reader's attention and makes the reader want to find out what's coming next. Every detail adds a little more to the main ideas. I ended at a good place and at just the right time.
Voice	I can't really hear my voice in this paper. It was hard for me to write this paper. I really need to know much more about my topic.	Although readers will understand what I mean, they may not "feel" what I mean. My personality comes through sometimes. I probably need to know a little more about my topic to show, rather than tell, the reader about it.	My paper has lots of personality. It really sounds like me. People who know me will know it is my paper.
Use of Language	Even when I read this paper, I have to go back, stop, and read over, just to figure out the sentences. A lot of my sentences seem to be the same. The words I chose don't seem to be very interesting.	Some of my sentences are choppy and awkward, but most are clear. Some words are very general, but most readers will figure out what I mean.	The sentences in my paper are clear and sound good when read aloud. Words fit just right.
Use of Conventions	There are a lot of spelling and grammar errors in my paper. Punctuation and capital letters seem to be missing. My paragraphs are not indented.	My spelling is correct on simple words. Most of my sentences begin with capital letters and end with the right punctuation.	There are very few errors in my paper; it wouldn't take long to get this ready to publish.

Conferencing with Writers

Providing a forum for children to talk about their writing is essential to understanding their motivations and intentions as writers. The writing process has response built into it through child-teacher conferences, response partners and groups, and editing partners and groups. Teachers should also conference with children while they are engaged in functional writing as another window into children's thinking. Talk can focus on how thinking is organized, why a particular format is chosen, other forms that are considered, and explaining the ideas/content of the writing. Assessment and evaluation must begin with and build on what children see in their writing.

Teachers who use the writing process extensively in their classrooms conference with children in a number of different ways (see writing conferences section on pages 356–358). From conferences during writer's workshop teachers have notes about each child. Conference notes may be kept in a separate folder or notebook or combined with the other anecdotal records made from observations. These records must be considered as teachers evaluate pieces of children's writing that are to be placed in an assessment portfolio, a folder of selected pieces that best illustrate a child's growth as a writer.

Notes from conferences help teachers understand how children think as writers. It may be difficult to adequately evaluate samples of children's writing unless teachers are able to go beyond the surface of the writing and into the processes children use as writers. For example, review the teacher's notes in

FIGURE 9.25
Making notes about writing conferences.

Writing Conference Notes		Name _Roberto_
1/25 Illustrations only. When asked to tell about his "story" he points to and identifies objects, partly in Spanish. I asked if I could write his words. Roberto agreed so I labeled objects in his drawing.	2/14 Roberto has been drawing pictures about blue houses for a week— family has moved out of apartment to house. I encouraged him to label his own picture. He wrote, "Mi Hs bl Hs" (my house blue house).	3/3 Roberto wrote "We wnt to se rs crz." When he reads his story he reads an elaborated version, with many details. He has a story in his head. His illustrations tell only a part. Roberto tells episodes (then, then).

Figure 9.25 about Roberto, a first-grade child. The conference notes suggest that Roberto has a concept of story that is limited both physically and linguistically for the time being. Discussions with Roberto should let a teacher know that his oral language is well ahead of his knowledge of written language at present. Conferences with Roberto provide a context for evaluating his drawings and spelling. Really listening to children can teach us a lot about themselves and their writing.

Collecting Samples of Writing

A portfolio of writing should be kept for each child and used to develop a comprehensive picture of each child as a writer. Teachers may actually keep three types of portfolios:

- A work folder containing most all of a child's work completed during a particular grading period,
- The child's portfolio for self-evaluation of selected pieces, and
- The teacher's portfolio for assessment and evaluation of growth.

Writing Folder

During a grading period, all writing that children have begun and/or completed should be kept. From the writing folder, the child and teacher can select writing to be placed in the child's portfolio and/or the teacher's assessment portfolio. Some teachers choose to divide this writing into two folders for ease of handling—work-in-progress and past work. Work-in-progress should remain in the writing folder so that it is not cluttered. A running list of ideas and self-assessment checklists can also be kept in the inside pocket of the folder. Past work that is not needed on a daily basis should be filed in a more permanent folder. This folder should be accessible to the child, as needed. Past writing might be divided between "completed pieces" and "drafts and ideas." Even if a piece is initially abandoned, the first attempts should be kept in case the child decides to return to the piece.

Child's Portfolio

During each marking period children should have the opportunity to select pieces of writing to go into their personal writing portfolio that will go home at the end of the school year. Graves (1994) suggests that along with selecting what children think is their "best" work, they should also be asked to select work that represents specific writing strategies or behaviors. For example, if developing detail or description has been a focus of that marking period, children are asked to select the piece that is their best example of using detail or description. In addition to focused selections, children should also have the option of selecting additional pieces they want to place in their portfolio.

To help children make selections, Graves (1994) suggests that children frequently spend time during writer's workshop reviewing past writing and reflecting on the merit of that writing. It is helpful to focus mini-lessons on how to reflect on one's own writing by modeling this activity. Mini-lessons may also

FIGURE 9.26
Forms to help children
monitor their own writing.

```
┌─────────────────────────────────────────────────────────┐
│  Checking my story . . .                                  │
│                                                           │
│  My story has       ____ a problem in the beginning       │
│                                                           │
│                     ____ a middle with 2 or 3 events      │
│                                                           │
│                     ____ an end that solves the problem   │
│                                                           │
└─────────────────────────────────────────────────────────┘
```

FIGURE 9.27
Form for child's self-
evaluation for portfolio
selection.

```
┌─────────────────────────────────────────────────────────┐
│  I chose this piece for my writing portfolio because it   │
│  shows...                                                 │
│  _____  │
│  _____  │
│  _____  │
│  _____  │
│                                                           │
│                     Signed _____  │
└─────────────────────────────────────────────────────────┘
```

encourage children to share their thinking as they reflect on their past writings. For each piece selected, children should provide an explanation for their selection. Self-evaluation is not a natural process and needs to be taught. Again, mini-lessons can focus on teaching the processes of self-evaluation. A child's self-evaluation should be attached to the finished piece of writing when it is placed in the portfolio. With very young children, the self-evaluation may be dictated to the teacher. For other children, a self-evaluation form may be provided on which children record their explanation. Sample evaluation forms for children are shown in Figures 9.26 and 9.27.

The self-evaluation that teachers encourage in children should be linked to observations of their writing behavior and the writing strategies that have been encouraged during that grading period. Children will learn more about themselves as writers if they focus on evaluating particular traits of their writing, instead of giving them the impression that "whatever they want to say about their writing is fine." Writing is a complex process and involves the use of many skills and strategies. Teachers can help children self-evaluate by focusing attention on particular strategies for some pieces, yet leaving the evaluation of at least one piece open for them to decide the focus.

```
┌─────────────────────────────────────────────────────────────┐
│  This piece was selected for  _____'s      │
│  assessment portfolio because it shows. . .                   │
│                                                               │
│  _____ │
│  _____ │
│  _____ │
│  _____ │
│  _____ │
│  _____ │
└─────────────────────────────────────────────────────────────┘
```

FIGURE 9.28
Form for teacher's evaluation of a portfolio selection.

Teacher's Assessment Portfolio

Teachers should keep a folder of writing that serves as the basis for evaluation and grading. This assessment portfolio should follow the child from grade to grade to document growth. During each marking period, the teacher selects samples of a child's work that document areas of growth as a writer, as well as areas of need. Selecting a piece for this portfolio constitutes assessment. How the piece is judged becomes the evaluation. The pieces that are selected should be photocopied so that originals can remain with the child. The teacher's evaluation of what each piece represents for the child should be clearly identified and should relate to instructional goals during that marking period. A sample evaluation form that might be attached to a child's writing is shown in Figure 9.28.

A child's writing should be evaluated according to the teacher's instructional goals that are reflected in:

- the topics of mini-lessons,
- shared/interactive writing topics,
- writing strategies suggested in conferences, and
- behaviors noted in anecdotal records of observations and conferences.

Instructional goals can be turned into a checklist format that will enable a quick and clear indication of a child's overall progress in areas such as using the writing process, types of writing, and writing traits. The best checklists are self-made, because they accurately reflect the goals of a particular literacy program. A sample checklist is provided in Figure 9.29.

Monitoring children's progress in writing is a continuous process and will require focused attention. Teachers cannot develop an appropriate writing program for children without knowing them as writers. A teacher cannot know a child as a writer without carefully observing and talking with that child over a period of time. Careful monitoring is a commitment teachers must make to have an effective writer's workshop.

FIGURE 9.29
Recording form for
children's progress in
writing processes.

Growth in Using Writing Processes			Name	
Date				
Getting Started . . . • uses informal writing strategies • explores new topics • uses background experience				
Finding a Focus . . . • focuses after exploring ideas • abandons unproductive topics				
Composing . . . • shows sustained effort • shows meaning is more important than conventions				
Editing for Meaning . . . • rereads to check meaning • receives input from others • uses input from others • changes words/sentences • changes order • adds on				
Editing for Correctness . . . • receives input from others • checks for capital letters • checks for punctuation • checks for spelling (in word knowledge stage)				

RESPECTING DIVERSITY IN WRITING DEVELOPMENT

If children come to school with different experiences, then teachers must assume that their knowledge of writing and interest in communicating through writing is also different. Like reading, writing is very personal. Writers develop through a personal desire to communicate with themselves and others. Teachers can support diversity by honoring children's thinking and supporting their independent development as writers.

Honoring Children's Thinking

When children are asked to put their thoughts on paper, making their ideas visible, they are entrusting teachers with their thoughts and feelings. How their ideas are treated tells children a great deal about how they are viewed as human beings and how they are valued as individuals. If writing is viewed as an extension of oneself, then children's writing must be treated with respect. It is very easy for adults to see what is missing from children's writing, what children might have included, or what the teacher believed the children know or should do. In such cases, teachers might be inclined to impose their ideas on the writing. This takes the writing out of the hands of the writer (Calkins, 1994).

When children write, they have intentions. Are teachers aware of those intentions? Response to children's writing should help them accomplish their intentions. When intentions are known, teachers can nudge the writing, offering suggestions that might be helpful. Care must be taken, however, not to impose the teacher's ideas on the writing.

Supporting Independence

Developmental learning environments promote independence, which can then strengthen one's view of self. During their preschool years, children learn to be quite independent in their activity, including dressing and feeding themselves and finding their way around the neighborhood. Developing as writers should also encourage independence. To support children's independence as writers, teachers must value children's ideas as individuals and provide many opportunities for them to show who they are as writers.

Young children believe they know much about writing (Calkins, 1994). Unlike reading, the products of writing have been quite visible to them. They most likely have experimented with their own writing in a variety of forms. Writing activities in primary-grade classrooms must encourage children to explore and experiment rather than merely copy and imitate. When children spend the majority of their writing time copying or imitating the writing of another, they learn that someone else's ideas are more valuable than their own.

Making Connections . . .

As you reflect on the content of this chapter, what ideas do you have about developing an environment that will support the development of children's writing processes in your classroom?

What do you think will be the most important things for you to consider as you plan for guided and independent writing experiences? How do you think you might balance the need to support children in their development with their need for independence? Record your thinking in a reflective journal. Share your thinking with your peers.

Part II
Making Connections:
Linking Children's
Learning Experiences within a
Balanced Literacy Program

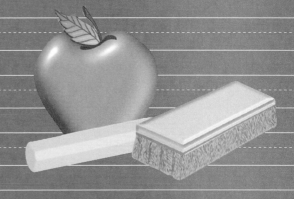

C H A P T E R

10

Teaching a Basal Reading/Language Arts Series: Integrating Instruction to Maximize Children's Learning

Linking the components in our literacy framework . . .

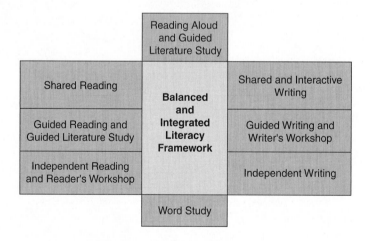

In this chapter we learn about . . .

- 🍎 organizing and using a basal reading/language arts series
- 🍎 planning a basal lesson

- guiding the development of children's reading and writing in a basal series
- modifying basal lessons to fit personal instructional goals

Focus Literature:

- *The Pine Park Mystery* by Tracey West
- An adopted basal reading/language arts series in a local school district(s)

Looking into Classrooms . . .

Kendra sits down to plan for next week's literacy activities with the newly adopted basal reading program. When she was hired by Midwest School District she was committed to teaching mainly with children's literature, but Midwest School District had adopted a new basal reading/language arts series in an effort to provide equal access for all children to a research-based literacy program. Since the No Child Left Behind Act (2001) became law, Kendra's school has been held accountable by the federal government for the academic progress of all children. The school district believes that it needs to standardized expectations for all children and that adopting a basal reading/language arts program is one step in that direction.

Last year Kendra taught reading primarily with small, leveled books (like Rigby and Wright Group) and other trade books, including both fiction and nonfiction. Guided reading and literature study groups were the centerpiece of her reading program. Reading aloud and shared reading occurred several times each day. She used shared/interactive writing and writer's workshop to model and guide writing processes and various forms of writing, as well as grammar and mechanics of language. Phonics and spelling were integrated throughout her literacy program, as well as highlighted in a daily word study time when she engaged children in word building and sorting patterns that were developmentally appropriate.

This year the school district has asked all teachers to use the newly adopted basal materials as their primary instructional materials. Kendra is finding that though the sequence of skills and strategies outlined in the basal series is slightly different than what she taught last year, the quality of the literature is good and some leveled materials are provided. She is able to use the same basic organization for her literacy block as last year—moving from whole-group activities to a small-group/independent work time, and then back to whole group. Sometimes she supplements the independent reading book boxes with her own leveled books. She continues to read aloud quality children's literature in addition to what is provided with the basal series. The one area where she has the most challenge is in spelling. Only one level of spelling materials is provided in the basal series. The English language learners and students who read below grade level in Kendra's class find the spelling words in the basal series quite challenging. Kendra adjusts the level of challenge for these students.

BUILDING A THEORY BASE . . .

Imagine that, like Kendra, you have accepted a position as a second-grade teacher in a school district that has recently adopted a basal reading/language arts series for teaching reading. In your new classroom you find copies of student books, teacher editions, and other support materials for the Harcourt Trophies Reading/Language Arts Program (Beck, Farr, & Strickland, 2005). As you leaf through the books you reflect back on your own reading experiences in elementary school and remember sitting around a table with other children while a teacher guided you through stories in reading books. You realize that basal series were a part of your own reading history.

WHAT IS A BASAL READING/LANGUAGE ARTS SERIES?

Read here to find a definition of *basal reading/language arts series.*

A *basal reading/language arts series* is a sequential set of instructional materials organized around a hierarchy of reading skills and strategies (Goodman, Shannon, Freeman, & Murphy, 1988). The definition of *basal* in this context is *basic* or *of primary importance.* A basal program is the *basic* or *primary program* for many school districts. Though teachers have historically used some type of printed materials to teach children to read, sets of basal reading materials have only been part of the American educational system since the early 1900s (Goodman et al., 1988). More recently, the basal series include attention to all of the language arts (reading, writing, listening, speaking, and sometimes viewing).

A Little History

Teachers have always been concerned with having appropriate reading materials for young children. Books for young readers, however, have not always been available. Early in our nation's history, reading was taught with a Hornbook, a 3″ × 5″ hand-held paddle with one page of text. Daily, children would recite the alphabet, phonetic syllables, and The Lord's Prayer from their Hornbook.

By the 1840s educators became concerned with carefully controlling the rate at which new words were introduced to young readers. *McGuffey Eclectic Readers* provide an example of early attempts to control vocabulary, a characteristic of most basal series (Bohning, 1986). A page in a McGuffey reader might have included the following words, letter patterns, and controlled text:

dŏg   Răb

Făt   Năt's

Nat's cap   a fat dog

Has the lad a dog?
The lad has a fat dog.
The dog has Nat's cap.
Nat and Rab ran.
Rab ran at a cat.

Children would pronounce words and sounds, then apply them to a simple text. The text itself bore great similarity to the basal series used in the 1950s and 1960s.

Around the turn of the century, with dramatic increases in the school-age population, elementary schools were organized into a graded system by age for more efficient instruction. During this time in our history, industrialization had great influence on our thinking and schools became concerned with efficiency and standardization of "product." Teachers at that time did not always have a high level of training and there was concern that all children would not receive similar instruction (Shannon, 1992). These concerns lead to the creation of sets of graded reading materials known as a *basal reading series* (Betts, 1946).

Since their inception, basal series have dominated reading instruction in the United States (McCallum, 1988). As early as 1935, basal series were seen as the foundation for classroom reading programs and the source of "expert" knowledge for instruction. Arthur Gates (1935), a well-known reading educator, suggested that basal series freed the teacher to give more attention to the proper selection of other reading materials and the proper guidance of children in their total reading program.

From the 1940s to the 1960s, classroom instruction was dominated by basal reading series, such as the *Dick and Jane New Basic Readers,* that conveyed stereotypic images of family life (Reutzel & Cooter, 1992). With rapidly expanding global competition in the 1960s and 1970s, basal series began to reflect a growing national concern for students' ability to demonstrate their knowledge of basic skills. The struggle for equality by various groups in the United States during that same period led to criticisms of stereotyped character portrayals in basal texts (Aukerman, 1981).

As a result of the whole language movement (1990s), the content of basal series changed to include higher-quality literature, less isolated skills instruction, more integration of reading with other language arts and content areas, and greater flexibility in decision making for teachers. More recently, as a result of the report of the National Institute of Child Health and Human Development Panel (2000) and the No Child Left Behind Act (2001) basal reading series are giving renewed attention to phonics instruction and fluency.

Basal reading/language arts series continue to dominate reading instruction in the United States. Textbook-adoption policies and funds for purchasing instructional materials have contributed greatly to this domination (Goodman et al., 1988). Textbook-adoption committees at state and local levels:

- Set acceptable standards for textbooks to be used in public schools,
- Review materials submitted by publishers, and
- Select materials that can be purchased with public school funds for use in schools. (Farr, Tulley, & Powell, 1987)

School districts often adopt a single series as the "district curriculum" and funds are provided for purchase of those materials. School districts may allow teachers to use authentic literature rather than an adopted reading/language arts series, but textbook funds for purchasing the literature may be limited. In such cases, literature-based teachers do not have equal access to funds for instructional materials.

A Call for Change

During the 1980s and 1990s basal reading/language arts series became the target of criticism by groups that advocate holistic philosophies (Goodman et al., 1988; Shannon, Reutzel & Cooter, 1992; 1992). The main areas of concern were the quality of literature, teaching of isolated skills, and the control of teachers' instructional decisions.

Authors of a basal reading/language arts series selct the literature that children read, provide direction to teachers in using the reading selections with children, and furnish prepared practice materials for children to use. The literature selected for children was not always authentic, but instead was often written by the editors of the series to control the level of readability and to avoid controversial issues. The controls on readability led to selections in which the language was stilted, uninteresting, and difficult to understand. Materials for emergent readers controlled the language to the point that without illustrations on each page, the text had little meaning. Controls on the content of the literature led to stories that were uninteresting and of little value.

Skill instruction suggested by a basal teacher edition often was isolated from the meaningful context of real reading. The workbooks were criticized because they provided practice that required children to "fill in" someone else's ideas. The number of different skills introduced or practiced in one lesson forced "reading" time to become a "skill and drill" time. In addition, the placement of skills instruction within the basal series seemed arbitrary and unrelated to the selections being read.

Another major criticism was that the organization and language of basal teacher editions led teachers to believe that educators who developed the series had "expert" knowledge about reading, more expert than their own knowledge about literacy. Consequently, teachers allowed the teacher edition to make decisions that should have been made at the classroom level. Michael Apple (1988) refers to this as *deskilling*, when teachers do not trust their own knowledge and instead defer to an outside "expert" as a better source of knowledge. If this type of thinking continues, eventually teachers become reskilled in basal approaches and techniques, becoming technicians who merely turn pages and follow directions rather than professionals who make their own informed decisions.

Originally a basal teacher edition was a few pages in the back of a student's book, highlighting the new words in a selection and offering a few suggestions for teaching each selection. During the 1970s, teacher editions became scripts to be read by the teacher during instruction. Scripting was seen as an attempt to provide teachers with information about new instructional strategies and to make teacher's actions during reading instruction more standardized across the country.

What do these concerns suggest for reading instruction today? Publishers of the current series have been responding to past criticisms:

🍎 Current basal series are incorporating higher-quality literature selections.

🍎 There is more balance between fiction, informational texts, and poetry.

🍎 There is an attempt to present skill instruction in more meaningful contexts and extension activities are provided.

🍎 Teachers are being encouraged to be decision makers and select activities that are appropriate for their children.

TEACHER DECISION MAKING AND THE BASAL SERIES

Given the strides that current basal reading series have made, have the concerns of the past disappeared? Whenever someone other than the teacher is making decisions about instruction that will occur in a particular classroom, there should be concern. Lesson plans and materials that are developed by the authors of basal reading series must be subjected to the same decision-making processes as the lesson plans and materials that teachers create.

Perhaps teachers should view a basal reading series as multiple copies of children's literature selections and a series of skills lessons. In that way, teachers might be better able to use their knowledge of literacy teaching and learning more effectively. Before teaching with basal materials, teachers should decide the types of experiences children need, just as when teacher-selected literature is being used. Keeping objectives in mind, teachers should then select the portions of the basal materials that best meet the objectives for their children.

In the sections that follow, opportunities are provided to become familiar with the organization of basal reading series . . . focusing on one series as an example. You will have opportunities to think about the decisions that need to be made in using such materials with young children. Basal reading series can be very effective for reading instruction if teachers make informed decisions for reading instruction.

Making Connections . . .

To increase your opportunities for learning in the remainder of this chapter, it is important that you have access to copies of the basal reading materials that are adopted by your local school district, especially a teacher's edition. This chapter provides an overview of the organization and content of the Harcourt Trophies Reading/Language Arts Program (2005), which you should compare and contrast to materials in use in your local schools.

PUTTING THEORY INTO PRACTICE . . .

Imagine once again that we are second-grade teachers and our school district has recently adopted a new basal reading/language arts series as the primary instructional materials. As we look over the materials, we realize that there are enormous amounts of information and activities to be covered if we follow all of the suggestions provided by the authors of the basal series. What we know about organizing literacy instruction (reading aloud, shared reading, guided reading, shared writing, etc.) are the same approaches to instruction we should use with the materials provided by a basal series. As we begin to plan a basal lesson, we must keep this in mind!

WHAT IS IN A BASAL READING/ LANGUAGE ARTS SERIES?

Current basal series are very comprehensive. Publishers typically provide anthologies of literature selections for children, consumable materials such as workbooks, supplemental materials to extend beyond the literature selection, an assessment program for monitoring children's progress, and a comprehensive teacher's edition that includes lesson plans and illustrations of student and supplemental materials.

The large spiral-bound teacher's edition for *Trophies: Banner Days, Theme 2* of the second-grade basal reading program (there are six themes in second grade) makes reference to components of the program, such as:

- a teacher's edition,
- a pupil edition of literature selections,
- decodable book selections,
- independent/self-selected books,
- a pupil practice book,
- teaching transparencies,
- word builders/letter cards,
- a spelling practice book,
- homework masters,
- library book collections,
- technology resources,
- reading and language skills assessment materials,
- end-of-selection tests,
- interventions resources kit, and
- an English language learners kit.

We can also see the impact of technology by the inclusion of CD ROM and other supporting media. Trophies is a comprehensive program with many materials, many of which can be purchased separately. We are fortunate that our school district purchased all of the essential materials for our grade level. (Be aware that this may not be true for all school districts.)

Typical of many basal series, the Harcourt Trophies program provides reading materials for kindergarten through sixth-grade students. The student anthology for each grade level is broken into a number of themes. Each theme includes a variety of literature selections with other supporting activities in the language arts.

HOW IS A THEME ORGANIZED IN A BASAL SERIES?

Most current basal reading/language arts series are organized around themes, or units of instruction, that contain literature selections, skill and strategy instruction, extension activities, and assessment materials. In the Harcourt Trophies series, for example, each of the six themed units in second grade has five main literature selections with additional poetry, magazine articles, and other supportive texts to extend children's engagement with the theme. (It is important to remember that most schools are usually in session about 36 weeks each year. The Harcourt Trophies program provides reading materials and lesson plans for at least 30 weeks.)

Understanding the organization of a theme, including the literature selections within the theme, is the key to understanding the organization of a grade level of instruction. With five main literature selections in a theme, we can focus on one theme for about 5 to 6 weeks. (Other basal series are similar.)

Let's consider the theme *Neighborhood News* to explore how a theme can be organized and the components of instruction that are typically included in a basal series. In the opening pages of the theme, the focus is explained, along with an overview of:

- skills/strategies for each selection,
- resources available for teaching selection in the theme,
- assessment materials to monitor children's progress,
- ways to provide support to all learners,
- homework ideas for each week, and
- a theme project.

The authors of the Harcourt Trophies series also suggest a framework for managing time and instructional activities. As you can see in Figure 10.1, the authors of the series suggest that we spend approximately 130 to 160 minutes per day engaging children in the basal materials. We have seen this type of organization of time throughout this text. This movement from whole-class work to a work time for small groups and individuals, then back to whole class is the same organization as whole-class or small-group guided literature study (Chapters 4 and 6), a reader's workshop (Chapter 7), or a writer's workshop (Chapter 9).

We could plan the time allocations suggested in Figure 10.1 in either three separate time periods (whole class, small group/independent, whole class) or one large "literacy block." That would depend on our daily schedule, but would probably vary somewhat from day to day because of school schedules for music, physical education, art, library, and/or computer skills.

The overview of the theme shows the literature selections that are included. Many basal series now incorporate authentic children's literature with authors and illustrators who are familiar. The main selections in the "Neighborhood News" unit are:

- *The Pine Park Mystery* by Tracey West,
- *Good-bye, Curtis* by Kevin Henkes,
- *Max Found Two Sticks* by Brian Pinkney,

FIGURE 10.1
Suggested organization and time allocation for a second grade basal reading/language arts series.

Daily Reading/Language Arts—Second Grade	
Whole Group (40 minutes)	Sharing literature Phonics Spelling Vocabulary High-frequency words

**Small Groups
& Independent
Work**
(60–90 minutes)
	Reading with teacher
	   Literature selections
	   Decodable books (two for this
	     theme)
	
	Independent
	   Practice pages
	   Cross-curricular centers
	   Books for all learners/leveled
	     books

Whole Group 30 minutes	Writing Grammar
Daily Routines	Morning message Journal writing prompts* Daily language practice*

*Place where most appropriate.

- *Anthony Reynoso: Born to Rope* by Martha Cooper and Ginger Gordon, and
- *Chinatown* by William Low.

The literature selections in this theme are all written and illustrated by published authors/illustrators.

To introduce the theme to the children, a poem titled "Our Block" by Lois Lenski is provided in the teacher's edition. The poem relates to the theme of how people in a community are connected in a variety of ways and that each person plays an important part in the community.

WHAT IS INCLUDED WITH EACH LITERATURE SELECTION?

Let's examine the first literature selection in the theme, *The Pine Park Mystery* by Tracey West, and the suggestions provided for teaching that selection. This selection is in the format of a play with six characters and a narrator. At the beginning of the selection there is an overview of resources for planning instruction that includes:

- a list of *practice and resource materials* to support the selection,
- a *Lesson Planner* that outlines suggested activities for 5 days, similar to a teacher's plan book, and

🍎 suggestions for *cross-curricular centers* for independent work and extending children's focus on the theme story and/or theme.

Practice and Resource Materials

Books for All Learners

Leveled books for independent or guided reading are available for use with each main literature selection. Multiple copies of these texts provide material that may be closer to each student's instructional reading level. There are four texts: below-level, on-level, advanced, and ELL (english language learners). The texts are related to vocabulary and skills and related to the literature selection and/or theme.

Consumable Practice Books

Practice materials for phonics, vocabulary, and comprehension are available in four levels: below-level, on-level, advanced, and ELL. Practice materials are also available for spelling and grammar, but in only one level.

Additional Resources

Because the Harcourt Trophies series is intended to provide comprehensive development in reading/language arts a variety of resources are available:

🍎 Read Aloud Literature (an anthology),
🍎 Teaching Transparencies for skill instruction,
🍎 Cross-Curricular Activity Cards to support the theme,
🍎 Comprehension cards,
🍎 Word builders/letter cards,
🍎 An intervention resource kit for specialized support of children who are below-level, and
🍎 An ELL Resource Kit.

Lesson Planner

The Lesson Planner, two facing pages in the teacher's edition at the beginning of each new literature selection, shows a listing of activities for each of the 5 days of instruction. The activities are divided into four categories: oral language, word work, reading, and language arts. Figure 10.2 shows the suggested contents of each category. Notice that the order of activities is similar to the overall organization suggested by the series authors (see Figure 10.1); however, the suggestions for the allocation of time are different. There is more time suggested for the whole-group activities (70 minutes versus 105 minutes) and a decrease of time for small groups/independent work (60 to 90 minutes versus 45 minutes). Remember, these are merely estimates of time needed. It should be noted that basal reading/language arts series such as Trophies by Harcourt, can be used within a variety of literacy models, including balanced literacy as advocated by this text.

In the end we, the teachers, should make the decision about what is appropriate for our particular classroom of children. Figure 10.2 also shows the match between the basal series and the elements of the literacy framework developed in this text.

FIGURE 10.2
Overview of a basal lesson planner.

Lesson Planner		Instructional Framework in this Text
Oral Language (30 minutes)	Sharing literature	Mediated read-aloud (Chapter 4)
Word Work (30 minutes)	Morning message	Interactive writing/shared reading (Chapters 5 and 8)
	Phonics	Word study (Chapters 2 and 3)
	Spelling	Word study (Chapter 3)
	Vocabulary	Mediated read-aloud/guided reading (Chapters 4 and 8)
	High-frequency words	Word study (Chapter 3)
Reading (45 minutes)	Comprehension	Mediated read-aloud/guided reading (Chapters 4 and 6)
	Fluency	
	Independent reading	Independent reading (Chapter 7)
Language Arts (45 minutes)	Writing	Shared writing/writer's workshop (Chapters 8 and 9)
	Grammar	

Cross-Curricular Centers

The authors of the Harcourt Trophies series suggest that second-grade teachers offer children time to work in five centers during the week. Looking back to Figure 10.1, we see that it is suggested that center time occur during the small-group/independent work time.

Content of the Centers

The Harcourt Trophies series provides suggestions for five centers. For the literature selection we will review, *The Pine Park Mystery,* the suggested centers are:

- Science—children draw, label, and write about birds.
- Writing—focus on what the characters in the literature selection might do to solve the mystery.
- Social Studies—focus on community jobs.
- Drama—practice scenes from the play.
- Computer—children prepare programs for the performance of the reader's theater version of *The Pine Park Mystery.*

Three of these centers rely on children having knowledge of the literature selection: the writing, drama, and computer centers. We should wait to introduce these centers until the children are familiar with the selection. Thus, we will introduce centers in a staggered manner. If we leave each center up for at least 5 days for children to have ample time to visit, then at any given time we will probably have new centers, as well as centers used with the previous literature selection. Staggering the introduction of centers will make it easier to give directions and make sure that children know what to do in each center so that they can work independently. Certainly children in the class can help each other

Group 1	Group 2	Group 3	Group 4
Small Group with Teacher	Independent reading	Centers	Independent reading
Practice to follow-up small group	**Small Group with Teacher**	Centers	Centers
Independent reading	Practice to follow-up small group	**Small Group with Teacher**	Centers
Centers	Centers	Practice to follow-up small group	**Small Group with Teacher**
Centers	Centers	Independent reading	Practice to follow-up small group

FIGURE 10.3
Rotation of small groups during reading time.

navigate the centers—that will be part of the management routines that we will need to teach.

Using Centers in the Classroom

Using centers in the classroom requires the teaching of routines for working independently while the teacher is meeting with a small group. Setting routines begins early in the school year as we establish other classroom routines. It is important that the first centers we use are independent for our children. We may want to begin by offering short "center times" during the day before including them with guided reading, so that we can reinforce appropriate behaviors in each center.

To have centers available during the time that we are reading with small groups, we might plan a system of rotating groups of children through the small-group, follow-up activities for the reading selection, independent reading, and centers. Some teachers allow children to choose activities after the responsibilities in the small-group and follow-up work are completed. Choice works best after routines are well established. How might it work if we rotated children between small reading groups and independent work? Figure 10.3 provides an overview of how four groups of children might rotate between small-group activities with the teacher and independent activities.

Imagine that we have 20 second-grade children in our classroom that we divide into four flexible groups because they have different needs as readers and are at different instructional reading levels. We would probably spend about 15 to 20 minutes with each group in guided reading activities and prepare them to practice specific skills after leaving the group. To keep children engaged throughout this "work time," we use independent reading and centers. The rotation

FIGURE 10.4
File-folder center.

All About Birds

1. Look at the bird books in the center. Find your favorite bird.

2. Draw a picture of your favorite bird. Write the name of your bird.

3. Label the parts of your bird.

beak	foot
wing	eye
tail	feathers

4. Write some things you know about birds. Tell why this bird is your favorite.

shown in Figure 10.3 would take at least 75 to 100 minutes to complete. Notice that by the last rotation we have met with all groups, so we are free to move about the room. We might want to meet our most challenging group last so that we are able to provide support during their practice/follow-up activities.

Preparing the Centers

To make our planning work more smoothly it is a good idea to prepare the five centers for this literature selection before we plan to teach the selection. The materials for most of the suggested centers are typically available in a classroom (paper, pencils, crayons, markers, rulers, etc.). The first year that we teach with this basal series it will be time consuming to prepare all of the centers. The second year of using the centers will be much easier if we prepare centers that can be easily stored. If we use the inside of a file folder to provide directions and examples for a center, the file folder can be easily stored when the center is no longer in use. Figure 10.4 shows an example of a file-folder center for use with this literature selection, *The Pine Park Mystery*.

TEACHING A BASAL LITERATURE SELECTION

If we are planning our own theme we would:

- determine what children need to learn,
- consider how to assess children's learning.
- gather and/or prepare the necessary resources, and
- plan activities that will help all children reach the desired learning goals/objectives.

All of these aspects of planning are included in a basal series. Our task is to clearly identify each step in planning and then to decide how well the basal suggestions meet the needs and interests of our children. As we make decisions, we may find that some basal activities:

- 🍎 are very appropriate and should be kept,
- 🍎 meet our goals but need to be modified to meet our students' needs, or
- 🍎 are inappropriate for our goals and/or our children's needs and should be delayed or discarded.

How can we evaluate the appropriateness of the suggestions made by the authors of this basal series? It will help to consider their ideas within a familiar framework. Let's return to the organizational framework presented in Figure 10.1. We are familiar with organizing learning experiences for children that move from whole class to small group/independent, then back to whole class, an organizational framework that works well for basal instruction. Using this framework will keep us focused on linking learning experiences for children, and not teaching skills that are isolated from meaningful reading and writing.

As we saw in Figure 10.2, the basal program can show children involved in four types of literacy activities each day: oral language, word work, reading, and language arts. We can do that using the whole class to small group independent to whole class framework. Figure 10.5 provides an overview of the 5 days of suggested activities placed into that framework. Notice that plans for each area of reading/language arts development are provided by the authors of the basal series.

Let's take a closer look at each section of the framework. As we examine the suggested plans of the Harcourt Trophies authors we must ask ourselves:

- 🍎 Will the activities help children learn through meaningful reading and writing activity?
- 🍎 If not, can we modify the activity to provide more meaningful engagement? **or**
- 🍎 Should we delay or discard the activity and find something more appropriate?

WHOLE GROUP: ORAL LANGUAGE AND WORD WORK (40 TO 60 MINUTES)

The purpose of this block of instructional time is twofold: to develop an ear for language and an eye for decoding print. The authors of the Harcourt Trophies series advocate reading aloud to children as a way of increasing their background knowledge; increasing their knowledge of written language, vocabulary, and comprehension; and encouraging a love of literature. We know these desired outcomes are more likely to occur when we engage children in a mediated read-aloud and scaffold their engagement with a text, so we will use that teaching technique when we plan.

The authors also advocate providing explicit and systematic instruction in phonics, spelling, and vocabulary to support children's comprehension of text. Though multilevel support is provided in phonics and vocabulary, only one level of spelling practice is provided. It is highly likely that a number of our children will

FIGURE 10.5
Overview of suggested activities for a basal lesson—second grade.

	Day 1	Day 2	Day 3	Day 4	Day 5
Whole Class	Read Aloud Story: *A History Mystery*	Read Aloud Poem: "Late for Breakfast"	Read Aloud Story: *A History Mystery*	Read Aloud Poem: "Late for Breakfast"	Compare setting, characters, plot: *History Mystery* and *Pine Park Mystery*
Oral Language & Word Work	Phonics: Prefixes *re-*, *pre-* (prefix + base)	Phonics: Review prefixes *re-*, *pre-*	Phonics: Review prefixes *re-*, *pre-*	Phonics: Syllable patterns prefix/base Prefixes: *mis-*, *under-*	Phonics: Maintain diphthongs *ou*, *ow*
	Spelling: Words with *re-*, *pre-* Pretest Word Sort	Spelling: building words	Spelling: Generalization about words with prefixes *re-*, *pre-*	Spelling: Review building words with prefixes *re-*, *pre-*	Spelling: Posttest
(40–60 minutes)		Vocabulary: (*caused, clasp, confused, cornered, removes, typical*) High-frequency words	Vocabulary: Words in context High-frequency words	Vocabulary: Synonyms for vocabulary High-frequency words	Vocabulary: Antonyms for vocabulary High-frequency words
Small-Group & Independent Work		Read *Pine Park Mystery*	Reread *Pine Park Mystery* for fluency	Comprehension: Story map (setting, characters, problem, events, resolution)	Reread *Pine Park Mystery* for fluency
Reading		*Comprehension:* Narrative elements (plot, beginning-middle-end)	Read science article, "Birds Do It! Recycle" Compare to *Pine Park Mystery*		
		Strategy: Use context to confirm meaning			
(60–90 minutes)	Independent Reading Books for All Learners	Independent Reading (leveled books/book boxes)	Independent Reading (leveled books/book boxes)	Independent Reading (leveled books/book boxes)	Independent Reading (leveled books/book boxes)
	Cross-Curricular Centers	Cross-Curricular Centers	Cross-Curricular Centers	Cross-Curricular Centers	Cross-Curricular Centers
Whole Class	Writer's Craft: Analyze descriptive paragraph, write short description of a favorite place (see, hear, taste, smell, feel)	Writer's Craft: Analyze descriptive paragraph, write short description of what children see, hear, taste, smell, feel when they first wake up	Writer's Craft: Introduce similes, look for description in *Pine Park Mystery*, choose a piece of writing from folder to revise, make description more vivid, add similes	Writer's Craft: Brainstorm, prewrite, draft descriptive paragraph	Writer's Craft: Peer conference, focus on revision of description from day 3, use scoring rubric
Language Arts					
(30–45 minutes)	Grammar: Identify action verbs in sentences	Grammar: Find action verbs in *Pine Park Mystery*	Grammar: Find action verbs in big book poem "Spoiled Roy"	Grammar: Make a verb book with magazine pictures, write sentences with action verbs	Grammar: Find action verbs in sentences, write sentences in present tense.

410

not be successful spelling the words suggested by the series authors. Based on our assessment of children's spelling (see Chapter 3) we will make decisions about words that will be more appropriate for the children who are below-level. We know that children who read at varying levels are likely to write at varying levels as well.

Imagine that we are starting the process of writing plans for next week's whole-class activities in read-aloud and word work. We begin to record activities for each day in our Teacher's Plan Book. As we record the suggestions made by the authors of the basal series, we also reflect on our own knowledge of balanced and integrated literature learning to decide whether the suggestions are appropriate for our children. Where needed, we make adjustments in what is suggested by the basal authors.

Making Connections . . .

Now take time to examine our Teacher's Plan Book (pages 412–416) for the 5 days of whole-group activities in which we will teach oral language and word work to prepare and support children while they read *The Pine Park Mystery*. Review the suggestions by the authors of the basal series that appear on the left side of each page of the plan book, then consider what our literacy framework might suggest (shown on the right). Make notations wherever you think that other additions or revisions are needed. Share your thinking with a peer.

From the whole-group lesson plans for days 1 through 5, we can clearly see that we are providing explicit and systematic instruction in skills that are needed by developing readers. We have modified lessons slightly to bring in children's literature or move an activity to another part of our literacy block. Our greatest concern is that there is only one level of spelling words. We know that we will probably need to provide more personalized instruction for our below-level readers, but we also know ways to plan for that (see Chapters 2 and 3).

Now let's turn our focus to the next part of our literacy block: small-group/independent work.

SMALL-GROUP/INDEPENDENT WORK: READING (60 TO 90 MINUTES)

Referring back to Figure 10.1, we see that small-group/independent work time includes time to read with the teacher, time to read independently, completing practice activities, and work in centers. The purpose of this block of time is to provide closer support to children as they read and discuss text. The authors of the Harcourt Trophies Reading/Language Arts Program discuss the importance of explicit and systematic instruction that develops vocabulary, decoding, fluency, and comprehension of text. Remember, in this context *explicit and systematic* means that we are direct with children about what they need to know and we engage them in a deliberate and planned manner. The time we spend in guided reading with small groups of children provides an important assessment opportunity.

Looking back at Figure 10.2 reminds us that we already know a great deal about what should take place during this period of time. We know how to design effective guided reading lessons, including determining teaching points that support

Teacher's Plan Book—Day 1
Whole Group: Oral Language and Word Work

Basal series authors suggest:	**Our thoughts, additions, and revisions:**

Basal series authors suggest:

Morning Message:
To prepare for reading aloud the story *The History Mystery,* guide children to write a short message about a make-believe pet, then read together. Enlist children's help in writing previously taught elements.
Sample in basal:

> Good Morning!
> Today is _____.
> Let's pretend someone mailed you a
> make-believe pet _____.
> It isn't like most pets. It _____.
> Maybe it causes problems because it _____.

Sharing Literature:
Read aloud *A History Mystery* (author unknown). Listen to find out what is special about the object the children find.

Phonics:
Introduce prefixes *re-* and *pre-*, develop meaning when combined with a base word (transparency):

regrouped	reopen	preheat
respelled	return	preschool
recall	replay	prepay

Practice pages available for below-level, on-level, advanced, and ELL.

Spelling:
Give pretest:

New words		Review	High-Frequency
remove	preheat	swimming	maybe
return	prepay	doing	near
recycle	preschool		park
replace	preview		
recall	prefix		

Word Sort:
Children write two lists of words, words with the prefix *re-* and words with the prefix *pre-*. Spelling practice book page available (one level only) for writing words by pattern.

Our thoughts, additions, and revisions:

Build Background for Theme:
Introduce theme—Develop web identifying the types of workers children see in the community. Model what to do in the social studies center.

Morning Message:
Use as suggested. Interactive writing and shared reading is a good way to start the day. Engages children and helps them focus on what is to be learned.

Sharing Literature:
Quality story. Use a mediated read-aloud to guide children's listening comprehension of text. Focus on making inferences about characters' actions that create the plot. Make inference about why the story is titled *A History Mystery.*

Phonics:
Begin with word *regrouped* from the story *A History Mystery:* "The next day after school the kids regrouped at Henry's house." Use story context to determine meaning, write word on board. Then proceed with basal lesson. Do practice page in independent work time.

Spelling:
Use suggested words for children on-level and advanced. Meet in spelling groups. Replace review with challenge words for advanced. Provide alternative new and review words for children below-level, probably one-syllable words with double- and/or variant-vowel patterns. Provide word cards for sorting during the week.

Word Sort:
Use with phonics lesson above. Provide cards for each child to actually sort, then write. Could also be completed during independent work time as a practice activity.

Vocabulary:
Not suggested until day 2, but introduce on day 1 in whole group, reinforce in guided reading. A School–Home Connection page is available to practice vocabulary at home.

412

Teacher's Plan Book—Day 2
Whole Group: Oral Language and Word Work

Basal series authors suggest:	Our thoughts, additions, and revisions:
Morning Message: To prepare for reading the poem *"Late for Breakfast,"* guide children to create a short message about getting ready for school, then read together. Enlist children's help in writing previously taught elements.	**Morning Message:** Use as suggested—use interactive writing.
Sharing Literature: Read aloud the poem *"Late for Breakfast"* by Mary Dawson. Discuss how children get ready for school and how it compares to the person in the poem.	**Sharing Literature:** Prepare poem on large chart for shared reading. Read aloud, then do shared reading. Write children's comparisons on a T-chart.

Poem	How We Get Ready

Basal series authors suggest:	Our thoughts, additions, and revisions:
Phonics: Review words made the prefixes *re-* and *pre-*. Words for the day: *retrace, remove, replace, prepay, prewrite,* and *preheat.* Listen for the number of syllables. Dictate words, children write on cards for word bank or in journal. Practice pages available for below-level, on-level, advanced, and ELL.	**Phonics:** Read and start words like day 1. Add new words. Glue word sort onto paper. The suggested dictation *may not be appropriate* for children below-level. Do practice pages during independent work time.
Spelling: Build words with *re-* and *pre-*. Teacher writes the word *return* on the board, covers all but *re-*, has a child name another spelling word that begins with *re-*. Child comes to the board and writes the word. For each word the teacher asks, "What are the two parts of the word _____?" Spelling practice book page available (one level only) for filling in the blank in sentences using spelling words.	**Spelling:** Do at end of whole-group time. Meet in spelling groups to support children below-level and observe. Closed sort for pattern.
Build Background for Theme: Develop a simple web identifying the types of workers children see in the community.	**Build Background for Theme:** Use web on day 1 to introduce theme.
Vocabulary: Introduce new words in story: *caused, clasp, confused, cornered, objects, removes, typical.* Read in context (transparency). Review high-frequency words: *near, park, sign, maybe, isn't.* Do Vocabulary Power (vocabulary in context in student book)—read paragraphs to practice new vocabulary and discuss. A School–Home Connection page is available to practice vocabulary at home.	**Vocabulary:** Use as suggested to develop meaning on day 1, but also discuss decoding of the words. Do Vocabulary Power in guided reading groups later in the day to practice strategies for decoding.

the literature. In addition, our knowledge of skills and strategies will help us make decisions about independent activities that are valuable to our students.

The center section of Figure 10.5 provides an overview of the suggested activities that will take place day 1 though day 5. Our Teacher's Plan Book will take a close look at the details suggested by the series authors.

Teacher's Plan Book—Day 3
Whole Group: Oral Language and Word Work

Basal series authors suggest:	**Our thoughts, additions, and revisions:**
Morning Message: To prepare for rereading the story *The History Mystery,* guide children to create a short message about the mystery they are reading and whether it could really happen. Then read together. Enlist children's help in writing previously taught elements.	**Morning Message:** Use as suggested—interactive writing
Sharing Literature: Reread *A History Mystery* (author unknown). Listen to find out how the children discover what kind of coin they have found. Discuss meaning of *design.*	**Sharing Literature:** Do as mediated read-aloud. Focus on how character's dialogue tells the story.
Phonics: Write *re-* and *pre-* words on board. Draw one line under the prefix and one line under the base word. Discuss how to decode *re-cy-cle.* Dictate sentences: *I remove my jacket when I return home. I do not preheat the oven when I buy premade cookies.*	**Phonics:** Guide children in word-building activity. Children write each word the class builds. Then use the underlining activity as suggested. Dictation may not be appropriate for children below-level.
Spelling: Children explain what generalization the spelling words have in common. Review high-frequency words. Note that *maybe* is a compound word. Spelling practice book page available (one level only) for writing words by pattern.	**Spelling:** Meet in spelling groups. Hunt for words that follow spelling pattern. Teacher moves between groups, helping children verbalize the generalization for the words they find.
Vocabulary: Read aloud sentences that use vocabulary words. Check comprehension by labeling as true or false. Example: *A clasp is used to keep a necklace closed.* (*true*)	**Vocabulary:** Use in guided reading groups and as follow-up activity during independent work time.

Making Connections . . .

Let's turn once again to our Teacher's Plan Book (pages 417–421). This time we examine the suggestions for supporting children as they read the literature selection, the skills and strategies we need to teach for comprehension and fluency, and how to organize independent work time. First review the suggestions by the authors of the basal series that appear on the left side of each chart, then consider what our literacy framework might suggest. Make notations wherever you think that additions or revisions are needed. Share your thinking with a peer.

The small-group/independent work time provides a block of time for children to practice skills and develop independence, as well as opportunities for assessment by the teacher. Setting classroom management routines early in the

Teacher's Plan Book—Day 4
Whole Group: Oral Language and Word Work

Basal series authors suggest:	Our thoughts, additions, and revisions:

Basal series authors suggest:

Our thoughts, additions, and revisions:

Morning Message:
To prepare for rereading the poem, *"Late for Breakfast,"* guide children to create a short message about the way to make the morning less hurried, then read together. Enlist children's help in writing previously taught elements.

Morning Message:
Use as suggested—interactive writing.

Sharing Literature:
Reread the poem "Late for Breakfast" by Mary Dawson. Discuss how the problem in the poem is similar/different from *The Pine Park Mystery.*

Sharing Literature:
Use as suggested. Add shared rereading of poem. Record (shared writing) similarities and differences on T-chart or Venn diagram.

Phonics:
Listen for number of syllables in *re-* and *pre-* words. Identify syllables. Draw a line between the syllables: *re/move.*

Review syllable generalizations:
- Words with prefixes have at least two syllables.
- Divide a word between the prefix and base word/root.

Sort *re-* and *pre-* words by number of syllables.

    <u>2 syllables</u>   <u>3 syllables</u>

Practice pages available for below-level, on-level, advanced, and ELL.

Introduce new prefixes: *mis-* and *under-*
Sort words: *misbehave, misbelieve, underhand, misfortune, undersea, underwater, misspell.* Discuss how prefixes can change meaning of the base/root. Build words with *mis-* and *under-*. Base words: *took, shirt, stand, lead, take, guide.* Practice pages available for below-level, on-level, advanced, and ELL.

Phonics:
Give children a list of prefix words. Partners read words, listen for syllables, then divide words in syllables. Discuss generalizations as a class. Give children a sheet of word cards to cut apart. Children complete the sort and glue onto paper.

Do not introduce *mis-* and *under-* prefixes today. This element is highlighted in two other stories in the theme.

Spelling:
Write base words on separate index cards. Tape each card to the board. Make cards with *re-* and *pre-*fixes. Children take turns matching the correct prefix card to a base word, then writing the word on the board. Spelling practice book page available (one level only) for writing words by pattern.

Spelling:
Meet in spelling groups. Partners place words found in word hunt on day 3 on small cards for sorting. Record sort in word study notebook.

Vocabulary:
Match vocabulary words to words/phrases on the board that have the same or nearly the same meaning:

    takes away, puts away = removes

Then children use words in a sentence that shows they understand the meaning.

Vocabulary:
Use in guided reading group and as follow-up activity.

Teacher's Plan Book—Day 5
Whole Group: Oral Language and Word Work

Basal series authors suggest:	**Our thoughts, additions, and revisions:**
Morning Message: Guide children to create a short message about what they learned this week about reading, writing, and mysteries. Enlist children's help in writing previously taught elements.	**Morning Message:** Use as suggested—use interactive writing.
Sharing Literature: Invite retellings of *A History Mystery* and *The Pine Park Mystery.* Reread *A History Mystery* after children set a purpose for listening. Compare and contrast the *problems* and *resolutions* in the story and the play.	**Sharing Literature:** Read aloud a community picture book, such as *City Green* (DyAnne DiSalvo-Ryan, 1994). Then compare the problems and solutions in *City Green, A History Mystery,* and *The Pine Park Mystery.* Record children's responses on a chart.

	City Green	History Mystery	Pine Park Mystery
problem			
solution			

Phonics: Review vowel diphthongs *ou-* (*pout*) and *ow-* (*how*) Which words in each group have the same sound? *about how* soil Word sort: *ou ow other* Use words in the sort to write sentences. Practice pages available for below-level, on-level, advanced, and ELL.	**Phonics:** Use as suggested with all students. Use practice pages during independent work time.
Spelling: Give posttest. Dictate all words on day 1 list. Also have children complete sentences by filling in the blanks. I _____ the oven and bake my pie.	**Spelling:** Spelling groups meet. Partners dictate words for posttest. Teacher observes.
Vocabulary: Explore antonyms. Help children generate antonyms for vocabulary words. Example: *confused/understands.*	**Vocabulary:** Use as suggested in guided reading.

school year will be absolutely essential to the success of having children work on their own or with a partner.

Let's turn our attention to the final block of instructional time. This block focuses on modeling and guiding children's development as writers.

WHOLE GROUP: LANGUAGE ARTS (30 TO 45 MINUTES)

Referring back to Figure 10.1, we see that the final whole-group instructional time includes attention to the writer's craft and grammar. Its purpose is to provide focused instruction on the writing process and the development of skills in

Teacher's Plan Book—Day 1
Small-Group and Independent Reading

Basal series authors suggest:

Reading with Teacher:
No suggested plans for reading with the teacher on day 1.

Our thoughts, additions, and revisions:

Guided Reading Groups:
Use leveled texts (Books for All Learners) for guided reading. Plans appear in teacher's edition. Then move texts to book boxes for independent reading. Introduce vocabulary for *The Pine Park Mystery.* Do Vocabulary Power (vocabulary in context in student book), read paragraphs to practice new vocabulary, discuss meaning and decoding.

Rotating Guided Reading Groups: (Figure 10.3)

Group 1	Ind. Read	Centers	Centers
Follow-up	**Group 2**	Centers	Centers
Ind. Read	Follow-up	**Group 3**	Ind. Read
Centers	Centers	Follow-up	**Group 4**
Centers	Centers	Ind. Read	Follow-up

Independence Practice:
Practice pages as appropriate. (See plans for whole-group instruction periods, such as phonics, vocabulary, grammar).

Journal Prompt: Think about a favorite place to go. Write several sentences describing that place.

Independent Practice:
Respond to guided reading text—draw favorite part and tell why.

Complete practice page for vocabulary (multilevel). Take Home–School Connection page home to practice vocabulary.

Independent Reading:
Independent reading in Books for All Learners (leveled texts) is suggested for day 1.

Below-Level: *Minnie, the Talking Bird*
On-Level: *Sam's Chase*
Advanced: *The Return of the Peregrine Falcon*
ELL: *Getting Around the City*

Independent Reading:
Book boxes (previous guided readings).

Cross-Curricular Centers:
Science—All About Birds
Draw and write about birds (part of the mystery in the selection).

Social Studies—Community Jobs
Construct a web of community jobs.

Writing—What Happens Next?
Partners write new scenes for the play, what characters do after the mystery is solved.

Drama—Scene Reading
Groups of children take parts and practice play for fluency.

Computer Center—Set Design
Create program for class performance of the play, experiment with font size and style.

Cross-Curricular Centers:
Carry over some centers from previous story/theme.

Science—All About Birds
Provide books about birds and file folder with directions (see Figure 10.4).

Social Studies Center—Community Jobs
Provide a variety of books about community workers. Place a community related book at the listening station. Children begin a web of community jobs.

Teacher's Plan Book—Day 2
Small-Group and Independent Reading

Basal series authors suggest:

Reading with Teacher:
Prepare to Read:
Preview the play. Discuss what children know about mysteries and how to read the script of a play.

Focus Skill—Narrative Elements
Present a problem/solution chart (transparency), a story map, which will be completed after reading. Discuss the story's problem.

Focus Strategy—Using context to confirm meaning
Teacher models, children apply during reading.

During Reading:
Below-Level—Teacher reads aloud as children read silently, then children take turns rereading. Guided comprehension.

On-Level—Read selection orally, children may take parts as they read the play. Guided comprehension.

Advanced—Introduce, share predictions, then read independently. Discussion follows.

ELL—Children imitate as teacher reads aloud. Encourage children to repeat lines. Guided comprehension.

After Reading:
Focus Skill—Narrative Elements
Retell and summarize story, complete a problem/solution chart (transparency), construct a story map (beginning-middle-end)

Practice pages—comprehension check (one level).

Independence Practice:
Practice pages as appropriate. (See plans for whole-group instruction periods, such as phonics, vocabulary, grammar)
Journal Prompt: Imagine you are on a walk in the woods. What do you see? Hear? Smell? Feel?

Independent Reading:
Books for All Learners
Self-selected reading is suggested each day.

Cross-Curricular Centers:
(See day 1.)

Our thoughts, additions, and revisions:

Guided Reading Groups:
Review vocabulary, meaning, and decoding.

Preview illustrations, paying special attention to the illustrations, make predictions about what the mystery might be.

Guide reading of text as suggested for each level, using mediated support.

Observe students' use of focus strategy (context) during reading.

Retell events and summarize plot. Shared writing of summary.

Delay completing problem/solution chart until day 3 when there is more time to focus on skill development.

Independent Practice:
Phonics practice page (multilevel)
Literature log—Is there another way the mystery could have been solved? Illustrate three vocabulary words and write a sentence.

Independent Reading:
Book boxes (previous guided readings).

Cross-Curricular Centers:
Introduce new centers for independent work. All centers are in use. See rotation chart on day 1.
Drama—Scene Reading
Writing—What Happens Next?
Computer Center—Set Design

Teacher's Plan Book—Day 3
Small-Group and Independent Reading

Basal series authors suggest:	Our thoughts, additions, and revisions:
Reading with Teacher:	**Guided Reading Groups:**
Reading for Fluency:	Retell story events from day 2 reading.
Below-Level—Independently, partners take turns rereading scene 3.	As a group, complete problem/solution chart that includes story events.
On-Level—Independently, group rereads a scene of choice, emphasize interpretation.	
Advanced—Children prepare and present scene 4, emphasize on interpretation and expression.	
ELL—Teacher rereads one scene, rereads again and children act it out, then children echo-read the scene.	
Companion Selection:	*Companion Selection:*
Read *Birds Do It! Recycle!* (two pages) Preview, predict, read, check for understanding. Compare to *Pine Park Mystery.* Cross-Curricular Activity Card—Make a Recycling Poster	Read companion text, *Birds Do It! Recycle!* (two pages) Use as suggested. Relate bird behavior to the problem in *The Pine Park Mystery.*
Independence Practice:	**Independent Practice:**
Practice pages as appropriate. (See plans for whole-group instruction periods, such as phonics, vocabulary, grammar)	Literature log—Partners help each other complete a problem/solution chart that includes story events. Illustrate three vocabulary words and write a sentence.
Journal Prompt: Look out window and describe what they see.	
Independent Reading:	**Independent Reading:**
Books for All Learners	Book boxes (previous guided readings). Reader's theater practice for day 5.
Cross-Curricular Centers:	**Cross-Curricular Centers:**
(See day 1.)	All centers are in use. See rotation chart on day 1.

conventional writing. The spelling lessons that occur in the first whole-group instructional period also contribute to conventional writing skills. The authors of the basal series also suggest sentences for daily practice in applying the conventions of language by correcting mistakes in grammar and spelling.

Reading and writing are reciprocal processes that build on the same foundation of language. Unlike reading, writing is an open-ended process. With teacher support, one open-ended writing assignment can fit a variety of levels of student needs and abilities. An open-ended task has multiple possibilities rather than one right answer. Children have some control over open-ended writing tasks, in which they determine the content, length, and complexity of their writing.

Teacher's Plan Book—Day 4
Small-Group and Independent Reading

Basal series authors suggest:	Our thoughts, additions, and revisions:
Reading with Teacher: *Focus Skill—Narrative Elements* Discuss elements of the plot. Read p. 174 in student text. Reread scene 3 of *The Pine Park Mystery*. Discuss how characters try to solve the mystery.	**Guided Reading Groups:** Share and discuss problem/solution charts that each student made. Reread scene 3 of *The Pine Park Mystery*. Discuss how characters try to solve the mystery. Focus on interpretation of characters' speech.

Independence Practice:
Practice pages as appropriate. (See plans for whole-group instruction periods, such as phonics, vocabulary, grammar)

Journal Prompt: Write a paragraph that describes a family holiday.

Independent Practice:
Practice pages for phonics and narrative elements (multilevel)

Literature log—Follow-up whole-group vocabulary activity. Match vocabulary words to words that have the same or nearly the same meaning (takes away = removes). Cut apart, match, glue in literature log.

caught	normal
thing	hook
made	removes
object	clasp
takes away	cornered
typical	caused

Independent Reading:
Books for All Learners

Independent Reading:
Book boxes (previous guided readings).
Reader's theater practice.

Cross-Curricular Centers:
Science—All About Birds
Writing—What Happened Next?
Social Studies—Community Jobs
Drama—Scene Reading
Computer Center—Set Design

Cross-Curricular Centers:
All centers are in use.
Add recycling poster (day 3) to the science center.

We already know quite a bit about helping children develop writing skills (see Figure 10.2). We can use shared/interactive writing and mini-lessons as demonstrations of the *writer's craft,* the term used by the authors of the Harcourt Trophies series to describe the processes for teaching the elements of writing. We have organized those same ideas into writer's workshop, enabling us to guide and support children's development as writers as they take pieces of their writing through the process of planning, writing, editing, and sharing.

The lower section of Figure 10.5 provides an overview of the activities suggested by the series authors for developing writing skills. These activities become the basis for making decisions for planning as shown in our Teacher's Plan Book in the next section.

Teacher's Plan Book—Day 5
Small-Group and Independent Reading

| Basal series authors suggest: | Our thoughts, additions, and revisions: |

Basal series authors suggest:

Reading with Teacher:
Teacher meets with advanced group, take parts, reread the play with feeling.

Other groups are rereading for fluency, working individually, with partners, or in small groups. Children may choose self-selected reading at this time.

Our thoughts, additions, and revisions:

Guided Reading Groups:
Each group performs one scene for the reader's theater in place of group meeting. Then begin rotation for remainder of activities:

Reader's Theater	Reader's Theater	Reader's Theater	Reader's Theater
Follow-up	Ind. Read	Centers	Centers
Ind. Read	Follow-up	Follow-up	Ind. Read
Centers	Centers	Ind. Read	Follow-up

Independent Practice:
Practice pages as appropriate. (See plans for whole-group instruction periods, such as phonics, vocabulary, grammar)

Journal Prompt: Child chooses topic for descriptive paragraph.

Independent Practice:
Practice pages for phonics (multilevel)

Literature log—Illustrate antonyms for vocabulary words from whole-group discussion (*confused/understand, typical/strange,* etc.)

Independent Reading:
Books for All Learners

Independent Reading:
Book boxes (previous guided readings).

Cross-Curricular Centers:
(See day 1.)

Cross-Curricular Centers:
All centers are in use.

Making Connections . . .

Let's turn our attention once again to our Teacher's Plan Book (pages 422–425), to the final stage of planning for these 5 days of instruction with *The Pine Park Mystery.* This time we examine the suggestions for supporting children as writers, to develop the skills and strategies they need to communicate their thinking in writing to others. As with the other phases of planning, review the suggestions by the authors of the basal series that appear on the left-hand side of each day's plans, then consider what our literacy framework might suggest. Make notations wherever you think that additions or revisions are needed. Share your thinking with a peer.

The pages of our Teacher's Plan Book demonstrate that current basal reading/language arts programs provide a myriad of materials and activities that teachers can use to plan a balanced and somewhat integrated approach to literacy for primary-grade students. Children are engaged in daily reading and writing that provides explicit and systematic instruction in the skills and strategies necessary to their development as readers and writers. As teachers, we are able to use our knowledge to personalize instruction for a particular group of children.

Teacher's Plan Book—Day 1
Whole Group: Language Arts

Basal series authors suggest:

Writers Craft:
Word Choice: Telling What Something Is Like
Recall description in *A History Mystery.* A descriptive paragraph has two parts. Read descriptive paragraph (transparency) to see

1. topic sentence and
2. describing words in detail sentences.

Children write description of a favorite place to go.

Grammar:
Introduce verbs that tell about now. Children display an action and others guess. Complete sentences to reinforce (transparency).

Daily Language Practice:
Children correct these sentences:

Lisa are tallest than me.

They is the funniest children in the class.

Our thoughts, additions, and revisions:

The focus this week is on descriptive writing, which requires facility with adjectives. However, the grammar lessons focus on verbs throughout this theme. We can support children's growth in language by concentrating more fully on the language of description. We will not focus on verbs this week.

We use writer's workshop to integrate instruction in writer's craft and grammar.

Writer's Workshop:
Whole Group
Mini-lesson—Read excerpts of quality descriptive writing from familiar texts (make transparency). Highlight descriptive phrases/sentences, discuss what makes them descriptive.

Writing Time
Getting started/finding focus—Describe a strong memory of person, place, or event that made you feel happy. Gather ideas (web, list, etc.) and begin to organize. Teacher circulates to provide support.

Whole Group
Share ideas children are focusing on and how they think they will develop their idea tomorrow when they begin to compose.

ASSESSMENT: MONITORING CHILDREN'S PROGRESS IN A BASAL SERIES

In previous chapters we have identified a variety of ways to assess children's progress, including:

🍎 observation of children's performance in a variety of settings,

🍎 evaluating samples of children's work, and

🍎 conducting teacher-student conferences.

A comprehensive basal reading/language arts series provides these types of assessments plus formal assessments, in the form of tests, to monitor children's progress.

The Harcourt Trophies program (2005) provides both formal and informal assessments throughout the year for each grade level. Formal assessments oc-

Teacher's Plan Book—Day 2
Whole Group: Language Arts

Basal series authors suggest:

Writers Craft:
Word Choice: Telling What Something Is Like
Read descriptive paragraph (transparency), notice different types of descriptions.

Children write two descriptive sentences telling what they see, hear, feel, or smell when they first wake up.

Grammar:
Model how to identify an action verb. Reread parts of p. 157 in student level. Listen for action verbs. Word-hunt for action verbs in story.

Practice page for action verbs (one level).

Daily Language Practice:
Children correct these sentences:
> *There is for children at the party.*
> *He put ate eggs in the cake.*

Our thoughts, additions, and revisions:

Writer's Workshop:
Whole Group
Demonstration of writing—Jointly develop a descriptive paragraph about the school (shared writing). Brainstorm descriptive words, develop several descriptive sentences, develop a topic sentence to introduce the main idea and a concluding sentence to close. Jointly identify the descriptive words, discuss role of adjectives in our language.

Writing Time
Composing—Children review their work from day 1, begin to develop descriptive sentences from their brainstormed ideas. Encourage them not to focus yet on a topic sentence.

Encourage them to seek response from a peer as they are drafting ideas. Help each other look for places of good description.

Teacher has "shoulder conferences" by circulating around the room to hear children's thinking.

Whole Group
Share a few descriptive sentences that students have developed. Encourage children to tell what they notice in the descriptions.

---

cur at a variety of points in the program. To support placement decisions, a Placement and Diagnostic Assessment is available. An End-of-Selection Test provides a formal assessment of vocabulary and comprehension, and the Oral Reading Fluency Assessment monitors progression of fluency skills.

In addition to formal assessments, there are numerous informal assessments, such as:

- 🍎 Performance assessments;
- 🍎 Diagnostic checklists for listening, speaking, reading, and writing;
- 🍎 Portfolio options, a working portfolio and a show portfolio; and
- 🍎 Reading notebooks to monitor children's independent reading.

Teachers know which skills are the focus skills in each theme. The skills that will be assessed at the end of a theme are indicated with an **T** on the "Theme at a Glance" and the Suggested Lesson Planner for each literature selection. If we are teaching a basal series, we should include assessment as a part of our planning.

Teacher's Plan Book—Day 3
Whole Group: Language Arts

Basal series authors suggest:

Writers Craft:
Word Choice: Telling What Something Is Like
Remind children about a special kind of description, similes. Discuss similes and how similes compare two things that seem unlike. Read descriptive paragraph (transparency). Have children recall description in selection, identify similes.

Apply—Have children look though their writing portfolio and choose a piece that has description. Revise sections to make more vivid, add similes.

Grammar:
Review verbs that tell about now. Children suggest verbs, teacher writes. Have children pantomime verbs. Listen to a rhyme. *Spoiled Roy* (big books). Read as shared reading. Reread and point to verbs that tell about now (*is, enjoys, puts, goes, pounds, annoys*).

Practice page—action verbs (one level).

Daily Language Practice:
Children correct these sentences:
> *The two kites fly hi.*
> *This won is softest than the other.*

Our thoughts, additions, and revisions:

Writer's Workshop:
Whole Group
Mini-lesson—Developing a topic sentence that is focused and grabs interest. Read topic sentences from familiar literature. Discuss what makes a good topic sentence.

Writing Time
Children continue to develop their descriptive sentences, then topic and concluding sentences.

Encourage children to respond to peers, helping them think about their descriptions, whether their topic sentence grabs interest and their concluding sentence sums up their main idea.

Whole Group
Children share topic sentence they have written, group predicts what the paragraph will be about.

Before we begin teaching a unit we should be well aware of which skills/strategies will be assessed and the form of that assessment.

RESPECTING DIVERSITY IN BASAL INSTRUCTION

Like most facets of our society, basal reading/language arts series are showing greater sensitivity to the diverse needs and interests of learners in a classroom. For example, in the lesson we reviewed, attention to the following was suggested:

- Diversity of characters in the literature selection,
- Language in the text for English language learners,
- Varying levels of materials for instruction, and
- Different types of groupings to meet student needs.

Current basal reading/language arts programs provide opportunities to address issues of diversity. We, the teachers, are the decision makers and must act in the best interest of our children.

Teacher's Plan Book—Day 4
Whole Group: Language Arts

Basal series authors suggest:

Writers Craft:
Word Choice: Telling What Something Is Like
Prewrite and Draft—Brainstorm possible topics for a descriptive paragraph.

Prewrite ideas, beginning with a topic sentence and a list of ideas.

Draft paragraph using colorful and precise words and similes. Conclude with a sentence that summarizes main idea.

Grammar:
Make a Verb Book. Cut pictures out of magazines and newspapers. Glue into book. Write a sentence that tells about the action. Share books.

Practice page—action verbs (one level).

Daily Language Practice:
Children correct these sentences:
  I like my to read shirts.
  This book is sillier.

Our thoughts, additions, and revisions:

Writer's Workshop:
Whole Group
Mini-lesson—Read aloud *Quick as a Cricket* (Wood, 1998). Listen for comparisons (similes) and how they create images, which is another form of description. Encourage children to consider how they might use a simile to create a more vivid image in their descriptive paragraph.

Writing Time
Children continue to develop and organize their descriptions.

Encourage conferences for response and editing for meaning and correctness.

Work toward final copy to share on day 5.

Whole Group
No sharing today in order to provide more writing time.

Teacher's Plan Book—Day 5
Whole Group: Language Arts

Basal series authors suggest:

Writers Craft:
Word Choice: Telling What Something Is Like
Revise/Peer Conference—Partners use checklist to revise: Does paragraph have a topic sentence, clearly stated ideas, exact words, precise details, a simile, concluding sentence?

Grammar:
Circle the action verb in sentences.
Write sentences with action verbs using *I, you, we, outside, bikes, quickly.*

Practice page—action verbs (one level).

Daily Language Practice:
Children correct these sentences:
  We played fiv greater games.
  She paint me a prettiest card.

Our thoughts, additions, and revisions:

Writer's Workshop:
Whole Group
Overview plans to complete compositions and sharing.

Writing Time
Complete final copy of compositions, edited and legible.

Whole Group
Author's chair for students who volunteer. All writing is displayed on the Writing Wall with the caption "We Tell What Something Is Like."

Making Connections . . .

As you reflect on the content of this chapter, what ideas do you have about planning and teaching lessons that are suggested by the authors of a basal reading/language arts series? Do you see how the elements of the literacy framework developed in this text can help you plan a balanced and integrated program of literacy skills and strategies for young children? This would be an important time for you to try developing some sample Teacher's Plan Book charts of your own. Work with a partner to become familiar with the format of a current basal series, then create several days of Teacher's Plan Book pages of your own. You will feel more confident if you are able to apply your own knowledge. Record your thinking in a reflective journal. Share your thinking with your peers.

Aa Bb Cc Dd Ee Ff Gg Hh Ii Jj Kk Ll Mm

C H A P T E R

11

Integrating Elements in a Literacy Framework: Teaching about Amphibians in Second Grade

Linking the components in our literacy framework . . .

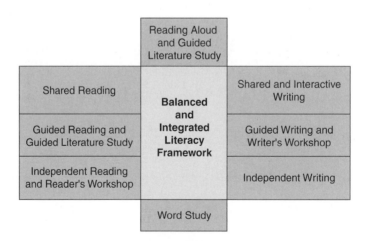

In this unit study, we learn about . . .

- 🍎 Organizing instruction around the components of a balanced literacy program
- 🍎 Considering how to link children's learning experiences to enhance literacy development

Focus Literature:

- A variety of texts about amphibians, both fiction and information
- *Frog and Toad Are Friends* by Arnold Lobel
- Versions of the story, *The Frog Prince*

Looking into Classrooms . . .

Jeana, Marcie, Nicki, and Mary, all second grade teachers who team-teach together, sit around a table in the school library with stacks of books. They are in the process of planning their next unit of study about amphibians that will begin in a few weeks. On a large chart they have a simple four-week calendar divided into blocks of time, the way they "chunk" the school day. Today they are focusing on selecting books for the times each day when they read aloud to the children, morning and afternoon. They want to be sure the children will find the texts engaging, so they carefully consider the quality of photographs and illustrations, along with the style of writing. Many of their children are English language learners so it is important to consider texts in which the language is comprehensible. They read portions of texts aloud to each other and discuss their impressions. Then they sort books into groups by the focus of the text. They decide that Weeks 1 and 2 of the unit will introduce the characteristics of amphibians. They select 20 books, two per day, information texts which will expose the children to essential vocabulary needed to understand amphibian characteristics and life cycles, and fictional texts to continue to develop children's sense of story. Read aloud for Weeks 3 and 4 will focus on whole-class literature study with a class set of Frog and Toad Are Friends *for children to read along with the teacher and versions of* The Frog Prince *for comparative study. Planning for read aloud is one step in the process that these teachers use to engage children in meaningful literacy activities. They are as energized as the children and look forward to the in-depth focus on amphibians as a vehicle for developing literacy skills and strategies.*

PUTTING THEORY INTO PRACTICE . . .

We began this text by considering the components of balanced literacy, how to create meaningful learning environments for young children, and the importance of our role as teachers. In each chapter that followed, we considered the purpose of particular literacy component and the possibilities for each component as it is implemented in the classroom. In this chapter, we take the opportunity to visit two second-grade team-teaching classrooms in which the teachers are working to develop and implement a more balanced and integrated approach to literacy learning.

 SETTING THE STAGE

Before we visit the classrooms, consider the following ideas. We know that the most meaningful learning experiences are integrated in natural ways, like the learning experiences we have outside of school. We also know that effective literacy learning is the central focus of instruction in the primary grades. Learning to integrate literacy components to enhance children's learning, however, is not an easy task and requires a great deal of study and reflection on the effectiveness of the instructional decisions we make in the classroom. Effective teachers strive to link learning experiences for children because they know that focusing instruction in this way provides more in-depth learning. Integrating instruction demonstrates to children that literacy is a tool for learning about the world, as well as themselves. In an integrated curriculum, oral and written language are tools for exploration and inquiry. Integrated learning experiences teach children that listening, speaking, reading, and writing are vehicles for exploring one's own thinking and inquiring into the thinking of others.

To make effective instructional decisions, teachers must realize that learning how to link literacy components for integration hinges on our ability to select the component(s) that provide the most appropriate levels of assistance to support and extend children's learning, moving them toward independence. Throughout this text we have considered components that provide varying levels of support for children's learning (see Figure 11.1).

To link instructional components, teachers begin by selecting those that provide high teacher support. Then, as children acquire background, skills, and strategy, teachers select components that enable children to be more independent, thus gaining control over their own learning.

 MEET THE TEACHERS

To observe the linking of components in our literacy framework, we visit two team-teaching second-grade classrooms in which the teachers deliberately select components to provide the appropriate support to children as they learn about the world of amphibians. Each team of teachers (Jeana and Marcie, Nicki and Mary) has a group of 30 to 32 children. Many of the children are English language learners. The school in which they teach has a high percentage of children

	Reading	Writing	Word Study
High Teacher Support	Read-Aloud	Shared Writing	Whole-Class Word Building
	Whole-Class Literature Study	Interactive Writing	Read-Aloud/ Literature Study
	Shared Reading		Shared Reading
			Shared/Interactive Writing
Moderate Teacher Support	Guided Reading	Guided Writing in Writer's Workshop	Small-Group Word Study
	Small-Group Literature Study		Guided Reading/ Literature Study
	Reader's Workshop		Reader's Workshop
			Guided Writing
Limited Teacher Support	Independent Reading	Independent Writing	Independent Reading
			Independent Writing

FIGURE 11.1
Level of teacher support provided by literacy components.

who receive free or reduced-cost breakfast and lunch. A number of years ago the faculty began investigating balanced literacy as a framework for a schoolwide literacy program. Jeana, Marcie, Nicki, and Mary have been working to implement a balanced literacy framework in ways that work best for their children. They believe that linking instructional experiences through the components maximizes language development and conceptual learning for all of their children.

GETTING STARTED WITH PLANNING

The units of study that these teachers create are driven by two factors:

- the school district's academic standards, and
- the importance of leading children's development in literacy.

Academic Standards in Language Arts

Language arts standards for second-grade children in this school district focus on helping children acquire language skills that encourage and support fluent reading and writing. Knowing that many children in their classrooms speak Spanish at home, these teachers focus intensely on the development of English through a unit of study such as amphibians. Learning about the world becomes an anchor for learning language. These experiences also provide motivation for extending skills and strategies in reading and writing. The teachers decide that this unit will focus on developing the necessary skills and strategies required to:

- 🍎 respond to ideas in fiction and poetry,
- 🍎 improve ability to decode unfamiliar words,
- 🍎 gather accurate information from texts,
- 🍎 compare/contrast ideas found in texts,
- 🍎 read texts fluently and with expression,
- 🍎 express ideas clearly and accurately through speaking and writing, and
- 🍎 organize written ideas around a topic.

Academic Standards in Science

Science standards for second-grade children in this school district focus on concepts about ecosystems and the diversity of living things. Experience has taught Jeana, Marcie, Nicki, and Mary that their children are fascinated with animals and very motivated to learn about the environments in which various animals live. They decide on a unit that will focus on:

- 🍎 amphibians—primarily frogs, toads, and salamanders—as an example of diversity within a classification of animals, and
- 🍎 how all living things move through life cycles.

Several weeks before a unit of study begins, the teachers brainstorm ideas together, share the materials they already have, and search for additional songs, poems, chants, and books to support the study. Their experience with second-grade children has taught them that a unit of approximately 3 to 4 weeks provides an appropriate amount of time to develop the language and concepts of a topic. Though the teachers want variety in their teaching materials, they also want to limit the number of different materials they use in order to provide ample time for revisiting some materials. They have learned that repeated exposure in meaningful contexts is a key to helping their children acquire language to support reading and writing skills/strategies. They use the Internet to gather information from sites such as *http://www.sandiegozoo.org/animalbytes/a-amphibians.html*.

The daily routine these teachers typically follow is shown in Figure 11.2. In these team-teaching classrooms instruction in science and social studies always occurs through the literacy components. Working in a school in which children are considered to be at risk for academic success causes these teachers to make each learning experience a literacy experience.

MAKING INSTRUCTIONAL DECISIONS

As the teachers plan together, they consider how to best use each component of the literacy framework to build children's background knowledge and teach literacy skills and strategies. Let's consider some of the ideas these teachers have for using each component in the amphibian unit.

Daily Routine

Morning:
 Shared Reading (poem of the week)

 Mediated Read-Aloud
 or
 Guided Literature Study

 Shared/Interactive Writing
 (to respond to or process the read-aloud)

 Guided Writing

 Word Study
 (building and sorting words, applying patterns)

Afternoon
 Guided Reading Block
  Flexible Guided Reading Groups
  Independent Reading/Book Boxes
  Activity Centers
  (includes independent writing)

 Math

 Mediated Read-Aloud (second of the day)

FIGURE 11.2
Daily routine in second grade.

Shared Reading—Poem of the Week (15–20 Minutes)

Each week, the children are introduced to a new poem that emphasizes oral language and vocabulary. The children practice all week and individually recite the poem on Friday. Frequently the poem is written to the tune of a familiar song. When this occurs, the teachers sing/read the words of the poem to emphasize the rhythm for the first few readings.

Monday

The children listen to the teachers read the poem aloud, pointing to the words. The teachers then reread the poem and encourage children to join in. Teachers and children discuss the meaning of the poem and any vocabulary the children are not sure about. When needed, teachers show visuals to support the poem and link back to children's experiences. The class creates movements and gestures to fit the poem, connecting language to action. Children receive a personal copy for practicing the poem at home.

Tuesday through Friday

The teachers illustrate favorite or important parts of the poem on a class chart and provide individual copies. The poem is reread in whole group, in guided reading, with a partner during independent reading, and during center time.

Children may also practice handwriting by writing the poem during the guided reading block. Children individually recite the poem on Friday.

Teaching Points

The teachers draw teaching points from what each text offers that might be new knowledge for the children or as an opportunity to reinforce skills/strategies. They also consider which teaching points are most emphasized by the language arts standards. Possible teaching points from the poem of the week may be emphasized during shared reading as well as shared and interactive writing.

Mediated Read-Aloud (20 Minutes, Twice Each Day)

To extend children's background knowledge and their engagement with the topic, the teachers read aloud both fiction and informational texts. Children are encouraged to be interactive during the read-aloud, as in the sample mediated read-aloud presented in Chapter 4. The discussion that grows out of the mediated read-aloud becomes the base for whole-class shared writings. Reading both fiction and informational text provides an additional opportunity to compare the depiction of reality and fantasy in literature, another language arts standard for second grade. As you can see in Figure 11.2, these teachers read books aloud twice a day, in the morning and afternoon.

Guided Literature Study (20 Minutes)

Guided literature study with the whole class is a variation of mediated read-aloud (see Chapter 4). During the third week of this unit the class studies *Frog and Toad Are Friends* by Arnold Lobel. The teachers have a class set of books so that all children can follow along. In contrast to guided reading of texts for fluency in small groups, the focus of this literature study is children's responses to the literature, especially to the characters and their actions. There is also discussion of reality versus fantasy, discussing what frogs and toads are like in the real world versus the characters portrayed in the book. Near the end of the unit, the children will study several versions of *The Frog Prince* and make comparisons between versions.

Shared/Interactive Writing (15–20 Minutes)

Following the read-aloud and/or guided literature study, the teachers engage the children in a variety of compositions that utilize children's growing knowledge base, and they model various composition styles identified in the second-grade language arts standards (compare/contrast, sequence, description, explanation). The teachers decide whether the composing process will be shared or interactive or both depending upon the nature of the text.

In general, it takes these second-grade children 20 to 30 minutes to interactively compose and write one to two sentences, depending on sentence length/complexity and the time of the school year. Texts are typically a cumulative composition, written over several days. Sequential compositions, such as retelling the life cycle of a frog, make excellent interactive writings. Interactive compositions provide opportunities for children to learn how to self-monitor writing, as well as ways to help themselves when they are "stuck" while writing. For example, the teachers encourage children to make analogies to familiar words to spell new words, such as asking, "If I know *long*, how can I figure out *song?*"

The teachers choose shared writing to label drawings of amphibians and engage children in discussion to develop vocabulary (a narrative drawing), model how to compare two things using a Venn diagram, create charts to compare attributes of amphibians, and compose paragraphs with a topic sentence and supporting details that explain or describe.

Guided Writing (30–40 Minutes)

Following read-aloud/guided literature study and shared/interactive writing, children are invited to work on their own compositions, with the teachers available to assist. While the children are gathered on the carpet at the end of shared writing, they are encouraged to verbalize ideas for their compositions that day, to say aloud the sentences as they might write them. The teachers find that having ideas in mind for the composition increases children's writing fluency. The children frequently have the opportunity to carry their writing over several days, to develop their ideas and practice monitoring their own writing so that it communicates what the child has in mind. If children encounter some difficulty in composing, whether it is ideas/content, organization, or the use of conventions, they are encouraged to search for ways to help themselves. They might find what they need on the word wall, in a past composition, somewhere else in the room, from a friend, and so forth. These teachers encourage children to believe they can solve their own writing problems, but the teachers always keep a watchful eye on how well the children are making decisions.

Word Study (15–20 Minutes)

Word building and sorting involves the whole class and occurs several times each week to support exploration of letter-sound patterns with their teachers' support. Remember, in word building, the letters of a word are used to make a number of other words that vary in length and complexity. To catch children's interest, the teachers often choose a word related to the unit. Selecting a variety of words during a unit of study enables the children to maintain familiar letter-sound patterns and, over time, practice new patterns in a supportive environment. The teachers consider the possible patterns that selecting a particular word provides. In addition to word building and sorting, the teachers lead the children to think about and examine words as part of daily literacy activities.

Guided Reading Block (60–90 Minutes)

Each afternoon the teachers provide time for children to meet in guided reading groups, practice reading with familiar texts from their book boxes, write independently, and work in one or more activity centers. Each guided reading group

FIGURE 11.3
Guided reading block.

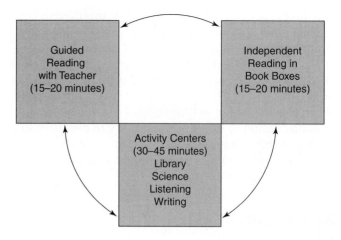

usually lasts about 20 minutes. In a team-teaching classroom with approximately 30 children, there are typically five to six guided reading groups. In these second-grade classrooms, children who read at first-grade level meet for guided reading every day. Children who read at grade level or above meet every other day. After a text is introduced and read in the group, it is moved to the independent book boxes. When children are not in a guided reading group, they are engaged in independent reading and activity centers that relate to the unit of study (see Figure 11.3).

While one team-teacher is with a guided reading group, the other team-teacher listens in on several children's independent reading. The activity centers are set up to be independent activities in which children explore or practice ideas/concepts from the unit or other current interests.

The teachers try to find multiple copies of texts that complement the unit and that are at the children's instructional level. Sometimes it is difficult, however, to find enough instructional-level texts for guided reading throughout a unit. These teachers know that it is more important for children to be in appropriate-level materials than to have all guided reading texts relate to the unit. When appropriate, personal copies of shared/interactive writings, as well as other instructional-level texts that are not related to the unit, are used for guided reading.

The teachers use resources such as *Matching Books to Readers* (Fountas & Pinnell, 1999) and *Guided Reading* (Fountas & Pinnell, 1996), published by Heinemann Books, to identify appropriate texts. Their school has purchased many of these texts in sets specifically for guided reading. The materials available for guided reading that relate to the unit are shown in Figure 11.4.

Independent Reading (15–20 Minutes)

Each day the children spend time rereading texts from their designated book boxes, the shared reading poem of the week, or other texts at their instructional level. Each text in their book boxes has been read during guided reading. Children select the texts they prefer to reread. The children practice fluent reading

Middle First Grade:
Frog's Lunch (Lillgard & Zimmerman, Scholastic)
Frogs on a Log (Teacher's Choice Series, Dominie)
Frogs (Pebble Books, Grolier)
Freddie the Frog (First Start, Troll)
The Frog and the Fly (Cat on the Mat Books, Oxford University Press)
Jog, Frog, Jog (Barbara Gregorich, School Zone)
Little Frog's Monster Story (Ready Readers, Modern Curriculum)
Toad on the Road (Susan Schade)

Late First Grade:
Frogs (Storyteller-First Snow, Shortland Publications)
Freddy Frog's Note (Ready Readers, Modern Curriculum)
How Do Frogs Grow? (Discovery Links, Newbridge)
Tale of a Tadpole (Karen Wallace, Dorling Kindersly)

Early Second Grade:
How Do Frogs Grow? (Discovery Links, Newbridge)
Days with Frog and Toad (Arnold Lobel, HarperTrophy)
Froggy Learns to Swim (Jonathan London, Scholastic)
The Show-and-Tell Frog (Bank Street Readers)

Middle Second Grade:
Commander Toad Series (Jane Yolen, Putnam & Grosset)
Frog and Toad Together (Arnold Lobel, HarperCollins)
Frog or Toad? (Ready Readers, Modern Curriculum Press)

Late Second Grade/Early Third Grade:
Encyclopedia Brown and the Case of the Slippery Salamander (Donald Sobol, Yearling)
The Magic School Bus: A Book About Warm- and Cold-Blooded Animals (Tracey West, Sagebrush)
The Frog Alphabet Book (Jerry Pallotta, Charlesbridge Publishing)

FIGURE 11.4
Guided reading texts for the amphibian unit.

with these familiar texts. Frequently children sit with another child from the guided reading group to partner-read, providing motivation and assistance for each other.

While one team-teacher is with a guided reading group, the other is listening to a few focus children read from their book boxes. These teachers know that focusing on children during independent reading is an excellent way to gauge how well children are independently using what they have been learning through other literacy components. This is an excellent time to make an unscripted reading record (see Assessment section in Chapter 6) to document the strategies children use independently. These teachers believe that children will become better readers by practicing fluent, skilled reading in familiar texts every day.

Independent Writing (Time Varies)

The teachers include independent writing in the afternoon activity centers. Children are invited to respond to unit experiences, such as writing facts about amphibians or continuing a piece they started in their journal. Children can also make their own amphibian books, record observations of the amphibians in the science center (frog, salamander, and newt), label illustrations of amphibians with appropriate vocabulary as modeled by a teacher, or create their own Venn diagram comparing two amphibians as modeled by a teacher. Another activity is "write the room," during which children look for ideas in the room to write about, such as on the word wall, shared writing charts, or the poem of the week.

 PLANNING KEY FEATURES OF THE UNIT

As the teachers begin to brainstorm the unit they chart the key features they want to take place over the course of the 4 weeks (see Figure 11.5). Placing the key features on a chart helps the teachers check the balance and flow of activities within the unit. They don't plot guided reading on the chart because appropriate books related to the unit are not always available. The unit will begin with building background about amphibians, especially the language needed to talk about amphibians. The initial focus on informational texts gives way in week 3 to guided literature study of a short chapter book from the *Frog and Toad* series by Arnold Lobel, then a variety of versions of the fairy tale *The Frog Prince* in week 4.

 PUTTING THE PIECES TOGETHER

Let's examine how these teachers develop their lesson plans for each week. With four teachers sharing ideas, they find that they begin to adjust activities throughout the unit as they discuss their observations of children's engagement and response. Sometimes they find that what they thought was a good idea does not work well with this particular group of children at this time. Over time they have learned that integrating the components well requires them to remain flexible and take their direction from the children's responses.

Making Connections . . .

Now take time to examine the second-grade Teacher's Plan Book (on pages 440 and 441) for the first week of the amphibian unit. The Teacher's Plan Book shows how they use their daily routine to develop reading and writing skills using the language needed for discussion of amphibians. Following the pages of the Teacher's Plan Book you will find Lesson Plans for each instructional component that provide more detail

FIGURE 11.5
Planning key features of the unit.

Key Features	Week 1	Week 2	Week 3	Week 4
Reading **Poem of the Week**	"Frogs and Toads"	"Salamanders, Salamanders"	"Tadpoles, Tadpoles"	"Five Little Bumpy Toads"
Mediated Read-Aloud—Informational Text	Build background for frogs, toads	Build background for salamanders Life cycle of amphibians	Variety of texts about amphibians	Variety of texts about amphibians
Mediated Read-Aloud—Fiction	Variety of texts about amphibians	Variety of texts about amphibians		
Guided Literature Study			*Frog and Toad Are Friends*	Versions of *The Frog Prince*
Writing **Shared Writing**	Narrated drawings—frog, toad Venn diagrams—frog, toad	Narrated drawing—salamander		Story map—problem/solution
Interactive Writing	T-chart—facts about frogs, toads	Chart comparing characteristics of frogs, toads, salamanders	T-chart—character of Frog and Toad	
Guided Writing	Amphibian facts	Word splash Compare/contrast amphibian characteristics	Group reports • characteristics • habitat • diet • life cycle	*The Frog Prince* • retellings • response • create own version
Word Study **Whole-Class Word Building & Word Sorting**	*jumping*—short *i*, short *u*	*salamander*—short *a*, long *e*, *r*-controlled	*tadpoles*—short/long *a*, short *e*, short/long *o*, plurals	*prince*—short/long *i*, soft *c*, blends

about how they use that component during the week. After you review each week of plans, take time to make connections to what occurred the week before. Be sure that you are noticing how the teachers connect student learning within each week, as well as from week to week. Also take time to make notations wherever you think of other ideas that might also fit with the goals of the unit. Share your thinking with a peer.

Teacher's Plan Book—Week 1

Monday

Shared Reading
Introduce "Frogs and Toads." *Teaching Point: -og, -oad*

Shared Writing
What do we think we know about frogs and toads? Begin a T-chart for frogs and toads.

Morning Mediated Read-Aloud (Informational Text)
Read *Very First Things to Know About Frogs. Teaching Point:* Listening for information, special words.

Interactive Writing (Continued from Shared Writing)
Add to/revise T-chart for details about frogs from reading.

Word Study
Build words with letters in *jumping.*

Guided Reading Block (See Group Rotation Schedule)
Group 1 (mid-1st): First reading of *Frog's Lunch. Teaching Point:* Decode *-og* words

Group 2 (late 1st): First reading of *Freddy Frog's Note. Teaching Point:* Possessive (Freddy Frog's).

Group 3 (early 2nd): First reading of *Froggy Learns to Swim. Teaching Point:* Base + suffix (*frog + g + y*).

Group 5 (mid 2nd): Begin reading and discussion of *Commander Toad in Space* (chapter book). *Teaching Point:* Decoding multisyllable words (*com/mand/er*).

Independent Reading
Book Boxes

Activity Centers
  Library Corner
  Science Center
  Listening Station
  Writing Center
  Computer Center

Afternoon Mediated Read-Aloud (Fiction)
It's Mine

Tuesday

Shared Reading
Reread "Frogs and Toads." *Teaching Point:* Describing words (*strong, webbed, bulging, sticky*).

Morning Mediated Read-Aloud (Informational Text)
Review T-chart. Read *Jumpy, Green, & Croaky. What Am I? Teaching Point:* Listening for information, special words.

Interactive Writing
Add to/revise details on T-chart for frogs. Reinforce details by completing a narrated drawing of a frog.

Guided Writing:
Journal Prompt—I think frogs are . . .

Word Study
Rebuild words with letters in *jumping.*

Guided Reading Block
Group 1 (mid 1st): Reread *Frog's Lunch. Teaching Point:* Fluency.

Group 2 (late 1st): Complete first reading of *Freddy Frog's Note. Teaching Point:* decode long *o (o_e).*

Group 4 (early 2nd): First reading of *Froggy Learns to Swim. Teaching Point:* Base + suffix (*frog + g + y*).

Group 6 (late 2nd/early 3rd): Begin reading *Encyclopedia Brown and the Case of the Slippery Salamander,* Ch. 1 & 2. *Teaching Points:* Using context to confirm decoding and word meaning; making inferences to solve a mystery.

Independent Reading
Book Boxes
Partner-Read Poem of the Week—"Frogs and Toads"

Activity Centers
Continue from Monday

Afternoon Mediated Read-Aloud (Fiction)
Jump, Frog, Jump

Teacher's Plan Book—Week 1

Wednesday	**Thursday**	**Friday**

Shared Reading
Reread "Frogs and Toads." *Teaching Point:* Base + inflectional suffix words.

Shared Reading
Reread "Frogs and Toads." *Teaching Point:* Plurals.

Shared Reading
Children individually perform "Frogs and Toads."

Morning Mediated Read-Aloud (Informational Text)
Read *Toad Overload. Teaching Point:* Listening for information, special words.

Mediated Read-Aloud (Informational Text)
Read *Hiding Toads. Teaching Point:* Listening for information, special words.

Mediated Read-Aloud (Informational Text)
Frog or Toad? Teaching Point: Listening for information, special words.

Interactive Writing
Review T-chart. Add to/revise for toads based on reading.

Shared Writing
Review T-chart. Use details to develop chart to compare/contrast frog and toad characteristics, habitat, and diet.

Interactive Writing
Review chart. Summarize how frogs and toads are different.

Guided Writing
Learning Log—What are you learning about frogs and toads? Time to share.

Guided Writing
Learning Log: What are you learning about frogs and toads? Provide time to share.

Guided Writing
Learning Log: What are you learning about frogs and toads? Time provided for sharing.

Word Study
Open sort, individual and pocket chart.

Word Study
Closed sort, individual and pocket chart.

Word Study
Assessment.

Guided Reading Block
Group 1 (mid 1st): First reading of *Frogs. Teaching Point:* Locating details.

Group 2 (late 1st): Rereading and discussion of *Freddie Frog's Note. Teaching Point:* Fluency.

Group 3 (early 2nd): Rereading and discussion of *Froggy Learns to Swim. Teaching Point:* Fluency.

Group 5 (mid 2nd): Continue reading and discussion of *Commander Toad. Teaching Point:* Understanding character.

Guided Reading Block
Group 1 (mid 1st): Reread *Frogs. Teaching Point:* Fluency.

Group 2 (late 1st): Begin first reading of *Frogs. Teaching Point:* Locating details.

Group 4 (early 2nd): Rereading and discussion of *Froggy Learns to Swim. Teaching Point:* Fluency.

Group 6 (late 2nd/early 3rd): Continue reading *Encyclopedia Brown and the Case of the Slippery Salamander*, Ch. 3 & 4. *Teaching Points:* Using context to confirm decoding and word meaning, making inferences to solve a mystery.

Guided Reading Block
Group 1 (mid 1st): First reading of *Frogs on a Log. Teaching Point:* Decoding -og words.

Group 2 (late 1st): Complete first reading of *Frogs. Teaching Point:* Locating details.

Group 3 (early 2nd): Begin reading *The Show-and-Tell Frog. Teaching Point:* Making Inferences.

Group 5 (mid 2nd): Continue reading and discussion of *Commander Toad in Space. Teaching Point:* Understanding character.

Independent Reading
Book Boxes
Partner-Read Poem of the Week—"Frogs and Toads"

Independent Reading
Book Boxes
Partner-Read Poem of the Week—"Frogs and Toads"

Independent Reading
Book Boxes

Activity Centers
(See Monday)

Activity Centers
(See Monday)

Activity Centers
(See Monday)

Afternoon Mediated Read-Aloud (Fiction)
If You Hopped Like a Frog

Afternoon Mediated Read-Aloud (Fiction)
Tuesday

Afternoon Mediated Read-Aloud (Fiction)
Frog in the Kitchen Sink

LESSON PLANS FOR WEEK I—INTRODUCTION TO AMPHIBIANS

Poem of the Week—"Frogs and Toads"

Text

- 🍎 Poem composed by the teachers, in the pattern of "The Farmer in the Dell" (see Figure 11.6).
- 🍎 Read and reread over the week with individual performances on Friday.

Teaching Points

- 🍎 Decode words using a familiar rime, such as *-og* (build the words *frog, bog, log* from poem, make analogy/apply to new word, *hog*).
- 🍎 Decode words with *-oad* (build the word *toad,* make analogy/apply to new word, *road*).
- 🍎 Identify and decode describing words (*strong, webbed, bulging, sticky*); discuss how these words make the poem more interesting and help the reader to make mental pictures.
- 🍎 Identify words that are base words + inflectional suffix (*jumping, looking, flicking, bulging* [*e* drop], *swimming* [consonant double]);

FIGURE 11.6
Poem of the week—"Frogs
and Toads."

Week 1—Poem of the Week

Frogs and Toads

Frogs and toads here,
Frogs and toads there,
Frogs and toads, frogs and toads,
everywhere.

Strong legs jumping
Webbed feet swimming
Bulging eyes looking
And sticky tongues flicking

Frogs near a bog
Toads under ground
Frogs on a lily pad
Toads on land

Frogs and toads here,
Frogs and toads there,
Frogs and toads, frogs and toads,
everywhere.

Frogs and toads!
Frogs and toads!
(to the tune of "Farmer in the Dell")

discuss how to decode the word by finding the base word inside, then adding the suffix.

- Identify words that are plurals (*frogs, toads, eyes, legs, tongues, feet* [irregular]).

Morning Mediated Read-Aloud (Informational Text)

Texts

Very First Things to Know About Frogs (Patricia Grossman)
Jumpy, Green, and Croaky. What am I? (Moira Butterfield & Wayne Ford)
Toad Overload (Patricia Seibert)
Hiding Toads (Suzanne Paul Dell'Oro)
Frog or Toad? (Ready Reader, Modern Curriculum Press)

Teaching Points

- Build background and extend personal knowledge of frogs and toads through read-aloud. Discussion before, during, and after the reading of a text provides time to build background.
- Use illustrations and language in context to relate to children's prior knowledge.
- Identify and discuss specialized vocabulary. Discuss decoding of words as needed.
- Identify details about frogs and toads, then confirm in text.

Interactive Writing—T-Chart of Facts

- Begin the week by tapping into children's prior knowledge of frogs and toads.
- After each reading of a text, process essential information in text by comparing/contrasting prior knowledge to a particular text.
- Add to and/or revise as needed so the chart reflects accurate information (see Figure 11.7).

Shared Writing—Narrated Drawing

- On a large chart, lightly sketch the outline of a frog and place penciled notes (or sticky notes) around the edge as reminders of attributes to be labeled on the drawing (see Figure 11.8).
- Following the mediated read-aloud, engage the children in discussion about frogs.
- As the discussion develops, use a marking pen to "draw" the frog, label its parts, and make notes about its behavior. To the children this appears to be a creation of the moment, not tracing by the teacher.
- The drawing serves as a review of facts about frogs and supports children's development of technical vocabulary.
- A blank copy of the frog outline is placed in the activity centers during week 2 for children to complete as a review.

FIGURE 11.7
T-chart to collect facts
about frogs and toads.

Frogs	Toads
two bulging eyes to see well	toads are actually frogs
long hind legs	stubby bodies
jump or leap	short hind legs
short front legs to balance	walk or short hops
webbed feet to swim	warty and dry skin
is an amphibian	like dryer climates
has a backbone	has a backbone
smooth or slimy skin	poison glands behind the eyes
lay eggs in clusters	lay eggs in long chains
tadpoles have gills	is an amphibian
many different sizes	spade feet, toes spread apart to walk
many different colors	usually nocturnal
some live in cold climate and hibernate	
most like warmer climate	
catch food with sticky tongue	
teeth in top jaw	
some are nocturnal	

FIGURE 11.8

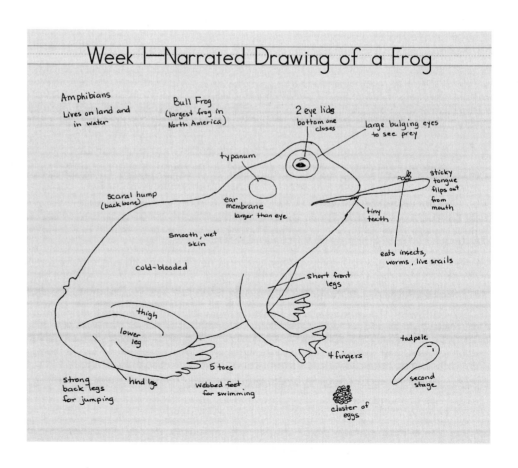

Week I—Narrated Drawing of a Frog

444

Shared Writing—Compare/Contrast Chart

🍎 Near the end of the first week, engage the children in comparing and contrasting what they know about frogs and toads.

🍎 Use information gathered on the T-chart as the basis for the compare/contrast.

🍎 Divide a chart into categories to show what is similar and what is different between frogs and toads. The categories are characteristics, diet, and habitat (see Figure 11.9). Salamanders, newts, and life cycles will be added in week 2.

🍎 The teacher records the composition to maximize time.

🍎 A blank copy of the chart is placed in the activity centers during week 2. Teachers prepare printed words and phrases about amphibians for children to cut out, sort, and glue on their personal chart.

Interactive Writing—Summarize Differences

🍎 At the end of the week help children summarize the contrasting they have been doing for several days (see Figure 11.10).

FIGURE 11.9
Week 1—comparing/contrasting frogs and toads.

	Frogs	Toads	Both
Characteristics	Long hind legs for jumping Slimy, smooth skin Webbed feet for swimming or sticky pads for climbing trees	Short hind legs for walking Dry, warty skin Feet have toes or claws Are actually frogs	Are amphibians Have a backbone No neck, cannot turn head Bulging eyes to see well Nocturnal Males have loud voices
Habitat	Live on land and in water Protect with poison skin and color camouflage	Live on land Protect with poison glands and color camouflage	Do not live in polar regions or very dry deserts Like a warm, wet climate In cold climate they burrow underground and hibernate in the winter
Diet			Tadpoles eat plants Adults are carnivorous Adults eat insects, spiders, worms, and slugs

FIGURE 11.10

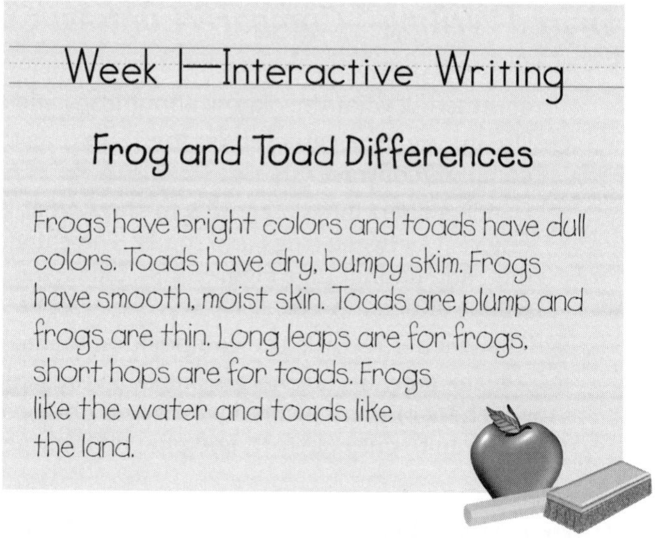

> Week I—Interactive Writing
>
> ## Frog and Toad Differences
>
> Frogs have bright colors and toads have dull colors. Toads have dry, bumpy skim. Frogs have smooth, moist skin. Toads are plump and frogs are thin. Long leaps are for frogs, short hops are for toads. Frogs like the water and toads like the land.

- 🍎 Verbalize each statement the class wants to write, then individual children are selected to come to the chart to write whole words, parts of words, or phrases.
- 🍎 One team-teacher supports the child who is writing on the chart, the other uses a small whiteboard and marker to engage the class in thinking about particular features of the words in the composition.

Guided Writing—Learning Logs

- 🍎 Guided writing begins on Tuesday of the first week. This gives extra time on Monday to tap into children's prior knowledge and to read an additional book during mediated read-aloud.
- 🍎 Children are encouraged to begin to record things they are learning about frogs and toads, adding new ideas each day (see excerpts from Ricardo's journal in Figure 11.11).

Word Study

Monday

- 🍎 Use the letters in the word *jumping* to build words as a class. Work from shortest to longest. The teacher guides the word building.
- 🍎 Build words in the following order to help children make connections between spelling patterns:

    up, in, pin, nip, pig, jug,

    mug, gum, gun, jump, jumping.
- 🍎 Building *pin,* then *nip (mug/gum)* emphasizes the importance of the left-to-right position of letters within a word.
- 🍎 Building *in/pin, pin/pig, gum/gun* emphasizes that new words are created by adding or substituting letters.

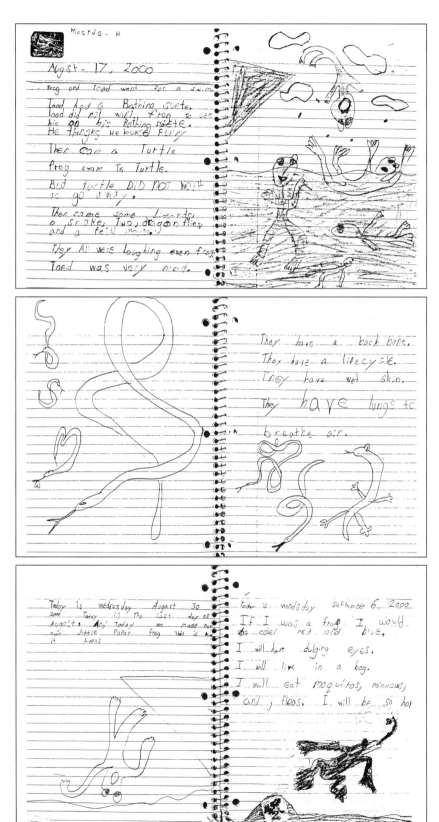

Excerpts from Ricardo's journal.

447

FIGURE 11.11 (continued)
Excerpts from Ricardo's journal.

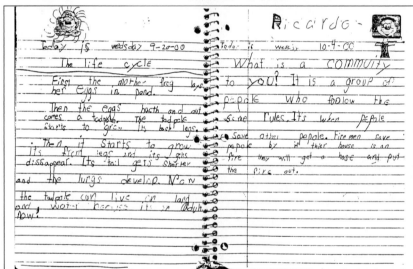

🍃 Building *jump/jumping* emphasizes that related words can be made by adding a meaningful chunk (in this case a suffix) to a base word.

🍃 Record the words for the week in a word study notebook.

🍃 Provide a take-home list of the words for study.

Tuesday

🍃 Rebuild each word from day 1. Children come to the pocket chart, build a word, and explain their thinking.

🍃 Apply to new words. Use *jump* to spell *bump.* Use *nip* to spell *sip,* then *slip.*

Wednesday

🍃 Show words on large cards. Place in pocket chart as children read each word aloud. Provide a sheet of small word cards. Read each word. Children cut words apart for sorting.

- Invite children to do an open sort, grouping words to show the patterns they see.
- Write the results of the sort in a word study notebook.
- Discuss the categories that emerge from their sort. Have children use the large cards in the pocket chart to show the categories they made and explain their thinking.

Thursday

- Review the results of the open sort from Wednesday, then ask children to do a closed sort for short *i* (*in*) and short *u* (*up*).

<u>in</u>	<u>up</u>
pin	*jug*
nip	*mug*
pig	*gum*
	gun
	jump
	jumping

- Record results of the closed sort in a word study notebook.

Friday

- Assess children's understanding of short *i* and *u* patterns. Give a spelling test. Dictate each word (in isolation, in a sentence, then again in isolation).
- Add two application words—*mud* (from *mug*), *stump* (from *jump*).
- Dictation sentence: *A big pig cannot jump up.*

Guided Reading Block

Rotation of Groups

- Teachers select appropriate level of text for each group of children.
- Each day the teachers meet with four groups.
  - Below-level groups meet every day; on-level and above groups meet every other day.
  - On-level at this time of the school year is early second grade.
  - Groups that are not meeting with a teacher on a particular day have additional time in independent reading and activity centers.
  - See Figure 11.12 for rotation of guided reading groups.
- All texts are read and discussed.
  - Children in below-level (First grade) and on-level groups (early second grade) typically read orally at their own pace.
  - Children in above-level groups (mid-to late-second and early third grade) typically read silently at their own pace.
- Rereading is oral and focused on interpretation/expression and developing comprehension by supporting answers with text.

FIGURE 11.12
Rotation of guided reading groups.

Group Meetings	Group 1 Mid-1st	Group 2 Late 1st	Group 3 Early 2nd	Group 4 Early 2nd	Group 5 Mid 2nd	Group 6 Late 2nd/ Early 3rd
Week 1	M–F	M–F	M, W, F	T, Th,	M, W, F	T, Th
Week 2	M–F	M–F	T, Th	M, W, F	T, Th	M, W, F
Week 3	M–F	M–F	M, W, F	T, Th,	M, W, F	T, Th
Week 4	M–F	M–F	T, Th	M, W, F	T, Th	M, W, F

Teaching Points

- Teaching points are determined by each individual text and teacher's observations of children's reading (see Teacher's Plan Book for week 1).
- Oral fluency and comprehension of text are emphasized.
- Part or all of each text is reread for fluency.
- Children are encouraged to apply teaching points in independent reading and writing.

Independent Reading

- During the first week of the unit, independent reading occurs in texts from the previous weeks' guided reading that are stored in a book box for each group.
- As guided reading books are completed they are added to the book boxes. Books are removed after children have had ample time to practice rereading and/or have lost interest.
- Children may also choose to partner-read the poem of the week to prepare for individual performance on Friday.

Activity Centers

- During the first week of the unit, activity centers include:
  - *Library Corner*—Displays a collection of unit books, including wordless books by Mercer Mayer. Books read aloud are also placed in the library and book boxes for rereading.
  - *Science Center*—Houses an aquarium set up as a habitat for several small frogs, an aquarium with tadpoles, and books with excellent photographs of frogs and toads.
  - *Listening Center*—Provides a tape-recorded copy of *Frogs* by Gail Gibbons, which presents information in an interesting and clear format. Following the reading, children are encouraged to illustrate and write about something new they learned.
  - *Writing Center*—Provides a variety of papers, writing implements, an interesting display of pictures of amphibians, and small blank books shaped like frogs or toads.

- *Computer Center*—Provides access to approved websites such as:
  - *http://www.homestead.com/kidstuff/,*
  - *http://www.kiddyhouse.com/Themes/frogs/,* and
  - *http://allaboutfrogs.org/froglnd.shtml.*

Afternoon Mediated Read-Aloud (Fiction)

- End the day by sharing a fictional account about frogs and/or toads. Encourage response to text.
- Compare/contrast the ways that frogs and toads are depicted in informational texts that have been read aloud.

Texts

Frog in the Kitchen Sink (Jim Post)

If You Hopped Like a Frog (David Schwartz)

Jump, Frog, Jump (Robert Kalan)

It's Mine (Leo Lionni)

Tuesday (David Wiesner)

LESSON PLANS FOR WEEK 2—SALAMANDERS AND AMPHIBIAN LIFE CYCLES

Poem of the Week—"Salamanders, Salamanders"

Text

- Adapted from a poem written by a parent volunteer (see Figure 11.13).
- Note: *caecilians* is pronounced seh-SILL-yens.

Teaching Points

- Decoding big words, *sal-a-man-der* and *am-phib-i-an*. Find familiar chunks in big words.
- Use a question mark to show a question. How to hear a question in voice intonation.
- Read, build, and write the contraction *you're*. Discuss the base words from which it is made and the letters that the apostrophe replaces. Use letter cards to show how the contraction is made.

Morning Mediated Read-Aloud (Informational Text)

Texts for Salamanders

A Salamander's Life (John Himmelman)

Salamanders Secret, Silent Lives (Sara Swan Miller)

Teacher's Plan Book—Week 2

Monday	Tuesday
Shared Reading/Poem of the Week Introduce "Salamander, Salamander." *Teaching Point:* Decoding big words.	**Shared Reading/Poem of the Week** Reread "Salamander Salamander." *Teaching Point:* How do we show a question?
Mediated Read-Aloud (Informational Text) Read *A Salamander's Life.*	**Mediated Read-Aloud (Informational Text)** Read *Salamanders Secret, Silent Lives.*
Interactive Writing Add salamanders to amphibian chart.	**Interactive Writing** Review chart. Add any new information about salamanders.
Guided Writing Learning Log: Word splash (*insects, egg, toad, smooth, tadpole, frog, amphibian, bulging, webbed, bumpy, sticky*).	**Guided Writing** Learning Log: Complete word splash.
Word Study Use the letters in *salamander* to build words.	**Word Study** Rebuild words using letters from *salamander.* Apply to new words.
Shared Writing Begin character map of Frog and Toad (T-chart comparing character traits).	**Shared Writing** Add to character map of Frog and Toad.
Guided Reading Block *Group 1 (mid 1st):* Rereading of *Frogs on a Log. Teaching Point:* Fluency. *Group 2 (late 1st):* Rereading and discussion of *Frogs. Teaching Points:* Fluency, identifying details. *Group 4 (early 2nd):* Begin reading *The Show-and-Tell Frog. Teaching Point:* Making inferences. *Group 6 (late 2nd/early 3rd):* Continue reading *Encyclopedia Brown and the Case of the Slippery Salamander,* Ch. 5 & 6. *Teaching Points:* Using context to confirm decoding and word meaning; making inferences to solve a mystery.	**Guided Reading Block** *Group 1 (mid 1st):* First reading of *Freddie the Frog. Teaching Point:* Using initial blends to decode words (*fr, Freddie, frog*). *Group 2 (late 1st):* First reading of *How Do Frogs Grow? Teaching Point: ow (how)* versus *ow (grow).* *Group 3 (early 2nd):* Rereading and discussion of *The Show-and-Tell Frog. Teaching Points:* Fluency; confirming inferences. *Group 5 (mid 2nd):* Continue reading and discussion of *Commander Toad in Space. Teaching Point:* Understanding character.
Independent Reading Book Boxes	**Independent Reading** Book Boxes Partner-Read "Salamander, Salamander"

Activity Centers
    Library Center
    Science Center
    Listening Center
    Writing Center
    Computer Center
	Activity Centers
	(See Monday)

Mediated Read-Aloud (Fiction) *The Adventures of Salamander Sam*	**Mediated Read-Aloud (Fiction)** *Would You Rather Be a Bull Frog?*

Teacher's Plan Book—Week 2

Wednesday	Thursday	Friday
Shared Reading/Poem of the Week Reread "Salamander, Salamander." *Teaching Point:* Contractions (*you're*).	**Shared Reading/Poem of the Week** Reread "Salamander, Salamander" *Teaching Point:* Nouns are naming words.	**Shared Reading/Poem of the Week** Individual performances of "Salamander, Salamander."
Mediated Read-Aloud (Informational Text) Read *A New Frog: My First Look at the Life Cycle of an Amphibian. Teaching Point:* Using words and illustrations to detect sequence of events.	**Mediated Read-Aloud (Informational Text)** Read *From Tadpole to Frog. Teaching Point:* Using words and illustrations to detect sequence of events.	**Mediated Read-Aloud (Informational Text)** Read *Frogs, Toads, Lizards, and Salamanders. Teaching Point:* Using words and illustrations to detect sequence of events.
Interactive Writing Add life cycle information to chart.	**Interactive Writing** Continue to add life cycle information to chart. Summarize life cycle of frogs.	**Shared Writing** Summarize information about amphibian characteristics from weeks 1 and 2.
Guided Writing Learning Log: Write facts about amphibians or imagine yourself as an amphibian.	**Guided Writing** Learning Log: Write facts about amphibians or imagine yourself as an amphibian	**Guided Writing** Learning Log: Write facts about amphibians or imagine yourself as an amphibian.
Word Study Open sort, individual and pocket chart.	**Word Study** Closed sort, individual and pocket chart.	**Word Study** Assessment.
Guided Reading Block *Group 1 (mid 1st):* Reread and discuss *Freddie the Frog. Teaching Points:* Fluency; identifying details. *Group 2 (late 1st):* Reread and discuss *How Do Frogs Grow? Teaching Points:* Fluency; identifying details. *Group 4 (early 2nd):* Rereading and discussion of *The Show-and-Tell Frog. Teaching Points:* Fluency, confirming inferences. *Group 6 (late 2nd/early 3rd):* Continue reading *Encyclopedia Brown and the Case of the Slippery Salamander,* Ch. 7 & 8. *Teaching Points:* Using context to confirm decoding and word meaning; making inferences to solve a mystery.	**Guided Reading Block** *Group 1 (mid 1st): The Frog and the Fly. Teaching Point:* Contrast blends (*fr, fl*). *Group 2 (late 1st):* First reading of *Tale of a Tadpole. Teaching Point:* Compare short *a* (*tad/pole*) and long *a* (*tale*). *Group 3 (early 2nd):* Begin reading *How Do Frogs Grow? Teaching Point:* Compare sounds of *ow* (*how, grow*). *Group 5 (mid 2nd):* Complete reading/discussion of *Commander Toad. Teaching Point:* Understanding character.	**Guided Reading Block** *Group 1 (mid 1st):* Reread and discuss *The Frog and the Fly. Teaching Points:* Fluency; identifying details. *Group 2 (late 1st):* Complete reading *Tale of a Tadpole. Teaching Points:* Identifying details; sequence. *Group 4 (early 2nd):* Begin reading *How Do Frogs Grow? Teaching Point:* Compare sounds of *ow* (*how, grow*). *Group 6 (late 2nd/early 3rd):* Continue reading *Encyclopedia Brown,* Ch. 9 & 10. *Teaching Points:* Using context to confirm decoding and word meaning; making inferences to solve a mystery.
Independent Reading Book Boxes Partner-Read "Salamander, Salamander"	**Independent Reading** Book Boxes Partner-Read "Salamander, Salamander"	**Independent Reading** Book Boxes Partner-Read "Salamander, Salamander."
Activity Centers (See Monday)	**Activity Centers** (See Monday)	**Activity Centers** (See Monday)
Mediated Read-Aloud (Fiction) *Tyler Toad and the Thunder*	**Mediated Read Aloud (Fiction)** *Frog Goes to Dinner*	**Mediated Read-Aloud (Fiction)** *Can You Jump Like a Frog?*

FIGURE 11.13

> ## Week 2—Poem of the Week
>
> ### Salamander, Salamander
>
> Salamander, salamander,
> Where do you hide?
> Under rocks in the woods,
> Wiggling side to side.
>
> You look like a lizard,
> But like frogs, toads, and caecilians,
> You're in a family
> Called amphibians.
>
> (adapted from a poem by Mrs. Cassas)

Teaching Points

🍎 Build background and develop vocabulary for salamanders.

🍎 Use illustrations and vocabulary to identify details about salamanders.

🍎 Begin to compare/contrast with frogs and toads to generalize amphibian characteristics.

Texts for Life Cycles

A New Frog: My First Look at the Life Cycle of an Amphibian (Pamela Hickman)

From Tadpole to Frog (Kathleen Zoehfeld)

Frogs, Toads, Lizards, and Salamanders (Nancy Winslow Parker)

(Reread portions of other texts as needed.)

Teaching Points

🍎 Use illustrations and vocabulary to identify details related to the sequence of development of a frog.

🍎 Identify words that signal sequence (*first, then, next, last,* etc.).

Interactive Writing—Salamander Characteristics and Life Cycle

🍎 Same procedures as week 1 for engaging children in writing the text. Verbal composition by children—children take turns writing a word or partial word while others discuss spelling patterns and word knowledge needed to compose (see Figure 11.14).

🍎 Encourage self-monitoring strategies for writing by modeling how to reread to check for meaning and correctness.

FIGURE 11.14
T-chart—add salamanders and life cycles in week 2.

	Frogs	Toads	Both Frogs and Toads	Salamanders
Characteristics	Long hind legs for jumping Slimy, smooth skin Webbed feet for swimming or sticky pads for climbing trees	Short hind legs for walking Dry, warty skin Feet have toes or claws Are actually frogs	Have a backbone No neck, cannot turn head Bulging eyes to see well Nocturnal Males have loud voices	Look like a cross between a frog and a lizard Use tail to swim Can have moist, smooth skin or dry, warty skin Some have lungs Some have gills Most breathe through their skin Webbed feet Short toes
Habitat	Live on land and in water Protect with poison skin and color camouflage	Live on land Protect with poison glands and color camouflage	Do not live in polar regions or very wet deserts Like a warm, dry climate In cold climate they burrow underground and hibernate in the winter	Some live in water On land need a shady, cool place near water Can live under rocks, up in trees, or burrow in damp earth
Diet			Tadpoles eat plants Adults are carnivorous Adults eat insects, spiders, worms, and slugs	Carnivores Eat earthworms, slugs, and snails Bigger salamanders eat small fish and mammals like mice
Life Cycle	Lay eggs in clusters in water	Lay eggs in chains, usually in the water	Tadpoles have gills Tadpoles grow back legs, then front legs Young frogs have tails Tails grow shorter, then disappear Adults have lungs Live 1–30 years	Some salamanders lay eggs on land, some in the water When larvae hatch they grow up in the water Some salamanders return to land

FIGURE 11.15

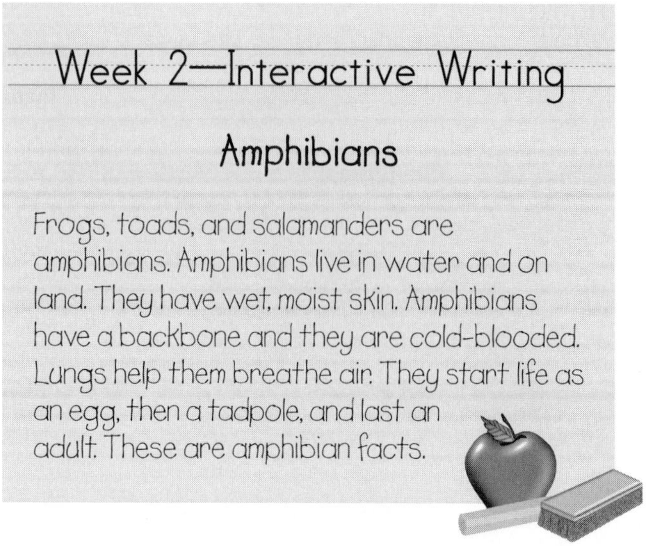

Week 2—Interactive Writing

Amphibians

Frogs, toads, and salamanders are
amphibians. Amphibians live in water and on
land. They have wet, moist skin. Amphibians
have a backbone and they are cold-blooded.
Lungs help them breathe air. They start life as
an egg, then a tadpole, and last an
adult. These are amphibian facts.

FIGURE 11.16

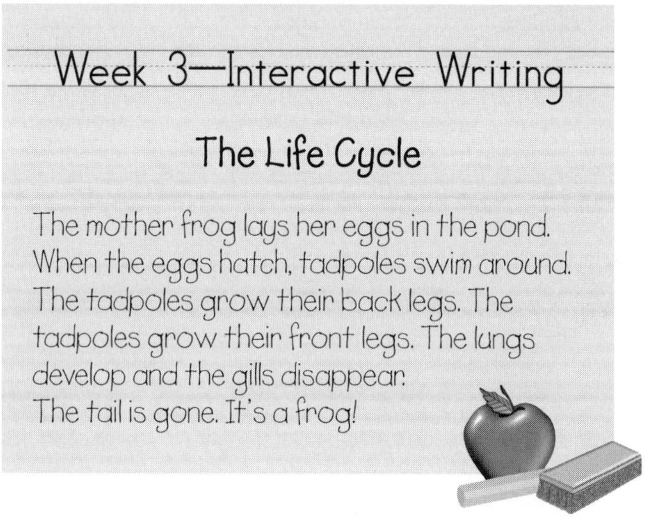

Week 3—Interactive Writing

The Life Cycle

The mother frog lays her eggs in the pond.
When the eggs hatch, tadpoles swim around.
The tadpoles grow their back legs. The
tadpoles grow their front legs. The lungs
develop and the gills disappear.
The tail is gone. It's a frog!

Interactive Writing—Summarize Amphibian Characteristics and Life Cycles

- 🍎 Verbal composition by children—children take turns writing a word or partial word while others discuss spelling patterns and word knowledge needed to compose (see Figures 11.15 and Figure 11.16).
- 🍎 Self-monitoring strategies for writing are encouraged.

Guided Writing—Learning Logs

- 🍎 Because children have had some opportunity to build vocabulary, the teachers provide a word splash for guided writing. A word splash is a

Karen's Word Splash

FIGURE 11.17

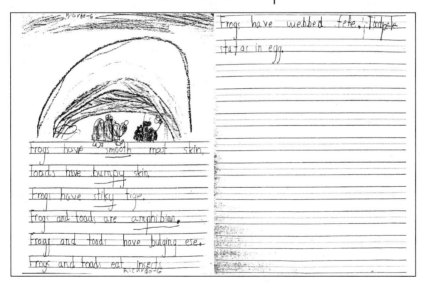

insects

egg   toad

tadpole

frog   amphibian   smooth

sticky

bulging

webbed

bumpy

frogs and toads have webbed feet.

Toads and frogs have bulging eyes.

Frogs, toads and salamanders are amphibians

Karen's word splash.

Tadpoles are baby frogs or toads.

Toads and frogs have sticky toungs.

Toads have bumpy skin.

Mother frog/toad lays her eggs in

the pond. Frogs have smooth skin.

Ricardo's Word Splash

Ricardo-6

Frogs have webbed fete. Tadpole start in egg.

frogs have smooth moot skin.

toads have bumpy skin.

frogs have stiky tige.

Frogs and toads are amphibian.

Frogs and toads have bulging ese.

Frogs and toads eat insects

Ricardo-6

half-page of words "splashed on to the paper." Children compose sentences using the vocabulary. They are encouraged to relate the sentences to the content of the unit (see Figure 11.17).

 Teachers encourage children to use their knowledge to write facts about amphibians.

 Teachers encourage children to imagine themselves as one of the amphibians being studied (see Figure 11.18).

 Children are asked to explain the life cycle of an amphibian.

FIGURE 11.18
Excerpts from Karen's journal.

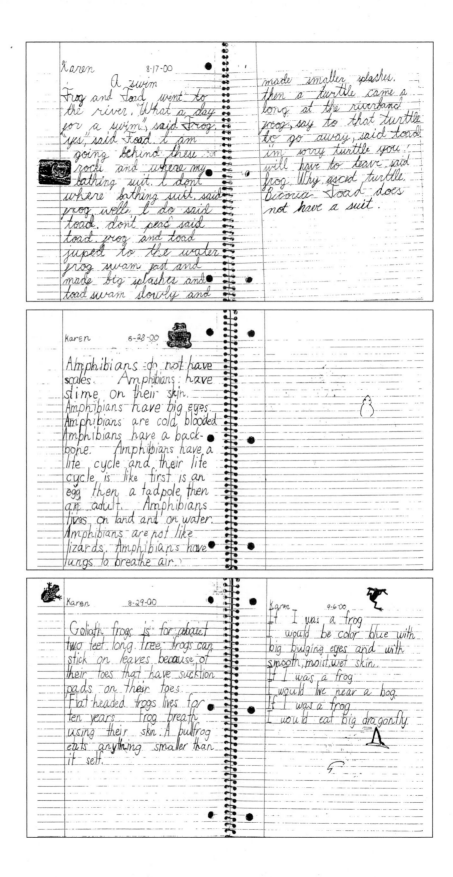

Karen   8-17-00

A swim

Frog and Toad went to the river. "What a day for a swim," said Frog. "Yes," said Toad. I am going behind these rocks and where my bathing suit. I dont where bathing suit, said Frog. well, I do said Toad. dont peac said Toad. Frog and Toad juped to the water Frog swam fast and made big splashes and Toad swam slowly and made smaller splashes. then a turtle came a long at the riverband Frog, say to that turtle to go away, said Toad. I'm sorry turtle you will have to leave, said Frog. Why asced turtle. Bicoua Toad does not have a suit.

Karen   8-28-00

Amphibians do not have scales. Amphibians have slime on their skin. Amphibians have big eyes. Amphibians are cold blooded Amphibians have a backbone. Amphibians have a life cycle and their life cycle is like first is an egg then a tadpole then an adult. Amphibians lives on land and on water. Amphibians are not like lizards. Amphibians have lungs to breathe air.

Karen   8-29-00

Goliath frogs is for abuact two feet long. tree frogs can stick on leaves because of their toes that have suction pads on their toes. Flat headed frogs lives for ten years frog breath using their skin. A bullfrog eats anything smaller than it self.

Karen   9-6-00

If I was a frog I would be color blue with big bulging eyes and with smooth, moist, wet skin. If I was a frog I would live near a bog. If I was a frog I would eat big dragonfly.

458

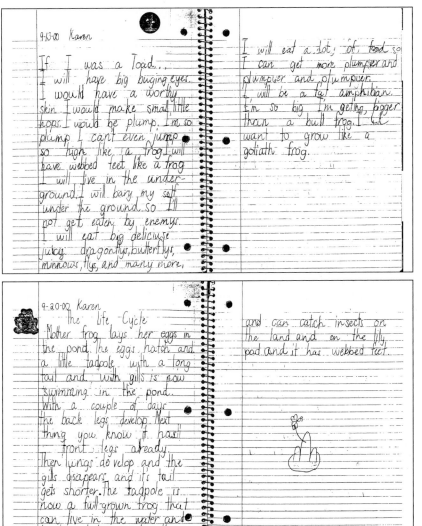

FIGURE 11.18 (continued)
Excerpts from Karen's journal.

Word Study

Monday

 Use the letters in the word *salamander* to build words as a class. Work from shortest to longest. The teacher guides the word building.

 Build words in the following order to help children make connections between spelling patterns:

> as, man, sand, land, sale, male,
>
> den, men, end, lend, mend, mean,
>
> lean, leans, dream, dreams, near,
>
> dear, dare, mare, salad, salamander.

🍎 When building *sand/land, mean/lean/dream,* and *near/dear,* discuss the impact on pronunciation of replacing phonemes in a word.

🍎 Build *dear/dare;* discuss how changing the order of letters changes the pronunciation of a word.

🍎 Record the words for the week in a word study notebook.

🍎 Provide a take-home list of the words for study.

Tuesday

🍎 Rebuild each word from Monday. Children build words at their seat, as well as at the pocket chart, and explain their thinking.

🍎 Apply patterns to new words. Use *mean* to spell *meat.* Use *sand* to spell *stand.*

Wednesday

🍎 Show words on large cards. Place in pocket chart as children read each word aloud. Provide a sheet of small word cards. Read each word. Children cut words apart for sorting.

🍎 Invite children to do an open sort, grouping words to show the patterns they see.

🍎 Discuss the categories that emerge from their sort. Have children use the large cards in the pocket chart to show the categories they made and explain their thinking.

🍎 Record results of open sort in word study notebook.

Thursday

🍎 Review the results of the open sort from Wednesday, then ask children to do two closed sorts.

🍎 Sort short versus long vowels. Discuss differences in vowel sounds and how a long-vowel sound can be spelled.

short a	long a	short e	long e
as	*sale*	*men*	*lean*
man	*male*	*den*	*leans*
land		*send*	*mean*
sand		*mend*	*dream*
salad		*lend*	*dreams*

🍎 Sort long versus *r*-controlled to reinforce the influence of the letter *r* on long-vowel spellings.

long vowels	r-controlled
sale	*dare*
male	*mare*
lean	*dear*
leans	*near*
mean	
dream	
dreams	

🍎 Record results of closed sort in word study notebook.

Friday

- Assess children's understanding of spelling patterns. Give a spelling test. Dictate each word (in isolation, in a sentence, then again in isolation).
- Add two application words—*fear* (from *dear*) and *clean* (from *lean*).
- Dictation sentence: *The mean man had a bad dream.*

Guided Reading Block

- Same basic procedure as week 1.
- During week 2 of the unit, independent reading texts are a combination of previous weeks' guided reading texts, including texts from week 1.
- During week 2 the activity centers include:
  - *Library Corner*—Displays a collection of unit books, with the addition of books about salamanders.
  - *Science Center*—Now houses three aquariums for observation. A new aquarium is set up as a habitat for a salamander. Children are encouraged to record observations in a science center log. Blank individual copies of frogs and toads are provided for children to label with vocabulary and factual information, similar to the narrated drawing from week 1.
  - *Listening Center*——Provides a tape recorded book about salamanders, *A Salamander's Life.*
  - *Writing Center*——Contains a variety of papers, writing implements, blank books shaped like salamanders, and an interesting display of pictures of amphibians.
  - *Computer Center*——See suggested websites in week 1.

Afternoon Mediated Read-Aloud (Fiction)

Texts

The Adventures of Salamander Sam (Donna Ebl)
Would You Rather Be a Bullfrog? (Dr. Seuss)
Frog Goes to Dinner (Mercer Mayer)
Can You Jump Like a Frog? (Mark Brown)
Tyler Toad and the Thunder (Robert Crowe)

Teaching Point

- Help children notice and articulate differences between the portrayal of amphibians in fiction and informational text.

Teacher's Plan Book—Week 3

Monday	Tuesday

Monday

Shared Reading/Poem of the Week
Introduce "Tadpoles, Tadpoles." *Teaching Point:* Signal words for sequence (*first, then, finally*).

Guided Literature Study
Whole-class study of *Frog and Toad Are Friends* (Ch. 1, "Spring." *Teaching Point:* Inferring character traits and theme (friendship).

Shared Writing
Begin a T-chart for character traits of Frog and Toad.

Guided Writing
Group report on an amphibian: characteristics, habitat, diet, life cycle. Getting started phase, brainstorming/planning writing.

Word Study
Use letters in *tadpoles* to build words.

Guided Reading Block
Group 1 (mid 1st): First reading of *Jog, Frog, Jog.* *Teaching Point:* Rhyming words, compare spelling patterns.

Group 2 (late 1st): Reread and discuss *Tale of a Tadpole.* *Teaching Points:* Fluency; identifying details and sequence.

Group 3 (early 2nd): Complete reading of *How Do Frogs Grow? Teaching Points:* Identifying details; sequence.

Group 5 (mid 2nd): Begin reading and discussion of *Frog or Toad? Teaching Point:* Inferring compare/contrast using language cues.

Independent Reading
Book Boxes

Activity Centers
    Library Center
    Science Center
    Listening Center
    Writing Center

Mediated Read-Aloud (Informational Text)
Frogs, Toads, Lizards, and Salamanders

Tuesday

Shared Reading/Poem of the Week
Reread "Tadpoles, Tadpoles." *Teaching Point:* Nouns as naming words.

Guided Literature Study
Continue study of *Frog and Toad Are Friends* (Ch. 2, "The Story." *Teaching Point:* Inferring character traits and theme (friendship).

Shared Writing
Add to T-chart of Frog and Toad.

Guided Writing
Group report—beginning to compose.

Word Study
Rebuild words with letters in *tadpoles.* Apply patterns to new words.

Guided Reading Block
Group 1 (mid 1st): Reread and discuss *Jog, Frog, Jog.* *Teaching Points:* Fluency; identifying details.

Group 2 (late 1st): Begin reading *Frogs. Teaching Point:* Identifying details.

Group 4 (early 2nd): Complete reading of *How Do Frogs Grow? Teaching Points:* Identifying details; sequence.

Group 6 (late 2nd/early 3rd): Begin reading *The Magic School Bus: A Book About Warm- and Cold-Blooded Animals. Teaching Point:* Comparing and contrasting fiction versus informational text; how to use format of a text to find information.

Independent Reading
Book Boxes
Rereading of "Tadpoles, Tadpoles."

Activity Centers
(See Monday)

Mediated Read-Aloud (Informational Text)
Lizards and Salamanders

Teacher's Plan Book—Week 3

Wednesday	**Thursday**	**Friday**

Shared Reading/Poem of the Week
Reread "Tadpoles, Tadpoles."
Teaching Point: Plural nouns.

Guided Literature Study
Continue study of *Frog and Toad Are Friends* (Ch. 3, "A Lost Button"). *Teaching Point:* Inferring character traits and theme (friendship).

Interactive Writing
Add to T-chart of Frog and Toad.

Word Study
Open sort for patterns children observe in words built from *tadpoles.*

Guided Writing
Group report—composing/editing.

Guided Reading Block
Group 1 (mid 1st): First reading of *Little Frog's Monster Story. Teaching Point.* Possessives (*Frog's*).

Group 2 (late 1st): Complete reading of *Frogs. Teaching Points:* Identifying details; sequence.

Group 3 (early 2nd): Rereading and discussion of *How Do Frogs Grow? Teaching Points:* Identifying details; sequence.

Group 5 (mid 2nd): Continue reading and discussion of *Frog or Toad? Teaching Points:* Inferring compare/contrast using language cues; fluency.

Independent Reading
Book Boxes
Rereading of "Tadpoles, Tadpoles"

Activity Centers
(See Monday)

**Mediated Read-Aloud
(Informational Text)**
Climbing Tree Frogs

Shared Reading/Poem of the Week
Reread "Tadpoles, Tadpoles."
Teaching Point: Verbs with *-ing.*

Guided Literature Study
Continue *Frog and Toad Are Friends* (Ch. 4, "A Swim"). *Teaching Point:* Inferring character traits and theme (friendship).

Interactive Writing
Add to T-chart of Frog and Toad.

Shared Writing
Begin brainstorming and drafting paragraph about the friendship between Frog and Toad.

Word Study
Closed sort for long/short-vowel patterns, plurals.

Guided Writing
Group report—composing/editing.

Guided Reading Block
Group 1 (mid 1st): Reread and discuss *Little Frog's Monster Story. Teaching Points:* Fluency; identifying plot sequence.

Group 2 (late 1st): Reread and discuss *Frogs. Teaching Points:* Fluency; sequence.

Group 4 (early 2nd): Rereading and discussion of *How Do Frogs Grow? Teaching Points:* Identifying details; sequence.

Group 6 (late 2nd/early 3rd): Rereading and discussion of *The Magic School Bus: A Book About Warm- and Cold-Blooded Animals. Teaching Points:* Comparing and contrasting fiction versus informational text; how to use format of a text to find information.

Independent Reading
Book Boxes
Rereading of "Tadpoles, Tadpoles"

Activity Centers
(See Monday)

**Mediated Read-Aloud
(Informational Text)**
A Wood Frog's Life

Shared Reading/Poem of the Week
Individual performances.

Guided Literature Study
Complete *Frog and Toad Are Friends* (Ch. 5, "The Letter"). *Teaching Point:* Inferring character traits and theme (friendship).

Shared Writing
Complete composition about the friendship between Frog and Toad.

Word Study
Assessment.

Guided Writing
Complete group report, prepare for presentations during week 4.

Guided Reading Block
Group 1 (mid 1st): First reading of *Toad on the Road. Teaching Point:* Decoding long *o (o_e, oa)*, compare to short *o.*

Group 2 (late 1st): Begin reading *Five Green and Speckled Frogs. Teaching Point:* Decoding big words (*speckled*).

Group 3 (early 2nd): Begin reading *Days with Frog and Toad. Teaching Point:* Inferring character.

Group 5 (mid 2nd): Complete reading and discussion of *Frog or Toad? Teaching Points:* Inferring compare/contrast using language cues; fluency.

Independent Reading
Book Boxes

Activity Centers
(See Monday)

**Mediated Read-Aloud
(Informational Text)**

LESSON PLANS FOR WEEK 3—<u>FROG AND TOAD ARE FRIENDS</u> AND GROUP REPORTS

Poem of the Week—"Tadpoles, Tadpoles"

Teaching Points

- 🍎 How to use a pronoun to stand for a noun (see Figure 11.19).
- 🍎 How words signal sequence (*first, then, finally*).
- 🍎 Longer words have more chunks (clap syllables, count chunks, compare long and short words).

Guided Literature Study—**Frog and Toad Are Friends**

- 🍎 Use a class set of texts to encourage whole-class read-along; read and discuss one chapter per day.
  - 🍎 Monday—Ch. 1, "Spring"
  - 🍎 Tuesday—Ch. 2, "The Story"
  - 🍎 Wednesday—Ch. 3, "A Lost Button"
  - 🍎 Thursday—Ch. 4, "A Swim"
  - 🍎 Friday—Ch. 5, "The Letter"
- 🍎 Infer character traits through dialogue between Frog and Toad and narrator's description.

FIGURE 11.19

Week 3—Poem of the Week

Tadpoles

Tadpoles, tadpoles,
First, they are eggs.

Then heads, then tails,
Then come legs.

Finally, in half a year,
They are sitting on logs.

Hopping and croaking,
As young, green frogs.

- Use understanding of character and personal experience to discuss/respond to the ways that Frog and Toad show their friendship for one another.
- As children gather background information about frogs and toads, discussion can also focus on comparing/contrasting real frogs and toads with make-believe ones. Extend discussion during afternoon read-aloud.
- Partner-rereading of chapters is encouraged during independent reading in the guided reading block.

Interactive Writing—Character T-Chart

- Following the reading of each chapter in *Frog and Toad Are Friends*, engage children in identifying what they have learned about each character and how that character acts as a friend to the other. Use a T-chart format (see Figure 11.20).
- Reread text as needed to confirm details and inferences about characters and friendship.
- Use the contents of the T-chart later in week 3 to compose a shared writing paragraph about the friendship between Frog and Toad.

	Frog	Toad
Ch. 1 "Spring"	Frog spends time with Toad. Frog doesn't give up trying to get Toad to get out of bed.	
Ch. 2 "The Story"	Frog tells Toad a story when he is feeling bad.	Toad helped Frog when he was sick. Toad made hot tea for Frog. Toad tried very hard to think of a story to tell Frog to make him feel better.
Ch. 3 "A Lost Button"	Frog helped Toad look in many places for a lost button.	Toad sewed all the buttons they found on his jacket and gave it to Frog.
Ch. 4 "The Swim"	Frog asked the animals not to look at Toad in his bathing suit.	
Ch. 5 "The Letter"	Frog wrote a letter to Toad so he could get some mail.	

FIGURE 11.20
T-chart—how do Frog and Toad show their friendship?

Shared Writing—Response to Frog and Toad's Friendship

🍎 Near the end of the week, children compose their responses to the friendship they have observed between Frog and Toad. The children decide to focus on how Toad helped Frog when Frog was sick (see Figure 11.21).

🍎 Shared writing is used to maximize instructional time.

🍎 Ideas in the composition have been discussed over the week of literature study.

🍎 The teachers model composing a well-organized paragraph with topic sentence, supporting details, and a concluding statement. The teachers introduce indenting the first word of a paragraph.

Guided Writing—Group Reports

🍎 Groups of mixed ability and interest are formed to write about frogs, toads, and salamanders.

🍎 The class decides that each report will include a section about:
  🍎 characteristics,
  🍎 habitat,
  🍎 diet, and
  🍎 life cycle (see Figure 11.22).

🍎 Large blocks of time during the week are devoted to rereading of informational texts, discussion, and writing to prepare the group reports.

🍎 The teachers guide the writing process, helping children use their participation in shared and interactive writing to make decisions about the writing traits that should be included:
  🍎 which *ideas and content* to include,
  🍎 the *organization* of their ideas,
  🍎 how to let their voice come through in the writing, and
  🍎 the appropriate use of *language,* including *conventions,* to communicate their ideas.

🍎 The group reports are presented to the class in an author's chair during week 4.

FIGURE 11.21
Shared writing—Frog and Toad.

Frog and Toad

Toad is a good friend to Frog. When Frog was sick, Toad gave him a cup of tea. Toad also shared his bed. He tried his best to tell Frog a story. Frog is lucky to have a friend like Toad.

FIGURE 11.22
Group book—amphibians.

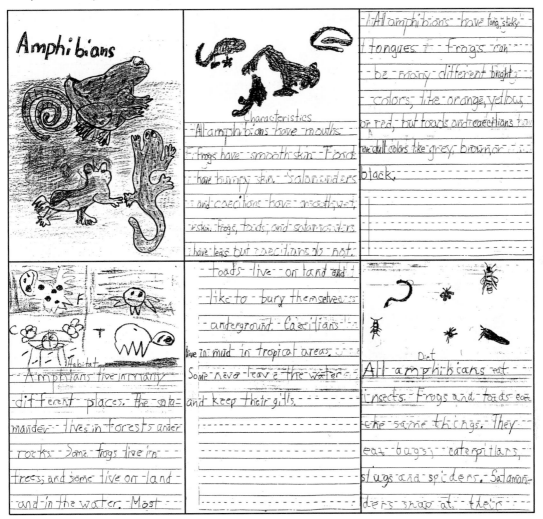

Word Study

Monday

🍎 Use the letters in the word *tadpoles* to build words as a class. Work from shortest to longest. The teacher guides the word building.

🍎 Build words in the following order to help children make connections between spelling patterns:

> sad, lad, pad, pads, let, pet,
>
> pets/step, pot/top, pots/spot/stop,
>
> tale, tales, late/plate, lead, leads,
>
> leap, leaps, pole, poles, toad, told,
>
> pedal, pedals, tadpole, tadpoles.

FIGURE 11.22 (continued)
Group book—amphibians.

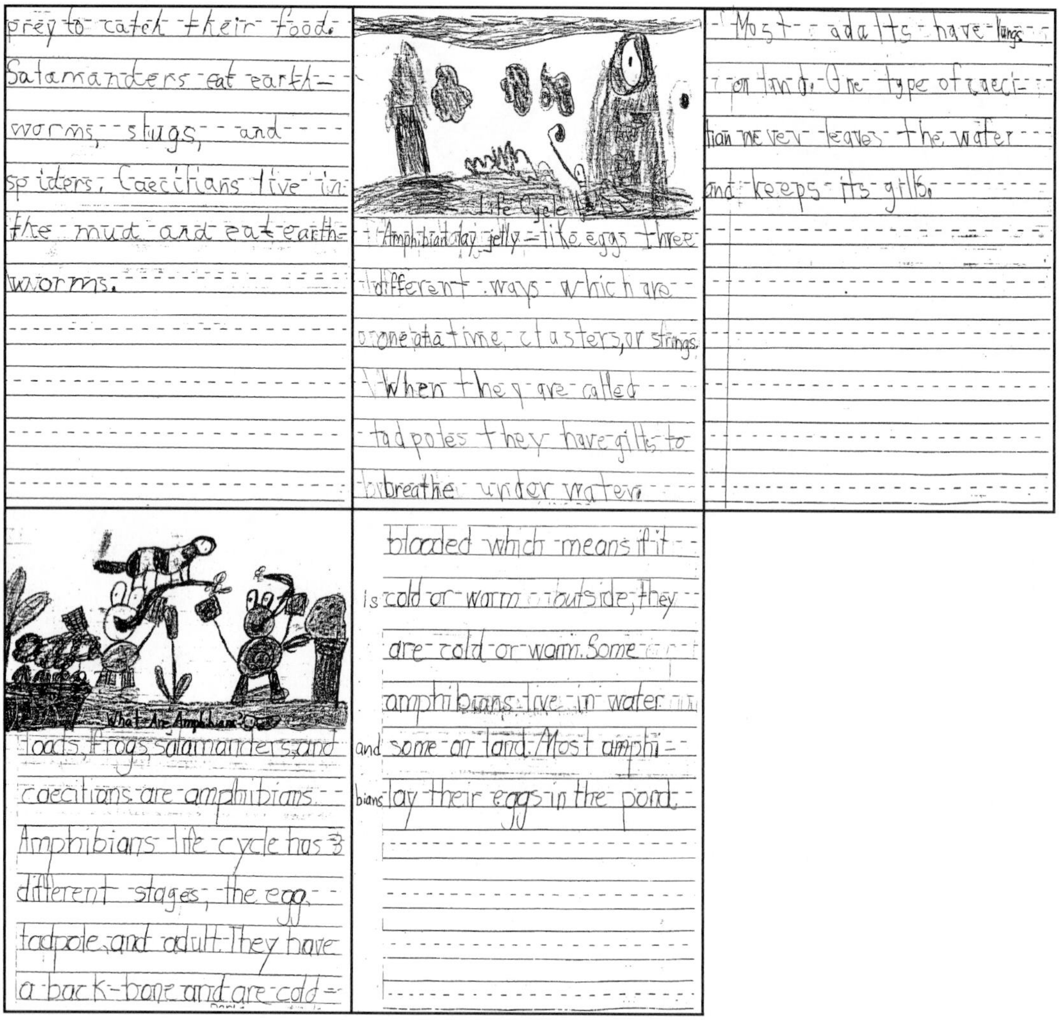

- Build *late/plate*, discuss the impact of adding phonemes to a word.
- Build *pots/spot/stop* and *pets/pest/step,* discuss how the order of letters changes the pronunciation of a word.
- Record the words for the week in a word study notebook.
- Provide a take-home list of the words for study.

Tuesday

- Rebuild each word from Monday. Children build words at their seat, as well as at the pocket chart, and explain their thinking.
- Apply patterns to new words. Use *tadpole* to make *flagpole.*

Wednesday

- Show words on large cards. Place in pocket chart as children read each word aloud. Provide a sheet of small word cards. Read each word. Children cut words apart for sorting.
- Invite children to do an open sort, grouping words to show the patterns they see.
- Discuss the categories that emerge from their sort. Have children use the large cards in the pocket chart to show the categories they made and explain their thinking.
- Record results of the open sort in word study notebook.

Thursday

- Review the results of the open sort from Wednesday, then ask children to do two closed sorts.
- Sort short vowels versus long vowels. Notice patterns. Discuss differences in vowel sounds, how certain spelling patterns usually signal (but not always, as in *told*) a long vowel.

short *a*	long *a*	short *e*	long *e*	short *o*	long *o*
sad	tale	let	lead	top	pole
lad	tales	pet	leads	pot	poles
pad	late	pets	leap	pots	told
pads	plate	pest	leaps	spot	toad
lads		step		stop	
tad/pole		ped/al			
tad/poles		ped/als			

- Sort singular versus plural.

singular	plural
pad	pads
pet	pets
pole	poles
tale	tales
pedal	pedals
tadpole	tadpoles

- Record results of closed sort in word study notebook.

Friday

- Assess children's understanding of spelling patterns. Give a spelling test. Dictate each word (in isolation, in a sentence, then again in isolation).
- Add two application words—use *told* to make *cold,* use *tale* to make *stale.*
- Dictation sentence: *My pet tadpole cannot leap.*

Teacher's Plan Book—Week 4

Monday

Shared Reading/Poem of the Week:
Introduce "Five Little Bumpy Toads." *Teaching Point:* adding *y* to a base word (*bump+y*).

Guided Literature Study
Read and discuss *The Princess and the Frog. Teaching Point:* Identifying story elements.

Shared Writing
Record story elements on the class chart.

Word Study
Build words with the letters in *prince.*

Guided Writing
Retelling or response to *The Princess and the Frog.*
Author's Chair: Present group reports.

Guided Reading Block
Group 1 (mid 1st): Rereading and discussion of *Toad on the Road. Teaching Points:* Fluency; plot sequence.

Group 2 (late 1st): Reread and discuss *Five Green and Speckled Frogs. Teaching Point:* Compare spelling patterns of rhyming words.

Group 4 (early 2nd): Begin reading *Days with Frog and Toad. Teaching Point:* Inferring character.

Group 6 (late 2nd/early 3rd): Begin reading *The Frog Alphabet Book. Teaching Point:* Identifying main ideas and supporting details.

Independent Reading
Book Boxes

Activity Centers
    Library Center
    Science Center
    Listening Center
    Writing Center
    Computer Center

Afternoon Mediated Read-Aloud
Read *Peach and Blue. Teaching Point:* Identifying story elements (problem/solution).

Tuesday

Shared Reading/Poem of the Week:
Reread "Five Little Bumpy Toads." *Teaching Point:* Using context for word meaning (*burrowed*).

Guided Literature Study
Read and discuss *The Frog Prince. Teaching Point:* Identifying story elements.

Shared Writing
Record story elements on the class chart.

Word Study
Rebuild words with letters in *tadpoles.* Apply patterns to new words.

Guided Writing
Retelling or response to *The Frog Prince.*
Author's Chair: Present group reports.

Guided Reading Block
Group 1 (mid 1st): Read/reread other leveled books not related to theme.

Group 2 (late 1st): Read/reread other leveled books not related to theme.

Group 3 (early 2nd): Continue reading *Days with Frog and Toad. Teaching Point:* Inferring character.

Group 5 (mid 2nd): Begin reading and discussion of *Frog and Toad Together.* Teaching Point: Understanding character.

Independent Reading
Book Boxes
Partner-Read "Five Little Bumpy Toads"

Activity Centers
(See Monday)

Afternoon Mediated Read-Aloud
Read *The Icky Sticky Frog. Teaching Point:* Identifying story elements (problem/solution).

Teacher's Plan Book—Week 4

Wednesday	Thursday	Friday
Shared Reading/Poem of the Week	**Shared Reading/Poem of the Week**	**Shared Reading/Poem of the Week**
Reread "Five Little Bumpy Toads." *Teaching Point:* Decoding double vowels (*oa, ou*).	Reread "Five Little Bumpy Toads." *Teaching Point:* Identifying describing words.	Individual performances.
Guided Literature Study	**Guided Literature Study**	**Guided Literature Study**
Reread *The Frog Prince* and *The Princess and the Frog. Teaching Point:* Comparing/contrasting story elements.	Reread *The Frog Prince* and *The Princess and the Frog.* Confirm story elements.	Read *The Frog Prince, Continued.* Compare/contrast to Venn's diagram.
Shared Writing	**Shared Writing**	**Shared Writing**
Begin a Venn diagram that compares/contrasts the two versions.	Complete Venn diagram that compares two versions of *The Frog Prince.*	Summarize the comparison of versions of *The Frog Prince.*
Word Study	**Word Study**	**Word Study**
Open sort for patterns children observe in words built from *prince.*	Closed sort for long/short-vowel patterns, blends, soft *c.*	Assessment.
Guided Writing	**Guided Writing**	**Guided Writing**
Retelling or response to *The Frog Prince.*	Retelling or response to *The Frog Prince.*	Retelling or response to *The Frog Prince.*
Author's Chair: Present group reports.	Author's chair: Present group reports.	Author's Chair: Present group reports.
Guided Reading Block	**Guided Reading Block**	**Guided Reading Block**
Group 1 (mid 1st): Read/reread other leveled books not related to theme.	*Group 1 (mid 1st):* Read/reread other leveled books not related to theme.	*Group 1 (mid 1st):* Read/reread other leveled books not related to theme.
Group 2 (late 1st): Read/reread other leveled books not related to theme.	*Group 2 (late 1st):* Read/reread other leveled books not related to theme.	*Group 2 (late 1st):* Read/reread other leveled books not related to theme.
Group 4 (early 2nd): Continue reading *Days with Frog and Toad. Teaching Point:* Inferring character.	*Group 3 (early 2nd):* Complete reading *Days with Frog and Toad. Teaching Point:* Inferring character.	*Group 4 (early 2nd):* Complete reading *Days with Frog and Toad. Teaching Point:* Inferring character.
Group 6 (late 2nd/early 3rd): Continue reading and discussion of *The Frog Alphabet Book. Teaching Point:* Identifying main ideas and supporting details.	*Group 5 (mid 2nd):* Continue reading and discussion of *Frog and Toad Together. Teaching Point:* Understanding character.	*Group 6 (late 2nd/early 3rd):* Complete reading and discussion of *The Frog Alphabet Book. Teaching Point:* Identifying main ideas and supporting details.
Independent Reading	**Independent Reading**	**Independent Reading**
Book Boxes	Book Boxes	Book Boxes
Partner-Read "Five Little Bumpy Toads"	Partner–Read "Five Little Bumpy Toads"	
Activity Centers	**Activity Centers**	**Activity Centers**
(See Monday)	(See Monday)	(See Monday)
Add Venn diagram for comparing/contrasting versions of *The Frog Prince.*		
Afternoon Mediated Read-Aloud	**Afternoon Mediated Read-Aloud**	**Afternoon Mediated Read-Aloud**
Reread class favorites.	Reread class favorites.	Reread class favorites.

Guided Reading Block

- 🍎 Same procedure as weeks 1 and 2.
- 🍎 During week 3 of the unit, independent reading texts are a combination of previous weeks' guided reading texts, including texts from weeks 1 and 2. Now children have many related texts to reread. Partner reading of *Frog and Toad Are Friends* is encouraged.
- 🍎 During week 3 the activity centers include:
  - 🍎 *Library Corner*—Displays a collection of other stories about Frog and Toad by Arnold Lobel.
  - 🍎 *Science Center*—Now houses two aquariums for observation. One is set up as a habitat for several small frogs and one for a salamander. Children are encouraged to record observations in a science center log. Provide blank copies of the amphibian chart and Venn diagrams (from week 2) for children to practice comparing/contrasting amphibians.
  - 🍎 *Listening Center*—Provides recordings of favorite read-alouds such as *Frog in the Kitchen Sink* or *Can You Hop Like a Frog?*
  - 🍎 *Writing Center*—Provides a variety of papers, writing implements, an interesting display of pictures of amphibians, and an accordion book (see Chapter 9) for showing sequence of events in a story. Children may choose to make a retelling of a part of *Frog and Toad Are Friends* or develop an episode of their own.
  - 🍎 *Computer Center*—Provides opportunities for children to compose, edit, and print responses to *Frog and Toad Are Friends.*

Afternoon Mediated Read-Aloud (Informational Text)

Texts

Climbing Tree Frogs (Ruth Berman)
A Wood Frog's Life (John Himmelman)
Lizards and Salamanders (Scott Foresman)
Frogs, Toads, Lizards, and Salamanders (Nancy Parker & Joan Wright)
(*Reread favorites as needed.*)

Teaching Points

- 🍎 Identifying important/relevant details.
- 🍎 Comparing and contrasting different amphibians using appropriate vocabulary.

LESSON PLANS FOR WEEK 4—VERSIONS OF <u>THE FROG PRINCE</u>

Poem of the Week—"Five Little Bumpy Toads"

Teaching Points

- What happens when we add *y* to words like *bump* to make *bumpy?* (see Figure 11.23).
- Using context to figure out the meaning of words like *burrowed.*
- Decoding double-vowel words (*toads, road, ground, found, croak*).
- Identifying descriptive words (*little, bumpy, most delicious*).

FIGURE 11.23

Week 4—Poem of the Week

Five Little Bumpy Toads

Five little bumpy toads
Hopped across a bumpy road
To find some most delicious bugs.
Yum! Yum!

One burrowed under ground
Where it could not be found
Now there are four little bumpy toads.
Croak! Croak!

Continue to count down to zero toads.
(adapted from the song, "Five Little Speckled Frogs")

Guided Literature Study—Versions of The Frog Prince

Texts

The Princess and the Frog (retold by Rachel Isadora)
A Frog Prince (Alex Berenzy)
The Frog Prince, Continued (Jon Scieszka)

Teaching Points

- 🍎 Following the reading of each text, discuss story elements (characters, setting, problem, solution).
- 🍎 Discuss the similarities and differences children are noticing between the versions read aloud.

Shared Writing—Story Elements Chart

- 🍎 Begin a story elements chart (also called *literary elements chart* for older students) to help children remember the characters, setting, problem, and solution for each of the books read aloud (see Figure 11.24).
- 🍎 The chart sets the stage for a Venn diagram during week 4 to carefully compare the two versions that emerge as the children's favorites.
- 🍎 Shared writing is chosen to maximize use of time.

FIGURE 11.24
Charting story elements.

	Characters	Setting	Problem	Solution
The Princess and the Frog	frog becomes a prince princess king	castle spring	The princess does not want to keep her promise to marry the frog.	The frog turned into a human prince.
The Frog Prince	frog princess becomes a frog king moon beetle turtle trolls dove	castle swamp	The princess does not want to keep her promise to marry the frog.	The princess is turned into a frog.
The Frog Prince, Continued	princess prince Miss Witch Fairy Godmother	castle forest tiny cottage	The princess does not want the Frog Prince to act like a frog.	The fairy godmother cast a spell that turned the Frog Prince into a real prince.

Shared Writing—Venn Diagram

- To prepare for writing a paragraph about comparing two texts, children participate in a shared writing to create a Venn diagram comparing the two versions (see Figure 11.25).

Shared Writing—Summarize Comparison

- At the end of the week children use ideas from the Venn diagram to explain the comparison between their two favorite versions of *The Frog Prince* (see Figure 11.26).

Guided Writing—Literature Logs

- Children are encouraged to write about the versions of *The Frog Prince* that have been studied (see Kaylo's journal in Figure 11.27).

FIGURE 11.25

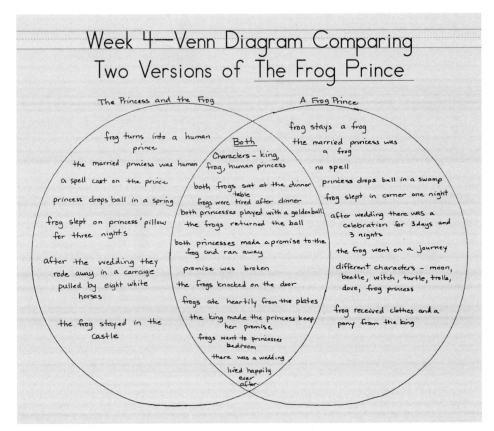

FIGURE 11.26

Week 4—Shared Writing

A Comparison

We compared two stories based on a book called <u>The Frog Prince</u>. In both stories some parts were different and some parts were the same. One difference was in one story the frog remains a frog, and in the other story the frog becomes a prince. One similarity was the king makes the princess keep her promise to the frog.

FIGURE 11.27
Excerpts from Kaylo's journal—responses to *The Frog Prince*.

The frog was nice because he got the golden ball for the princess. He was brave because he went to the palace and knocked on the door.

He was helpful because because he got the ball. The frog was annoying to the princess because he talked and ate and sleept in her bed. The frog was friendly because he started talking to the princes.

In both stories of The Frog Prince the frogs knocked on the door of the casil. Both princesses ran away from the frog. The frog returned the

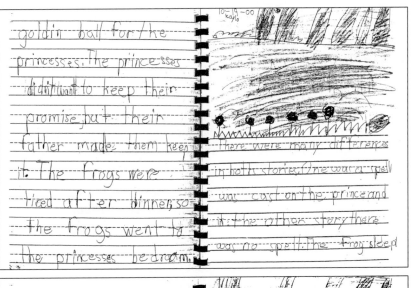

goldin ball for the princesses. The princesses didn't want to keep their promise but their father made them keep it. The frogs were tired after dinner, so the frogs went to the princesses bedroom.

there were many differences in both stories. One was a spell was cast on the prince and in the other story there was no spell. The frog sleep

on the princesses pillow for three nights and the other frog slept in the corner. One frog stayed in the casil and one went on a journey. In one story the princess drops her ball in a spring and the other one drops her ball in a clam.

Once there was a frog. He lived in a bog. One day he went to his friends house to see how he was doing.

When he got there, he knocked on the door. "Come in" said his friend. He went in. He saw his friend. He knew he was sick. He said "you will get better soon."

Word Study

Monday

🍎 Use the letters in the word *prince* to build words as a class. Work from shortest to longest. The teacher guides the word building.

🍎 Build words in the following order to help children make connections between spelling patterns:

in, pin/pine, rip, pen, ice, nice, rice/price, cried, price/prince.

🍎 Build *pin/pine, rice/price, price/prince,* discuss the impact of adding phonemes to a word.

🍎 Build *cried,* discuss the impact of adding the suffix *-ed* to *cry.*

🍎 Record the words for the week in a word study notebook.

🍎 Provide a take-home list of the words for study.

Tuesday

🍎 Rebuild each word from Monday. Children build words at their seat, as well as at the pocket chart, and explain their thinking.

🍎 Apply patterns to new words. Use *cried* to make *tried.* Use *prince* to make *princes* and *princess.*

Wednesday

🍎 Show words on large cards. Place in pocket chart as children read each word aloud. Provide a sheet of small word cards. Read each word. Children cut words apart for sorting.

🍎 Invite children to do an open sort, grouping words to show the patterns they see.

🍎 Discuss the categories that emerge from their sort. Have children use the large cards in the pocket chart to show the categories they made and explain their thinking.

🍎 Record results of open sort in word study notebook.

Thursday

🍎 Review the results of the open sort from Wednesday, then ask children to do two closed sorts.

🍎 Sort short vowels versus long vowels. Notice patterns. Discuss differences in vowel sounds and how certain spelling patterns usually signal a long vowel.

short *e*	short *i*	long *i*
pen	in	ice
	pin	rice
	rip	nice
	prince	pine
		cried
		price

- Sort for blend, no blend.

blend	**no blend**
price	*rice*
prince	*nice*
cried	*pine*
	pen
	ice

- Record results of closed sort in word study notebook.

Friday

- Assess children's understanding of spelling patterns. Give a spelling test. Dictate each word (in isolation, in a sentence, then again in isolation).
- Add two application words—use *rip* to make *ripe,* use *ice* to make *slice.*
- Dictation sentence: *The prince got rice and pine nuts for a good price.*

Guided Reading Block

- Same basic procedure as previous weeks.
- During this final week of the unit, independent reading texts are a combination of previous weeks' guided reading texts. Children have at least six related texts in the book box to reread.
- During week 4 the activity centers include:
  - *Library Center*——Displays a collection of unit books, including the versions of *The Frog Prince.*
  - *Science Center*——Houses two aquariums for observation. One set up as a habitat for several small frogs and one for a salamander. Children are encouraged to record observations in a science center log. Add pocket chart activity for putting sentence strips with the stages of the life cycle in order. Make individual copies of a cut-and-paste activity to put the stages of the life cycle in order and illustrate.
  - *Listening Center*——Provides tape-recorded copies of the favorite books of the unit.
  - *Writing Center*——Contains a variety of papers, writing implements, an interesting display of pictures of amphibians, and blank copies of a Venn diagram to compare/contrast versions of *The Frog Prince.*
  - *Computer Center*——Children compose, edit, and print responses to versions of *The Frog Prince* or create own version.

Afternoon Mediated Read-Aloud (Fiction)

Texts

Peach and Blue (Sarah Kilborne, Bantam Doubleday)

The Icky Sticky Frog (Dawn Bentley, Intervisual Books) (*Reread other class favorites as needed.*)

ASSESSMENT: MONITORING CHILDREN'S LEARNING IN A THEMATIC UNIT

The teachers began this unit with a focus on helping children develop and/or improve the skills and strategies necessary to:

- respond to ideas in fiction and poetry,
- improve ability to decode unfamiliar words,
- gather accurate information from texts,
- compare/contrast ideas found in texts,
- read texts fluently and with expression,
- express ideas clearly and accurately through speaking and writing, and
- organize written ideas around a topic.

How well did they accomplish these goals? How can student learning in this unit be documented?

Documenting Student Learning

As we discussed at the end of each of the previous chapters, it is essential that teachers continually monitor student progress. Adjusting our instruction is possible only when we are keenly aware of children's responses to our instructional decisions.

Throughout the unit, the second-grade team-teachers:

- discuss and make notes about what they observe,
- collect and evaluate samples of student work, and
- engage children in self-evaluation of their own progress.

Teacher Observations during the Unit

Shared Reading

- Accuracy of decoding unfamiliar words in texts
- Accuracy of making connections between new words and familiar words and/or spelling patterns
- Fluency and expression when reading text

Mediated Read-Aloud

- Frequency and quality of children's responses to readings and rereadings (accurate details, main ideas, inferences, summarize ideas)
- Types of connections verbalized by children about ideas within and between texts (inferences)
- Accuracy of the vocabulary children use to express their ideas

Shared/Interactive Writing Experiences

- Frequency and quality of children's contributions to group writing experiences

🍎 Accuracy of the vocabulary children use to express their ideas

🍎 Structure of sentences children offer during joint compositions

🍎 Accuracy of spelling patterns and other conventions children use during interactive writing

Guided Writing

🍎 Frequency and nature of children's requests for assistance

🍎 Relationship between children's expressed ideas and what they actually write

Word Study

🍎 Accuracy of children's spelling and sorting

🍎 Confidence displayed in selecting and arranging letters to spell words or sorting words into categories

🍎 Application of spelling patterns to other reading and writing activities

Guided Reading Groups

🍎 Ability to use letter-sound knowledge to make meaning with text

🍎 Quality of comprehension exhibited during discussion of texts (identify details, sequence, and main ideas; make inferences)

🍎 Application of skills and strategies from teaching points to reading of text

🍎 Fluency of reading and rereading

Student Work Produced during the Unit

Guided Writing

🍎 Week 1—Accuracy and organization of ideas expressed about amphibians, sentence structures, spelling of high-frequency words, and capitalization and punctuation

🍎 Week 2—Accuracy and organization of ideas expressed about amphibian vocabulary (word splash) and life cycles, sentence structures, spelling of high-frequency words, and capitalization and punctuation

🍎 Week 3—Writing traits demonstrated in the planning, drafting, and editing of the group report:

  🍎 Ideas/Content—accurate, detailed, supported.

  🍎 Organization—focused on topic, clear beginning/middle/end.

  🍎 Voice—enough knowledge of topic to make writing personal and interesting.

  🍎 Language—appropriate sentence structures and word choice.

  🍎 Conventions—accurate use of punctuation, capitalization, and spelling.

🍎 Week 4—Quality and organization of ideas expressed related to versions of *The Frog Prince* or creation of own version, sentence structures, spelling of high-frequency words, and capitalization and punctuation

Word Study

- 🍎 Accurate spelling of words recorded in word study notebook
- 🍎 Appropriateness of categories in open sort
- 🍎 Accuracy of categories in closed sort
- 🍎 Application to other writing contexts such as the group report

Activity Centers

- 🍎 Accuracy and quality of observations recorded in the science center
- 🍎 Writing traits exhibited in independent writing from writing center and computer center
- 🍎 Quality of ideas expressed in response to books in listening center

Student Self-Evaluations

Have children use simple rubrics to evaluate their participation and/or performance in the following:

Poem of the Week

- 🍎 Accuracy of recitation
- 🍎 Fluency and expression

Guided Literature Study

- 🍎 Participation in discussion

Group Report

- 🍎 Evaluate writing traits
- 🍎 Collaboration with group members to complete the report

Student work and teacher observations provide a bounty of evidence to document student learning throughout the unit. At the end of the unit, representative samples of work are placed in each child's portfolio. Over the course of the school year the portfolio becomes an excellent tool for conferencing with parents/guardians about children's progress, as well as for teachers to demonstrate to their principal the effectiveness of their instruction.

Making Connections . . .

What understandings do you now have about using the various elements of our literacy framework in a balanced and integrated manner? Do you think these four second-grade teachers provide their students with a rich and meaningful learning experience? If so, what stands out for you? This is a good time to compare your understandings of the potential of the elements in our literacy framework with the ways in which the teachers in this chapter utilized each. It is important to remember that orchestrating literacy components in a balanced and effective manner develops slowly over time as you continue to gain a greater understanding of children's literacy development. Record your reflections in your journal. Share your thinking with your peers.

A Concluding Thought . . .

As you look back over your reflections at the end of each chapter in this text, how has your understanding of young children's literacy development grown and changed? What seems to be the most significant change(s) for you? What area(s) may need your greatest attention as you prepare to teach? As you think about setting up a primary-grade classroom that supports young children's literacy development, what will your classroom look like? Sound like? Feel like?

Appendix A

Handbook of Children's Literature

I. Genres of Children's Literature

Lukens (1998) defines genre as a "kind or type of literature in which the members share a common set of characteristics" (p. 13). There are different genres in literature because writing is used for different purposes or intentions. You will encounter the following genres in children's literature:

- contemporary realistic fiction,
- historical fiction,
- fantasy,
- folk literature,
- biography and autobiography,
- informational, and
- poetry.

An author's intention or purpose influences the organization of ideas in particular ways and the selection of words to serve particular purposes. With each genre, you may find similarities and differences in the ways that authors share their ideas, but you will also find that each genre is unique in some way.

Contemporary Realistic Fiction

It is necessary for each of us to learn about our own world. Realistic fiction enables children to explore the reality of their lives and the lives of others. In quality realistic fiction, authors create the following:

- Believable characters who think and act like people who are or could be known to us,
- Contemporary settings that could exist and support the telling of a believable story,
- Plots and themes that reflect contemporary issues, problems, and values, and
- Stories that are appropriate for the audience for whom they are intended.

Realistic fiction is found in both picture book and chapter book forms and should be an essential part of your literature program. Picture storybooks such as *The Wednesday Surprise* (Bunting, 1989) let children explore the role they can have in helping a relative learn to read. As children follow the actions of the characters, they can think about people who care about and help others, do everyday things that we all do to live our lives, and work to solve problems to make their lives more satisfying. All of this is wrapped in a story of usually no more than 32 pages of print and illustrations.

In chapter books, children encounter more complex plot and character development, and continue to explore life situations. The Ramona series, including *Ramona Quimby, Age 8* (1981), by Beverly Cleary, has been a favorite of many schoolchildren. Primary-grade children watch Ramona grow and change through her own primary-grade years. Ramona's feelings and predicaments are often familiar and humorous. Similarly, the story of *Felita* (Mohr, 1989) lets children explore the dilemmas of a young Puerto Rican girl when her family decides to leave their old neighborhood. Both books are chapter books, and children are able to follow Ramona and Felita through 100+ pages of people and events that affect their lives. Chapter books bring contemporary realistic fiction to life for a reader.

Historical Fiction

Historical fiction bears a strong resemblance to contemporary fiction. Both are realistic, differing mainly in the impact of the setting on the telling of the story. When authors move to a time period other than their own, they are obligated to help readers understand how the time of the story affects the characters and the events of the plot. Writers of historical fiction must be true to the period in which they set the story. The characters do not have to be people that actually lived, but they must be realistic.

Historical picture books are available in limited number. One excellent example is *Nettie's Trip South* (Turner, 1987). The setting is the South, during pre–Civil War days. Although Nettie is a fictional character, the life that she lived is in keeping with lives of White children during that time. Through Nettie's letter to her friend Addie, children can explore what it might have been like to be confronted with the realities of slavery. Turner creates a fictional character in Nettie to share actual events from the life of Turner's great-grandmother as told in diary entries from 1859.

Many wonderful pieces of historical fiction are available in chapter book form. However, many will be challenging for the majority of primary-grade readers. One example of historical fiction that is appropriate for the primary grades is *Sarah, Plain and Tall* (MacLachlan, 1985), which tells the story of a mail-order bride from Maine who comes to be mother and wife for a pioneer family living on the plains. Through this family, children can not only experience life in a time when modern conveniences were not available, but may also see that family relationships have always been important.

Fantasy

Fiction that contains elements not found in the natural world is called *fantasy*. Early fantasy comes in the form of picture books, with illustrations that help children develop images of fantasitc people and places. Fantasy helps young children begin to distinguish what is real from what may be imaginary. Fantasy also helps young children think of possibilities beyond their everyday lives. In the picture storybook fantasy *Sylvester and the Magic Pebble* (Steig, 1969), a donkey family and a magic pebble help children explore the theme that love conquers all.

As children advance as readers, fantasy becomes more of an issue of other worlds and times, as in *James and the Giant Peach* (Dahi, 1961). Living in the imaginary world becomes a delight in itself, letting children explore the possibilities of what could be, without needing to distinguish what is "real." Children (and adults) may enjoy the fantasy for its own sake. Description takes the place of illustration, freeing children to create their own images of imaginary characters and worlds.

Quality fantasy rests on the author's ability to create a willing suspension of disbelief—imaginary worlds and characters must seem possible to the reader. In *Charlotte's Web* (1952), E. B. White roots his fantasy in the reality of farm life. He creates characters that seem so believable that the reader accepts animals talking and thinking as if they were human. Though the reader knows that animals cannot actually behave in this way, the behavior is so integral to the story that the fantasy is not questioned.

Folk Literature

For as long as people have lived their lives with others, telling stories has been part of sharing the lessons of life. Folk literature has its roots in the oral storytelling tradition. You are probably quite familiar with this genre of literature from your own background of reading in school. This category includes folktales, fairy tales, fables, tall tales, myths, and legends. Myths and legends, however, are not widely used in primary-grade classrooms because of the frequent maturity of their content.

When storytellers share a story, they often concentrate on the development of the plot, using recognizable characters and settings. Because folk literature comes out of an oral tradition, it often has simple plots, rather stock characters with easily identifiable characteristics, and settings in "long ago" or "far away" times. Such stories usually have strong, clear, and often explicit themes that clearly teach a lesson or moral. Such explicit themes are helpful to young children, who are usually not yet able to judge behavior according to situational conditions.

One of the greatest values of folk literature is the possibility of sharing stories across cultures. For example, Cinderella stories coming to us from different countries let us see commonalities, as well as differences, across cultures. We can see similarities to the Cinderella tale that is familiar to most of us (Perrault, 1981) in such stories as the following:

- 🍎 *Tattercoats* from England (Steele, 1976),
- 🍎 *Mufaro's Beautiful Daughters* from Africa (Steptoe, 1987),
- 🍎 *Moss Gown* from eastern North Carolina (Hooks, 1987), and
- 🍎 *Yen-Shen* from China (Louie, 1982).

Through folk literature, we are able to see that, across other time periods and cultures, life has taught many others the same lessons that we, too, have learned.

Biography and Autobiography

Biography, in which an author tells the story of another person's life, often mixes the accuracy of informational texts with the literary elements of fiction. The writer of biography is obliged to accurately present the facts of a person's life while using an interesting writing style to bring that person to life for the reader. *Autobiography* is a firsthand account of a person's own life, and should be an accurate retelling.

The difficulty for the writer of biography for young children lies in telling stories out of a time period that is unknown to the young reader. To be appropriate and appealing to primary-grade children, authors often present biographies in picture book format with illustrations to support the text. Illustration can fill in information the reader needs to relate to unfamiliar settings and circumstances. David Adler has created a fine series of picture book biographies of famous Americans, such as Martin Luther King, Jr. and John F. Kennedy.

Authors of biographies for developing readers in third and fourth grade must also consider the match between the reader's life and the time period addressed in the biography. Through careful development of setting, character, and plot, biographers should help readers connect to time periods and living conditions that may be dramatically different from what they personally know. A good example is *Sadako and the Thousand Paper Cranes* (Coerr, 1977), the story of a young Japanese girl who survived the bombing of Hiroshima in 1945, but later died as a result of radiation from the bomb.

Autobiographies are more difficult to find for primary-grade children. A new series, called Meet the Author (published by Richard C. Owens), offers autobiographies of children's authors with particular emphasis on aspects of their lives that have influenced their writing. One example is *A Letter from Phoenix Farm* by Jane Yolen (1992).

Informational Books

Children are curious about the world. Informational books offer children opportunities to explore the world through both images and ideas. Quality informational books should have photographs and/or illustrations that accurately depict a topic, such as Aliki's *How a Book Is Made* (1986). Young children should be able to gain content background through close inspection of the illustrations. The text of informational books should be well organized, allowing developing readers to successfully think their way through text as you share it aloud.

Children's first informational books often focus on familiar people, objects, or events. As children become acquainted with books, we want them to see that familiar things can be represented, first through photographs and illustrations and eventually through words. Alphabet, counting, and concept books for young children typically have limited amounts of text. Photographs or illustrations carry a great deal of the "message" of the book. The absence of text encourages interaction between the reader and the illustrations, particularly in early read-aloud experiences. For a good example, examine books by Tana Hoban or Bruce McMillan. These two authors use photography to help children relate to information available in the environment, such as shapes and pairs of things. For excellent infromational books with simple, clear drawings, consider books by Gail Gibbons, Richard Scarry, and Sandra Boynton.

Young children need extensive experiences with quality informational books before you can expect them to read such books independently. Children must learn that the writing in informational books is different from that in other genres. An author's intention for writing an informational book about spiders and how they live is different than an author's intention when retelling a folktale about a spider, such as *Anansi and the Moss-Covered Rock* (Kimmel, 1988), in which Anansi uses his cleverness to outwit much larger animals. Different intentions lead to different styles of writing. Because the writing in informational books is different, children should approach informational books with different expectations than they have for stories. Later in this appendix you will have the opportunity to consider how different genres give us different types of writing.

Poetry

Children and poetry are a natural match. The sensations created by the ways that poets use language appeal to the sensory nature of young children. Watching young children at work and play has probably taught you that children love the sounds and the feel of language. Young children pick up a new word or jingle and repeat it many times to experience the sounds and sensations it produces. Poetic elements such as rhythm, rhyme, and repetition help to make language seem more concrete to young children because they can *feel* it.

Poetry that is appropriate for young children should invite them to become involved in "trying on" language. For young children, poetry should contain familiar objects and experiences, tell stories of the familiar, express familiar feelings, and contain rhythm, rhyme, and repetition. Poetic language for young children should be concrete, using words from children's background experience. Abstract poetry forms such as haiku or cinquain are best saved until children have developed their ability to deal with abstraction.

Children's favorite poets are often humorous ones, such as Jack Prelutsky and Shel Silverstein. Illustrated picture books of poetry such as *Tyrannosaurus Was a Beast* by Jack Prelutsky (1988) not only provide images through language but also through colorful illustrations. Collections of poetry can offer an in-depth exploration of one topic or a wide variety of topics and styles. Silverstein's collection *Where the Sidewalk Ends* (1974) is "credited with bringing more converts to poetry than any other volume" (Cullinan, 1989, p. 347).

Poetry has made its way into emergent-reading instruction through predictable, patterned texts, such as *Brown Bear, Brown Bear, What Do You See?* (Martin, 1983) and *The Napping House* (Wood & Wood, 1984). Developing readers meet poetry in book form through examples such as *Dancing with the Indians* (Medearis, 1991). You will find that the rhythm and rhyme of poetry provide support as children are learning the ins and outs of written language.

II. Narrative Writing: Becoming Aware of Literary Elements

You will often find narrative writing in the picture books and chapter books that primary-grade children will read. This writing is characterized by the use of the following literary elements:

- setting,
- characters,

🍎 plot,

🍎 point of view,

🍎 theme, and

🍎 style.

In this section, we examine the literary elements used in children's literature and consider the importance of each. We will consider both picture and chapter books from the perspective of both literature and reading instruction. We will draw our examples most often from picture storybooks, because they provide excellent samples in a short text.

Setting

One of the first elements that a reader might notice in any text is the author's use of setting. Simply speaking, *setting* helps you develop a sense of time and place, but it is in reality much more. If you consider an author's intention for writing, you will understand setting's potential.

Types of Settings. In some stories, the author focuses on the development of characters, and where the story is taking place seems somewhat unimportant. In such cases, the setting is merely a *backdrop* and you may not pay much attention to it. The author probably intends for you to devote your attention to other elements in the story. The author creates a setting that does not exert much influence on the characters or plot. *The Terrible Thing That Happened at Our House* (Blaine, 1975) provides an example of a backdrop setting. As a reader, you realize where and when the story is taking place, but you also realize that the setting does not influence your attention to the conflict the main character is experiencing.

Functions of Setting. In contrast, the author may choose to use the setting in a more integral way. When settings are integral to the telling of the story, the setting actually plays a part in the story and can serve several different functions. Lukens (1998) writes that authors might use integral settings to (1) affect the mood of the story, (2) show a particular side of a character, (3) act as an antagonist, or (4) symbolize a figurative meaning. To explore these functions of integral settings, we focus on one picture storybook, *The Ghost-Eye Tree* (Martin & Archambault, 1985). In it, we may observe all of the functions of setting.

How setting affects the mood of the story is easy to see in *The Ghost-Eye Tree* because of the power of Ted Rand's illustrations. The placement of the illustrations on the page and the predominance of black and grays give an eerie feel to the story as you begin to read: "One dark and windy autumn night when the sun had long gone down. . . . " The teller of the story, a young boy, continues as we hear, "Oooo . . . . I dreaded to go. . . . I dreaded the tree. . . . " The mood is set. The setting already affects you as reader. You have expectations that the setting will be important to the upcoming events.

Sometimes an author uses a setting to illuminate a character, or show you a side of a character that might not be evident in any other way. You often see this when there is a person-against-nature conflict in a story. As you are introduced to the older sister in *The Ghost-Eye Tree,* you hear her call her younger brother a "fraidy cat," the beginning of a conversation that shows the older sister's impatience with her brother's fear. As they return from fetching a bucket of milk and must pass by the dreaded tree, both children are scared by noises from the tree and run the rest of the way home. The boy discovers that he has lost his hat. The sister, realizing how important the hat is to her brother, returns to the tree to find it. Without the influence of this setting you might not have seen the softer, sympathetic side of the sister.

Settings can also act as an antagonist. Lukens (1998) defines *antagonist* as an opposing force to the *protagonist,* or main character. It is the conflict between the protagonist and antagonist that creates plot in most stories. In *The Ghost-Eye Tree,* the tension in the plot is based on the conflict between the setting and the characters. Without a setting that scared the children, they would likely not have behaved as they did.

Though the setting creates a mood and brings out certain behaviors in the characters, you also realize that it represents more, that it symbolizes a figurative meaning. In *The Ghost-Eye Tree,* the darkness, the wind, and the cloudy sky suggest fear of the unknown. The ghost-eye tree itself, looking like the eye of a terrible monster, symbolizes evil. The reader senses the evil as the illustrations and the text reinforce the young boy's fear.

Characters

Many writers would say that characters are at the heart of their writing. Through the characters' actions and reactions the plot is created. Authors reveal their characters through description and dialogue. Characters come in a variety of types and serve different functions.

Learning about Characters. Readers learn about characters through description and dialogue. As you read an author's description of a character, you learn about the character's physical appearance and actions, possibly the character's thoughts, and, if the author is narrating the story, what the author thinks about the character. Through dialogue, you "listen" to the character's words and also to what others say about the character. It is then your job as the reader to put these pieces of information together to form your own understanding of the character. As you begin to read *The Ghost-Eye Tree,* for example, you immediately meet the main character, a young boy, who will be narrating the story. To learn about the character of this young boy you will need to attend carefully to his words as he tells you about the dark autumn night, his older sister, and the task of getting a bucket of milk for his mother, which will take him by the dreaded ghost-eye tree.

Types of Characters. Characters are described in part by how much the reader knows about them. When an author focuses a story around one or two characters, you often know much about them. Characters about which readers come to know many different aspects are referred to as *round* characters. Main characters are often round, because readers need information about them to buy into the plot. In picture story books that focus mainly on developing the plot or that are drawn from a genre such as folk literature that uses stock characters, you may learn very little about some characters. Such characters are called *flat* characters. Both the sister and brother in *The Ghost-Eye Tree* are round characters; you learn a great deal about them through dialogue and the brother's telling of the story. In contrast, the mother is a flat character; you really don't need to know much about her to understand her role in the story.

Characters can also be described by how much they change during the development of the plot. The events of the plot affect some characters, and you can see how they grow and change as a result of their experiences. Characters that change are referred to as *dynamic* characters. In contrast, some characters show consistent traits throughout a story. These *static* characters can be like the people in your life you depend on to always be a certain way, or like the type of people who remain unchanged by life's events. Depending on the duration of the plot, the author may need both types of characters to tell a believable story. As you follow the brother and sister in *The Ghost-Eye Tree* as they get a bucket of milk, you see two consistent characters: The young boy tries to overcome his fears while the older sister keeps trying to show him that his fear is in his mind. Throughout the episode you see glimpses of softness and caring in the older sister, especially when she goes back to get her brother's hat. You do not see a (dynamic) character change because the duration of the plot, one night, is too short to realistically expect to see change in a person.

Two other types of characters that you are likely to meet in various genres are the stereotyped and the anthropomorphic characters. When authors describe characters as if they represent generalized characteristics of a group rather than as developed individuals, we say the character is *stereotyped*. In folk literature, stereotyped characters such as evil witches are common because one intent of the genre is to teach lessons about life and readers must easily identify character traits. In contrast, you would not want stereotyped characters in realistic fiction because the author should be developing individuals who are unique and believable. Any characters, whether round, flat, or stereotyped, that are animals that act like humans are called *anthropomorphic* characters. This type of character is often found in fantasies when the author wants the reader to suspend disbelief and respond to a world created by the author.

Functions of Characters.　　As part of using characters to create an interesting story, an author can consciously use characters to serve specific purposes. The author will usually develop a main character, referred to as the *protagonist,* who leads or propels the action. To keep the plot moving along, the author will also create an *antogonist,* an opposing force(s) that pushes or challenges the main character. Sometimes (as noted previously) the opposing force is the setting, but most often it is another character.

Characters also serve a third function, that of a *foil.* When the author needs to push the protagonist in a particular direction or cause characters to show a particular side of themselves, but the antagonist cannot serve that purpose, the author will create a character with a limited and short-lived role. This character, a foil, has a specific purpose and will usually disappear after serving that purpose.

Unity between Characters and Actions.　　As you read, you look for consistency between characters and their actions. A well-developed character's actions should fit with what you have learned about that person. How you view the character should suggest possible behaviors that you would expect. This unity of character and action is part of what makes a story believable. If an author wants the reader to invest belief in a character, unity is vitally important, especially in the genres of realistic and historical fiction, fantasy, and biography.

Plot

Plot gives structure to a story. Plot organizes the telling of the story in a chronological fashion. The actions and reactions of the characters create problems and tensions that build toward a resolution.

Types of Plots.   As authors move characters through a series of actions and reactions, two basic types of plots emerge: progressive and episodic. In a *progressive* plot you sense when the author builds the tension between characters and events as the plot develops. *Where the Wild Things Are* (Sendak, 1963) is a good example of a progressive plot in a picture book. You follow Max from his bedroom to the island where he finds the wild things, then back to his bedroom. In a chapter book, a progressive plot usually keeps you involved from chapter to chapter, anticipating what will happen next. *Charlotte's Web* (White, 1952) is an example of a progressive plot in which the author involves you in the trials and tribulations of life, friendship, and death.

In contrast, an *episodic* plot focuses on one life event in a picture book, and seems to begin anew with each new chapter in a chapter book. As a reader, you probably do not feel the same type of tension in the development of an episode. Though you do follow a main character or two, each chapter is usually a new episode in the character's life and is not necessarily linked directly to the previous chapter. *The Ghost-Eye Tree* is a good example of one episode that is developed into a picture storybook. The Little House books by Laura Ingalls Wilder are examples of episodic plots in chapter books, with each chapter beginning a new episode that may or may not be connected to the previous episode/chapter.

Order in Plots.   Probably one of the most noticeable aspects of plot is order. For most stories, it makes sense for an author to tell the story in a *chronological* order. *The Ghost-Eye Tree* is an example of a chronological plot. You have a stronger interest in the feelings of the brother and sister after following their milk-getting adventure that takes them past the dreaded tree. A chronological plot allows you to have time to build a relationship with the author and characters. Sometimes it is easier for an author to "hook" you by beginning the telling of a story after the event has taken place, then reconstructing a portion or all past events for you. Such a *flashback* plot can be seen in *The Day Jimmie's Boa Ate the Wash* (Noble, 1980), where the story opens at home after a school field trip is over, then reconstructs the story a young girl tells her mother about the exciting day. The illustrator, Steven Kellogg, helps to make the flashback understandable to young children by showing the beginning of the retelling in thought bubbles above the heads of the characters. The thought bubbles gradually enlarge to become a full-page display of the flashback.

Action in Plots.   Good stories keep readers or listeners engaged, waiting to find out what happens. The "what happens" is usually tied to the solving of a problem or dilemma that faces a significant character. As you follow the character through the plot, a skillful author builds in just enough action or tension to keep you wanting to see how the character resolves the problem. The author may structure the story using several literacy devices. Tension may build to a breaking point, called the *climax,* as you follow the characters. Some authors may choose to leave you at that exciting point, letting you decide how the problem resolved itself. Such as story is called a *cliff-hanger*. Adults often enjoy this type of participation in a plot, but children can find the lack of closure unsettling. Consequently, you will not find many books for young children written in a cliff-hanger style.

Realistically, most of the events of our lives do not climax, yet are interesting and can help us learn about life. Stories written in this manner have *tension*, but no climax. Exposure to such stories can help children appreciate the drama of their own lives as they watch others live. Realistic fiction is a genre that contains many such stories. *Nettie's Trip South* (Turner, 1987) is an example of a historical story with tension, but no climax. The author's intention was perhaps to help children consider the seriousness of slavery, and perhaps felt this was best accomplished without the added emotion of climactic events. Beverly Cleary's series of chapter books about Ramona also let children consider the realism and humor of life without dramatic conclusions. There is a building of tensions, however, that are a part of everyday life.

Some readers like the exhilaration of a climax, but prefer for the author to show how the characters reacted to the climax. This reaction, usually the conclusion of the story, is called the *resolution*. Authors can resolve a story in two ways: closed and open. A *closed resolution* leaves little doubt in your mind about what followed the climax. Bringing closure can be very comforting for young children who still see life as definitive and want to know "the answer." As a genre, folk literature, which developed out of telling stories about life, provides many good examples of closed resolutions. In *The Paper Crane* (Bang, 1985) for example, the author provides closure with the words, "But neither the stranger nor the dancing crane has ever been seen again." Realistic fiction also provides many good examples of closed resolutions in contemporary settings. *The Ghost-Eye Tree* lets you know how the young boy resolved his fear of having to go by the dreaded tree to get milk for his mother. In *The Terrible Thing That Happened at Our House,* you find out how the family coped with working parents.

In contrast, some authors end with an *open resolution,* leaving some doubt about the outcomes and letting you contribute to the ending. *The Day Jimmie's Boa Ate the Wash* and *Jumanji* (Van Allsburg, 1981) are examples of an open resolution following a climax. In both of these books you are aware of possibilities for future events, but the authors allow you to complete the story. Open resolutions are very effective with older children who are able to use their knowledge of life and story characters to carry on the story.

Conflict in Plots.
Conflicts in our everyday lives influence many of our actions and reactions. You are probably aware of things that you do that are motivated by struggles and desires within yourself, with other people, with your environment, or with the conventions of society. Your life is influenced by the ways that you act and react with the conflicts you encounter. Because narrative tells the stories of people's lives, it naturally centers around the conflicts in which people find themselves. There are at least four types of conflict found in narrative: conflict *with self, with people, with nature,* and *with society.* Without these conflicts, there can be no tension in a plot, because tension could not build to a point that requires a climax to resolve it. Without conflict, what would keep you interested in reading to find out what happens next?

As you read *The Ghost-Eye Tree,* did you sense the conflicts that helped the plot develop? You may see the conflict the boy had with himself, coping with his fear of the tree, and the conflicts he had with his older sister, not wanting her to think he was afraid. You also may see conflicts the children had with the dreaded tree and the spooky effects of wind and darkness. When you recognize these conflicts, you can better understand the actions of the boy and identify with him from times in your life when you experienced similar conflicts. By recognizing the conflicts and associating them with conflicts from your own life, you anticipate what he would do and can better understand his reasons for acting as he did.

The Ghost-Eye Tree shows you conflicts characters have with self, other people, and nature. *Nettie's Trip South* clearly shows you conflict with society. Nettie could not understand how the people of the South could treat slaves as they did. In her letter to her friend, Addie, Nettie expresses her conflict with Southern society's views of slaves.

Point of View

Types of Point of View.
Considering who is telling the story becomes increasingly important as children are able to see things from the perspective of another. Young children see the world through their own eyes and often do not realize that others may see that same world differently. At this stage of development, it may be best to engage children with literature written from an objective perspective, allowing them to see all sides of an issue and not be influenced by the view of a particular individual who may be telling a personal version of the story. Sendak tells *Where the Wild Things Are* (1963) through an *objective narrator,* who seems to be suspended over the characters and setting, with the ability to see and hear all that goes on. The narrator introduces the characters and the setting, then proceeds to retell the dialogue and events as they happen. It is then up to you, the reader, to judge the value or meaning of the characters' actions.

If the narrator had allowed you to know the thoughts of one or more of the characters, in addition to knowing and hearing all that was done and said, the point of view would have been that of a *limited omniscient* narrator. In some plots it is important for you to know what a character, often the main character, is thinking to become more involved with the characters or to better understand a character's motivations.

As a contrast to the narrator's point of view, *The Ghost-Eye Tree* is told from the point of view of the young boy, a *first-person* point of view. You see all of the events of plot through his eyes. He interprets his sister's actions, the mood of the night, the fear of the tree, and his own feelings and actions. Is it possible that his view influences your reactions to the story? When you read a story written from a first-person point of view, it is important to realize that you are seeing one view of the events and that that view is influenced by the teller's feelings. Very young children may not understand the difference between a narrator's view and a single person's view of story events.

Point of view can influence the interpretations that children make about characters and story events. When you share literature with children, you must consider who is telling the story and whether children will be able to detect the influence of point of view on their personal interpretation of character actions and reactions.

Theme

Types of Themes. The themes of stories help us think about important aspects of life: friendships, loyalty, death, courage, cleverness, and so on. In some genres and among certain writers, the theme is rather *explicit*—its point is easy to detect. Folk literature often has explicit themes, especially in fables, which usually state a moral at the end. *Miss Rumphius* (Cooney, 1982) is an example of realistic fiction that provides an explicit theme: Do something to leave the world more beautiful. While very young, Alice Rumphius is told by her grandfather that during her life she must do something to make the world more beautiful. Through all of her travels Miss Rumphius remembers her grandfather's words, and finally discovers something she can do. You hear the theme again at the end of the story when Miss Rumphius tells her niece, "You must do something to make the world more beautiful."

The theme of *The Ghost-Eye Tree* is more of an *implicit* theme—one that you must infer from the characters' actions. As a reader, you make inferences based upon what you think is important about a story, influenced by your experience as a reader and in life. Because inference is involved in interpreting implicit themes, it is possible for different readers to "see" these themes differently.

As you select literature to share with children, you will want to consider the clarity of the theme or themes in a story and the possible interpretations that your students may make based on their experiences as readers and in life. Your expectations for what students will take from a story may be based on their ability to infer about life themes. Explicit themes are most appropriate for very young children, who see the world as either right or wrong. Implicit themes become more appropriate as children are able to understand and see the world from more than one perspective.

Style

For many of us, a writer's style can have a tremendous impact on our response to a story. Writers use language in distinctive ways, ways that can draw us in as readers or push us away. Style is an important element to consider when selecting literature for young children. Reading involves meaning making, which will be difficult for young children who cannot relate to the way that an author is using language.

Sentence Structure and Patterns. One of the first things you may notice about writing is the sentence *structure*. Are sentences complicated and confusing or fairly easy to follow? This is an important consideration when you are selecting literature to share with young children. Book language is more formal than spoken language, and books often introduce young children to sentence structures that they do not hear frequently in the language spoken in familiar surroundings. As you select literature you must consider how familiar your children will be with the sentence structures that a particular author uses.

Consider the sentence structure used by Eric Kimmel to introduce the folktale of *Anansi and the Moss-Covered Rock* (1988): "Once upon a time Anansi the Spider was walking, walking, walking through the forest when something caught his eye. It was a strange moss-covered rock." If you have read much folk literature this is probably a familiar opening to you. The nature of folk literature, drawn from storytelling, brings with it certain uses of language that can affect the structure and pattern of sentences. You would select this folktale to share with children in part on the basis of your children's experience with the language of folk literature.

Authors use words and sentence structures purposefully. For example, in *The Wednesday Surprise* (1989), Eve Bunting lets you know how Anna feels about her Grandmother when she says, "I show Grandma my breath picture, if it's still there. Mostly she knows what it is. Mostly she's the only one who does." In *The Snowy Day* (1962), Ezra Jack Keats arranges his sentences to show the reader something about the meaning of the words. For example, describing what Peter does in the snow, Keats says, "Then he dragged his feet s-l-o-w-l-y to make tracks."

Sentence *patterns,* found more and more frequently in books intended for very young children, provide children with repeated exposure to particular sentence structures. For example, you find the following pattern in *Brown Bear, Brown Bear, What Do You See?* (Martin, 1983):

> *Brown Bear, Brown Bear,*
> *What do you see?*
> *I see a redbird*
> *Looking at me.*

The same pattern continues as each new animal is introduced. Continuing the pattern allows young children time to develop comfort with understanding the structure of the sentences. Though this is a simplistic example of pattern, you can see how predictability in sentence structure could aid a child's understanding.

Uses of Language.

As you consider the maturity and experience that your children have with language, particularly book language, you will also consider the ways in which authors use words. Some authors will use words to help readers make mental images, or comparisons that are more concrete. Some authors will play with language in new and creative ways. Some authors will appeal to your senses through the use of language.

Imagery is the term most frequently used to describe an author's use of words to appeal to your senses. Imagery that reminds you of pleasant memories is likely to draw you in to listen to an author's ideas. You are reminded of childhood treasures when you read about Sylvester finding a pebble that "was flaming red, shiny, and perfectly round, like a marble" (*Sylvester and the Magic Pebble* [Steig, 1969]). Imagery can also be instrumental when an author is trying to help you understand situations in which you may lack firsthand experience. In *Nettie's Trip South,* Nettie struggles to explain in her letter to Addie her reaction to seeing slaves sold at auction: "Someone called out a price and she was gone. Gone, Addie, like a sack of flour pushed across a store counter." In each example, imagery helps the author reach out to you, encouraging you to respond to the sensations that words can evoke.

You may wonder why imagery would be important for young children. You might ask, "Aren't primary-grade children too young to think about imagery?" The children with whom you will share literature are still very sensory in their responses to the world around them. They are curious about their world. If you are aware of an author's use of imagery to appeal to a reader's senses, you will be able to help children use their sensory responses with literature. You will call attention to interesting images as you read aloud. You will emphasize language that appeals to the senses. You will help children use images to build new understandings of the world they know and the world they are learning about each day. Imagery is especially important for primary-grade children.

Figurative language can be thought of as "using words in a nonliteral way, giving them meaning beyond their usual, everyday definitions" (Lukens, 1998, p. 143). For young children, figurative language will also include personification and simile. Other figurative devices, such as metaphor, hyperbole, understatement, allusion, symbol, and puns, will require further maturation and are more appropriate for intermediate and middle school–age students.

Our language is full of multiple meanings and phrases that cannot be interpreted literally. Young children will need experience with language to appreciate an author's use of figurative language. In *The Wednesday Surprise,* Grandma surprises everyone by showing that she has learned how to read. To describe this situation Bunting writes, "Grandma *has the floor.* She . . . gives back the book and *beams all over her face*" (emphasis added). Bunting has used contemporary, yet figurative, language that cannot be interpreted literally. Young children will need experience with figurative language to fully appreciate many stories. Figurative language can also create humorous situations. When Amelia Bedelia, the maid, is asked to draw the drapes, she sits down with crayons and makes a picture of curtains at the window.

Young children who have been read to already have experience with *personification.* Many books for young children use anthropomorphic animal characters, which take on human qualities. Think of the classic tales of childhood—"Goldilocks and the Three Bears," "The Three Little Pigs," and "Little Red Riding Hood." The animals in these classic tales speak as humans, show human feelings, and live human lives. As young children interact with these anthropomorphic, personified characters, it is possible that they will consider the realities of human behavior. Personification accentuates human behavior, calling attention to what might otherwise go unnoticed.

To accentuate the qualities of an object or person, an author may use a comparative relationship between unlike things. This comparison, called a *simile,* usually includes the words *as, like,* or *than* to show the relationship in a directly stated comparison. To accentuate the atmosphere on a plantation in *Nettie's Trip South,* Turner says, "Trees were like old men with tattered gray coats." Trees and old men are certainly unlike things, yet Turner uses this comparison to help you sense what Nettie might have been feeling about the plantation. To emphasize the color of snow in *Owl Moon,* Yolen states that it "was whiter than the milk in a cereal bowl." Similes, which are rather explicit comparisons, are excellent stylistic devices to introduce to young children.

Devices of *sound* appeal to what readers find pleasing, such as onomatopoeia, alliteration, and rhythm. Children's interest in sound is evident in their play, as they chant jingles from television commercials and the like.

You will want to use books that feature *onomatopoeia,* descriptive words that mimic the sounds that people and objects make. In *The Snowy Day,* Peter hears his feet make *crunch, crunch, crunch* sounds as he walks in the snow. The wind *swishes* and *swooshes* around the housetops in *Mirandy and Brother Wind.* Onomatopoeia can make descriptions more concrete for young children.

Alliteration is the repetition of initial consonant sounds to accentuate particular words and phrases. In *Owl Moon,* to set the mood for going owling on a cold winter night, Yolen writes, "Somewhere behind us a train whistle blew, long and low, like a sad, sad song." Do you notice how her repetition of words that begin with *l* and *s* adds to the mood she is trying to create? Alliteration is most effective when read aloud to children so they can appreciate the beauty of the language.

Using words to create *rhythm,* repeating cadences of sounds and syllables, in the phrases and sentences of a story can also appeal to the senses of young children and add to their appreciation of literature. Some rhythms are so obvious that children join the author and chant a particular part of a story. Children cannot resist the rhythm of, "they roared their terrible roars and gnashed their terrible teeth and . . . " in *Where the Wild Things Are.* This portion of the story soon becomes a chant that is often repeated long after the reading is over. A more subtle, yet equally effective, use of rhythm is found in *The Ghost-Eye Tree.* The young narrator asks,

> *Why does Mama always choose me*
> *when the night is so dark*
> *and the mind runs free?*

Rhythm combined with predictable sentence patterns makes excellent literature for emerging readers. The rhythm of language makes language patterns easier to remember for young children as they are learning to read.

As you select literature to share with children, you will want to consider the author's style of using words and anticipate how your students will respond to that particular style. Selecting appropriate literature for young children means more than finding content or plots that will be interesting or that focus on a particular topic. If children cannot relate to an author's style, they may miss much of what a book has to offer.

We have been discussing literary elements that authors use to develop narrative texts. Although this may be the dominant type of writing that children read before school, you will want to provide more balance in your class between narrative and informational writing because informational writing is the writing most used for life purposes.

III. Informational Writing: Becoming Aware of Text Structures

Information is available in many genres. *Bread Bread Bread* (Morris, 1989) and *What Will the Weather Be Like Today?* (Rogers, 1989) offer information embedded in poetic writing. The *Magic School Bus Inside the Human Body* (Cole, 1989) teaches science information through fantasy. Children learn about the act of writing through fiction in *If You Were a Writer* (Nixon, 1988). When compared with other genres, however, informational writing offers contrasting structures for sharing an author's ideas. As informational writers organize their ideas to describe, inform, persuade, respond, or compare, their writing takes on structures that are different from those of narrative writing.

Common Text Structures

Authors use several common structures or organization patterns repeatedly in informational writing (Meyer & Freedle, 1984; Niles, 1974):

- 🍎 comparison,
- 🍎 cause and effect,
- 🍎 description,
- 🍎 problem and solution or question and answer, and
- 🍎 ordered list or sequence.

Narrative writers describe life situations and problems by skillfully using literary elements to develop believable settings, plots, and characters that will touch your emotions and draw you into the story. Informational writers also arrange ideas to serve their purpose(s) for writing. For example, to inform you about the dangers of pollution, an informational writer may identify causes of pollution and inform you about the harmful effects or potential harm for humans and for nature. In contrast, an informational writer whose purpose is to teach you how to determine if water is polluted will need to organize ideas differently, to list the procedures for testing samples of water.

Description. Paragraph A is an example of descriptive writing.

> [A] Life in a high desert town is quite nice. The sky is almost always blue and the sun shines more than 300 days of the year. The air is dry, so that even on hot days your skin does not perspire. The nights are cool, making summer evenings especially pleasant. Winters are mild, with limited snowfall. Snow melts quickly in the valley, but stays on the mountains that surround us to make a very pleasing sight.

In paragraph A, we find out about the characteristics of a desert town. The description does not have to be presented in a particular order for us to have an image of the town. In descriptive writing, there typically are very few clues to tell us how to arrange the ideas in a way that makes sense to us. All of the ideas together relate to the topic, but in no particular order. Descriptive writing requires us, the readers, to link the ideas. We know the topic and the details from the author. We must decide how the ideas are related.

Description can be difficult writing for children because they must establish the relationships among the details and the main idea. If the topic of the writing is unfamiliar, the task of linking ideas is more difficult. Unfortunately, much information writing in school is descriptive writing, in which children must learn to link the ideas.

Ordered List or Sequence. Paragraph B provides an ordered list of directions to follow.

> [B] The best way to see Lake Tahoe for the first time is to go west from Reno on Hwy, 431. As you twist and turn your way up the Mount Rose Highway, you will pass two downhill ski areas and several rustic restaurants. Soon you will pass the mountain summit and begin your descent into the Tahoe Basin. Next you will pass a large open meadow that is excellent for cross-country skiing. Just after you get your first glimpse of Lake Tahoe there will be a scenic overlook on the left side of the road. Stop there for a breathtaking view of the lake.

In paragraph B, we can follow the order of the directions for the best way to get to Lake Tahoe. The author uses language suggesting that there is an order to follow. The directional words help us sense that order, such as "As you twist and turn . . . , Soon you . . . . , Next . . . . , and Just after . . . . " Directions are usually sequences of steps. Ordered lists or sequences are most understandable when they include language related to sequence or time. Without such language, we would need firsthand experience to understand the order.

Comparison.   Paragraph C is an example of comparison text.

> [C] When I am driving in my town, I can always tell what direction I am going by looking at the mountains. On the west side of town the mountains are higher and more rugged looking, and have more trees than the mountains to the east. Two of the mountains on the west stay snow covered most of the year and trees have been cut to make ski runs. The mountains on the east are very dry, brown, and rounded compared to the mountains on the west.

Paragraph C compares and contrasts the mountains on the east and west sides of a city to show how they are used to tell direction. Comparative words help us understand: *higher, more rugged, more tress*. Distinctive features that set each mountain apart are described. Do you see those contrasts? In comparison writing, the author establishes relationships between the objects or ideas being compared.

Cause and Effect.   Paragraph D is an example of text that sets up a cause/effect relationship.

> [D] A desert is considered to be a dry climate, with limited precipitation and low humidity. The result of limited precipitation is often a shortage of water in the hot, dry summer months when trees and grass most need moisture. The low humidity causes moisture to evaporate quickly from skin. The effect of this evaporation is dry, flaky, and sometimes cracking skin.

In paragraph D, the cause-and-effect relationship is evident as the author explains the effects of a dry desert climate. We can infer that the cause is the dry climate, because the effects of that climate are described. The order of the cause and the effects could have been reversed without altering the meaning of the paragraph. The emphasis in this paragraph, however, is on the effects. Sometimes in cause-and-effect writing, the author gives clues by using words such as *cause, effect, result,* or *because*. These clue words help us know which ideas to link together.

Problem and Solution.   In paragraph E a problem and its solution are presented in the same text.

> [E] During the winter months our town has "red" days when the air quality is hazardous to living things. To alleviate this problem, the city council requires that from November to March gas stations must sell a special gasoline that helps to reduce the particles that car exhaust puts into the air. People are also encouraged to car pool. In addition, no burning is allowed on "red" days because the particles in the smoke further contaminate the air.

In paragraph E, by the time that we read the second sentence we are aware of being asked to think about a particular problem and some possible solutions. When we read the phrase, "to alleviate this problem," we might question whether we understand what the problem is and if more than one solution is possible. The author does not explicitly state what the problem is, although we do know the effect of the problem. In addition, we do know about solutions for the problem. Problem/solution and question/answer structures suggest that at least two parts must be understood. As the reader, we need to be sure that we understand what the parts are.

Text Structures in Children's Literature

Let us shift our focus to the actual use of different text structures in informational books used by primary-grade children. In this section, you will consider two informational texts, *Fire Fighters* (Maass, 1989) and *Rain Forest Secrets* (Dorros, 1990), as examples of how authors use text structures in book-length writings.

Fire Fighters beings with a question-and-answer paragraph about what firefighters do. What follows in just the first 10 pages is a mixture of structures:

- 🍎 A descriptive section about what firefighters must learn about hoses,
- 🍎 An ordered list to help the reader understand the procedure firefighters use to get water from hydrants to the fire,
- 🍎 A descriptive section about the tools that firefighters use, and
- 🍎 An ordered list of a firefighter's training.

Each time Maass changes the structure of the writing, you must adjust your thinking as a reader to follow his ideas. This means that in the first 10 pages of *Fire Fighters* you have to change your thinking at least four times. These changes are part of what makes informational writing so challenging for children.

As in *Fire Fighters,* in *Rain Forest Secrets,* Dorros tries to capture your interest in rain forests by first asking a question: "Have you ever been to a rain forest?" He then gives the following descriptions:

- 🍎 a general rain forest environment,
- 🍎 rain forest location,
- 🍎 rainfall,
- 🍎 the Amazon River,
- 🍎 the ecology of the forest floor,
- 🍎 the canopy,
- 🍎 the understory, and
- 🍎 uses of rain forest plants.

The first 23 pages of text consist of detailed description, details about which the reader may lack experience and knowledge.

You will remember that in descriptive writing, the reader generally must link the ideas together. This means that the reader must be able to tell which ideas go together and which do not. Being aware that the structure of this book is predominantly description might lead you to help children learn how to organize the information in the descriptions so they may then use that information. *Rain Forest Secrets* contains information that is important for children to have, but the structure of the writing may make the text inaccessible for many primary-grade children.

In thinking about these two examples, you can see that informational writing will present challenges to you in your teaching of reading and writing. You must consider the structure of the writing and what readers must know to make sense of the author's ideas. Look carefully at how well the author helps readers to do this. Children deserve informational writing that is considerate of their background as readers and that supports them as they try to learn from informational text.

Description, ordered lists or sequences, cause and effect, problem/solution or question/answer, and comparison are the major text structures that you will encounter in informational books for young children. Spend some time with your favorite informational books to identify their structures. Try to become aware of how you detect and use the different informational writing structures in learning.

Children's Literature

Adler, D. (1989). *A picture book of Martin Luther King, Jr.* New York: Holiday House.

Aliki. (1982). *We are best friends.* New York: Greenwillow Books.

Aliki (1986). *How a book is made.* New York: Cromwell.

Bang, M. (1983). *Ten, nine, eight.* New York: Crowell.

Bang, M. (1985). *The paper crane.* New York: Greenwillow Books.

Bayer, J. (1984). *A my name is Alice.* New York: Dial.

Blaine, M. (1975). *The terrible thing that happened at our house.* New York: Scholastic.

Blume, J. (1974). *The pain and the great one.* New York: Dell.

Blume, J. (1981). *The one in the middle is a green kangaroo,* New York: Dell.

Brett, J. (1989). *The mitten.* New York: Scholastic.

Bulla, C. R. (1955). *The poppy seeds.* New York: Penguin.

Bunting, E. (1989). *The Wednesday surprise.* New York: Clarion.

Byars, B. (1988). *Beans on the roof.* New York: Bantam Doubleday.

Carle, E. (1969). *The very hungry caterpillar.* New York: Scholastic.

Carle, E. (1971). *Do you want to be my friend?* New York: Crowell-Collier.

Charles, O. (1988). *How is a crayon made?* New York: Simon Schuster.

Cleary, B. (1981). *Ramona Quimby, age 8.* New York: Dell.

Coerr, E. (1977). *Sadako and the thousand paper cranes.* New York: Putnam.

Cole, J. (1989). *The magic school bus inside the human body.* New York: Scholastic.

Conrad, P. (1988). *Staying nine.* New York: HarperCollins.

Cooney, B. (1982). *Miss Rumphius.* New York: Scholastic.

Crews, D. (1978). *Fright train.* New York: William Morrow & Company.

Dahl, R. (1961). *James and the giant peach.* New York: Knopf.

dePaola, T. (1979). *Oliver Button is a sissy.* New York: Harcourt Brace Jovanovich.

dePaola, T. (1981). *Now one foot, now the other.* New York: Putnam.

Dorros, A. (1990). *Rain forest secrets.* New York: Scholastic.

Fox, M. (1986). *Hattie and the fox.* New York: Bradbury Press.

Galdone, P. (1973). *The little red hen.* New York: Clarion.

Gardiner, J. R. (1980). *Stone fox.* New York: Harper & Row.

Gibbons, G. (1987). *Trains.* New York: Holiday House.

Gibbons, G. (1990). *Weather words and what they mean.* New York: Holiday House.

Ginsburg, M. (1972). *The chick and the duckling.* New York: Macmillan.

Hoffman, M., & Binch, C. (1991). *Amazing Grace.* New York: Dial Books.

Hooks, W. (1987). *Moss gown.* New York: Clarion.

Hutchins, P. (1968). *Rosie's walk.* New York: Simon & Schuster.

Keats, E. J. (1962). *The snowy day.* New York: Viking Press.

Kimmel, E. (1988). *Anansi and the moss-covered rock.* New York: Scholastic.

Lear, E. (1983). *An Edward Lear alphabet.* New York: Mulberry Books.

Lobel, A. (1981). *On Market Street.* New York: Greenwillow.

Louie, A. (1982). *Yen-Shen: A Cinderella story from China.* New York: Philomel.

Maass, R. (1989). *Fire fighters.* New York: Scholastic.

MacLachlan, P. (1985). *Sarah, plain and tall.* New York: Harper & Row.

Martin, B. (1983). *Brown bear, brown bear, what do you see?* New York: Henry Holt and Company.

Martin, B., & Archambault, J. (1989). *Chicka chicka boom boom.* New York: Holt, Rinehart & Winston.

Martin, B., & Archambault, J. (1985). *The ghost-eye tree.* New York: Scholastic.

McKissack, P. (1988). *Mirandy and brother wind.* New York: Alfred A. Knopf.

Medearis, A. S. (1991). *Dancing with the Indians.* New York: Scholastic.

Mohr, N. (1989). *Felita.* New York: Bantam Skylark.

Morris, A. (1989). *Bread, bread, bread.* New York: Lathrop, Lee, & Shepard.

Nixon, J. L. (1988). *If you were a writer.* New York: Simon & Schuster.

Noble, T. H. (1980). *The day Jimmie's boa ate the wash.* New York: Dial.

Pallotta, J. (1986). *The icky bug alphabet book.* New York: Trumpet.

Perrault, C. (1981). *Cinderella.* Illustrated by Marcia Brown. New York: Simon & Schuster.

Prelutsky, J. (1988). *Tyrannosaurus was a beast.* New York: Greenwillow.

Rees, M. (1988). *Ten in a bed.* Boston, MA: Little Brown.

Rogers, P. (1989). *What will the weather be like today?* New York: Scholastic.

Scott, A. H. (1990). *One good cow: A cowpuncher's counting book.* New York: Greenwillow.

Sendak, M. (1963). *Where the wild things are.* New York: Harper & Row.

Shaw, C. G. (1947). *It looked like spilt milk.* New York: Harper & Row.

Silverstein, S. (1974). *Where the sidewalk ends.* New York: Harper & Row.

Slepian, J., & Seidler, A. (1967). *The hungry thing.* New York: Scholastic.

Slepian, J., & Seidler, A. (1990). *The hungry thing returns.* New York: Scholastic.

Smith, R. K. (1972). *Chocolate fever.* New York: Dell Publishing.

Steele, F. A. (1976). *Tattercoats: An old English tale.* New York: Bradbury.

Steig, W. (1969). *Sylvester and the magic pebble.* New York: Simon & Schuster, Inc.

Steptoe, J. (1987). *Mufaro's beautiful daughters.* New York: Scholastic.

Talanda, S. (1983). *Dad told me not to.* Milwaukee, WI: Raintree.

Turner, A. (1987). *Nettie's trip South.* New York: Scholastic.

Van Allsburg, C. (1981). *Jumanji.* New York: Scholastic.

White, E. B. (1952). *Charlotte's web.* New York: Harper & Row.

Wells, R. (1985). *Hazel's amazing mother.* New York: Trumpet.

Williams, V. B. (1982). *A chair for my mother.* New York: Greenwillow.

Wood, A., & Wood, D. (1984). *The napping house.* San Diego, CA: Harcourt Brace Jovanovich.

Yolen, J. (1972). *The girl who loved the wind.* New York: Crowell.

Yolen, J. (1987a). *Owl moon.* New York: Scholastic.

Yolen, J. (1987b). *The Three Bears rhyme book.* San Diego: Hardcourt Brace Jovanovich.

Yolen, J. (1992). *A letter from Phoenix Farm.* Katonah, NY: Richard C. Owens.

References

Cullinan, B. (1989). *Literature and the child.* San Diego, CA: Hardcourt Brace Jovanovich.

Gonzalez, R. D. (1990). When minority becomes majority: The changing face of English classrooms. *English Journal, 79,* 16–23.

Lukens, R. (1990). *A critical handbook of children's literature.* Glenview, IL: Scott, Foresman.

Martinez, M., & Nash, M. F. (1990). Bookalogues: Talking about children's literature. *Language Arts, 67,* 599–606.

Meyer, B. J., & Freedle, R. O. (1984). Effects of discourse type on recall. *American Educational Research Journal, 21,* 121–143.

Morrow, L. (1989). *Literacy developement in the early years.* Englewood Cliffs, NJ: Prentice Hall.

Niles, O. S. (1974). Organization perceived. In H. L. Herber (Ed.), *Perspectives in reading: Developing study skills in secondary schools* (pp. 57–76). Newark, DE: International Reading Association.

Rasinski, T., & Padak, N. D. (1990). Multicultural learning through children's literature. *Lanuage Arts, 67,* 576–580.

Reimer, K. M. (1992). Multiethnic literature: Holding fast to dreams. *Language Arts, 69,* 14–21.

Sims, R. (1983). What has happened to the "all White" world of children's books? *Phi Delta Kappa, 64,* 650–653.

Sulzby, E. (1995). Children's emergent reading of favorite storybooks. *Reading Research Quarterly, 20,* 458–481.

Appendix B

Sample Word Lists and Word Sorts

The word lists and sorts that follow are appropriate examples for developing and transitional readers and writers. The words are drawn from high-frequency word lists and current basal reading series. Before sorting words, children should be able to segment a specific phonetic element through picture sorts. Word sorts should contain words that are sight words and that appear frequently in independent and instructional reading materials.

Word Lists and Sorting for Phonic Patterns

Children in the developing stage refine their knowledge of single consonants, developed in the emergent stage through picture sorting, as they add new knowledge about short vowels and consonant teams. Transitional readers and writers continue to develop their phonics knowledge, but typically in multisyllable words.

Notice that in the suggested sequence for word sorts, short vowels. consonant blends/clusters, and consonant digraphs are mixed to provide a constant review of basic phonic elements.

Suggested Sequence for Word Study—Short Vowels, Consonant Blends, and Digraphs

short *a*	not short *a*				
short *i*	not short *i*				
short *a*	short *i*	neither			
l blend	not *l* blend				
bl	*cl*	*fl*	*gl*	*pl*	*sl*
sh (initial)	*sh* (final)	neither			
short *o*	not short *o*				
short *a*	short *i*	short *o*	none		
r blends	not *r* blends				
br	*cr*	*dr*	*fr*	*gr*	*pr*	*tr*
ch	*sh*	neither			
short *u*	not short *u*				

short *o*	short *u*	neither				
s blands	not *s* blends					
sk	*sn*	*sp*	*st*	*sw*	*scr*	*spl*
th (voiced)	*th* (voiceless)	neither				

Note: Words are selected so that the focus of the sort is the only new phonetic element in the word. Words chosen for the crazy (discard) pile are always sight words or known words from previous sorts.

Sample Word Sorts *(in suggested sequence)*

short *a* (only single consonants)

had	ham	at
bad	jam	cat
mad	am	sat
sad	map	hat
rag	nap	an
bag	cap	can
tag	man	ran

not short *a* (sight words)

the	is
to	me
I	be
go	in
my	you

short *i* (only single consonants)

did	dip	hit
pin	tip	kit
in	zip	fit
sit	big	if
it	dig	six

not short *i* (sight words/short *a*)

I	tan
go	zap
the	pad
me	bag
to	ax

short *o* (only single consonants)

not	on	pop
got	box	hop
pot	fox	top
hot	job	log
lot	dog	mom

not short *o* (sight words/short *a*/*i*)

hip	was
lap	am
sip	did
six	rag

l blend (only short *a* and *i*)

clap	glad
clip	plan
flip	slap
flag	slam
flat	slip

not *l* blend

lap	fat
lip	pan
can	sip
tag	pig

same *l* blend

bl	*cl*	*fl*	*gl*	*pl*	*sl*
black	clap	flag	glad	plan	slam
	clip	flat			slap
		flip			slip

initial *sh*	final *sh*	neither
ship	wish	and
shin	fish	of
she	dish	flip
shot	dash	
shop	flash	

r blend		not *r* blend
brag	drop	bag
brat	drag	plan
crab	frog	shop
crop	grin	have
drip	trip	was
trap	prop	pop

same *r* blend

br	*cr*	*dr*	*fr*	*gr*	*pr*	*tr*
brag	crab	drag	frog	grin	prop	trip
brat	crop	drip	trap			trap
		drop				

ch		*sh*		neither
chop	rich	shin	fish	crab
chat	much	she	flash	grin
chip	such	ship		glad
chin				slip

short *u*			not short *u*	
but	fun	rug	chop	hat
cut	run	bug	frog	cab
up	sun	us	stop	drag
cup	bun	bus		
rub	tub	mud		

short *e*			not short *e*	
get	bed	jet	fun	glad
let	red	met	she	big
yet	hen	leg	mud	ship
pet	men	beg		
set	ten	yes		

s blend		not *s* blend	
scrub	spot	bus	yes
skin	spit	sun	chat
skip	splash	men	frog
snap	stop		
spin	step		
split	swim		

same *s* blend

sk	*sn*	*sp*	*st*	*sw*	*scr*	*spl*
skin	snap	spin	stop	swim	scrub	splash
skip		spot	step			split
						spit

th (voiced)		*th* (voiceless)	neither
then	the	thin	chin
them	that	bath	chat
this	three	both	shin
than		with	are

Suggested Sequence for Word Study—Adding Single Long Vowels

long *a_e*	short *a*		
long *i_e*	short *i*		
long *a_e*	long *i_e*	neither	
long *o_e*	short *o*		
long *o_e*	long *a_e*	long *i_e*	none
long *u_e*	short *u*		
long *e*	short *e*		
long *u_e*	long *e*	neither	

Sample Word Sorts (in suggested sequence)

long *a_e*			**short *a***	
name	tape	plate	mad	bath
same	shape	plane	at	snap
game	make	grade	plan	that
gave	lake	brave	jam	tap
late	case	made		
gate	chase	skate		

long *i_e*		**short *i***	
I	bike	big	if
time	slide	six	slid
wife	smile	drip	rid
five	nine		
like	ride		

long *a_e*	**long *i_e***	**neither**
game	nine	had
skate	smile	lip
plane	time	six
lake	five	bag
chase	bike	

long *o_e*		short *o*	
so	pole	not	
no	bone	stop	
go	stone	mom	
rope	joke	hop	
home	broke	dot	
note	stove	frog	

long *o_e*	long *a_e*	long *i_e*	none
no	gate	wife	do
joke	shape	ride	him
stove	made	hike	ham
home	name		
bone			

long *u_e*		short *u*
cute	tube	plug
cube	June	cup
mule	rude	bus
rule	flute	drum
tune		sun

long *e*		short *e*
he	tree	them
we	sweet	then
me	free	yes
be	see	red
she	feet	step

long *u*	long *e*	neither
cube	tree	but
flute	she	sun
rule	feet	red
June	green	
me		

Suggested Sequence for Word Study—Adding Variant Consonants, Variant Vowels, and Silent Letters

final double consonant		not double consonant	
single and double consonants (same sound)			
hard *c/g*	soft *c/g*		
final *s* as *z*	*s* as *s*		
ar	short *a*	neither	
or/ore	short *o*	neither	
er/ir/ur	short *e*	short *i*	short *u*
ai/ay	*a_e*	short *a*	
oa	*o_e*	short *o*	
igh/ight	*i_e*	short *i*	
ea (long *e*)	*ea* (short *e*)	*ea* (long *a*)	short *e*

silent consonant digraph		no silent consonant digraph	
final consonant blend		no final blend	

oo (long)	*oo* (short)	long *o*	short *o*
ow (*ow*)	*ow* (long *o*)	short *o*	
au/aw	long *a*	short *a*	
oi/oy	long *o*	short *o*	
ou (*ow*)	(long *oo*)	(short *oo*)	(long *o*) (short *u*) (*au*)
ui/ue/ew/u_e		short *u*	

are/air	*ar*	neither	
ear/eer/ere (*eer*)	*ear* (*er*)	*ear* (*air*)	*ear* (*ar*)
ire	*ir*	neither	
ure	*ur*	neither	

long *a* (*a_e, ai, ay, ea, ei, ey*)	short *a*
long *e* (*e, ee, ea, ie, ey*)	short *e*
long *i* (*i_e, y, ie, igh*)	short *i*

Sample Word Sorts *(in suggested sequence)*

double consonant			**not double consonant**	
will	dress	mess	sled	if
all	off	class	leg	pal
small	sniff	add	bus	is
well	egg	buzz		

final *l/ll*	**final *s/ss***	**final *f/ff***	**final *g/gg***	**final *d/dd***
will	bus	off	leg	mad
pal	dress	if	egg	slid
small	class	sniff	bag	add
well	yes			odd
pill				
doll				

	soft *c/g*	**hard *c/g***
face	mice	cat
place	cage	cape
race	age	bag
nice	stage	frog
ice	huge	game

initial *s/s/*	**final *s/s/***		**final *s/z/***	
said	dress	yes	his	has
sing	glass	us	as	nose
six	kiss	bus	wise	use
sun			these	was

ar		**short *a***	**neither**
car	barn	ran	run
star	arm	jam	frog
jar	far	fan	game
farm	mark	flag	
sharp		bath	

or/ore	**short *o***	**neither**
for	on	rob
more	pot	rope
store	stop	crab
or	frog	
chore		
fork		

er/ir/ur		**short *e***	**short *i***	**short *u***
her	first	hen	did	fun
bird	dirt	bed	slip	bud
girl	stir	step		gun
fur	burn			

ai/ay		*a_e*	**short *a***
train	tray	gate	pat
rain	may	game	ran
stain	play	made	clap
mail	say	shake	plan
pail	day	shave	
wait	way		

oa		*o_e*	**short *o***
boat	road	joke	drop
coat	toad	rope	spot
float	loaf	stove	dog
goat	goal	home	
soap	toast		

igh/ight		*i_e*	**short *i***
sigh	tight	five	big
high	might	smile	him
right	sight	nine	sit
light	flight	kite	grin
fight	night		clip

ea (long *a*)	*ea* (short *e*)	*ea* (long *a*)	short *e*
clean	spread	great	step
team	dead	break	red
beat	head	steak	then
sea	deaf		
teach	bread		
please			
each			
meat			

silent consonant digraph

			no silent digraph
write	white	lamb	ride
wrote	witch	comb	way
know	catch	fudge	no
knife	wheel	bridge	grin
knit	match	sign	make
ghost	whale	half	with
who	black	calf	
when	trick	duck	

same silent digraphs (initial)

wr(w)	*kn*(k)	*gh*(g)	*wh*(w)	*wh*(h)
write	know	ghost	when	who
wrote	knife	ghost	white	
	knit		whale	
			wheel	

same silent digraphs (final)

ck(k)	*mb*(m)	*gn*(n)	*lf*(f)	*tch*(ch)	*dge*(j)
duck	comb	sign	calf	match	fudge
trick	lamb	reign	half	witch	bridge
black				catch	

final blend (short vowel)

			not final blend	
belt	next	fast	mat	hike
milk	left	must	hid	had
help	pink	ask	cap	let
and	think	plant		
hand	bank	thank		

final blend (long vowel)

		not final blend	
old	kind	odd	that
cold	wild	fin	thin
told	child	kid	pin
find			

oo (long)		**oo (short)**		**long o**	**short o**
boot	tool	foot	good	stone	hop
soon	cool	look	wood	robe	not
boom	shoot	book	hook	road	got
moon	tooth	took		goat	
hoop	broom				

ow (ow)		**ow (long o)**		**short o**
cow	down	row	throw	hot
now	crown	bow	slow	box
bow	brown	know	show	sock
how	plow	grow	flow	

au/aw		**long a**	**short a**
haul	jaw	lake	snap
law	crawl	day	chat
draw	dawn	clay	match
paw	saw	rain	
saw		snail	

oi/oy		**long o**	**short o**
oil	toy	bone	on
coin	boy	road	not
boil	joy	rope	box
noise		stove	job
join		boat	stop

ou(ow)	**(long oo)**	**(short oo)**	**(long o)**	**(short u)**	**(au)**
out	you	would	though	tough	ought
cloud	through	could	soul	rough	fought
mouse	soup	should		young	bought
sound	group				
shout					
bounce					
round					
couch					
mouth					

ue/ui	**ew/u_e**	**short u**
blue	flute	bug
true	tube	sun
suit	use	club
fruit	stew	crush
juice	blew	

are/air		*ar*		**neither**
care	stairs	far	mark	game
rare	chair	car	cart	can
share	pair	barn	dark	glad
scare	fair	start		flake

ear/eer/ere (eer)		*ear* (er)	*ear* (air)	*ear* (ar)
ear	here	earth	bear	heart
dear	deer	learn	pear	
fear	clear	earn	wear	
near	year			

ire	*ir*	**neither**
fire	dirt	bike
wire	girl	hide
tire	first	fit
hire	third	clip

ure	*ur*	**neither**
pure	fur	cute
sure	burn	suit
cure	turn	fun
	nurse	

a_e, ai, ay, ea, ei, ey (long *a*)		**short *a***
cape	they	sand
shake	eight	rag
mail	rein	clap
rain	great	that
stay	break	chat
play	steak	

e, ee, ea, ie, ey (long *e*)		**short *e***
she	key	step
need	field	net
sheep	chief	egg
sweet	dream	when
each	treat	left

i_e, y, ie, igh (long *i*)		**short *i***
five	light	will
smile	high	stick
pipe	knight	fish
drive	tie	which
fly	lie	hip
try	pie	with
sky		

o_e, oa, ou, ow (long o)

		short o
bone	home	rock
boat	float	plop
soap	toast	box
joke	know	spot
stove	show	frog
though	grow	

Word Lists and Sorts for Structural Patterns

Suggested Sequence of Word Sorts—Structural Units:

compound word	not a compound	
compound—literal	compound—implied	
contraction	not a contraction	
contractions by families		
inflected ending	no inflected ending	
e drop	no e drop	
consonant double	no consonant double	
ends with y	y changes to i	y does not change
independent prefix	no independent prefix	
same prefix		
derivational suffix	no derivational suffix	
dependent prefix	no dependent prefix	

Sample Word Sorts (in suggested sequence)

compound word		**not a compound word**
bedroom	snowman	room
goldfish	baseball	dog
houseboat	daydream	house
doghouse	playground	ground
armchair	wheelchair	chair

compound—literal meaning		**compound—implied meaning**	
bedroom	cheerleader	starfish	runaway
doghouse	salesperson	butterfly	breakfast
wheelchair	shipyard	homesick	fallout
daytime	eyesight	software	everywhere
weekend	newscast	overdrawn	

contraction		**not a contraction**	
can't	you'll	can	have
didn't	haven't	did	her
you're	we've	you	I
we'll	he's	not	will
I'm			

contractions by families

not		are	will	is	have
aren't	shouldn't	you're	I'll	he's	I've
can't	couldn't	we're	you'll	she's	you've
didn't	wouldn't	they're	we'll	it's	we've
don't	hadn't	they'll	I'm		they've
won't	haven't				

inflected suffix

dogs	smartest
horses	taller
dishes	barking
hits	washed
writes	jumped

no inflected suffix

dog	smart
horse	tall
dish	bark
hit	wash
write	jump

e drop

raked	making
baking	liking
nicer	smiling
hoping	using

no *e* drop

jumped
washed
thinking
sleeping
playing

consonant double

hitting	rubbed
runner	chopped
hottest	hopping
stopping	bigger

no consonant double

thinking
watching
shorter
tallest
smartest

ends with *y*

baby	ugly
fly	puppy
pretty	cry
try	candy

y changes to *i*

babies	tried
candies	flies
prettiest	uglier
cried	puppies

y does not change

flying
trying
crying

independent prefix

untie	forget
preview	forgive
reuse	unload
prepay	unkind
repay	undo
recall	

no independent prefix

tie	get
view	load
use	give
pay	kind
call	do

same prefix (meaning)

un	re	pre	for
untie	reuse	preview	forgive
unkind	review	prepay	forget
unload	repay		
undo	recall		

derivational suffix		no derivational suffix	
careful	helpful	care	help
slowly	wisely	slow	wise
sleepy	waiter	sleep	kind
cloudy	really	cloud	real
painless	kindness	pain	wait
friendly		friend	

dependent prefix		no dependent prefix	
insist	recognize	unload	disagree
inspire	proposal	repay	recall
infection	reluctant	unkind	reappear
assure	disturb	preview	incorrect
embarrass	relieve		

Word Lists and Sorts for Syllabication Generalizations

Suggested Sequence for Word Study: Integrating Phonics and Structure

structural word	phonetic word	
base + base	prefix + base	base + suffix
VC/CV (same letters)	VC/CV (different letters)	
V/CV	VC/V	
VC/CV	V/CV VC/V	C+le

Sample Word Sorts (in suggested sequence)

structural word		phonetic word	
floating	starlight	towel	family
thirsty	friendly	river	butter
winner	dresses	bubble	early
carefully	repay	giant	squirrel
we're	driver	dollar	buffalo
untie			

base + base	prefix + base	base + suffix
starfish	untie	swimming
didn't	prepay	horses
I'll	recall	washed
daydream	forgive	careful
you're	unkind	slowly
houseboat		kindness
weekend		

VC/CV (same letters)

kitten	dollar
summer	hammer
rabbit	lesson
pillow	yellow
little	pretty

VC/CV (different letters)

picnic	signal
pencil	person
garden	monkey
circus	winter
doctor	

V/CV

cider	open
pilot	secret
later	student
water	apart
music	father

VC/V

river	rocket
second	linen
clever	lizard
sugar	pocket
ticket	radish

VC/CV — V/CV — VC/V — C+le

VC/CV	V/CV	VC/V	C+le
after	recess	brother	purple
balloon	cement	cousin	eagle
basket	diner	never	fable
carrot	equal	travel	fiddle
chimney	hotel	visit	pebble
dinner	music	lizard	turtle
harvest	open	pocket	candle
hungry		river	cycle

Appendix C

Pictures for Sorting Activities

Suggested Sequence for Word Study and Picture Sorting: Initial Consonants

b	not *b*			
f	not *f*			
b	*f*	neither		
m	not *m*			
b	*f*	*m*	none	
s	not *s*			
t	not *t*			
s	*t*	neither		
d	not *d*			
s	*t*	*d*	none	
l	not *l*			
s	*t*	*d*	*l*	none
n	not *n*			
l	*n*	neither		
r	not *r*			
l	*n*	*r*	none	
p	not *p*			
n	*l*	*r*	*p*	none
j	not *j*			
k	not *k*			
j	*k*	neither		
v	not *v*			
j	*k*	*v*	none	
z	not *z*			
j	*k*	*v*	*z*	none
h	not *h*			
w	not *w*			
h	*w*	neither		
y	not *y*			
h	*w*	*y*	none	

Suggested Sequence for Word Study and Picture Sorts: Final Consonants

final *d*	not final *d*	
initial *d*	final *d*	neither
final *g*	not final *g*	
initial *g*	final *g*	neither
final *d*	final *g*	neither
final *b*	not final *b*	
initial *b*	final *b*	neither
final *t*	not final *t*	
initial *t*	final *t*	neither
final *b*	final *t*	neither
final *n*	not final *n*	
initial *n*	final *n*	neither
final *p*	not final *p*	
initial *p*	final *p*	neither
final *n*	final *p*	neither
final *m*	not final *m*	
initial *m*	final *m*	neither
final *r*	not final *r*	
initial *r*	final *r*	neither
final *m*	final *r*	neither

initial b		initial c (hard)	

bell	bird	cat	cake
box	barn	car	comb
bus	bat	cup	camel
ball	book	can	coat
bed	boat	candle	cap

522

initial d		initial f	
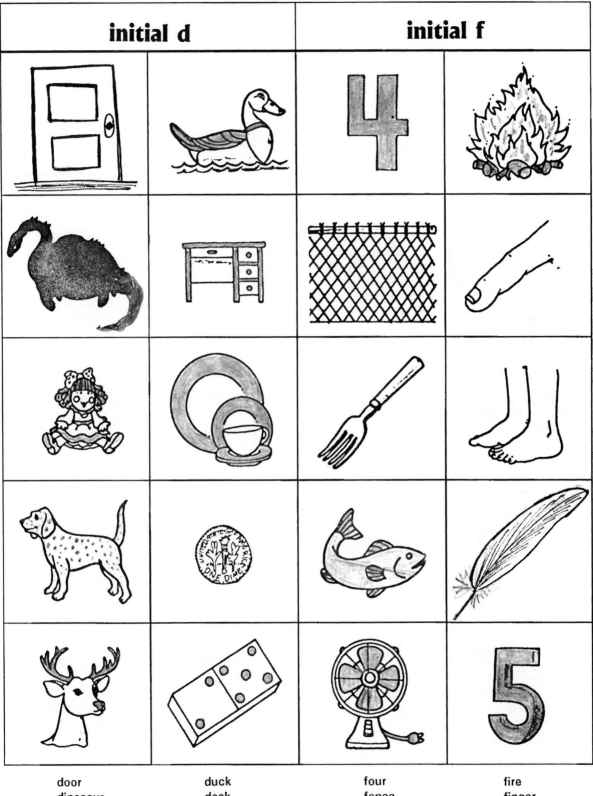			

door   duck   four   fire
dinosaur   desk   fence   finger
doll   dishes   fork   feet
dog   dime   fish   feather
deer   domino   fan   five

523

initial g (hard)		initial h	

ghost	gum	hamburger	hanger
goat	gorilla	heart	hair
girl	gate	hammer	hat
garden	gun	hook	horse
game	goose	hand	hose

initial j		initial k	

jar	jack-o-lantern	ketchup	kitten
jet	jacket	kangaroo	kettle
jacks	jack-in-the-box	king	kitchen
jeep	jug	key	kite
jam	jumprope	kick	kiss

525

initial l	initial m

lion	ladder	money	mop
lock	lemon	mail	mouse
lightbulb	legs	monkey	mailbox
leaf	lamp	map	man
lizard	lawn mower	mitten	matches

526

initial n		initial p	

newspaper	nose
nail	nuts
nest	net
nickel	needle
nine	night

pin	pan
pencil	pie
pig	purse
pear	pitcher
pillow	paper

527

initial q		initial r	

question mark   queen   rug   ring
quarter   quilt   rabbit   rake
quack   rain   radio
                                     rat   rooster
                                     rocket   road

initial s		initial t	

sandbox	saw	two	tent
suit	sun	turtle	table
sandwich	seven	telephone	television
six	sink	tire	toaster
soap	sock	top	ten

529

initial w		initial v	

whale	watch	vacuum	vase
web	window	vine	valentine
well	watermelon	violin	veterinarian (vet)
windmill	witch	vegetables	vest
wagon	worm	volcano	van

initial y		initial z	
color			

yolk	yawn	zero	zebra
yoyo	yarn	zipper	zoo
yard	yell	zigzag	
yellow			

final b		final d	

tub   bulb   bread   bird
crib   cab   bed   sled
scrub   web   red   lid
bib   tube   hand   lizard
globe   road   record

final f		final g	

leaf	wolf	bug	leg
scarf	knife	egg	frog
giraffe	roof	pig	tag
cuff	chef	bag	dog
		rug	log

533

final k	final l

duck	fork	well	kettle
rake	rock	mail	camel
sink	lake	ball	turtle
hook	book	shell	hill
cake	lock	bell	doll

final m		final n	

jam	arm	ten	pan
broom	steam	lion	fan
gum	thumb	wagon	pin
drum	swim	seven	man
ham		sun	mitten

535

final p		final r	

mop	top	door	hammer
cap	map	bear	four
sleep	jeep	pear	deer
clap	stamp	jar	car
cup	rope	hair	

final s		final t	

horse	vase	boat	bat
goose	house	goat	cat
glass	dress	suit	heart
lips	mouse	foot	mat
bus		net	hat

537

final v		final x	

glove	cave	box	six
five	wave	fox	wax
shave	twelve	ax	ox
dive		mix	

538

bl	cl	fl	gl

block	clown	fly	glasses
blind	cloud	flowers	glove
blanket	club	flashlight	globe
blouse	clock	flag	glue
blade	clam	flute	glass

pl	sl	br	cr

plate   slide   broom   crayon
pliers   slippers   bread   crack
plane   sled   brush   cry
plug   slingshot   bride   crab
plant   sling   bridge   crib

dr	fr	gr	pr

dr	fr	gr	pr
dress	frame	grasshopper	present
drawer	frog	grin	pretzel
dragon	fruit	groceries	prince
drum	freckles	grapes	prize
drive	fry	green	press

541

tr	sc/sk	sm	sn

tr	sc/sk	sm	sn
track	skis	smile	snake
truck	scout	smoke	snail
tree	skull	smell	snowman
train	skate		
triangle	skunk		

sp	st	sw	scr

sp	st	sw	scr
spill	stamp	sweater	screw
spoon	stove	swing	scrub
spear	store	swim	screen
spider	star	switch	scroll
space	stairs	sweep	

spr	str	initial sh	final sh

spr	str	initial sh	final sh
sprinkler	straw	shell	dish
spring	street	ship	brush
spray	strainer	shoe	bush
	strawberry	shovel	trash
		sheep	fish

544

(voiceless)

initial th	final th	initial ch	final ch

three
thumb
thimble
throne
thermometer

wreath
tooth
teeth
moth

chin
chick
chair
check
cheese

match
sandwich
watch
peach
catch

545

short a		long a	

short a		long a	
crab	flag	cane	rain
glass	fan	whale	skate
hat	man	train	snake
bat	hand	cape	chain
map	apple	frame	tape

546

short e		long e	

desk	ten	three	sheep
dress	web	teeth	cheese
well	bed	street	key
net	shell	queen	jeep
belt	bell	leaf	tree

547

short i		long i	

chick	whip	kite	five
ship	milk	cube	spider
brick	swim	prize	tire
spill	chin	nine	bride
hill	crib	bike	slide

short o		long o	

frog	stop	nose	rope
clock	box	hose	globe
block	top	bow	road
dog	fox	hoe	coat
lock	cross	cone	smoke

short u		long u	

scrub	cup	tube	suit
plug	drum	fruit	cube
skunk	duck	music	mule
bus	truck	ruler	tulip
rug	brush		

References

Adams, J., & Collins, A. (1985). A schematic-theoretic view of reading. In H. Singer & R. B. Ruddell (Eds.), *Theoretical models and processes of reading* (3rd ed., pp. 404–425). Newark, DE: International Reading Association.

Adams, M. J. (1994). *Beginning to read: Thinking and learning about print.* Cambridge, MA: MIT press.

Adams, M. J., & Bruck, M. (1995). Resolving the "great debate." *American Educator, 8,* 7–20.

Adams, M. J., & Osborn, J. (1990). Beginning reading instruction in the United States. Paper presented at the Meeting of the Educational Policy Group, Washington, DC: (ERIC Document Reproduction Service No. ED 320 128)

Allington, R. (1977). If they don't read much, how they ever gonna get good? *Journal of Reading, 21*(2), 57–61.

Allington, R., & McGill-Franzen, A. (1989). Different programs, indifferent instruction. In D. K. Lipsky & A. Gartner (Eds.), *Beyond separate education: Quality education for all* (pp. 75–98). Baltimore, MD: Paul H. Brooks.

Allington, R. L. (1984). Oral reading. In P. D. Pearson (Ed.), *Handbook of reading research* (pp. 829–864). New York: Longman.

Allington, R. L. (1994). The schools we have. The schools we need. *The Reading Teacher, 48*(1), 14–29.

Anderson, K. (2000, June 18). The reading wars: Understanding the debate over how best to teach children to read. *Los Angeles Times.*

Anderson, R. A., & Pearson, P. D. (1984). A schematic-theoretic view of reading comprehension. In P. D. Pearson (Ed.), *Handbook of reading research* (pp. 255–291). New York: Longman.

Anderson, R. C., Hiebert, E. H., Scott, J., & Wilkinson, I. A. G. (1985). *Becoming a nation of readers.* Champaign-Urbana, IL: Center for the Study of Reading.

Anderson, R. C., Wilson, P. T., & Fielding, L. G. (1992). Growth in reading and how children spend their time outside of school. *Reading Research Quarterly, 23,* 285–303.

Apple, M. (1988). *Teachers and texts.* New York: Routledge.

Armbruster, B. B., Lehr, F., & Osborn, J. (2001). *Put reading first: The research building blocks for teaching children to read. Kindergarten through grade 3.* Washington, DC: National Institute for Literacy.

Ashton-Warner, S. (1963). *Teacher.* New York: Simon & Schuster.

Atwell, N. (1998). In the middle: Writing, reading and learning with adolescents (2nd ed.). Portsmouth, NH: Heinemann.

Aukerman, R.C., & Aukerman, L. R. (1981). *How do I teach reading?* New York: John Wiley and Sons.

Barbe, W. B, Wasylyk, T. M., Hackney, C. S., & Braun, L. A. (1984). *Zaner-Bloser creative growth in handwriting (Grades K–8).* Columbus, OH: Zaner-Bloser.

Barnitz, J. (1986). *Reading development of nonnative speakers of English.* Orlando, FL: Harcourt, Brace Jovanovich and the Center for Applied Linguistics.

Barone, D. (1990). The written responses of young children: Beyond comprehension to story understanding. *The New Advocate, 3,* 49–56.

Barrett, F. L. (1982). *A teacher's guide to shared reading.* Ontario, Canada: Scholastic-TAB.

Bartlett, F. C. (1932). *Remembering.* Cambridge: Cambridge University Press.

Beach, S. A. (1990, May). The interrelationship of phonemic segmentation, auditory abstraction and word recognition. A paper presented at the annual meeting of the International Reading Association, Atlanta, GA.

Bear, D. R., & Barone, D. (1989). Using children's spellings to group for word study and directed reading in the primary classroom. *Reading Psychology, 10,* 275–292.

Beaver, J. M. (1982). Say it! Over and over. *Language Arts, 59*(2), 143–148.

Beck, I., & Juel, C. (1995). The role of decoding in learning to read. *American Educator, 8,* 21–25, 39–42.

Beck, I., & McKeown, M. (1990). Conditions of vocabulary acquisition. In R. Barr, M. L. Kamil, P. B. Mosenthal, and P. D. Pearson (Eds.), *Handbook of Reading Research* (Vol. 2, pp. 789–814). New York: Longman.

Beck, I. L., Farr, R. C., & Strickland, D. S. (2005). *Trophies: A Harcourt reading/language arts program.* Orlando, FL: Harcourt.

Beck, I. L., Perfetti, C. A., & McKeown, M. G. (1982). The effects of long-term vocabulary instruction on lexical access and reading comprehension. *Journal of Educational Psychology, 74,* 506–521.

Bedrova, E., & Leong, D. J. (1996). *Tools of the mind: The Vygotskian approach of early childhood education.* Englewood Cliffs, NJ: Merrill/Prentice-Hall.

Beldin, H. L. (1970). Informal reading tests: Historical review and review of the research. In W. D. Durr (Ed.), *Reading difficulties: Diagnosis, correction and remediation.* Newark, DE: International Reading Association.

Bernstein, R. (2005). Foreign-born population tops 34 million, Census Bureau estimates. *U.S. Census Bureau News.* Washington, DC: U.S. Department of Commerce. Retrieved March 9, 2005, from http://www.census.gov/Press-Release/www/releases/archives/foreignborn_population/003969.html

Betts, E. A. (1946). *Foundations of reading instruction.* New York: American Book Company.

Biemiller, A. (1970). The development and use of graphic and contextual information as children learn to read. *Reading Research Quarterly, 6,* 75–96.

Biemiller, A. (1977/1978). Relationships between oral reading rates for letters, words, and simple text in the development of reading achievement. *Reading Research Quarterly, 13,* 223–253.

Bissex, G. L. (1980). *Gnys at wrk: A child learns to read and write.* Cambridge, MA: Harvard University Press.

Blachman, B. (1991). Getting ready to read: Learning how print maps to speech. In J. Kavanagh (Ed.), *The language continuum: From infancy to literacy.* Parkton, MD: York Press.

Blackburn, E. (1985). Stories never end. In J. Hansen, T. Newkirk, & D. Graves (Eds.), *Breaking ground: Teachers relate reading and writing in the elementary school.* Portsmouth, NH: Heinemann.

Bode, B. A. (1989). Dialogue journal writing. *The Reading Teacher, 42,* 568–571.

Bond, G. L., & Dykstra, R. (1967). The cooperative program in first grade reading instruction. *Reading Research Quarterly, 2,* 5–142.

Bowyer, T. (1988). Implementing the language experience approach in an E. M. H. classroom. Creative component completed in partial fulfillment of master's degree. Oklahoma State University.

Bridge, C. A., Winograd, P. N., & Haley, D. (1983). Using predictable materials vs. preprimers to teach beginning sight words. *The Reading Teacher, 36,* 884–891.

Britton, J. (1970). *Language and learning.* New York: Penguin.

Brown, H., & Cambourne, B. (1992). *Read and retell.* Portsmouth, NH: Heinemann.

Brown, K. J. (1999/2000). What kind of text—For whom and when? Textual scaffolding for beginning readers. *The Reading Teacher, 53,* 292–307.

Butler, A. (1987). *Shared book experience.* Crystal Lake, IL: Rigby.

Byrne, B., Freebody, P., & Gates, A. (1992). Longitudinal data on the relations of word-reading strategies to comprehension, reading time, and phonemic awareness. *Reading Research Quarterly, 27,* 141–151.

Calkins, L. M. (1986). *The art of teaching writing.* Portsmouth, NH: Heinemann.

Calkins, L. M.(1994).*The art of teaching writing* (Rev. ed). Portsmouth, NH: Heinemann.

Carter, B., & Abrahamson, R. F. (1998). Castles to Colin Powell: The truth about nonfiction. In K. Beers & B. G. Samuels (Eds.), *Into focus: Understanding and creating middle school readers* (pp. 313–322). Norwood, MA: Christopher Gordon Publishers.

Center for the Study of Reading. (1990). *Teachers and independent reading: Suggestions for the classroom.* Urbana, IL: Author.

Chall, J. S. (1967). *Learning to read: The great debate.* New York: McGraw-Hill.

Chall, J. S. (1979). The great debate: Ten years later, with a modest proposal for reading stages. In L. B. Resnick & P. A. Weaver (Eds.), *Theory and practice of early reading* (Vol. 1, pp. 29–54). Hillsdale, NJ: Lawrence Erlbaum.

Chall, J. S. (1983). *Stages of reading development.* New York: McGraw-Hill.

Chomsky, N. (1975). *Reflections on language.* New York: Pantheon Books.

Clay, M. M. (1966). Emergent reading behavior. Unpublished doctoral dissertation. University of Aukland, NZ.

Clay, M. M. (1967). The reading behavior of five-year-old children: A research report. *New Zealand Journal of Educational Studies, 2,* 11–31.

Clay, M. M. (1975). *What did I write? Beginning writing behaviour.* Portsmouth, NH: Heinemann.

Clay, M. M. (1979). *Reading: The patterning of complex behavior.* Portsmouth, NH: Heinemann.

Clay, M. M. (1985). *Early detection of reading difficulties* (3rd ed.). Portsmouth, NH: Heinemann.

Clay, M. M. (1991). *Becoming literate: The construction of inner control.* Portsmouth, NH: Heinemann.

Clay, M. M. (1998). *By different paths to common outcomes.* York, ME: Stenhouse Publishers.

Clay, M. M. (2002). *An observation survey of early literacy achievement.* Portsmouth, NH: Heinemann.

Clay, M. (2004). Stirring the waters. Presentation at the International Reading Association Annual Convention, Reno, NV.

Cooper, J. D. (1993). *Literacy: Helping children construct meaning.* Boston, MA: Houghton Mifflin.

Cullinan, B. E. (1989). *Literature and the child.* San Diego, CA: Harcourt Brace Jovanovich.

Cummins, J. (1981) The role of primary language development in promoting educational success for language minority students. In California State Department of Education (Ed.), *Schooling and language minority students: A theoretical framework* (pp. 3–50). Los Angeles, CA: California State University, Los Angeles; Evaluation, Dissemination and Assessment Center.

Cunningham, P. M. (2005). *Phonics they use: Words for reading and writing* (3rd ed.). New York: HarperCollins.

Cunningham, P. M., & Cunningham, J. W. (1992). Making words: Enhancing the spelling-decoding connection. *The Reading Teacher, 46*(2), 106–115.

Cunningham, P. M., & Hall, D. P. (1994). *Making words: Multilevel, hands-on, developmentally appropriate spelling and phonics activities.* Torrance, CA: Good Apple.

Cunningham, P. M., Moore, S. A., Cunningham, J. W., & Moore, D. W. (2003). *Reading and Writing in Elementary Classrooms: Research-Based K–4 Instruction.* Boston, MA: Allyn & Bacon.

Daniel, T. B., Fehrenbach, C. R., & Greer, F. S. (1986). Supporting concept development with LEA. *Science and Children, 3,* 15–17.

Daniels, H. (2002). *Literature circles: Voice and choice in book clubs and reading groups.* Portland, ME: Stenhouse.

D'Arcy, P. (1989). *Making sense, shaping meaning: Writing in the context of a capacity-based approach to learning.* Portsmouth, NH: Heinemann.

Davey, B. (1983). Think-aloud–modeling the cognitive processes of reading comprehension. *Journal of Reading, 27,* 44–47.

DeFord, D. (1981). Literacy: Reading, writing and other essentials. *Language Arts, 58*(6), 652–658.

Dixon-Krauss, L. A., & Powell, W. R. (1995). Lev Semyonovich Vygotsky: The scholar/teacher. In Dixon-Krauss, L. (Ed.), *Vygotsky in the classroom: Mediated literacy instruction and assessment.* New York: Longman.

Dolch, E. W. (1949). *Problems in reading.* New York: The Garrard Press.

Donahue, P. L., Voelkl, K. E., Campbell, J. R., & Mazzeo, J. (1999, March). *NAEP 1998 reading report card for the nation and states.* Washington, DC: Department of Education.

Douglas, D. J. (1988). Factors related to choice of topic in a first grade process writing classroom. Unpublished doctoral dissertation, Oklahoma State University.

Dowhower, S. (1987). Effects of repeated reading on second-grade transitional readers' fluency and comprehension. *Reading Research Quarterly, 22,* 389–406.

Driscoll, M. P. (1994). *Psychology of learning for instruction.* Needham, MA: Allyn & Bacon.

Duke, N. K., & Pursell-Gates, V. (2003). Genres at home and school: Bringing the known to the new. *The Reading Teacher, 57*(1), pp. 30–37.

Durkin, D. (1966). *Children who read early.* New York: Teachers College Press.

Durrell, D. D. (1937). *Durrell analysis of reading difficulties.* New York: Harcourt Brace Jovanovich.

Dykstra, R. (1968). Summary of the second grade phase of the cooperative research program in primary reading instruction. *Reading Research Quarterly, 4,* 49–70.

Eeds, M., & Wells, D. (1989). Grand conversations: An exploration of meaning construction in literature study groups. *Research in the Teaching of English, 23,* 4–29.

Ehri, L. C. (1991). Development of the ability to read words. In R. Barr, M. L. Kamii, P. Mosenthal, & P. D. Pearson (Eds.), *Handbook of reading research* (Vol. 2, pp. 383–417). Mahway, NJ: Lawrence Erlbaum.

Ehri, L. C. (1998). Grapheme-phoneme knowledge is essential for learning to read words in English. In J. L. Metsala & L. C. Ehri (Eds.), *Word recognition in beginning literacy* (pp. 3–40). Mahwah, NJ: Lawrence Erlbaum.

Ehri, L. C., Duffner, N. D., & Wilce, L. S. (1984). Pictorial mnemonics for phonics. *Journal of Educational Psychology, 76,* 880–893.

Eldredge, J. L., Reutzel, D. R., & Hollingsworth, P. M. (1996). Comparing the effectiveness of two oral reading practices: Round-robin reading and the shared book experience. *Journal of Literacy Research, 28*(2), pp. 201–225.

Elster, C. A. (1995). Importations in preschoolers' emergent readings. *Journal of Reading Behavior, 27,* 65–84.

Elster, C. A. (1998). Influences of text and pictures on shared and emergent readings. *Research in the Teaching of English, 32,* 43–78.

Ewoldt, C., & Hammermeister, F. (1986). The language-experience approach to facilitating reading and writing for hearing-impaired students. *American Annal of the Deaf, 131,* 271–274.

Farr, R., Tulley, M. A., & Powell, D. (1987). The evaluation and selection of basal readers. *Elementary School Journal, 87,* 267–282.

Farris, P. J. (1991). Handwriting instruction should not be extinct. *Language Arts, 68,* 312–314.

Ferguson, A. M., & Fairburn, J. (1985). Language experience for problem solving in mathematics. *The Reading Teacher, 38,* 504–506.

Fielding, L. G., Wilson, P. T., & Anderson, R. (1984). A new focus on free reading: The role of trade books in reading instruction. In T. E. Raphael (Ed.), *The contexts of school-based literacy.* New York: Random House.

Filby, N., Barnett, B., & Bossart, S. (1982). *Grouping practices and their consequences.* San Francisco, CA: Far West Laboratory for Educational Research and Development.

Fillmore, L. W., & Snow, C. E. (2000). *What teachers need to know about language.* Washington, DC: ERIC Clearinghouse on Languages and Linguistics.

Five, C. L. (1988, Spring). From workbooks to workshop: Increasing children's involvement in the reading process. *The New Advocate, 1,* 103–113.

Fountas, I. C., & Pinnell, G. S. (1996). *Guided reading: Good first teaching for all children.* Portsmouth, NH: Heinemann.

Fountas, I. C., & Pinnell, G. S. (1999). *Matching books to readers.* Portsmouth; NH: Heinemann.

Fox, B., & Routh, D. (1984). Phonemic analysis and synthesis as word attack skills: Revisited. *Journal of Educational Psychology, 76,* 1059–1064.

Freeman, J. (1992). Reading aloud: A few tricks of the trade. *School Library Journal, 38*(7), 26–29.

Freppon, P. A., & Dahl, K. L. (1991). Learning about phonics in a whole-language classroom. *Language Arts, 68,* 190–197.

Fry, E. B., Kress, J. E., & Fountoukidis, D. L. (2000). *The reading teacher's book of lists.* Englewood Clifs, NJ: Prentice Hall.

Fulwiler, T. (1985). Writing and learning, grade 3. *Language Arts, 62,* 55–59.

Furner, B. A. (1985). Handwriting instruction for a high-tech society: Will handwriting be necessary? Paper presented at the National Council of Teachers of English Spring Conference, Houston, Texas. (ERIC Document Reproduction Service No. ED 257 119)

Gambrell, L. B. (1978). Getting started with sustained silent reading and keeping it going. *The Reading Teacher, 32*(3) 328–331.

Gambrell, L. B. (1985). Dialogue journals: Reading-writing interaction. *The Reading Teacher, 38,* 512–515.

Gates, A. I. (1935). *The improvement of reading.* New York: Macmillan.

Gilmore, J. V., & Gilmore, E. C. (1951). *Gilmore oral reading tests.* New York: Harcourt, Brace Jovanovich.

Goodman, K. S., Shannon, P., Freeman, Y., & Murphy, S. (1988). *Report card on basal readers.* Katonah, NY: Richard C. Owen.

Goodman, Y. (1985). Kidwatching: Observing children in the classroom. In A. Jaggar & M. T. Smith-Burke (Eds.), *Observing the Language Learner* (pp. 9–18). New York: International Reading Association and the National Council of Teachers of English.

Goodman, Y. M., & Burke, C. L. (1970). *Reading miscues inventory.* New York: Macmillan.

Gough, P. B., & Tunmer, W. E. (1986). Decoding, reading, and reading disability. *Remedial and Special Education, 7,* 6–10.

Gould, J. S., & Gould, E. J. (2002). *Four-square writing method: The total writing classroom for grades 1–4.* Carthage, IL: Teaching & Learning Company.

Graves, D. H. (1973). Children's writing: Research directions and hypotheses based upon an examination of the writing processes of seven-year-old children. Unpublished doctoral dissertation. State University of New York at Buffalo.

Graves, D. H. (1983). *Teaching writing.* Portsmouth, NH: Heinemann.

Graves, D. H. (1994). *A fresh look at writing.* Portsmouth, NH: Heinemann.

Gray, W. S. (1915). *Standardized oral reading paragraphs.* Bloomington, IL: Public School Publishing Company.

Griffith, P. L. (1991). Phonemic awareness helps first graders invent spellings and third graders remember correct spellings. *Journal of Reading Behavior, 23,* 215–233.

Griffith, P. L., & Klesius, J. P. (1990, November). The effect of phonemic awareness ability and reading instructional approach on first grade children's acquisition of spelling and decoding skills. A paper presented at the National Reading Conference.

Griffith, P. L., & Olson, M. W. (1992). Phonemic awareness helps beginning readers break the code. *The Reading Teacher, 45,* 516–523.

Hagerty, P. (1992). *Reader's workshop: Real reading.* Ontario, Canada: Scholastic Canada Ltd.

Hall, M. (1978). *The language experience approach for teaching reading, a research perspective.* Newark, DE: International Reading Association.

Hall, M. (1981). *Teaching reading as a language experience* (3rd ed.). Columbus, OH: Merrill.

Halliday, M. A. K. (1975). *Learning how to mean: Exploration in the development of language.* London: Edward Arnold.

Hansen, J. (1987). *When writers read.* Portsmouth, NH: Heinemann.

Harris, V. J. (1994). Multiculturalism and children's literature. In F. Lehr & J. Osborn (Eds.), *Reading, language and literacy* (pp. 201–214). Mahwah, NJ: Lawrence Erlbaum.

Hart, B., & Risley, T. R. (1995). *Meaningful differences in the everyday experience of young American children.* Baltimore: Brookes.

Hauerwas, L. B., & Walker, J. (2004). What can children's spelling of *sunning* and *jumped* tell us about their need for spelling instruction? *The Reading Teacher, 58*(2), 168–176.

Heald-Taylor, G. (1987). How to use predictable books for K–2 language arts instruction. *The Reading Teacher, 40,* 656–661.

Heibert, E. H., & Colt, J. (1989). Patterns of literature-based reading instruction. *The Reading Teacher, 43,* 14–20.

Helman, L. A. (2004). Building on the sound system of Spanish: Insights from the alphabetic spellings of English-language learners. *The Reading Teacher, 57*(5), 452–460.

Henderson, E. (1985). *Teaching spelling.* Boston, MA: Houghton Mifflin.

Henderson, E. H., & Beers, J. W: (1980). *Developmental and cognitive aspects of learning to spell: A reflection of word knowledge.* Newark, DE: International Reading Association.

Herman, P. A. (1985). The effect of repeated readings on reading rate, speech pauses, and word recognition accuracy. *Reading Research Quarterly, 20,* 553–564.

Hill, B. C., Johnson, N. J., & Schlick Noe, K. L. (Eds.) (1995). *Literature circles and response.* Norwood, MA: Christopher-Gordon Publishers.

Hilliard, A. (1994). Foreword. In E. W. King, M. Chipman, & M. Cruz-Janzen (Eds.), *Educating young children in a diverse society* (p. x). Boston, MA: Allyn & Bacon.

Holdaway, D. (1979). *Foundations of literacy.* Sydney, Australia: Ashton Scholastic.

Holdaway, D. (1980). *Independence in reading.* Portsmouth, NH: Heinemann.

Holdaway, D. (1984). *Stability and change in literacy learning.* Portsmouth, NH: Heinemann.

Individuals with Disabilities Education Act, Public Law 105–17. Washington, DC: U.S. Department of Education.

Johnson, D. M. (1981). The effects of cooperative, competitive and individualistic goal structures on achievement: A meta-analysis. *Psychological Bulletin, 89,* 47–62.

Johnston, F. R. (1998). The reader, the text, and the task: Learning words in first grade. *The Reading Teacher, 51,* 666–675.

Jones, N. K. (1995). Learning to read: Insights from reading recovery. *Literacy, Teaching, and Learning, 1*(2), 41–56.

Juel, C. (1991). Beginning reading. In R. Barr, M. Kamil, P. Mosenthal, & P. D. Pearson (Eds.), *Handbook of reading research* (Vol. 2, pp. 759–788). New York: Longman.

Juel, C., Griffith, P. L., & Gough, P. B. (1986). Acquisition of literacy: A longitudinal study of children in first and second grade. *Journal of Educational Psychology, 78,* 243–255.

Kawakami, A. J. (1985). A study of the effects of repeated story reading on kindergarten children's story comprehension. Paper presented at the annual meeting of the National Reading Conference, San Diego.

Kelleher, M. E. (1997). Readers' theater and metacognition. *The New England Reading Association Journal, 33,* 4–12.

Kozub, R. (2000, May). Reader's theater and its effect on oral reading fluency. *Reading OnLine.* Retrieved March 9, 2005, from http://www.Readingonline.org

Kreeft, J. (1984). Dialogue writing—bridge from talk to essay writing. *Language Arts, 651,* 141–150.

Kristo, J. (1993). Reading aloud in a primary classroom: Reaching and teaching young readers. In K. E. Holland, R. A. Hungerford, & S. B. Ernst (Eds.), *Journeying: Students responding to literature* (pp. 54–71). Portsmouth, NH: Heinemann.

Ladson-Billings, G. (2001). *Crossing over to Canaan: The Journey of new teachers in diverse classrooms.* San Francisco: Jossey-Bass.

Lindfors, J. W. (1987). *Children's language and learning* (2nd ed.). Englewood Cliffs, NJ: Prentice-Hall.

Lukens, R. (1998). *A critical handbook of children's literature.* Glenview, IL: Scott Foresman.

Lynch, P. (1986). *Using big books and predictable books.* New York: Scholastic.

Maclean, M., Bryant, P., & Bradley, L. (1987). Rhymes, nursery rhymes, and reading in early childhood. *Merrill-Palmer Quarterly, 33,* 255–282.

Madura, S. (1995). The line and texture of aesthetic response: Primary children study authors and illustrators. *The Reading Teacher, 49,* 110–118.

Marr, D., Windsor, M. M., & Chermak, S. (2001). Handwriting readiness: Locatives and visuomotor skills in the kindergarten year. *Early Childhood Research and Practice, 3*(1). Retrieved September 11, 2004, from http://ecrp.uiuc.edu/v3n1/marr.html

Martinez, M., & Nash, M. F. (1990). Bookalogues: Talking about children's literature. *Language Arts, 67*(6), 599–606.

Mason, J. (1984). Early reading: A developmental perspective. In P. D. Pearson (Ed.), *Handbook of reading research* (pp. 505–544). New York: Longman.

McCallum, R. D. (1988). *Don't throw the basals out with the bath water.* The Reading Teacher, 42, 204–209.

McCarrier, A., Pinnell, G. S., & Fountas, I. C. (2000). *Interactive writing: How language and literacy come together, K–2.* Portsmouth, NH: Heinemann.

McKenzie, M. G. (1985). *Shared writing: Apprenticeship in written language matters.* London: Centre for Language in Primary Education.

McMahon, S. I. (1991). Book club: How written and oral discourse influence the development of ideas as children respond to literature. Paper presented at the annual meeting of the American Educational Research Association.

Merriam-Webster. (2003). *Merriam-Webster collegiate dictionary.* New York: Merriam-Webster.

Meyer, B. F. (1985). Prose analysis: Purposes, procedures, and problems. In B. K. Britton & J. B. Back (Eds.), *Understanding expository text* (pp. 11–64). Hillsdale, NJ: Lawrence Erlbaum.

Meyer, B. J., & Freedle, R. O. (1984). Effects of discourse type on recall. *American Educational Research Journal, 21,* 121–143.

Mooney, M. E. (1990). *Reading to, with, and by children.* Katonah, NY: Richard C. Owens.

Morris, D., Bloodgood, J., & Perney, J. (2003). Kindergarten predictors of first- and second-grade reading achievement. *The Elementary School Journal, 104*(2), 93–108.

Morrow, L. M. (1985). Retelling stories: A strategy for improving young children's comprehension of story structures and oral language complexity. *Elementary School Journal, 85,* 647–661.

Morrow, L. M. (2005). *Literacy development in the early years: Helping children read and write* (5th ed.). Boston: Allyn & Bacon.

Morrow, L. M., & Gambrell, L. B. (2004). *Using children's literature in preschool: Comprehending and enjoying books.* Newark, NJ: International Reading Association.

Morrow, L. M., & Weinstein, C. S. (1986). Encouraging voluntary reading: The impact of a literature program on children's use of library centers. *Reading Research Quarterly, 21,* 330–346.

Mullis, I. V. S., Campbell, J. R., & Farstrup, A. E. (1993). *NAEP 1992 reading report card for the nation and states.* Washington, DC: Office of Education Research and Improvement.

Murray, D. (1985). *A writer teaches writing* (2nd ed). Boston: Houghton Mifflin.

Nagy, W. E., Herman, P. A., & Anderson, R. C. (1985). Learning words from context. *Reading Research Quarterly, 20,* 233–253.

National Assessment of Educational Progress 2002 (NAEP). (2002). Washington, DC: Office of Education Research and Improvement.

National Assessment Of Educational Progress 2003 (*NAEP*). (2003). Washington, DC: Office of Education Research and Improvement.

National Center for Education Statistics. (2000). *The condition of education.* Washington, DC: U.S. Department of Education, Office of Education Research and Improvement.

National Institute of Child Health and Human Development (NICHD). (2000). *Report of the National Reading Panel: Teaching children to read.* Washington, DC: U.S. Department of Health and Human Services.

National Literacy Standards for Language Arts. (1996). Urbana-Champaign, IL: National Council for Teachers of English and International Reading Association.

Nessel, D. D., & Jones, M. B. (1981). *The language-experience approach to reading.* New York: Teachers College Press.

Neuman, S. B. (1999). Creating continuity in early literacy: Linking home and school with a culturally responsive approach. In L. B. Gambrell, L. M. Morrow, S. B. Neuman, & M. Pressley (Eds.), *Best practices in literacy instruction* (pp. 258–270). New York: The Guildford Press.

Niles, O. S. (1974). Organization perceived. In H. L. Herber (Ed.), *Perspectives in reading: Developing study skills in secondary schools* (pp. 57–76). Newark, DE: International Reading Association.

Northwest Regional Educational Laboratory, Equity Center. (2004). *Improving education for immigrant students: A guide for K–12 educators in the Northwest and Alaska.* Portland, OR: Northwest Regional Educational Laboratory.

Ogle, D. (1986). The K–W–L: A teaching model that develops active reading of expository text. *The Reading Teacher, 39,* 364–370.

Opitz, M. F., & Rasinski, T. V. (1998). *Goodbye round robin.* Portsmouth, NH: Heinemann.

Orehovec, B., & Alley, M. (2004). *Revisiting the reading workshop: Management, mini-lessons, and strategies.* Thousand Oaks, CA: Teaching Resources.

O'Shea, L. J., Sindelar, P. T., and O'Shea, D. J. (1985). The effects of repeated readings and attentional cues on reading fluency and comprehension. *Journal of Reading Behavior, 17*(2) 129–142.

Pappas, C. C., Kiefer, B. Z., & Levstik, L. S. (1999). *An integrated language perspective in the elementary school* (2nd ed.). New York: Longman.

Paris, S. G., Wasik, B. A., & Turner, J. C. (1991). The development of strategic readers. In R. Barr, M. L. Kamil, P. Mosenthal, & P. D. Pearson (Eds.), *Handbook of reading research* (Vol. 2). New York: Longman.

Peck, M., Askov, E. N., & Fairchild, D. H. (1980). Another decade of research in handwriting: Progress and prospect in the 1970s. *Journal of Educational Research, 73*(2), 283–298.

Pennington, B. F., Grossier, D., & Welsh, M. C. (1993). Contrasting cognitive deficits in attention deficit hyperactivity disorder versus reading disability. *Developmental Psychology, 29,* 511–523.

Perfetti, C. A. (1985). *Reading ability.* New York: Oxford University Press.

Person, M. E. (1990). Say it right! *The Reading Teacher, 43,* 428–429.

Peterson, R., & Eeds, M. (1990). *Grand conversations: Literature groups in action.* Ontario, Canada: Scholastic-TAB.

Piaget, J., & Inhelder, B. (1969). *The psychology of the child.* New York: Basic Books.

Pinnell, G. S., Pikulski, J. J., Wixson, K. K., Campbell, J. R., Gough, P. B., & Beatty, A. S. (1995). *Listening to children read aloud: Oral fluency.* Washington, DC: National Center for Education Statistics, U.S. Department of Education. Retrieved June 25, 2003, from www.ncrel.org/rf/components.pdf

Powell, W. R. (1993). Classroom literacy instruction and assessment from the Vygotskian perspective. Paper presented at the Thirty-Eighth Annual Convention of the International Reading Association, San Antonio, TX.

Pressley, M. (1997). The cognitive science of reading. *Contemporary Educational Psychology, 22,* 247–259.

Pressley, M. (1998). *Reading instruction that works: A case for balanced teaching.* New York: The Guilford Press.

Rack, J., Snowling, M., & Olsen, R. (1992). The nonword reading deficits in developmental dyslexia: A review. *Reading Research Quarterly, 27,* 28–53.

Ramirez, G., & Ramirez, J. L. (1994). *Multiethnic children's literature.* Albany, NY: Delmar.

Rameriz, J. D., Pasts, D. J., Yuen, S., Billings, D. K., & Ramey, D. R. (1991). *Final report: Longitudinal study of structural immersion strategy, early-exit, and late-exit transitional bilingual education programs for language minority children.* San Mateo, CA: Aguirre International.

Raphael, T. E., & McMahon, S. I. (1994). "Book clubs": An alternative framework for reading instruction. *The Reading Teacher, 48,* 102–116.

Rasinski, T. V. (1990). Effects of repeated reading and listening-while-reading on reading fluency. *Journal of Educational Research, 83,* (pp. 147–150). New York: Scholastic.

Rasinski, T. V. (2003). The fluent reader: Oral reading strategies for building word recognition, fluency, and comprehension. New York: Scholastic.

Rasinski, T. V., & Padak, N. D. (1990). Multicultural learning through children's literature. *Language Arts, 67*(6), 576–580.

Read, C. (1975). Children's categorizations of speech sounds in English (NCTE Res. Rep. No. 17). Urbana, IL: National Council of Teachers of English.

Reimer, K. M. (1992). Multiethnic literature: Holding fast to dreams. Technical Report No. 551. (ERIC Document Service Reproduction No: ED 343 128)

Rhodes, L. K. (1981). I can read! Predictable books as resources for reading and writing instruction. *The Reading Teacher, 34,* 511–518.

Reutzel, R. D., & Cooter, R. B., Jr. (1992). *Teaching children to Read: From basals to books.* Macmillan Publishing Company. New York: New York.

Rigg, P. (1986). Reading in ESL: Learning from kids. In P. Rigg & D. S. Enright (Eds.), *Children and ESL: Integrating perspectives* (pp. 14–27). Washington, DC: Teachers of English to Speakers of Other Languages.

Rigg, P. (1989). Language experience approach: Reading naturally. In P. Rigg & R. Van Allen (Eds.), *When they don't all speak English: Integrating the ESL student into the regular classroom* (pp. 35–51). Urbana, IL: National Council of Teachers of English.

Rinsky, L. A. (1993). *Teaching word recognition skills* (5th ed.). Scottsdale, AZ: Gorsuch Scarisbrick.

Rosen, H., & Rosen, C. (1973). *The language of primary school children.* London: Penguin/Education for the Schools Council.

Rosenblatt, L. M. (1978). *The reader, the text, the poem: The transactional theory of the literary work.* Carbondale, IL: Southern Illinois University Press.

Routman, R. (1991). *Invitations: Changing teaching and learning K–12.* Portsmouth, NH: Heinemann.

Samuels, S. J. (1979). The method of repeated reading. *The Reading Teacher, 32,* 403–408.

Schank, R., & Abelson, R. (1975). *Knowledge structures.* Mahwah, NJ: Lawrence Erlbaum.

Senick, G. J. (Ed.). (1976–1995). *Children's literature review* (Vol. 1–34). New York: Gale Research.

Shanklin, N. K. (1982). *Relating reading and writing: Developing a transitional model of the writing process.* Bloomington, IN: Monographs in Teaching and Learning, School of Education, Indiana University.

Shannon, P. (Ed.). (1992). *Becoming political: Reading and writing in the politics of literacy education.* Portsmouth, NH: Heinemann.

Siera, M., & Combs, M. (1990). Transitions in reading instruction: Handling contradictions in beliefs and practice. *Reading Horizons, 31,* 113–126.

Sims, R. (1983). What has happened to the "all white" world of children's books? *Phi Delta Kappan, 64,* 650–653.

Slavin, R. E., Madden, N. A., Karweit, N. L., Dolan, L. J., & Wasik, B. A. (1991). Success for all: Ending reading failure from the beginning. *Language Arts, 68,* 404–409.

Slocum, T. A., O'Connor, R. E., & Jenkins, J. R. (1993). Transfer among phonological manipulation skills. *Journal of Educational Psychology, 85,* 618–630.

Smith, F. (1982). *Writing and the writer.* New York: Holt, Rinehart & Winston.

Snow, C. E., Burns, M. S., & Griffin, P. (Eds.). (1998). *Preventing reading difficulties in young children.* Washington, DC: National Academy Press.

Soderman, A. K., Gregory, K. M., & O'Neill, L. T. (1999). *Scaffolding emergent literacy: A child-centered approach for preschool through grade 5.* Boston, MA: Allyn & Bacon.

Spache, G. D. (1963). *Diagnostic reading scales.* Monterey, CA: CTB/McGraw-Hill.

Speigel, D. L. (1985). Developing independence in decoding. *Reading World,* 75–80.

Stahl, S., & Miller, P. (1989). Whole language and language experience approaches for beginning reading: A quantative research synthesis. *Review of Educational Research, 59,* 87–116.

Stahl, S. A., & Murray, B. A. (1994). Defining phonological awareness and its relationship to early reading. *Journal of Educational Psychology, 86,* 221–234.

Standards for the english language arts. (1996). Newark, DE & Urbana, IL: International Reading Association and the National Council of Teachers of English.

Stanovich, K. (1986). Matthew effects in reading: Some consequences of individual differences in the acquisition of literacy. *Reading Research Quarterly, 21,* 360–407.

Stanovich, K. E. (1982). Individual differences in the cognitive processes of reading: I. Word decoding. *Journal of Learning Disabilities, 15,* 485–493.

Stanovich, K. E., Cunningham, A. E., & West, R. F. (1981). A longitudinal study of the development of automatic recognition skills in first graders. *Journal of Reading Behavior, 13,* 57–74.

Staton, J. (1980). Writing and counseling: Using a dialogue journal. *Language Arts, 57,* 514–518.

Staton, J. (1987). The power of responding in dialogue journals. In T. Fulwiler (Ed.), *The journal book* (pp. 47–63). Portsmouth, NH: Heinemann.

Stauffer, R. G. (1975). *Directing the reading-thinking process.* New York: Harper & Row.

Stauffer, R. G. (1980). *The language experience approach to the teaching of reading.* New York: Harper & Row.

Stauffer, R. G., & Hammond, W. D. (1967). The effectiveness of language arts and basal reader approaches to first grade reading instruction. *The Reading Teacher, 20,* 740–746.

Stauffer, R. S. (1959). A directed reading-thinking plan. *Education, 79,* 527–532.

Sulzby, E. (1985). Children's emergent reading of favorite storybooks. *Reading Research Quarterly, 20,* 458–481.

Sulzby, E., & Teale, W. H. (1991). Emergent literacy. In R. Barr, M. L. Kamil, P. Mosenthal, & P. D. Pearson (Eds.), *Handbook of reading research* (Vol. 2, pp. 727–757). New York: Longman.

Tan-Lin, Amy. (1981). An investigation into the developmental course of preschool/kindergarten aged children's handwriting behavior. *Dissertation Abstracts International, 42,* 4287A.

Taylor, B. M., Frye, B. J., & Maruyama, G. M. (1990). Time spent reading and reading growth. *American Educational Research Journal, 27,* 351–362.

Taylor, N. E., Wade, M., & Yekovich, F. R. (1985, Fall). The effect of manipulation and multiple reading strategies on the reading performance of good and poor readers. *Reading Research Quarterly,* 566–574.

Taylor, W. L. (1953). Cloze procedure: A new tool for measuring readability. *Journalism Quarterly, 30,* 414–438.

Teale, W. H. (1986). Home background and children's literacy development. In W. H. Teale & E. Sulzby (Eds.), *Emergent literacy: Writing and reading* (pp. 173–206). Norwood, NJ: Ablex.

Telgen, D. (Ed.). (1971–1994). *Something about the author* (Vol. 1–76). Detroit, MI: Gale Research.

Temple, C., Nathan, R., Temple, F., & Burris, N. (1993). *The beginnings of writing* (2nd ed.). Boston, MA: Allyn & Bacon.

Tharp, R. G., & Gallimore, R. (1988). *Rousing minds to life: Teaching, learning, and schooling in social context.* Cambridge, UK: Cambridge University Press.

Thomson, J. (1987). *Understanding teenagers' reading.* Urbana, IL: National Council of Teachers of English.

Tompkins, G. E. (2000). *Teaching writing: Balancing process and product* (2nd ed.). New York: Macmillan.

Trachtenburg, P., & Ferruggia, A. (1989). Big books from little voices: Reaching high-risk readers. *The Reading Teacher, 43,* 284–289.

Treadway, J. (1993). Language experience and whole language for the second language student. Unpublished course materials, San Diego State University.

Trelease, J. (2001). *The new read-aloud handbook.* New York: Viking Penguin.

Tunnell, M. O., & Jacobs, J. S. (1989). Using "real" books: Research findings on literature based reading instruction. *The Reading Teacher, 42,* 470–477.

Van Allen, R. (1974). *Language experiences in reading.* Chicago, IL: Encyclopedia Britannica Press.

Veatch, J. (1959). *Individualizing your reading program: Self-selection in action.* New York: Putman.

Vygotsky, L. S. (1962). *Thought and language* (E. Hanfmann & G. Vakar, Eds. & Trans.). Cambridge, MA: MIT Press.

Vygotsky, L. S. (1978). *Mind in society* (M. Cole, V. John-Steiner, S. Scribner, & E. Sounerman, Eds. & Trans.). Cambridge, MA: Harvard University Press.

Wagner, R. K., Torgenson, J. K., Laughon, P., Simmons, K., & Rashotti, C. A. (1993). Development of young readers' phonological processing abilities. *Journal of Educational Psychology, 85,* 83–103.

Walmsley, S. (1992). Reflections on the state of elementary literature instruction. *Language Arts, 69,* 508–514.

Wells, G. (1986). *The meaning makers: Children learning language and using language to learn.* Portsmouth, NH: Heinemann.

White, K. R. (1982). The relation between socioeconomic status and academic achievement. *Psychological Bulletin, 91,* 461–481.

Whitehurst, G. J., Falco, F. L., Lonigan, C., Fischel, J. E., DeBaryshe, B. D., Valdez-Menchaca, M. C., & Caulfield, M. (1988). Accelerating language development through picture book reading. *Developmental Psychology, 24,* 552–588.

Wood, S. S., Bruner, J. S., & Ross, G. (1976). The role of tutoring in problem solving. *Journal of Child Psychology, 17,* 89–100.

Wren, S. (2004). Reading comprehension. Developing research-based resources for the balanced reading teacher. Retrieved March 8, 2005, from http://www.balancedreading.com/readingcomprehension.html

Yaden, D. (1988). Understanding stories through repeated read-alouds: How many does it take? *The Reading Teacher, 41,* 556–560.

Yopp, H. (1988). The validity and reliability of phonemic awareness tests. *Reading Research Quarterly, 23,* 159–177.

Yopp, H. K. (1992). Developing phonemic awareness in young children. *The Reading Teacher, 45,* 696–703.

Yopp, H. K., & Yopp, R. H. (2000). Supporting phonemic awareness development in the classroom. *The Reading Teacher, 54,* 130–143.

Name Index

Abelson, R., 28, 557
Abrahamson, R.F., 163, 552
Ada, A.F., 173
Adams, J., 28, 551
Adams, M.J., 26, 27, 37, 39, 43, 44,
    47, 48, 78, 190, 551
Adler, D., 488, 504
Ainsworth, L., 62
Aliki, 488, 504
Alley, M., 269, 556
Allington, R.L., 73, 225, 271, 551
Altlman, L.J., 173
Andersen, H.C., 317
Anderson, K., 6, 551
Anderson, R.A., 135, 271, 551
Anderson, R.C., 6, 137, 268, 269,
    271, 551, 553, 556
Andrews-Goebel, N., 173
Apple, M., 400, 551
Archambault, J., 490, 491, 494,
    495, 504
Armbruster, B.B., 191, 551
Aruego, J., 194
Ashton-Warner, S., 551
Askov, E.N., 47, 556
Atwell, N., 269, 355, 551
Aukerman, R.C., 399

Baker, A., 62
Bang, M., 494, 504
Barbe, W.B., 551
Barnett, B., 225, 553
Barnitz, J., 331, 551
Barone, D., 120, 363, 364, 551
Barrett, F.L., 186, 551
Bartlett, F.C., 271, 551
Bayer, J., 61, 62, 504
Baylor, B., 346, 347
Beach, S.A., 39, 551
Bear, D.R., 120, 551
Beatty, A.S., 262, 556
Beaver, J.M., 139, 153, 201, 551
Beck, I.L., 48, 78, 190, 398, 551

Bedrova, E., 9, 17, 32, 552
Beers, J.W., 92, 554
Beldin, H.L., 253, 552
Bentley, D., 479
Berenzy, A., 474
Berman, R., 472
Bernstein, R., 552
Betts, E.A., 253, 399, 552
Biemiller, A., 26, 77, 552
Billings, D.K., 15, 556
Binch, C., 129, 376, 504
Bissex, G.L., 26, 552
Bjorkman, S., 173
Blachman, B., 58, 552
Blackburn, E., 131, 552
Blaine, M., 490, 504
Bloodgood, J., 37, 39, 64, 211, 555
Blume, J., 353, 504
Bode, B.A., 361, 552
Bond, G.L., 299, 552
Bossart, S., 115, 553
Bowyer, T., 333, 552
Boyntan, S., 488
Bradley, L., 39, 555
Braine, S., 173
Branley, F.M., 177, 178
Braun, L.A., 551
Brett, J., 504
Bridge, C.A., 186, 552
Britton, J., 131, 552
Brown, H., 155, 552
Brown, K.J., 26, 76, 77, 552
Brown, M., 461
Bruck, M., 48, 551
Bruner, J.S., 16, 558
Bryant, P., 39, 555
Bulla, C.R., 218, 245, 504
Bunting, E., 173, 486, 497, 504
Burke, C.L., 115, 227, 253, 554
Burns, M.S., 6, 26, 557
Burris, N., 104, 558
Butler, A., 185, 552
Butterfield, M., 443

Byars, B., 218, 245, 504
Byrne, B., 78, 552

Calkins, L.M., 295, 302, 303, 304,
    337, 343, 350, 351, 356, 357,
    358, 393, 552
Cambourne, B., 155, 552
Campbell, J.R., 136, 269, 553, 556
Carle, E., 155, 187, 504
Carter, B., 163, 552
Caulfield, M., 190, 558
Center for the Study of Reading,
    271, 552
Chall, J.S., 26, 76, 190, 552
Charles, O., 132, 504
Cheng, A., 173
Chermak, S., 555, 48
Choi, S.N., 173
Chomsky, N., 11, 552
Cisneros, S., 173
Clay, M.M., 9, 10, 13, 26, 27, 28, 29,
    30, 32, 67, 78, 137, 206, 224,
    226, 253, 297, 303, 552
Cleary, B., 486, 504
Coerr, E., 488, 504
Cole, J., 499, 504
Collins, A., 28, 551
Colt, J., 554
Combs, M., 557
Conrad, P., 218, 245, 504
Cooney, B., 496, 504
Cooper, J.D., 208, 552
Cooper, M., 404
Cooter, R.B., Jr., 399, 400, 557
Cousins, L., 62
Crews, D., 504
Crowe, R., 461
Cullinan, B.E., 131, 489, 505, 552
Cummins, J., 11, 15, 31, 182, 224, 552
Cunningham, 1995, 57, 305
Cunningham, A.E., 77, 557
Cunningham, J.W., 60, 95, 553
Cunningham, P.M., 35, 94, 95, 553

Dahl, K.L., 554
Dahl, R., 504, 587
Daniel, T.B., 319, 553
Daniels, 247
D'Arcy, P., 300, 302, 303, 337, 338, 553
Davey, B., 249, 284, 553
DeBaryshe, B.D., 190, 558
DeFord, D., 131, 553
Dell'Oro, S.P., 443
dePaola, T., 139, 335, 504
Dewey, A., 194
Dixon-Krauss, L.A., 142, 236, 553
Dolan, L.J., 270, 557
Dolch, E.W., 35, 553
Donahue, P.L., 269, 553
Dooley, N., 173
Dorros, A., 173, 502, 504
Douglas, D.J., 356, 366, 553
Dowhower, S., 191, 271, 553
Dr. Seuss, 461
Dragonwagon, C., 62
Driscoll, M.P., 28, 553
Duffner, N.D., 45, 553
Duke, N.K., 132, 553
Durkin, D., 131, 553
Durrell, D.D., 253, 553
Dykstra, R., 299, 552, 553

Ebl, D., 461
Eeds, M., 131, 169, 553, 556
Ehlert, L., 62
Ehri, L.C., 26, 35, 45, 78, 190, 553
Eldredge, J.L., 190, 204, 553
Elster, C.A., 12, 131, 132, 137, 553
Ewoldt, C., 333, 553

Fairburn, J., 319, 553
Fairchild, D.H., 47, 556
Falco, F.L., 190, 558
Falwell, C., 173
Farr, R.C., 398, 399, 551, 553
Farris, P.J., 384, 553
Farstrup, A.E., 136, 556
Feelings, M., 62
Feelings, T., 62
Fehrenbach, C.R., 319, 553
Ferguson, A.M., 319, 553
Ferruggia, A., 207, 208, 558
Fielding, L.G., 268, 551, 553
Filby, N., 225, 553
Fillmore, L.W., 15, 553
Fischel, J.E., 190, 558

Five, C.L., 249, 269, 343, 553
Ford, W., 443
Fountas, I.C., 219, 222, 226, 295, 297, 299, 342, 436, 553, 555
Fountoukidis, D.L., 35, 554
Fox, B., 39, 554
Fox, M., 139, 504
Freebody, P., 78, 552
Freedle, R.O., 500, 505, 555
Freeman, J., 141, 554
Freeman, Y., 398, 399, 400, 554
Freppon, P.A., 554
Fry, E.B., 35, 554
Frye, B.J., 268, 269, 558
Fulwiler, T., 365, 554
Furner, B.A., 47, 554

Galdone, P., 139, 504
Gallimore, R., 17, 558
Gambrell, L.B., 13, 269, 361, 554, 555
Gardiner, J., 217, 218, 245
Gates, A.I., 78, 253, 399, 552, 554
Gibbons, G., 129, 139, 148-152, 155, 171, 189, 504
Gilmore, E.C., 253, 554
Gilmore, J.V., 253, 554
Ginsburg, M., 177, 194, 504
Gonzalez, R.D., 505
Goodman, K.S., 398, 399, 400, 554
Goodman, Y.M., 112, 115, 227, 253, 554
Gordon, G., 404
Gough, P.B., 37, 77, 262, 554, 555, 556
Gould, E.J., 344, 554
Gould, J.S., 344, 554
Graves, D.H., 131, 303, 337, 341, 343, 350, 356, 360, 366, 384, 389, 554
Gray, W.S., 253, 554
Greenfield, E., 173
Greer, F.S., 319, 553
Gregory, K.M., 337, 342, 557
Griffin, P., 6, 26, 557
Griffith, P.L., 37, 39, 49, 554, 555
Grossier, D., 27, 556
Grossman, P., 443

Hackney, T.M., 551
Hagerty, P., 249, 269, 270, 271, 554
Haley, D., 186, 552

Hall, D.P., 94, 95, 553
Hall, M., 182, 299, 328, 554
Halliday, M.A.K., 10, 554
Hamanaka, S., 173
Hamilton, V., 173
Hammermeister, F., 333, 553
Hammond, W.D., 295, 299, 557
Hansen, J., 131, 269, 343, 554
Harjo, J., 173
Harris, V.J., 554
Hart, B., 10, 554
Hauerwas, L.B., 79, 88, 554
Heald-Taylor, G., 179, 554
Heibert, E.H., 554
Heiman, L.A., 554
Henderson, E.H., 92, 554
Henkes, K., 403
Heo, Y., 273
Herman, P.A., 191, 271, 554, 556
Hickman, P., 454
Hiebert, E.H., 6, 137, 269, 551
Hill, B.C., 554
Hilliard, A., 7, 555
Himmelman, J., 451, 472
Hoban, T., 488
Hoffman, M., 129, 376, 504
Holdaway D., 17, 35, 36, 76, 78, 137, 178, 186, 189, 208, 269, 270, 271, 285, 555
Hollingsworth, P.M., 190, 204, 553
Hooks, W., 487, 504
Hutchins, P., 504

Individuals with Disabilities Education Act, 555
Ingalls, L.W., 493
Inhelder, B., 92, 300, 556
Isadora, R., 474

Jacobs, J.S., 131, 271, 558
Jay, A., 62
Jenkins, J.R., 37, 557
Johnson, D.M., 270, 555
Johnson, N.J., 554
Johnson, S.T., 62
Johnston, F.R., 190, 555
Jones, M.B., 182, 295, 299, 556
Jones, N.K., 4, 555
Juel, C., 26, 37, 48, 551, 555

Kalan, R., 451
Karweit, N.L., 270, 557
Kawakami, A.J., 190, 555

Keats, E.J., 129, 139, 164–165, 335, 372, 497, 504
Kelleher, M.E., 183, 555
Kellogg, S., 493
Kiefer, B.Z., 290, 556
Kilborne, S., 479
Kimmel, E., 489, 496, 504
Kirk, D., 62
Klesius, J.P., 39, 554
Kozub, R., 191, 555
Kreeft, J., 363, 555
Kress, J.E., 35, 554
Kristo, J., 137, 139, 555

Ladson-Billings, G., 15, 555
Laughon, P., 37, 558
Lear, E., 504
Lehr, F., 191, 551
Lenski, L., 404
Leong, D.J., 9, 17, 32, 552
Levine, E., 173
Levstik, L.S., 290, 556
Lindfors, J.W., 10, 555
Lionni, L., 62, 451
Lobel, A., 61, 62, 371, 434, 438, 472, 504
Lonigan, C., 190, 558
Louie, A., 487, 504
Low, W., 404
Lukens, R., 485, 490, 491, 498, 505, 555
Lynch, P., 555

Maass, R., 502, 504
MacLachlan, P., 486, 504
Maclean, M., 39, 555
Madden, N.A., 270, 557
Madura, S., 161, 555
Marr, D., 48, 555
Martin, B., 61, 62, 132, 187, 489, 490, 491, 494, 495, 497, 504
Martinez, E., 217, 242, 243
Martinez, M., 132, 505, 555
Maruyama, G.M., 268, 269, 558
Mason, J., 26, 555
Mayer, M., 461
Mazzeo, J., 269, 553
McCallum, R.D., 399
McCarrier, A., 295, 297, 299, 342, 555
McCloskey, R., 376
McGill-Franzen, A., 225, 551
McKenzie, M.G., 295, 555

McKeown, M.G., 78, 190, 551
McKissack, P., 173, 504
McMahon, S.I., 131, 247, 269, 555, 556
McMillan, B., 488
Medearis, A.S., 489, 504
Merriam-Webster, 28, 130, 131, 555
Meyer, B.J., 163, 500, 505, 555
Miller, J., 62
Miller, P., 299, 557
Miller, S.S., 451
Mochizuki, K., 173
Mohr, N., 486, 504
Mooney, M.E., 19, 555
Moore, D.W., 60, 553
Moore, S.A., 60, 553
Morris, A., 499, 504
Morris, D., 37, 39, 64, 211, 555
Morrow, L., 505
Morrow, L.M., 12, 13, 142, 155, 268, 555
Mullis, I.V.S., 136, 556
Murphy, S., 398, 399, 400, 554
Murray, B.A., 37, 557
Murray, D., 338, 556
Murray, M., 62

Nagy, W.E., 271, 556
Nash, M.F., 132, 505, 555
Nathan, R., 558
National Assessment of Educational Progress 2002, 5, 556
National Assessment of Educational Progress 2003, 5, 556
National Center for Education Statistics, 556
National Institute of Child Health and Human Development, 6, 18, 35, 191, 556
National Literacy Standards for Language Arts, 4, 556
Nessel, D.D., 182, 295, 299, 556
Neuman, S.B., 15, 556
Niles, O.S., 500, 505, 556
Nixon, J.L., 499, 505
Noble, T.H., 493, 505
Northwest Regional Educational Laboratory, 14, 556

O'Connor, R.E., 37, 557
Ogle, D., 310, 322, 556
Olsen, R., 556
Olson, M.W., 49, 77, 554

O'Neill, L.T., 337, 342, 557
Opitz, M.F., 191, 556
Orehovec, B., 269, 556
Ortiz, S., 173
Osborn, J., 78, 191, 551
Osens, R.C., 488
O'Shea, D.J., 189, 556
O'Shea, L.J., 189, 556
Owens, R.C., 488

Padak, N.D., 133, 505, 557
Pallotta, J., 505
Pappas, C.C., 290, 556
Paris, S.G., 226, 556
Parker, N., 472
Parker, N.W., 454
Pasts, D.J., 15, 556
Pearson, P.D., 135, 271, 551
Peck, M., 47, 556
Pennington, B.F., 27, 556
Perfetti, C.A., 77, 78, 190, 551, 556
Perney, J., 37, 39, 64, 211, 555
Perrault, C., 505, 587
Person, M.E., 183, 556
Peterson, R., 169, 556
Piaget, J., 92, 300, 556
Pikulski, J.J., 262, 556
Pinkney, B., 403
Pinnell, G.S., 219, 222, 226, 262, 295, 297, 299, 342, 436, 553, 555, 556
Polacco, P., 173, 376
Post, J., 451
Powell, D., 399, 553
Powell, W.R., 142, 191, 236, 553, 556
Prelutsky, J., 371, 489, 505
Pressley, M., 27, 45, 556
Pursell-Gates, V., 132, 553

Rack, J., 77, 556
Ramey, D.R., 15, 556
Ramirez, G., 7, 556
Ramirez, J.D., 15, 556
Ramirez, J.L., 7, 556
Rand, T., 490
Raphael, T.E., 131, 269, 556
Rashotti, C.A., 37, 558
Rasinski, T., 505
Rasinski, T.V., 133, 191, 262, 556, 557
Read, C., 557
Rees, M., 186, 188, 505
Reimer, K.M., 133, 505, 557

Reiser, L., 173
Reutzel, D.R., 190, 204, 553
Reutzel, R.D., 399, 400, 557
Rey, H.A., 62
Rey, M., 62
Rhodes, L.D., 186, 187, 189, 557
Rigg, P., 331, 557
Ringgold, F., 173
Rinsky, L.A., 557
Risley, T.R., 10, 554
Rogers, P., 499, 505
Rosen, C., 131, 557
Rosen, H., 131, 557
Rosenblatt, L.M., 4, 270, 557
Ross, G., 16, 558
Routh, D., 39, 554
Routman, R., 269, 557

Samuels, S.J., 191, 557
Sanchez, E.O., 173
Scarry, R., 488
Schank, R., 28, 557
Schlick Noe, K.L., 554
Schwartz, D., 451
Scieszka, J., 474
Scott, A.H., 505
Scott, J., 6, 137, 269, 551
Seibert, P., 443
Seidler, A., 62-64, 505
Sendak, M., 62, 353, 493, 495,
    499, 505
Senick, G.J., 139, 557
Seuss, Dr., 62
Shanklin, N.K., 28, 557
Shannon, G., 62
Shannon, P., 4, 398, 399, 400, 554,
    557
Shaw, C.G., 321, 505
Siera, M., 557
Silverstein, S., 505
Simmons, K., 37, 558
Sims, R., 133, 505, 557
Sindelar, P.T., 189, 556
Slavin, R.E., 270, 557
Slepian, J., 62-64, 505
Slocum, T.A., 37, 557
Smith, F., 357, 557
Smith, R.K., 129, 130, 166,
    251, 505
Snow, C.E., 6, 15, 26, 553, 557
Snowling, M., 77, 556

Soderman, A.K., 337, 342, 557
Soto, G., 173, 217, 242, 243
Spache, G.D., 253, 557
Speigel, D.L., 145, 557
Stahl, S.A., 37, 299, 557
Standards for the English
    Language Arts, 557
Stanley, G.E., 177, 205
Stanovich, K.E., 27, 77, 557
Staton, J., 361, 363, 557
Stauffer, R.G., 142, 182, 295, 299,
    316, 327, 557, 558
Steele, F.A., 487, 505
Steig, W., 181, 217, 236, 237, 372,
    376, 487, 497, 505
Steptoe, J., 132, 173, 487, 505
Strickland, D.S., 398, 551
Sulzby, E., 13, 26, 132, 185,
    505, 558

Talanda, S., 505
Tan-Lin, Amy, 48, 558
Tarpley, N.A., 173
Taylor, B.M., 268, 269, 558
Taylor, N.E., 189, 558
Taylor, W.L., 558
Te Ata, 173
Teale, W.H., 11, 26, 558
Telgen, D., 139, 558
Temple, C., 104, 558
Temple, F., 104, 558
Tharp, R.G., 17, 558
Thiele, B., 173
Thomas, J.C., 173
Thomson, J., 4, 558
Thong, R., 173
Thornton, P., 173
Tompkins, G.E., 361, 363, 379, 558
Torgenson, J.K., 37, 558
Trachtenburg, P., 207, 208, 558
Treadway, J., 333, 558
Trelease, J., 141, 558
Tulley, M.A., 399, 553
Tunmer, W.E., 554, 77
Tunnell, M.O., 131, 271, 558
Turner, A, 486, 494, 495, 498, 505
Turner, J.C., 226, 556

Valdez-Menchaca, M.C., 190, 558
Van Allen, R., 182, 558
Van Allsburg, C., 494, 505

Vaughn, M., 173
Veatch, J., 269, 558
Voelkl, K.E., 269, 553
Vygotsky, L.S., 8, 10, 16, 17, 31, 104,
    142, 270, 558

Waboose, J.B., 173
Wade, M., 189, 558
Wagner, R.K., 37, 558
Walker, J., 79, 88, 554
Walmsley, S., 131, 558
Wasik, B.A., 226, 270, 556, 557
Wasylyk, T.M., 551
Weatherford, C.B., 173
Weinstein, C.S., 268, 555
Weiss, G.D., 173
Wells, D., 131, 553
Wells, G., 13, 131, 558
Wells, R., 505
Welsh, M.C., 27, 556
West, R.F., 77, 557
West, T., 397, 403, 404
White, E.B., 487, 493, 505
White, K.R., 7, 558
Whitehurst, G.J., 190, 558
Wiesner, D., 183, 451
Wilce, L.S., 45, 553
Wilkinson, I.A.G., 6, 137, 269, 551
Williams, V.B., 129, 134, 142,
    144–148, 505
Wilson, P.T., 268, 551, 553
Windsor, M.M., 555, 48
Winograd, P.N., 186, 552
Wixon, K.K., 262, 556
Wolf, B., 173
Wong, J.S., 173
Wood, A., 187, 489, 505
Wood, D., 489, 505
Wood, S.S., 16, 558
Wren, S., 130, 558
Wright, J., 472

Yaden, D., 189, 201, 558
Yekovich, F.R., 189, 558
Yolen, J., 365, 488, 498, 505
Yopp, H.K., 37, 39, 48, 50, 51, 52,
    53, 558
Yopp, R.H., 37, 39, 48, 50, 53, 558
Yuen, S., 15, 556

Zoehfeld, K., 454

Subject Index

A My Name Is Alice (Bayer), 61
A to Zoo (Lima & Lima), 164
Accuracy rate for oral reading, 256
Acrostic poem, 371
Activities to promote language and
    literacy development, 11–12
Activity centers, 380–381,
    450–451
Adequate Yearly Progress (AYP),
    No Child Left Behind Act
    (NCLB), 15, 18
*Adventures of Salamander Sam,
    The* (Ebl), 461
Affixes, 86–87
Alliteration, 499
Alphabet books, 61–62
Alphabet letters
    in the emergent stage, 43–45
    and phonemes, 83
    recognition, 325–326
    and sounds, 45–47
    writing, 47–48, 383–385
"Alphabet Song", 43
Amazing Grace (Hoffman and
    Binch), 129
Amphibians. *See* Teaching about
    amphibians in second grade
Anansi and the Moss-Covered Rock
    (Kimmel), 489, 496
Annotated drawings, 209–210, 307
Antagonist, 491, 492
Anthologies of literature
    selections, 402
Anthony Reynoso: Born To Rope
    (Cooper & Gordon), 404
Anthropomorphic characters, 492
Art, 288, 330
Art response to literature, 161
Assessment
    basal reading/language arts
      series, 422–424
    child's portfolio, 389–390

collecting samples of writing,
    389–391
in comprehension of text,
    136–137
conferences with children,
    280–284, 289
conferencing with writers,
    388–389
documenting student
    learning, 480
in the emergent stage, 64–70
evaluating writing traits, 386–387
focusing students, 289
guided and independent
    writing, 385–392
guided reading, 250, 253–263
independent reading, 288–289
informal reading inventories, 253
miscues analysis, 253
observing children's
    progress, 277
observing writers at work,
    385–386
reading records, 253, 288–289
in reading to children, 171, 172
recording form for children's
    progress in writing, 392
running records, 253
samples of student work, 289
shared and interactive writing,
    330–331, 332
student self-evaluations, 482
student work produced,
    481–482
teacher observations, 480–481
teacher's assessment
    portfolio, 3391
teaching about amphibians in
    second grade, 480–482
of word knowledge, 112–122
year-at-a-glance reading
    record, 261

Assisted writing, 295
Aural context, 36
Authentic literature and
    reading/language arts series,
    400–401
Author or illustrator focus, 164
Author studies, 279
Author's chair, 360
Author's intentions, 134
Autobiography, 131, 488
AYP. *See* Adequate Yearly
    Progress

Background knowledge and
    independent reading, 271
Balanced and integrated literacy
    framework. *See* Framework
    for literacy teaching and
    learning
Basal reading/language arts series,
    396–426
    assessment, 422–424
    components of, 402
    concerns and criticisms,
      400–401
    definition, 398
    diversity in students, 424
    history, 398–400
    included in each literature
      selection, 404–408
    small-group/independent work,
      411, 412–421
    teacher decision making, 401
    teaching a basal literature
      selection, 408–409
    themes in, 403–404
    whole group: language arts, 416,
      419–425
    whole group: oral language and
      word work, 409–411,
      412–416
Base words, 85

Beans on the Roof (Byars), 218, 245
Becoming a Nation of Readers, Commission on Reading, 6
Bedtime stories, 12
Big books, 179, 180, 194–197, 208
Biography, 131, 488
Biopoem, 371–372
Book boxes or tubs, 273
Book clubs, 247
    mail-order, 277
Book language, 154, 496
Book-reading experiences, 12
Book talks, 272, 273, 279
Bookmaking, 381–383
Bound morphemes, 85
Bread Bread Bread (Morris), 499
Brown Bear, Brown Bear, What Do You See? (Martin), 489, 497
Building background before reading, 321

Caldecott Award, 161
Can You Jump Like a Frog? (Brown), 461
Cause and effect, 378, 501
CD ROM, 402
Chair for My Mother, A (Williams), 129, 134, 135, 136, 142, 144–148, 152, 155, 159, 160–161
Challenging text for shared reading, 204–206
Chants and rhythms response to literature, 160–161, 372
Chapter books, 166–170, 243–249
Characters, 164, 491–492
Charlotte's Web (White), 487, 493
Charts, 180–184, 197–200, 209, 307–308
Chick and the Duckling, The (Ginsburg), 177, 192, 194–197, 200, 201–204, 209, 210
Chicka Chicka Boom Boom (Martin & Archambault), 61, 187
Child Health and Human Development Panel, 399
Child-led groups, 247
Children's literature in the emergent stage, 61–64
Children's Literature Review (Senick), 139
Child's portfolio, 389–390

Chinatown (Low), 404
Chocolate Fever (Smith), 129, 130, 166–170, 251
Chronological order in plots, 493
Chunks, 88, 92
"Clap, Clap, Clap Your Hands", 50
Class-made big book, 327
Classroom library, 276–277
Cliffhangers in plots, 494
Climax in plots, 493–494
Climbing Tree Frogs (Berman), 472
Closed resolution in plot, 494
Closure for the day, 360
Cloze procedure, 196
Clusters, 306–307
Code-breaking strategies, 77
Commission on Reading, *Becoming a Nation of Readers*, 6
Committee on the Prevention of Reading Difficulties in Young Children, 6
Compare/contrast chart, 445
Comparing levels of text, 221
Comparisons, 376–378, 501
Composing, 338–339
Composition processes, 317–319
Comprehension of text, 19, 130, 133–134, 190
Computer center, 451, 472
Concept of word (COW), 211–213
Concept of word in print, 324
Concepts about print, 189, 206–207
Concrete poem, 372, 373
Confidence and sense of control, 189
Conflict in plots, 494–495
Consonant blends, 79
Consonant diagraphs, 79
Consonants, 79–80
Contemporary realistic fiction, 131, 485–486
Context clues, 207–209
Context in decoding print, 36–37
Context/written cloze, 325
Controversial issues, 400
COW. *See* Concept of word
Creative movement response to literature, 161
Cross-curricular centers, 406–408
Cueing strategies, 258
Cultural conglomerates, 133
Cultural heritage, 7, 10, 13
Culturally conscious literature, 133
Cumulative pattern, 186–187, 188

Daily independent reading time (DIRT), 268
Daily routine, 432, 433
Dancing with the Indians (Medearis), 489
Day Jimmie's Boa Ate the Wash, The (Noble), 493, 494
DEAR. *See* Drop everything and read
Decoding in the emergent stage, 38–43
Decoding print, 34–38
Decoding skills, 190
Decoding words, 209
Demographics of United States population, 8
Dependent prefixes, 86
Derivational suffixes, 87
Descriptions, 305–306, 375–376, 500
"Deskilling", 400
Developing stage
    guided reading teaching points, 240
    independent reading, 275
    and levels of difficulty, 222
    of readers and writers, 76–77, 89, 90
Developmental levels, 73
Diagraphs in consonants, 79
Diagraphs in vowels, 82
Dialogue journals, 361, 363
Diamonte, 372
Dick and Jane New Basic Readers, 399
Directed Listening-Thinking Activity (Stauffer), 142
Directionality of print, 30–31, 34, 206
DIRT. *See* Daily independent reading time
Discussion skills and guide, 169–170
Diversity in students, 7–8, 13
    basal reading/language arts series, 424
    experience sets children apart, 73
    experiential background of learners, 333
    honoring children's thinking, 393
    inclusivity, 8
    independent reading, 290–291
    language of instruction, 73

language of learners, 331
learning words, 122
multicultural literature,
132–133, 173
reading ability, 263
reading interests, 263
reading to children, 171–177
segregation, 7
shared reading, 213–214
special learning needs, 333
supporting independence, 393
text and comprehension,
263, 265
thinking of learners, 333
see also English as a second
language
Do You Want to Be My Friend?
(Carle), 155
Dolch 220 list, 35
Double-entry journals, 364–365
Down Comes the Rain (Branley),
177, 178, 182, 192, 193,
197–200
Drama, 158, 288
Drawings, 156
Drop everything and read
(DEAR), 268
Duplicated text in shared and
interactive writing, 326–330
Dynamic characters, 492

*Early Detection of Reading
Difficulties* (Clay), 67
Editing for meaning and
correctness, 339–341
Editing partners/groups, 359
Editing text, 324
Edward Lear Alphabet, An
(Newsom), 61
Elements of literature, 164, 320
Embedded instruction, 93–94
Emergent literacy, 26–28
Emergent stage
guided reading teaching points,
239–240
independent reading, 275
and levels of difficulty, 221–222
words in, 24–73
English Language Learners, 5, 10
Adequate Yearly Progress
(AYP), 15
advanced fluency, 15
concept of word (COW),
211–213

early production stage, 14
intermediate fluency, 15
key word vocabulary, 35
language of instruction, 73
preproduction stage, 14
selecting texts for, 185
speech emergence stage, 14
stages of learning, 14–15
Teaching English to Speakers of
Other Languages
(TESOL), 15
see also Diversity in students
Enlarged text for wall stories,
202–203
Environmental print to focus on
letters and sounds, 60–61
print books, 60
word wall, 60–61
Ethnic groups, 7, 13
Everybody Needs a Rock
(Baylor), 346
Explanations, 308
Explicit instruction, 92–93
Explicit theme, 496
Expository texts, 142–152, 185
Expressions of learning, 309–310
Extending engagement with books,
286–288

Familiar sequences and content,
187, 188
"Families Are Alike and Different",
241, 242
Fantasy, 131, 486–487
Federal reading education policy, 6
Fiction, 131, 344–346, 485–486
and plot, 368–371
Figurative language, 498
Final consonants, 79
Fire Fighters (Maass), 502
First-person point of view, 495
Five-finger test, 274
Five senses poem, 373
Flannel boards, 157
Flashbacks in plots, 493
Flat characters, 491
Flexibility principle, 33–34
Flexible groups, 225, 228–229,
285–286
Floor puzzles, 203
Fluency, 19, 190–191, 261–263
and independent reading, 271
Focused writing sample, 118–119
Foils (characters), 492

Folk literature, 131, 487
Form for recording reading
record, 258
Forms of writing, 319–320,
366–380
fiction and plot, 368–371
informational writing, 375–380
personal narratives, 366–368
poetry, 371–375
Four-Square Writing Method (Gould
& Gould), 344
Framework for literacy teaching
and learning, 18–22
components of the framework,
18–19
instructional strategies in the
framework, 19–22
Free and bound morphemes, 85
Frog and Toad (Lobel), 438
Frog Goes to Dinner (Mayer), 461
Frog or Toad?, 443
Frog Prince, A (Berenzy), 474
Frog Prince, Continued
(Scieszka), 474
Frog Prince, The, 75
*Frogs, Toads, Lizards, and
Salamanders* (Parker &
Wright), 454, 472
From Tadpole to Frog
(Zoehfeld), 454
Frog in the Kitchen Sink
(Post), 451
Frustration level, 220
Fry's Instant Words, 35
Functional writing, 320
Functional writing forms, 304–308

Games, 329
in the emergent stage, 53
Gender differences, 7
Generative principle, 33
Genres of children's literature,
131–133, 164, 223–224, 319,
485–489
Ghost-Eye Tree, The (Martin &
Archambault), 490, 491, 492,
493, 494, 495, 496, 499
Goldilocks test, 275
Good-bye, Curtis (Henkes), 403
Graphemes, 18–19
Graphophonics, 226–227
Graphs, 308
Group literature log, 322
Group reports, 466, 467

Guided and independent writing, 334–393
  activity centers, 380–381
  assessment, 385–392
  bookmaking, 381–383
  diversity in students, 392–393
  handwriting, 383–385
  independence as writers, 341–343, 361–366
  organizing a writer's workshop, 350–351
  phases of writing, 337–341
  whole-class closing meeting, 359–361
  whole-class opening meeting, 351–355
  writer's workshop, 343–350
  writing time, 356–359
  see also Forms of writing
Guided literature study in small groups, 240–249
Guided reading, 216–265, 324–325
  assessment, 250, 253–263
  definition of, 218–219
  diversity of students, 263, 265
  flexible grouping, 225
  guided literature study in small groups, 240–249
  matching children and texts, 219–222
  mini-lessons, 249–250, 251–252
  planning for, 228–231
  sample guided reading lesson/*Sylvester and the Magic Pebble*, 236–239
  sample guided reading lesson/*Three Little Ducks*, 231–235
  selecting text, 222–225
  self-monitoring strategies, 226–227
  small-group setting, 225
  strategic reading/"in-the-head" processes, 227
  teaching points for, 239–240
Guided reading block, 435–436
Guided writing, 435

Handbook of Children's Literature, 485–505
  genres of children's literature, 485–489
  literary elements in narrative writing, 489–499
  text structures in informational writing, 499–503
Handwriting, 383–385
Harcourt Trophies program, 402, 403, 422
Hattie and the Fox (Fox), 139
High-frequency sight words, 34–35, 115–116, 207
Hispanics, 133
Historical fiction, 131, 486
History of basal reading/language arts series, 398–400
Home language, 13
Hornbooks, 398
How a Book Is Made (Aliki), 488
Hungry Thing Returns, The (Slepian & Seidler), 62–64
Hungry Thing, The (Slepian & Seidler), 62–64
Hurricane (Wiesner), 183

Icky Sticky Frog, The (Bentley), 479
Idea clusters, 210
Ideas in print, 12
If You Hopped Like a Frog (Schwartz), 451
If You Were a Writer (Nixon), 499
Illustrations, 185, 223
Illustrator focus, 164
Imagery, 497
Implicit theme, 496
"In-the-head" processes, 227
Inclusivity of students, 8
Independence as writers, 341–343, 361–366
Independent level, 221
Independent prefixes, 86
Independent readers, 225
Independent reading, 266–291, 436–437
  assessment, 288–289
  benefits of, 271–272
  conferences with children, 280–284
  definition of, 268–269
  diversity of students, 290–291
  extending engagement with books, 286–288
  instruction in reader's workshops, 284–286
  planning for, 276–277
  reader's workshop, 269–271, 278–284
  a reading atmosphere, 272–275

Independent writing, 438
Individual books, 327
Individual writing, 356
Individualized reading, 269
Individuals with Disabilities Education Amendments Act, 8
Inferential comprehension—text-implicit thinking, 134–135
Inflectional suffixes, 86–87
Informal reading inventories, 253
Informational books, 131, 488–489
Informational charts, 323
Informational text structures, 320
Informational writing, 375–380, 499–503
Initial consonants, 79
Innovating with the text, 210, 321
Instruction in the emergent stage, 49
Instructional level, 220
Instructional strategies in the framework for literacy teaching and learning, 19–22
Integrating elements in a literacy framework. *See* Teaching about amphibians in second grade
Intensive reading experiences, 178
Interactions in language and literacy development, 10–13
Internal mental processes, 10

James and the Giant Peach (Dahl), 487
Journal response to literature, 159–160
Journals, 210, 361–366
Jump, Frog, Jump (Kalan), 451
Jumpy, Green, and Croaky, What Am I? (Butterfield and Ford), 443

K-W-L charts, 322–323
Key word vocabulary, 35

Labeled drawings, 323
Language
  rules of, 11
  symbolic power of, 13
Language and literacy development, 8, 9–14
  activities to promote, 11–12
  English as a second language, 14–15

and interactions, 10–13
in preschool years, 10–13
in primary grades (K-4), 13–14
Language and literacy foundations, 2–22
achievement levels in reading and writing, 5
fourth grade reading and writing levels, 5
literacy defined, 4–5
literacy instruction, 5–7
student diversity, 7–8
see also English as a second language; Teaching and learning principles; Written language
Language arts, 416, 419–425
Language arts academic standards, 431–432
Language cues/syntax, 226
Language experience approach (LEA), 295, 299
Language experience charts, 182–183
Language of print, 207
Language to talk about print, 31–32
Lau v. Nichols, 14
LEA. See Language experience approach
Learning about self as reader, 290
Learning environments, 9, 17–18
encouraging independence, 17
respecting and valuing individuals, 17–18
Learning logs, 365–366, 446, 447, 456–459
Learning styles, 7
Least restrictive educational environment, 8
Length of text, 223
Lesson planner, 405–406
Lesson plans (week 1), 442–451
Lesson plans (week 2), 451–463
Lesson plans (week 3), 464–473
Lesson plans (week 4), 473–479
Letter from Phoenix Farm, A (Yolen), 488
Levels of difficulty, 221–222
Library, classroom, 276–277
Library corner, 450
Library location, 272
Lifelong readers, 225
Limited omniscient narrator point of view, 495

Linking learning experiences, 224–225
List poem, 374
Listening center, 450, 472
Lists, 305
Literacy. See Language and literacy foundations
Literal comprehension—text-explicit thinking, 134
Literary elements, 164, 320, 489–499
Literature circles, 247
Literature logs, 286–287, 475–477
Little House books, 493
Little Red Hen, The (Galdone), 139
Lizards and Salamanders, 472
Locater devices, 209

Magic School Bus Inside the Human Body (Cole), 499
Magic window words, 329
Mail-order book clubs, 277
"Mary Had a Little Lamb", 212
Masking text, 208
Matching children and texts, 219–222
Max Found Two Sticks (Pinkney), 403
McGuffey Eclectic Readers, 398–399
Meaning chunks, 88
Meaning cues/semantics, 226
Mediated read-aloud, 140–142, 143, 434
Metalinguistic awareness, 32
Mini-lessons, 249–250, 251–252, 284–285, 322, 351–354
Minority children
and achievement levels in reading and writing, 5
see also Diversity in students
Mirandy and Brother Wind, 498
Miscues analysis, 253
Miss Rumphius (Cooney), 496
Modeling and guided participation, 214
Morphemes
bound morphemes, 85
dependent prefix, 86
derivational suffix, 86
free morpheme, 85
independent prefix, 86
inflectional suffix, 86–87
morphemic analysis, 38
in the developing and transitional stages, 83–87
patterns, 326

Morphemic word building, 98–101
Moss Gown (Hooks), 487
"Mother May I?", 53
Motivation and independent reading, 271
Mrs. Piggie Wiggie, 159
Mufaro's Beautiful Daughters (Steptoe), 487
Multicultural literature, 132–133, 173
Multiple copies of a text, 184–185, 204
Music to focus on sounds, 49–53

NAEP. See National Assessment of Educational Progress
Napping House, The (Wood & Wood), 187, 489
Narrated drawing, 443, 444
Narrative texts, 142–148, 185
Narrative writing, 489–499
National Assessment of Educational Progress (NAEP), 5, 136
National Institute of Child Health and Human Development, 18
National Literacy Standards for Language Arts, 4
National Reading Panel, 6, 18
Nation's Report Card, 5
NCLB. See No Child Left Behind Act
Nettie's Trip South (Turner), 486, 494, 495, 497, 498
New Frog, A: My First Look at the Life Cycle of an Amphibian (Hickman), 454
New literature, 138–139
No Child Left Behind Act (NCLB), 6, 397, 399
Adequate Yearly Progress (AYP), 15, 18
Reading First (program), 6–7
Nonfiction, 131, 346–350

Objective narrator point of view, 495
Observation Survey, The (Clay), 67
Old favorites, 139
"Old MacDonald Had a Farm", 51, 181
Oliver Buttons Is a Sissy (dePaola), 139
On Market Street (Lobel), 61
Onomatopoeia, 498
Onset, 41–42
Oral language and word work, 409–411, 412–416

Oral reading miscues, 115
Ordered list or sequence, 305, 376, 500–501
Organization of thinking, 310–313
Original text, 324–326
Overhead transparencies, 179–180, 209
Owl Moon (Yolen), 365, 498

Pain and the Great One, The (Blume), 353
Paper Crane, The (Bang), 494
Peach and Blue (Kilborne), 479
Permanence of print, 30, 206
Personal and/or critical comprehension—scriptal thinking about text, 135–136
Personal journals, 361, 362
Personal narratives, 366–368
Personal reading interests, 290
Personalized reading, 269
Personification, 498
Persuasion, 379–380
Phases of writing, 337–341
Phoneme and word recognition, 116
Phonemes, 18, 42–43, 83
Phonemic awareness, 18, 37
Phonetic word building, 97–98
Phonic patterns, 326
    sample word lists and word sorts, 506–516
Phonics
    chunks, 88, 92
    code-breaking strategies, 77
    consonant blend, 79
    consonant diagraphs, 79
    consonants, 79–80
    definition of, 18–19
    in the developing and transitional stages, 79–83
    diphthongs, 82
    explicit instruction, 92–93
    phonemes, 18, 42–43, 83
    "reading wars", 5–6
    r-controlled vowels, 81
    short vowels, 81
    single long vowels, 81
    syllabication generalizations, 518–519
    visual cues/graphophonics, 197, 209, 226–227
    vowel diagraphs, 82
    vowels, 80–82

Phonics analysis, 37–38
Phonological awareness, 37
Picture books, 164–166, 241–243
Picture dictionary, 329
Pictures for sorting activities, 520–550
Pine Park Mystery, The (West), 397, 403, 404
Plot, 164, 493–495
Pocket charts, 183, 209
Poems/chants, 181
Poetry, 131, 371–375, 489
Poetry books, 181
Point of view, 164, 495
Pointers, 209
Popcorn reading, 204
Poppy Seeds (Bulla), 218, 245
Population, demographics of, 8
Positive outcomes while enjoying reading (POWER), 269
POWER. *See* Positive outcomes while enjoying reading
Practice and resource materials, 405
Predictability of text, 186–188, 214, 224
Predictions before reading, 321
Prefixes, 86
Preschool years in language and literacy development, 10–13
Prewriting or rehearsal, 338
Primary grades (K-4) in language and literacy development, 13–14
Princess and the Frog, The (Isadora), 474
Print, size and amount of print, 185–186, 223
Print concepts, 29–32
Private speech, 10
Problem/solution or question/answer, 378–379, 501–502
Problems in Reading (Dolch), 5
Protagonist, 491, 492
Publishers, 400–401
Purposes of print, 206

Question/answer, 378–379

R-controlled vowels, 81
Racial groups, 7
Rain Forest Secrets (Dorros), 502
Ramona Quimby, Age 8 (Cleary), 486

Random House Book of Poetry for Children, The (Prelutsky and Lobel), 371
Re-presenting the writing, 341
Read-aloud literature study, 162–164
Readability formulas, 224
Readability level, 400
Reader's intentions, 133
Reader's theater, 183–184, 203–204
Reader's workshops, 269–271, 278–284, 284–286
Reading aloud, 279
Reading atmosphere, 272–275
Reading by children, 21
Reading education, federal reading education policy, 6
Reading First (program), No Child Left Behind Act (NCLB), 6–7
Reading levels and interests, 276
Reading potential, 220
Reading records, 253
Reading to children, 20, 128–174
    assessment, 171, 172
    comprehension of text, 130, 133–134
    discussion skills and guide, 169–170
    diversity in students, 171–177
    expository texts, 142–152
    genres in literature, 131–133
    guidelines for, 138–141
    mediated read-aloud, 140–142, 143
    multicultural literature, 132–133, 173
    narrative texts, 142–148
    read-aloud literature study, 162–164
    reasons for reading and studying literature, 131
    rereading texts, 153–155
    responses to literature, 158–162
    retelling, 155–158
"Reading wars", 5–6
Reading with children, 20–21, 138–140
Reconstructing text, 327
Recurring principle, 32
Repeated readings of familiar stories, 187, 188
Repetitive pattern, 186, 188
Rereading texts, 153–155, 187, 327

Resolution in plot, 494
Response journals, 363–364
Response partners/groups, 358–359
Responses to literature, 158–162
Retelling and responding, 202
Retelling stories in literature, 155–158, 321
Rhyming words, 39–40
Rhythmic and rhyming pattern, 187, 188, 499
Rigby (publisher), 179, 223
Rime, 41–42
Root words, 85–86
Rosie's Walk (Hutchins), 155
Round characters, 491
Round-robin reading, 204
Rules of language, 11
Running records, 253

Sadako and the Thousand Paper Cranes (Coerr), 488
Safety and support of a group, 214
Salamander's Life, A (Himmelman), 451
Salamanders Secret, Silent Lives (Miller), 451
Sample guided reading lesson/*Sylvester and the Magic Pebble*, 236–239
Sample guided reading lesson/*Three Little Ducks*, 231–235
Sample Word Lists and Word Sorts, 506–519
   for phonic patterns, 506–516
   for structural patterns, 516–518
   for syllabication generalizations, 518–519
Sarah, Plain and Tall (MacLachlan), 486
Scaffolding children's learning, 10, 16, 205
Scaffolding children's reading. *See* Guided reading
Schema for words and print, 28–29
Scholastic, 179
Science academic standards, 432
Science center, 450, 472
Scriptal thinking about text, 135–136
Scripted reading record, 253–255
Scripts for reader's theater, 183–184

Segregation of students, 7
Selecting text, 222–225, 229–230
   genre and text structure, 223–224
   illustration support, 223
   language structures and concepts, 224
   length of text, 223
   linking learning experiences, 224–225
   predictability and pattern, 224
   print size and layout on page, 223
   for shared reading, 185–189
Self-confidence, 225
Self-correction rate, 256–257
Self-esteem, 225
Self-monitoring, 290
Self-monitoring strategies, 226–227, 290
   language cues/syntax, 226
   meaning cues/semantics, 226
   visual cues/graphophonics, 226–227
Self-regulated behaviors, 16–17
Self-selecting books, 273–274, 278–279
Semantics, 226
Sense of control, 189
Sentence building, 327
Sentence structure and patterns, 496–497
Setting, 164, 490–491
Shape books, 210
Shared and interactive writing, 292–333, 354–355, 434–435
   assessment, 330–331, 332
   composition processes, 317–319
   definition of interactive writing, 297–298
   definition of shared writing, 295–296
   diversity in students, 331, 333
   duplicated text, 326–330
   forms of writing, 319–320
   functional writing forms, 304–308
   by grade level, 309–313
   grouping for, 313–314
   original text, 324–326
   procedures for, 314–317
   reasons for using, 299–302
   shared/interactive compositions, 320–324
   use in classrooms, 302–304

Shared reading, 176–214
   assessment—concept of word (COW), 211–213
   challenging text, 204–206
   diversity of students, 213–214
   extending shared reading, 200–204
   organizing, 193–194
   planning, 191–193
   reasons for, 189–191
   sample shared reading—big book, 194–197
   sample shared reading—experience chart, 197–200
   selecting texts, 185–189
   texts for, 179–185
   word knowledge development through, 206–209
   and writing, 209–211
Shared reading—poem of the week, 433–434
Shared rereading, 187
Shared writing—story elements chart, 474–475
Shared writing or language experience charts, 182–183
Sharing book choices, 274
Sheltered text, 214
Short vowels, 81
Sight words, 34–35, 115–116, 325
Sign concept, 33
Silent reading, 269
Similes, 498
Single long vowels, 81
Skill instruction, 400, 401
Small-group approach to word study, 101–105
Small-group/independent work, 411, 412–421
Small-group setting, 225
Snowy Day, The (Keats), 129, 139, 164–166, 372, 497, 498
Social interactions, 11
Socioeconomic status, 10
   and achievement levels in reading and writing, 5
Something About the Author (Telgen), 139
Song frame, 374
Songs, 181
Sorting activities, 53–58
Sorting words, 101–102, 106–111
Sound boxes, 58–60
Sound chunks, 88

Sound devices, 498
Sound poem, 374–375
Speech versus text, 12
Spelling assessment, 121
SQUIRT. *See* Sustained quiet uninterrupted reading time
SSR. *See* Sustained silent reading
Stages of development and levels of difficulty, 221–222
Static characters, 492
Staying Nine (Conrad), 218, 245
Stereotyped character portrayals, 399, 492
Stone Fox (Gardiner), 217, 218, 245, 246, 247, 249
Story maps, 156
Strategic reading "in-the-head" processes, 227
Structural patterns in morphemes, 84
Structural patterns sample word lists and word sorts, 516–518
Structure or predictability of text, 186–188
Students. *See* Diversity in students
Style, 496–499
Styles of letter formation, 384
Suffixes, 86–87
Sustained quiet uninterrupted reading time (SQUIRT), 296
Sustained silent reading (SSR), 268, 279
Syllabication generalizations for sample word lists and word sorts, 518–519
Syllable units, 40–41
Sylvester and the Magic Pebble (Steig), 156, 157, 181, 217, 236–239, 368, 372, 487, 497
Syntax, 226
Synthetic approach, 92
Systematic instruction, 92

T-chart of characters, 465
T-chart of facts, 443, 444
Tape-recorded books, 288
Tattercoats (Steele), 487
Teacher decision making, 401
Teacher-led groups, 246–247
Teacher support, 430–431
Teacher's assessment portfolio, 391
Teacher's editions, 402

Teacher's plan book, 440–444, 452–453, 462–463, 470–471
Teaching a basal literature selection, 408–409
Teaching about amphibians in second grade, 428–483
assessment, 480–482
instructional decisions, 432–438
lesson plans (week 1), 442–451
lesson plans (week 2), 451–463
lesson plans (week 3), 464–473
lesson plans (week 4), 473–479
level of teacher support, 430–431
planning, 431–432
setting the stage, 430
teacher's plan book, 440–444, 452–453, 462–463, 470–471
Teaching and learning principles, 8–18
language and literacy development, 8, 9–14
learning environments, 9, 17–18
teaching-learning relationships, 8, 15–17
see also Framework for literacy teaching and learning
Teaching English to Speakers of Other Languages (TESOL), 15
see also English as a second language
Teaching-learning relationships, 8, 15–17
guidance toward self-regulated behaviors, 16–17
scaffolding children's learning, 16
zone of proximal development (ZPD), 16
Technology, 402
Ten in the Bed (Rees), 186
Terrible Thing That Happened at Our House, The (Blaine), 490, 494
TESOL. *See* Teaching English to Speakers of Other Languages
Text-explicit thinking, 134
Text illustrations, 155
Text-implicit thinking, 134–135
Text structure, 223–224, 499–503
Textbook adoption, 399–400
Texts for shared reading, 179–185
Theme, 164, 496
Themes, in basal reading/language arts series, 403–404

Third-Grade Detectives #1: The Clue of the Left-Handed Envelope (Stanley), 205
Three Little Ducks, 231–235, 255
Three Little Pigs, 159, 160, 498
Toad Overload (Seibert), 443
Too Many Tamales (Soto and Martinez), 217, 242, 243
Topic or theme focus, 163
Trains (Gibbons), 129, 148–152, 155, 159, 171
Transitional stage
guided reading teaching points, 240
independent reading, 275
and levels of difficulty, 222
of readers and writers, 77, 89, 91
Trophies: Banner Days, Theme 2, 402
Tuesday (Wiesner), 451
"Twinkle, Twinkle, Little Star", 212, 213
Tyler Toad and the Thunder (Crowe), 461
Tyrannosaurus Was a Beast (Prelutsky), 489

Ugly Duckling, The (Andersen), 317–319
Unfocused writing sample, 116–117
Uninterrupted sustained silent reading, 268
United States, demographics of United States population, 8
Unscripted reading rate, 253, 257–261

Venn diagram, 475
Very First Things to Know About Frogs (Grossman), 443
Very Hungry Caterpillar, The (Carle), 187
Visual cues/graphophonics, 197, 209, 226–227
Vocabulary, 19, 154
and independent reading, 271
Vocabulary development, 190
Vowel diagraphs, 82
Vowel diphthongs, 22
Vowels, 80–82

Wall stories, 202–203
Wednesday Surprise, The (Bunting), 486, 497, 498

What Will the Weather Be Like Today? (Rogers), 499
Where the Wild Things Are (Sendek), 353, 493, 495, 499
Whiteboards, 209
Whole-class approach to word study, 94–101
Whole-class closing meeting, 359–361
Whole-class opening meeting, 351–355
Whole group: language arts, 416, 419–425
Whole group: oral language and word work, 409–411, 412–416
Whole language movement, 399
Whole language versus phonics, 5–6
Wikki sticks, 209
Wood Frog's Life, A (Himmelman), 472
Word bank, 207
Word bank books, 328
Word building, 328
Word concepts, 206
Word hunts, 329
Word knowledge assessment, 112–122
Word knowledge development, 206–209
Word posters, 329
Word recognition, 116
Word recognition assessment, 118
Word selection for study, 105–106
Word sorts, 328
Word study, 435
Word study notebooks, 108, 111–112, 113
Word wall, 329
Word work, 409–411, 412–416
Words in context, 119–120
Words in isolation, 120–121
Words in phonics and morphemic analysis, 74–126
    assessment, 112–122
    developing readers and writers, 76–77

diversity in students, 122
guiding principles for instruction, 91–94
importance of learning about words, 77–78
instruction in the developing and transitional stages, 88–89, 88–91
morphemes in the developing and transitional stages, 83–87
phonics in the developing and transitional stages, 79–83
small-group approach to word study, 101–105
techniques for learning about words, 78–79
transitional readers and writers, 77
types of sorts, 106–111
whole-class approach to word study, 94–101
word selection for study, 105–106
word study notebooks, 108, 111–112, 113
Words in the emergent stage, 24–73
    alphabet letters, 43–45
    assessment of early concepts, 64–70
    children's literature to focus on sounds and letters, 61–64
    connecting letters to sounds, 45–47
    decoding in the emergent stage, 38–43
    decoding print, 34–38
    diversity in students, 70, 73
    emergent literacy, 26–28
    environmental print to focus on letters and sounds, 60–61
    games, 53
    instruction in the emergent stage, 49

music to focus on sounds, 49–53
print concepts, 29–32
schema for words and print, 28–29
sorting activities, 53–58
sound boxes, 58–60
writing alphabet letters, 47–48
written language principles, 32–34
Would You Rather Be a Bullfrog? (Dr. Seuss), 461
Wright Group, 179, 223
Writer's workshop, 343–350, 350–351
    fiction, 344–346
    nonfiction, 346–350
Writing, 288
    by children, 21
    with children, 21
    retelling with, 147–158
    samples of focused, 118–119
    samples of unfocused, 116–117
    and shared reading, 209–211
    see also Guided and independent writing; Shared and interactive writing
Writing center, 450
Writing conferences, 356–358
Writing folder, 389
Writing time, 356–359
Written language concepts, 12–13
Written language principles, 32–34
    directionality, 34
    flexibility principle, 33–34
    generative principle, 33
    recurring principle, 32
    sign concept, 33

Year-at-a-glance reading record, 261
Yen-Shen (Louie), 487

Zone of performance, 225
Zone of proximal development (ZPD), 16